FIXED INCOME AND DERIVATIVES

CFA® Program Curriculum
2017 • LEVL II • VOLUME 5

Photography courtesy of Hector Emanuel.

ISBN 978-1-942471-77-6 (paper)
ISBN 978-1-942471-98-1 (ebk)

10 9 8 7 6 5 4 3 2 1

Please visit our website at
www.WileyGlobalFinance.com.

FSC
www.fsc.org

MIX
Paper from
responsible sources

FSC® C101537

CONTENTS

⊡ indicates an optional segment

◙ indicates an optional segment

Contents

◘ indicates an optional segment

Derivatives

◙ indicates an optional segment

Contents

◙ indicates an optional segment

How to Use the CFA Program Curriculum

Congratulations on reaching Level II of the Chartered Financial Analyst® (CFA®) Program. This exciting and rewarding program of study reflects your desire to become a serious investment professional. You are embarking on a program noted for its high ethical standards and the breadth of knowledge, skills, and abilities it develops. Your commitment to the CFA Program should be educationally and professionally rewarding.

The credential you seek is respected around the world as a mark of accomplishment and dedication. Each level of the program represents a distinct achievement in professional development. Successful completion of the program is rewarded with membership in a prestigious global community of investment professionals. CFA charterholders are dedicated to life-long learning and maintaining currency with the ever-changing dynamics of a challenging profession. The CFA Program represents the first step toward a career-long commitment to professional education.

The CFA examination measures your mastery of the core skills required to succeed as an investment professional. These core skills are the basis for the Candidate Body of Knowledge (CBOK™). The CBOK consists of four components:

- A broad outline that lists the major topic areas covered in the CFA Program (www.cfainstitute.org/cbok);
- Topic area weights that indicate the relative exam weightings of the top-level topic areas (www.cfainstitute.org/level_II);
- Learning outcome statements (LOS) that advise candidates about the specific knowledge, skills, and abilities they should acquire from readings covering a topic area (LOS are provided in candidate study sessions and at the beginning of each reading); and
- The CFA Program curriculum, which contains the readings and end-of-reading questions, that candidates receive upon exam registration.

Therefore, the key to your success on the CFA examinations is studying and understanding the CBOK. The following sections provide background on the CBOK, the organization of the curriculum, and tips for developing an effective study program.

CURRICULUM DEVELOPMENT PROCESS

The CFA Program is grounded in the practice of the investment profession. Beginning with the Global Body of Investment Knowledge (GBIK), CFA Institute performs a continuous practice analysis with investment professionals around the world to determine the knowledge, skills, and abilities (competencies) that are relevant to the profession. Regional expert panels and targeted surveys are conducted annually to verify and reinforce the continuous feedback from the GBIK collaborative website. The practice analysis process ultimately defines the CBOK. The CBOK reflects the competencies that are generally accepted and applied by investment professionals. These competencies are used in practice in a generalist context and are expected to be demonstrated by a recently qualified CFA charterholder.

The Education Advisory Committee, consisting of practicing charterholders, in conjunction with CFA Institute staff, designs the CFA Program curriculum in order to deliver the CBOK to candidates. The examinations, also written by charterholders, are designed to allow you to demonstrate your mastery of the CBOK as set forth in the CFA Program curriculum. As you structure your personal study program, you should emphasize mastery of the CBOK and the practical application of that knowledge. For more information on the practice analysis, CBOK, and development of the CFA Program curriculum, please visit www.cfainstitute.org.

ORGANIZATION OF THE CURRICULUM

The Level II CFA Program curriculum is organized into 10 topic areas. Each topic area begins with a brief statement of the material and the depth of knowledge expected.

Each topic area is then divided into one or more study sessions. These study sessions—17 sessions in the Level II curriculum—should form the basic structure of your reading and preparation.

Each study session includes a statement of its structure and objective and is further divided into specific reading assignments. An outline illustrating the organization of these 18 study sessions can be found at the front of each volume of the curriculum.

The readings and end-of-reading questions are the basis for all examination questions and are selected or developed specifically to teach the knowledge, skills, and abilities reflected in the CBOK. These readings are drawn from content commissioned by CFA Institute, textbook chapters, professional journal articles, research analyst reports, and cases. All readings include problems and solutions to help you understand and master the topic areas.

Reading-specific Learning Outcome Statements (LOS) are listed at the beginning of each reading. These LOS indicate what you should be able to accomplish after studying the reading. The LOS, the reading, and the end-of-reading questions are dependent on each other, with the reading and questions providing context for understanding the scope of the LOS.

You should use the LOS to guide and focus your study because each examination question is based on the assigned readings and one or more LOS. The readings provide context for the LOS and enable you to apply a principle or concept in a variety of scenarios. The candidate is responsible for the entirety of the required material in a study session, which includes the assigned readings as well as the end-of-reading questions and problems.

We encourage you to review the information about the LOS on our website (www.cfainstitute.org/programs/cfaprogram/courseofstudy/Pages/study_sessions.aspx), including the descriptions of LOS "command words" (www.cfainstitute.org/programs/Documents/cfa_and_cipm_los_command_words.pdf).

FEATURES OF THE CURRICULUM

OPTIONAL
SEGMENT

Required vs. Optional Segments   You should read all of an assigned reading. In some cases, though, we have reprinted an entire chapter or article and marked certain parts of the reading as "optional." The CFA examination is based only on the required segments, and the optional segments are included only when it is determined that they might help you to better understand the required segments (by seeing the required material in its full context). When an optional segment begins, you will see an icon and a dashed vertical bar in the outside margin that will continue until the optional segment ends, accompanied by another icon. *Unless the material is specifically marked as optional, you should assume it is required.* You should rely on the required segments and the reading-specific LOS in preparing for the examination.

END OPTIONAL SEGMENT

End-of-Reading Problems/Solutions   *All problems in the readings as well as their solutions (which are provided directly following the problems) are part of the curriculum and are required material for the exam.* When appropriate, we have included problems within and after the readings to demonstrate practical application and reinforce your understanding of the concepts presented. The problems are designed to help you learn these concepts and may serve as a basis for exam questions. Many of these questions are adapted from past CFA examinations.

Glossary and Index   For your convenience, we have printed a comprehensive glossary in each volume. Throughout the curriculum, a **bolded** word in a reading denotes a term defined in the glossary. The curriculum eBook is searchable, but we also publish an index that can be found on the CFA Institute website with the Level II study sessions.

Source Material   The authorship, publisher, and copyright owners are given for each reading for your reference. We recommend that you use the CFA Institute curriculum rather than the original source materials because the curriculum may include only selected pages from outside readings, updated sections within the readings, and problems and solutions tailored to the CFA Program. Note that some readings may contain a web address or URL. The referenced sites were live at the time the reading was written but may have been deactivated since then.

LOS Self-Check   We have inserted checkboxes next to each LOS that you can use to track your progress in mastering the concepts in each reading.

DESIGNING YOUR PERSONAL STUDY PROGRAM

Create a Schedule   An orderly, systematic approach to exam preparation is critical. You should dedicate a consistent block of time every week to reading and studying. Complete all reading assignments and the associated problems and solutions in each study session. Review the LOS both before and after you study each reading to ensure that you have mastered the applicable content and can demonstrate the knowledge, skill, or ability described by the LOS and the assigned reading. Use the LOS self-check to track your progress and highlight areas of weakness for later review.

As you prepare for your exam, we will e-mail you important exam updates, testing policies, and study tips. Be sure to read these carefully. Curriculum errata are periodically updated and posted on the study session page at www.cfainstitute.org.

Successful candidates report an average of more than 300 hours preparing for each exam. Your preparation time will vary based on your prior education and experience. The 2017 Level II curriculum has 17 study sessions, so a good plan is to devote 15–20 hours per week for 17 weeks to studying the material. Use the final four to six weeks before the exam to review what you have learned and practice with topic tests and mock exams. This recommendation, however, may underestimate the hours needed for appropriate examination preparation depending on your individual circumstances, relevant experience, and academic background. You will undoubtedly adjust your study time to conform to your own strengths and weaknesses and to your educational and professional background.

You will probably spend more time on some study sessions than on others, but on average you should plan on devoting 15–20 hours per study session. You should allow ample time for both in-depth study of all topic areas and additional concentration on those topic areas for which you feel the least prepared.

An interactive study planner is available in the candidate resources area of our website to help you plan your study time. The interactive study planner recommends completion dates for each topic of the curriculum. Dates are determined based on study time available, exam topic weights, and curriculum weights. As you progress through the curriculum, the interactive study planner dynamically adjusts your study plan when you are running off schedule to help you stay on track for completion prior to the examination.

CFA Institute Topic Tests   The CFA Institute topic tests are intended to assess your mastery of individual topic areas as you progress through your studies. After each test, you will receive immediate feedback noting the correct responses and indicating the relevant assigned reading so you can identify areas of weakness for further study. For more information on the topic tests, please visit www.cfainstitute.org.

CFA Institute Mock Exams   The three-hour mock exams simulate the morning and afternoon sessions of the actual CFA examination, and are intended to be taken after you complete your study of the full curriculum so you can test your understanding of the curriculum and your readiness for the exam. You will receive feedback at the end of the mock exam, noting the correct responses and indicating the relevant assigned readings so you can assess areas of weakness for further study during your review period. We recommend that you take mock exams during the final stages of your preparation for the actual CFA examination. For more information on the mock examinations, please visit www.cfainstitute.org.

Preparatory Providers   After you enroll in the CFA Program, you may receive numerous solicitations for preparatory courses and review materials. When considering a prep course, make sure the provider is in compliance with the CFA Institute Prep Provider Guidelines Program (www.cfainstitute.org/utility/examprep/Pages/index.aspx). Just remember, there are no shortcuts to success on the CFA examinations; reading and studying the CFA curriculum is the key to success on the examination. The CFA examinations reference only the CFA Institute assigned curriculum—no preparatory course or review course materials are consulted or referenced.

SUMMARY

Every question on the CFA examination is based on the content contained in the required readings and on one or more LOS. Frequently, an examination question is based on a specific example highlighted within a reading or on a specific end-of-reading question and/or problem and its solution. To make effective use of the CFA Program curriculum, please remember these key points:

1   All pages of the curriculum are required reading for the examination except for occasional sections marked as optional. You may read optional pages as background, but you will not be tested on them.

2   All questions, problems, and their solutions—found at the end of readings—are part of the curriculum and are required study material for the examination.

3   You should make appropriate use of the topic tests and mock examinations and other resources available at www.cfainstitute.org.

4 Use the interactive study planner to create a schedule and commit sufficient study time to cover the 17 study sessions, review the materials, and take topic tests and mock examinations.

5 Some of the concepts in the study sessions may be superseded by updated rulings and/or pronouncements issued after a reading was published. Candidates are expected to be familiar with the overall analytical framework contained in the assigned readings. Candidates are not responsible for changes that occur after the material was written.

FEEDBACK

At CFA Institute, we are committed to delivering a comprehensive and rigorous curriculum for the development of competent, ethically grounded investment professionals. We rely on candidate and member feedback as we work to incorporate content, design, and packaging improvements. You can be assured that we will continue to listen to your suggestions. Please send any comments or feedback to info@cfainstitute.org. Ongoing improvements in the curriculum will help you prepare for success on the upcoming examinations and for a lifetime of learning as a serious investment professional.

Fixed Income

STUDY SESSIONS

Study Session 12   Valuation Concepts

Study Session 13   Topics in Fixed Income Analysis

TOPIC LEVEL LEARNING OUTCOME

The candidate should be able to estimate the risks and expected returns for fixed income instruments, analyze the term structure of interest rates and yield spreads, and evaluate fixed income instruments with embedded options and unique features.

12

Fixed Income

Valuation Concepts

This study session covers essential knowledge and skills needed for the valuation of fixed-income investments. The first reading discusses the term structure of interest rates and interest rate dynamics. The second reading addresses arbitrage-free valuation of fixed-income securities.

READING ASSIGNMENTS

Reading 35	The Term Structure and Interest Rate Dynamics by Thomas S.Y. Ho, PhD, Sang Bin Lee, PhD, and Stephen E. Wilcox, PhD, CFA
Reading 36	The Arbitrage-Free Valuation Framework by Steven V. Mann, PhD

The Term Structure and Interest Rate Dynamics

by Thomas S.Y. Ho, PhD, Sang Bin Lee, PhD, and
Stephen E. Wilcox, PhD, CFA

Thomas S.Y. Ho, PhD, is at Thomas Ho Company Ltd (USA). Sang Bin Lee, PhD, is at Hanyang University (South Korea). Stephen E. Wilcox, PhD, CFA, is at Minnesota State University, Mankato (USA).

LEARNING OUTCOMES

Mastery	The candidate should be able to:
☐	a. describe relationships among spot rates, forward rates, yield to maturity, expected and realized returns on bonds, and the shape of the yield curve;
☐	b. describe the forward pricing and forward rate models and calculate forward and spot prices and rates using those models;
☐	c. describe how zero-coupon rates (spot rates) may be obtained from the par curve by bootstrapping;
☐	d. describe the assumptions concerning the evolution of spot rates in relation to forward rates implicit in active bond portfolio management;
☐	e. describe the strategy of riding the yield curve;
☐	f. explain the swap rate curve and why and how market participants use it in valuation;
☐	g. calculate and interpret the swap spread for a given maturity;
☐	h. describe the Z-spread;
☐	i. describe the TED and Libor–OIS spreads;
☐	j. explain traditional theories of the term structure of interest rates and describe the implications of each theory for forward rates and the shape of the yield curve;
☐	k. describe modern term structure models and how they are used;
☐	l. explain how a bond's exposure to each of the factors driving the yield curve can be measured and how these exposures can be used to manage yield curve risks;
☐	m. explain the maturity structure of yield volatilities and their effect on price volatility.

1 INTRODUCTION

Interest rates are both a barometer of the economy and an instrument for its control. The term structure of interest rates—market interest rates at various maturities—is a vital input into the valuation of many financial products. The goal of this reading is to explain the term structure and interest rate dynamics—that is, the process by which the yields and prices of bonds evolve over time.

A spot interest rate (in this reading, "spot rate") is a rate of interest on a security that makes a single payment at a future point in time. The forward rate is the rate of interest set today for a single-payment security to be issued at a future date. Section 2 explains the relationship between these two types of interest rates and why forward rates matter to active bond portfolio managers. Section 2 also briefly covers other important return concepts.

The swap rate curve is the name given to the swap market's equivalent of the yield curve. Section 3 describes in more detail the swap rate curve and a related concept, the swap spread, and describes their use in valuation.

Sections 4 and 5 describe traditional and modern theories of the term structure of interest rates, respectively. Traditional theories present various largely qualitative perspectives on economic forces that may affect the shape of the term structure. Modern theories model the term structure with greater rigor.

Section 6 describes yield curve factor models. The focus is a popular three-factor term structure model in which the yield curve changes are described in terms of three independent movements: level, steepness, and curvature. These factors can be extracted from the variance–covariance matrix of historical interest rate movements.

A summary of key points concludes the reading.

2 SPOT RATES AND FORWARD RATES

In this section, we will first explain the relationships among spot rates, forward rates, yield to maturity, expected and realized returns on bonds, and the shape of the yield curve. We will then discuss the assumptions made about forward rates in active bond portfolio management.

At any point in time, the price of a risk-free single-unit payment (e.g., $1, €1, or £1) at time T is called the **discount factor** with maturity T, denoted by $P(T)$. The yield to maturity of the payment is called a **spot rate**, denoted by $r(T)$. That is,

$$P(T) = \frac{1}{\left[1 + r(T)\right]^T} \tag{1}$$

The discount factor, $P(T)$, and the spot rate, $r(T)$, for a range of maturities in years $T > 0$ are called the **discount function** and the **spot yield curve** (or, more simply, **spot curve**), respectively. The spot curve represents the term structure of interest rates at any point in time. Note that the discount function completely identifies the spot curve and vice versa. The discount function and the spot curve contain the same set of information about the time value of money.

The spot curve shows, for various maturities, the annualized return on an option-free and default-risk-free **zero-coupon bond** (**zero** for short) with a single payment of principal at maturity. The spot rate as a yield concept avoids the complications associated with the need for a reinvestment rate assumption for coupon-paying securities. Because the spot curve depends on the market pricing of these option-free zero-coupon bonds at any point in time, the shape and level of the spot yield curve are dynamic—that is, continually changing over time.

As Equation 1 suggests, the default-risk-free spot curve is a benchmark for the time value of money received at any future point in time as determined by the market supply and demand for funds. It is viewed as the most basic term structure of interest rates because there is no reinvestment risk involved; the stated yield equals the actual realized return if the zero is held to maturity. Thus, the yield on a zero-coupon bond maturing in year T is regarded as the most accurate representation of the T-year interest rate.

A **forward rate** is an interest rate that is determined today for a loan that will be initiated in a future time period. The term structure of forward rates for a loan made on a specific initiation date is called the **forward curve**. Forward rates and forward curves can be mathematically derived from the current spot curve.

Denote the forward rate of a loan initiated T^* years from today with tenor (further maturity) of T years by $f(T^*,T)$. Consider a forward contract in which one party to the contract, the buyer, commits to pay the other party to the contract, the seller, a forward contract price, denoted by $F(T^*,T)$, at time T^* years from today for a zero-coupon bond with maturity T years and unit principal. This is only an agreement to do something in the future at the time the contract is entered into; thus, no money is exchanged between the two parties at contract initiation. At T^*, the buyer will pay the seller the contracted forward price value and will receive from the seller at time $T^* + T$ the principal payment of the bond, defined here as a single currency unit.

The **forward pricing model** describes the valuation of forward contracts. The no-arbitrage argument that is used to derive the model is frequently used in modern financial theory; the model can be adopted to value interest rate futures contracts and related instruments, such as options on interest rate futures.

The no-arbitrage principle is quite simple. It says that tradable securities with identical cash flow payments must have the same price. Otherwise, traders would be able to generate risk-free arbitrage profits. Applying this argument to value a forward contract, we consider the discount factors—in particular, the values $P(T^*)$ and $P(T^* + T)$ needed to price a forward contract, $F(T^*,T)$. This forward contract price has to follow Equation 2, which is known as the forward pricing model.

$$P(T^* + T) = P(T^*)F(T^*,T) \qquad \text{(2)}$$

To understand the reasoning behind Equation 2, consider two alternative investments: (1) buying a zero-coupon bond that matures in $T^* + T$ years at a cost of $P(T^*+ T)$, and (2) entering into a forward contract valued at $F(T^*,T)$ to buy at T^* a zero-coupon bond with maturity T at a cost today of $P(T^*)F(T^*,T)$. The payoffs for the two investments at time $T^* + T$ are the same. For this reason, the initial costs of the investments have to be the same, and therefore, Equation 2 must hold. Otherwise, any trader could sell the overvalued investment and buy the undervalued investment with the proceeds to generate risk-free profits with zero net investment.

Working the problems in Example 1 should help confirm your understanding of discount factors and forward prices. Please note that the solutions in the examples that follow may be rounded to two or four decimal places.

EXAMPLE 1

Spot and Forward Prices and Rates (1)

Consider a two-year loan ($T = 2$) beginning in one year ($T^* = 1$). The one-year spot rate is $r(T^*) = r(1) = 7\% = 0.07$. The three-year spot rate is $r(T^* + T) = r(1 + 2) = r(3) = 9\% = 0.09$.

1   Calculate the one-year discount factor: $P(T^*) = P(1)$.

2   Calculate the three-year discount factor: $P(T^* + T) = P(1 + 2) = P(3)$.

3 Calculate the forward price of a two-year bond to be issued in one year: $F(T^*,T) = F(1,2)$.

4 Interpret your answer to Problem 3.

Solution to 1:

Using Equation 1,

$$P(1) = \frac{1}{(1+0.07)^1} = 0.9346$$

Solution to 2:

$$P(3) = \frac{1}{(1+0.09)^3} = 0.7722$$

Solution to 3:

Using Equation 2,

$$0.7722 = 0.9346 \times F(1,2).$$

$$F(1,2) = 0.7722 \div 0.9346 = 0.8262.$$

Solution to 4:

The forward contract price of $F(1,2) = 0.8262$ is the price, agreed on today, that would be paid one year from today for a bond with a two-year maturity and a risk-free unit-principal payment (e.g., \$1, €1, or £1) at maturity. As shown in the solution to 3, it is calculated as the three-year discount factor, $P(3) = 0.7722$, divided by the one-year discount factor, $P(1) = 0.9346$.

2.1 The Forward Rate Model

This section uses the forward rate model to establish that when the spot curve is upward sloping, the forward curve will lie above the spot curve, and that when the spot curve is downward sloping, the forward curve will lie below the spot curve.

The forward rate $f(T^*,T)$ is the discount rate for a risk-free unit-principal payment $T^* + T$ years from today, valued at time T^*, such that the present value equals the forward contract price, $F(T^*,T)$. Then, by definition,

$$F(T^*,T) = \frac{1}{\left[1 + f(T^*,T)\right]^T} \tag{3}$$

By substituting Equations 1 and 3 into Equation 2, the forward pricing model can be expressed in terms of rates as noted by Equation 4, which is the **forward rate model**:

$$\left[1 + r(T^* + T)\right]^{(T^*+T)} = \left[1 + r(T^*)\right]^{T^*}\left[1 + f(T^*,T)\right]^T \tag{4}$$

Thus, the spot rate for $T^* + T$, which is $r(T^* + T)$, and the spot rate for T^*, which is $r(T^*)$, imply a value for the T-year forward rate at T^*, $f(T^*,T)$. Equation 4 is important because it shows how forward rates can be extrapolated from spot rates; that is, they are implicit in the spot rates at any given point in time.[1]

---

1 An approximation formula that is based on taking logs of both sides of Equation 4 and using the approximation $\ln(1 + x) \approx x$ for small x is $f(T^*,T) \approx [(T^* + T)r(T^* + T) - T^*r(T^*)]/T$. For example, $f(1,2)$ in Example 2 could be approximated as $(3 \times 11\% - 1 \times 9\%)/2 = 12\%$, which is svery close to 12.01%.

Equation 4 suggests two interpretations or ways to look at forward rates. For example, suppose $f(7,1)$, the rate agreed on today for a one-year loan to be made seven years from today, is 3%. Then 3% is the

- reinvestment rate that would make an investor indifferent between buying an eight-year zero-coupon bond or investing in a seven-year zero-coupon bond and at maturity reinvesting the proceeds for one year. In this sense, the forward rate can be viewed as a type of breakeven interest rate.

- one-year rate that can be locked in today by buying an eight-year zero-coupon bond rather than investing in a seven-year zero-coupon bond and, when it matures, reinvesting the proceeds in a zero-coupon instrument that matures in one year. In this sense, the forward rate can be viewed as a rate that can be locked in by extending maturity by one year.

Example 2 addresses forward rates and the relationship between spot and forward rates.

EXAMPLE 2

Spot and Forward Prices and Rates (2)

The spot rates for three hypothetical zero-coupon bonds (zeros) with maturities of one, two, and three years are given in the following table.

Maturity (T)	1	2	3
Spot rates	$r(1) = 9\%$	$r(2) = 10\%$	$r(3) = 11\%$

1 Calculate the forward rate for a one-year zero issued one year from today, $f(1,1)$.

2 Calculate the forward rate for a one-year zero issued two years from today, $f(2,1)$.

3 Calculate the forward rate for a two-year zero issued one year from today, $f(1,2)$.

4 Based on your answers to 1 and 2, describe the relationship between the spot rates and the implied one-year forward rates.

Solution to 1:

$f(1,1)$ is calculated as follows (using Equation 4):

$$\left[1 + r(2)\right]^2 = \left[1 + r(1)\right]^1 \left[1 + f(1,1)\right]^1$$

$$(1 + 0.10)^2 = (1 + 0.09)^1 \left[1 + f(1,1)\right]^1$$

$$f(1,1) = \frac{(1.10)^2}{1.09} - 1 = 11.01\%$$

Solution to 2:

$f(2,1)$ is calculated as follows:

$$\left[1 + r(3)\right]^3 = \left[1 + r(2)\right]^2 \left[1 + f(2,1)\right]^1$$

$$(1 + 0.11)^3 = (1 + 0.10)^2 \left[1 + f(2,1)\right]^1$$

$$f(2,1) = \frac{(1.11)^3}{(1.10)^2} - 1 = 13.03\%$$

Solution to 3:

$f(1,2)$ is calculated as follows:

$$[1 + r(3)]^3 = [1 + r(1)]^1[1 + f(1,2)]^2$$

$$(1 + 0.11)^3 = (1 + 0.09)^1[1 + f(1,2)]^2$$

$$f(1,2) = \sqrt[2]{\frac{(1.11)^3}{1.09}} - 1 = 12.01\%$$

Solution to 4:

The upward-sloping zero-coupon yield curve is associated with an upward-sloping forward curve (a series of increasing one-year forward rates because 13.03% is greater than 11.01%). This point is explained further in the following paragraphs.

The analysis of the relationship between spot rates and one-period forward rates can be established by using the forward rate model and successive substitution, resulting in Equations 5a and 5b:

$$[1 + r(T)]^T = [1 + r(1)][1 + f(1,1)][1 + f(2,1)][1 + f(3,1)]\ldots$$
$$[1 + f(T-1,1)] \tag{5a}$$

$$r(T) = $$
$$\{[1 + r(1)][1 + f(1,1)][1 + f(2,1)][1 + f(3,1)]\ldots[1 + f(T-1,1)]\}^{(1/T)} - 1 \tag{5b}$$

Equation 5b shows that the spot rate for a security with a maturity of $T > 1$ can be expressed as a geometric mean of the spot rate for a security with a maturity of $T = 1$ and a series of $T - 1$ forward rates.

Whether the relationship in Equation 5b holds in practice is an important consideration for active portfolio management. If an active trader can identify a series of short-term bonds whose actual returns will exceed today's quoted forward rates, then the total return over his or her investment horizon would exceed the return on a maturity-matching, buy-and-hold strategy. Later, we will use this same concept to discuss dynamic hedging strategies and the local expectations theory.

Examples 3 and 4 explore the relationship between spot and forward rates.

EXAMPLE 3

Spot and Forward Prices and Rates (3)

Given the data and conclusions for $r(1)$, $f(1,1)$, and $f(2,1)$ from Example 2:

$r(1) = 9\%$

$f(1,1) = 11.01\%$

$f(2,1) = 13.03\%$

Show that the two-year spot rate of $r(2) = 10\%$ and the three-year spot rate of $r(3) = 11\%$ are geometric averages of the one-year spot rate and the forward rates.

Solution:

Using Equation 5a,

$$\left[1 + r(2)\right]^2 = \left[1 + r(1)\right]\left[1 + f(1,1)\right]$$

$$r(2) = \sqrt[2]{(1 + 0.09)(1 + 0.1101)} - 1 \approx 10\%$$

$$\left[1 + r(3)\right]^3 = \left[1 + r(1)\right]\left[1 + f(1,1)\right]\left[1 + f(2,1)\right]$$

$$r(3) = \sqrt[3]{(1 + 0.09)(1 + 0.1101)(1 + 0.1303)} - 1 \approx 11\%$$

We can now consolidate our knowledge of spot and forward rates to explain important relationships between the spot and forward rate curves. The forward rate model (Equation 4) can also be expressed as Equation 6.

$$\left\{ \frac{\left[1 + r(T^* + T)\right]}{\left[1 + r(T^*)\right]} \right\}^{\frac{T^*}{T}} \left[1 + r(T^* + T)\right] = \left[1 + f(T^*,T)\right] \tag{6}$$

To illustrate, suppose $T^* = 1$, $T = 4$, $r(1) = 2\%$, and $r(5) = 3\%$; the left-hand side of Equation 6 is

$$\left(\frac{1.03}{1.02}\right)^{\frac{1}{4}} (1.03) = (1.0024)(1.03) = 1.0325$$

so $f(1,4) = 3.25\%$. Given that the yield curve is upward sloping—so, $r(T^* + T) > r(T^*)$—Equation 6 implies that the forward rate from T^* to T is greater than the long-term $(T^* + T)$ spot rate: $f(T^*,T) > r(T^* + T)$. In the example given, 3.25% > 3%. Conversely, when the yield curve is downward sloping, then $r(T^* + T) < r(T^*)$ and the forward rate from T^* to T is lower than the long-term spot rate: $f(T^*,T) < r(T^* + T)$. Equation 6 also shows that if the spot curve is flat, all one-period forward rates are equal to the spot rate. For an upward-sloping yield curve—$r(T^* + T) > r(T^*)$—the forward rate rises as T^* increases. For a downward-sloping yield curve—$r(T^* + T) < r(T^*)$—the forward rate declines as T^* increases.

EXAMPLE 4

Spot and Forward Prices and Rates (4)

Given the spot rates $r(1) = 9\%$, $r(2) = 10\%$, and $r(3) = 11\%$, as in Examples 2 and 3:

1   Determine whether the forward rate $f(1,2)$ is greater than or less than the long-term rate, $r(3)$.

2   Determine whether forward rates rise or fall as the initiation date, T^*, for the forward rate is increased.

Solution to 1:

The spot rates imply an upward-sloping yield curve, $r(3) > r(2) > r(1)$, or in general, $r(T^* + T) > r(T^*)$. Thus, the forward rate will be greater than the long-term rate, or $f(T^*,T) > r(T^* + T)$. Note from Example 2 that $f(1,2) = 12.01\% > r(1 + 2) = r(3) = 11\%$.

Solution to 2:

The spot rates imply an upward-sloping yield curve, $r(3) > r(2) > r(1)$. Thus, the forward rates will rise with increasing T^*. This relationship was shown in Example 2, in which $f(1,1) = 11.01\%$ and $f(2,1) = 13.03\%$.

These relationships are illustrated in Exhibit 1, using actual data. The spot rates for US Treasuries as of 31 July 2013 are represented by the lowest curve in the exhibit, which was constructed using interpolation between the data points, shown in the table following the exhibit. Note that the spot curve is upward sloping. The spot curve and the forward curves for the end of July 2014, July 2015, July 2016, and July 2017 are also presented in Exhibit 1. Because the yield curve is upward sloping, the forward curves lie above the spot curve and increasing the initiation date results in progressively higher forward curves. The highest forward curve is that for July 2017. Note that the forward curves in Exhibit 1 are progressively flatter at later start dates because the spot curve flattens at the longer maturities.

Exhibit 1	Spot Curve vs. Forward Curves, 31 July 2013

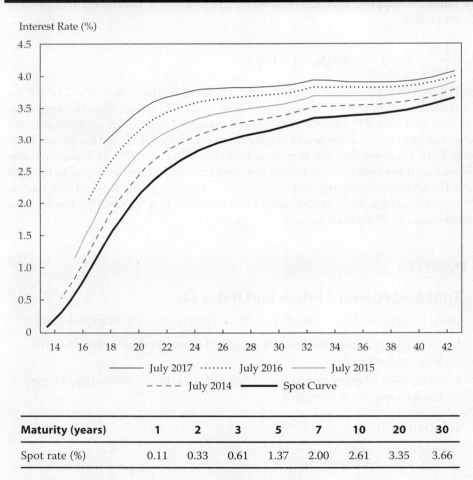

Maturity (years)	1	2	3	5	7	10	20	30
Spot rate (%)	0.11	0.33	0.61	1.37	2.00	2.61	3.35	3.66

When the spot yield curve is downward sloping, the forward yield curve will be below the spot yield curve. Spot rates for US Treasuries as of 31 December 2006 are presented in the table following Exhibit 2. We used linear interpolation to construct the spot curve based on these data points. The yield curve data were also somewhat modified to make the yield curve more downward sloping for illustrative purposes. The spot curve and the forward curves for the end of December 2007, 2008, 2009, and 2010 are presented in Exhibit 2.

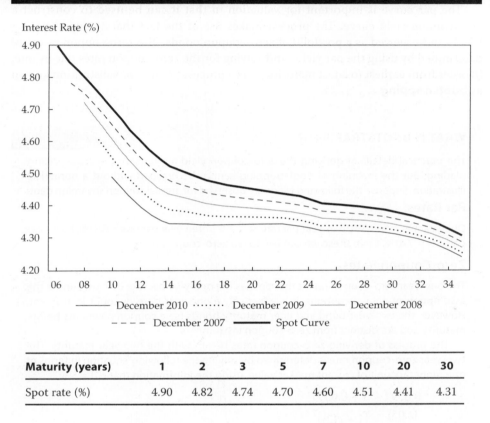

| Exhibit 2 | Spot Curve vs. Forward Curves, 31 December 2006 (Modified for Illustrative Purposes) |

Maturity (years)	1	2	3	5	7	10	20	30
Spot rate (%)	4.90	4.82	4.74	4.70	4.60	4.51	4.41	4.31

The highest curve is the spot yield curve, and it is downward sloping. The results show that the forward curves are lower than the spot curve. Postponing the initiation date results in progressively lower forward curves. The lowest forward curve is that dated December 2010.

An important point that can be inferred from Exhibit 1 and Exhibit 2 is that forward rates do not extend any further than the furthest maturity on today's yield curve. For example, if yields extend to 30 years on today's yield curve, then three years hence, the most we can model prospectively is a bond with 27 years to final maturity. Similarly, four years hence, the longest maturity forward rate would be $f(4,26)$.

In summary, when the spot curve is upward sloping, the forward curve will lie above the spot curve. Conversely, when the spot curve is downward sloping, the forward curve will lie below the spot curve. This relationship is a reflection of the basic mathematical truth that when the average is rising (falling), the marginal data point must be above (below) the average. In this case, the spot curve represents an average over a whole time period and the forward rates represent the marginal changes between future time periods.[2]

We have thus far discussed the spot curve and the forward curve. Another curve important in practice is the government par curve. The **par curve** represents the yields to maturity on coupon-paying government bonds, priced at par, over a range of maturities. In practice, recently issued ("on the run") bonds are typically used to create the par curve because new issues are typically priced at or close to par.

The par curve is important for valuation in that it can be used to construct a zero-coupon yield curve. The process makes use of the fact that a coupon-paying bond can be viewed as a portfolio of zero-coupon bonds. The zero-coupon rates are determined by using the par yields and solving for the zero-coupon rates one by one, in order from earliest to latest maturities, via a process of forward substitution known as **bootstrapping**.

WHAT IS BOOTSTRAPPING?

The practical details of deriving the zero-coupon yield are outside the scope of this reading. But the meaning of bootstrapping cannot be grasped without a numerical illustration. Suppose the following yields are observed for annual coupon sovereign debt:

Par Rates:

One-year par rate = 5%, Two-year par rate = 5.97%, Three-year par rate = 6.91%, Four-year par rate = 7.81%. From these we can bootstrap zero-coupon rates.

Zero-Coupon Rates:

The one-year zero-coupon rate is the same as the one-year par rate because, under the assumption of annual coupons, it is effectively a one-year pure discount instrument. However, the two-year bond and later-maturity bonds have coupon payments before maturity and are distinct from zero-coupon instruments.

The process of deriving zero-coupon rates begins with the two-year maturity. The two-year zero-coupon rate is determined by solving the following equation in terms of one monetary unit of current market value, using the information that $r(1) = 5\%$:

$$1 = \frac{0.0597}{(1.05)} + \frac{1 + 0.0597}{\left[1 + r(2)\right]^2}$$

In the equation, 0.0597 and 1.0597 represent payments from interest and principal and interest, respectively, per one unit of principal value. The equation implies that $r(2) = 6\%$. We have bootstrapped the two-year spot rate. Continuing with forward substitution, the three-year zero-coupon rate can be bootstrapped by solving the following equation, using the known values of the one-year and two-year spot rates of 5% and 6%:

$$1 = \frac{0.0691}{(1.05)} + \frac{0.0691}{(1.06)^2} + \frac{1 + 0.0691}{\left[1 + r(3)\right]^3}$$

Thus, $r(3) = 7\%$. Finally the four-year zero-coupon rate is determined to be 8% by using

$$1 = \frac{0.0781}{(1.05)} + \frac{0.0781}{(1.06)^2} + \frac{0.0781}{(1.07)^3} + \frac{1 + 0.0781}{\left[1 + r(4)\right]^4}$$

In summary, $r(1) = 5\%$, $r(2) = 6\%$, $r(3) = 7\%$, and $r(4) = 8\%$.

---

2 Extending this discussion, one can also conclude that when a spot curve curve rises and then falls, the forward curves will also rise and then fall.

In the preceding discussion, we considered an upward-sloping (spot) yield curve (Exhibit 1) and an inverted or downward-sloping (spot) yield curve (Exhibit 2). In developed markets, yield curves are most commonly upward sloping with diminishing marginal increases in yield for identical changes in maturity; that is, the yield curve "flattens" at longer maturities. Because nominal yields incorporate a premium for expected inflation, an upward-sloping yield curve is generally interpreted as reflecting a market expectation of increasing or at least level future inflation (associated with relatively strong economic growth). The existence of risk premiums (e.g., for the greater interest rate risk of longer-maturity bonds) also contributes to a positive slope.

An inverted yield curve (Exhibit 2) is somewhat uncommon. Such a term structure may reflect a market expectation of declining future inflation rates (because a nominal yield incorporates a premium for expected inflation) from a relatively high current level. Expectations of declining economic activity may be one reason that inflation might be anticipated to decline, and a downward-sloping yield curve has frequently been observed before recessions.[3] A flat yield curve typically occurs briefly in the transition from an upward-sloping to a downward-sloping yield curve, or vice versa. A humped yield curve, which is relatively rare, occurs when intermediate-term interest rates are higher than short- and long-term rates.

2.2 Yield to Maturity in Relation to Spot Rates and Expected and Realized Returns on Bonds

Yield to maturity (YTM) is perhaps the most familiar pricing concept in bond markets. In this section, our goal is to clarify how it is related to spot rates and a bond's expected and realized returns.

How is the yield to maturity related to spot rates? In bond markets, most bonds outstanding have coupon payments and many have various options, such as a call provision. The YTM of these bonds with maturity T would not be the same as the spot rate at T. But, the YTM should be mathematically related to the spot curve. Because the principle of no arbitrage shows that a bond's value is the sum of the present values of payments discounted by their corresponding spot rates, the YTM of the bond should be some weighted average of spot rates used in the valuation of the bond.

Example 5 addresses the relationship between spot rates and yield to maturity.

EXAMPLE 5

Spot Rate and Yield to Maturity

Recall from earlier examples the spot rates $r(1) = 9\%$, $r(2) = 10\%$, and $r(3) = 11\%$. Let $y(T)$ be the yield to maturity.

1   Calculate the price of a two-year annual coupon bond using the spot rates. Assume the coupon rate is 6% and the face value is $1,000. Next, state the formula for determining the price of the bond in terms of its yield to maturity. Is $r(2)$ greater than or less than $y(2)$? Why?

2   Calculate the price of a three-year annual coupon-paying bond using the spot rates. Assume the coupon rate is 5% and the face value is £100. Next, write a formula for determining the price of the bond using the yield to maturity. Is $r(3)$ greater or less than $y(3)$? Why?

---

3 The US Treasury yield curve inverted in August 2006, more than a year before the recession that began in December 2007. See Haubrich (2006).

Solution to 1:

Using the spot rates,

$$Price = \frac{\$60}{(1 + 0.09)^1} + \frac{\$1{,}060}{(1 + 0.10)^2} = \$931.08$$

Using the yield to maturity,

$$Price = \frac{\$60}{\left[1 + y(2)\right]^1} + \frac{\$1{,}060}{\left[1 + y(2)\right]^2} = \$931.08$$

Note that $y(2)$ is used to discount both the first- and second-year cash flows. Because the bond can have only one price, it follows that $r(1) < y(2) < r(2)$ because $y(2)$ is a weighted average of $r(1)$ and $r(2)$ and the yield curve is upward sloping. Using a calculator, one can calculate the yield to maturity $y(2) = 9.97\%$, which is less than $r(2) = 10\%$ and greater than $r(1) = 9\%$, just as we would expect. Note that $y(2)$ is much closer to $r(2)$ than to $r(1)$ because the bond's largest cash flow occurs in Year 2, thereby giving $r(2)$ a greater weight than $r(1)$ in the determination of $y(2)$.

Solution to 2:

Using the spot rates,

$$Price = \frac{£5}{(1 + 0.09)^1} + \frac{£5}{(1 + 0.10)^2} + \frac{£105}{(1 + 0.11)^3} = £85.49$$

Using the yield to maturity,

$$Price = \frac{£5}{\left[1 + y(3)\right]^1} + \frac{£5}{\left[1 + y(3)\right]^2} + \frac{£105}{\left[1 + y(3)\right]^3} = £85.49$$

Note that $y(3)$ is used to discount all three cash flows. Because the bond can have only one price, $y(3)$ must be a weighted average of $r(1)$, $r(2)$, and $r(3)$. Given that the yield curve is upward sloping in this example, $y(3) < r(3)$. Using a calculator to compute yield to maturity, $y(3) = 10.93\%$, which is less than $r(3) = 11\%$ and greater than $r(1) = 9\%$, just as we would expect because the weighted yield to maturity must lie between the highest and lowest spot rates. Note that $y(3)$ is much closer to $r(3)$ than it is to $r(2)$ or $r(1)$ because the bond's largest cash flow occurs in Year 3, thereby giving $r(3)$ a greater weight than $r(2)$ and $r(1)$ in the determination of $y(3)$.

Is the yield to maturity the expected return on a bond? In general, it is not, except under extremely restrictive assumptions. The expected rate of return is the return one anticipates earning on an investment. The YTM is the expected rate of return for a bond that is held until its maturity, assuming that all coupon and principal payments are made in full when due and that coupons are reinvested at the original YTM. However, the assumption regarding reinvestment of coupons at the original yield to maturity typically does not hold. The YTM can provide a poor estimate of expected return if (1) interest rates are volatile; (2) the yield curve is steeply sloped, either upward or downward; (3) there is significant risk of default; or (4) the bond has one or more embedded options (e.g., put, call, or conversion). If either (1) or (2) is the case, reinvestment of coupons would not be expected to be at the assumed rate (YTM). Case (3) implies that actual cash flows may differ from those assumed in the YTM calculation, and in case (4), the exercise of an embedded option would, in general, result in a holding period that is shorter than the bond's original maturity.

The realized return is the actual return on the bond during the time an investor holds the bond. It is based on actual reinvestment rates and the yield curve at the end of the holding period. With perfect foresight, the expected bond return would equal the realized bond return.

To illustrate these concepts, assume that $r(1) = 5\%$, $r(2) = 6\%$, $r(3) = 7\%$, $r(4) = 8\%$, and $r(5) = 9\%$. Consider a five-year annual coupon bond with a coupon rate of 10%. The forward rates extrapolated from the spot rates are $f(1,1) = 7.0\%$, $f(2,1) = 9.0\%$, $f(3,1) = 11.1\%$, and $f(4,1) = 13.1\%$. The price, determined as a percentage of par, is 105.43.

The yield to maturity of 8.62% can be determined using a calculator or by solving

$$105.43 = \frac{10}{\left[1 + y(5)\right]} + \frac{10}{\left[1 + y(5)\right]^2} + \cdots + \frac{110}{\left[1 + y(5)\right]^5}$$

The yield to maturity of 8.62% is the bond's expected return assuming no default, a holding period of five years, and a reinvestment rate of 8.62%. But what if the forward rates are assumed to be the future spot rates?

Using the forward rates as the expected reinvestment rates results in the following expected cash flow at the end of Year 5:

$10(1 + 0.07)(1 + 0.09)(1 + 0.111)(1 + 0.131) + 10(1 + 0.09)(1 + 0.011)(1 + 0.131)$
$+ 10(1 + 0.111)(1 + 0.131) + 10(1 + 0.131) + 110 \approx 162.2.2$

Therefore, the expected bond return is $(162.22 - 105.43)/105.43 = 53.87\%$ and the expected annualized rate of return is 9.00% [solve $(1 + x)^5 = 1 + 0.5387$].

From this example, we can see that the expected rate of return is not equal to the YTM even if we make the generally unrealistic assumption that the forward rates are the future spot rates. Implicit in the determination of the yield to maturity as a potentially realistic estimate of expected return is a flat yield curve; note that in the formula just used, every cash flow was discounted at 8.62% regardless of its maturity.

Example 6 will reinforce your understanding of various yield and return concepts.

EXAMPLE 6

Yield and Return Concepts

1 When the spot curve is upward sloping, the forward curve:
   A lies above the spot curve.
   B lies below the spot curve.
   C is coincident with the spot curve.

2 Which of the following statements concerning the yield to maturity of a default-risk-free bond is *most* accurate? The yield to maturity of such a bond:
   A equals the expected return on the bond if the bond is held to maturity.
   B can be viewed as a weighted average of the spot rates applying to its cash flows.
   C will be closer to the realized return if the spot curve is upward sloping rather than flat through the life of the bond.

3 When the spot curve is downward sloping, an increase in the initiation date results in a forward curve that is:
   A closer to the spot curve.
   B a greater distance above the spot curve.
   C a greater distance below the spot curve.

Solution to 1:

A is correct. Points on a spot curve can be viewed as an average of single-period rates over given maturities whereas forward rates reflect the marginal changes between future time periods.

Solution to 2:

B is correct. The YTM is the discount rate that, when applied to a bond's promised cash flows, equates those cash flows to the bond's market price and the fact that the market price should reflect discounting promised cash flows at appropriate spot rates.

Solution to 3:

C is correct. This answer follows from the forward rate model as expressed in Equation 6. If the spot curve is downward sloping (upward sloping), increasing the initiation date (T^*) will result in a forward curve that is a greater distance below (above) the spot curve. See Exhibit 1 and Exhibit 2.

2.3 Yield Curve Movement and the Forward Curve

This section establishes several important results concerning forward prices and the spot yield curve in anticipation of discussing the relevance of the forward curve to active bond investors.

The first observation is that the forward contract price remains unchanged as long as future spot rates evolve as predicted by today's forward curve. Therefore, a change in the forward price reflects a deviation of the spot curve from that predicted by today's forward curve. Thus, if a trader expects that the future spot rate will be lower than what is predicted by the prevailing forward rate, the forward contract value is expected to increase. To capitalize on this expectation, the trader would buy the forward contract. Conversely, if the trader expects the future spot rate to be higher than what is predicted by the existing forward rate, then the forward contract value is expected to decrease. In this case, the trader would sell the forward contract.

Using the forward pricing model defined by Equation 2, we can determine the forward contract price that delivers a T-year-maturity bond at time T^*, $F(T^*,T)$ using Equation 7 (which is Equation 2 solved for the forward price):

$$F(T^*,T) = \frac{P(T^* + T)}{P(T^*)} \qquad (7)$$

Now suppose that after time t, the new discount function is the same as the forward discount function implied by today's discount function, as shown by Equation 8.

$$P^*(T) = \frac{P(t + T)}{P(t)} \qquad (8)$$

Next, after a lapse of time t, the time to expiration of the contract is $T^* - t$, and the forward contract price at time t is $F^*(t,T^*,T)$. Equation 7 can be rewritten as Equation 9:

$$F^*(t,T^*,T) = \frac{P^*(T^* + T - t)}{P^*(T^* - t)} \qquad (9)$$

Substituting Equation 8 into Equation 9 and adjusting for the lapse of time t results in Equation 10:

$$F^*(t,T^*,T) = \frac{\dfrac{P(t + T^* + T - t)}{P(t)}}{\dfrac{P(t + T^* - t)}{P(t)}} = \frac{P(T^* + T)}{P(T^*)} = F(T^*,T) \qquad (10)$$

Equation 10 shows that the forward contract price remains unchanged as long as future spot rates are equal to what is predicted by today's forward curve. Therefore, a change in the forward price is the result of a deviation of the spot curve from what is predicted by today's forward curve.

To make these observations concrete, consider a flat yield curve for which the interest rate is 4%. Using Equation 1, the discount factors for the one-year, two-year, and three-year terms are, to four decimal places,

$$P(1) = \frac{1}{(1 + 0.04)^1} = 0.9615$$

$$P(2) = \frac{1}{(1 + 0.04)^2} = 0.9246$$

$$P(3) = \frac{1}{(1 + 0.04)^3} = 0.8890$$

Therefore, using Equation 7, the forward contract price that delivers a one-year bond at Year 2 is

$$F(2,1) = \frac{P(2 + 1)}{P(2)} = \frac{P(3)}{P(2)} = \frac{0.8890}{0.9246} = 0.9615$$

Suppose the future discount function at Year 1 is the same as the forward discount function implied by the Year 0 spot curve. The lapse of time is $t = 1$. Using Equation 8, the discount factors for the one-year and two-year terms one year from today are

$$P^*(1) = \frac{P(1 + 1)}{P(1)} = \frac{P(2)}{P(1)} = \frac{0.9246}{0.9615} = 0.9616$$

$$P^*(2) = \frac{P(1 + 2)}{P(1)} = \frac{P(3)}{P(1)} = \frac{0.8890}{0.9615} = 0.9246$$

Using Equation 9, the price of the forward contract one year from today is

$$F^*(1,2,1) = \frac{P^*(2 + 1 - 1)}{P^*(2 - 1)} = \frac{P^*(2)}{P^*(1)} = \frac{0.9246}{0.9616} = 0.9615$$

The price of the forward contract has not changed. This will be the case as long as future discount functions are the same as those based on today's forward curve.

From this numerical example, we can see that if the spot rate curve is unchanged, then each bond "rolls down" the curve and earns the forward rate. Specifically, when one year passes, a three-year bond will return (0.9246 – 0.8890)/0.8890 = 4%, which is equal to the spot rate. Furthermore, if another year passes, the bond will return (0.9615 – 0.9246)/0.9246 = 4%, which is equal to the implied forward rate for a one-year security one year from today.

2.4 Active Bond Portfolio Management

One way active bond portfolio managers attempt to outperform the bond market's return is by anticipating changes in interest rates relative to the projected evolution of spot rates reflected in today's forward curves.

Some insight into these issues is provided by the forward rate model (Equation 4). By re-arranging terms in Equation 4 and letting the time horizon be one period, $T^* = 1$, we get

$$\frac{\left[1 + r(T+1)\right]^{T+1}}{\left[1 + f(1,T)\right]^{T}} = \left[1 + r(1)\right]$$

(11)

The numerator of the left hand side of Equation 11 is for a bond with an initial maturity of $T + 1$ and a remaining maturity of T after one period passes. Suppose the prevailing spot yield curve after one period is the current forward curve; then, Equation 11 shows that the total return on the bond is the one-period risk-free rate. The following sidebar shows that the return of bonds of varying tenor over a one-year period is always the one-year rate (the risk-free rate over the one-year period) if the spot rates evolve as implied by the current forward curve at the end of the first year.

WHEN SPOT RATES EVOLVE AS IMPLIED BY THE CURRENT FORWARD CURVE

As in earlier examples, assume the following:

   $r(1) = 9\%$

   $r(2) = 10\%$

   $r(3) = 11\%$

   $f(1,1) = 11.01\%$

   $f(1,2) = 12.01\%$

If the spot curve one year from today reflects the current forward curve, the return on a zero-coupon bond for the one-year holding period is 9%, regardless of the maturity of the bond. The computations below assume a par amount of 100 and represent the percentage change in price. Given the rounding of price and the forward rates to the nearest hundredth, the returns all approximate 9%. However, with no rounding, all answers would be precisely 9%.

The return of the one-year zero-coupon bond over the one-year holding period is 9%. The bond is purchased at a price of 91.74 and is worth the par amount of 100 at maturity.

$$\left(100 \div \frac{100}{1 + r(1)}\right) - 1 = \left(100 \div \frac{100}{1 + 0.09}\right) - 1 = \frac{100}{91.74} - 1 = 9\%$$

The return of the two-year zero-coupon bond over the one-year holding period is 9%. The bond is purchased at a price of 82.64. One year from today, the two-year bond has a remaining maturity of one year. Its price one year from today is 90.08, determined as the par amount divided by 1 plus the forward rate for a one-year bond issued one year from today.

$$\left(\frac{100}{1 + f(1,1)} \div \frac{100}{\left[1 + r(2)\right]^2}\right) - 1 = \left(\frac{100}{1 + 0.1101} \div \frac{100}{\left(1 + 0.10\right)^2}\right) - 1$$

$$= \frac{90.08}{82.64} - 1 = 9\%$$

EXAMPLE 7

Active Bond Portfolio Management

1 The "riding the yield curve" strategy is executed by buying bonds whose maturities are:

  A equal to the investor's investment horizon.

  B longer than the investor's investment horizon.

  C shorter than the investor's investment horizon.

2 A bond will be overvalued if the expected spot rate is:

  A equal to the current forward rate.

  B lower than the current forward rate.

  C higher than the current forward rate.

3 Assume a flat yield curve of 6%. A three-year £100 bond is issued at par paying an annual coupon of 6%. What is the bond's expected return if a trader predicts that the yield curve one year from today will be a flat 7%?

  A 4.19%

  B 6.00%

  C 8.83%

4 A forward contract price will increase if:

  A future spot rates evolve as predicted by current forward rates.

  B future spot rates are lower than what is predicted by current forward rates.

  C future spot rates are higher than what is predicted by current forward rates.

Solution to 1:

B is correct. A bond with a longer maturity than the investor's investment horizon is purchased but then sold prior to maturity at the end of the investment horizon. If the yield curve is upward sloping and yields do not change, the bond will be valued at successively lower yields and higher prices over time. The bond's total return will exceed that of a bond whose maturity is equal to the investment horizon.

Solution to 2:

C is correct. If the expected discount rate is higher than the forward rate, then the bond will be overvalued. The expected price of the bond is lower than the price obtained from discounting using the forward rate.

Solution to 3:

A is correct. Expected return will be less than the current yield to maturity of 6% if yields increase to 7%. The expected return of 4.19% is computed as follows:

$$\frac{6 + \dfrac{6}{1 + 0.07} + \dfrac{106}{\left(1 + 0.07\right)^2}}{100} - 1 \approx 4.19\%$$

> **Solution to 4:**
>
> B is correct. The forward rate model can be used to show that a change in the forward contract price requires a deviation of the spot curve from that predicted by today's forward curve. If the future spot rate is lower than what is predicted by the prevailing forward rate, the forward contract price will increase because it is discounted at an interest rate that is lower than the originally anticipated rate.

3 THE SWAP RATE CURVE

Section 2 described the spot rate curve of default-risk-free bonds as a measure of the time value of money. The swap rate curve, or swap curve for short, is another important representation of the time value of money used in the international fixed-income markets. In this section, we will discuss how the swap curve is used in valuation.

3.1 The Swap Rate Curve

Interest rate swaps are an integral part of the fixed-income market. These derivative contracts, which typically exchange, or swap, fixed-rate interest payments for floating-rate interest payments, are an essential tool for investors who use them to speculate or modify risk. The size of the payments reflects the floating and fixed rates, the amount of principal—called the notional amount, or notional—and the maturity of the swap. The interest rate for the fixed-rate leg of an interest rate swap is known as the **swap rate**. The level of the swap rate is such that the swap has zero value at the initiation of the swap agreement. Floating rates are based on some short-term reference interest rate, such as three-month or six-month dollar Libor (London Interbank Offered Rate); other reference rates include euro-denominated Euribor (European Interbank Offered Rate) and yen-denominated Tibor (Tokyo Interbank Offered Rate). Note that the risk inherent in various floating reference rates varies according to the risk of the banks surveyed; for example, the spread between Tibor and yen Libor was positive as of October 2013, reflecting the greater risk of the banks surveyed for Tibor. The yield curve of swap rates is called the **swap rate curve**, or, more simply, the **swap curve**. Because it is based on so-called **par swaps**, in which the fixed rates are set so that no money is exchanged at contract initiation—the present values of the fixed-rate and benchmark floating-rate legs being equal— the swap curve is a type of par curve. When we refer to the "par curve' in this reading, the reference is to the government par yield curve, however.

The swap market is a highly liquid market for two reasons. First, unlike bonds, a swap does not have multiple borrowers or lenders, only counterparties who exchange cash flows. Such arrangements offer significant flexibility and customization in the swap contract's design. Second, swaps provide one of the most efficient ways to hedge interest rate risk. The Bank for International Settlements (BIS) estimated that the notional amount outstanding on interest rate swaps was about US$370 trillion in December 2012.[5]

---

5 Because the amount outstanding relates to notional values, it represents far less than $370 trillion of default exposure.

Many countries do not have a liquid government bond market with maturities longer than one year. The swap curve is a necessary market benchmark for interest rates in these countries. In countries in which the private sector is much bigger than the public sector, the swap curve is a far more relevant measure of the time value of money than is the government's cost of borrowing.

In Asia, the swap markets and the government bond markets have developed in parallel, and both are used in valuation in credit and loan markets. In Hong Kong and South Korea, the swap markets are active out to a maturity of 10 years, whereas the Japanese swap market is active out to a maturity of 30 years. The reason for the longer maturity in the Japanese government market is that the market has been in existence for much longer than those in Hong Kong and South Korea.

According to the *2013 CIA World Fact Book*, the size of the government bond market relative to GDP is 214.3% for Japan but only 33.7% and 46.9% for Hong Kong and South Korea, respectively. For the United States and Germany, the numbers are 73.6% and 81.7%, and the world average is 64%. Even though the interest rate swap market in Japan is very active, the US interest rate swap market is almost three times larger than the Japanese interest rate swap market, based on outstanding amounts.

3.2 Why Do Market Participants Use Swap Rates When Valuing Bonds?

Government spot curves and swap rate curves are the chief reference curves in fixed-income valuation. The choice between them can depend on multiple factors, including the relative liquidity of these two markets. In the United States, where there is both an active Treasury security market and a swap market, the choice of a benchmark for the time value of money often depends on the business operations of the institution using the benchmark. On the one hand, wholesale banks frequently use the swap curve to value assets and liabilities because these organizations hedge many items on their balance sheet with swaps. On the other hand, retail banks with little exposure to the swap market are more likely to use the government spot curve as their benchmark.

Let us illustrate how a financial institution uses the swap market for its internal operations. Consider the case of a bank raising funds using a certificate of deposit (CD). Assume the bank can borrow $10 million in the form of a CD that bears interest of 1.5% for a two-year term. Another $10 million CD offers 1.70% for a three-year term. The bank can arrange two swaps: (1) The bank receives 1.50% fixed and pays three-month Libor minus 10 bps with a two-year term and $10 million notional, and (2) the bank receives 1.70% fixed and pays three-month Libor minus 15 bps with a three-year term and a notional amount of $10 million. After issuing the two CDs and committing to the two swaps, the bank has raised $20 million with an annual funding cost for the first two years of three-month Libor minus 12.5 bps applied to the total notional amount of $20 million. The fixed interest payments received from the counterparty to the swap are paid to the CD investors; in effect, fixed-rate liabilities have been converted to floating-rate liabilities. The margins on the floating rates become the standard by which value is measured in assessing the total funding cost for the bank.

By using the swap curve as a benchmark for the time value of money, the investor can adjust the swap spread so that the swap would be fairly priced given the spread. Conversely, given a swap spread, the investor can determine a fair price for the bond. We will use the swap spread in the following section to determine the value of a bond.

3.3 How Do Market Participants Use the Swap Curve in Valuation?

Swap contracts are non-standardized and are simply customized contracts between two parties in the over-the-counter market. The fixed payment can be specified by an amortization schedule or to be coupon paying with non-standardized coupon payment dates. For this section, we will focus on zero-coupon bonds. The yields on these bonds determine the swap curve, which, in turn, can be used to determine bond values. Examples of swap par curves are given in Exhibit 3.

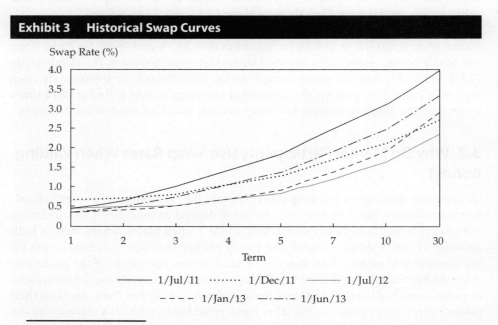

Exhibit 3   Historical Swap Curves

Note: Horizontal axis is not drawn to scale. (Such scales are commonly used as an industry standard because most of the distinctive shape of yield curves is typically observed before 10 years.)

Each forward date has an associated discount factor that represents the value today of a hypothetical payment that one would receive on the forward date, expressed as a fraction of the hypothetical payment. For example, if we expect to receive ₩10,000 (10,000 South Korean won) in one year and the current price of the security is ₩9,259.30, then the discount factor for one year would be 0.92593 (= ₩9,259.30/₩10,000). Note that the rate associated with this discount factor is 1/0.92593 −1 ≈ 8.00%.

To price a swap, we need to determine the present value of cash flows for each leg of the transaction. In an interest rate swap, the fixed leg is fairly straightforward because the cash flows are specified by the coupon rate set at the time of the agreement. Pricing the floating leg is more complex because, by definition, the cash flows change with future changes in interest rates. The forward rate for each floating payment date is calculated by using the forward curves.

Let $s(T)$ stand for the swap rate at time T. Because the value of a swap at origination is set to zero, the swap rates must satisfy Equation 12. Note that the swap rates can be determined from the spot rates and the spot rates can be determined from the swap rates.

$$\sum_{t=1}^{T} \frac{s(T)}{\left[1 + r(t)\right]^t} + \frac{1}{\left[1 + r(T)\right]^T} = 1 \qquad \text{(12)}$$

The right side of Equation 12 is the value of the floating leg, which is always 1 at origination. The swap rate is determined by equating the value of the fixed leg, on the left-hand side, to the value of the floating leg.

Example 8 addresses the relationship between the swap rate curve and spot curve.

EXAMPLE 8

Determining the Swap Rate Curve

Suppose a government spot curve implies the following discount factors:

$P(1) = 0.9524$

$P(2) = 0.8900$

$P(3) = 0.8163$

$P(4) = 0.7350$

Given this information, determine the swap rate curve.

Solution:

Recall from Equation 1 that $P(T) = \dfrac{1}{\left[1 + r(T)\right]^T}$. Therefore,

$$r(T) = \left\{\frac{1}{\left[P(T)\right]}\right\}^{(1/T)} - 1$$

$$r(1) = \left(\frac{1}{0.9524}\right)^{(1/1)} - 1 = 5.00\%$$

$$r(2) = \left(\frac{1}{0.8900}\right)^{(1/2)} - 1 = 6.00\%$$

$$r(3) = \left(\frac{1}{0.8163}\right)^{(1/3)} - 1 = 7.00\%$$

$$r(4) = \left(\frac{1}{0.7350}\right)^{(1/4)} - 1 = 8.00\%$$

Using Equation 12, for $T = 1$,

$$\frac{s(1)}{\left[1 + r(1)\right]^1} + \frac{1}{\left[1 + r(1)\right]^1} = \frac{s(1)}{(1 + 0.05)^1} + \frac{1}{(1 + 0.05)^1} = 1$$

Therefore, $s(1) = 5\%$.

For $T = 2$,

$$\frac{s(2)}{\left[1 + r(1)\right]^1} + \frac{s(2)}{\left[1 + r(2)\right]^2} + \frac{1}{\left[1 + r(2)\right]^2} = \frac{s(2)}{(1 + 0.05)^1} + \frac{s(2)}{(1 + 0.06)^2} + \frac{1}{(1 + 0.06)^2}$$

$$= 1$$

Therefore, $s(2) = 5.97\%$.

For $T = 3$,

$$\frac{s(3)}{\left[1 + r(1)\right]^1} + \frac{s(3)}{\left[1 + r(2)\right]^2} + \frac{s(3)}{\left[1 + r(3)\right]^3} + \frac{1}{\left[1 + r(3)\right]^3} =$$

$$\frac{s(3)}{\left(1 + 0.05\right)^1} + \frac{s(3)}{\left(1 + 0.06\right)^2} + \frac{s(3)}{\left(1 + 0.07\right)^3} + \frac{1}{\left(1 + 0.07\right)^3} = 1$$

Therefore, $s(3) = 6.91\%$.

For $T = 4$,

$$\frac{s(4)}{\left[1 + r(1)\right]^1} + \frac{s(4)}{\left[1 + r(2)\right]^2} + \frac{s(4)}{\left[1 + r(3)\right]^3} + \frac{s(4)}{\left[1 + r(4)\right]^4} + \frac{1}{\left[1 + r(4)\right]^4} =$$

$$\frac{s(4)}{\left(1 + 0.05\right)^1} + \frac{s(4)}{\left(1 + 0.06\right)^2} + \frac{s(4)}{\left(1 + 0.07\right)^3} + \frac{s(4)}{\left(1 + 0.08\right)^4} + \frac{1}{\left(1 + 0.08\right)^4} = 1$$

Therefore, $s(4) = 7.81\%$.

Note that the swap rates, spot rates, and discount factors are all mathematically linked together. Having access to data for one of the series allows you to calculate the other two.

3.4 The Swap Spread

The swap spread is a popular way to indicate credit spreads in a market. The **swap spread** is defined as the spread paid by the fixed-rate payer of an interest rate swap over the rate of the "on-the-run" (most recently issued) government security with the same maturity as the swap.[6]

Often, fixed-income prices will be quoted in SWAPS +, for which the yield is simply the yield on an equal-maturity government bond plus the swap spread. For example, if the fixed rate of a five-year fixed-for-float Libor swap is 2.00% and the five-year Treasury is yielding 1.70%, the swap spread is 2.00% − 1.70% = 0.30%, or 30 bps.

For euro-denominated swaps, the government yield used as a benchmark is most frequently bunds (German government bonds) with the same maturity. Gilts (UK government bonds) are used as a benchmark in the United Kingdom. CME Group began clearing euro-denominated interest rate swaps in 2011.

A Libor/swap curve is probably the most widely used interest rate curve because it is often viewed as reflecting the default risk of private entities at a rating of about A1/A+, roughly the equivalent of most commercial banks. (The swap curve can also be influenced by the demand and supply conditions in government debt markets, among other factors.) Another reason for the popularity of the swap market is that it is unregulated (not controlled by governments), so swap rates are more comparable across different countries. The swap market also has more maturities with which to construct a yield curve than do government bond markets. Libor is used for short-maturity yields, rates derived from eurodollar futures contracts are used for mid-maturity

---

6 The term "swap spread" is sometimes also used as a reference to a bond's basis point spread over the interest rate swap curve and is a measure of the credit and/or liquidity risk of a bond. In its simplest form, the swap spread in this sense can be measured as the difference between the yield to maturity of the bond and the swap rate given by a straight-line interpolation of the swap curve. These spreads are frequently quoted as an I-spread, ISPRD, or interpolated spread, which is a reference to a linearly interpolated yield. In this reading, the term "swap spread" refers to an excess yield of swap rates over the yields on government bonds and I-spreads to refer to bond yields net of the swap rates of the same maturities.

yields, and swap rates are used for yields with a maturity of more than one year. The swap rates used are the fixed rates that would be paid in swap agreements for which three-month Libor floating payments are received.[7]

HISTORY OF THE US SWAP SPREAD, 2008–2013

Normally, the Treasury swap spread is positive, which reflects the fact that governments generally pay less to borrow than do private entities. However, the 30-year Treasury swap spread turned negative following the collapse of Lehman Brothers Holdings Inc. in September 2008. Liquidity in many corners of the credit markets evaporated during the recent financial crisis, leading investors to doubt the safety and security of their counterparties in some derivatives transactions. The 30-year Treasury swap spread tumbled to a record low of −62 bps in November 2008. The 30-year Treasury swap spread again turned positive in the middle of 2013. A dramatic shift in sentiment regarding the Federal Reserve outlook since early May 2013 was a key catalyst for a selloff in most bonds. The sharp rise in Treasury yields at that time pushed up funding and hedging costs for companies, which was reflected in a rise in swap rates.

To illustrate the use of the swap spread in fixed-income pricing, consider a US$1 million investment in GE Capital (GECC) notes with a coupon rate of 1 5/8% (1.625%) that matures on 2 July 2015. Coupons are paid semiannually. The evaluation date is 12 July 2012, so the remaining maturity is 2.97 years [= 2 + (350/360)]. The Treasury rates for two-year and three-year maturities are 0.525% and 0.588%, respectively. By simple interpolation between these two swap rates, the swap rate for 2.97 years is 0.586% [= 0.525% + (350/360)(0.588% − 0.525%)]. If the swap spread for the same maturity is 0.918%, then the yield to maturity on the bond is 1.504% (= 0.918% + 0.586%). Given the yield to maturity, the invoice price (price including accrued interest) for US$1 million face value is

$$\frac{1,000,000\left(\dfrac{0.01625}{2}\right)}{\left(1+\dfrac{0.01504}{2}\right)^{\left(1-\frac{10}{180}\right)}} + \frac{1,000,000\left(\dfrac{0.01625}{2}\right)}{\left(1+\dfrac{0.01504}{2}\right)^{\left(2-\frac{10}{180}\right)}} + \cdots +$$

$$\frac{1,000,000\left(\dfrac{0.01625}{2}\right)}{\left(1+\dfrac{0.01504}{2}\right)^{\left(6-\frac{10}{180}\right)}} + \frac{1,000,000}{\left(1+\dfrac{0.01504}{2}\right)^{\left(6-\frac{10}{180}\right)}} = US\$1,003,954.12$$

The left side sums the present values of the semiannual coupon payments and the final principal payment of US$1,000,000. The accrued interest rate amount is US$451.39 [= 1,000,000 × (0.01625/2)(10/180)]. Therefore, the clean price (price not including accrued interest) is US$1,003,502.73 (= 1,003,954.12 − 451.39).

The swap spread helps an investor to identify the time value, credit, and liquidity components of a bond's yield to maturity. If the bond is default free, then the swap spread could provide an indication of the bond's liquidity or it could provide evidence of market mispricing. The higher the swap spread, the higher the return that investors require for credit and/or liquidity risks.

Although swap spreads provide a convenient way to measure risk, a more accurate measure of credit and liquidity is called the zero-spread (Z-spread). The **Z-spread** is the constant basis point spread that would need to be added to the implied spot yield

---

7 The US dollar market uses three-month Libor, but other currencies may use one-month or six-month Libor.

curve so that the discounted cash flows of a bond are equal to its current market price. This spread will be more accurate than a linearly interpolated yield, particularly with steep interest rate swap curves.

USING THE Z-SPREAD IN VALUATION

Consider again the GECC semi-annual coupon note with a maturity of 2.97 years and a par value of US$1,000,000. The spot yield curve is

$r(0.5) = 0.16\%$

$r(1) = 0.21\%$

$r(1.5) = 0.27\%$

$r(2) = 0.33\%$

$r(2.5) = 0.37\%$

$r(3) = 0.41\%$

The Z-spread is given as 109.6 bps. Using the spot curve and the Z-spread, the invoice price is

$$\frac{1,000,000\left(\dfrac{0.01625}{2}\right)}{\left(1+\dfrac{0.0016+0.01096}{2}\right)^{\left(1-\frac{10}{180}\right)}} + \frac{1,000,000\left(\dfrac{0.01625}{2}\right)}{\left(1+\dfrac{0.00021+0.01096}{2}\right)^{\left(2-\frac{10}{180}\right)}} + \cdots +$$

$$\frac{1,000,000\left(\dfrac{0.01625}{2}\right)}{\left(1+\dfrac{0.0041+0.01096}{2}\right)^{\left(6-\frac{10}{180}\right)}} +$$

$$\frac{1,000,000}{\left(1+\dfrac{0.0041+0.01096}{2}\right)^{\left(6-\frac{10}{180}\right)}} = US\$1,003,954.12$$

3.5 Spreads as a Price Quotation Convention

We have discussed both Treasury curves and swap curves as benchmarks for fixed-income valuation, but they usually differ. Therefore, quoting the price of a bond using the bond yield net of either a benchmark Treasury yield or swap rate becomes a price quote convention.

The Treasury rate can differ from the swap rate for the same term for several reasons. Unlike the cash flows from US Treasury bonds, the cash flows from swaps are subject to much higher default risk. Market liquidity for any specific maturity may differ. For example, some parts of the term structure of interest rates may be more actively traded with swaps than with Treasury bonds. Finally, arbitrage between these two markets cannot be perfectly executed.

Swap spreads to the Treasury rate (as opposed to the **I-spreads**, which are bond rates net of the swap rates of the same maturities) are simply the differences between swap rates and government bond yields of a particular maturity. One problem in defining swap spreads is that, for example, a 10-year swap matures in exactly 10 years whereas there typically is no government bond with exactly 10 years of remaining maturity. By convention, therefore, the 10-year swap spread is defined as the difference between the 10-year swap rate and the 10-year on-the-run government bond. Swap spreads of other maturities are defined similarly.

To generate the curves in Exhibit 4, we used the constant-maturity Treasury note to exactly match the corresponding swap rate. The 10-year swap spread is the 10-year swap rate less the 10-year constant-maturity Treasury note yield. Because counterparty risk is reflected in the swap rate and US government debt is considered nearly free of default risk, the swap rate is usually greater than the corresponding Treasury note rate and the 10-year swap spread is usually, but not always, positive.

Exhibit 4   10-Year Swap Rate vs. 10-Year Treasury Rate

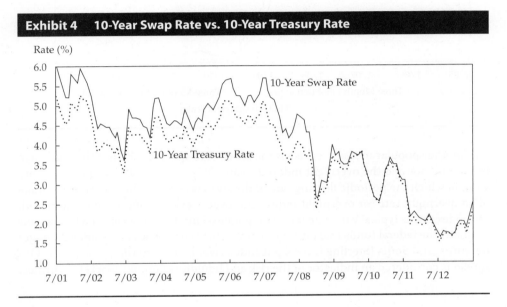

The **TED spread** is an indicator of perceived credit risk in the general economy. TED is an acronym formed from US T-bill and ED, the ticker symbol for the eurodollar futures contract. The TED spread is calculated as the difference between Libor and the yield on a T-bill of matching maturity. An increase (decrease) in the TED spread is a sign that lenders believe the risk of default on interbank loans is increasing (decreasing). Therefore, as it relates to the swap market, the TED spread can also be thought of as a measure of counterparty risk. Compared with the 10-year swap spread, the TED spread more accurately reflects risk in the banking system, whereas the 10-year swap spread is more often a reflection of differing supply and demand conditions.

Exhibit 5   TED Spread

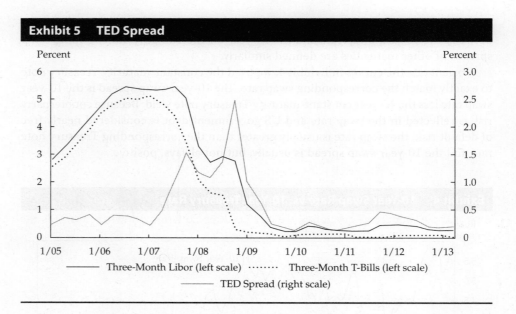

Another popular measure of risk is the **Libor–OIS spread**, which is the difference between Libor and the overnight indexed swap (OIS) rate. An OIS is an interest rate swap in which the periodic floating rate of the swap is equal to the geometric average of an overnight rate (or overnight index rate) over every day of the payment period. The index rate is typically the rate for overnight unsecured lending between banks—for example, the federal funds rate for US dollars, Eonia (Euro OverNight Index Average) for euros, and Sonia (Sterling OverNight Index Average) for sterling. The Libor–OIS spread is considered an indicator of the risk and liquidity of money market securities.

4

TRADITIONAL THEORIES OF THE TERM STRUCTURE OF INTEREST RATES

This section presents four traditional theories of the underlying economic factors that affect the shape of the yield curve.

4.1 Local Expectations Theory

One branch of traditional term structure theory focuses on interpreting term structure shape in terms of investors' expectations. Historically, the first such theory is known as the **unbiased expectations theory** or **pure expectations theory**. It says that the forward rate is an unbiased predictor of the future spot rate; its broadest interpretation is that bonds of any maturity are perfect substitutes for one another. For example, buying a bond with a maturity of five years and holding it for three years has the same expected return as buying a three-year bond or buying a series of three one-year bonds.

The predictions of the unbiased expectations theory are consistent with the assumption of risk neutrality. In a risk-neutral world, investors are unaffected by uncertainty and risk premiums do not exist. Every security is risk free and yields the risk-free rate for that particular maturity. Although such an assumption leads to interesting results, it clearly is in conflict with the large body of evidence that shows that investors are risk averse.

A theory that is similar but more rigorous than the unbiased expectations theory is the **local expectations theory**. Rather than asserting that every maturity strategy has the same expected return over a given investment horizon, this theory instead contends that the expected return for every bond over short time periods is the risk-free rate. This conclusion results from an assumed no-arbitrage condition in which bond pricing does not allow for traders to earn arbitrage profits.

The primary way that the local expectations theory differs from the unbiased expectations theory is that it can be extended to a world characterized by risk. Although the theory requires that risk premiums be nonexistent for very short holding periods, no such restrictions are placed on longer-term investments. Thus, the theory is applicable to both risk-free as well as risky bonds.

Using the formula for the discount factor in Equation 1 and the variation of the forward rate model in Equation 5, we can produce Equation 13, where $P(t,T)$ is the discount factor for a T-period security at time t.

$$\frac{1}{P(t,T)} = \left[1 + r(1)\right]\left[1 + f(1,1)\right]\left[1 + f(2,1)\right]\left[1 + f(3,1)\right]\ldots\left[1 + f(T-1,1)\right] \qquad (13)$$

Using Equation 13, we can show that if the forward rates are realized, the one-period return of a long-term bond is $r(1)$, the yield on a one-period risk-free security, as shown in Equation 14.

$$\frac{P(t+1,T-1)}{P(t,T)} = 1 + r(1) \qquad (14)$$

The local expectations theory extends this equation to incorporate uncertainty while still assuming risk neutrality in the short term. When we relax the certainty assumption, then Equation 14 becomes Equation 15, where the tilde (~) represents an uncertain outcome. In other words, the one-period return of a long-term risky bond is the one-period risk-free rate.

$$\frac{E\left[\tilde{P}(t+1,T-1)\right]}{P(t,T)} = 1 + r(1) \qquad (15)$$

Although the local expectations theory is economically appealing, it is often observed that short-holding-period returns on long-dated bonds do exceed those on short-dated bonds. The need for liquidity and the ability to hedge risk essentially ensure that the demand for short-term securities will exceed that for long-term securities. Thus, both the yields and the actual returns for short-dated securities are typically lower than those for long-dated securities.

4.2 Liquidity Preference Theory

Whereas the unbiased expectations theory leaves no room for risk aversion, liquidity preference theory attempts to account for it. **Liquidity preference theory** asserts that **liquidity premiums** exist to compensate investors for the added interest rate risk they face when lending long term and that these premiums increase with maturity.[8] Thus, given an expectation of unchanging short-term spot rates, liquidity preference theory predicts an upward-sloping yield curve. The forward rate provides an estimate of the expected spot rate that is biased upward by the amount of the liquidity premium, which invalidates the unbiased expectations theory.

---

8 The wording of a technical treatment of this theory would be that these premiums increase monotonically with maturity. A sequence is said to be monotonically increasing if each term is greater than or equal to the one before it. Define $LP(T)$ as the liquidty premium at maturity T. If premiums increase monotonically with maturity, then $LP(T+t) \geq LP(T)$ for all $t > 0$.

For example, the US Treasury offers bonds that mature in 30 years. However, the majority of investors have an investment horizon that is shorter than 30 years.[9] For investors to hold these bonds, they would demand a higher return for taking the risk that the yield curve changes and that they must sell the bond prior to maturity at an uncertain price. That incrementally higher return is the liquidity premium. Note that this premium is not to be confused with a yield premium for the lack of liquidity that thinly traded bonds may bear. Rather, it is a premium applying to all long-term bonds, including those with deep markets.

Liquidity preference theory fails to offer a complete explanation of the term structure. Rather, it simply argues for the existence of liquidity premiums. For example, a downward-sloping yield curve could still be consistent with the existence of liquidity premiums if one of the factors underlying the shape of the curve is an expectation of deflation (i.e., a negative rate of inflation due to monetary or fiscal policy actions). Expectations of sharply declining spot rates may also result in a downward-sloping yield curve if the expected decline in interest rates is severe enough to offset the effect of the liquidity premiums.

In summary, liquidity preference theory claims that lenders require a liquidity premium as an incentive to lend long term. Thus, forward rates derived from the current yield curve provide an upwardly biased estimate of expected future spot rates. Although downward-sloping or hump-shaped yield curves may sometimes occur, the existence of liquidity premiums implies that the yield curve will typically be upward sloping.

4.3 Segmented Markets Theory

Unlike expectations theory and liquidity preference theory, **segmented markets theory** allows for lender and borrower preferences to influence the shape of the yield curve. The result is that yields are not a reflection of expected spot rates or liquidity premiums. Rather, they are solely a function of the supply and demand for funds of a particular maturity. That is, each maturity sector can be thought of as a segmented market in which yield is determined independently from the yields that prevail in other maturity segments.

The theory is consistent with a world where there are asset/liability management constraints, either regulatory or self-imposed. In such a world, investors might restrict their investment activity to a maturity sector that provides the best match for the maturity of their liabilities. Doing so avoids the risks associated with an asset/liability mismatch.

For example, because life insurers sell long-term liabilities against themselves in the form of life insurance contracts, they tend to be most active as buyers in the long end of the bond market. Similarly, because the liabilities of pension plans are long term, they typically invest in long-term securities. Why would they invest short term given that those returns might decline while the cost of their liabilities stays fixed? In contrast, money market funds would be limited to investing in debt with maturity of one year or less, in general.

In summary, the segmented markets theory assumes that market participants are either unwilling or unable to invest in anything other than securities of their preferred maturity. It follows that the yield of securities of a particular maturity is determined entirely by the supply and demand for funds of that particular maturity.

---

9 This view can be confirmed by examining typical demand for long-term versus short-term Treasuries at auctions.

4.4 Preferred Habitat Theory

The **preferred habitat theory** is similar to the segmented markets theory in proposing that many borrowers and lenders have strong preferences for particular maturities but it does not assert that yields at different maturities are determined independently of each other.

However, the theory contends that if the expected additional returns to be gained become large enough, institutions will be willing to deviate from their preferred maturities or habitats. For example, if the expected returns on longer-term securities exceed those on short-term securities by a large enough margin, money market funds will lengthen the maturities of their assets. And if the excess returns expected from buying short-term securities become large enough, life insurance companies might stop limiting themselves to long-term securities and place a larger part of their portfolios in shorter-term investments.

The preferred habitat theory is based on the realistic notion that agents and institutions will accept additional risk in return for additional expected returns. In accepting elements of both the segmented markets theory and the unbiased expectations theory, yet rejecting their extreme polar positions, the preferred habitat theory moves closer to explaining real-world phenomena. In this theory, both market expectations and the institutional factors emphasized in the segmented markets theory influence the term structure of interest rates.

PREFERRED HABITAT AND QE

The term "quantitative easing" (QE) refers to an unconventional monetary policy used by central banks to increase the supply of money in an economy when central bank and/or interbank interest rates are already close to zero. The first of three QE efforts by the US Federal Reserve began in late 2008, following the establishment of a near-zero target range for the federal funds rate. Since then, the Federal Reserve has greatly expanded its holdings of long-term securities via a series of asset purchase programs, with the goal of putting downward pressure on long-term interest rates thereby making financial conditions even more accommodative. Exhibit 6 presents information regarding the securities held by the Federal Reserve on 20 September 2007 (when all securities held by the Fed were US Treasury issuance) and 19 September 2013 (one year after the third round of QE was launched).

Exhibit 6 Securities Held by the US Federal Reserve		
(US$ millions)	20 Sept. 2007	19 Sept. 2013
Securities held outright	779,636	3,448,758
US Treasury	779,636	2,047,534
Bills	267,019	0
Notes and bonds, nominal	472,142	1,947,007
Notes and bonds, inflation indexed	35,753	87,209
Inflation compensation	4,723	13,317
Federal agency	0	63,974
Mortgage-backed securities	0	1,337,520

As Exhibit 6 shows, the Federal Reserve's security holdings on 20 September 2007 consisted entirely of US Treasury securities and about 34% of those holdings were short term in the form of T-bills. On 19 September 2013, only about 59% of the Federal

Reserve's security holdings were Treasury securities and none of those holdings were T-bills. Furthermore, the Federal Reserve held well over US$1.3 trillion of mortgage-backed securities (MBS), which accounted for almost 39% of all securities held.

Prior to the QE efforts, the yield on MBS was typically in the 5%–6% range. It declined to less than 2% by the end of 2012. Concepts related to preferred habitat theory could possibly help explain that drop in yield.

The purchase of MBS by the Federal Reserve essentially reduced the supply of these securities that was available for private purchase. Assuming that many MBS investors are either unwilling or unable to withdraw from the MBS market because of their investment in gaining expertise in managing interest rate and repayment risks of MBS, MBS investing institutions would have a "preferred habitat" in the MBS market. If they were unable to meet investor demand without bidding more aggressively, these buyers would drive down yields on MBS.

The case can also be made that the Federal Reserve's purchase of MBS helped reduced prepayment risk, which also resulted in a reduction in MBS yields. If a homeowner pre-pays on a mortgage, the payment is sent to MBS investors on a pro-rata basis. Although investors are uncertain about when such a prepayment will be received, prepayment is more likely in a declining interest rate environment.

Use Example 9 to test your understanding of traditional term structure theories.

EXAMPLE 9

Traditional Term Structure Theories

1 In 2010, the Committee of European Securities Regulators created guidelines that restricted weighted average life (WAL) to 120 days for short-term money market funds. The purpose of this restriction was to limit the ability of money market funds to invest in long-term, floating-rate securities. This action is *most* consistent with a belief in:

   A the preferred habitat theory.

   B the segmented markets theory.

   C the local expectations theory.

2 The term structure theory that asserts that investors cannot be induced to hold debt securities whose maturities do not match their investment horizon is *best* described as the:

   A preferred habitat theory.

   B segmented markets theory.

   C unbiased expectations theory.

3 The unbiased expectations theory assumes investors are:

   A risk averse.

   B risk neutral.

   C risk seeking.

4 Market evidence shows that forward rates are:

   A unbiased predictors of future spot rates.

   B upwardly biased predictors of future spot rates.

   C downwardly biased predictors of future spot rates.

5 Market evidence shows that short holding-period returns on short-maturity bonds *most* often are:

   A less than those on long-maturity bonds.

B about equal to those on long-maturity bonds.

C greater than those on long-maturity bonds.

Solution to 1:

A is correct. The preferred habitat theory asserts that investors are willing to move away from their preferred maturity if there is adequate incentive to do so. The proposed WAL guideline was the result of regulatory concern about the interest rate risk and credit risk of long-term, floating-rate securities. An inference of this regulatory action is that some money market funds must be willing to move away from more traditional short-term investments if they believe there is sufficient compensation to do so.

Solution to 2:

B is correct. Segmented markets theory contends that asset/liability management constraints force investors to buy securities whose maturities match the maturities of their liabilities. In contrast, preferred habitat theory asserts that investors are willing to deviate from their preferred maturities if yield differentials encourage the switch. The unbiased expectations theory makes no assumptions about maturity preferences. Rather, it contends that forward rates are unbiased predictors of future spot rates.

Solution to 3:

B is correct. The unbiased expectations theory asserts that different maturity strategies, such as rollover, maturity matching, and riding the yield curve, have the same expected return. By definition, a risk-neutral party is indifferent about choices with equal expected payoffs, even if one choice is riskier. Thus, the predictions of the theory are consistent with the existence of risk-neutral investors.

Solution to 4:

B is correct. The existence of a liquidity premium ensures that the forward rate is an upwardly biased estimate of the future spot rate. Market evidence clearly shows that liquidity premiums exist, and this evidence effectively refutes the predictions of the unbiased expectations theory.

Solution to 5:

A is correct. Although the local expectations theory predicts that the short-run return for all bonds will be equal to the risk-free rate, most of the evidence refutes that claim. Returns from long-dated bonds are generally higher than those from short-dated bonds, even over relatively short investment horizons. This market evidence is consistent with the risk–expected return trade-off that is central to finance and the uncertainty surrounding future spot rates.

MODERN TERM STRUCTURE MODELS

5

Modern term structure models provide quantitatively precise descriptions of how interest rates evolve. A model provides a sometimes simplified description of a real-world phenomenon on the basis of a set of assumptions; models are often used to solve particular problems. These assumptions cannot be completely accurate in depicting the real world, but instead, the assumptions are made to explain real-world phenomena sufficiently well to solve the problem at hand.

Interest rate models attempt to capture the statistical properties of interest rate movements. The detailed description of these models depends on mathematical and statistical knowledge well outside the scope of the investment generalist's technical preparation. Yet, these models are very important in the valuation of complex fixed-income instruments and bond derivatives. Thus, we provide a broad overview of these models in this reading. Equations for the models and worked examples are given for readers who are interested.

5.1 Equilibrium Term Structure Models

Equilibrium term structure models are models that seek to describe the dynamics of the term structure using fundamental economic variables that are assumed to affect interest rates. In the modeling process, restrictions are imposed that allow for the derivation of equilibrium prices for bonds and interest rate options. These models require the specification of a drift term (explained later) and the assumption of a functional form for interest rate volatility. The best-known equilibrium models are the **Cox–Ingersoll–Ross model**[10] and the **Vasicek model**,[11] which are discussed in the next two sections.

Equilibrium term structure models share several characteristics:

- *They are one-factor or multifactor models.* One-factor models assume that a single observable factor (sometimes called a state variable) drives all yield curve movements. Both the Vasicek and CIR models assume a single factor, the short-term interest rate, r. This approach is plausible because empirically, parallel shifts are often found to explain more than 90% of yield changes. In contrast, multifactor models may be able to model the curvature of a yield curve more accurately but at the cost of greater complexity.

- *They make assumptions about the behavior of factors.* For example, if we focus on a short-rate single-factor model, should the short rate be modeled as mean reverting? Should the short rate be modeled to exhibit jumps? How should the volatility of the short rate be modeled?

- *They are, in general, more sparing with respect to the number of parameters that must be estimated compared with arbitrage-free term structure models.* The cost of this relative economy in parameters is that arbitrage-free models can, in general, model observed yield curves more precisely.[12]

An excellent example of an equilibrium term structure model is the Cox–Ingersoll–Ross (CIR) model discussed next.

5.1.1 *The Cox–Ingersoll–Ross Model*

The CIR model assumes that every individual has to make consumption and investment decisions with their limited capital. Investing in the productive process may lead to higher consumption in the following period, but it requires sacrificing today's consumption. The individual must determine his or her optimal trade-off assuming that he or she can borrow and lend in the capital market. Ultimately, interest rates will reach a market equilibrium rate at which no one needs to borrow or lend. The CIR model can explain interest rate movements in terms of an individual's preferences for investment and consumption as well as the risks and returns of the productive processes of the economy.

---

10 Cox, Ingersoll, and Ross (1985).
11 Vasicek (1977).
12 Other contrasts are more technical. They include that equilibrium models use real probabilities whereas arbitrage-free models use so-called risk-neutral probabilities. See footnote 9 for another contrast.

As a result of this analysis, the model shows how the short-term interest rate is related to the risks facing the productive processes of the economy. Assuming that an individual requires a term premium on the long-term rate, the model shows that the short-term rate can determine the entire term structure of interest rates and the valuation of interest rate–contingent claims. The CIR model is presented in Equation 16.

In Equation 16, the terms "dr" and "dt" mean, roughly, an infinitely small increment in the (instantaneous) short-term interest rate and time, respectively; the CIR model is an instance of a so-called continuous-time finance model. The model has two parts: (1) a deterministic part (sometimes called a "drift term"), the expression in dt, and (2) a stochastic (i.e., random) part, the expression in dz, which models risk.

$$dr = a(b - r)dt + \sigma\sqrt{r}\,dz \tag{16}$$

The way the deterministic part, $a(b - r)dt$, is formulated in Equation 16 ensures mean reversion of the interest rate toward a long-run value b, with the speed of adjustment governed by the strictly positive parameter a. If a is high (low), mean reversion to the long-run rate b would occur quickly (slowly). In Equation 16, for simplicity of presentation we have assumed that the **term premium** of the CIR model is equal to zero.[13] Thus, as modeled here, the CIR model assumes that the economy has a constant long-run interest rate that the short-term interest rate converges to over time.

Mean reversion is an essential characteristic of the interest rate that sets it apart from many other financial data series. Unlike stock prices, for example, interest rates cannot rise indefinitely because at very high levels, they would hamper economic activity, which would ultimately result in a decrease in interest rates. Similarly, with rare historical exceptions, nominal interest rates are non-negative. As a result, short-term interest rates tend to move in a bounded range and show a tendency to revert to a long-run value b.

Note that in Equation 16, there is only one stochastic driver, dz, of the interest rate process; very loosely, dz can be thought of as an infinitely small movement in a "random walk." The stochastic or volatility term, $\sigma\sqrt{r}\,dz$, follows the random normal distribution for which the mean is zero, the standard deviation is 1, and the standard deviation factor is $\sigma\sqrt{r}$. The standard deviation factor makes volatility proportional to the square root of the short-term rate, which allows for volatility to increase with the level of interest rates. It also avoids the possibility of non-positive interest rates for all positive values of a and b.[14]

Note that a, b, and σ are model parameters that have to be specified in some manner.

AN ILLUSTRATION OF THE CIR MODEL

Assume again that the current short-term rate is $r = 3\%$ and the long-run value for the short-term rate is $b = 8\%$. As before, assume that the speed of the adjustment factor is $a = 0.40$ and the annual volatility is $\sigma = 20\%$. Using Equation 16, the CIR model provides the following formula for the change in short-term interest rates, dr:

$$dr = 0.40(8\% - r)dt + (20\%)\sqrt{r}\,dz$$

Assume that a random number generator produced standard normal random error terms, dz, of 0.50, –0.10, 0.50, and –0.30. The CIR model would produce the evolution of interest rates shown in Exhibit 7. The bottom half of the exhibit shows the pricing of bonds consistent with the evolution of the short-term interest rate.

---

13 Equilibrium models, but not arbitrage-free models, assume that a term premium is required on long-term interest rates. A term premium is the additional return required by lenders to invest in a bond to maturity net of the expected return from continually reinvesting at the short-term rate over that same time horizon.
14 As long as $2ab > \sigma^2$, per Yan (2001, p. 65).

	Time				
Parameter	**$t = 0$**	**$t = 1$**	**$t = 2$**	**$t = 3$**	**$t = 4$**
r	3.000%	6.732%	6.720%	9.825%	7.214%
$a(b - r) = 0.40(8\% - r)$	2.000%	0.507%	0.512%	−0.730%	
dz	0.500	−0.100	0.500	−0.300	
$\sigma\sqrt{r}dz = 20\%\sqrt{r}dz$	1.732%	−0.519%	2.592%	−1.881%	
dr	3.732%	−0.012%	3.104%	−2.611%	
$r(t + 1) = r + dr$	6.732%	6.720%	9.825%	7.214%	
YTM for Zero-Coupon Bonds Maturing in					
1 Year	3.862%	6.921%	6.911%	9.456%	7.316%
2 Years	4.499%	7.023%	7.015%	9.115%	7.349%
5 Years	5.612%	7.131%	7.126%	8.390%	7.327%
10 Years	6.333%	7.165%	7.162%	7.854%	7.272%
30 Years	6.903%	7.183%	7.182%	7.415%	7.219%

Exhibit 7   Evolution of the Short-Term Rate in the CIR Model

The simulation of interest rates starts with an interest rate of 3%, which is well below the long-run value of 8%. Interest rates generated by the model quickly move toward this long-run value. Note that the standard normal variable dz is assumed to be 0.50 in time periods $t = 0$ and $t = 2$ but the volatility term, $\sigma\sqrt{r}dz$, is much higher in $t = 2$ than in $t = 0$ because volatility increases with the level of interest rates in the CIR model.

This example is stylized and intended for illustrative purposes only. The parameters used in practice typically vary significantly from those used here.

5.1.2 The Vasicek Model

Although not developed in the context of a general equilibrium of individuals seeking to make optimal consumption and investment decisions, as was the case for the CIR model, the Vasicek model is viewed as an equilibrium term structure model. Similar to the CIR model, the Vasicek model captures mean reversion.

Equation 17 presents the Vasicek model:

$$dr = a(b - r)dt + \sigma dz \tag{17}$$

The Vasicek model has the same drift term as the CIR model and thus tends toward mean reversion in the short rate, r. The stochastic or volatility term, σdz, follows the random normal distribution for which the mean is zero and the standard deviation is 1. Unlike the CIR Model, interest rates are calculated assuming that volatility remains constant over the period of analysis. As with the CIR model, there is only one stochastic driver, dz, of the interest rate process and a, b, and σ are model parameters that have to be specified in some manner. The main disadvantage of the Vasicek model is that it is theoretically possible for the interest rate to become negative.

AN ILLUSTRATION OF THE VASICEK MODEL

Assume that the current short-term rate is $r = 3\%$ and the long-run value for the short-term rate is $b = 8\%$. Also assume that the speed of the adjustment factor is $a = 0.40$ and the annual volatility is $\sigma = 2\%$. Using Equation 17, the Vasicek model provides the following formula for the change in short-term interest rates, dr:

$$dr = 0.40(8\% - r)dt + (2\%)dz$$

The stochastic term, dz, is typically drawn from a standard normal distribution with a mean of zero and a standard deviation of 1. Assume that a random number generator produced standard normal random error terms of 0.45, 0.18, −0.30, and 0.25. The Vasicek model would produce the evolution of interest rates shown in Exhibit 8.

Exhibit 8   Evolution of the Short-Term Rate in the Vasicek Model

Parameter	t = 0	t = 1	t =2	t = 3	t = 4
r	3.000%	5.900%	7.100%	6.860%	7.816%
$a(b - r)$	2.000%	0.840%	0.360%	0.456%	
dz	0.450	0.180	−0.300	0.250	
σdz	0.900%	0.360%	−0.600%	0.500%	
dr	2.900%	1.200%	−0.240%	0.956%	
$r(t + 1) = r + dr$	5.900%	7.100%	6.860%	7.816%	
YTM for Zero-Coupon Bonds Maturing in					
1 Year	3.874%	6.264%	7.253%	7.055%	7.843%
2 Years	4.543%	6.539%	7.365%	7.200%	7.858%
5 Years	5.791%	7.045%	7.563%	7.460%	7.873%
10 Years	6.694%	7.405%	7.670%	7.641%	7.876%
30 Years	7.474%	7.716%	7.816%	7.796%	7.875%

Note that the simulation of interest rates starts with an interest rate of 3%, which is well below the long-run value of 8%. Interest rates generated by the model move quickly toward this long-run value despite declining in the third time period, which reflects the mean reversion built into the model via the drift term $a(b - r)dt$.

This example is stylized and intended for illustrative purposes only. The parameters used in practice typically vary significantly from those used here.

Note that because both the Vasicek model and the CIR model require the short-term rate to follow a certain process, the estimated yield curve may not match the observed yield curve. But if the parameters of the models are believed to be correct, then investors can use these models to determine mispricings.

5.2 Arbitrage-Free Models: The Ho–Lee Model

In **arbitrage-free models**, the analysis begins with the observed market prices of a reference set of financial instruments and the underlying assumption is that the reference set is correctly priced. An assumed random process with a drift term and volatility factor is used for the generation of the yield curve. The computational process that determines the term structure is such that the valuation process generates the market prices of the reference set of financial instruments. These models are called "arbitrage-free" because the prices they generate match market prices.

The ability to calibrate models to market data is a desirable feature of any model, and this fact points to one of the main drawbacks of the Vasicek and CIR models: They have only a finite number of free parameters, and so it is not possible to specify these parameter values in such a way that model prices coincide with observed market prices. This problem is overcome in arbitrage-free models by allowing the parameters to vary deterministically with time. As a result, the market yield curve can be modeled with the accuracy needed for such applications as valuing derivatives and bonds with embedded options.

The first arbitrage-free model was introduced by Ho and Lee.[15] It uses the relative valuation concepts of the Black–Scholes–Merton option-pricing model. Thus, the valuation of interest rate contingent claims is based solely on the yield curve's shape and its movements. The model assumes that the yield curve moves in a way that is consistent with a no-arbitrage condition.

In the **Ho–Lee model**, the short rate follows a normal process, as shown in Equation 18:

$$dr_t = \theta_t dt + \sigma dz_t \tag{18}$$

The model can be calibrated to market data by inferring the form of the time-dependent drift term, θ_t, from market prices, which means the model can precisely generate the current term structure. This calibration is typically performed via a binomial lattice-based model in which at each node the yield curve can move up or down with equal probability. This probability is called the "implied risk-neutral probability." Often it is called the "risk-neutral probability," which is somewhat misleading because arbitrage-free models do not assume market professionals are risk neutral as does the local expectations theory. This is analogous to the classic Black–Scholes–Merton option model insofar as the pricing dynamics are simplified because we can price debt securities "as if" market investors were risk neutral.

To make the discussion concrete, we illustrate a two-period Ho–Lee model. Assume that the current short-term rate is 4%. The time step is monthly, and the drift terms, which are determined using market prices, are $\theta_1 = 1\%$ in the first month and $\theta_2 = 0.80\%$ in the second month. The annual volatility is 2%. Below, we create a two-period binomial lattice-based model for the short-term rate. Note that the monthly volatility is

$$\sigma\sqrt{\frac{1}{t}} = 2\%\sqrt{\frac{1}{12}} = 0.5774\%$$

and the time step is

$$dt = \frac{1}{12} = 0.0833$$

$$dr_t = \theta_t dt + \sigma dz_t = \theta_t(0.0833) + (0.5774)dz_t$$

If the rate goes up in the first month,

$r = 4\% + (1\%)(0.0833) + 0.5774\% = 4.6607\%$

If the rate goes up in the first month and up in the second month,

$r = 4.6607\% + (0.80\%)(0.0833) + 0.5774\% = 5.3047\%$

If the rate goes up in the first month and down in the second month,

$r = 4.6607\% + (0.80\%)(0.0833) - 0.5774\% = 4.1499\%$

---

15 Ho and Lee (1986).

If the rate goes down in the first month,

$r = 4\% + (1\%)(0.0833) - 0.5774\% = 3.5059\%$

If the rate goes down in the first month and up in the second month,

$r = 3.5059\% + (0.80\%)(0.0833) + 0.5774\% = 4.1499$

If the rate goes down in the first month and down in the second month,

$r = 3.5059\% + (0.80\%)(0.0833) - 0.5774\% = 2.9951\%$

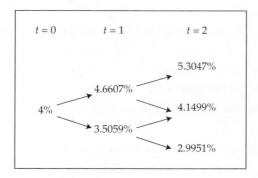

The interest rates generated by the model can be used to determine zero-coupon bond prices and the spot curve. By construction, the model output is consistent with market prices. Because of its simplicity, the Ho–Lee model is useful for illustrating most of the salient features of arbitrage-free interest rate models. Because the model generates a symmetrical ("bell-shaped" or normal) distribution of future rates, negative interest rates are possible. Note that although the volatility of the one-period rate is constant at each node point in the illustration, time-varying volatility—consistent with the historical behavior of yield curve movements—can be modeled in the Ho–Lee model because sigma (interest rate volatility) can be specified as a function of time. A more sophisticated example using a term structure of volatilities as inputs is outside the scope of this reading.

As mentioned before, models are assumptions made to describe certain phenomena and to provide solutions to problems at hand. Modern interest rate theories are proposed for the most part to value bonds with embedded options because the values of embedded options are frequently contingent on interest rates. The general equilibrium models introduced here describe yield curve movement as the movement in a single short-term rate. They are called one-factor models and, in general, seem empirically satisfactory. Arbitrage-free models do not attempt to explain the observed yield curve. Instead, these models take the yield curve as given. For this reason, they are sometimes labeled as **partial equilibrium models**.

The basic arbitrage-free concept can be used to solve much broader problems. These models can be extended to value many bond types, allowing for a term structure of volatilities, uncertain changes in the shape of the yield curve, adjustments for the credit risk of a bond, and much more. Yet, these many extensions are still based on the concept of arbitrage-free interest rate movements. For this reason, the principles of these models form a foundation for much of the modern progress made in financial modeling.

Example 10 addresses several basic points about modern term structure models.

EXAMPLE 10

Modern Term Structure Models

1   Which of the following would be expected to provide the *most* accurate modeling with respect to the observed term structure?

   A   CIR model

   B   Ho–Lee model

   C   Vasicek model

2   Which of the following statements about the Vasicek model is *most* accurate? It has:

   A   a single factor, the long rate.

   B   a single factor, the short rate.

   C   two factors, the short rate and the long rate.

3   The CIR model:

   A   assumes interest rates are not mean reverting.

   B   has a drift term that differs from that of the Vasicek model.

   C   assumes interest rate volatility increases with increases in the level of interest rates.

Solution to 1:

B is correct. The CIR model and the Vasicek model are examples of equilibrium term structure models, whereas the Ho–Lee model is an example of an arbitrage-free term structure model. A benefit of arbitrage-free term structure models is that they are calibrated to the current term structure. In other words, the starting prices ascribed to securities are those currently found in the market. In contrast, equilibrium term structure models frequently generate term structures that are inconsistent with current market data.

Solution to 2:

B is correct. Use of the Vasicek model requires assumptions for the short-term interest rate, which are usually derived from more general assumptions about the state variables that describe the overall economy. Using the assumed process for the short-term rate, one can determine the yield on longer-term bonds by looking at the expected path of interest rates over time.

Solution to 3:

C is correct. The drift term of the CIR model is identical to that of the Vasicek model, and both models assume that interest rates are mean reverting. The big difference between the two models is that the CIR model assumes that interest rate volatility increases with increases in the level of interest rates. The Vasicek model assumes that interest rate volatility is a constant.

6   YIELD CURVE FACTOR MODELS

The effect of yield volatilities on price is an important consideration in fixed-income investment, particularly for risk management and portfolio evaluation. In this section, we will describe measuring and managing the interest rate risk of bonds.

6.1 A Bond's Exposure to Yield Curve Movement

Shaping risk is defined as the sensitivity of a bond's price to the changing shape of the yield curve. The shape of the yield curve changes continually, and yield curve shifts are rarely parallel. For active bond management, a bond investor may want to base trades on a forecasted yield curve shape or may want to hedge the yield curve risk on a bond portfolio. Shaping risk also affects the value of many options, which is very important because many fixed-income instruments have embedded options.

Exhibits 9 through 11 show historical yield curve movements for US, Japanese, and South Korean government bonds from August 2005 to July 2013. The exhibits show that the shape of the yield curve changes considerably over time. In the United States and South Korea, central bank policies in response to the Great Recession led to a significant decline in short-term yields during the 2007–2009 time period. Long-term yields eventually followed suit, resulting in a flattening of the yield curve. Short-term Japanese yields have been low for quite some time, and recent long-term yields are the lowest of any developed market. Note that the vertical axis values of the three exhibits differ.

Exhibit 9   Historical US Yield Curve Movements

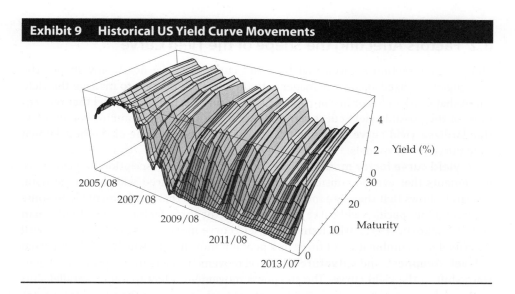

Exhibit 10   Historical Japanese Yield Curve Movements

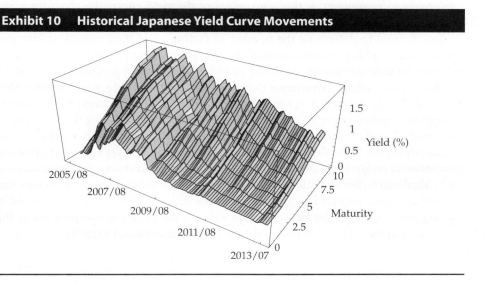

Exhibit 11   Historical Korean Yield Curve Movements

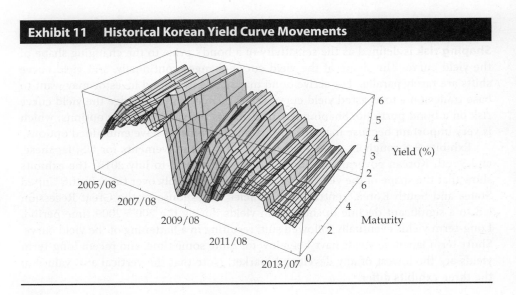

6.2 Factors Affecting the Shape of the Yield Curve

The previous section showed that the yield curve can take nearly any shape. The challenge for a fixed-income manager is to implement a process to manage the yield curve shape risk in his or her portfolio. One approach is to find a model that reduces most of the possible yield curve movements to a probabilistic combination of a few standardized yield curve movements. This section presents one of the best-known yield curve factor models.

A **yield curve factor model** is defined as a model or a description of yield curve movements that can be considered realistic when compared with historical data. Research shows that there are models that can describe these movements with some accuracy. One specific yield curve factor model is the three-factor model of Litterman and Scheinkman (1991), who found that yield curve movements are historically well described by a combination of three independent movements, which they interpreted as **level**, **steepness**, and **curvature**. The level movement refers to an upward or downward shift in the yield curve. The steepness movement refers to a non-parallel shift in the yield curve when either short-term rates change more than long-term rates or long-term rates change more than short-term rates. The curvature movement is a reference to movement in three segments of the yield curve: the short-term and long-term segments rise while the middle-term segment falls or vice versa.

The method to determine the number of factors—and their economic interpretation—begins with a measurement of the change of key rates on the yield curve, in this case 10 different points along the yield curve, as shown in Exhibits 12 and 13. The historical variance/covariance matrix of these interest rate movements is then obtained. The next step is to try to discover a number of independent factors (not to exceed the number of variables—in this case, selected points along the yield curve) that can explain the observed variance/covariance matrix. The approach that focuses on identifying the factors that best explain historical variances is known as **principal components analysis** (PCA). PCA creates a number of synthetic factors defined as (and calculated to be) statistically independent of each other; how these factors may be interpreted economically is a challenge to the researcher that can be addressed by relating movements in the factors (as we will call the principal components in this discussion) to movements in observable and easily understood variables.

In applying this analysis to historical data for the period of August 2005–July 2013, very typical results were found, as expressed in Exhibit 12 and graphed in Exhibit 13. The first principal component explained about 77% of the total variance/covariance, and the second and third principal components (or factors) explained 17% and 3%, respectively. These percentages are more commonly recognized as R^2s, which, by the underlying assumptions of principal components analysis, can be simply summed to discover that a linear combination of the first three factors explains almost 97% of the total yield curve changes in the sample studied.

Exhibit 12	The First Three Yield Curve Factors, US Treasury Securities, August 2005–July 2013 (Entries are percents)									
Time to Maturity (Years)	**0.25**	**0.5**	**1**	**2**	**3**	**5**	**7**	**10**	**20**	**30**
Factor 1 "Level"	−0.2089	−0.2199	−0.2497	−0.2977	−0.3311	−0.3756	−0.3894	−0.3779	−0.3402	−0.3102
Factor 2 "Steepness"	0.5071	0.4480	0.3485	0.2189	0.1473	−0.0371	−0.1471	−0.2680	−0.3645	−0.3514
Factor 3 "Curvature"	0.4520	0.2623	0.0878	−0.3401	−0.4144	−0.349	−0.1790	0.0801	0.3058	0.4219

Note that in Exhibit 13, the x-axis represents time to maturity in years.

Exhibit 13	The First Three Yield Curve Factors for US Treasury Securities, August 2005–July 2013

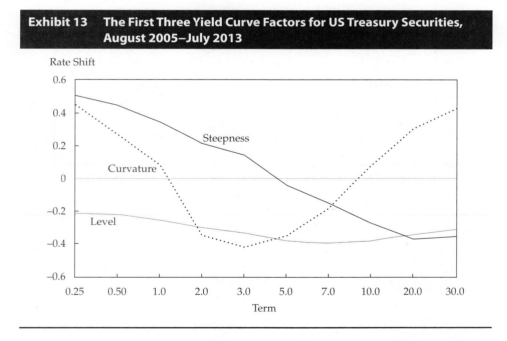

How should Exhibit 12 be interpreted? Exhibit 12 shows that for a one standard deviation positive change in the first factor (normalized to have unit standard deviation), the yield for a 0.25-year bond would decline by 0.2089%, a 0.50-year bond by 0.2199%, and so on across maturities, so that a 30-year bond would decline by 0.3102%.

Because the responses are in the same direction and by similar magnitudes, a reasonable interpretation of the first factor is that it describes (approximately) parallel shifts up and down the entire length of the yield curve.

Examining the second factor, we notice that a unitary positive standard deviation change appears to raise rates at shorter maturities (e.g., +0.5071% for 0.25-year bonds) but lowers rates at longer maturities (e.g., −0.3645% and −0.3514% for 20- and 30-year bonds, respectively). We can reasonably interpret this factor as one that causes changes in the steepness or slope of the yield curve. We note that the R^2 associated with this factor of 17% is much less important than the 77% R^2 associated with the first factor, which we associated with parallel shifts in the yield curve.

The third factor contributes a much smaller R^2 of 3%, and we associate this factor with changes in the curvature or "twist" in the curve because a unitary positive standard deviation change in this factor leads to positive yield changes at both short and long maturities but produces declines at intermediate maturities.

PCA shows similar results when applied to other government bond markets during the August 2005–July 2013 time period. Exhibits 14 and 15 reflect the results graphically for the Japanese and South Korean markets. In these instances, results can also be well explained by factors that appear to be associated, in declining order of importance, with parallel shifts, changes in steepness, and changes in curvature. Note that in Exhibits 14 and 15, as in Exhibit 13, the x-axis represents time to maturity in years.

Exhibit 14   The First Three Yield Curve Factors for Japanese Government Securities, August 2005–July 2013

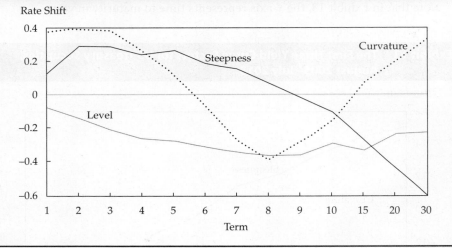

Exhibit 15   The First Three Yield Curve Factors for South Korean Government Securities, August 2005–July 2013

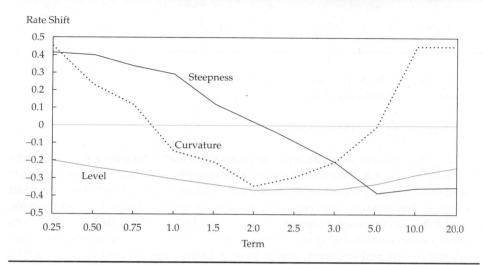

As in any other time series or regression model, the impact of the factors may change depending on the time period selected for study. However, if the reader selects any date within the sample period used to estimate these factors, a linear combination of the factors should explain movements of the yield curve on that date well.

6.3 The Maturity Structure of Yield Curve Volatilities

In modern fixed-income management, quantifying interest rate volatilities is important for at least two reasons. First, most fixed-income instruments and derivatives have embedded options. Option values, and hence the values of the fixed-income instrument, crucially depend on the level of interest rate volatilities. Second, fixed-income interest rate risk management is clearly an important part of any management process, and such risk management includes controlling the impact of interest rate volatilities on the instrument's price volatility.

The term structure of interest rate volatilities is a representation of the yield volatility of a zero-coupon bond for every maturity of security. This volatility curve (or "vol") or volatility term structure measures yield curve risk.

Interest rate volatility is not the same for all interest rates along the yield curve. On the basis of the typical assumption of a lognormal model, the uncertainty of an interest rate is measured by the annualized standard deviation of the proportional change in a bond yield over a specified time interval. For example, if the time interval is a one-month period, then the specified time interval equals 1/12 years. This measure is called interest rate volatility, and it is denoted $\sigma(t,T)$, which is the volatility of the rate for a security with maturity T at time t. The term structure of volatilities is given by Equation 19:

$$\sigma(t,T) = \frac{\sigma\left[\Delta r(t,T)/r(t,T)\right]}{\sqrt{\Delta t}}$$

(19)

In Exhibit 16, to illustrate a term structure of volatility, the data series is deliberately chosen to end before the 2008 financial crisis, which was associated with some unusual volatility magnitudes.

Exhibit 16	Historical Volatility Term Structure: US Treasuries, August 2005–December 2007									
Maturity (years)	0.25	0.50	1	2	3	5	7	10	20	30
$\sigma(t,T)$	0.3515	0.3173	0.2964	0.2713	0.2577	0.2154	0.1885	0.1621	0.1332	0.1169

For example, the 35.15% standard deviation for the three-month T-bill in Exhibit 16 is based on a monthly standard deviation of 0.1015 = 10.15%, which annualizes as

$$0.1015 \div \sqrt{\frac{1}{12}} = 0.3515 = 35.15\%$$

The volatility term structure typically shows that short-term rates are more volatile than long-term rates. Research indicates that short-term volatility is most strongly linked to uncertainty regarding monetary policy whereas long-term volatility is most strongly linked to uncertainty regarding the real economy and inflation. Furthermore, most of the co-movement between short-term and long-term volatilities appears to depend on the ever-changing correlations between these three determinants (monetary policy, the real economy, and inflation). During the period of August 2005–December 2007, long-term volatility was lower than short-term volatility, falling from 35.15% for the 0.25-year rate to 11.69% for the 30-year rate.

6.4 Managing Yield Curve Risks

Yield curve risk—risk to portfolio value arising from unanticipated changes in the yield curve—can be managed on the basis of several measures of sensitivity to yield curve movements. Management of yield curve risk involves changing the identified exposures to desired values by trades in security or derivative markets (the details fall under the rubric of fixed-income portfolio management and thus are outside the scope of this reading).

One available measure of yield curve sensitivity is effective duration, which measures the sensitivity of a bond's price to a small parallel shift in a benchmark yield curve. Another is based on key rate duration, which measures a bond's sensitivity to a small change in a benchmark yield curve at a specific maturity segment. A further measure can be developed on the basis of the factor model developed in Section 6.3. Using one of these last two measures allows identification and management of "shaping risk"—that is, sensitivity to changes in the shape of the benchmark yield curve—in addition to the risk associated with parallel yield curve changes, which is addressed adequately by effective duration.

To make the discussion more concrete, consider a portfolio of 1-year, 5-year, and 10-year zero-coupon bonds with $100 value in each position; total portfolio value is therefore $300. Also consider the hypothetical set of factor movements shown in the following table:

Year	1	5	10
Parallel	1	1	1
Steepness	−1	0	1
Curvature	1	0	1

In the table, a parallel movement or shift means that all the rates shift by an equal amount—in this case, by a unit of 1. A steepness movement means that the yield curve steepens with the long rate shifting up by one unit and the short rate shifting down by one unit. A curvature movement means that both the short rate and the long rate shift up by one unit whereas the medium-term rate remains unchanged. These movements need to be defined, as they are here, such that none of the movements can be a linear combination of the other two movements. Next, we address the calculation of the various yield curve sensitivity measures.

Because the bonds are zero-coupon bonds, the effective duration of each bond is the same as the maturity of the bonds.[16] The portfolio's effective duration is the weighted sum of the effective duration of each bond position; for this equally weighted portfolio, effective duration is $0.333(1 + 5 + 10) = 5.333$.

To calculate **key rate durations**, consider various yield curve movements. First, suppose that the one-year rate changes by 100 bps while the other rates remain the same; the sensitivity of the portfolio to that shift is $1/[(300)(0.01)] = 0.3333$. We conclude that the key rate duration of the portfolio to the one-year rate, denoted D_1, is 0.3333. Likewise, the key rate durations of the portfolio to the 5-year rate, D_5, and the 10-year rate, D_{10}, are 1.6667 and 3.3333, respectively. Note that the sum of the key rate durations is 5.333, which is the same as the effective duration of the portfolio. This fact can be explained intuitively. Key rate duration measures the portfolio risk exposure to each key rate. If all the key rates move by the same amount, then the yield curve has made a parallel shift, and as a result, the proportional change in value has to be consistent with effective duration. The related model for yield curve risk based on key rate durations would be

$$\left(\frac{\Delta P}{P}\right) \approx -D_1 \Delta r_1 - D_5 \Delta r_5 - D_{10} \Delta r_{10}$$

(20)

$$= -0.3333\Delta r_1 - 1.6667\Delta r_5 - 3.3333\Delta r_{10}$$

Next, we can calculate a measure based on the decomposition of yield curve movements into parallel, steepness, and curvature movements made in Section 6.3. Define D_L, D_S, and D_C as the sensitivities of portfolio value to small changes in the level, steepness, and curvature factors, respectively. Based on this factor model, Equation 21 shows the proportional change in portfolio value that would result from a small change in the level factor (Δx_L), the steepness factor (Δx_S), and the curvature factor (Δx_C).

$$\left(\frac{\Delta P}{P}\right) \approx -D_L \Delta x_L - D_S \Delta x_S - D_C \Delta x_C$$

(21)

Because D_L is by definition sensitivity to a parallel shift, the proportional change in the portfolio value per unit shift (the line for a parallel movement in the table) is $5.3333 = 16/[(300)(0.01)]$. The sensitivity for steepness movement can be calculated as follows (see the line for steepness movement in the table). When the steepness makes an upward shift of 100 bps, it would result in a downward shift of 100 bps for the 1-year rate, resulting in a gain of $1, and an upward shift for the 10-year rate, resulting in a loss of $10. The change in value is therefore $(1 - 10)$. D_S is the negative of the proportional change in price per unit change in this movement and in this case is $3.0 = -(1 - 10)/[(300)(0.01)]$. Considering the line for curvature movement in the table, $D_C = 3.6667 = (1 + 10)/[(300)(0.01)]$. Thus, for our hypothetical bond portfolio, we can analyze the portfolio's yield curve risk using

$$\left(\frac{\Delta P}{p}\right) \approx -5.3333\Delta x_L - 3.0\Delta x_S - 3.6667\Delta x_C$$

(22)

---

16 Exactly so under continuous compounding.

For example, if $\Delta x_L = -0.0050$, $\Delta x_S = 0.002$, and $\Delta x_C = 0.001$, the predicted change in portfolio value would be +1.7%. It can be shown that key rate durations are directly related to level, steepness, and curvature in this example and that one set of sensitivities can be derived from the other. One can use the numerical example to verify that[17]

$$D_L = D_1 + D_5 + D_{10}$$
$$D_S = -D_1 + D_{10}$$
$$D_C = D_1 + D_{10}$$

Example 11 reviews concepts from this section and the preceding sections.

EXAMPLE 11

Term Structure Dynamics

1 The most important factor in explaining changes in the yield curve has been found to be:

   A level.

   B curvature.

   C steepnesss.

2 A movement of the yield curve in which the short rate decreases by 150 bps and the long rate decreases by 50 bps would *best* be described as a:

   A flattening of the yield curve resulting from changes in level and steepness.

   B steepening of the yield curve resulting from changes in level and steepness.

   C steepening of the yield curve resulting from changes in steepness and curvature.

3 A movement of the yield curve in which the short- and long-maturity sectors increase by 100 bps and 75 bps, respectively, but the intermediate-maturity sector increases by 10 bps, is *best* described as involving a change in:

   A level only.

   B curvature only.

   C level and curvature.

4 Typically, short-term interest rates:

   A are less volatile than long-term interest rates.

   B are more volatile than long-term interest rates.

   C have about the same volatility as long-term rates.

---

[17] To see this, decompose Δr_1, Δr_5, and Δr_{10} into three factors—parallel, steepness, and curvature—based on the hypothetical movements in the table.

$$\Delta r_1 = \Delta x_L - \Delta x_s + \Delta x_C$$
$$\Delta r_5 = \Delta x_L$$
$$\Delta r_{10} = \Delta x_L + \Delta x_S + \Delta x_C$$

When we plug these equations into the expression for portfolio change based on key rate duration and simplify, we get

$$\frac{\Delta P}{P} = -D_1(\Delta x_L - \Delta x_S + \Delta x_C) - D_5(\Delta x_L) - D_{10}(\Delta x_L + \Delta x_S + \Delta x_C)$$
$$= -(D_1 + D_5 + D_{10})\Delta x_L - (-D_1 + D_{10})\Delta x_S - (D_1 + D_{10})\Delta x_C$$

> **5** Suppose for a given portfolio that key rate changes are considered to be changes in the yield on 1-year, 5-year, and 10-year securities. Estimated key rate durations are $D_1 = 0.50$, $D_2 = 0.70$, and $D_3 = 0.90$. What is the percentage change in the value of the portfolio if a parallel shift in the yield curve results in all yields declining by 50 bps?
>
> **A** −1.05%.
>
> **B** +1.05%
>
> **C** +2.10%.

Solution to 1:

A is correct. Research shows that upward and downward shifts in the yield curve explain more than 75% of the total change in the yield curve.

Solution to 2:

B is correct. Both the short-term and long-term rates have declined, indicating a change in the level of the yield curve. Short-term rates have declined more than long-term rates, indicating a change in the steepness of the yield curve.

Solution to 3:

C is correct. Both the short-term and long-term rates have increased, indicating a change in the level of the yield curve. However, intermediate rates have increased less than both short-term and long-term rates, indicating a change in curvature.

Solution to 4:

B is correct. A possible explanation is that expectations for long-term inflation and real economic activity affecting longer-term interest rates are slower to change than those related to shorter-term interest rates.

Solution to 5:

B is correct. A decline in interest rates would lead to an increase in bond portfolio value: $-0.50(-0.005) - 0.70(-0.005) - 0.90(-0.005) = 0.0105 = 1.05\%$.

SUMMARY

- The spot rate for a given maturity can be expressed as a geometric average of the short-term rate and a series of forward rates.

- Forward rates are above (below) spot rates when the spot curve is upward (downward) sloping, whereas forward rates are equal to spot rates when the spot curve is flat.

- If forward rates are realized, then all bonds, regardless of maturity, will have the same one-period realized return, which is the first-period spot rate.

- If the spot rate curve is upward sloping and is unchanged, then each bond "rolls down" the curve and earns the forward rate that rolls out of its pricing (i.e., a T^*-period zero-coupon bond earns the T^*-period forward rate as it rolls down to be a $T^* - 1$ period security). This implies an expected return in excess of short-maturity bonds (i.e., a term premium) for longer-maturity bonds if the yield curve is upward sloping.

- Active bond portfolio management is consistent with the expectation that today's forward curve does not accurately reflect future spot rates.

- The swap curve provides another measure of the time value of money.

- The swap markets are significant internationally because swaps are frequently used to hedge interest rate risk exposure.

- The swap spread, the I-spread, and the Z-spread are bond quoting conventions that can be used to determine a bond's price.

- Swap curves and Treasury curves can differ because of differences in their credit exposures, liquidity, and other supply/demand factors.

- The local expectations theory, liquidity preference theory, segmented markets theory, and preferred habitat theory provide traditional explanations for the shape of the yield curve.

- Modern finance seeks to provide models for the shape of the yield curve and the use of the yield curve to value bonds (including those with embedded options) and bond-related derivatives. General equilibrium and arbitrage-free models are the two major types of such models.

- Arbitrage-free models are frequently used to value bonds with embedded options. Unlike equilibrium models, arbitrage-free models begin with the observed market prices of a reference set of financial instruments, and the underlying assumption is that the reference set is correctly priced.

- Historical yield curve movements suggest that they can be explained by a linear combination of three principal movements: level, steepness, and curvature.

- The volatility term structure can be measured using historical data and depicts yield curve risk.

- The sensitivity of a bond value to yield curve changes may make use of effective duration, key rate durations, or sensitivities to parallel, steepness, and curvature movements. Using key rate durations or sensitivities to parallel, steepness, and curvature movements allows one to measure and manage shaping risk.

REFERENCES

Cox, John C., Jonathan E. Ingersoll, and Stephen A. Ross. 1985. "An Intertemporal General Equilibrium Model of Asset Prices." *Econometrica*, March:363–384.

Haubrich, Joseph G. 2006. "Does the Yield Curve Signal Recession?" Federal Reserve Bank of Cleveland (15 April).

Ho, Thomas S.Y., and Sang Bin Lee. 1986. "Term Structure Movements and Pricing Interest Rate Contingent Claims." *Journal of Finance*, December:1011–1029.

Litterman, Robert, and José Scheinkman. 1991. "Common Factors Affecting Bond Returns." *Journal of Fixed Income*, vol. 1, no. 1 (June):54–61.

Vasicek, Oldrich. 1977. "An Equilibrium Characterization of the Term Structure." *Journal of Financial Economics*, November:177–188.

Yan, Hong. 2001. "Dynamic Models of the Term Structure." *Financial Analysts Journal*, vol. 57, no. 4 (July/August):60–76.

PRACTICE PROBLEMS

1 Given spot rates for one-, two-, and three-year zero coupon bonds, how many forward rates can be calculated?

2 Give two interpretations for the following forward rate: The two-year forward rate one year from now is 2%.

3 Describe the relationship between forward rates and spot rates if the yield curve is flat.

4 **A** Define the yield to maturity for a coupon bond.

   B Is it possible for a coupon bond to earn less than the yield to maturity if held to maturity?

5 If a bond trader believes that current forward rates overstate future spot rates, how might he or she profit from that conclusion?

6 Explain the strategy of riding the yield curve.

7 What are the advantages of using the swap curve as a benchmark of interest rates relative to a government bond yield curve?

8 Describe how the Z-spread can be used to price a bond.

9 What is the TED spread and what type of risk does it measure?

10 According to the local expectations theory, what would be the difference in the one-month total return if an investor purchased a five-year zero-coupon bond versus a two-year zero-coupon bond?

11 Compare the segmented market and the preferred habitat term structure theories.

12 **A** List the three factors that have empirically been observed to affect Treasury security returns and explain how each of these factors affects returns on Treasury securities.

   B What has been observed to be the most important factor in affecting Treasury returns?

   C Which measures of yield curve risk can measure shaping risk?

13 Which forward rate cannot be computed from the one-, two-, three-, and four-year spot rates? The rate for a:

   A one-year loan beginning in two years.

   B two-year loan beginning in two years.

   C three-year loan beginning in two years.

14 Consider spot rates for three zero-coupon bonds: $r(1) = 3\%$, $r(2) = 4\%$, and $r(3) = 5\%$. Which statement is correct? The forward rate for a one-year loan beginning in one year will be:

   A less than the forward rate for a one-year loan beginning in two-years.

   B greater than the forward rate for a two-year loan beginning in one-year.

   C greater than the forward rate for a one-year loan beginning in two-years.

15 If one-period forward rates are decreasing with maturity, the yield curve is *most likely*:

   A flat.

    B upward-sloping.

    C downward sloping.

The following information relates to Questions 16–29

A one-year zero-coupon bond yields 4.0%. The two- and three-year zero-coupon bonds yield 5.0% and 6.0% respectively.

16 The rate for a one-year loan beginning in one year is *closest* to:

    A 4.5%.

    B 5.0%.

    C 6.0%.

17 The forward rate for a two-year loan beginning in one year is *closest* to:

    A 5.0%

    B 6.0%

    C 7.0%

18 The forward rate for a one-year loan beginning in two years is *closest* to:

    A 6.0%

    B 7.0%

    C 8.0%

19 The five-year spot rate is not given above; however, the forward price for a two-year zero-coupon bond beginning in three years is known to be 0.8479. The price today of a five-year zero-coupon bond is *closest* to:

    A 0.7119.

    B 0.7835.

    C 0.9524.

20 The one-year spot rate $r(1) = 4\%$, the forward rate for a one-year loan beginning in one year is 6%, and the forward rate for a one-year loan beginning in two years is 8%. Which of the following rates is *closest* to the three-year spot rate?

    A 4.0%

    B 6.0%

    C 8.0%

21 The one-year spot rate $r(1) = 5\%$ and the forward price for a one-year zero-coupon bond beginning in one year is 0.9346. The spot price of a two-year zero-coupon bond is *closest* to:

    A 0.87.

    B 0.89.

    C 0.93.

22 In a typical interest rate swap contract, the swap rate is *best* described as the interest rate for the:

    A fixed-rate leg of the swap.

    B floating-rate leg of the swap.

    C difference between the fixed and floating legs of the swap.

23 A two-year fixed-for-floating Libor swap is 1.00% and the two-year US Treasury bond is yielding 0.63%. The swap spread is *closest* to:

A   37 bps.

B   100 bps.

C   163 bps.

24 The swap spread is quoted as 50 bps. If the five-year US Treasury bond is yielding 2%, the rate paid by the fixed payer in a five-year interest rate swap is *closest* to:

A   0.50%.

B   1.50%.

C   2.50%.

25 If the three-month T-bill rate drops and the Libor rate remains the same, the relevant TED spread:

A   increases.

B   decreases.

C   does not change.

26 Given the yield curve for US Treasury zero-coupon bonds, which spread is *most* helpful pricing a corporate bond? The:

A   Z-Spread.

B   TED spread.

C   Libor–OIS spread.

27 A four-year corporate bond with a 7% coupon has a Z-spread of 200 bps. Assume a flat yield curve with an interest rate for all maturities of 5% and annual compounding. The bond will *most likely* sell:

A   close to par.

B   at a premium to par.

C   at a discount to par.

28 The Z-spread of Bond A is 1.05% and the Z-spread of Bond B is 1.53%. All else equal, which statement *best* describes the relationship between the two bonds?

A   Bond B is safer and will sell at a lower price.

B   Bond B is riskier and will sell at a lower price.

C   Bond A is riskier and will sell at a higher price.

29 Which term structure model can be calibrated to closely fit an observed yield curve?

A   The Ho–Lee Model

B   The Vasicek Model

C   The Cox–Ingersoll–Ross Model

The following information relates to Questions 30–36

Jane Nguyen is a senior bond trader and Christine Alexander is a junior bond trader for an investment bank. Nguyen is responsible for her own trading activities and also for providing assignments to Alexander that will develop her skills and create profitable trade ideas. Exhibit 1 presents the current par and spot rates.

Exhibit 1	Current Par and Spot Rates	
Maturity	**Par Rate**	**Spot Rate**
One year	2.50%	2.50%
Two years	2.99%	3.00%
Three years	3.48%	3.50%
Four years	3.95%	4.00%
Five years	4.37%	

Note: Par and spot rates are based on annual-coupon sovereign bonds.

Nguyen gives Alexander two assignments that involve researching various questions:

Assignment 1: What is the yield to maturity of the option-free, default risk–free bond presented in Exhibit 2? Assume that the bond is held to maturity, and use the rates shown in Exhibit 1.

Exhibit 2	Selected Data for $1,000 Par Bond	
Bond Name	**Maturity (T)**	**Coupon**
Bond Z	Three years	6.00%

Note: Terms are today for a *T*-year loan.

Assignment 2: Assuming that the projected spot curve two years from today will be below the current forward curve, is Bond Z fairly valued, undervalued, or overvalued?

After completing her assignments, Alexander asks about Nguyen's current trading activities. Nguyen states that she has a two-year investment horizon and will purchase Bond Z as part of a strategy to ride the yield curve. Exhibit 1 shows Nguyen's yield curve assumptions implied by the spot rates.

30 Based on Exhibit 1, the five-year spot rate is *closest to*:

   A   4.40%

   B   4.45%

   C   4.50%

31 Based on Exhibit 1, the market is *most likely* expecting:

   A   deflation.

   B   inflation.

   C   no risk premiums.

32 Based on Exhibit 1, the forward rate of a one-year loan beginning in three years is *closest to*:

A 4.17%.

B 4.50%.

C 5.51%.

33 Based on Exhibit 1, which of the following forward rates can be computed?

A A one-year loan beginning in five years

B A three-year loan beginning in three years

C A four-year loan beginning in one year

34 For Assignment 1, the yield to maturity for Bond Z is *closest* to the:

A one-year spot rate.

B two-year spot rate.

C three-year spot rate.

35 For Assignment 2, Alexander should conclude that Bond Z is currently:

A undervalued.

B fairly valued.

C overvalued.

36 By choosing to buy Bond Z, Nguyen is *most likely* making which of the following assumptions?

A Bond Z will be held to maturity.

B The three-year forward curve is above the spot curve.

C Future spot rates do not accurately reflect future inflation.

The following information relates to Questions 37–41

Laura Mathews recently hired Robert Smith, an investment adviser at Shire Gate Advisers, to assist her in investing. Mathews states that her investment time horizon is short, approximately two years or less. Smith gathers information on spot rates for on-the-run annual-coupon government securities and swap spreads, as presented in Exhibit 1. Shire Gate Advisers recently published a report for its clients stating its belief that, based on the weakness in the financial markets, interest rates will remain stable, the yield curve will not change its level or shape for the next two years, and swap spreads will also remain unchanged.

Exhibit 1   Government Spot Rates and Swap Spreads

	Maturity (years)			
	1	2	3	4
Government spot rate	2.25%	2.70%	3.30%	4.05%
Swap spread	0.25%	0.30%	0.45%	0.70%

Smith decides to examine the following three investment options for Mathews:

Investment 1:	Buy a government security that would have an annualized return that is nearly risk free. Smith is considering two possible implementations: a two-year investment or a combination of two one-year investments.
Investment 2:	Buy a four-year, zero-coupon corporate bond and then sell it after two years. Smith illustrates the returns from this strategy using the swap rate as a proxy for corporate yields.
Investment 3:	Buy a lower-quality, two-year corporate bond with a coupon rate of 4.15% and a Z-spread of 65 bps.

When Smith meets with Mathews to present these choices, Mathews tells him that she is somewhat confused by the various spread measures. She is curious to know whether there is one spread measure that could be used as a good indicator of the risk and liquidity of money market securities during the recent past.

37 In his presentation of Investment 1, Smith could show that under the no-arbitrage principle, the forward price of a one-year government bond to be issued in one year is *closest* to:

    A 0.9662.

    B 0.9694.

    C 0.9780.

38 In presenting Investment 1, using Shire Gate Advisers' interest rate outlook, Smith could show that riding the yield curve provides a total return that is *most likely*:

    A lower than the return on a maturity-matching strategy.

    B equal to the return on a maturity-matching strategy.

    C higher than the return on a maturity-matching strategy.

39 In presenting Investment 2, Smith should show a total return *closest* to:

    A 4.31%.

    B 5.42%.

    C 6.53%.

40 The bond in Investment 3 is *most likely* trading at a price of:

    A 100.97.

    B 101.54.

    C 104.09.

41 The *most* appropriate response to Mathews question regarding a spread measure is the:

    A Z-spread.

    B Treasury–Eurodollar (TED) spread.

    C Libor–OIS (overnight indexed swap) spread.

The following information relates to Questions 42–48

Rowan Madison is a junior analyst at Cardinal Capital. Sage Winter, a senior portfolio manager and Madison's supervisor, meets with Madison to discuss interest rates and review two bond positions in the firm's fixed-income portfolio.

Winter begins the meeting by asking Madison to state her views on the term structure of interest rates. Madison responds:

> "Yields are a reflection of expected spot rates and risk premiums. Investors demand risk premiums for holding long-term bonds, and these risk premiums increase with maturity."

Winter next asks Madison to describe features of equilibrium and arbitrage-free term structure models. Madison responds by making the following statements:

Statement 1   "Equilibrium term structure models are factor models that use the observed market prices of a reference set of financial instruments, assumed to be correctly priced, to model the market yield curve."

Statement 2   "In contrast, arbitrage-free term structure models seek to describe the dynamics of the term structure by using fundamental economic variables that are assumed to affect interest rates."

Winter asks Madison about her preferences concerning term structure models. Madison states:

> "I prefer arbitrage-free models. Even though equilibrium models require fewer parameters to be estimated relative to arbitrage-free models, arbitrage-free models allow for time-varying parameters. In general, this allowance leads to arbitrage-free models being able to model the market yield curve more precisely than equilibrium models."

Winter tells Madison that, based on recent changes in spreads, she is concerned about a perceived increase in counterparty risk in the economy and its effect on the portfolio. Madison asks Winter:

> "Which spread measure should we use to assess changes in counterparty risk in the economy?"

Winter is also worried about the effect of yield volatility on the portfolio. She asks Madison to identify the economic factors that affect short-term and long-term rate volatility. Madison responds:

> "Short-term rate volatility is mostly linked to uncertainty regarding monetary policy, whereas long-term rate volatility is mostly linked to uncertainty regarding the real economy and inflation."

Finally, Winter asks Madison to analyze the interest rate risk portfolio positions in a 5-year and a 20-year bond. Winter requests that the analysis be based on level, slope, and curvature as term structure factors. Madison presents her analysis in Exhibit 1.

Exhibit 1	Three-Factor Model of Term Structure	
	Time to Maturity (years)	
Factor	5	20
Level	−0.4352%	−0.5128%
Steepness	−0.0515%	−0.3015%
Curvature	0.3963%	0.5227%

Note: Entries indicate how yields would change for a one standard deviation increase in a factor.

Winter asks Madison to perform two analyses:

Analysis 1:   Calculate the expected change in yield on the 20-year bond resulting from a two standard deviation increase in the steepness factor.

Analysis 2:   Calculate the expected change in yield on the five-year bond resulting from a one standard deviation decrease in the level factor and a one standard deviation decrease in the curvature factor.

42   Madison's views on the term structure of interest rates are *most* consistent with the:

   A   local expectations theory.

   B   segmented markets theory.

   C   liquidity preference theory.

43   Which of Madison's statement(s) regarding equilibrium and arbitrage-free term structure models is *incorrect*?

   A   Statement 1 only

   B   Statement 2 only

   C   Both Statement 1 and Statement 2

44   Is Madison correct in describing key differences in equilibrium and arbitrage-free models as they relate to the number of parameters and model accuracy?

   A   Yes

   B   No, she is incorrect about which type of model requires fewer parameter estimates

   C   No, she is incorrect about which type of model is more precise at modeling market yield curves

45   The *most appropriate* response to Madison's question regarding the spread measure is the:

   A   Z-spread.

   B   Treasury–Eurodollar (TED) spread.

   C   Libor–OIS (overnight indexed swap) spread.

46   Is Madison's response regarding the factors that affect short-term and long-term rate volatility correct?

   A   Yes

   B   No, she is incorrect regarding factors linked to long-term rate volatility

   C   No, she is incorrect regarding factors linked to short-term rate volatility

47   Based on Exhibit 1, the results of Analysis 1 should show the yield on the 20-year bond decreasing by:

A 0.3015%.

B 0.6030%.

C 0.8946%.

48 Based on Exhibit 1, the results of Analysis 2 should show the yield on the five-year bond:

A decreasing by 0.8315%.

B decreasing by 0.0389%.

C increasing by 0.0389%.

SOLUTIONS

1   Three forward rates can be calculated from the one-, two- and three-year spot rates. The rate on a one-year loan that begins at the end of Year 1 can be calculated using the one- and two-year spot rates; in the following equation one would solve for $f(1,1)$:

$$[1 + r(2)]^2 = [1 + r(1)]^1[1 + f(1,1)]^1$$

The rate on a one-year loan that starts at the end of Year 2 can be calculated from the two- and three-year spot rates; in the following equation one would solve for $f(2,1)$:

$$[1 + r(3)]^3 = [1 + r(2)]^2[1 + f(2,1)]^1$$

Additionally, the rate on a two-year loan that begins at the end of Year 1 can be computed from the one- and three-year spot rates; in the following equation one would solve for $f(1,2)$:

$$[1 + r(3)]^3 = [1 + r(1)]^1[1 + f(1,2)]^2$$

2   For the two-year forward rate one year from now of 2%, the two interpretations are as follows:

- 2% is the rate that will make an investor indifferent between buying a three-year zero-coupon bond or investing in a one-year zero-coupon bond and when it matures reinvesting in a zero-coupon bond that matures in two years.

- 2% is the rate that can be locked in today by buying a three-year zero-coupon bond rather than investing in a one-year zero-coupon bond and when it matures reinvesting in a zero-coupon bond that matures in two years.

3   A flat yield curve implies that all spot interest rates are the same. When the spot rate is the same for every maturity, successive applications of the forward rate model will show all the forward rates will also be the same and equal to the spot rate.

4   **A**   The yield to maturity of a coupon bond is the expected rate of return on a bond if the bond is held to maturity, there is no default, and the bond and all coupons are reinvested at the original yield to maturity.

   B   Yes, it is possible. For example, if reinvestment rates for the future coupons are lower than the initial yield to maturity, a bond holder may experience lower realized returns.

5   If forward rates are higher than expected future spot rates the market price of the bond will be lower than the intrinsic value. This is because, everything else held constant, the market is currently discounting the bonds cash flows at a higher rate than the investor's expected future spot rates. The investor can capitalize on this by purchasing the undervalued bond. If expected future spot rates are realized, then bond prices should rise, thus generating gains for the investor.

6   The strategy of riding the yield curve is one in which a bond trader attempts to generate a total return over a given investment horizon that exceeds the return to bond with maturity matched to the horizon. The strategy involves buying a bond with maturity more distant than the investment horizon. Assuming an upward sloping yield curve, if the yield curve does not change level or shape, as

the bond approaches maturity (or rolls down the yield curve) it will be priced at successively lower yields. So as long as the bond is held for a period less than maturity, it should generate higher returns because of price gains.

7 Some countries do not have active government bond markets with trading at all maturities. For those countries without a liquid government bond market but with an active swap market, there are typically more points available to construct a swap curve than a government bond yield curve. For those markets, the swap curve may be a superior benchmark.

8 The Z-spread is the constant basis point spread added to the default-free spot curve to correctly price a risky bond. A Z-spread of 100bps for a particular bond would imply that adding a fixed spread of 100bps to the points along the spot yield curve will correctly price the bond. A higher Z-spread would imply a riskier bond.

9 The TED spread is the difference between a Libor rate and the US T-Bill rate of matching maturity. It is an indicator of perceived credit risk in the general economy. I particular, because sovereign debt instruments are typically the benchmark for the lowest default risk instruments in a given market, and loans between banks (often at Libor) have some counterparty risk, the TED spread is considered to at least in part reflect default (or counterparty) risk in the banking sector.

10 The local expectations theory asserts that the total return over a one-month horizon for a five-year zero-coupon bond would be the same as for a two-year zero-coupon bond.

11 Both theories attempt to explain the shape of any yield curve in terms of supply and demand for bonds. In segmented market theory, bond market participants are limited to purchase of maturities that match the timing of their liabilities. In the preferred habitat theory, participants have a preferred maturity for asset purchases, but may deviate from it if they feel returns in other maturities offer sufficient compensation for leaving their preferred maturity segment.

12 A Studies have shown that there have been three factors that affect Treasury returns: (1) changes in the level of the yield curve, (2) changes in the slope of the yield curve, and (3) changes in the curvature of the yield curve. Changes in the level refer to upward or downward shifts in the yield curve. For example, an upward shift in the yield curve is likely to result in lower returns across all maturities. Changes in the slope of the yield curve relate to the steepness of the yield curve. Thus, if the yield curve steepens it is likely to result in higher returns for short maturity bonds and lower returns for long maturity bonds. An example of a change in the curvature of the yield curve is a situation where rates fall at the short and long end of the yield curve while rising for intermediate maturities. In this situation returns on short and long maturities are likely to rise to rise while declining for intermediate maturity bonds.

B Empirically, the most important factor is the change in the level of interest rates.

C Key rate durations and a measure based on sensitivities to level, slope, and curvature movements can address shaping risk, but effective duration cannot.

13 C is correct. There is no spot rate information to provide rates for a loan that terminates in five years. That is $f(2,3)$ is calculated as follows:

$$f(2,3) = \sqrt[3]{\frac{\left[1 + r(5)\right]^5}{\left[1 + r(2)\right]^2}}$$

The equation above indicates that in order to calculate the rate for a three-year loan beginning at the end of two years you need the five year spot rate $r(5)$ and the two-year spot rate $r(2)$. However $r(5)$ is not provided.

14 A is correct. The forward rate for a one-year loan beginning in one-year $f(1,1)$ is $1.04^2/1.03 - 1 = 5\%$. The rate for a one-year loan beginning in two-years $f(2,1)$ is $1.05^3/1.04^2 - 1 = 7\%$. This confirms that an upward sloping yield curve is consistent with an upward sloping forward curve.

15 C is correct. If one-period forward rates are decreasing with maturity then the forward curve is downward sloping. This turn implies a downward sloping yield curve where longer term spot rates $r(T + T^*)$ are less than shorter term spot rates $r(T)$.

16 C is correct. From the forward rate model, we have

$$[1 + r(2)]^2 = [1 + r(1)]^1[1 + f(1,1)]^1$$

Using the one- and two-year spot rates, we have

$$(1 + .05)^2 = (1 + .04)^1[1 + f(1,1)]^1, \text{ so } \frac{(1 + .05)^2}{(1 + .04)^1} - 1 = f(1,1) = 6.010\%$$

17 C is correct. From the forward rate model,

$$[1 + r(3)]^3 = [1 + r(1)]^1[1 + f(1,2)]^2$$

Using the one and three-year spot rates, we find

$$(1 + 0.06)^3 = (1 + 0.04)^1[1 + f(1,2)]^2, \text{ so } \sqrt{\frac{(1 + 0.06)^3}{(1 + 0.04)^1}} - 1 = f(1,2) = 7.014\%$$

18 C is correct. From the forward rate model,

$$[1 + r(3)]^3 = [1 + r(2)]^2[1 + f(2,1)]^1$$

Using the two and three-year spot rates, we find

$$(1 + 0.06)^3 = (1 + 0.05)^2[1 + f(2,1)]^1, \text{ so } \frac{(1 + 0.06)^3}{(1 + 0.05)^2} - 1 = f(2,1) = 8.029\%$$

19 A is correct. We can convert spot rates to spot prices to find $P(3) = \dfrac{1}{(1.06)^3} = 0.8396$. The forward pricing model can be used to find the price of the five-year zero as $P(T^* + T) = P(T^*)F(T^*,T)$, so $P(5) = P(3)F(3,2) = 0.8396 \times 0.8479 = 0.7119$.

20 B is correct. Applying the forward rate model, we find

$$[1 + r(3)]^3 = [1 + r(1)]^1[1 + f(1,1)]^1[1 + f(2,1)]^1$$

So $[1 + r(3)]^3 = (1 + 0.04)^1(1 + 0.06)^1(1 + 0.08)^1$, $\sqrt[3]{1.1906} - 1 = r(3) = 5.987\%$.

21 B is correct. We can convert spot rates to spot prices and use the forward pricing model, so have $P(1) = \dfrac{1}{(1.05)^1} = 0.9524$. The forward pricing model is

$P(T^* + T) = P(T^*)F(T^*,T)$ so $P(2) = P(1)F(1,1) = 0.9524 \times 0.9346 = 0.8901$.

22 A is correct. The swap rate is the interest rate for the fixed-rate leg of an interest rate swap.

23 A is correct. The swap spread = 1.00% – 0.63% = 0.37% or 37 bps.

24 C is correct. The fixed leg of the five-year fixed-for-floating swap will be equal to the five-year Treasury rate plus the swap spread: 2% + 0.5% = 2.5%.

25 A is correct. The TED spread is the difference between the three-month Libor rate and the three-month Treasury bill rate. If the T-bill rate falls and Libor does not change, the TED spread will increase.

26 A is correct. The Z-spread is the single rate which, when added to the rates of the spot yield curve, will provide the correct discount rates to price a particular risky bond.

27 A is correct. The 200bps Z-spread can be added to the 5% rates from the yield curve to price the bond. The resulting 7% discount rate will be the same for all of the bond's cash-flows, since the yield curve is flat. A 7% coupon bond yielding 7% will be priced at par.

28 B is correct. The higher Z-spread for Bond B implies it is riskier than Bond A. The higher discount rate will make the price of Bond B lower than Bond A.

29 A is correct. The Ho–Lee model is arbitrage-free and can be calibrated to closely match the observed term structure.

30 B is correct. The five-year spot rate is determined by using forward substitution and using the known values of the one-year, two-year, three-year, and four-year spot rates as follows:

$$1 = \frac{0.0437}{(1.025)} + \frac{0.0437}{(1.030)^2} + \frac{0.0437}{(1.035)^3} + \frac{0.0437}{(1.040)^4} + \frac{1+0.0437}{\left[1+r(5)\right]^5}$$

$$r(5) = \sqrt[5]{\frac{1.0437}{0.8394}} - 1 = 4.453\%$$

31 B is correct. The spot rates imply an upward-sloping yield curve, $r(3) > r(2) > r(1)$. Because nominal yields incorporate a premium for expected inflation, an upward-sloping yield curve is generally interpreted as reflecting a market expectation of increasing, or at least level, future inflation (associated with relatively strong economic growth).

32 C is correct. A one-year loan beginning in three years, or $f(3,1)$, is calculated as follows:

$$\left[1+r(3+1)\right]^{(3+1)} = \left[1+r(3)\right]^3\left[1+f(3,1)\right]^1$$

$$[1.040]^4 = [1.035]^3\left[1+f(3,1)\right]^1$$

$$f(3,1) = \frac{(1.04)^4}{(1.035)^3} - 1 = 5.514\%$$

33 C is correct. Exhibit 1 provides five years of par rates, from which the spot rates for $r(1)$, $r(2)$, $r(3)$, $r(4)$, and $r(5)$ can be derived. Thus the forward rate $f(1,4)$ can be calculated as follows:

$$f(1,4) = \sqrt[4]{\frac{[1+r(5)]^5}{[1+r(1)]}} - 1$$

34 C is correct. The yield to maturity, $y(3)$, of Bond Z should be a weighted average of the spot rates used in the valuation of the bond. Because the bond's largest cash flow occurs in Year 3, $r(3)$ will have a greater weight than $r(1)$ and $r(2)$ in determining $y(3)$.

Using the spot rates:

$$\text{Price} = \frac{\$60}{(1.025)^1} + \frac{\$60}{(1.030)^2} + \frac{\$1,060}{(1.035)^3} = \$1,071.16$$

Using the yield to maturity:

$$\text{Price} = \frac{\$60}{[1+y(3)]^1} + \frac{\$60}{[1+y(3)]^2} + \frac{\$1,060}{[1+y(3)]^3} = \$1,071.16$$

Using a calculator, the compute result is $y(3) = 3.46\%$, which is closest to the three-year spot rate of 3.50%.

35 A is correct. Alexander projects that the spot curve two years from today will be below the current forward curve, which implies that her expected future spot rates beyond two years will be lower than the quoted forward rates. Alexander would perceive Bond Z to be undervalued in the sense that the market is effectively discounting the bond's payments at a higher rate than she would and the bond's market price is below her estimate of intrinsic value.

36 B is correct. Nguyen's strategy is to ride the yield curve, which is appropriate when the yield curve is upward sloping. The yield curve implied by Exhibit 1 is upward sloping, which implies that the three-year forward curve is above the current spot curve. When the yield curve slopes upward, as a bond approaches maturity or "rolls down the yield curve," the bond is valued at successively lower yields and higher prices.

37 B is correct. The forward pricing model is based on the no-arbitrage principle and is used to calculate a bond's forward price based on the spot yield curve. The spot curve is constructed by using annualized rates from option-free and default risk–free zero-coupon bonds.

Equation 2: $P(T^* + T) = P(T^*)F(T^*,T)$; we need to solve for $F(1,1)$.

$P(1) = 1/(1 + 0.0225)^1$ and $P(2) = 1/(1 + 0.0270)^2$,

$F(1,1) = P(2)/P(1) = 0.9481/0.9780 = 0.9694$.

38 C is correct. When the spot curve is upward sloping and its level and shape are expected to remain constant over an investment horizon (Shire Gate Advisers' view), buying bonds with a maturity longer than the investment horizon (i.e., riding the yield curve) will provide a total return greater than the return on a maturity-matching strategy.

39 C is correct. The swap spread is a common way to indicate credit spreads in a market. The four-year swap rate (fixed leg of an interest rate swap) can be used as an indication of the four-year corporate yield. Riding the yield curve by purchasing a four-year zero-coupon bond with a yield of 4.75% {i.e., 4.05% + 0.70%, $[P_4 = 100/(1 + 0.0475)^4 = 83.058]$} and then selling it when it becomes a two-year zero-coupon bond with a yield of 3.00% {i.e., 2.70% + 0.30%, $[P_2 = 100/(1 + 0.0300)^2 = 94.260]$} produces an annual return of 6.53%: $(94.260/83.058)^{0.5} - 1.0 = 0.0653$.

40 B is correct. The Z-spread is the constant basis point spread that is added to the default-free spot curve to price a risky bond. A Z-spread of 65 bps for a particular bond would imply adding a fixed spread of 65 bps to maturities along the spot curve to correctly price the bond. Therefore, for the two-year bond, $r(1) = 2.90\%$ (i.e., 2.25% + 0.65%), $r(2) = 3.35\%$ (i.e., 2.70% + 0.65%), and the price of the bond with an annual coupon of 4.15% is as follows:

$$P = 4.15/(1 + 0.029)^1 + 4.15/(1 + 0.0335)^2 + 100/(1 + 0.0335)^2,$$

$$P = 101.54.$$

41 C is correct. The Libor–OIS spread is considered an indicator of the risk and liquidity of money market securities. This spread measures the difference between Libor and the OIS rate.

42 C is correct. Liquidity preference theory asserts that investors demand a risk premium, in the form of a liquidity premium, to compensate them for the added interest rate risk they face when buying long-maturity bonds. The theory also states that the liquidity premium increases with maturity.

43 C is correct. Both statements are incorrect because Madison incorrectly describes both types of models. Equilibrium term structure models are factor models that seek to describe the dynamics of the term structure by using fundamental economic variables that are assumed to affect interest rates. Arbitrage-free term structure models use observed market prices of a reference set of financial instruments, assumed to be correctly priced, to model the market yield curve.

44 A is correct. Consistent with Madison's statement, equilibrium term structure models require fewer parameters to be estimated relative to arbitrage-free models, and arbitrage-free models allow for time-varying parameters. Consequently, arbitrage-free models can model the market yield curve more precisely than equilibrium models.

45 B is correct. The TED spread, calculated as the difference between Libor and the yield on a T-bill of matching maturity, is an indicator of perceived credit risk in the general economy. An increase (decrease) in the TED spread signals that lenders believe the risk of default on interbank loans is increasing (decreasing). Therefore, the TED spread can be thought of as a measure of counterparty risk.

46 A is correct. Madison's response is correct; research indicates that short-term rate volatility is mostly linked to uncertainty regarding monetary policy, whereas long-term rate volatility is mostly linked to uncertainty regarding the real economy and inflation.

47 B is correct. Because the factors in Exhibit 1 have been standardized to have unit standard deviations, a two standard deviation increase in the steepness factor will lead to the yield on the 20-year bond decreasing by 0.6030%, calculated as follows:

Change in 20-year bond yield = −0.3015% × 2 = −0.6030%.

48 C is correct. Because the factors in Exhibit 1 have been standardized to have unit standard deviations, a one standard deviation decrease in both the level factor and the curvature factor will lead to the yield on the five-year bond increasing by 0.0389%, calculated as follows:

Change in five-year bond yield = 0.4352% − 0.3963% = 0.0389%.

The Arbitrage-Free Valuation Framework

by Steven V. Mann, PhD

Steven V. Mann, PhD, is at the University of South Carolina (USA).

LEARNING OUTCOMES

Mastery	The candidate should be able to:
☐	**a.** explain what is meant by arbitrage-free valuation of a fixed-income instrument;
☐	**b.** calculate the arbitrage-free value of an option-free, fixed-rate coupon bond;
☐	**c.** describe a binomial interest rate tree framework;
☐	**d.** describe the backward induction valuation methodology and calculate the value of a fixed-income instrument given its cash flow at each node;
☐	**e.** describe the process of calibrating a binomial interest rate tree to match a specific term structure;
☐	**f.** compare pricing using the zero-coupon yield curve with pricing using an arbitrage-free binomial lattice;
☐	**g.** describe pathwise valuation in a binomial interest rate framework and calculate the value of a fixed-income instrument given its cash flows along each path;
☐	**h.** describe a Monte Carlo forward-rate simulation and its application.

INTRODUCTION

1

The idea that market prices will adjust until there are no opportunities for arbitrage underpins the valuation of fixed-income securities, derivatives, and other financial assets. It is as intuitive as it is well-known. For a given investment, if the net proceeds are zero (e.g., buying and selling the same dollar amount of stocks) and the risk is zero, the return should be zero. Valuation tools must produce a value that is arbitrage free. The purpose of this reading is to develop a set of valuation tools for bonds that are consistent with this notion.

The reading is organized around the learning objectives. After this brief introduction, Section 2 defines an arbitrage opportunity and discusses the implications of no arbitrage for the valuation of fixed-income securities. Section 3 presents some essential ideas and tools from yield curve analysis needed to introduce the binomial interest rate tree. In this section, the binomial interest rate tree framework is developed and used to value an option-free bond. The process used to calibrate the interest rate tree to match the current yield curve is introduced. This step ensures that the interest rate tree is consistent with pricing using the zero-coupon (i.e., spot) curve. The final topic presented in the section is an introduction of pathwise valuation. Section 4 describes a Monte Carlo forward-rate simulation and its application. A summary of the major results is given in Section 5.

2   THE MEANING OF ARBITRAGE-FREE VALUATION

Arbitrage-free valuation refers to an approach to security valuation that determines security values that are consistent with the absence of an **arbitrage opportunity**, which is an opportunity for trades that earn riskless profits without any net investment of money. In well-functioning markets, prices adjust until there are no arbitrage opportunities, which is the **principle of no arbitrage** that underlies the practical validity of arbitrage-free valuation. This principle itself can be thought of as an implication of the idea that identical assets should sell at the same price.

These concepts will be explained in greater detail shortly, but to indicate how they arise in bond valuation, consider first an imaginary world in which financial assets are free of risk and the benchmark yield curve is flat. A flat yield curve implies that the relevant yield is the same for all cash flows regardless of when the cash flows are delivered in time.[1] Accordingly, the value of a bond is the present value of its certain future cash flows. In discounting those cash flows—determining their present value—investors would use the risk-free interest rate because the cash flows are certain; because the yield curve is assumed to be flat, one risk-free rate would exist and apply to all future cash flows. This is the simplest case of bond valuation one can envision. When we exit this imaginary world and enter more realistic environs, bonds' cash flows are risky (i.e., there is some chance the borrower will default) and the benchmark yield curve is not flat. How would our approach change?

A fundamental principle of valuation is that the value of any financial asset is equal to the present value of its expected future cash flows. This principle holds for any financial asset from zero-coupon bonds to interest rate swaps. Thus, the valuation of a financial asset involves the following three steps:

Step 1   Estimate the future cash flows.

Step 2   Determine the appropriate discount rate or discount rates that should be used to discount the cash flows.

Step 3   Calculate the present value of the expected future cash flows found in Step 1 by applying the appropriate discount rate or rates determined in Step 2.

The traditional approach to valuing bonds is to discount all cash flows with the same discount rate as if the yield curve were flat. However, a bond is properly thought of as a package or portfolio of zero-coupon bonds. Each zero-coupon bond in such a package can be valued separately at a discount rate that depends on the shape of the

---

1 The terms yield, interest rate, and discount rate will be used interchangeably.

yield curve and when its single cash flow is delivered in time. The term structure of these discount rates is referred to as the spot curve. Bond values derived by summing the present values of the individual zeros (cash flows) determined by such a procedure can be shown to be arbitrage free.[2] Ignoring transaction costs for the moment, if the bond's value was much less than the sum of the values of its cash flows individually, a trader would perceive an arbitrage opportunity and buy the bond while selling claims to the individual cash flows and pocketing the excess value. Although the details bear further discussion (see Section 2.3), the valuation of a bond as a portfolio of zeros based on using the spot curve is an example of arbitrage-free valuation. Regardless of the complexity of the bond, each component must have an arbitrage-free value. A bond with embedded options can be valued in parts as the sum of the arbitrage-free bond without options (that is, a bond with no embedded options) and the arbitrage-free value of each of the options.

2.1 The Law of One Price

The central idea of financial economics is that market prices will adjust until there are no opportunities for arbitrage. We will define shortly what is meant by an arbitrage opportunity, but for now think of it as "free money." Prices will adjust until there is no free money to be acquired. Arbitrage opportunities arise as a result of violations of the **law of one price**. The law of one price states that two goods that are perfect substitutes must sell for the same current price in the absence of transaction costs. Two goods that are identical, trading side by side, are priced the same. Otherwise, if it were costless to trade, one would simultaneously buy at the lower price and sell at the higher price. The riskless profit is the difference in the prices. An individual would repeat this transaction without limit until the two prices converge. An implication of these market forces is deceptively straightforward and basic. If you do not put up any of your own money and take no risk, your expected return should be zero.

2.2 Arbitrage Opportunity

With this background, let us define arbitrage opportunity more precisely. An arbitrage opportunity is a transaction that involves no cash outlay that results in a riskless profit. There are two types of arbitrage opportunities. The first type of arbitrage opportunity is often called **value additivity** or, put simply, the value of the whole equals the sum of the values of the parts. Consider two risk-free investments with payoffs one year from today and the prices today provided in Exhibit 1. Asset A is a simple risk-free zero-coupon bond that pays off one dollar and is priced today at 0.952381 ($1/1.05). Asset B is a portfolio of 105 units of Asset A that pays off $105 one year from today and is priced today at $95. The portfolio does not equal the sum of the parts. The portfolio (Asset B) is cheaper than buying 105 units of Asset A at a price of $100 and then combining. An astute investor would sell 105 units of Asset A for 105 × $0.952381 = $100 while simultaneously buying one portfolio Asset B for $95. This position generates a certain $5 today ($100-95) and generates net $0 one year from today because cash inflow for Asset B matches the amount for the 105 units of Asset A sold. An investor would engage in this trade over and over again until the prices adjust.

The second type of arbitrage opportunity is often called **dominance**. A financial asset with a risk-free payoff in the future must have a positive price today. Consider two assets, C and D, that are risk-free zero-coupon bonds. Payoffs in one year and prices today are displayed in Exhibit 1. On careful review, it appears that Asset D is cheap relative to Asset C. If both assets are risk-free, they should have the same

---

2 A zero is a zero-coupon bond or discount instrument.

discount rate. To make money, sell two units of Asset C at a price of $200 and use the proceeds to purchase one unit of Asset D for $200. The construction of the portfolio involves no net cash outlay today. Although it requires zero dollars to construct today, the portfolio generates $10 one year from today. Asset D will generate a $220 cash inflow whereas the two units of Asset C sold will produce a cash outflow of $210.

Exhibit 1	Price Today and Payoffs in One Year for Sample Assets	
Asset	**Price Today**	**Payoff in One Year**
A	$0.952381	$1
B	$95	$105
C	$100	$105
D	$200	$220

This existence of both types of arbitrage opportunities is transitory. Investors aware of this mispricing will demand the securities in question in unlimited quantities. Something must change in order to restore stability. Prices will adjust until there are no arbitrage opportunities.

EXAMPLE 1

Arbitrage Opportunities

Which of the following investment alternatives includes an arbitrage opportunity?

> **Bond A:** The yield for a 3% coupon 10-year annual-pay bond is 2.5% in New York City. The same bond sells for $104.376 per $100 face value in Chicago.

> **Bond B:** The yield for a 3% coupon 10-year annual-pay bond is 3.2% in Hong Kong. The same bond sells for RMB97.220 per RMB100 face value in Shanghai.

Solution:

Bond B is correct. Bond B's arbitrage-free price is $3/1.032 + 3/1.032^2 + ... + 103/1.032^{10} = 98.311$, which is higher than the price in Shanghai. Therefore, an arbitrage opportunity exists. Buy bonds in Shanghai for RMB97.220 and sell them in Hong Kong for RMB98.311. You make RMB1.091 per RMB100 of bonds traded.

　　Bond A's arbitrage-free price is $3/1.025 + 3/1.025^2 + ... + 103/1.025^{10} = 104.376$, which matches the price in Chicago. Therefore, no arbitrage opportunity exists in this market.

2.3 Implications of Arbitrage-Free Valuation for Fixed-Income Securities

Using the arbitrage-free approach, any fixed-income security should be thought of as a package or portfolio of zero-coupon bonds. Thus, a five-year 2% coupon Treasury issue should be viewed as a package of eleven zero-coupon instruments (10 semiannual coupon payments, one of which is made at maturity, and one principal value payment at maturity) The market mechanism for US Treasuries that enables this approach is the dealer's ability to separate the bond's individual cash flows and trade them as zero-coupon securities. This process is called **stripping**. In addition, dealers can recombine the appropriate individual zero-coupon securities and reproduce the underlying coupon Treasury. This process is called **reconstitution**. Dealers in sovereign debt markets around the globe are free to engage in the same process.

Arbitrage profits are possible when value additivity does not hold. The arbitrage-free valuation approach does not allow a market participant to realize an arbitrage profit through stripping and reconstitution. By viewing any security as a package of zero-coupon securities, a consistent and coherent valuation framework can be developed. Viewing a security as a package of zero-coupon bonds means that two bonds with the same maturity and different coupon rates are viewed as different packages of zero-coupon bonds and valued accordingly. Moreover, two cash flows that have identical risks delivered at the same time will be valued using the same discount rate even though they are attached to two different bonds.

INTEREST RATE TREES AND ARBITRAGE-FREE VALUATION   **3**

The goal of this section is to develop a method to produce an arbitrage-free value for an option-free bond and to provide a framework—based on interest rate trees–that is rich enough to be applied to the valuation of bonds with embedded options.

For bonds that are option-free, the simplest approach to arbitrage-free valuation involves determining the arbitrage-free value as the sum of the present values of expected future values using the benchmark spot rates. Benchmark securities are liquid, safe securities whose yields serve as building blocks for other interest rates in a particular country or currency. Sovereign debt is the benchmark in many countries. For example, on-the-run Treasuries serve as benchmark securities in the United States. Par rates derived from the Treasury yield curve can be used to obtain spot rates by means of bootstrapping. Gilts serve as a benchmark in the United Kingdom. In markets where the sovereign debt market is not sufficiently liquid, the swaps curve is a viable alternative.

In this reading, benchmark bonds are assumed to be correctly priced by the market. The valuation model we develop will be constructed so as to reproduce exactly the prices of the benchmark bonds.

EXAMPLE 2

The Arbitrage-Free Value of an Option-Free Bond

The yield to maturity ("par rate") for a benchmark one-year annual-pay bond is 2%, for a benchmark two-year annual-pay bond is 3%, and for a benchmark three-year annual-pay bond is 4%. A three year, 5% coupon, annual-pay bond with the same risk and liquidity as the benchmarks is selling for $102.7751 today (time zero) to yield 4%. Is this value correct for the bond given the current term structure?

Solution:

The first step in the solution is to find the correct spot rate (zero-coupon rates) for each year's cash flow.[3] The spot rates may be determined using bootstrapping, which is an iterative process. Using the bond valuation equation below, one can solve iteratively for the spot rates, z_t (rate on a zero-coupon bond of maturity t), given the periodic payment, PMT, on the relevant benchmark bond.

$$100 = \frac{PMT}{(1 + z_1)^1} + \frac{PMT}{(1 + z_2)^2} + \cdots + \frac{PMT + 100}{(1 + z_N)^N}$$

A revised equation, which uses the par rate rather than PMT, may also be used to calculate the spot rates. The revised equation is:

$$1 = \frac{\text{Par rate}}{[1 + r(1)]^1} + \frac{\text{Par rate}}{[1 + r(2)]^2} + \cdots + \frac{\text{Par rate} + 1}{[1 + r(N)]^N}$$

where par rate is PMT divided by 100 and represents the par rate on the benchmark bond and $r(t)$ is the t-period zero-coupon rate.

In this example, the one-year spot rate, $r(1)$, is 2%, which is the same as the one-year par rate. To solve for $r(2)$:

$$1 = \frac{0.03}{[1 + r(1)]^1} + \frac{0.03 + 1}{[1 + r(2)]^2} = \frac{0.03}{(1 + 0.02)^1} + \frac{0.03 + 1}{[1 + r(2)]^2}$$

$$r(2) = 3.015\%$$

To solve for $r(3)$:

$$1 = \frac{0.04}{(1 + 0.02)^1} + \frac{0.04}{(1 + 0.03015)^2} + \frac{0.04 + 1}{[1 + r(3)]^3}$$

$$r(3) = 4.055\%$$

The spot rates are 2%, 3.015%, and 4.055%. The correct arbitrage-free price for the bond, then, is

$$P_0 = 5/1.02 + 5/1.03015^2 + 105/1.04055^3 = \$102.8102$$

To be arbitrage-free, each cash flow of a bond must be discounted by the spot rate for zero-coupon bonds maturing on the same date as the cash flow. Discounting early coupons by the bond's yield to maturity gives too much discounting with an upward sloping yield curve and too little discounting for a downward sloping yield curve. The bond is mispriced by $0.0351 per $100 of par value.

For option-free bonds, performing valuation discounting with spot rates produces an arbitrage-free valuation. For bonds that have embedded options, we need a different approach. The challenge one faces when developing a framework for valuing bonds with embedded options is that their expected future cash flows are interest rate dependent. If the bonds are option-free, changes in interest rates have no impact on the size and timing of the bond's cash flows. For bonds with options attached, changes in future interest rates impact the likelihood the option will be exercised and in so doing impact the cash flows. Therefore, in order to develop a framework that values both bonds without and with embedded options, we must allow interest rates to take on different potential values in the future based on some assumed level of volatility. The vehicle to portray this information is an interest rate "tree" representing possible future interest rates consistent with the assumed volatility. Because the interest rate

---

3 Par, spot, and forward interest rates were discussed in Level I.

tree resembles a lattice, these models are often called "lattice models." The interest rate tree performs two functions in the valuation process: (1) generate the cash flows that are interest rate dependent and (2) supply the interest rates used to determine the present value of the cash flows. This approach will be used in later readings when considering learning outcome statements involving callable bonds.

An interest rate model seeks to identify the elements or *factors* that are believed to explain the dynamics of interest rates. These factors are random or *stochastic* in nature, so we cannot predict the path of any particular factor. An interest rate model must, therefore, specify a statistical process that describes the stochastic property of these factors in order to arrive at a reasonably accurate representation of the behavior of interest rates. What is important to understand is that the interest rate models commonly used are based on how short-term interest rates can evolve (i.e., change) over time. Consequently, these interest rate models are referred to as one-factor models because only one interest rate is being modeled over time. More complex models consider how more than one interest rate changes over time (e.g., the short rate and the long rate) and are referred to as two-factor models.

Our task at hand is to describe the binomial interest rate tree framework. The valuation model we are attempting to build is the binomial lattice model. It is so named because the short interest rate can take on one of two possible values consistent with the volatility assumption and an interest rate model. As we will soon discover, the two possible interest rates next period will be consistent with the following three conditions: (1) an interest rate model that governs the random process of interest rates, (2) the assumed level of interest rate volatility, and (3) the current benchmark yield curve. We take the prices of the benchmark bonds as given such that when these bonds are valued in our model we recover the market values for each benchmark bond. In this way, we tie the model to the current yield curve that reflects the underlying economic reality.

3.1 The Binomial Interest Rate Tree

The first stop for demonstrating the binomial valuation method is to present the benchmark par curve by using bonds of a particular country or currency. For simplicity in our illustration, we will use US dollars. The same principles hold with equal force regardless of the country or currency. The benchmark par curve is presented in Exhibit 2. For simplicity, we assume that all bonds have annual coupon payments. Benchmark bonds are conveniently priced at par so the yields to maturity and the coupon rates on the bonds are the same. From these par rates, we use the bootstrapping methodology to uncover the underlying spot rates shown in Exhibit 3. Because the par curve is upward sloping, it comes as no surprise that after Year 1 the spot rates are higher than the par rates. In Exhibit 4 we present the one-year implied forward rates derived from the spot curve using no arbitrage. Because the par, spot, and forward curves reflect the same information about interest rates, if one of the three curves is known, it is possible to generate the other two curves. The three curves are only identical if the yield curve is flat.

Exhibit 2 Benchmark Par Curve		
Maturity (Years)	**Par Rate**	**Bond Price**
1	1.00%	100
2	1.20%	100
3	1.25%	100

(continued)

Exhibit 2   (Continued)

Maturity (Years)	Par Rate	Bond Price
4	1.40%	100
5	1.80%	100

Exhibit 3   Underlying One-Year Spot Rates of Par Rates

Maturity (Years)	One-Year Spot Rate
1	1.000%
2	1.201%
3	1.251%
4	1.404%
5	1.819%

Exhibit 4   One-Year Implied Forward Rates

Maturity (Years)	Forward Rate
Current one-year rate	1.000%
One-year rate, one year forward	1.400%
One-year rate, two years forward	1.350%
One-year rate, three years forward	1.860%
One-year rate, four years forward	3.500%

Recall from our earlier discussion that if we value the benchmark bonds using rates derived from these curves, we will recover the market price of par for all five bonds in Exhibit 2. Specifically, par rates represent the single interest applied to all the cash flows that will produce the market prices. Discounting each cash flow separately with the set of spot rates will also give the same answer. Finally, forward rates are the discount rates of a single cash flow over a single period. If we discount each cash flow with the appropriate discount rate for each period, the computed values will match the observed prices.

When we approach the valuation of bonds with cash flows that are interest rate dependent, we must explicitly allow interest rates to change. We accomplish this task by introducing interest rate volatility and generating an interest rate tree (see Section 3.2 for a discussion of interest rate volatility). An interest rate tree is simply a visual representation of the possible values of interest rates based on an interest rate model and an assumption about interest rate volatility.

A binomial interest rate tree is presented in Exhibit 5. Our goal is to learn how to populate this structure with interest rates. Notice the *i*'s, which represent different potential values one-year interest rates may take over time. As we move from left to right on the tree, the number of possible interest rates increases. The first is the current time (in years), or formally Time 0. The interest rate displayed at Time 0 is the discount rate that converts Time 1 payments to Time 0 present-free values. At the bottom of the graph, time is the unit of measurement. Notice that there is one year between possible interest rates. This is called the "time step" and, in our illustration, it matches the frequency of the annual cash flows. The i's in Exhibit 5 are called nodes. The first node is called the root of the tree and is simply the current one-year rate at Time 0.

Exhibit 5   Binomial Interest Rate Tree

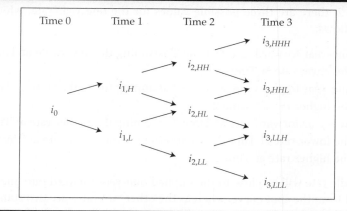

We now turn to the question of how to obtain the two possible values for the one-year interest rate one year from today. Two assumptions are required: an interest rate model and a volatility of interest rates. Recall an interest rate model puts structure on the randomness. We are going to use the lognormal random walk, and the resulting tree structure is often referred to as a lognormal tree. A lognormal model of interest rates insures two appealing properties: (1) non-negativity of interest rates and (2) higher volatility at higher interest rates. At each node, there are two possible rates one year forward at Time 1. We will assume for the time being that each has an equal probability of occurring. The two possible rates we will calculate are going to be higher and lower than the one-year forward rate at Time 1 one year from now.

We denote i_L to be the rate lower than the implied forward rate and i_H to be the higher forward rate. The lognormal random walk posits the following relationship between $i_{1,L}$ and $i_{1,H}$:

$$i_{1,H} = i_{1,L}e^{2\sigma}$$

where σ is the standard deviation and e is Euler's number, the base of natural logarithms, which is a constant 2.7183.[4] The random possibilities each period are (nearly) centered on the forward rates calculated from the benchmark curve. The intuition of this relationship is deceptively quick and simple. Think of the one-year forward implied interest rate from the yield curve as the average of possible values for the one-year rate at Time 1. The lower of the two rates, i_L, is one standard deviation below the mean (one-year implied forward rate) and i_H is one standard deviation above the mean. Thus, the higher and lower values (i_L and i_H) are multiples of each other and the multiplier is $e^{2\sigma}$. Note that as the standard deviation (i.e., volatility) increases, the multiplier increases and the two rates will grow farther apart but will still be (nearly) centered on the implied forward rate derived from the spot curve. We will demonstrate this soon.

---

4 The number e is transcendental and continues infinitely without repeating.

We use the following notation to describe the tree at Time 1. Let

σ = assumed volatility of the one-year rate,

$i_{1,L}$ = the lower one-year forward rate one year from now at Time 1, and

$i_{1,H}$ = the higher one-year forward rate one year from now at Time 1.

For example, suppose that $i_{1,L}$ is 1.194% and σ is 15% per year, then $i_{1,H}$ = 1.194%($e^{2\times0.15}$) = 1.612%.

At Time 2, there are three possible values for the one-year rate, which we will denote as follows:

$i_{2,LL}$ = one-year forward rate at Time 2 assuming the lower rate at Time 1 and the lower rate at Time 2

$i_{2,HH}$ = one-year forward rate at Time 2 assuming the higher rate at Time 1 and the higher rate at Time 2

$i_{2,HL}$ = one-year forward rate at Time 2 assuming the higher rate at Time 1 and the lower rate at Time 2, or equivalently, the lower rate at Time 1 and the higher rate at Time 2

The middle rate will be close to the implied one-year forward rate one year from now derived from the spot curve, whereas the other two rates are two standard deviations above and below this value. (Recall that the multiplier for adjacent rates on the tree differs by a multiple of e raised to the 2σ.) This type of tree is called a recombining tree because there are two paths to get to the middle rate. This feature of the model results in faster computation because the number of possible outcomes each period grows linearly rather than exponentially.

The relationship between $i_{2,LL}$ and the other two one-year rates is as follows:

$$i_{2,HH} = i_{2,LL}(e^{4\sigma}) \text{ and } i_{2,HL} = i_{2,LL}(e^{2\sigma})$$

In a given period, adjacent possible outcomes in the tree are two standard deviations apart. So, for example, if $i_{2,LL}$ is 0.980%, and assuming once again that σ is 15%, we calculate

$$i_{2,HH} = 0.980\%(e^{4\times0.15}) = 1.786\%$$

and

$$i_{2,HL} = 0.980\%(e^{2\times0.15}) = 1.323\%.$$

There are four possible values for the one-year forward rate at Time 3. These are represented as follows: $i_{3,HHH}$, $i_{3,HHL}$, $i_{3,LLH}$ and $i_{3,LLL}$. Once again all the forward rates in the tree are multiples of the lowest possible rates each year. The lowest possible forward rate at Time 3 is $i_{3,LLL}$ and is related to the other three as given below:

$$i_{3,HHH} = (e^{6\sigma})i_{3,LLL}$$

$$i_{3,HHL} = (e^{4\sigma})i_{3,LLL}$$

$$i_{3,LLH} = (e^{2\sigma})i_{3,LLL}$$

Exhibit 6 shows the notation for a four-year binomial interest rate tree. We can simplify the notation by centering the one-year rates on the tree on implied forward rates on the benchmark yield curve and letting i_t be the one-year rate t years from now be the centering rates. The subscripts indicate the rates at the end of the year, so in the second year, it is the rate at the end of Time 2 to the end of Time 3. Exhibit 6 uses this uniform notation. Note that adjacent forward rates in the tree are two standard deviations (σs) apart.

Exhibit 6   Four-Year Binomial Tree

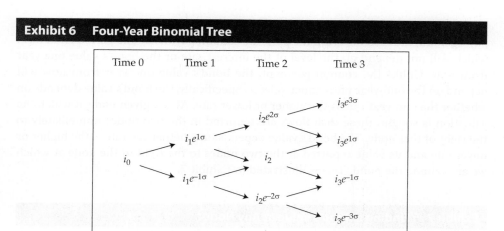

Before we attempt to build an interest rate tree, two additional tools are needed. These tools are introduced in the next two sections.

3.2 What Is Volatility and How Is It Estimated?

Recall that variance is a measure of dispersion of a probability distribution. The standard deviation is the square root of the variance and it is a statistical measure of volatility in the same units as the mean. With a simple lognormal distribution, the changes in interest rates are proportional to the level of the one-period interest rates each period. Volatility is measured relative to the current level of rates. It can be shown that for a lognormal distribution the standard deviation of the one-year rate is equal to $i_0\sigma$.[5] For example, if σ is 10% and the one-year rate (i_0) is 2%, then the standard deviation of the one-year rate is 2% × 10% = 0.2% or 20 bps. As a result, interest rate moves are larger when interest rates are high and are smaller when interest rates are low. One of the benefits of a lognormal distribution is that if interest rates get too close to zero, the absolute change in interest rates becomes smaller and smaller. Negative interest rates are not possible.

There are two methods commonly used to estimate interest rate volatility. The first method is by estimating historical interest rate volatility; volatility is calculated by using data from the recent past with the assumption that what has happened recently is indicative of the future. A second method to estimate interest rate volatility is based on observed market prices of interest rate derivatives (e.g., swaptions, caps, floors). This approach is called implied volatility.

3.3 Determining the Value of a Bond at a Node

To find the value of the bond at a particular node, we use the backward induction valuation methodology. Barring default, we know that at maturity the bonds will be valued at par. So, we start at maturity, fill in those values, and work back from right to left to find the bond's value at the desired node. Suppose we want to determine the bond's value at the lowest node at Time 1. To find this value, we must first calculate the bond's value at the two nodes to the right of the node we selected. The bond's value at the two nodes immediately to the right must be available.

---

5 Given that $e^{2\sigma} \approx 1 + 2\sigma$, the standard deviation of the one-year rate is $\dfrac{re^{2\sigma} - r}{2} \approx \dfrac{r + 2\sigma r - r}{2} = \sigma r$.

A bond's value at any node will depend on the future cash flows. For a coupon-paying bond, the cash flows are the periodic coupon payments one period from now, which will not depend on the level of the interest rate or the bond's value one year from now. Unlike the coupon payment, the bond's value one year from now will depend on the one-year rate chance selects. Specifically, the bond's value depends on whether the one-year rate is the higher or lower rate. At any given node at which the valuation is sought, these cash flows are reported in the two nodes immediately to the right of that node. The bond's value depends on whether the rate is the higher or lower rate and its value reported at the two nodes to the right of the node at which we are valuing the bond. This is illustrated in Exhibit 7.

Exhibit 7   Finding a Bond's Value at Any Node

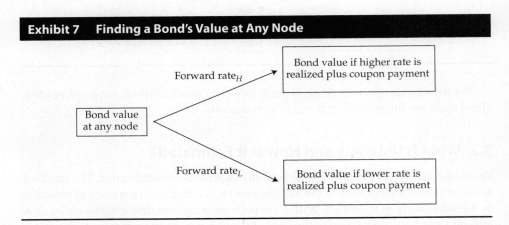

Now that we have specified the cash flows, the next step is to determine the present value of those cash flows. The relevant discount rate to use is the one-year forward rate at the node. Because there are two possible interest rates one year from today, there are two present values to calculate. The two states of the world are whether chance selects the higher or lower one-year forward rate one year hence. Because it is assumed that either outcome is equally likely, the average of the two present values is computed. This same procedure holds for any node with forward rates discounting cash flows moving from node to node.

Let us make this process more complete by introducing some notation. Assume that the one-year forward rate is i at a particular node and let

  VH = the bond's value if the higher forward rate is realized one year hence,
  VL = the bond's value if the lower forward rate is realized one year hence, and
  C = coupon payment that is not dependent on interest rates.

At any node, the cash flows one year from today are the coupon payment plus the bond's value if chance chooses the higher one-year forward rate ($C + VH$) and the coupon payment plus the bond's value if chance chooses the lower forward rate ($C + VL$). A bond's value at any node is determined by the following expression:

$$\text{Bond value at a node} = 0.50 \times \left[\frac{VH + C}{(1 + i)} + \frac{VL + C}{(1 + i)} \right]$$ (1)

EXAMPLE 3

Pricing a Bond Using a Binomial Tree

Using the interest rate tree below, find the correct price for a three-year, annual-pay bond with a coupon rate of 5%.

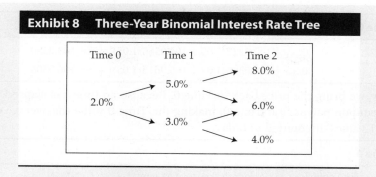

Exhibit 8   Three-Year Binomial Interest Rate Tree

Solution:

Calculating the bond's value includes being careful with the timing of cash flows. A three-year bond pays coupons and returns principal at the *end* of each year. When we state an annual interest rate, that rate is effective as of the *beginning* of that year.

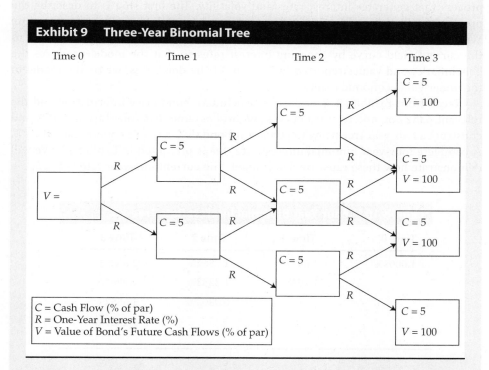

Exhibit 9   Three-Year Binomial Tree

C = Cash Flow (% of par)
R = One-Year Interest Rate (%)
V = Value of Bond's Future Cash Flows (% of par)

No matter what level interest rates move to at Time 3, the cash flow from a three-year bond at Time 3 will be the same: par plus a final coupon payment. In addition, a coupon payment will be made at Time 2. Consequently, Time 2 values will be:

Time 0	Time 1	Time 2
		0.5 × [(105/1.08 + 105/1.08)] + 5 = 102.2222
		0.5 × [(105/1.06 + 105/1.06)] + 5 = 104.0566
		0.5 × [(105/1.04 + 105/1.04)] + 5 = 105.9615

Time 1 values will be the average of Time 2 discounted plus the coupon payment:

Time 0	Time 1
	$0.5 \times [(102.2222/1.05 + 104.0566/1.05)] + 5 = 103.2280$
	$0.5 \times [(104.0566/1.03 + 105.9615/1.03)] + 5 = 106.9506$

Finally, we bring the price back to Time 0. Because no time has elapsed, there is no coupon payment at Time 0, making the Time 0 value the average of the Time 1 values discounted to today:

Time 0
$0.5 \times [(103.2280/1.02 + 106.9506/1.02)] = 103.0287$

3.4 Constructing the Binomial Interest Rate Tree

The construction of a binomial interest rate tree requires multiple steps, but keep in mind what we are trying to accomplish. We are making an assumption about the process that generates interest rates and volatility. The first step is to describe the process of calibrating a binomial interest rate tree to match a specific term structure. We do this to ensure that the model is arbitrage free. We fit the interest rate tree to the current yield curve by choosing interest rates so that the model produces the benchmark bond values reported in Section 3.1. By doing this, we tie the model to the underlying economic reality.

Recall from Exhibits 2, 3, and 4 the benchmark bond price information and the relevant par, spot, and forward curves. We will assume that volatility, σ, is 15% and construct a two-year tree using the two-year bond that carries a coupon rate of 1.2%. A complete four-year binomial interest rate tree is presented in Exhibit 10. We will demonstrate how these rates are determined. The current one-year rate is 1%, i_0.

Exhibit 10	Four-Year Binomial Interest Rate Tree			
	Time 0	**Time 1**	**Time 2**	**Time 3**
	1.0000%	1.6121%	1.7862%	2.8338%
		1.1943%	1.3233%	2.0994%
			0.9803%	1.5552%
				1.1521%

Finding the rates in the tree is an iterative process, and the interest rates are found numerically. There are two possible rates that will discount cash flows from Time 2 to Time 1—the higher rate and the lower rate. We observe these rates one year from today. These two rates must be consistent with the volatility assumption, the interest rate model, and the observed market value of the benchmark bond. Assume that the interest rate volatility is 15%. From our discussion earlier, we know that at Time 1 the lower one-year rate is lower than the implied one-year forward rate and the higher rate is a multiple of the lower rate. We iterate to a solution with constraints in mind. Once we select these rates, how will we know the rates are correct? The answer is when we discount the cash flows using the tree and produce a value that matches the price of the two-year benchmark bond. If the model does not produce the correct price with this result, we need to select another forward rate and repeat the process. The process of calibrating a binomial interest rate tree to match a specific term structure is illustrated in the following paragraphs.

Suppose we use an analytic tool, such as Solver in Excel, to carry out this calculation and it produces a value for $i_{1,L}$ of 1.1943%. This is the lower one-year rate. The higher one-year rate is 1.6121% [= $1.1943\%(e^{2\times0.15})$]. Recall from the information on the benchmark bonds, that the two-year bond will pay its maturity value of $100 in Time 2 and an annual coupon payment of $1.20. The bond's value at Time 2 is $101.20. The present value of the coupon payment plus the bond's maturity value if the higher one-year rate is realized, *VH*, is $99.59444 (= $101.20/1.016121). Alternatively, the present value of the coupon payment plus the bond's maturity value if the lower one-year rate is realized, *VL*, is $100.00563 (= $101.20/1.011943). These two calculations determine the bond's value one year forward. Effectively, the forward rates move the bond's value from Time 2 to Time 1.

100	99.59444 + 1.20	100 + 1.20
	100.00563 + 1.20	100 + 1.20
		100 + 1.20

To find the value today, we discount the coupon payment and bond values just obtained (*VH* and *VL*). Including the coupon payment, we obtain $100.79444 ($99.59444 + $1.20) as the cash flow for the higher rate and $101.20563 ($100.00563 + $1.20) as the cash flow for the lower rate. We use the current one year rate to obtain the present value of the two cash flows as follows:

$$\frac{VH + C}{1 + i} = \frac{\$100.79444}{1.01000} = \$99.79647$$

and

$$\frac{VL + C}{1 + i} = \frac{\$101.20563}{1.01} = 100.20360$$

Multiplying each present value by 0.5, we obtain a bond value of $100, which is the price of the two-year benchmark bond. The model produces the same value as the market, so we take rates 1.1943% and 1.6121% as the forward rates at Time 1.

1%	1.6122%
	1.1943%

To build out the tree one more year, we repeat the same process, this time using a three-year benchmark bond with a coupon rate of 1.25%. Now, we are looking for three forward rates that are consistent with (1) the interest rate model assumed, (2) the assumed volatility of 15%, (3) a current one-year rate of 1.0%, and (4) the two possible forward rates one year from now (at Time 1) of 1.1943% (the lower rate) and 1.6121% (the higher rate), as shown in Exhibit 11.

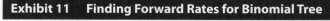

Exhibit 11   Finding Forward Rates for Binomial Tree

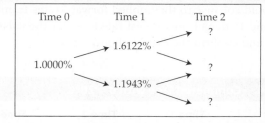

At Time 3, we receive the final coupon payment and maturity value. In Exhibit 12, we see these values filled in for the three-year benchmark bond and three forward rates we must find. These are the rates from previous calculations. We simply work backward from right to left to obtain these values.

Exhibit 12	Working Backward to Find Forward Rates		
Time 0	**Time 1**	**Time 2**	**Time 3**
100	?	?	101.25
	?	?	101.25
		?	101.25
			101.25

We selected a value for $i_{2,LL}$, which is 0.9803% and is below the implied one-year forward rate, two years hence. All of the other forward rates are multiples of this rate. The corresponding rates for $i_{2,HL}$ and $i_{2,HH}$ would be 1.3233% and 1.7863%, respectively. To demonstrate that these are the correct values, we simply work backward from the four nodes at Time 3 of the tree in Exhibit 12. The same procedure is used to obtain the values at the other nodes. The completed tree is shown in Exhibit 13.

Exhibit 13	Completed Binomial Tree with Calculated Forward Rates

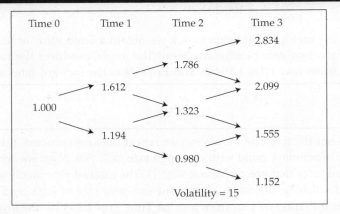

Let us focus on the impact of volatility on the possible forward rates in the tree. If we were to use a higher estimate of volatility, say 20%, the possible forward rates should spread out on the tree. If we were to use a lower estimate of volatility, say 0.01%, the rates should collapse to the implied forward rates from the current yield curve. Exhibits 14 and 15 depict the interest rate trees for the volatilities of 20% and 0.01%, respectively, and confirm the expected outcome.

Exhibit 14	Completed Tree with σ = 20%		
Time 0	**Time 1**	**Time 2**	**Time 3**
1.0000%	1.6806%	1.9415%	3.2134%
	1.1265%	1.3014%	2.1540%

Exhibit 14	(Continued)		
Time 0	Time 1	Time 2	Time 3
		0.8724%	1.4439%
			0.9678%

Exhibit 15	Completed Tree with $\sigma = 0.01\%$		
Time 0	Time 1	Time 2	Time 3
1.0000%	1.4029%	1.3523%	1.8653%
	1.4026%	1.3521%	1.8649%
		1.3518%	1.8645%
			1.8641%

EXAMPLE 4

Calibrating a Binomial Tree to Match a Specific Term Structure

As in Example 2, the one-year par rate is 2.0%, the two-year par rate is 3.0%, and the three-year par rate is 4.0%. Consequently, the spot rates are $S_1 = 2.0\%$, $S_2 = 3.015\%$ and $S_3 = 4.055\%$. Zero-coupon bond prices are $P_1 = 1/1.020 = 0.9804$, $P_2 = 1/(1.03015)^2 = 0.9423$, and $P_3 = 1/(1.04055)^3 = 0.8876$. Interest volatility is 15% for all years.

Calibrate the binomial tree in Exhibit 16.

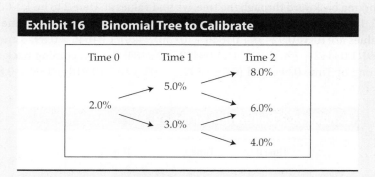

Exhibit 16   Binomial Tree to Calibrate

Solution:

Time 0

The par, spot, and forward rates are all the same for the first period in a binomial tree. Consequently, $Y_0 = S_0 = F_0 = 2.0\%$.

Time 1

Because the two-year spot rate is the geometric average of the one-year forward rate at Time 0 and the one-year forward rate at Time 1, we can infer the average forward rate for Time 2. $1.03015^2 = (1.02)(1+F_{1,1})$ implies $F_{1,1} = 4.040\%$. In addition, because we have chosen to impose a lognormal model on interest rate changes, $F_{1,1u} = (F_{1,1d})(e^{2\sigma})$. So, the two numbers average to 4.040% and one is $e^{2\sigma}$ greater than the other.

Beginning at $F_{1,1d} = (4.040\%)(e^{-0.15}) = 3.477\%$ and $F_{1,1u} = (4.040\%)(e^{0.15})$ = 4.694% gives a price for the two-year zero of $[(0.5)(1/1.03477) + (0.5)(1/1.04694)]/1.02 = 0.9419$. Notice that the price is quite close to the correct value of 0.9423. By using numeric methods (in this case, Excel's Solver), we find that the actual number for $F_{1,1d} = 3.442\%$ instead of 3.477%, making $F_{1,1u}$ = 4.646% instead of 4.694%.

Exhibit 17   Calibration of Time 1

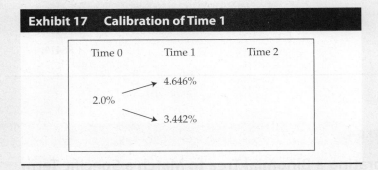

Time 2

We will begin with the average forward rate for Time 2, $F_{2,1} = (1.04055^3/1.03015^2)$ – 1 = 6.167% as the middle value with $(6.167\%)(e^{-0.3}) = 4.569\%$ and $(6.167\%)(e^{0.3})$ = 8.325% as the lower and upper values. Those values give a price for a three-year zero-coupon bond of 0.8866, which is close to the correct price of 0.8876. Using numerical methods (again, Excel's Solver), we find that the three correct one-year forwards are 4.482%, 6.051%, and 8.167%.

Working backward through the tree, we find values at Time 2 to be 1/1.08167 = 0.9245, 1/1.06051 = 0.9429, and 1/1.04482 = 0.9571. Coming back to Time 1, the tree values are (0.5)(0.9245)/1.04646 + (0.5)(0.9429)/1.04646 = 0.8923 and (0.5)(0.9429)/1.03442 + (0.5)(0.9571)/1.03442 = 0.9184. Finally, coming back to the beginning of Time 0, we find (0.5)(0.8923)/1.02 + (0.5)(0.9184)/1.02 = 0.8876.

Exhibit 18   Calibration of Time 2

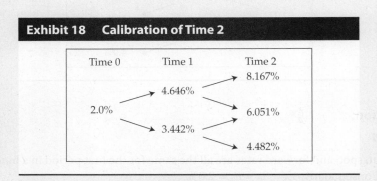

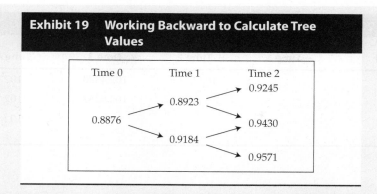

Exhibit 19 Working Backward to Calculate Tree Values

Now that our tree gives the correct prices for zero-coupon bonds maturing in one, two, and three years, we say that our tree is calibrated to be arbitrage free. It will price option-free bonds correctly, including par prices for the par bonds used to find the spot rates and, to the extent that we have chosen an appropriate interest rate process and interest rate volatility, it will provide insights into the value of bonds with embedded options and their risk parameters.

3.5 Valuing an Option-Free Bond with the Tree

Our next task is twofold. First, we calculate the arbitrage-free value of an option-free, fixed-rate coupon bond. Second, we compare the pricing using the zero-coupon yield curve with the pricing using an arbitrage-free binomial lattice. Because these two valuation methods are arbitrage-free, these two values must be the same.

Now, consider an option-free bond with four years remaining to maturity and a coupon rate of 2%. Note that this is not a benchmark bond and it carries a higher coupon than the four-year benchmark bond, which is priced at par. The value of this bond can be calculated by discounting the cash flow at the spot rates in Exhibit 3 as shown in the following equation:

$$\frac{\$2}{(1.01)^1} + \frac{\$2}{(1.01201)^2} + \frac{\$2}{(1.01251)^3} + \frac{\$100 + \$2}{(1.01404)^4} = \$102.33$$

The binomial interest rate tree should produce the same value as discounting the cash flows with the spot rates. An option-free bond that is valued by using the binomial interest rate tree should have the same value as discounting by the spot rates, which is true because the binomial interest rate tree is arbitrage-free.

Let us give the tree a test run and use the 2% option-free bond with four years remaining to maturity. Also assume that the issuer's benchmark yield curve is the one given in Exhibit 2, hence the appropriate binomial interest rate tree is the one in Exhibit 13. Exhibit 20 shows the various values in the discounting process and produces a bond value of $102.3254. The tree produces the same value for the bond as the spot rates and is therefore consistent with our standard valuation model.[6]

Exhibit 20 Sample Valuation for an Option-Free Bond using a Binomial Tree

Time 0	Time 1	Time 2	Time 3	Time 4
102.3254	102.6769	101.7639	101.1892	102
	104.0204	102.8360	101.9027	102

(continued)

---

6 There is a slight difference in price due to rounding at intermediate steps.

Exhibit 20	(Continued)			
Time 0	**Time 1**	**Time 2**	**Time 3**	**Time 4**
		103.6417	102.4380	102
			102.8382	102
				102

EXAMPLE 5

Confirming the Arbitrage-Free Value of a Bond

Using the par curve from Example 2 and Example 4, the yield to maturity for a one-year annual-pay bond is 2%, for a two-year annual-pay bond is 3%, and for a three-year annual-pay bond is 4%. Because this is the same curve as that used in Example 4, we can use the calibrated tree from that example to price a bond. Let us use a three-year annual-pay bond with a 5% coupon, just as we did in Example 2. We know that if the calibrated tree was built correctly and we perform calculations to value the bond with that tree (Exhibit 18, shown here again), its price should be $102.8102.

Exhibit 18   (repeated)

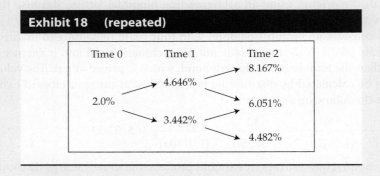

Exhibit 21

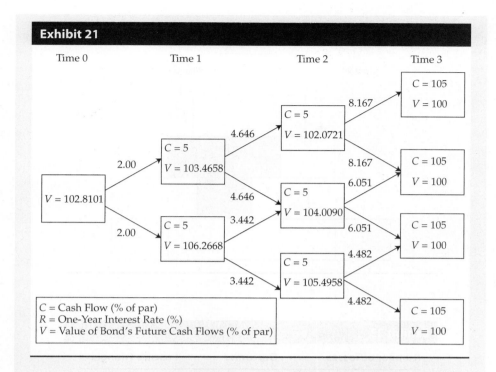

C = Cash Flow (% of par)
R = One-Year Interest Rate (%)
V = Value of Bond's Future Cash Flows (% of par)

Because the tree was calibrated to the same par curve (and spot curve) that was used to price this option-free bond using spot rates only, the tree gives the same price as the spot rate pricing.

3.6 Pathwise Valuation

An alternative approach to backward induction in a binomial tree is called pathwise valuation. The binomial interest rate tree specifies all potential rate paths in the model, whereas an interest rate path is the route an interest rate takes from the current time to the security's maturity. Pathwise valuation calculates the present value of a bond for each possible interest rate path and takes the average of these values across paths. We will use the pathwise valuation approach to produce the same value as the backward induction method for an option-free bond. Pathwise valuation involves the following steps: (1) specify a list of all potential paths through the tree, (2) determine the present value of a bond along each potential path, and (3) calculate the average across all possible paths.

Determining all potential paths is just like the following experiment. Suppose you are tossing a fair coin and are keeping track of the number of ways heads and tails can be combined. We will use a device called Pascal's Triangle, displayed in Exhibit 22. Pascal's Triangle can be built as follows: Start with the number 1 at the top of the triangle. The numbers in the boxes below are the sum of the two numbers above it except that the edges on each side are all 1. The shaded numbers show that 3 is the sum of 2 and 1. Now toss the coin while keeping track of the possible outcomes. The possible groupings are listed in Exhibit 23 where H stands for heads and T stands for tails.

Exhibit 22

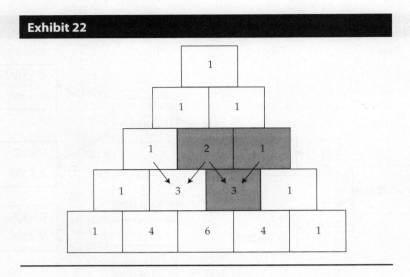

Exhibit 23

Number of Tosses	Outcomes	Pascal's Triangle
1	H T	1, 1
2	HH HT TH TT	1,2,1
3	HHH HHT HTH THH HTT THT TTH TTT	1, 3, 3, 1

This experiment mirrors exactly the number of interest rate paths in our binomial interest rate tree. The total number of paths for each period/year can be easily determined by using Pascal's Triangle. Let us work through an example for a three-year zero-coupon bond. From Pascal's Triangle, there are four possible paths to arrive at Year 3: HH, HT, TH, TT. Using the same binomial tree from Section 3.4, we specify the four paths as well as the possible forward rates along those paths. In Exhibit 24, the last column on the right shows the present value for each path. In the bottom right corner is the average present value across all paths.

Exhibit 24   Four Interest Rate Paths for a Three-Year Zero-Coupon Bond

Path	Forward Rate Year 1	Forward Rate Year 2	Forward Rate Year 3	Present Value
1	1.0000%	1.6122%	1.7862%	95.72908
2	1.0000%	1.6122%	1.323%	96.16670
3	1.0000%	1.1943%	1.323%	96.56384
4	1.0000%	1.1943%	0.9803%	96.89155
				96.33779

Now, we can use the binomial tree to confirm our calculations for the three-year zero-coupon bond. The analysis is presented in Exhibit 25. The interest rate tree does indeed produce the same value.

Exhibit 25	Binomial Tree to Confirm Bond's Value		
Time 0	**Time 1**	**Time 2**	**Time 3**
96.338	96.907	98.245	100.000
	97.695	98.694	100.000
		99.029	100.000
			100.000

EXAMPLE 6

Pathwise Valuation Based on a Binomial Interest Rate Tree

Using the par curve from Example 2, Example 4, and Example 5, the yield to maturity for a one-year annual-pay bond is 2%, for a two-year annual-pay bond is 3%, and for a three-year annual-pay bond is 4%. We know that if we generate the paths in the tree correctly and discount the cash flows directly, the three-year, annual-pay, 5% coupon bond should still be priced at $102.8102.

There are eight paths through the three-year tree, four of which are unique. We discount the cash flows along each of the eight paths and take their average, as shown in Exhibits 26, 27, and 28.

Exhibit 26	Cash Flows			
Path	**Time 0**	**Time 1**	**Time 2**	**Time 3**
1	0	5	5	105
2	0	5	5	105
3	0	5	5	105
4	0	5	5	105
5	0	5	5	105
6	0	5	5	105
7	0	5	5	105
8	0	5	5	105

Exhibit 27	Discount Rates			
Path	**Time 0**	**Time 1**	**Time 2**	**Time 3**
1	2%	4.646%	8.167%	
2	2%	4.646%	8.167%	
3	2%	4.646%	6.051%	

(continued)

Exhibit 27	(Continued)			
Path	Time 0	Time 1	Time 2	Time 3
4	2%	4.646%	6.051%	
5	2%	3.442%	6.051%	
6	2%	3.442%	6.051%	
7	2%	3.442%	4.482%	
8	2%	3.442%	4.482%	

Exhibit 28	Present Values
Path	Time 0
1	100.5296
2	100.5296
3	102.3449
4	102.3449
5	103.4792
6	103.4792
7	104.8876
8	104.8876
Average	**102.8103**

4   MONTE CARLO METHOD

The Monte Carlo method is an alternative method for simulating a sufficiently large number of potential interest rate paths in an effort to discover how a value of a security is affected. This method involves randomly selecting paths in an effort to approximate the results of a complete pathwise valuation. Monte Carlo methods are often used when a security's cash flows are path dependent. Cash flows are path dependent when the cash flow to be received in a particular period depends on the path followed to reach its current level as well as the current level itself. For example, the valuation of mortgage-backed securities depends to a great extent on the level of prepayments, which are interest rate path dependent. Interest rate paths are generated based on some probability distribution, an assumption about volatility, and the model is fit to the current benchmark term structure of interest rates. The benchmark term structure is represented by the current spot rate curve such that the average present value across all scenario interest rate paths for each benchmark bond equals its actual market value. By using this approach, the model is rendered arbitrage free, which is equivalent to calibrating the interest rate tree as discussed in Section 3.

Suppose we intend to value a 30-year bond with the Monte Carlo method. For simplicity, assume the bond has monthly coupon payments (e.g., mortgage-backed securities). The following steps are taken: (1) simulate numerous (say, 500) paths of one-month interest rates under some volatility assumption and probability distribution, (2) generate spot rates from the simulated future one-month interest rates, (3) determine the cash flow along each interest rate path, (4) calculate the present value for each path, and (5) calculate the average present value across all interest rate paths.

Using the procedure just described, the model will produce benchmark bond values equal to the market prices only by chance. We want to ensure this is the case, otherwise the model will neither fit the current spot curve nor be arbitrage free. A constant is added to all interest rates on all paths such that the average present value for each benchmark bond equals its market value. The constant added to all short interest rates is called a drift term. When this technique is used, the model is said to be drift adjusted.

A question that arises concerns how many paths are appropriate for the Monte Carlo method. Increasing the number of paths increases the accuracy of the estimate in a statistical sense. It does not mean the model is closer to the true fundamental value of the security. The Monte Carlo method is only as good as the valuation model used and the accuracy of the inputs.

One other element that yield curve modelers often include in their Monte Carlo estimation is mean reversion. Mean reversion starts with the common-sense notion that history suggests that interest rates almost never get "too high" or "too low." What is meant by "too high" and "too low" is left to the discretion of the modeler. We implement mean reversion by implementing upper and lower bounds on the random process generating future interest rates. Mean reversion has the effect of moving the interest rate toward the implied forward rates from the yield curve.

EXAMPLE 7

The Application of Monte Carlo Simulation to Bond Pricing

Replace the interest rate paths from Example 6 with randomly generated paths that have been calibrated to the same initial par and spot curves, as shown in Exhibit 29.

Exhibit 29   Discount Rates

Path	Time 0	Time 1	Time 2	Time 3
1	2%	2.500%	4.548%	
2	2%	3.600%	6.116%	
3	2%	4.600%	7.766%	
4	2%	5.500%	3.466%	
5	2%	3.100%	8.233%	
6	2%	4.500%	6.116%	
7	2%	3.800%	5.866%	
8	2%	4.000%	8.233%	

Exhibit 30	Present Values
Path	**Time 0**
1	105.7459
2	103.2708
3	100.91064
4	103.8543
5	101.9075
6	102.4236
7	103.3020
8	101.0680
Average	**102.8103**

Because we continue to get $102.8103, as shown in Exhibit 30, as the price for our three-year, annual-pay, 5% coupon bond, we know that the Monte Carlo simulation has been calibrated correctly. The paths are now different enough such that path dependent securities, such as mortgage-backed securities, can be analyzed in ways that provide insights not possible in binomial trees.

SUMMARY

This reading presents the principles and tools for arbitrage valuation of fixed-income securities. Much of the discussion centers on the binomial interest rate tree, which can be used extensively to value both option-free bonds and bonds with embedded options. The following are the main points made in the reading:

- A fundamental principle of valuation is that the value of any financial asset is equal to the present value of its expected future cash flows.

- A fixed-income security is a portfolio of zero-coupon bonds.

- Each zero-coupon bond has its own discount rate that depends on the shape of the yield curve and when the cash flow is delivered in time.

- In well-functioning markets, prices adjust until there are no opportunities for arbitrage.

- The law of one price states that two goods that are perfect substitutes must sell for the same current price in the absence of transaction costs.

- An arbitrage opportunity is a transaction that involves no cash outlay yet results in a riskless profit.

- Using the arbitrage-free approach, viewing a security as a package of zero-coupon bonds means that two bonds with the same maturity and different coupon rates are viewed as different packages of zero-coupon bonds and valued accordingly.

- For bonds that are option free, an arbitrage-free value is simply the present value of expected future values using the benchmark spot rates.

- A binomial interest rate tree permits the short interest rate to take on one of two possible values consistent with the volatility assumption and an interest rate model.

- An interest rate tree is a visual representation of the possible values of interest rates (forward rates) based on an interest rate model and an assumption about interest rate volatility.

- The possible interest rates for any following period are consistent with the following three assumptions: (1) an interest rate model that governs the random process of interest rates, (2) the assumed level of interest rate volatility, and (3) the current benchmark yield curve.

- From the lognormal distribution, adjacent interest rates on the tree are multiples of e raised to the 2σ power.

- One of the benefits of a lognormal distribution is that if interest rates get too close to zero, then the absolute change in interest rates becomes smaller and smaller.

- We use the backward induction valuation methodology that involves starting at maturity, filling in those values, and working back from right to left to find the bond's value at the desired node.

- The interest rate tree is fit to the current yield curve by choosing interest rates that result in the benchmark bond value. By doing this, the bond value is arbitrage free.

- An option-free bond that is valued by using the binomial interest rate tree should have the same value as discounting by the spot rates.

- Pathwise valuation calculates the present value of a bond for each possible interest rate path and takes the average of these values across paths.

- The Monte Carlo method is an alternative method for simulating a sufficiently large number of potential interest rate paths in an effort to discover how the value of a security is affected and involves randomly selecting paths in an effort to approximate the results of a complete pathwise valuation.

PRACTICE PROBLEMS

The following information relates to Questions 1–6

Katrina Black, portfolio manager at Coral Bond Management, Ltd., is conducting a training session with Alex Sun, a junior analyst in the fixed income department. Black wants to explain to Sun the arbitrage-free valuation framework used by the firm. Black presents Sun with Exhibit 1, showing a fictitious bond being traded on three exchanges, and asks Sun to identify the arbitrage opportunity of the bond. Sun agrees to ignore transaction costs in his analysis.

Exhibit 1	Three-Year, €100 par, 3.00% Coupon, Annual Pay Option-Free Bond		
	Eurex	NYSE Euronext	Frankfurt
Price	€103.7956	€103.7815	€103.7565

Black shows Sun some exhibits that were part of a recent presentation. Exhibit 3 presents most of the data of a binomial lognormal interest rate tree fit to the yield curve shown in Exhibit 2. Exhibit 4 presents most of the data of the implied values for a four-year, option-free, annual pay bond with a 2.5% coupon based on the information in Exhibit 3.

Exhibit 2	Yield to Maturity Par Rates for One-, Two-, and Three-Year Annual Pay Option-Free Bonds	
One-year	Two-year	Three-year
1.25%	1.50%	1.70%

Exhibit 3	Binomial Interest Rate Tree Fit to the Yield Curve (Volatility = 10%)			
Current	Year 1	Year 2	Year 3	Year 4
1.2500%	1.8229%	1.8280%	2.6241%	Node 4–1
	1.4925%	Node 2–2	Node 3–2	4.2009%
		1.2254%	1.7590%	3.4394%
			Node 3–4	2.8159%
				Node 4–5

Exhibit 4	Implied Values (in Euros) for a 2.5%, Four-Year, Option-Free, Annual Pay Bond Based on Exhibit 3			
Year 0	Year 1	Year 2	Year 3	Year 4
103.4960	104.2876	103.2695	102.3791	102.5000
	Node 1–2	104.0168	102.8442	102.5000
		104.6350	103.2282	102.5000
			103.5448	102.5000
				102.5000

Black asks about the missing data in Exhibits 3 and 4 and directs Sun to complete the following tasks related to those exhibits:

Task 1   Test that the binomial interest tree has been properly calibrated to be arbitrage-free.

Task 2   Develop a spreadsheet model to calculate pathwise valuations. To test the accuracy of the spreadsheet, use the data in Exhibit 3 and calculate the value of the bond if it takes a path of lowest rates in Year 1 and Year 2 and the second lowest rate in Year 3.

Task 3   Identify a type of bond where the Monte Carlo calibration method should be used in place of the binomial interest rate method.

Task 4   Update Exhibit 3 to reflect the current volatility, which is now 15%.

1 Based on Exhibit 1, the *best* action that an investor should take to profit from the arbitrage opportunity is to:
   A buy on Frankfurt, sell on Eurex.
   B buy on NYSE Euronext, sell on Eurex.
   C buy on Frankfurt, sell on NYSE Euronext.

2 Based on Exhibits 1 and 2, the exchange that reflects the arbitrage-free price of the bond is:
   A Eurex.
   B Frankfurt.
   C NYSE Euronext.

3 Which of the following statements about the missing data in Exhibit 3 is correct?
   A Node 3–2 can be derived from Node 2–2.
   B Node 4–1 should be equal to Node 4–5 multiplied by $e^{0.4}$.
   C Node 2–2 approximates the implied one-year forward rate one year from now.

4 Based on the information in Exhibits 3 and 4, the bond price in euros at Node 1–2 in Exhibit 4 is *closest* to:
   A 102.7917.
   B 104.8640.
   C 105.2917.

5 A benefit of performing Task 1 is that it:
   A enables the model to price bonds with embedded options.
   B identifies benchmark bonds that have been mispriced by the market.

   C allows investors to realize arbitrage profits through stripping and reconstitution.

6 If the assumed volatility is changed as Black requested in Task 4, the forward rates shown in Exhibit 3 will *most likely*:

   A spread out.

   B remain unchanged.

   C converge to the spot rates.

The following information relates to Questions 7–10

Betty Tatton is a fixed income analyst with the hedge fund Sailboat Asset Management (SAM). SAM invests in a variety of global fixed-income strategies, including fixed-income arbitrage. Tatton is responsible for pricing individual investments and analyzing market data to assess the opportunity for arbitrage. She uses two methods to value bonds:

   Method 1   Discount each year's cash flow separately using the appropriate interest rate curve.

   Method 2   Build and use a binomial interest rate tree.

Tatton compiles pricing data for a list of annual pay bonds (Exhibit 1). Each of the bonds will mature in two years, and Tatton considers the bonds as being risk-free; both the one-year and two-year benchmark spot rates are 2%. Tatton calculates the arbitrage-free prices and identifies an arbitrage opportunity to recommend to her team.

Exhibit 1	Market Data for Selected Bonds	
Asset	**Coupon**	**Market Price**
Bond A	1%	98.0584
Bond B	3%	100.9641
Bond C	5%	105.8247

Next, Tatton uses the benchmark yield curve provided in Exhibit 2 to consider arbitrage opportunities of both option-free corporate bonds and corporate bonds with embedded options. The benchmark bonds in Exhibit 2 pay coupons annually, and the bonds are priced at par.

Exhibit 2	Benchmark Par Curve
Maturity (years)	**Yield to Maturity (YTM)**
1	3.0%
2	4.0%
3	5.0%

Tatton then identifies three mispriced three-year annual-pay bonds and compiles data on the bonds (see Exhibit 3).

Exhibit 3	Market Data of Annual-Pay Corporate Bonds			
Company	**Coupon**	**Market Price**	**Yield**	**Embedded Option?**
Hutto-Barkley Inc.	3%	94.9984	5.6%	No
Luna y Estrellas Intl.	0%	88.8996	4.0%	Yes
Peaton Scorpio Motors	0%	83.9619	6.0%	No

Lastly, Tatton identifies two mispriced Swiss bonds, Bond X, a three-year bond, and Bond Y, a five-year bond. Both are annual-pay bonds with a coupon rate of 6%. To calculate the bonds' values, Tatton devises the first three years of the interest rate lognormal tree presented in Exhibit 4 using historical interest rate volatility data. Tatton considers how this data would change if implied volatility, which is higher than historical volatility, were used instead.

Exhibit 4	Interest Rate Tree; Forward Rates Based on Swiss Market	
Year 1	**Year 2**	**Year 3**
	4%	6%
1%		5%
	2%	3%

7   Based on Exhibit 1, which of the following bonds *most likely* includes an arbitrage opportunity?

   A   Bond A

   B   Bond B

   C   Bond C

8   Based on Exhibits 2 and 3 and using Method 1, the amount (in absolute terms) by which the Hutto-Barkley corporate bond is mispriced is *closest* to:

   A   0.3368 per 100 of par value.

   B   0.4682 per 100 of par value.

   C   0.5156 per 100 of par value.

9   Method 1 would *most likely* **not** be an appropriate valuation technique for the bond issued by:

   A   Hutto-Barkley Inc.

   B   Luna y Estrellas Intl.

   C   Peaton Scorpio Motors.

10 Based on Exhibit 4 and using Method 2, the correct price for Bond X is *closest* to:

   A   97.2998.

   B   109.0085.

   C   115.0085.

SOLUTIONS

1 A is correct. This is the same bond being sold at three different prices so an arbitrage opportunity exists by buying the bond from the exchange where it is priced lowest and immediately selling it on the exchange that has the highest price. Accordingly, an investor would maximize profit from the arbitrage opportunity by buying the bond on the Frankfurt exchange (which has the lowest price of €103.7565) and selling it on the Eurex exchange (which has the highest price of €103.7956) to generate a risk-free profit of €0.0391 (as mentioned, ignoring transaction costs) per €100 par.

B is incorrect because buying on NYSE Euronext and selling on Eurex would result in an €0.0141 profit per €100 par (€103.7956 − €103.7815 = €0.0141), which is not the maximum arbitrage profit available. A greater profit would be realized if the bond were purchased in Frankfurt and sold on Eurex.

C is incorrect because buying on Frankfurt and selling on NYSE Euronext would result in an €0.0250 profit per €100 par (€103.7815 − €103.7565 = €0.0250). A greater profit would be realized if the bond were purchased in Frankfurt and sold on Eurex.

2 C is correct. The bond from Exhibit 1 is selling for its calculated value on the NYSE Euronext exchange. The arbitrage-free value of a bond is the present value of its cash flows discounted by the spot rate for zero coupon bonds maturing on the same date as each cash flow. The value of this bond, 103.7815, is calculated as follows:

	Year 1	Year 2	Year 3	Total PV
Yield to maturity	1.2500%	1.500%	1.700%	
Spot rate[1]	1.2500%	1.5019%	1.7049%	
Cash flow	3.00	3.00	103.00	
Present value of payment[2]	2.9630	2.9119	97.9066	103.7815

	Eurex	NYSE Euronext	Frankfurt
Price	€103.7956	€103.7815	€103.7565
Mispricing (per 100 par value)	0.141	0	−0.025

Notes:

1 Spot rates calculated using bootstrapping; for example: Year 2 spot rate (z_2): 100 = 1.5/1.0125 + 101.5/$(1+z_2)^2$ = 0.015019.

2 Present value calculated using the formula PV = FV/$(1+r)^n$, where n = number of years until cash flow, FV=cash flow amount, and r = spot rate.

A is incorrect because the price on the Eurex exchange, €103.7956, was calculated using the yield to maturity rate to discount the cash flows when the spot rates should have been used. C is incorrect because the price on the Frankfurt exchange, €103.7565, uses the Year 3 spot rate to discount all the cash flows.

3 C is correct. Because Node 2–2 is the middle node rate in Year 2, it will be close to the implied one-year forward rate one year from now (as derived from the spot curve). Node 4–1 should be equal to the product of Node 4–5 and $e^{0.8}$.

Lastly, Node 3–2 cannot be derived from Node 2–2; it can be derived from any other Year 3 node; for example, Node 3–2 can be derived from Node 3–4 (equal to the product of Node 3–4 and $e^{4\sigma}$).

4   C is correct. The value of a bond at a particular node, in this case Node 1–2, can be derived by working backwards from the two nodes to the right of that node on the tree. In this case, those two nodes are the middle node in Year 2, equal to 104.0168, and the lower node in Year 2, equal to 104.6350. The bond value at Node 1–2 is calculated as follows:

Value = 0.5 × [(104.0168/1.014925 + 104.6350/1.014925)] + 2.5
      = 0.5 × [102.4872 + 103.0963] + 2.5
      = 105.2917

A is incorrect because the calculation does not include the coupon payment. B is incorrect because the calculation incorrectly uses the Year 0 and Year 1 node values.

5   A is correct. Calibrating a binomial interest rate tree to match a specific term structure is important because we can use the known valuation of a benchmark bond from the spot rate pricing to verify the accuracy of the rates shown in the binomial interest rate tree. Once its accuracy is confirmed, the interest rate tree can then be used to value bonds with embedded options. While discounting with spot rates will produce arbitrage-free valuations for option-free bonds, this spot rate method will not work for bonds with embedded options where expected future cash flows are interest-rate dependent (as rate changes impact the likelihood of options being exercised). The interest rate tree allows for the alternative paths that a bond with embedded options might take.

B is incorrect because calibration does not identify mispriced benchmark bonds. In fact, benchmark bonds are employed to prove the accuracy of the binomial interest rate tree, as they are assumed to be correctly priced by the market.

C is incorrect because the calibration of the binomial interest rate tree is designed to produce an arbitrage-free valuation approach and such an approach does not allow a market participant to realize arbitrage profits though stripping and reconstitution.

6   A is correct. Volatility is one of the two key assumptions required to estimate rates for the binomial interest rate tree. Increasing the volatility from 10% to 15% would cause the possible forward rates to spread out on the tree as it increases the exponent in the relationship multiple between nodes ($e^{x\sigma}$, where x = 2 times the number of nodes above the lowest node in a given year in the interest rate tree). Conversely, using a lower estimate of volatility would cause the forward rates to narrow or converge to the implied forward rates from the prevailing yield curve.

B is incorrect because volatility is a key assumption in the binomial interest rate tree model. Any change in volatility will cause a change in the implied forward rates.

C is incorrect because increasing the volatility from 10% to 15% causes the possible forward rates to spread out on the tree, not converge to the implied forward rates from the current yield curve. Rates will converge to the implied forward rates when lower estimates of volatility are assumed.

7   B is correct. Bond B's arbitrage-free price is calculated as follows:

$$\frac{3}{1.02} + \frac{103}{1.02^2} = 101.9416$$

which is higher than the bond's market price of 100.9641. Therefore, an arbitrage opportunity exists. Since the bond's value (100.9641) is less than the sum of the values of its discounted cash flows individually (101.9416), a trader would perceive an arbitrage opportunity and could buy the bond while selling claims to the individual cash flows (zeros), capturing the excess value. The arbitrage-free prices of Bond A and Bond C are equal to the market prices of the respective bonds, so there is no arbitrage opportunity for these two bonds:

$$\text{Bond A: } \frac{1}{1.02} + \frac{101}{1.02^2} = 98.0584$$

$$\text{Bond C: } \frac{5}{1.02} + \frac{105}{1.02^2} = 105.8247$$

8 C is correct. The first step in the solution is to find the correct spot rate (zero-coupon rates) for each year's cash flow. The benchmark bonds in Exhibit 2 are conveniently priced at par so the yields to maturity and the coupon rates on the bonds are the same. Because the one-year issue has only one cash flow remaining, the YTM equals the spot rate of 3% (or z_1 = 3%). The spot rates for Year 2 (z_2) and Year 3 (z_3) are calculated as follows:

$$100 = \frac{4}{1.0300} + \frac{104}{(1 + z_2)^2}; z_2 = 4.02\%$$

$$100 = \frac{5}{1.0300} + \frac{5}{(1.0402)^2} + \frac{105}{(1 + z_3)^3}; z_3 = 5.07\%$$

The correct arbitrage-free price for the Hutto-Barkley Inc. bond is:

$$P_0 = \frac{3}{(1.0300)} + \frac{3}{(1.0402)^2} + \frac{103}{(1.0507)^3} = 94.4828$$

Therefore, the bond is mispriced by 94.4828 − 94.9984 = −0.5156 per 100 of par value.

A is incorrect because the correct spot rates are not calculated and instead the Hutto-Barkley Inc. bond is discounted using the respective YTM for each maturity. Therefore, this leads to an incorrect mispricing of 94.6616 − 94.9984 = −0.3368 per 100 of par value.

B is incorrect because the spot rates are derived using the coupon rate for Year 3 (maturity) instead of using each year's respective coupon rate to employ the bootstrap methodology. This leads to an incorrect mispricing of 94.5302 − 94.9984 = −0.4682 per 100 of par value.

9 B is correct. The Luna y Estrellas Intl. bond contains an embedded option. Method 1 will produce an arbitrage-free valuation for option-free bonds; however, for bonds with embedded options, changes in future interest rates impact the likelihood the option will be exercised and so impact future cash flows. Therefore, to develop a framework that values bonds with embedded options, interest rates must be allowed to take on different potential values in the future based on some assumed level of volatility (Method 2).

A and C are incorrect because the Hutto-Barkley Inc. bond and the Peaton Scorpio Motors bond are both option-free bonds and can be valued using either Method 1 or Method 2 to produce an arbitrage-free valuation.

10 B is correct. The first step is to identify the cash flows:

Time 0	Time 1	Time 2	Time 3
			106
		6	
	6		106
0		6	
	6		106
		6	
			106

Next, calculate the cash flows for each year beginning with Year 3 and move backwards to Year 1:

Year 3:

$$0.5 \times \left[\left(\frac{106}{1.06} \right) + \left(\frac{106}{1.06} \right) \right] + 6 = 106.0000$$

$$0.5 \times \left[\left(\frac{106}{1.05} \right) + \left(\frac{106}{1.05} \right) \right] + 6 = 106.9524$$

$$0.5 \times \left[\left(\frac{106}{1.03} \right) + \left(\frac{106}{1.03} \right) \right] + 6 = 108.9126$$

Year 2:

$$0.5 \times \left[\left(\frac{106.0000}{1.04} \right) + \left(\frac{106.9524}{1.04} \right) \right] + 6 = 108.3810$$

$$0.5 \times \left[\left(\frac{106.9524}{1.02} \right) + \left(\frac{108.9126}{1.02} \right) \right] + 6 = 111.8162$$

Year 1:

$$0.5 \times \left[\left(\frac{108.3810}{1.01} \right) + \left(\frac{111.8162}{1.01} \right) \right] = 109.0085$$

A is incorrect because the coupon payment is not accounted for at each node calculation. C is incorrect because it assumes that a coupon is paid in Year 1 (time zero) when no coupon payment is paid at time zero.

13

Topics in Fixed Income Analysis

This study session builds on the valuation concepts introduced in the previous study session. The first reading introduces valuation techniques for valuing bonds with embedded options. The second reading discusses credit risk and how it affects the valuation of fixed-income securities, credit analysis models, and how credit spreads are affected by liquidity. The final reading discusses credit default swaps.

READING ASSIGNMENTS

Reading 37	Valuation and Analysis: Bonds with Embedded Options by Leslie Abreo, MFE, Ioannis Georgiou, CFA, and Andrew Kalotay, PhD
Reading 38	Credit Analysis Models by Robert A. Jarrow, PhD, and Donald R. van Deventer, PhD
Reading 39	Credit Default Swaps by Brian Rose and Don M. Chance, PhD, CFA

READING
37

Valuation and Analysis: Bonds with Embedded Options

by Leslie Abreo, MFE, Ioannis Georgiou, CFA, and Andrew Kalotay, PhD

Leslie Abreo, MFE, is at Andrew Kalotay Associates, Inc. (USA). Ioannis Georgiou, CFA (Cyprus). Andrew Kalotay, PhD, is at Andrew Kalotay Associates, Inc. (USA).

LEARNING OUTCOMES

Mastery	The candidate should be able to:
☐	a. describe fixed-income securities with embedded options;
☐	b. explain the relationships between the values of a callable or putable bond, the underlying option-free (straight) bond, and the embedded option;
☐	c. describe how the arbitrage-free framework can be used to value a bond with embedded options;
☐	d. explain how interest rate volatility affects the value of a callable or putable bond;
☐	e. explain how changes in the level and shape of the yield curve affect the value of a callable or putable bond;
☐	f. calculate the value of a callable or putable bond from an interest rate tree;
☐	g. explain the calculation and use of option-adjusted spreads;
☐	h. explain how interest rate volatility affects option-adjusted spreads;
☐	i. calculate and interpret effective duration of a callable or putable bond;
☐	j. compare effective durations of callable, putable, and straight bonds;
☐	k. describe the use of one-sided durations and key rate durations to evaluate the interest rate sensitivity of bonds with embedded options;
☐	l. compare effective convexities of callable, putable, and straight bonds;
☐	m. describe defining features of a convertible bond;
☐	n. calculate and interpret the components of a convertible bond's value;

(continued)

1 INTRODUCTION

The valuation of a fixed-rate option-free bond generally requires determining its future cash flows and discounting them at the appropriate rates. Valuation becomes more complicated when a bond has one or more embedded options because the values of embedded options are typically contingent on interest rates.

Understanding how to value and analyze bonds with embedded options is important for practitioners. Issuers of bonds often manage interest rate exposure with embedded options such as call provisions. Investors in callable bonds must appreciate the risk of being called. The perception of this risk is collectively represented by the premium, in terms of increased coupon or yield, that the market demands for callable bonds relative to otherwise identical option-free bonds. Issuers and investors must also understand how other types of embedded options, such as put provisions, conversion options, caps, and floors, affect bond values and the sensitivity of these bonds to interest rate movements.

We begin this reading with a brief overview in Section 2 of various types of embedded options. We then discuss bonds that include a call or put provision. Taking a building-block approach, we show in Section 3 how the arbitrage-free valuation framework discussed in a previous reading can be applied to the valuation of callable and putable bonds, first in the absence of interest rate volatility and then when interest rates fluctuate. We also discuss how option-adjusted spreads are used to value risky callable and putable bonds. Section 4 covers interest rate sensitivity. It highlights the need to use effective duration, including one-sided durations and key rate durations, as well as effective convexity to assess the effect of interest rate movements on the value of callable and putable bonds.

We then turn to bonds that include other familiar types of embedded options. Section 5 focuses on the valuation of capped and floored floating-rate bonds (floaters). Convertible bonds are discussed in Section 6. The valuation of convertible bonds, which are typically callable and may also be putable, is complex because it depends not only on interest rate movements but also on future price movements of the issuer's underlying common stock.

Section 7 briefly highlights the importance of analytics software in bond valuation and analysis. Section 8 summarizes the reading.

2 OVERVIEW OF EMBEDDED OPTIONS

The term "embedded bond options" or **embedded options** refers to contingency provisions found in the bond's indenture or offering circular. These options represent rights that enable their holders to take advantage of interest rate movements. They can be exercised by the issuer or the bondholder, or they may be exercised automatically depending on the course of interest rates. For example, a call option allows the issuer to benefit from lower interest rates by retiring the bond issue early and refinancing at a lower cost. In contrast, a put option allows the bondholder to benefit from higher interest rates by putting back the bonds to the issuer and reinvesting the proceeds of the retired bond at a higher yield. These options are not independent of the bond and thus cannot be traded separately—hence the adjective "embedded." In this section, we provide a review of familiar embedded options.

Corresponding to every embedded option, or combination of embedded options, is an underlying bond with a specified issuer, issue date, maturity date, principal amount and repayment structure, coupon rate and payment structure, and currency denomination. In this reading, this underlying option-free bond is also referred to as the **straight bond**. The coupon of an underlying bond can be fixed or floating. Fixed-coupon bonds may have a single rate for the life of the bond, or the rate may step up or step down according to a coupon schedule. The coupons of floaters are reset periodically according to a formula based on a reference rate plus a credit spread—for example, six-month Libor + 100 basis points (bps). Except when we discuss capped and floored floaters, this reading focuses on fixed-coupon, single-rate bonds, also referred to as fixed-rate bonds.

2.1 Simple Embedded Options

Call and put options are standard examples of embedded options. In fact, the vast majority of bonds with embedded options are callable, putable, or both. The call provision is by far the most prevalent type of embedded option.

2.1.1 *Call Options*

A **callable bond** is a bond that includes an embedded call option. The call option is an issuer option—that is, the right to exercise the option is at the discretion of the bond's issuer. The call provision allows the issuer to redeem the bond issue prior to maturity. Early redemption usually happens when the issuer has the opportunity to replace a high-coupon bond with another bond that has more favorable terms, typically when interest rates have fallen or when the issuer's credit quality has improved.

Until the 1990s, most long-term corporate bonds in the United States were callable after either five or 10 years. The initial call price (exercise price) was typically at a premium above par, the premium depended on the coupon, and the call price gradually declined to par a few years prior to maturity. Today, most investment-grade corporate bonds are essentially non-refundable. They may have a "make-whole call," so named because the call price is such that the bondholders are more than "made whole" (compensated) in exchange for surrendering their bonds. The call price is calculated at a narrow spread to a benchmark security, usually an on-the-run sovereign bond such as Treasuries in the United States or gilts in the United Kingdom. Thus, economical refunding is virtually out of question, and investors need have no fear of receiving less than their bonds are worth.

Most callable bonds include a **lockout period** during which the issuer cannot call the bond. For example, a 10-year callable bond may have a lockout period of three years, meaning that the first potential call date is three years after the bond's issue date. Lockout periods may be as short as one month or extend to several years. For example, high-yield corporate bonds are often callable a few years after issuance. Holders of such bonds are usually less concerned about early redemption than about possible default. Of course, this perspective can change over the life of the bond—for example, if the issuer's credit quality improves.

Callable bonds include different types of call features. The issuer of a European-style callable bond can only exercise the call option on a single date at the end of the lockout period. An American-style callable bond is continuously callable from the end of the lockout period until the maturity date. A Bermudan-style call option can be exercised only on a predetermined schedule of dates after the end of the lockout period. These dates are specified in the bond's indenture or offering circular.

With a few exceptions, bonds issued by government-sponsored enterprises in the United States (e.g., Fannie Mae, Freddie Mac, Federal Home Loan Banks, and Federal Farm Credit Banks) are callable. These bonds tend to have relatively short maturities (5–10 years) and very short lockout periods (three months to one year). The call price is almost always at 100% of par, and the call option is often Bermudan style.

Tax-exempt municipal bonds (often called "munis"), a type of non-sovereign (local) government bond issued in the United States, are almost always callable at 100% of par any time after the end of the 10th year. They may also be eligible for advance refunding—a highly specialized topic that is not discussed here.

Although the bonds of US government-sponsored enterprises and municipal issuers account for most of the callable bonds issued and traded globally, bonds that include call provisions are also found in other countries in Asia Pacific, Europe, Canada, and Central and South America. The vast majority of callable bonds are denominated in US dollars or euros because of investors' demand for securities issued in these currencies. Australia, the United Kingdom, Japan, and Norway are examples of countries where there is a market for callable bonds denominated in local currency.

2.1.2 *Put Options and Extension Options*

A **putable bond** is a bond that includes an embedded put option. The put option is an investor option—that is, the right to exercise the option is at the discretion of the bondholder. The put provision allows the bondholders to put back the bonds to the issuer prior to maturity, usually at par. This usually happens when interest rates have risen and higher-yielding bonds are available.

Similar to callable bonds, most putable bonds include lockout periods. They can be European or, rarely, Bermudan style, but there are no American-style putable bonds.

Another type of embedded option that resembles a put option is an extension option: At maturity, the holder of an **extendible bond** has the right to keep the bond for a number of years after maturity, possibly with a different coupon. In this case, the terms of the bond's indenture or offering circular are modified, but the bond remains outstanding. Examples of extendible bonds can be found among Canadian issuers such as Royal Bank of Canada, which, as of July 2013, has a 1.125% semi-annual coupon bond outstanding that matures on 22 July 2016 but is extendible to 21 July 2017. We will discuss the resemblance between a putable and an extendible bond in Section 3.5.2.

2.2 Complex Embedded Options

Although callable and putable bonds are the most common types of bonds with embedded options, there are bonds with other types of options or combinations of options.

For instance, a bond can be both callable and putable. For example, as of July 2013, DIC Asset AG, a German corporate issuer, has a 5.875% annual coupon bond outstanding that matures on 16 May 2016. This bond can be either called by the issuer or put by the bondholders.

Convertible bonds are another type of bond with an embedded option. The conversion option allows bondholders to convert their bonds into the issuer's common stock. Convertible bonds are usually also callable by the issuer; the call provision enables the issuer to take advantage of lower interest rates or to force conversion. We will discuss convertible bonds thoroughly in Section 6.

Another layer of complexity is added when the option is contingent on some particular event. An example is the estate put or survivor's option that may be available to retail investors. For example, as of July 2013, GE Capital, a US corporate issuer, has a 5% semi-annual coupon callable bond outstanding that matures on 15 March 2018. In the event of its holder's death, this bond can be put at par by his or her heirs. Because the estate put comes into play only in the event of the bondholder's death, the value of a bond with an estate put is contingent on the life expectancy of its holder, which is uncertain.

BONDS WITH ESTATE PUTS

Colloquially known as "death-put" bonds, bonds with an estate put or survivor's option can be redeemed at par by the heirs of a deceased bondholder. The bonds should be put only if they sell at a discount—that is, if the prevailing price is below par. Otherwise, they should be sold in the market at a premium.

There is usually a ceiling on the principal amount of the bond the issuer is required to accept in a given year, such as 1% of the original principal amount. Estates giving notice of a put that would result in exceeding this ceiling go into a queue in chronological order.

The value of the estate put depends on the bondholder's life expectancy. The shorter the life expectancy, the greater the value of the estate put. A complicating factor is that most bonds with an estate put are also callable, usually at par and within five years of the issue date. If the issuer calls the bond early, the estate put is extinguished. Needless to say, valuing a callable bond with an estate put requires specialized tools. The key concept to keep in mind is that the value of such a bond depends not only on interest rate movements, like any bond with an embedded option, but also on the investor's life expectancy.

Bonds may contain several interrelated issuer options without any investor option. A prime example is a **sinking fund bond** (sinker), which requires the issuer to set aside funds over time to retire the bond issue, thus reducing credit risk. Such a bond may be callable and may also include options unique to sinking fund bonds, such as an acceleration provision and a delivery option.

SINKING FUND BONDS

The underlying bond has an amortizing structure—for example, a 30-year maturity with level annual principal repayments beginning at the end of the 11th year. In this case, each payment is 5% of the original principal amount. A typical sinking fund bond may include the following options:

- A standard *call option* above par, with declining premiums, starting at the end of Year 10. Thus, the entire bond issue could be called from Year 10 onward.

- An *acceleration provision*, such as a "triple up." Such a provision allows the issuer to repurchase at par three times the mandatory amount, or in this case 15% of the original principal amount, on any scheduled sinking fund date. Assume that the issuer wants to retire the bonds at the end of Year 11. Instead of calling the entire outstanding amount at a premium, it would be more cost effective to "sink" 15% at par and call the rest at a premium. Thus, the acceleration provision provides an additional benefit to the issuer if interest rates decline.

■ A *delivery option*, which allows the issuer to satisfy a sinking fund payment by delivering bonds to the bond's trustee in lieu of cash.[1] If the bonds are currently trading below par, say at 90% of par, it is more cost effective for the issuer to buy back bonds from investors to meet the sinking fund requirements than to pay par. The delivery option benefits the issuer if interest rates rise. Of course, the benefit can be materialized only if there is a liquid market for the bonds. Investors can take defensive action by accumulating the bonds and refusing to sell them at a discount.

From the issuer's perspective, the combination of the call option and the delivery option is effectively a "long straddle."[2] As a consequence, a sinking fund bond benefits the issuer not only if interest rates decline but also if they rise. Determining the combined value of the underlying bond and the three options is quite challenging.

EXAMPLE 1

Types of Embedded Options

1   Investors in putable bonds *most likely* seek to take advantage of:
    A   interest rate movements.
    B   changes in the issuer's credit rating.
    C   movements in the price of the issuer's common stock.

2   The decision to exercise the option embedded in an extendible bond is made by:
    A   the issuer.
    B   the bondholder.
    C   either the issuer or the bondholder.

3   The conversion option in a convertible bond is a right held by:
    A   the issuer.
    B   the bondholders.
    C   jointly by the issuer and the bondholders.

Solution to 1:

A is correct. A putable bond offers the bondholder the ability to take advantage of a rise in interest rates by putting back the bond to the issuer and reinvesting the proceeds of the retired bond in a higher-yielding bond.

---

1 A bond's trustee is typically a financial institution with trust powers. It is appointed by the issuer, but it acts in a fiduciary capacity with the bondholders. In public offerings, it is the trustee that determines, usually by lot, which bonds are to be retired.
2 A long straddle is an option strategy involving the purchase of a put option and a call option on the same underlying with the same exercise price and expiration date. At expiration, if the underlying price is above the exercise price, the put option is worthless but the call option is in the money. In contrast, if the underlying price is below the exercise price, the call option is worthless but the put option is in the money. Thus, a long straddle benefits the investor when the underlying price moves up or down. The greater the move up or down (i.e., the greater the volatility), the greater the benefit for the investor.

> **Solution to 2:**
>
> B is correct. An extendible bond includes an extension option that gives the bondholder the right to keep the bond for a number of years after maturity, possibly with a different coupon.
>
> **Solution to 3:**
>
> B is correct. A conversion option is a call option that gives the bondholders the right to convert their bonds into the issuer's common stock.

The presence of embedded options affects a bond's value. To quantify this effect, financial theory and financial technology come into play. The following section presents basic valuation and analysis concepts for bonds with embedded options.

VALUATION AND ANALYSIS OF CALLABLE AND PUTABLE BONDS

3

Under the arbitrage-free framework, the value of a bond with embedded options is equal to the sum of the arbitrage-free values of its parts. We first identify the relationships between the values of a callable or putable bond, the underlying option-free (straight) bond, and the call or put option, and then discuss how to value callable and putable bonds under different risk and interest rate volatility scenarios.

3.1 Relationships between the Values of a Callable or Putable Bond, Straight Bond, and Embedded Option

The value of a bond with embedded options is equal to the sum of the arbitrage-free value of the straight bond and the arbitrage-free values of the embedded options.

For a callable bond, the decision to exercise the call option is made by the issuer. Thus, the investor is long the bond but short the call option. From the investor's perspective, therefore, the value of the call option *decreases* the value of the callable bond relative to the value of the straight bond.

Value of callable bond = Value of straight bond − Value of issuer call option

The value of the straight bond can be obtained by discounting the bond's future cash flows at the appropriate rates, as described in Section 3.2. The hard part is valuing the call option because its value is contingent on future interest rates—specifically, the issuer's decision to call the bond depends on its ability to refinance at a lower cost. In practice, the value of the call option is often calculated as the difference between the value of the straight bond and the value of the callable bond:

Value of issuer call option
  = Value of straight bond − Value of callable bond   (1)

For a putable bond, the decision to exercise the put option is made by the investor. Thus, the investor has a long position in both the bond and the put option. As a consequence, the value of the put option *increases* the value of the putable bond relative to the value of the straight bond.

Value of putable bond = Value of straight bond + Value of investor put option

It follows that

Value of investor put option
= Value of putable bond − Value of straight bond   (2)

Although most investment professionals do not need to be experts in bond valuation, they should have a solid understanding of the basic analytical approach, presented in the following sections.

3.2 Valuation of Default-Free and Option-Free Bonds: A Refresher

An asset's value is the present value of the cash flows the asset is expected to generate in the future. In the case of a default-free and option-free bond, the future cash flows are, by definition, certain. Thus, the question is, at which rates should these cash flows be discounted? The answer is that each cash flow should be discounted at the spot rate corresponding to the cash flow's payment date. Although spot rates might not be directly observable, they can be inferred from readily available information, usually from the market prices of actively traded on-the-run sovereign bonds of various maturities. These prices can be transformed into spot rates, par rates (i.e., coupon rates of hypothetical bonds of various maturities selling at par), or forward rates. Recall from Level I that spot rates, par rates, and forward rates are equivalent ways of conveying the same information; knowing any one of them is sufficient to determine the others.

Suppose we want to value a three-year 4.25% annual coupon bond. Exhibit 1 provides the equivalent forms of a yield curve with maturities of one, two, and three years.

Exhibit 1	Equivalent Forms of a Yield Curve			
Maturity (year)	Par Rate (%)	Spot Rate (%)	One-Year Forward Rate (%)	
1	2.500	2.500	0 years from now	2.500
2	3.000	3.008	1 year from now	3.518
3	3.500	3.524	2 years from now	4.564

We start with the par rates provided in the second column of Exhibit 1. Because we are assuming annual coupons and annual compounding, the one-year spot rate is simply the one-year par rate. The hypothetical one-year par bond implied by the given par rate has a single cash flow of 102.500 (principal plus coupon) in Year 1.[3] In order to have a present value of par, this future cash flow must be divided by 1.025. Thus, the one-year spot rate or discount rate is 2.500%.

A two-year 3.000% par bond has two cash flows: 3 in Year 1 and 103 in Year 2. By definition, the sum of the two discounted cash flows must equal 100. We know that the discount rate appropriate for the first cash flow is the one-year spot rate (2.500%). We now solve the following equation to determine the two-year spot rate (S_2):

$$\frac{3}{(1.025)} + \frac{103}{(1 + S_2)^2} = 100$$

---

3 In this reading, all cash flows and values are expressed as a percentage of par.

We can follow a similar approach to determine the three-year spot rate (S_3):

$$\frac{3.500}{(1.02500)} + \frac{3.500}{(1.03008)^2} + \frac{103.500}{(1 + S_3)^3} = 100$$

The one-year forward rates are determined by using indifference equations. Assume an investor has a two-year horizon. She could invest for two years either at the two-year spot rate, or at the one-year spot rate for one year and then reinvest the proceeds at the one-year forward rate one year from now ($F_{1,1}$). The result of investing using either of the two approaches should be the same. Otherwise, there would be an arbitrage opportunity. Thus,

$$(1 + 0.03008)^2 = (1 + 0.02500) \times (1 + F_{1,1})$$

Similarly, the one-year forward rate two years from now ($F_{2,1}$) can be calculated using the following equation:

$$(1 + 0.03524)^3 = (1 + 0.03008)^2 \times (1 + F_{2,1})$$

The three-year 4.25% annual coupon bond can now be valued using the spot rates:[4]

$$\frac{4.25}{(1.02500)} + \frac{4.25}{(1.03008)^2} + \frac{104.25}{(1.03524)^3} = 102.114$$

An equivalent way to value this bond is to discount its cash flows one year at a time using the one-year forward rates:

$$\frac{4.25}{(1.02500)} + \frac{4.25}{(1.02500)(1.03518)} + \frac{104.25}{(1.02500)(1.03518)(1.04564)} = 102.114$$

3.3 Valuation of Default-Free Callable and Putable Bonds in the Absence of Interest Rate Volatility

When valuing bonds with embedded options, the approach relying on one-period forward rates provides a better framework than that relying on the spot rates because we need to know the value of the bond at different points in time in the future to determine whether the embedded option will be exercised at those points in time.

3.3.1 Valuation of a Callable Bond at Zero Volatility

Let us apply this framework to the valuation of a Bermudan-style three-year 4.25% annual coupon bond that is callable at par one year and two years from now. The decision to exercise the call option is made by the issuer. Because the issuer borrowed money, it will exercise the call option when the value of the bond's future cash flows is higher than the call price (exercise price). Exhibit 2 shows how to calculate the value of this callable bond using the one-year forward rates calculated in Exhibit 1.

---

4 The examples in this reading were created in Microsoft Excel. Numbers may differ from the results obtained using a calculator because of rounding.

Exhibit 2	Valuation of a Default-Free Three-Year 4.25% Annual Coupon Bond Callable at Par One Year and Two Years from Now at Zero Volatility			
	Today	Year 1	Year 2	Year 3
Cash Flow		4.250	4.250	104.250
Discount Rate		2.500%	3.518%	4.564%
Value of the Callable Bond	$\dfrac{100 + 4.250}{1.02500} = 101.707$	$\dfrac{99.700 + 4.250}{1.03518} = \cancel{100.417}$	$\dfrac{104.250}{1.04564} = 99.700$	
		Called at 100	Not called	

We start by discounting the bond's cash flow at maturity (104.250) to Year 2 using the one-year forward rate two years from now (4.564%). The present value at Year 2 of the bond's future cash flows is 99.700. This value is lower than the call price of 100, so a rational borrower will not call the bond at that point in time. Next, we add the cash flow in Year 2 (4.250) to the present value of the bond's future cash flows at Year 2 (99.700) and discount the sum to Year 1 using the one-year forward rate one year from now (3.518%). The present value at Year 1 of the bond's future cash flows is 100.417. Here, a rational borrower will call the bond at 100 because leaving it outstanding would be more expensive than redeeming it. Last, we add the cash flow in Year 1 (4.250) to the present value of the bond's future cash flows at Year 1 (100.000), and we discount the sum to today at 2.500%. The result (101.707) is the value of the callable bond.

We can apply Equation 1 to calculate the value of the call option embedded in this callable bond. The value of the straight bond is the value of the default-free and option-free three-year 4.25% annual coupon bond calculated in Section 3.2 (102.114). Thus,

Value of issuer call option = 102.114 − 101.707 = 0.407

Recall from the earlier discussion about the relationships between the value of a callable bond, straight bond, and call option that the investor is long the bond and short the call option. Thus, the value of the call option decreases the value of the callable bond relative to that of an otherwise identical option-free bond.

3.3.2 *Valuation of a Putable Bond at Zero Volatility*

We now apply this framework to the valuation of a Bermudan-type three-year 4.25% annual coupon bond that is putable at par one year and two years from now. The decision to exercise the put option is made by the investor. Because the investor lent money, he will exercise the put option when the value of the bond's future cash flows is lower than the put price (exercise price). Exhibit 3 shows how to calculate the value of the three-year 4.25% annual coupon bond putable at par one year and two years from today.

Exhibit 3	Valuation of a Default-Free Three-Year 4.25% Annual Coupon Bond Putable at Par One Year and Two Years from Now at Zero Volatility			
	Today	**Year 1**	**Year 2**	**Year 3**
Cash Flow		4.250	4.250	104.250
Discount Rate		2.500%	3.518%	4.564%
Value of the Putable Bond	$\frac{100.707 + 4.250}{1.02500} = 102.397$	$\frac{100 + 4.250}{1.03518} = 100.707$	$\frac{104.250}{1.04564} = 99.700$	
		Not put	Put at 100	

We can apply Equation 2 to calculate the value of the put option:

Value of investor put option = 102.397 − 102.114 = 0.283

Because the investor is long the bond and the put option, the value of the put option increases the value of the putable bond relative to that of an otherwise identical option-free bond.

OPTIMAL EXERCISE OF OPTIONS

The holder of an embedded bond option can extinguish (or possibly modify the terms of) the bond. Assuming that the option is currently exercisable, the obvious question is, does it pay to exercise? Assuming that the answer is affirmative, the follow-up question is whether it is better to exercise the option at present or to wait.

Let us consider the first question: Would it be profitable to exercise the option? The answer is usually straightforward: Compare the value of exercising with the value of not exercising. For example, suppose that a bond is currently putable at 100. If the bond's market price is above 100, putting the bond makes no sense because the cash value from selling the bond would exceed 100. In contrast, if the bond's market price is 100, putting the bond should definitely be considered. Note that the market price of the bond cannot be less than 100 because such a situation creates an arbitrage opportunity: Buy the bond below 100 and immediately put it at 100.

The logic of a call decision by the issuer is similar. If a bond's market price is significantly less than the call price, calling is foolish because the bonds could be simply repurchased in the market at a lower price. Alternatively, if the price is very close to the call price, calling may make sense.

Assume that we have determined that exercising the option would be profitable. If the option under consideration is European style, it is obvious that it should in fact be exercised: There is no justification for not doing so. But if it is an American-style or Bermudan-style option, the challenge is to determine whether it is better to act now or to wait for a better opportunity in the future. The problem is that although circumstances may become more favorable, they may also get worse. So, option holders must consider the odds and decide to act or wait, depending on their risk preference.

The approach presented in this reading for valuing bonds with embedded options assumes that the option holders, be they issuers or investors, are risk neutral. They exercise if, and only if, the benefit from exercise exceeds the expected benefit from waiting. In reality, option holders may be risk averse and may exercise early even if the option is worth more alive than dead.

EXAMPLE 2

Valuation of Default-Free Callable and Putable Bonds

George Cahill, a portfolio manager, has identified three five-year annual coupon bonds issued by a sovereign government. The three bonds have identical characteristics, except that Bond A is an option-free bond, Bond B is callable at par in two years and three years from today, and Bond C is callable and putable at par two years and three years from today.

1 Relative to the value of Bond A, the value of Bond B is:

    A lower.

    B the same.

    C higher.

2 Relative to the value of Bond B, the value of Bond C is:

    A lower.

    B the same.

    C higher.

3 Under a steeply upward-sloping yield curve scenario, Bond C will *most likely*:

    A be called by the issuer.

    B be put by the bondholders.

    C mature without exercise of any of the embedded options.

Solution to 1:

A is correct. Bond B is a callable bond, and Bond A is the underlying option-free (straight) bond. The call option embedded in Bond B is an issuer option that decreases the bond's value for the investor. If interest rates decline, bond prices usually increase, but the price appreciation of Bond B will be capped relative to the price appreciation of Bond A because the issuer will call the bond to refinance at a lower cost.

Solution to 2:

C is correct. Relative to Bond B, Bond C includes a put option. A put option is an investor option that increases the bond's value for the investor. Thus, the value of Bond C is higher than that of Bond B.

Solution to 3:

B is correct. As interest rates rise, bond prices decrease. Thus, the bondholders will have an incentive to exercise the put option so that they can reinvest the proceeds of the retired bond at a higher yield.

Exhibits 2 and 3 show how callable and putable bonds are valued in the absence of interest rate volatility. In real life, however, interest rates do fluctuate. Thus, the option holder must consider possible evolutions of the yield curve over time.

3.4 Effect of Interest Rate Volatility on the Value of Callable and Putable Bonds

In this section, we discuss the effects of interest rate volatility as well as the level and shape of the yield curve on the value of embedded options.

3.4.1 *Interest Rate Volatility*

The value of any embedded option, regardless of the type of option, increases with interest rate volatility. The greater the volatility, the more opportunities exist for the embedded option to be exercised. Thus, it is critical for issuers and investors to understand the effect of interest rate volatility on the value of bonds with embedded options.

The effect of interest rate volatility is represented in an interest rate tree or lattice, as illustrated in Exhibit 4. From each node on the tree starting from today, interest rates could go up or down. From these two states, interest rates could again go up or down. The dispersion between these up and down states anywhere on the tree is determined by the process generating interest rates based on a given yield curve and interest rate volatility assumptions.

Exhibit 4   Building an Interest Rate Tree

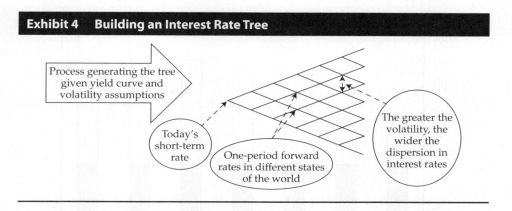

Exhibits 5 and 6 show the effect of interest rate volatility on the value of a callable bond and putable bond, respectively.

Exhibit 5   Value of a 30-Year 4.50% Bond Callable at Par in 10 Years under Different Volatility Scenarios Assuming a 4% Flat Yield Curve

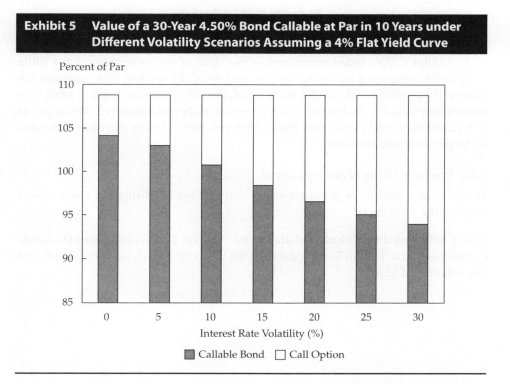

The stacked bars in Exhibit 5 represent the value of the straight bond, which is unaffected by interest rate volatility. The white component is the value of the call option which, when taken away from the value of the straight bond, gives the value of the callable bond—the shaded component. All else being equal, the call option increases in value with interest rate volatility. At zero volatility, the value of the call option is 4.60% of par; at 30% volatility, it is 14.78% of par. Thus, as interest rate volatility increases, the value of the callable bond decreases.

Exhibit 6   Value of a 30-Year 3.75% Bond Putable at Par in 10 Years under Different Volatility Scenarios Assuming a 4% Flat Yield Curve

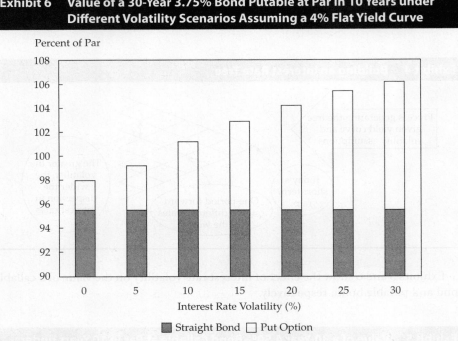

Percent of Par

Interest Rate Volatility (%)

▨ Straight Bond   ☐ Put Option

In Exhibit 6, the shaded component is the value of the straight bond, the white component is the value of the put option, and, thus, the stacked bars represent the value of the putable bond. All else being equal, the put option increases in value with interest rate volatility. At zero volatility, the value of the put option is 2.30% of par; at 30% volatility, it is 10.54% of par. Thus, as interest rate volatility increases, the value of the putable bond increases.

3.4.2 Level and Shape of the Yield Curve

The value of a callable or putable bond is also affected by changes in the level and shape of the yield curve.

3.4.2.1 Effect on the Value of a Callable Bond   Exhibit 7 shows the value of the same callable bond as in Exhibit 5 under different flat yield curve levels assuming an interest rate volatility of 15%.

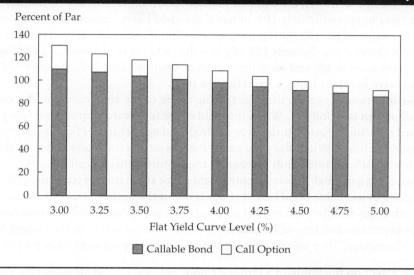

Exhibit 7   Value of a 30-Year 4.50% Bond Callable at Par in 10 Years under Different Flat Yield Curve Levels at 15% Interest Rate Volatility

Percent of Par

Flat Yield Curve Level (%)

■ Callable Bond   □ Call Option

Exhibit 7 shows that as interest rates decline, the value of the straight bond rises, but the rise is partially offset by the increase in the value of the call option. For example, if the yield curve is 5% flat, the value of the straight bond is 92.27% of par and the value of the call option is 5.37% of par, so the value of the callable bond is 86.90% of par. If the yield curve declines to 3% flat, the value of the straight bond rises by 40% to 129.54% of par, but the value of the callable bond only increases by 27% to 110.43% of par. Thus, the value of the callable bond rises less rapidly than the value of the straight bond, limiting the upside potential for the investor.

The value of a call option, and thus the value of a callable bond, is also affected by changes in the shape of the yield curve, as illustrated in Exhibit 8.

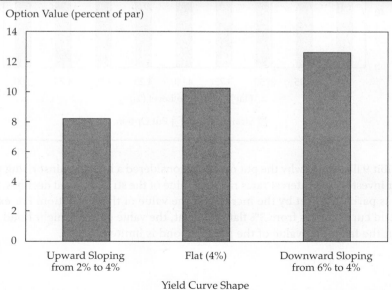

Exhibit 8   Value of a Call Option Embedded in a 30-Year 4.50% Bond Callable at Par in 10 Years under Different Yield Curve Shapes at 15% Interest Rate Volatility

Option Value (percent of par)

Yield Curve Shape

Upward Sloping from 2% to 4%   Flat (4%)   Downward Sloping from 6% to 4%

All else being equal, the value of the call option increases as the yield curve flattens. If the yield curve is upward sloping with short-term rates at 2% and long-term rates at 4% (the first bar), the value of the call option represents approximately 8% of par. It rises to approximately 10% of par if the yield curve flattens to 4% (the second bar). The value of the call option increases further if the yield curve actually inverts. Exhibit 8 shows that it exceeds 12% of par if the yield curve is downward sloping with short-term rates at 6% and long-term rates at 4% (the third bar). An inverted yield curve is rare but does happen from time to time.

The intuition to explain the effect of the shape of the yield curve on the value of the call option is as follows. When the yield curve is upward sloping, the one-period forward rates on the interest rate tree are high and opportunities for the issuer to call the bond are fewer. When the yield curve flattens or inverts, many nodes on the tree have lower forward rates, thus increasing the opportunities to call.

Assuming a normal, upward-sloping yield curve at the time of issue, the call option embedded in a callable bond issued at par is out of the money. It would not be called if the arbitrage-free forward rates at zero volatility prevailed. Callable bonds issued at a large premium, as happens frequently in the municipal sector in the United States, are in the money. They will be called if the arbitrage-free forward rates prevail.

3.4.2.2 Effect on the Value of a Putable Bond

Exhibits 9 and 10 show how changes in the level and shape of the yield curve affect the value of the putable bond used in Exhibit 6.

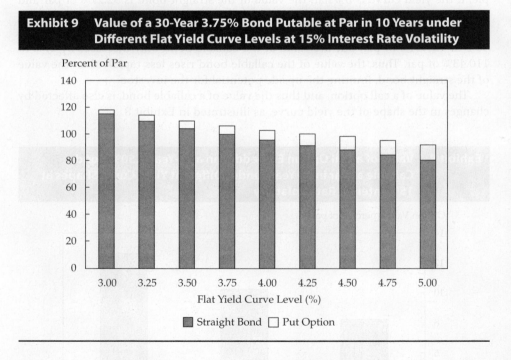

Exhibit 9   Value of a 30-Year 3.75% Bond Putable at Par in 10 Years under Different Flat Yield Curve Levels at 15% Interest Rate Volatility

Exhibit 9 illustrates why the put option is considered a hedge against rising interest rates for investors. As interest rates rise, the value of the straight bond declines, but the decline is partially offset by the increase in the value of the put option. For example, if the yield curve moves from 3% flat to 5% flat, the value of the straight bond falls by 30%, but the fall in the value of the putable bond is limited to 22%.

Exhibit 10 Value of the Put Option Embedded in a 30-Year 3.75% Bond Putable at Par in 10 Years under Different Yield Curve Shapes at 15% Interest Rate Volatility

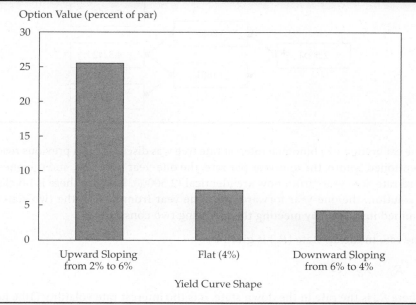

All else being equal, the value of the put option decreases as the yield curve moves from being upward sloping, to flat, to downward sloping. When the yield curve is upward sloping, the one-period forward rates in the interest rate tree are high, which creates more opportunities for the investor to put the bond. As the yield curve flattens or inverts, the number of opportunities declines.

3.5 Valuation of Default-Free Callable and Putable Bonds in the Presence of Interest Rate Volatility

The procedure to value a bond with an embedded option in the presence of interest rate volatility is as follows:

- Generate a tree of interest rates based on the given yield curve and interest rate volatility assumptions.

- At each node of the tree, determine whether the embedded options will be exercised.

- Apply the backward induction valuation methodology to calculate the bond's present value. This methodology involves starting at maturity and working back from right to left to find the bond's present value.

Let us return to the default-free three-year 4.25% annual coupon bonds discussed in Sections 3.3.1 (callable) and 3.3.2 (putable) to illustrate how to apply this valuation procedure. The bonds' characteristics are identical. The yield curve given in Exhibit 1 remains the same with one-year, two-year, and three-year par yields of 2.500%, 3.000%, and 3.500%, respectively. But we now assume an interest rate volatility of 10% instead of 0%. The resulting binomial interest rate tree showing the one-year forward rates zero, one, and two years from now is shown in Exhibit 11. The branching from each node to an up state and a down state is assumed to occur with equal probability.

Exhibit 11   Binomial Interest Rate Tree at 10% Interest Rate Volatility

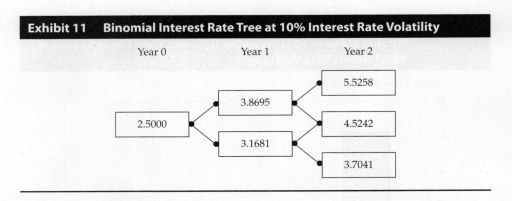

The calibration of a binomial interest rate tree was discussed in a previous reading. As mentioned before, the one-year par rate, the one-year spot rate, and the one-year forward rate zero years from now are identical (2.500%). Because there is no closed-form solution, the one-year forward rates one year from now in the two states are determined iteratively by meeting the following two constraints:

1   The rate in the up state (R_u) is given by

$$R_u = R_d \times e^{2\sigma\sqrt{t}}$$

where R_d is the rate in the down state, σ is the interest rate volatility (10% here), and t is the time in years between "time slices" (a year, so here $t = 1$).

2   The discounted value of a two-year par bond (bearing a 3.000% coupon rate in this example) equals 100.

In Exhibit 11, at the one-year time slice, R_d is 3.1681% and R_u is 3.8695%. Having established the rates that correctly value the one-year and two-year par bonds implied by the given par yield curve, we freeze these rates and proceed to iterate the rates in the next time slice to determine the one-year forward rates in the three states two years from now. The same constraints as before apply—that is, (1) each rate must be related to its neighbor by the factor $e^{2\sigma\sqrt{t}}$, and (2) the rates must discount a three-year par bond (bearing a 3.500% coupon rate in this example) to a value of 100.

Now that we have determined all the one-year forward rates, we can value the three-year 4.25% annual coupon bonds that are either callable or putable at par one year and two years from now.

3.5.1 *Valuation of a Callable Bond with Interest Rate Volatility*

Exhibit 12 depicts the valuation of a callable bond at 10% volatility.

Exhibit 12 Valuation of a Default-Free Three-Year 4.25% Annual Coupon Bond Callable at Par One Year and Two Years from Now at 10% Interest Rate Volatility

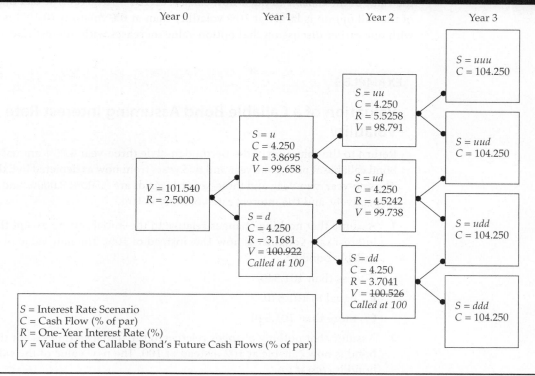

S = Interest Rate Scenario
C = Cash Flow (% of par)
R = One-Year Interest Rate (%)
V = Value of the Callable Bond's Future Cash Flows (% of par)

From the one-year rate, the two interest rate scenario branches in the tree are labeled *u* for an up state and *d* for a down state. Because this is a recombining binomial tree, the interest rate scenarios can be both the up state from the previous down state, and the down state from the previous up state. We use a single designation from the alternatives, if any. Thus, in Year 1, the states are *u* and *d*; in Year 2, *uu*, *ud*, and *dd*; and in Year 3, *uuu*, *uud*, *udd*, and *ddd*.

Starting from Year 3, we note that the bond's cash flow at maturity is 104.250 in the four states of the world. Each of the four cash flows in Year 3 is simply discounted at the appropriate one-year forward rate to Year 2. For example, the 104.250 in the state *uuu* is discounted at the one-year forward rate two years from now (5.5258%), which gives a value of 98.791. Because the bond is callable at par in Year 2, we check each scenario to determine whether the present value of the future cash flows is higher than the call price, in which case the issuer calls the bond. Exercise happens only in state *dd*, and so we reset the value from 100.526 to 100 in that state.

The value in each state of Year 1 is calculated by discounting the values in the two future states emanating from the present state plus the coupon at the appropriate rate in the present state. The probability-weighted average of these two discounted values is the value in the present state in Year 1. Because we assume equal probability for the two branches from any state, we simply divide the sum of the two discounted values by two. For example, the value in state *d* of Year 1 is given by

$$\frac{1}{2} \times \left(\frac{99.738 + 4.250}{1.031681} + \frac{100 + 4.250}{1.031681} \right) = 100.922$$

Finally, in Year 0, the value of the callable bond is 101.540. The value of the call option, obtained by taking the difference between the value of the straight bond and the value of the callable bond, is now 0.574 (102.114 − 101.540). The fact that the value of the call option is larger at 10% volatility than at 0% volatility (0.407) is consistent with our earlier discussion that option value increases with interest rate volatility.

EXAMPLE 3

Valuation of a Callable Bond Assuming Interest Rate Volatility

Return to the valuation of the Bermudan-style three-year 4.25% annual coupon bond callable at par in one year and two years from now as depicted in Exhibit 12. The one-year, two-year, and three-year par yields are 2.500%, 3.000%, and 3.500%, respectively, and the interest rate volatility is 10%.

1 Assume that nothing changes relative to the initial setting except that the interest rate volatility is now 15% instead of 10%. The new value of the callable bond is:

   A less than 101.540.

   B equal to 101.540.

   C more than 101.540.

2 Assume that nothing changes relative to the initial setting except that the bond is now callable at 102 instead of 100. The new value of the callable bond is *closest to*:

   A 100.000.

   B 102.000.

   C 102.114.

Solution to 1:

A is correct. A higher interest rate volatility increases the value of the call option. Because the value of the call option is subtracted from the value of the straight bond to obtain the value of the callable bond, a higher value for the call option leads to a lower value for the callable bond. Thus, the value of the callable bond at 15% volatility is less than that at 10% volatility—that is, less than 101.540.

Solution to 2:

C is correct. Looking at Exhibit 12, the call price is too high for the call option to be exercised in any scenario. Thus, the value of the call option is zero, and the value of the callable bond is equal to the value of the straight bond—that is, 102.114.

3.5.2 *Valuation of a Putable Bond with Interest Rate Volatility*

The valuation of the three-year 4.25% annual coupon bond putable at par in one year and two years from now at 10% volatility is depicted in Exhibit 13. The procedure for valuing a putable bond is very similar to that described earlier for valuing a callable bond, except that in each state, the bond's value is compared with the put price. The investor puts the bond only when the present value of the bond's future cash flows is lower than the put price. In this case, the value is reset to the put price (100). It happens twice in Year 2, in states *uu* and *ud*.

Exhibit 13	Valuation of a Default-Free Three-Year 4.25% Annual Coupon Bond Putable at Par One Year and Two Years from Now at 10% Interest Rate Volatility

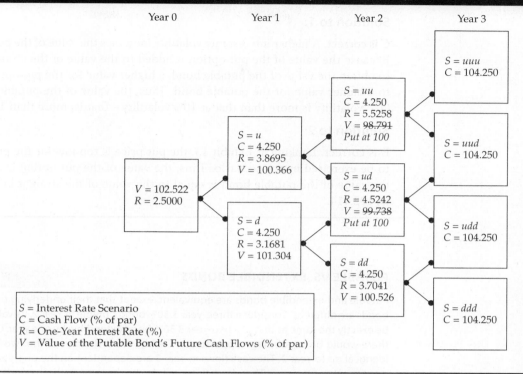

S = Interest Rate Scenario
C = Cash Flow (% of par)
R = One-Year Interest Rate (%)
V = Value of the Putable Bond's Future Cash Flows (% of par)

The value of the putable bond is 102.522. The value of the put option, obtained by taking the difference between the value of the putable bond and the value of the straight bond, is now 0.408 (102.522 – 102.114). As expected, the value of the put option is larger at 10% volatility than at 0% volatility (0.283).

EXAMPLE 4

Valuation of a Putable Bond Assuming Interest Rate Volatility

Return to the valuation of the Bermudan-style three-year 4.25% annual coupon bond putable at par in one year and two years from now, as depicted in Exhibit 13. The one-year, two-year, and three-year par yields are 2.500%, 3.000%, and 3.500%, respectively, and the interest rate volatility is 10%.

1 Assume that nothing changes relative to the initial setting except that the interest rate volatility is now 20% instead of 10%. The new value of the putable bond is:

A less than 102.522.

B equal to 102.522.

C more than 102.522.

2 Assume that nothing changes relative to the initial setting except that the bond is now putable at 95 instead of 100. The new value of the putable bond is *closest to*:

A 97.522.

B   102.114.

C   107.522.

Solution to 1:

C is correct. A higher interest rate volatility increases the value of the put option. Because the value of the put option is added to the value of the straight bond to obtain the value of the putable bond, a higher value for the put option leads to a higher value for the putable bond. Thus, the value of the putable bond at 20% volatility is more than that at 10% volatility—that is, more than 102.522.

Solution to 2:

B is correct. Looking at Exhibit 13, the put price is too low for the put option to be exercised in any scenario. Thus, the value of the put option is zero, and the value of the putable bond is equal to the value of the straight bond—that is, 102.114.

PUTABLE VS. EXTENDIBLE BONDS

Putable and extendible bonds are equivalent, except that their underlying option-free bonds are different. Consider a three-year 3.30% bond putable in Year 2. Its value should be exactly the same as that of a two-year 3.30% bond extendible by one year. Otherwise, there would be an arbitrage opportunity. Clearly, the cash flows of the two bonds are identical up to Year 2. The cash flows in Year 3 are dependent on the one-year forward rate two years from now. These cash flows will also be the same for both bonds regardless of the level of interest rates at the end of Year 2.

If the one-year forward rate at the end of Year 2 is higher than 3.30%, the putable bond will be put because the bondholder can reinvest the proceeds of the retired bond at a higher yield, and the extendible bond will not be extended for the same reason. So, both bonds pay 3.30% for two years and are then redeemed. Alternatively, if the one-year forward rate at the end of Year 2 is lower than 3.30%, the putable bond will not be put because the bondholder would not want to reinvest at a lower yield, and the extendible bond will be extended to hold onto the higher interest rate. Thus, both bonds pay 3.30% for three years and are then redeemed.

EXAMPLE 5

Valuation of Bonds with Embedded Options Assuming Interest Rate Volatility

Sidley Brown, a fixed income associate at KMR Capital, is analyzing the effect of interest rate volatility on the values of callable and putable bonds issued by Weather Analytics (WA). WA is owned by the sovereign government, so its bonds are considered default free. Brown is currently looking at three of WA's bonds and has gathered the following information about them:

Characteristic	Bond X	Bond Y	Bond Z
Times to maturity	Three years from today	Three years from today	Three years from today
Coupon	5.2% annual	Not available	4.8% annual

Characteristic	Bond X	Bond Y	Bond Z
Type of bond	Callable at par one year and two years from today	Callable at par one year and two years from today	Putable at par two years from today
Price (as a % of par)	Not available	101.325	Not available

The one-year, two-year, and three-year par rates are 4.400%, 4.700%, and 5.000%, respectively. Based on an estimated interest rate volatility of 15%, Brown has constructed the following binomial interest rate tree:

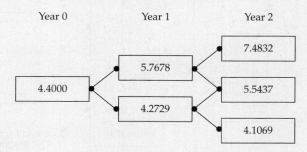

1 The price of Bond X is *closest to*:
   A 96.057% of par.
   B 99.954% of par.
   C 100.547% of par.

2 The coupon rate of Bond Y is *closest to*:
   A 4.200%.
   B 5.000%.
   C 6.000%.

3 The price of Bond Z is *closest to*:
   A 99.638% of par.
   B 100.340% of par.
   C 100.778% of par.

Brown is now analyzing the effect of interest rate volatility on the price of WA's bonds.

4 Relative to its price at 15% interest rate volatility, the price of Bond X at a lower interest rate volatility will be:
   A lower.
   B the same.
   C higher.

5 Relative to its price at 15% interest rate volatility, the price of Bond Z at a higher interest rate volatility will be:
   A lower.
   B the same.
   C higher.

Solution to 1:

B is correct.

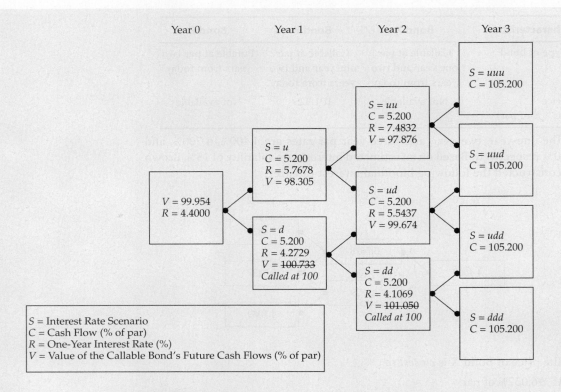

S = Interest Rate Scenario
C = Cash Flow (% of par)
R = One-Year Interest Rate (%)
V = Value of the Callable Bond's Future Cash Flows (% of par)

Solution to 2:

C is correct.

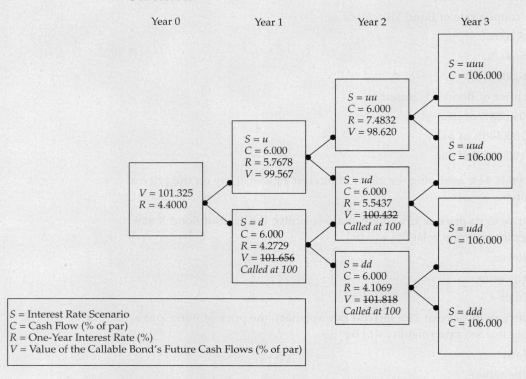

S = Interest Rate Scenario
C = Cash Flow (% of par)
R = One-Year Interest Rate (%)
V = Value of the Callable Bond's Future Cash Flows (% of par)

Although the correct answer can be found by using the interest rate tree depicted, it is possible to identify it by realizing that the other two answers are clearly incorrect. The three-year 5% straight bond is worth par given that the three-year par rate is 5%. Because the presence of a call option reduces the price of a callable bond, a three-year 5% bond callable at par can only be worth less than par, and certainly less than 101.325 given the yield curve and interest rate volatility assumptions, so B is incorrect. The value of a bond with a coupon rate of 4% is even less, so A is incorrect. Thus, C must be the correct answer.

Solution to 3:

B is correct.

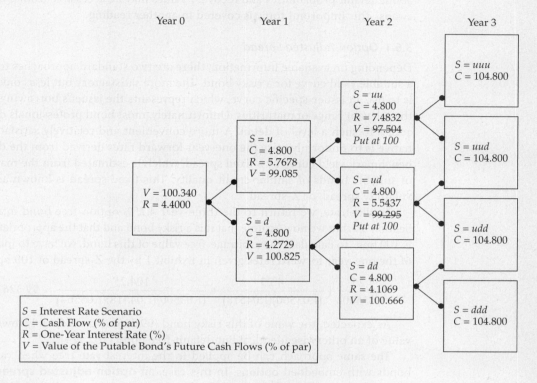

Solution to 4:

C is correct. Bond X is a callable bond. As shown in Equation 1, the value of the call option decreases the value of Bond X relative to the value of the underlying option-free bond. As interest rate volatility decreases, the value of the call option decreases, and thus the value of Bond X increases.

Solution to 5:

C is correct. Bond Z is a putable bond. As shown in Equation 2, the value of the put option increases the value of Bond Z relative to the value of the underlying option-free bond. As interest rate volatility increases, the value of the put option increases, and thus the value of Bond Z increases.

3.6 Valuation of Risky Callable and Putable Bonds

Although the approach described earlier for default-free bonds may apply to securities issued by sovereign governments in their local currency, the fact is that most bonds are subject to default. Accordingly, we have to extend the framework to the valuation of risky bonds.

There are two distinct approaches to valuing bonds that are subject to default risk. The industry-standard approach is to increase the discount rates above the default-free rates to reflect default risk. Higher discount rates imply lower present values, and thus the value of a risky bond will be lower than that of an otherwise identical default-free bond. How to obtain an appropriate yield curve for a risky bond is discussed in Section 3.6.1.

The second approach to valuing risky bonds is by making the default probabilities explicit—that is, by assigning a probability to each time period going forward. For example, the probability of default in Year 1 may be 1%; the probability of default in Year 2, conditional on surviving Year 1, may be 1.25%; and so on. This approach requires specifying the recovery value given default (e.g., 40% of par). Information about default probabilities and recovery values may be accessible from credit default swaps. This important topic is covered in another reading.

3.6.1 *Option-Adjusted Spread*

Depending on available information, there are two standard approaches to construct a suitable yield curve for a risky bond. The more satisfactory but less convenient one is to use an issuer-specific curve, which represents the issuer's borrowing rates over the relevant range of maturities. Unfortunately, most bond professionals do not have access to such a level of detail. A more convenient and relatively satisfactory alternative is to uniformly raise the one-year forward rates derived from the default-free benchmark yield curve by a fixed spread, which is estimated from the market prices of suitable bonds of similar credit quality. This fixed spread is known as the zero-volatility spread, or Z-spread.

To illustrate, we return to the three-year 4.25% option-free bond introduced in Section 3.2, but we now assume that it is a risky bond and that the appropriate Z-spread is 100 bps. To calculate the arbitrage-free value of this bond, we have to increase each of the one-year forward rates given in Exhibit 1 by the Z-spread of 100 bps:

$$\frac{4.25}{(1.03500)} + \frac{4.25}{(1.03500)(1.04518)} + \frac{104.25}{(1.03500)(1.04518)(1.05564)} = 99.326$$

As expected, the value of this risky bond (99.326) is considerably lower than the value of an otherwise identical but default-free bond (102.114).

The same approach can be applied to the interest rate tree when valuing risky bonds with embedded options. In this case, an **option-adjusted spread** (OAS) is used. As depicted in Exhibit 14, the OAS is the constant spread that, when added to all the one-period forward rates on the interest rate tree, makes the arbitrage-free value of the bond equal to its market price. Note that the Z-spread for an option-free bond is simply its OAS at zero volatility.

Exhibit 14   Interest Rate Tree and OAS

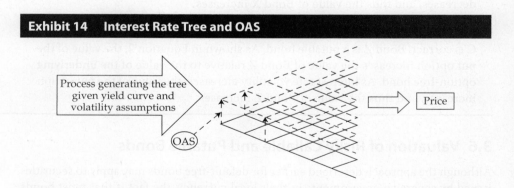

If the bond's price is given, the OAS is determined by trial and error. For example, suppose that the market price of a three-year 4.25% annual coupon bond callable in one year and two years from now, identical to the one valued in Exhibit 12 except that it is risky instead of default-free, is 101.000. To determine the OAS, we try shifting all the one-year forward rates in each state by adding a constant spread. For example, when we add 30 bps to all the one-year forward rates, we obtain a value for the callable bond of 100.973, which is lower than the bond's price. Because of the inverse relationship between a bond's price and its yield, this result means that the discount rates are too high, so we try a slightly lower spread. Adding 28 bps results in a value for the callable bond of 101.010, which is slightly too high. As illustrated in Exhibit 15, the constant spread added uniformly to all the one-period forward rates that justifies the given market price of 101.000 is 28.55 bps; this number is the OAS.

Exhibit 15   OAS of a Risky Three-Year 4.25% Annual Coupon Bond Callable at Par One Year and Two Years from Now at 10% Interest Rate Volatility

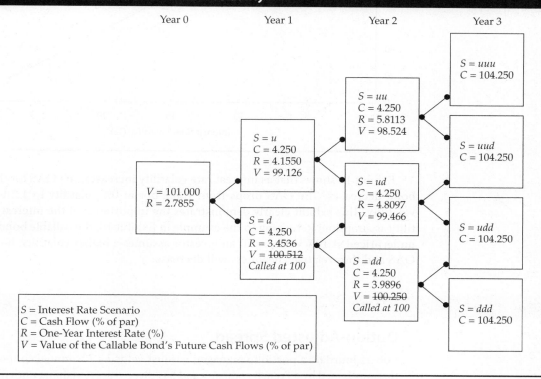

As illustrated in Exhibit 15, the value at each node is adjusted based on whether the call option is exercised. Thus, the OAS removes the amount that results from the option risk, which is why this spread is called "option adjusted."

OAS is often used as a measure of value relative to the benchmark. An OAS lower than that for a bond with similar characteristics and credit quality indicates that the bond is likely overpriced (rich) and should be avoided. A larger OAS than that of a bond with similar characteristics and credit quality means that the bond is likely underpriced (cheap). If the OAS is close to that of a bond with similar characteristics and credit quality, the bond looks fairly priced. In our example, the OAS at 10% volatility is 28.55 bps. This number should be compared with the OAS of bonds with similar characteristics and credit quality to make a judgment about the bond's attractiveness.

3.6.2 *Effect of Interest Rate Volatility on Option-Adjusted Spread*

The dispersion of interest rates on the tree is volatility dependent, and so is the OAS. Exhibit 16 shows the effect of volatility on the OAS for a callable bond. The bond is a 5% annual coupon bond with 23 years left to maturity, callable in three years, priced at 95% of par, and valued assuming a flat yield curve of 4%.

Exhibit 16   Effect of Interest Rate Volatility on the OAS for a Callable Bond

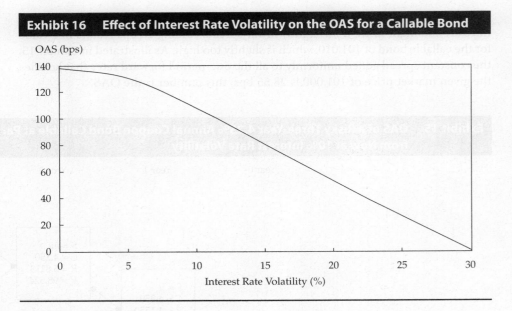

Exhibit 16 shows that as interest rate volatility increases, the OAS for the callable bond decreases. The OAS drops from 138.2 bps at 0% volatility to 1.2 bps at 30% volatility. This exhibit clearly demonstrates the importance of the interest rate volatility assumption. Returning to the example in Exhibit 15, the callable bond may look underpriced at 10% volatility. If an investor assumes a higher volatility, however, the OAS and thus relative cheapness will decrease.

EXAMPLE 6

Option-Adjusted Spread

Robert Jourdan, a portfolio manager, has just valued a 7% annual coupon bond that was issued by a French company and has three years remaining until maturity. The bond is callable at par one year and two years from now. In his valuation, Jourdan used the yield curve based on the on-the-run French government bonds. The one-year, two-year, and three-year par rates are 4.600%, 4.900%, and 5.200%, respectively. Based on an estimated interest rate volatility of 15%, Jourdan constructed the following binomial interest rate tree:

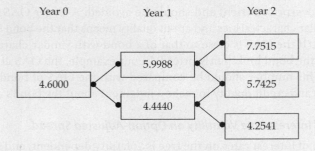

Jourdan valued the callable bond at 102.294% of par. However, Jourdan's colleague points out that because the corporate bond is more risky than French government bonds, the valuation should be performed using an OAS of 200 bps.

1   To update his valuation of the French corporate bond, Jourdan should:

   A   subtract 200 bps from the bond's annual coupon rate.

    B add 200 bps to the rates in the binomial interest rate tree.

    C subtract 200 bps from the rates in the binomial interest rate tree.

2 All else being equal, the value of the callable bond at 15% volatility is *closest to*:

    A 99.198% of par.

    B 99.247% of par.

    C 104.288% of par.

3 Holding the price calculated in the previous question, the OAS for the callable bond at 20% volatility will be:

    A lower.

    B the same.

    C higher.

Solution to 1:

B is correct. The OAS is the constant spread that must be *added* to all the one-period forward rates given in the binomial interest rate tree to justify a bond's given market price.

Solution to 2:

B is correct.

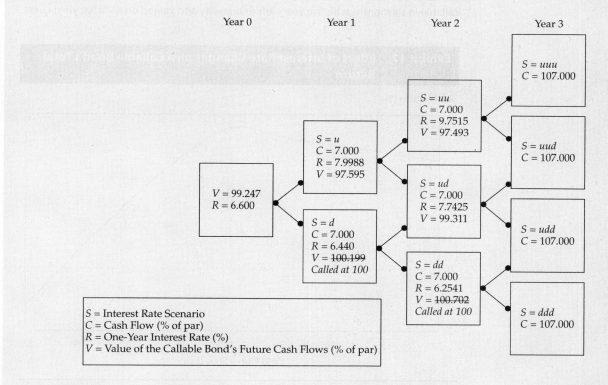

S = Interest Rate Scenario	
C = Cash Flow (% of par)	
R = One-Year Interest Rate (%)	
V = Value of the Callable Bond's Future Cash Flows (% of par)	

Solution to 3:

A is correct. If interest rate volatility increases from 15% to 20%, the OAS for the callable bond will decrease.

SCENARIO ANALYSIS OF BONDS WITH OPTIONS

Another application of valuing bonds with embedded options is scenario analysis over a specified investment horizon. In addition to reinvestment of interest and principal, option valuation comes into play in that callable and putable bonds can be redeemed and their proceeds reinvested during the holding period. Making scenario-dependent, optimal option-exercise decisions involves computationally intensive use of OAS technology because the call or put decision must be evaluated considering the evolution of interest rate scenarios during the holding period.

Performance over a specified investment horizon entails a trade-off between reinvestment of cash flows and change in the bond's value. Let us take the example of a 4.5% bond with five years left to maturity and assume that the investment horizon is one year. If the bond is option free, higher interest rates increase the reinvestment income but result in lower principal value at the end of the investment horizon. Because the investment horizon is short, reinvestment income is relatively insignificant, and performance will be dominated by the change in the value of the principal. Accordingly, lower interest rates will result in superior performance.

If the bond under consideration is callable, however, it is not at all obvious how the interest rate scenario affects performance. Suppose, for example, that the bond is first callable six months from now and that its current market price is 99.74. Steeply rising interest rates would depress the bond's price, and performance would definitely suffer. But steeply declining interest rates would also be detrimental because the bond would be called and *both interest and principal* would have to be reinvested at lower interest rates. Exhibit 17 shows the return over the one-year investment horizon for the 4.5% bond first callable in six months with five years left to maturity and valued on a 4% flat yield curve.

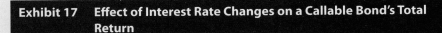

Exhibit 17   Effect of Interest Rate Changes on a Callable Bond's Total Return

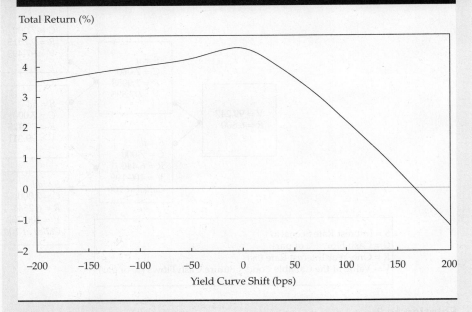

Exhibit 17 clearly shows that lower interest rates do not guarantee higher returns for callable bonds. The point to keep in mind is that the bond may be called long before the end of the investment horizon. Assuming that it is called on the horizon date would overestimate performance. Thus, a realistic prediction of option exercise is essential when performing scenario analysis of bonds with embedded options.

INTEREST RATE RISK OF BONDS WITH EMBEDDED OPTIONS

4

Measuring and managing exposure to interest rate risk are two essential tasks of fixed-income portfolio management. Applications range from hedging a portfolio to asset–liability management of financial institutions. Portfolio managers, whose performance is often measured against a benchmark, also need to monitor the interest rate risk of both their portfolio and the benchmark. In this section, we cover two key measures of interest rate risk: duration and convexity.

4.1 Duration

The duration of a bond measures the sensitivity of the bond's full price (including accrued interest) to changes in the bond's yield to maturity (in the case of *yield* duration measures) or to changes in benchmark interest rates (in the case of yield-curve or *curve* duration measures). Yield duration measures, such as modified duration, can be used only for option-free bonds because these measures assume that a bond's expected cash flows do not change when the yield changes. This assumption is in general false for bonds with embedded options because the values of embedded options are typically contingent on interest rates. Thus, for bonds with embedded options, the only appropriate duration measure is the curve duration measure known as effective (or option-adjusted) duration. Because effective duration works for straight bonds as well as for bonds with embedded options, practitioners tend to use it regardless of the type of bond being analyzed.

4.1.1 Effective Duration

Effective duration indicates the sensitivity of the bond's price to a 100 bps parallel shift of the benchmark yield curve—in particular, the government par curve—assuming no change in the bond's credit spread.[5] The formula for calculating a bond's effective duration is

$$\text{Effective duration} = \frac{(PV_-) - (PV_+)}{2 \times (\Delta \text{Curve}) \times (PV_0)} \tag{3}$$

where

ΔCurve = the magnitude of the parallel shift in the benchmark yield curve (in decimal);

PV_- = the full price of the bond when the benchmark yield curve is shifted down by ΔCurve;

PV_+ = the full price of the bond when the benchmark yield curve is shifted up by ΔCurve; and

PV_0 = the current full price of the bond (i.e., with no shift).

How is this formula applied in practice? Without a market price, we would need an issuer-specific yield curve to compute PV_0, PV_-, and PV_+. But practitioners usually have access to the bond's current price and thus use the following procedure:

1 Given a price (PV_0), calculate the implied OAS to the benchmark yield curve at an appropriate interest rate volatility.

---

5 Although it is possible to explore how arbitrary changes in interest rates affect the bond's price, in practice, the change is usually specified as a parallel shift of the benchmark yield curve.

2   Shift the benchmark yield curve down, generate a new interest rate tree, and then revalue the bond using the OAS calculated in Step 1. This value is PV_-.

3   Shift the benchmark yield curve up by the same magnitude as in Step 2, generate a new interest rate tree, and then revalue the bond using the OAS calculated in Step 1. This value is PV_+.

4   Calculate the bond's effective duration using Equation 3.

Let us illustrate using the same three-year 4.25% bond callable at par one year and two years from now, the same par yield curve (i.e., one-year, two-year, and three-year par yields of 2.500%, 3.000%, and 3.500%, respectively), and the same interest rate volatility (10%) as before. As in Section 3.6, we assume that the bond's current full price is 101.000. We apply the procedure just described:

1   As shown in Exhibit 15, given a price (PV_0) of 101.000, the OAS at 10% volatility is 28.55 bps.

2   We shift the par yield curve down by, say, 30 bps, generate a new interest rate tree, and then revalue the bond at an OAS of 28.55 bps. As shown in Exhibit 18 below, PV_- is 101.599.

3   We shift the par yield curve up by the same 30 bps, generate a new interest rate tree, and then revalue the bond at an OAS of 28.55 bps. As shown in Exhibit 19 below, PV_+ is 100.407.

4   Thus,

$$\text{Effective duration} = \frac{101.599 - 100.407}{2 \times 0.003 \times 101.000} = 1.97$$

An effective duration of 1.97 indicates that a 100-bps increase in interest rate would reduce the value of the three-year 4.25% callable bond by 1.97%.

Exhibit 18   Valuation of a Three-Year 4.25% Annual Coupon Bond Callable at Par One Year and Two Years from Now at 10% Interest Rate Volatility with an OAS of 28.55 bps When Interest Rates Are Shifted Down by 30 bps

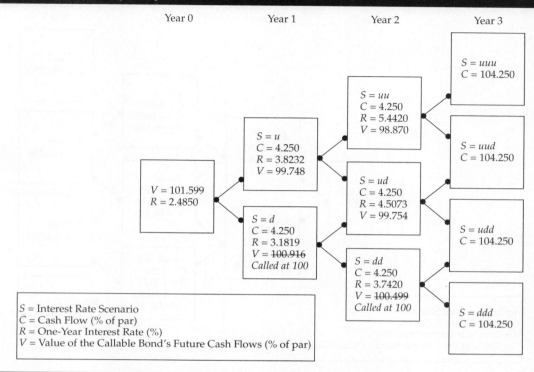

Year 0   Year 1   Year 2   Year 3

S = Interest Rate Scenario
C = Cash Flow (% of par)
R = One-Year Interest Rate (%)
V = Value of the Callable Bond's Future Cash Flows (% of par)

Exhibit 19   Valuation of a Three-Year 4.25% Annual Coupon Bond Callable at Par One Year and Two Years from Now at 10% Interest Rate Volatility with an OAS of 28.55 bps When Interest Rates Shifted Are Shifted Up by 30 bps

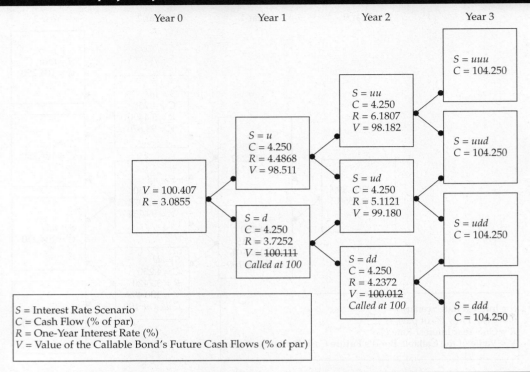

S = Interest Rate Scenario
C = Cash Flow (% of par)
R = One-Year Interest Rate (%)
V = Value of the Callable Bond's Future Cash Flows (% of par)

The effective duration of a callable bond cannot exceed that of the straight bond. When interest rates are high relative to the bond's coupon, the call option is out of the money, so the bond is unlikely to be called. Thus, the effect of an interest rate change on the price of a callable bond is very similar to that on the price of an otherwise identical option-free bond—the callable and straight bonds have very similar effective durations. In contrast, when interest rates fall, the call option moves into the money. Recall that the call option gives the issuer the right to retire the bond at the call price and thus limits the price appreciation when interest rates decline. As a consequence, the call option reduces the effective duration of the callable bond relative to that of the straight bond.

The effective duration of a putable bond also cannot exceed that of the straight bond. When interest rates are low relative to the bond's coupon, the put option is out of the money, so the bond is unlikely to be put. Thus, the effective duration of the putable bond is in this case very similar to that of an otherwise identical option-free bond. In contrast, when interest rates rise, the put option moves into the money and limits the price depreciation because the investor can put the bond and reinvest the proceeds of the retired bond at a higher yield. Thus, the put option reduces the effective duration of the putable bond relative to that of the straight bond.

When the embedded option (call or put) is deep in the money, the effective duration of the bond with an embedded option resembles that of the straight bond maturing on the first exercise date, reflecting the fact that the bond is highly likely to be called or put on that date.

Exhibit 20 compares the effective durations of option-free, callable, and putable bonds. All bonds are 4% annual coupon bonds with a maturity of 10 years. Both the call option and the put option are European-like and exercisable two months from now. The bonds are valued assuming a 4% flat yield curve and an interest rate volatility of 10%.

Exhibit 20   Comparison of the Effective Durations of Option-Free, Callable, and Putable Bonds

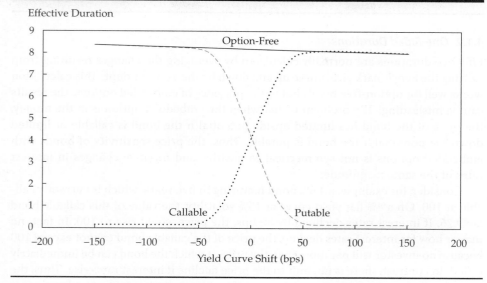

Exhibit 20 shows that the effective duration of an option-free bond changes very little in response to interest rate movements. As expected, when interest rates rise, the put option moves into the money, which limits the price depreciation of the putable bond and shortens its effective duration. In contrast, the effective duration of the callable bond shortens when interest rates fall, which is when the call option moves into the money, limiting the price appreciation of the callable bond.

EFFECTIVE DURATION IN PRACTICE

Effective duration is a concept most practically used in the context of a portfolio. Thus, an understanding of the effective durations of various types of instruments helps manage portfolio duration. In the following table, we show some properties of the effective duration of cash and the common types of bonds:[6]

Type of Bond	Effective Duration
Cash	0
Zero-coupon bond	≈ Maturity
Fixed-rate bond	< Maturity
Callable bond	≤ Duration of straight bond
Putable bond	≤ Duration of straight bond
Floater (Libor flat)	≈ Time (in years) to next reset

In general, a bond's effective duration does not exceed its maturity. There are a few exceptions, however, such as tax-exempt bonds when analyzed on an after-tax basis.

Knowing the effective duration of each type of bond is useful when one needs to change portfolio duration. For example, if a portfolio manager wants to shorten the effective duration of a portfolio of fixed-rate bonds, he or she can add floaters. For the

---

6 Because the curve shift unit in the denominator of the effective duration formula in Equation 3 is expressed per year, it turns out that the unit of effective duration is in years. In practice, however, effective duration is not viewed as a time measure but as an interest rate risk measure—that is, it reflects the percentage change in price per 100-bps change in interest rates.

debt manager of a company or other issuing entity, another way of shortening effective duration is to issue callable bonds. The topic of changing portfolio duration is covered thoroughly in Level III.

4.1.2 *One-Sided Durations*

Effective durations are normally calculated by averaging the changes resulting from shifting the benchmark yield curve up and down by the same amount. This calculation works well for option-free bonds but in the presence of embedded options, the results can be misleading. The problem is that when the embedded option is in the money, the price of the bond has limited upside potential if the bond is callable or limited downside potential if the bond is putable. Thus, the price sensitivity of bonds with embedded options is not symmetrical to positive and negative changes in interest rates of the same magnitude.

Consider, for example, a 4.5% bond maturing in five years, which is currently callable at 100. On a 4% flat yield curve at 15% volatility, the value of this callable bond is 99.75. If interest rates declined by 30 bps, the price would rise to 100. In fact, no matter how far interest rates decline, the price of the callable bond cannot exceed 100 because no investor will pay more than the price at which the bond can be immediately called. In contrast, there is no limit to the price decline if interest rates rise. Thus, the average price response to up- and down-shifts of interest rates (effective duration) is not as informative as the price responses to the up-shift (one-sided up-duration) and the down-shift (one-sided down-duration) of interest rates.

Exhibits 21 and 22 illustrate why **one-sided durations**—that is, the effective durations when interest rates go up or down—are better at capturing the interest rate sensitivity of a callable or putable bond than the (two-sided) effective duration, particularly when the embedded option is near the money.

Exhibit 21	Durations for a 4.5% Annual Coupon Bond Maturing in Five Years and Immediately Callable at Par on a 4% Flat Yield Curve at 15% Interest Rate Volatility		
	At a 4% Flat Yield Curve	Interest Rate up by 30 bps	Interest Rate down by 30 bps
Value of the Bond	99.75	99.17	100.00
Duration Measure	Effective duration 1.39	One-sided up-duration 1.94	One-sided down-duration 0.84

Exhibit 21 shows that a 30 bps increase in the interest rate has a greater effect on the value of the callable bond than a 30 bps decrease in the interest rate. The fact that the one-sided up-duration is higher than the one-sided down-duration confirms that the callable bond is more sensitive to interest rate rises than to interest rate declines.

Exhibit 22	Durations for a 4.1% Annual Coupon Bond Maturing in Five Years and Immediately Putable at Par on a 4% Flat Yield Curve at 15% Interest Rate Volatility		
	At a 4% Flat Yield Curve	Interest Rate up by 30 bps	Interest Rate down by 30 bps
Value of the Bond	100.45	100.00	101.81
Duration Measure	Effective duration 3.00	One-sided up-duration 1.49	One-sided down-duration 4.51

The one-sided durations in Exhibit 22 indicate that the putable bond is more sensitive to interest rate declines than to interest rate rises.

4.1.3 *Key Rate Durations*

Effective duration is calculated by assuming parallel shifts in the benchmark yield curve. In reality, however, interest rate movements are not as neat. Many portfolio managers and risk managers like to isolate the price responses to changes in the rates of key maturities on the benchmark yield curve. For example, how would the price of a bond be expected to change if only the two-year benchmark rate moved up by 5 bps? The answer is found by using **key rate durations** (also known as partial durations), which reflect the sensitivity of the bond's price to changes in specific maturities on the benchmark yield curve. Thus, key rate durations help portfolio managers and risk managers identify the "shaping risk" for bonds—that is, the bond's sensitivity to changes in the shape of the yield curve (e.g., steepening and flattening).

The valuation procedure and formula applied in the calculation of key rate durations are identical to those used in the calculation of effective duration, but instead of shifting the entire benchmark yield curve, only key points are shifted, one at a time. Thus, the effective duration for each maturity point shift is calculated in isolation.

Exhibits 23, 24, and 25 show the key rate durations for bonds valued at a 4% flat yield curve. Exhibit 23 examines option-free bonds, and Exhibits 24 and 25 extend the analysis to callable and putable bonds, respectively.

Exhibit 23	Key Rate Durations of 10-Year Option-Free Bonds Valued at a 4% Flat Yield Curve					
Coupon (%)	Price (% of par)	Key Rate Durations				
		Total	2-Year	3-Year	5-Year	10-Year
0	67.30	9.81	−0.07	−0.34	−0.93	11.15
2	83.65	8.83	−0.03	−0.13	−0.37	9.37
4	100.00	8.18	0.00	0.00	0.00	8.18
6	116.35	7.71	0.02	0.10	0.27	7.32
8	132.70	7.35	0.04	0.17	0.47	6.68
10	149.05	7.07	0.05	0.22	0.62	6.18

As shown in Exhibit 23, for option-free bonds not trading at par (the white rows), shifting any par rate has an effect on the value of the bond, but shifting the maturity-matched (10-year in this example) par rate has the greatest effect. This is simply because the largest cash flow of a fixed-rate bond occurs at maturity with the payment of both the final coupon and the principal.

For an option-free bond trading at par (the shaded row), the maturity-matched par rate is the only rate that affects the bond's value. It is a definitional consequence of "par" rates. If the 10-year par rate on a curve is 4%, then a 4% 10-year bond valued on that curve at zero OAS will be worth par, regardless of the par rates of the other maturity points on the curve. In other words, shifting any rate other than the 10-year rate on the par yield curve will not change the value of a 10-year bond trading at par. Shifting a par rate up or down at a particular maturity point, however, respectively increases or decreases the *discount rate* at that maturity point. These facts will be useful to remember in the following paragraph.

As illustrated in Exhibit 23, key rate durations can sometimes be negative for maturity points that are shorter than the maturity of the bond being analyzed if the bond is a zero-coupon bond or has a very low coupon. We can explain why this is the case by using the zero-coupon bond (the first row of Exhibit 23). As discussed in the previous paragraph, if we increase the five-year par rate, the value of a 10-year bond trading at par must remain unchanged because the 10-year par rate has not changed. But the five-year zero-coupon rate has increased because of the increase in the five-year par rate. Thus, the value of the five-year coupon of the 10-year bond trading at par will be lower than before the increase. But because the value of the 10-year bond trading at par must remain par, the remaining cash flows, including the cash flow occurring in Year 10, must be discounted at slightly *lower* rates to compensate. This results in a lower 10-year zero-coupon rate, which makes the value of a 10-year zero-coupon bond (whose only cash flow is in Year 10) *rise* in response to an *upward* change in the five-year par rate. Consequently, the five-year key rate duration for a 10-year zero-coupon bond is negative (−0.93).

Unlike for option-free bonds, the key rate durations of bonds with embedded options depend not only on the *time to maturity* but also on the *time to exercise*. Exhibits 24 and 25 illustrate this phenomenon for 30-year callable and putable bonds. Both the call option and the put option are European-like exercisable 10 years from now, and the bonds are valued assuming a 4% flat yield curve and a volatility of 15%.

Exhibit 24	Key Rate Durations of 30-Year Bonds Callable in 10 Years Valued at a 4% Flat Yield Curve with 15% Interest Rate Volatility						
Coupon (%)	Price (% of par)	Key Rate Durations					
		Total	2-Year	3-Year	5-Year	10-Year	30-Year
2	64.99	19.73	−0.02	−0.08	−0.21	−1.97	22.01
4	94.03	13.18	0.00	0.02	0.05	3.57	9.54
6	114.67	9.11	0.02	0.10	0.29	6.00	2.70
8	132.27	7.74	0.04	0.17	0.48	6.40	0.66
10	148.95	7.14	0.05	0.22	0.62	6.06	0.19

The bond with a coupon of 2% (the first row of Exhibit 24) is unlikely to be called, and thus it behaves more like a 30-year option-free bond, whose effective duration depends primarily on movements in the 30-year par rate. Therefore, the rate that has the highest effect on the value of the callable bond is the maturity-matched (30-year) rate. As the bond's coupon increases, however, so does the likelihood of the bond being called. Thus, the bond's total effective duration shortens, and the rate that has the highest effect on the callable bond's value gradually shifts from the 30-year rate to the 10-year rate. At the very high coupon of 10%, because of the virtual certainty of being called, the callable bond behaves like a 10-year option-free bond; the 30-year key rate duration is negligible (0.19) relative to the 10-year key rate duration (6.06).

Exhibit 25   Key Rate Durations of 30-Year Bonds Putable in 10 Years Valued at a 4% Flat Yield Curve with 15% Interest Rate Volatility

Coupon (%)	Price (% of par)	Key Rate Durations					
		Total	2-Year	3-Year	5-Year	10-Year	30-Year
2	83.89	9.24	−0.03	−0.14	−0.38	8.98	0.81
4	105.97	12.44	0.00	−0.01	−0.05	4.53	7.97
6	136.44	14.75	0.01	0.03	0.08	2.27	12.37
8	169.96	14.90	0.01	0.06	0.16	2.12	12.56
10	204.38	14.65	0.02	0.07	0.21	2.39	11.96

If the 30-year bond putable in 10 years has a high coupon, its price is more sensitive to the 30-year rate because it is unlikely to be put and thus behaves like an otherwise identical option-free bond. The 10% putable bond (the last row of Exhibit 25), for example, is most sensitive to changes in the 30-year rate, as illustrated by a 30-year key rate duration of 11.96. At the other extreme, a low-coupon bond is most sensitive to movements in the 10-year rate. It is almost certain to be put and so behaves like an option-free bond maturing on the put date.

4.2 Effective Convexity

Duration is an approximation of the expected bond price responses to changes in interest rates because actual changes in bond prices are not linear, particularly for bonds with embedded options. Thus, it is useful to measure **effective convexity**—that is, the sensitivity of duration to changes in interest rates—as well. The formula to calculate a bond's effective convexity is

$$\text{Effective convexity} = \frac{(PV_-) + (PV_+) - \left[2 \times (PV_0)\right]}{(\Delta \text{Curve})^2 \times (PV_0)} \tag{4}$$

where

   ΔCurve = the magnitude of the parallel shift in the benchmark yield curve (in decimal);
   PV_- = the full price of the bond when the benchmark yield curve is shifted down by ΔCurve;
   PV_+ = the full price of the bond when the benchmark yield curve is shifted up by ΔCurve; and
   PV_0 = the current full price of the bond (i.e., with no shift).

Let us return to the three-year 4.25% bond callable at par in one year and two years from now. We still use the same par yield curve (i.e., one-year, two-year, and three-year par yields of 2.500%, 3.000%, and 3.500%, respectively) and the same interest rate volatility (10%) as before, but we now assume that the bond's current full price is 100.785 instead of 101.000. Thus, the implied OAS is 40 bps. Given 30 bps shifts in the benchmark yield curve, the resulting PV_- and PV_+ are 101.381 and 100.146, respectively. Using Equation 4, the effective convexity is:

$$\frac{101.381 + 100.146 - 2 \times 100.785}{(0.003)^2 \times 100.785} = -47.41$$

Exhibit 20 in Section 4.1.1, although displaying effective durations, also illustrates the effective convexities of option-free, callable, and putable bonds. The option-free bond exhibits low positive convexity—that is, the price of an option-free bond rises slightly more when interest rates move down than it declines when interest rates move up by the same amount.

When interest rates are high and the value of the call option is low, the callable and straight bond experience very similar effects from changes in interest rates. They both have positive convexity. However, the effective convexity of the callable bond turns negative when the call option is near the money, as in the example just presented, which indicates that the upside for a callable bond is much smaller than the downside. The reason is because when interest rates decline, the price of the callable bond is capped by the price of the call option if it is near the exercise date.

Conversely, putable bonds always have positive convexity. When the option is near the money, the upside for a putable bond is much larger than the downside because the price of a putable bond is floored by the price of the put option if it is near the exercise date.

Compared side by side, putable bonds have more upside potential than otherwise identical callable bonds when interest rates decline. In contrast, when interest rates rise, callable bonds have more upside potential than otherwise identical putable bonds.

EXAMPLE 7

Interest Rate Sensitivity

Erna Smith, a portfolio manager, has two fixed-rate bonds in her portfolio: a callable bond (Bond X) and a putable bond (Bond Y). She wants to examine the interest rate sensitivity of these two bonds to a parallel shift in the benchmark yield curve. Assuming an interest rate volatility of 10%, her valuation software shows how the prices of these bonds change for 30-bps shifts up or down:

	Bond X	Bond Y
Time to maturity	Three years from today	Three years from today
Coupon	3.75% annual	3.75% annual
Type of bond	Callable at par one year from today	Putable at par one year from today
Current price (% of par)	100.594	101.330
Price (% of par) when shifting the benchmark yield curve down by 30 bps	101.194	101.882
Price (% of par) when shifting the benchmark yield curve up by 30 bps	99.860	100.924

1 The effective duration for Bond X is *closest* to:

   A   0.67.

   B   2.21.

   C   4.42.

2 The effective duration for Bond Y is *closest* to:

   A   0.48.

   B   0.96.

    C 1.58.

3 When interest rates rise, the effective duration of:

    A Bond X shortens.

    B Bond Y shortens.

    C the underlying option-free (straight) bond corresponding to Bond X lengthens.

4 When the option embedded in Bond Y is in the money, the one-sided durations *most likely* show that the bond is:

    A more sensitive to a decrease in interest rates.

    B more sensitive to an increase in interest rates.

    C equally sensitive to a decrease or to an increase in interest rates.

5 The price of Bond X is affected:

    A only by a shift in the one-year par rate.

    B only by a shift in the three-year par rate.

    C by all par rate shifts but is most sensitive to shifts in the one-year and three-year par rates.

6 The effective convexity of Bond X:

    A cannot be negative.

    B turns negative when the embedded option is near the money.

    C turns negative when the embedded option moves out of the money.

7 Which of the following statements is *most* accurate?

    A Bond Y exhibits negative convexity.

    B For a given decline in interest rate, Bond X has less upside potential than Bond Y.

    C The underlying option-free (straight) bond corresponding to Bond Y exhibits negative convexity.

Solution to 1:

B is correct. The effective duration for Bond X is

$$\text{Effective duration} = \frac{101.194 - 99.860}{2 \times 0.003 \times 100.594} = 2.21$$

A is incorrect because the duration of a bond with a single cash flow one year from now is approximately one year, so 0.67 is too low, even assuming that the bond will be called in one year with certainty. C is incorrect because 4.42 exceeds the maturity of Bond X (three years).

Solution to 2:

C is correct. The effective duration for Bond Y is

$$\text{Effective duration} = \frac{101.882 - 100.924}{2 \times 0.003 \times 101.330} = 1.58$$

Solution to 3:

B is correct. When interest rates rise, a put option moves into the money, and the putable bond is more likely to be put. Thus, it behaves like a shorter-maturity bond, and its effective duration shortens. A is incorrect because when interest rates rise, a call option moves out of the money, so the callable bond is less likely to be called. C is incorrect because the effective duration of an option-free bond changes very little in response to interest rate movements.

Solution to 4:

A is correct. If interest rates rise, the investor's ability to put the bond at par limits the price depreciation. In contrast, there is no limit to the increase in the bond's price when interest rates decline. Thus, the price of a putable bond whose embedded option is in the money is more sensitive to a decrease in interest rates.

Solution to 5:

C is correct. The main driver of the call decision is the two-year forward rate one year from now. This rate is most significantly affected by changes in the one-year and three-year par rates.

Solution to 6:

B is correct. The effective convexity of a callable bond turns negative when the call option is near the money because the price response of a callable bond to lower interest rates is capped by the call option. That is, in case of a decline in interest rates, the issuer will call the bonds and refund at lower rates, thus limiting the upside potential for the investor.

Solution to 7:

B is correct. As interest rates decline, the value of a call option increases whereas the value of a put option decreases. The call option embedded in Bond X limits its price appreciation, but there is no such cap for Bond Y. Thus, Bond X has less upside potential than Bond Y. A is incorrect because a putable bond always has positive convexity—that is, Bond Y has more upside than downside potential. C is incorrect because an option-free bond exhibits low positive convexity.

5 VALUATION AND ANALYSIS OF CAPPED AND FLOORED FLOATING-RATE BONDS

Options in floating-rate bonds (floaters) are exercised automatically depending on the course of interest rates—that is, if the coupon rate rises or falls below the threshold, the cap or floor automatically applies. Similar to callable and putable bonds, capped and floored floaters can be valued by using the arbitrage-free framework.

5.1 Valuation of a Capped Floater

The cap provision in a floater prevents the coupon rate from increasing above a specified maximum rate. As a consequence, a **capped floater** protects the issuer against rising interest rates and is thus an issuer option. Because the investor is long the bond but short the embedded option, the value of the cap decreases the value of the capped floater relative to the value of the straight bond:

> Value of capped floater
>   = Value of straight bond − Value of embedded cap   (5)

To illustrate how to value a capped floater, consider a floating-rate bond that has a three-year maturity. The floater's coupon pays the one-year Libor annually, set in arrears, and is capped at 4.500%. The term "set in arrears" means that the coupon rate is set at the beginning of the coupon period—that is, the coupon to be paid in one year is determined now. For simplicity, we assume that the issuer's credit quality closely matches the Libor swap curve (i.e., there is no credit spread) and that the

Libor swap curve is the same as the par yield curve given in Exhibit 1 (i.e., one-year, two-year, and three-year par yields of 2.500%, 3.000%, and 3.500%, respectively). We also assume that the interest rate volatility is 10%.

The valuation of the capped floater is depicted in Exhibit 26.

Exhibit 26   Valuation of a Three-Year Libor Floater Capped at 4.500% at 10% Interest Rate Volatility

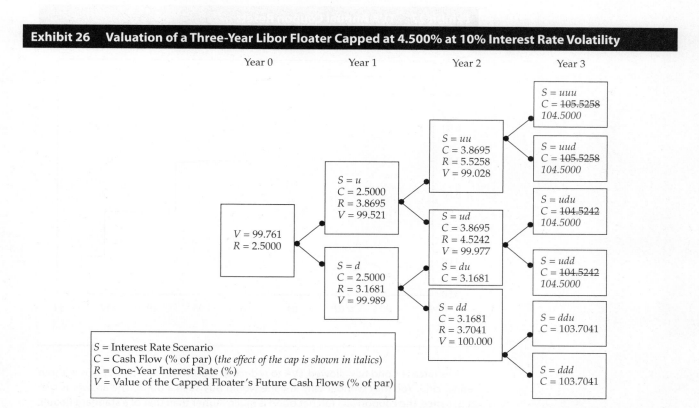

Without a cap, the value of this floater would be 100 because in every scenario, the coupon paid would be equal to the discount rate. But because the coupon rate is capped at 4.500%, which is lower than the highest interest rates in the tree, the value of the capped floater will be lower than the value of the straight bond.

For each scenario, we check whether the cap applies, and if it does, the cash flow is adjusted accordingly. For example, in state *uuu*, Libor is higher than the 4.500% cap. Thus, the coupon is capped at the 4.500 maximum amount, and the cash flow is adjusted downward from the uncapped amount (105.5258) to the capped amount (104.5000). The coupon is also capped for three other scenarios in Year 3.

As expected, the value of the capped floater is lower than 100 (99.761). The value of the cap can be calculated by using Equation 5:

Value of embedded cap = 100 − 99.761 = 0.239

RATCHET BONDS: DEBT MANAGEMENT ON AUTOPILOT

Ratchet bonds are floating-rate bonds with both issuer and investor options. As with conventional floaters, the coupon is reset periodically according to a formula based on a reference rate and a credit spread. A capped floater protects the issuer against rising interest rates. Ratchet bonds offer extreme protection: At the time of reset, the coupon can only decline; it can never exceed the existing level. So, over time, the coupon "ratchets down."

The Tennessee Valley Authority (TVA) was the first issuer of ratchet bonds. In 1998, it issued $575 million 6.75% "PARRS" due 1 June 2028. The coupon rate was resettable on 1 June 2003 and annually thereafter. Exhibit 27 shows annual coupon resets since 2003:[7]

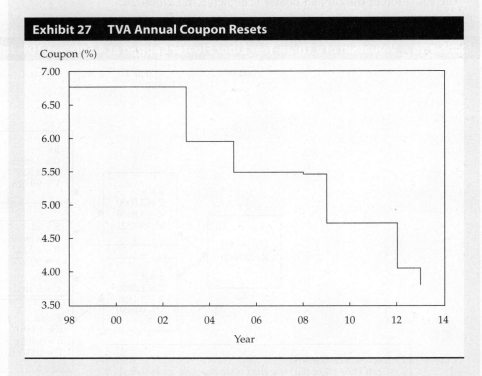

Exhibit 27   TVA Annual Coupon Resets

This ratchet bond has allowed TVA to reduce its borrowing rate by 292 bps without refinancing. You may wonder why anyone would buy such a bond. The answer is that at issuance, the coupon of a ratchet bond is much higher than that of a standard floater. In fact, the initial coupon is set well above the issuer's long-term option-free borrowing rate in order to compensate investors for the potential loss of interest income over time. In this regard, a ratchet bond is similar to a conventional callable bond: When the bond is called, the investor must purchase a replacement in the prevailing lower rate environment. The initial above-market coupon of a callable bond reflects this possibility.

A ratchet bond can be thought of as the lifecycle of a callable bond through several possible calls, in which the bond is replaced by one that is itself callable, to the original maturity. The appeal for the issuer is that these "calls" entail no transaction cost, and the call decision is on autopilot.

Ratchet bonds also contain investor options. Whenever a coupon is reset, the investor has the right to put the bonds back to the issuer at par. The embedded option is called a "contingent put" because the right to put is available to the investor *only* if the coupon is reset. The coupon reset formula of ratchet bonds is designed to assure that the market price at the time of reset is above par, provided that the issuer's credit quality does not deteriorate. Therefore, the contingent put offers investors protection against an adverse credit event. Needless to say, the valuation of a ratchet bond is rather complex.

7 See A. Kalotay and L. Abreo, "Ratchet Bonds: Maximum Refunding Efficiency at Minimum Transaction Cost," *Journal of Applied Corporate Finance*, vol. 12, no. 1 (Spring 1999):40–47.

5.2 Valuation of a Floored Floater

The floor provision in a floater prevents the coupon rate from decreasing below a specified minimum rate. As a consequence, a **floored floater** protects the investor against declining interest rates and is thus an investor option. Because the investor is long both the bond and the embedded option, the value of the floor increases the value of the floored floater relative to the value of the straight bond:

Value of floored floater
= Value of straight bond + Value of embedded floor   **(6)**

To illustrate how to value a floored floater, we return to the example we used for the capped floater but assume that the embedded option is now a 3.500% floor instead of a 4.500% cap. The other assumptions remain the same. The valuation of the floored floater is depicted in Exhibit 28.

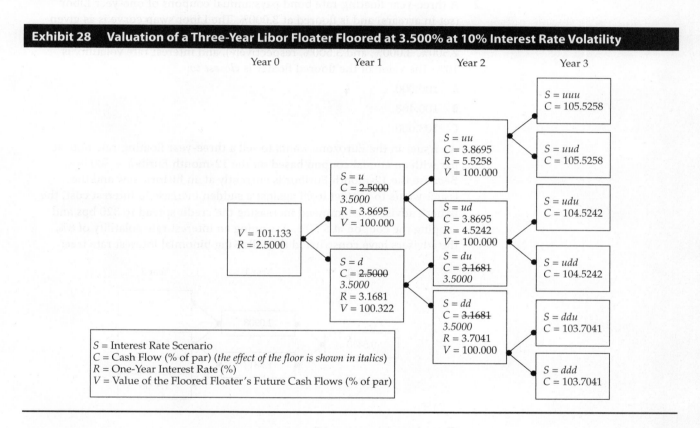

Exhibit 28   Valuation of a Three-Year Libor Floater Floored at 3.500% at 10% Interest Rate Volatility

Year 0   Year 1   Year 2   Year 3

S = uuu
C = 105.5258

S = uu
C = 3.8695
R = 5.5258
V = 100.000

S = uud
C = 105.5258

S = u
C = 2.5000
3.5000
R = 3.8695
V = 100.000

S = ud
C = 3.8695
R = 4.5242
V = 100.000

S = udu
C = 104.5242

V = 101.133
R = 2.5000

S = du
C = 3.1681
3.5000

S = udd
C = 104.5242

S = d
C = 2.5000
3.5000
R = 3.1681
V = 100.322

S = dd
C = 3.1681
3.5000
R = 3.7041
V = 100.000

S = ddu
C = 103.7041

S = ddd
C = 103.7041

S = Interest Rate Scenario
C = Cash Flow (% of par) (*the effect of the floor is shown in italics*)
R = One-Year Interest Rate (%)
V = Value of the Floored Floater's Future Cash Flows (% of par)

Recall from the discussion about the capped floater that if there were no cap, the value of the floater would be 100 because the coupon paid would equal the discount rate. The same principle applies here: If there were no floor, the value of this floater would be 100. Because the presence of the floor potentially increases the cash flows, however, the value of the floored floater must be equal to or higher than the value of the straight bond.

Exhibit 28 shows that the floor applies in four scenarios in Years 1 and 2, thus increasing the cash flows to the minimum amount of 3.500. As a consequence, the value of the floored floater exceeds 100 (101.133). The value of the floor can be calculated by using Equation 6:

Value of embedded floor = 101.133 − 100 = 1.133

EXAMPLE 8

Valuation of Capped and Floored Floaters

1   A three-year floating rate bond pays annual coupons of one-year Libor (set in arrears) and is capped at 5.600%. The Libor swap curve is as given in Exhibit 1 (i.e., the one-year, two-year, and three-year par yields are 2.500%, 3.000%, and 3.500%, respectively), and interest rate volatility is 10%. The value of the capped floater is *closest to*:

   A   100.000.

   B   105.600.

   C   105.921.

2   A three-year floating-rate bond pays annual coupons of one-year Libor (set in arrears) and is floored at 3.000%. The Libor swap curve is as given in Exhibit 1 (i.e., the one-year, two-year, and three-year par yields are 2.500%, 3.000%, and 3.500%, respectively), and interest rate volatility is 10%. The value of the floored floater is *closest to*:

   A   100.000.

   B   100.488.

   C   103.000.

3   An issuer in the Eurozone wants to sell a three-year floating-rate note at par with an annual coupon based on the 12-month Euribor + 300 bps. Because the 12-month Euribor is currently at an historic low and the issuer wants to protect itself against a sudden increase in interest cost, the issuer's advisers recommend increasing the credit spread to 320 bps and capping the coupon at 5.50%. Assuming an interest rate volatility of 8%, the advisers have constructed the following binomial interest rate tree:

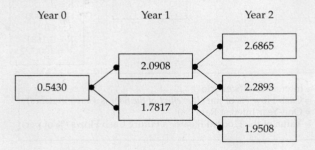

The value of the capped floater is *closest to*:

   A   92.929.

   B   99.916.

   C   109.265.

Solution to 1:

A is correct. As illustrated in Exhibit 26, the cap is higher than any of the rates at which the floater is reset on the interest rate tree. Thus, the value of the bond is the same as if it had no cap—that is, 100.

Solution to 2:

B is correct. One can eliminate C because as illustrated in Exhibit 28, all else being equal, the bond with a higher floor (3.500%) has a value of 101.133. The value of a bond with a floor of 3.000% cannot be higher. Intuitively, B is the likely correct answer because the straight bond is worth 100. However, it is still necessary to calculate the value of the floored floater because if the floor is low enough, it could be worthless.

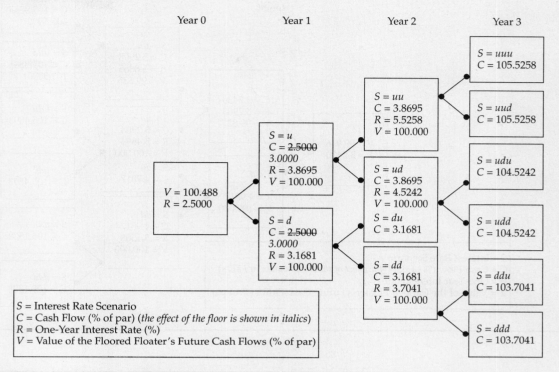

Here, it turns out that the floor adds 0.488 in value to the straight bond. Had the floor been 2.500%, the floored floater and the straight bond would both be worth par.

Solution to 3:

B is correct.

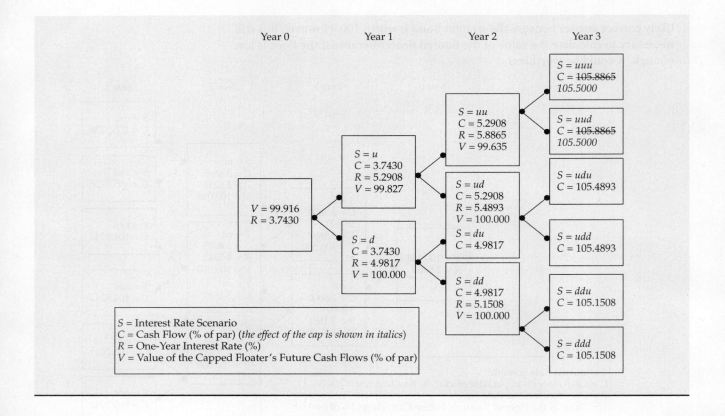

S = Interest Rate Scenario
C = Cash Flow (% of par) (*the effect of the cap is shown in italics*)
R = One-Year Interest Rate (%)
V = Value of the Capped Floater's Future Cash Flows (% of par)

6   VALUATION AND ANALYSIS OF CONVERTIBLE BONDS

So far, we have discussed bonds for which the exercise of the option is at the discretion of the issuer (callable bond), at the discretion of the bondholder (putable bond), or set through a pre-defined contractual arrangement (capped and floored floaters). What distinguishes a convertible bond from the bonds discussed earlier is that exercising the option results in the change of the security from a bond to a common stock. This section describes defining features of convertible bonds and discusses how to analyze and value these bonds.

6.1 Defining Features of a Convertible Bond

A **convertible bond** is a hybrid security. In its traditional form, it presents the characteristics of an option-free bond and an embedded conversion option. The conversion option is a call option on the issuer's common stock, which gives bondholders the right to convert their debt into equity during a pre-determined period (known as the **conversion period**) at a pre-determined price (known as the **conversion price**).

Convertible bonds have been issued and traded since the 1880s. They offer benefits to both the issuer and the investors. Investors usually accept a lower coupon for convertible bonds than for otherwise identical non-convertible bonds because they can participate in the potential upside through the conversion mechanism—that is, if the share price of the issuer's common stock (underlying share price) exceeds the conversion price, the bondholders can convert their bonds into shares at a cost lower than market value. The issuer benefits from paying a lower coupon. In case of conversion, an added benefit for the issuer is that it no longer has to repay the debt that was converted into equity.

However, what might appear as a win–win situation for both the issuer and the investors is not a "free lunch" because the issuer's existing shareholders face dilution in case of conversion. In addition, if the underlying share price remains below the conversion price and the bond is not converted, the issuer must repay the debt or refinance it, potentially at a higher cost. If conversion is not achieved, the bondholders will have lost interest income relative to an otherwise identical non-convertible bond that would have been issued with a higher coupon and would have thus offered investors an additional spread.

We will use the information provided in Exhibit 29 to describe the features of a convertible bond and then illustrate how to analyze it. This exhibit refers to a callable convertible bond issued by Waste Management Utility PLC (WMU), a company listed on the London Stock Exchange.

Exhibit 29   WMU £100,000,000 4.50% Callable Convertible Bonds Due 3 April 2017

Excerpt from the Bond's Offering Circular

- **Issue Date:** 3 April 2012
- **Status:** Senior unsecured, unsubordinated
- **Interest:** 4.50% of nominal value (par) per annum payable annually in arrears, with the first interest payment date on 3 April 2013 unless prior redeemed or converted
- **Issue Price:** 100% of par denominated into bonds of £100,000 each and integral multiples of £1,000 each thereafter
- **Conversion Period:** 3 May 2012 to 5 March 2017
- **Initial Conversion Price:** £6.00 per share
- **Conversion Ratio:** Each bond of par value of £100,000 is convertible to 16,666.67 ordinary shares
- **Threshold Dividend:** £0.30 per share
- **Change of Control Conversion Price:** £4.00 per share
- **Issuer Call Price:** From the second anniversary of issuance: 110%; from the third anniversary of issuance: 105%; from the fourth anniversary of issuance: 103%

Market Information

- **Convertible Bond Price on 4 April 2013:** £127,006
- **Share Price on Issue Date:** £4.58
- **Share Price on 4 April 2013:** £6.23
- **Dividend per Share:** £0.16
- **Share Price Volatility per annum as of 4 April 2013:** 25%

The applicable share price at which the investor can convert the bonds into ordinary (common) shares is called the conversion price. In the WMU example provided in Exhibit 29, the conversion price was set at £6 per share.

The number of shares of common stock that the bondholder receives from converting the bonds into shares is called the **conversion ratio**. In the WMU example, bondholders who have invested the minimum stipulated of £100,000 and convert their bonds into shares will receive 16,666.67 shares each (£100,000/£6) per £100,000 of nominal value. The conversion may be exercised during a particular period or at set intervals during the life of the bond. To accommodate share price volatility and technical settlement requirements, it is not uncommon to see conversion periods similar to the one in Exhibit 29—that is, beginning shortly after the issuance of the convertible bond and ending shortly prior to its maturity.

The conversion price in Exhibit 29 is referred to as the *initial* conversion price because it reflects the conversion price *at issuance*. Corporate actions, such as stock splits, bonus share issuances, and rights or warrants issuances, affect a company's share price and may reduce the benefit of conversion for the convertible bondholders. Thus, the terms of issuance of the convertible bond contain detailed information defining how the conversion price and conversion ratio are adjusted should such a corporate action occur during the life of the bond. For example, suppose that WMU performs a 2:1 stock split to its common shareholders. In this case, the conversion price would be adjusted to £3.00 per share and the conversion ratio would then be adjusted to 33,333.33 shares per £100,000 of nominal value.

As long as the convertible bond is still outstanding and has not been converted, the bondholders receive interest payments (annually in the WMU example). Meanwhile, if the issuer declares and pays dividends, common shareholders receive dividend payments. The terms of issuance may offer no compensation to convertible bondholders for dividends paid out during the life of the bond at one extreme, or they may offer full protection by adjusting the conversion price downward for any dividend payments at the other extreme. Typically, a threshold dividend is defined in the terms of issuance (£0.30 per share in the WMU example). Annual dividend payments below the threshold dividend have no effect on the conversion price. In contrast, the conversion price is adjusted downward for annual dividend payments above the threshold dividend to offer compensation to convertible bondholders.

Should the issuer be acquired by or merged with another company during the life of the bond, bondholders might no longer be willing to continue lending to the new entity. Change-of-control events are defined in the prospectus or offering circular and, if such an event occurs, convertible bondholders usually have the choice between

- a put option that can be exercised during a specified period following the change-of-control event and that provides full redemption of the nominal value of the bond; or
- an adjusted conversion price that is lower than the initial conversion price. This downward adjustment gives the convertible bondholders the opportunity to convert their bonds into shares earlier and at more advantageous terms, and thus allows them to participate in the announced merger or acquisition as common shareholders.

In addition to a put option in case of a change-of-control event, it is not unusual for a convertible bond to include a put option that convertible bondholders can exercise during specified periods. Put options can be classified as "hard" puts or "soft" puts. In the case of a hard put, the issuer must redeem the convertible bond for cash. In the case of a soft put, the investor has the right to exercise the put but the issuer chooses how the payment will be made. The issuer may redeem the convertible bond for cash, common stock, subordinated notes, or a combination of the three.

It is more frequent for convertible bonds to include a call option that gives the issuer the right to call the bond during a specified period and at specified times. As discussed earlier, the issuer may exercise the call option and redeem the bond early if interest rates are falling or if its credit rating is revised upward, thus enabling the issuance of debt at a lower cost. The issuer may also believe that its share price will increase significantly in the future because of its performance or because of events that will take place in the economy or in its sector. In this case, the issuer may try to maximize the benefit to its existing shareholders relative to convertible bondholders and call the bond. To offer convertible bondholders protection against early repayment, convertible bonds usually have a lockout period. Subsequently, they can be called but at a premium, which decreases as the maturity of the bond approaches. In the WMU example, the convertible bond is not callable until its second anniversary, when it is callable at a premium of 10% above par value. The premium decreases to 5% at its third anniversary and 3% at its fourth anniversary.

If a convertible bond is callable, the issuer has an incentive to call the bond when the underlying share price increases above the conversion price in order to avoid paying further coupons. Such an event is called **forced conversion** because it forces bondholders to convert their bonds into shares. Otherwise, the redemption value that bondholders would receive from the issuer calling the bond would result in a disadvantageous position and a loss compared with conversion. Even if interest rates have not fallen or the issuer's credit rating has not improved, thus not allowing refinancing at a lower cost, the issuer might still proceed with calling the bond when the underlying share price exceeds the conversion price. Doing so allows the issuer to take advantage of the favorable equity market conditions and force the bondholders to convert their bonds into shares. The forced conversion strengthens the issuer's capital structure and eliminates the risk that a subsequent correction in equity prices prevents conversion and requires redeeming the convertible bonds at maturity.

6.2 Analysis of a Convertible Bond

There are a number of investment metrics and ratios that help in analyzing and valuing a convertible bond.

6.2.1 Conversion Value

The **conversion value** or parity value of a convertible bond indicates the value of the bond if it is converted at the market price of the shares.

Conversion value = Underlying share price × Conversion ratio

Based on the information provided in Exhibit 29, we can calculate the conversion value for WMU's convertible bonds at the issuance date and on 4 April 2013:

Conversion value at the issuance date = £4.58 × 16,666.67 = £76,333.33

Conversion value on 4 April 2013 = £6.23 × 16,666.67 = £103,833.33

6.2.2 Minimum Value of a Convertible Bond

The minimum value of a convertible bond is equal to the greater of

- the conversion value and
- the value of the underlying option-free bond. Theoretically, the value of the straight bond (straight value) can be estimated by using the market value of a non-convertible bond of the issuer with the same characteristics as the convertible bond but without the conversion option. In practice, such a bond rarely exists. Thus, the straight value is found by using the arbitrage-free framework and by discounting the bond's future cash flows at the appropriate rates.

The minimum value of a convertible bond can also be described as a floor value. It is a *moving* floor, however, because the straight value is not fixed; it changes with fluctuations in interest rates and credit spreads. If interest rates rise, the value of the straight bond falls, making the floor fall. Similarly, if the issuer's credit spread increases as a result, for example, of a downgrade of its credit rating from investment grade to non-investment grade, the floor value will fall too.

Using the conversion values calculated in Section 6.2.1, the minimum value of WMU's convertible bonds at the issuance date is

Minimum value at the issuance date = Maximum(£76,333.33;£100,000)
= £100,000

The straight value at the issuance date is £100,000 because the issue price is set at 100% of par. But after this date, this value will fluctuate. Thus, to calculate the minimum value of WMU's convertible bond on 4 April 2013, it is first necessary to calculate the value of the straight bond that day using the arbitrage-free framework. From Exhibit 29, the coupon is 4.50%, paid annually. Assuming a 2.5% flat yield curve, the straight value on 4 April 2013 is:

$$\frac{£4,500}{(1.02500)} + \frac{£4,500}{(1.02500)^2} + \frac{£4,500}{(1.02500)^3} + \frac{£100,000 + £4,500}{(1.02500)^4} = £107,523.95$$

It follows that the minimum value of WMU's convertible bonds on 4 April 2013 is

Minimum value on 4 April 2013 = Maximum(£103,833.33;£107,523.95)
= £107,523.95

If the value of the convertible bond were lower than the greater of the conversion value and the straight value, an arbitrage opportunity would ensue. Two scenarios help illustrate this concept. Returning to the WMU example, suppose that the convertible bond is selling for £103,833.33 on 4 April 2013—that is, at a price that is lower than the straight value of £107,523.95. In this scenario, the convertible bond is cheap relative to the straight bond; put another way, the convertible bond offers a higher yield than an otherwise identical non-convertible bond. Thus, investors will find the convertible bond attractive, buy it, and push its price up until the convertible bond price returns to the straight value and the arbitrage opportunity disappears.

Alternatively, assume that on 4 April 2013, the yield on otherwise identical non-convertible bonds is 5.00% instead of 2.50%. Using the arbitrage-free framework, the straight value is £98,227.02. Suppose that the convertible bond is selling at this straight value—that is, at a price that is lower than its conversion value of £103,833.33. In this case, an arbitrageur can buy the convertible bond for £98,227.02, convert it into 16,666.67 shares, and sell the shares at £6.23 each or £103,833.33 in total. The arbitrageur makes a profit equal to the difference between the conversion value and the straight value—that is, £5,606.31 (£103,833.33 – £98,227.02). As more arbitrageurs follow the same strategy, the convertible bond price will increase until it reaches the conversion value and the arbitrage opportunity disappears.

6.2.3 *Market Conversion Price, Market Conversion Premium per Share, and Market Conversion Premium Ratio*

Many investors do not buy a convertible bond at issuance on the primary market but instead buy such a bond later in its life on the secondary market. The **market conversion premium per share** allows investors to identify the premium or discount payable when buying the convertible bond rather than the underlying common stock.[8]

$$\text{Market conversion premium per share} = \text{Market conversion price} - \text{Underlying share price}$$

where

$$\text{Market conversion price} = \frac{\text{Convertible bond price}}{\text{Conversion ratio}}$$

The market conversion price represents the price that investors effectively pay for the underlying common stock if they buy the convertible bond and then convert it into shares. It can be viewed as a break-even price. Once the underlying share price exceeds the market conversion price, any further rise in the underlying share price is certain to increase the value of the convertible bond by at least the same percentage (we will discuss why this is the case in Section 6.4).

Based on the information provided in Exhibit 29,

$$\text{Market conversion price on 4 April 2013} = \frac{£127,006}{16,666.67} = £7.62$$

and

$$\text{Market conversion premium per share on 4 April 2013} = £7.62 - £6.23 = £1.39$$

The **market conversion premium ratio** expresses the premium or discount investors have to pay as a percentage of the current market price of the shares:

$$\text{Market conversion premium ratio} = \frac{\text{Market conversion premium per share}}{\text{Underlying share price}}$$

In the WMU example,

$$\text{Market conversion premium ratio on 4 April 2013} = \frac{£1.39}{£6.23} = 22.32\%$$

Why would investors be willing to pay a premium to buy the convertible bond? Recall that the straight value acts as a floor for the convertible bond price. Thus, as the underlying share price falls, the convertible bond price will not fall below the straight value. Viewed in this context, the market conversion premium per share resembles the price of a call option. Investors who buy a call option limit their downside risk to the price of the call option (premium). Similarly, the premium paid when buying a convertible bond allows investors to limit their downside risk to the straight value. There is a fundamental difference, however, between the buyers of a call option and the buyers of a convertible bond. The former know exactly the amount of the downside risk, whereas the latter know only that the most they can lose is the difference between the convertible bond price and the straight value because the straight value is not fixed.

---

8 Although discounts are rare, they can theoretically happen given that the convertible bond and the underlying common stock trade in different markets with different types of market participants. For example, highly volatile share prices may result in the market conversion price being lower than the underlying share price.

6.2.4 Downside Risk with a Convertible Bond

Many investors use the straight value as a measure of the downside risk of a convertible bond, and calculate the following metric:

$$\text{Premium over straight value} = \frac{\text{Convertible bond price}}{\text{Straight value}} - 1$$

All else being equal, the higher the premium over straight value, the less attractive the convertible bond. In the WMU example,

$$\text{Premium over straight value} = \frac{£127,006}{£107,523.95} - 1 = 18.11\%$$

Despite its use in practice, the premium over straight value is a flawed measure of downside risk because, as mentioned earlier, the straight value is not fixed but rather fluctuates with changes in interest rates and credit spreads.

6.2.5 Upside Potential of a Convertible Bond

The upside potential of a convertible bond depends primarily on the prospects of the underlying common stock. Thus, convertible bond investors should be familiar with the techniques used to value and analyze common stocks. These techniques are covered in other readings.

6.3 Valuation of a Convertible Bond

Historically, the valuation of convertible bonds has been challenging because these securities combine characteristics of bonds, stocks, and options, thus requiring an understanding of what affects the value of fixed income, equity, and derivatives. The complexity of convertible bonds has also increased over time as a result of market innovations as well as additions to the terms and conditions of these securities. For example, convertible bonds have evolved into contingent convertible bonds and convertible contingent convertible bonds, which are even more complex to value and analyze.[9]

The fact that many bond's prospectuses or offering circulars frequently provide for an independent financial valuer to determine the conversion price (and in essence the value of the convertible bond) under different scenarios is evidence of the complexity associated with valuing convertible bonds. Because of this complexity, convertible bonds in many markets come with selling restrictions. They are typically offered in very high denominations and only to professional or institutional investors. Regulators perceive them as securities that are too risky for retail investors to invest in directly.

As with any fixed-income instrument, convertible bond investors should perform a diligent risk–reward analysis of the issuer, including its ability to service the debt and repay the principal, as well as a review of the bond's terms of issuance (e.g., collateral, credit enhancements, covenants, and contingent provisions). In addition, convertible bond investors must analyze the factors that typically affect bond prices, such as interest rate movements. Because most convertible bonds have lighter covenants than otherwise similar non-convertible bonds and are frequently issued as subordinated securities, the valuation and analysis of some convertible bonds can be complex.

---

9 Contingent convertible bonds, or "CoCos," pay a higher coupon than otherwise identical non-convertible bonds, but they are usually deeply subordinated and may be converted into equity or face principal write-downs if regulatory capital ratios are breached. Convertible contingent convertible bonds, or "CoCoCos," combine a traditional convertible bond and a CoCo. They are convertible at the discretion of the investor, thus offering upside potential if the share price increases, but they are also converted into equity or face principal write-downs in the event of a regulatory capital breach. CoCos and CoCoCos are usually issued by financial institutions, particularly in Europe.

The investment characteristics of a convertible bond depend on the underlying share price, so convertible bond investors must also analyze factors that may affect the issuer's common stock, including dividend payments and the issuer's actions (e.g., acquisitions or disposals, rights issues). Even if the issuer is performing well, adverse market conditions might depress share prices and prevent conversion. Thus, convertible bond investors must also identify and analyze the exogenous reasons that might ultimately have a negative effect on convertible bonds.

Academics and practitioners have developed advanced models to value convertible bonds, but the most commonly used model remains the arbitrage-free framework. A traditional convertible bond can be viewed as a straight bond and a call option on the issuer's common stock, so

Value of convertible bond = Value of straight bond
+ Value of call option on the issuer's stock

Many convertible bonds include a call option that gives the issuer the right to call the bond during a specified period and at specified times. The value of such bonds is

Value of callable convertible bond = Value of straight bond + Value of call option on the issuer's stock − Value of issuer call option

Suppose that the callable convertible bond also includes a put option that gives the bondholder the right to require that the issuer repurchases the bond. The value of such a bond is

Value of callable putable convertible bond = Value of straight bond + Value of call option on the issuer's stock − Value of issuer call option + Value of investor put option

No matter how many options are embedded into a bond, the valuation procedure remains the same. It relies on generating a tree of interest rates based on the given yield curve and interest rate volatility assumptions, determining at each node of the tree whether the embedded options will be exercised, and then applying the backward induction valuation methodology to calculate the present value of the bond.

6.4 Comparison of the Risk–Return Characteristics of a Convertible Bond, the Straight Bond, and the Underlying Common Stock

In its simplest form, a convertible bond can be viewed as a straight bond and a call option on the issuer's common stock. When the underlying share price is well below the conversion price, the convertible bond is described as "busted convertible" and exhibits mostly bond risk–return characteristics—that is, the risk–return characteristics of the convertible bond resemble those of the underlying option-free (straight) bond. In this case, the call option is out of the money, so share price movements do not significantly affect the price of the call option and, thus, the price of the convertible bond. Consequently, the price movement of the convertible bond closely follows that of the straight bond, and such factors as interest rate movements and credit spreads significantly affect the convertible bond price. The convertible bond exhibits even stronger bond risk–return characteristics when the call option is out of the money and the conversion period is approaching its end because the time value component of the option decreases toward zero, and it is highly likely that the conversion option will expire worthless.

In contrast, when the underlying share price is above the conversion price, a convertible bond exhibits mostly stock risk–return characteristics—that is, the risk–return characteristics of the convertible bond resemble those of the underlying common stock. In this case, the call option is in the money, so the price of the call option and thus the price of the convertible bond is significantly affected by share price movements but mostly unaffected by factors driving the value of an otherwise identical option-free bond, such as interest rate movements. When the call option is in the money, it is more likely to be exercised by the bondholder and the value of the shares resulting from the conversion is higher than the redemption value of the bond. Such convertible bonds trade at prices that follow closely the conversion value of the convertible bond, and their price exhibits similar movements to that of the underlying stock.

In between the bond and the stock extremes, the convertible bond trades like a hybrid instrument. It is important to note the risk–return characteristics of convertible bonds (1) when the underlying share price is below the conversion price and increases toward it and (2) when the underlying share price is above the conversion price but decreases toward it.

In the first case, the call option component increases significantly in value as the underlying share price approaches the conversion price. The return on the convertible bond during such periods increases significantly but at a lower rate than the increase in the underlying share price because the conversion price has not been reached yet. When the share price exceeds the conversion price and goes higher, the change in the convertible bond price converges toward the change in the underlying share price—this is why we noted in Section 6.2.4 that when the underlying share price exceeds the market conversion price, any further rise in the underlying share price is certain to increase the value of the convertible bond by at least the same percentage.

In the second case (that is, when the underlying share price is above the conversion price but decreases toward it), the relative change in the convertible bond price is less than the change in the underlying share price because the convertible bond has a floor. As mentioned earlier, this floor is the minimum value of the convertible bond, which in this case is equal to the value of the underlying option-free bond.

Exhibit 30 illustrates graphically the price behavior of a convertible bond and the underlying common stock.

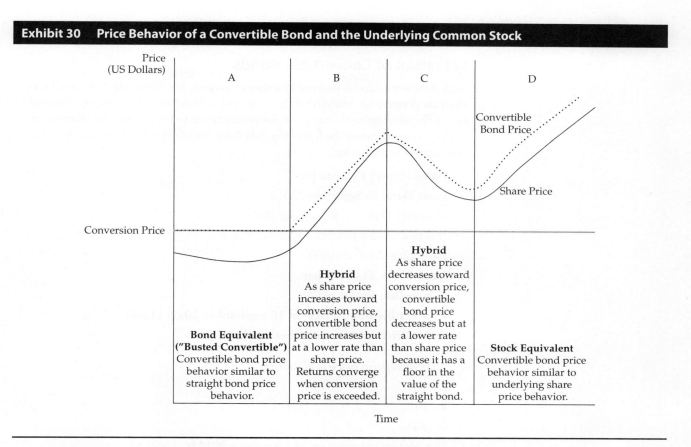

Exhibit 30   Price Behavior of a Convertible Bond and the Underlying Common Stock

Price
(US Dollars)

	A	B	C	D

Conversion Price

Convertible
Bond Price

Share Price

Bond Equivalent ("Busted Convertible")
Convertible bond price behavior similar to straight bond price behavior.

Hybrid
As share price increases toward conversion price, convertible bond price increases but at a lower rate than share price. Returns converge when conversion price is exceeded.

Hybrid
As share price decreases toward conversion price, convertible bond price decreases but at a lower rate than share price because it has a floor in the value of the straight bond.

Stock Equivalent
Convertible bond price behavior similar to underlying share price behavior.

Time

Why would an investor not exercise the conversion option when the underlying share price is above the conversion price, as in areas B, C, and D? The call option on the issuer's common stock may be a European-style option that cannot be exercised now but only at the end of a pre-determined period. Even if the call option is an American-style option, making it possible to convert the bond into equity, it may not be optimal for the convertible bondholder to exercise prior to the expiry of the conversion period; as discussed in Section 3.3.2, it is sometimes better to wait than to exercise an option that is in the money. The investor may also prefer to sell the convertible bond instead of exercising the conversion option.

Except for busted convertibles, the most important factor in the valuation of convertible bonds is the underlying share price. However, it is worth mentioning that large movements in interest rates or in credit spreads may significantly affect the value of convertible bonds. For a convertible bond with a fixed coupon, all else being equal, a significant fall in interest rates would result in an increase in its value and price, whereas a significant rise in interest rates would lead in a decrease in its value and price. Similarly, all else being equal, a significant improvement in the issuer's credit quality would result in an increase in the value and price of its convertible bonds, whereas a deterioration of the issuer's credit quality would lead to a decrease in the value and price of its convertible bonds.

EXAMPLE 9

Valuation of Convertible Bonds

Nick Andrews, a fixed-income investment analyst, has been asked by his supervisor to prepare an analysis of the convertible bond issued by Heavy Element Inc., a chemical industry company, for presentation to the investment committee. Andrews has gathered the following data from the convertible bond's prospectus and market information:

Issuer: Heavy Element Inc.

Issue Date: 15 September 2010

Maturity Date: 15 September 2015

Interest: 3.75% payable annually

Issue Size: $100,000,000

Issue Price: $1,000 at par

Conversion Ratio: 23.26

Convertible Bond Price on 16 September 2012: $1,230

Share Price on 16 September 2012: $52

1   The conversion price is *closest to*:

   A $19.

   B $43.

   C $53.

2   The conversion value on 16 September 2012 is *closest to*:

   A $24.

   B $230.

   C $1,209.

3   The market conversion premium per share on 16 September 2012 is *closest to*:

   A $0.88.

   B $2.24.

   C $9.00.

4   The risk–return characteristics of the convertible bond on 16 September 2012 *most likely* resemble that of:

   A   a busted convertible.

   B   Heavy Element's common stock.

   C   a bond of Heavy Element that is identical to the convertible bond but without the conversion option.

5   As a result of favorable economic conditions, credit spreads for the chemical industry narrow, resulting in lower interest rates for the debt of companies such as Heavy Element. All else being equal, the price of Heavy Element's convertible bond will *most likely*:

   A   decrease significantly.

   B   not change significantly.

   C   increase significantly.

6 Suppose that on 16 September 2012, the convertible bond is available in the secondary market at a price of $1,050. An arbitrageur can make a risk-free profit by:

    A buying the underlying common stock and shorting the convertible bond.

    B buying the convertible bond, exercising the conversion option, and selling the shares resulting from the conversion.

    C shorting the convertible bond and buying a call option on the underlying common stock exercisable at the conversion price on the conversion date.

7 A few months have passed. Because of chemical spills in lake water at the site of a competing facility, the government has introduced very costly environmental legislation. As a result, share prices of almost all publicly traded chemical companies, including Heavy Element, have decreased sharply. Heavy Element's share price is now $28. Now, the risk–return characteristics of the convertible bond *most likely* resemble that of:

    A a bond.

    B a hybrid instrument.

    C Heavy Element's common stock.

Solution to 1:

B is correct. The conversion price is equal to the par value of the convertible bond divided by the conversion ratio—that is, $1,000/23.26 = $43 per share.

Solution to 2:

C is correct. The conversion value is equal to the underlying share price multiplied by the conversion ratio—that is, $52 × 23.26 = $1,209.

Solution to 3:

A is correct. The market conversion premium per share is equal to the convertible bond price divided by the conversion ratio, minus the underlying share price—that is, ($1,230/23.26) – $52 = $52.88 – $52 = $0.88.

Solution to 4:

B is correct. The underlying share price ($52) is well above the conversion price ($43). Thus, the convertible bond exhibits risk–return characteristics that are similar to those of the underlying common stock. A is incorrect because a busted convertible is a convertible bond for which the underlying common stock trades at a significant discount relative to the conversion price. C is incorrect because it describes a busted convertible.

Solution to 5:

B is correct. The underlying share price ($52) is well above the conversion price ($43). Thus, the convertible bond exhibits mostly stock risk–return characteristics, and its price is mainly driven by the underlying share price. Consequently, the decrease in credit spreads will have little effect on the convertible bond price.

Solution to 6:

B is correct. The convertible bond price ($1,050) is lower than its minimum value ($1,209). Thus, the arbitrageur can buy the convertible bond for $1,050; convert it into 23.26 shares; and sell the shares at $52 each, or $1,209 in total, making a profit of $159. A and C are incorrect because in both scenarios, the arbitrageur is short the underpriced asset (convertible bond) and long an overpriced asset, resulting in a loss.

Solution to 7:

A is correct. The underlying share price ($28) is now well below the conversion price ($43), so the convertible bond is a busted convertible and exhibits mostly bond risk–return characteristics. B is incorrect because the underlying share price would have to be close to the conversion price for the risk–return characteristics of the convertible bond to resemble that of a hybrid instrument. C is incorrect because the underlying share price would have to be in excess of the conversion price for the risk–return characteristics of the convertible bond to resemble that of the company's common stock.

7   BOND ANALYTICS

The introduction of OAS analysis in the mid-1980s marked the dawn of modern bond valuation theory. The approach is mathematically elegant, robust, and widely applicable. The typical implementation, however, relies heavily on number crunching. Whether it involves calculating the OAS corresponding to a price, valuing a bond with embedded options, or estimating key rate durations, computers are essential to the process. Needless to say, practitioners must have access to systems that can execute the required calculations correctly and in a timely manner. Most practitioners rely on commercially available systems, but some market participants, in particular financial institutions, may develop analytics in-house.

How can a practitioner tell if such a system is adequate? First, the system should be able to report the correct cash flows, discount rates, and present value of the cash flows. The discount rates can be verified by hand or on a spreadsheet. In practice, it is impossible to examine every calculation, but there are a few relatively simple tests that can be useful, and we present three of these tests below. Also, even if it is difficult to verify that a result is correct, it may be possible to establish that it is wrong.

Check that the put–call parity holds. A simple test for option valuation is to check for put–call parity—that is, the important relationship for European-type options discussed in a previous reading on derivatives. According to put–call parity,

$$\text{Value}(C) - \text{Value}(P) = PV(\text{Forward price of bond on exercise date} - \text{Exercise price})$$

C and P refer to the European-type call option and put option on the same underlying bond and have the same exercise date and the same exercise price, respectively. If the system fails this test, look for an alternative.

Check that the value of the underlying option-free bond does not depend on interest rate volatility. To test the integrity of the interest rate tree calibration, set up and value a callable bond with a very high call price, say 150% of par. This structure should have the same value as that of the straight bond independent of interest rate volatility. The same should be true for a putable bond with a very low put price, say 50% of par.

Check that the volatility term structure slopes downward. As discussed earlier, the specified interest rate volatility is that of the short-term rate. This volatility, in turn, implies the volatilities of longer-term rates. In order for the interest rate process to be stable, the implied volatilities should decline as the term lengthens.

SUMMARY

This reading covers the valuation and analysis of bonds with embedded options. The following are the main points made in this reading:

- An embedded option represents a right that can be exercised by the issuer, by the bondholder, or automatically depending on the course of interest rates. It is attached to, or embedded in, an underlying option-free bond called a straight bond.

- Simple embedded option structures include call options, put options, and extension options. Callable and putable bonds can be redeemed prior to maturity, at the discretion of the issuer in the former case and of the bondholder in the latter case. An extendible bond gives the bondholder the right to keep the bond for a number of years after maturity. Putable and extendible bonds are equivalent, except that the underlying option-free bonds are different.

- Complex embedded option structures include bonds with other types of options or combinations of options. For example, a convertible bond includes a conversion option that allows the bondholders to convert their bonds into the issuer's common stock. A bond with an estate put can be put by the heirs of a deceased bondholder. Sinking fund bonds make the issuer set aside funds over time to retire the bond issue and are often callable, may have an acceleration provision, and may also contain a delivery option. Valuing and analyzing bonds with complex embedded option structures is challenging.

- According to the arbitrage-free framework, the value of a bond with an embedded option is equal to the arbitrage-free values of its parts—that is, the arbitrage-free value of the straight bond and the arbitrage-free values of each of the embedded options.

- Because the call option is an issuer option, the value of the call option decreases the value of the callable bond relative to an otherwise identical but non-callable bond. In contrast, because the put option is an investor option, the value of the put option increases the value of the putable bond relative to an otherwise identical but non-putable bond.

- In the absence of default and interest rate volatility, the bond's future cash flows are certain. Thus, the value of a callable or putable bond can be calculated by discounting the bond's future cash flows at the appropriate one-period forward rates, taking into consideration the decision to exercise the option. If a bond is callable, the decision to exercise the option is made by the issuer, which will exercise the call option when the value of the bond's future cash flows is higher than the call price. In contrast, if the bond is putable, the decision to exercise the option is made by the bondholder, who will exercise the put option when the value of the bond's future cash flows is lower than the put price.

- In practice, interest rates fluctuate, and interest rate volatility affects the value of embedded options. Thus, when valuing bonds with embedded options, it is important to consider the possible evolution of the yield curve over time.

- Interest rate volatility is modeled using a binomial interest rate tree. The higher the volatility, the lower the value of the callable bond and the higher the value of the putable bond.

- Valuing a bond with embedded options assuming an interest rate volatility requires three steps: (1) Generate a tree of interest rates based on the given yield curve and volatility assumptions; (2) at each node of the tree, determine whether the embedded options will be exercised; and (3) apply the backward induction valuation methodology to calculate the present value of the bond.

- The most commonly used approach to valuing risky bonds is to add a spread to the one-period forward rates used to discount the bond's future cash flows.

- The option-adjusted spread is the single spread added uniformly to the one-period forward rates on the tree to produce a value or price for a bond. OAS is sensitive to interest rate volatility: The higher the volatility, the lower the OAS for a callable bond.

- For bonds with embedded options, the best measure to assess the sensitivity of the bond's price to a parallel shift of the benchmark yield curve is effective duration. The effective duration of a callable or putable bond cannot exceed that of the straight bond.

- The effective convexity of a straight bond is negligible, but that of bonds with embedded options is not. When the option is near the money, the convexity of a callable bond is negative, indicating that the upside for a callable bond is much smaller than the downside, whereas the convexity of a putable bond is positive, indicating that the upside for a putable bond is much larger than the downside.

- Because the prices of callable and putable bonds respond asymmetrically to upward and downward interest rate changes of the same magnitude, one-sided durations provide a better indication regarding the interest rate sensitivity of bonds with embedded options than (two-sided) effective duration.

- Key rate durations show the effect of shifting only key points, one at a time, rather than the entire yield curve.

- The arbitrage-free framework can be used to value capped and floored floaters. The cap provision in a floater is an issuer option that prevents the coupon rate from increasing above a specified maximum rate. Thus, the value of a capped floater is equal to or less than the value of the straight bond. In contrast, the floor provision in a floater is an investor option that prevents the coupon from decreasing below a specified minimum rate. Thus, the value of a floored floater is equal to or higher than the value of the straight bond.

- The characteristics of a convertible bond include the conversion price, which is the applicable share price at which the bondholders can convert their bonds into common shares, and the conversion ratio, which reflects the number of shares of common stock that the bondholders receive from converting their bonds into shares. The conversion price is adjusted in case of corporate actions, such as stock splits, bonus share issuances, and rights and warrants issuances. Convertible bondholders may receive compensation when the issuer pays dividends to its common shareholders, and they may be given the opportunity to either put their bonds or convert their bonds into shares earlier and at more advantageous terms in the case of a change of control.

- There are a number of investment metrics and ratios that help analyze and value convertible bonds. The conversion value indicates the value of the bond if it is converted at the market price of the shares. The minimum value of a convertible bond sets a floor value for the convertible bond at the greater of the conversion value or the straight value. This floor is moving, however, because the straight value is not fixed. The market conversion premium represents the price investors effectively pay for the underlying shares if they buy the convertible bond and then convert it into shares. Scaled by the market price of the shares, it represents the premium payable when buying the convertible bond rather than the underlying common stock.

■ Because convertible bonds combine characteristics of bonds, stocks, and options, as well as potentially other features, their valuation and analysis is challenging. Convertible bond investors should consider the factors that affect not only bond prices but also the underlying share price.

■ The arbitrage-free framework can be used to value convertible bonds, including callable and putable ones. Each component (straight bond, call option of the stock, and call and/or put option on the bond) can be valued separately.

■ The risk–return characteristics of a convertible bond depend on the underlying share price relative to the conversion price. When the underlying share price is well below the conversion price, the convertible bond is "busted" and exhibits mostly bond risk–return characteristics. Thus, it is mainly sensitive to interest rate movements. In contrast, when the underlying share price is well above the conversion price, the convertible bond exhibits mostly stock risk–return characteristics. Thus, its price follows similar movements to the price of the underlying stock. In between these two extremes, the convertible bond trades like a hybrid instrument.

PRACTICE PROBLEMS

The following information relates to Questions 1–10

Samuel & Sons is a fixed-income specialty firm that offers advisory services to investment management companies. On 1 October 20X0, Steele Ferguson, a senior analyst at Samuel, is reviewing three fixed-rate bonds issued by a local firm, Pro Star, Inc. The three bonds, whose characteristics are given in Exhibit 1, carry the highest credit rating.

Exhibit 1	Fixed-Rate Bonds Issued by Pro Star, Inc.		
Bond	**Maturity**	**Coupon**	**Type of Bond**
Bond #1	1 October 20X3	4.40% annual	Option-free
Bond #2	1 October 20X3	4.40% annual	Callable at par on 1 October 20X1 and on 1 October 20X2
Bond #3	1 October 20X3	4.40% annual	Putable at par on 1 October 20X1 and on 1 October 20X2

The one-year, two-year, and three-year par rates are 2.250%, 2.750%, and 3.100%, respectively. Based on an estimated interest rate volatility of 10%, Ferguson constructs the binomial interest rate tree shown in Exhibit 2.

Exhibit 2	Binomial Interest Rate Tree

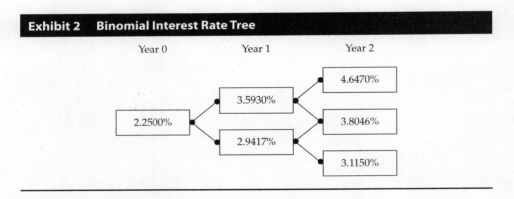

On 19 October 20X0, Ferguson analyzes the convertible bond issued by Pro Star given in Exhibit 3. That day, the market prices of Pro Star's convertible bond and common stock are $1,060 and $37.50, respectively.

Exhibit 3	Convertible Bond Issued by Pro Star, Inc.
Issue Date:	6 December 20X0
Maturity Date:	6 December 20X4
Coupon Rate:	2%
Issue Price:	$1,000
Conversion Ratio:	31

1   The call feature of Bond #2 is *best* described as:

  A   European style.

  B   American style.

  C   Bermudan style.

2   The bond that would *most likely* protect investors against a significant increase in interest rates is:

  A   Bond #1.

  B   Bond #2.

  C   Bond #3.

3   A fall in interest rates would *most likely* result in:

  A   a decrease in the effective duration of Bond #3.

  B   Bond #3 having more upside potential than Bond #2.

  C   a change in the effective convexity of Bond #3 from positive to negative.

4   The value of Bond #2 is *closest* to:

  A   102.103% of par.

  B   103.121% of par.

  C   103.744% of par.

5   The value of Bond #3 is *closest* to:

  A   102.103% of par.

  B   103.688% of par.

  C   103.744% of par.

6   All else being equal, a rise in interest rates will *most likely* result in the value of the option embedded in Bond #3:

  A   decreasing.

  B   remaining unchanged.

  C   increasing.

7   All else being equal, if Ferguson assumes an interest rate volatility of 15% instead of 10%, the bond that would *most likely* increase in value is:

  A   Bond #1.

  B   Bond #2.

  C   Bond #3.

8   All else being equal, if the shape of the yield curve changes from upward sloping to flattening, the value of the option embedded in Bond #2 will *most likely*:

  A   decrease.

  B   remain unchanged.

  C   increase.

9 The conversion price of the bond in Exhibit 3 is *closest* to:

   A $26.67.

   B $32.26.

   C $34.19.

10 If the market price of Pro Star's common stock falls from its level on 19 October 20X0, the price of the convertible bond will *most likely*:

   A fall at the same rate as Pro Star's stock price.

   B fall but at a slightly lower rate than Pro Star's stock price.

   C be unaffected until Pro Star's stock price reaches the conversion price.

The following information relates to Question 11–19

Rayes Investment Advisers specializes in fixed-income portfolio management. Meg Rayes, the owner of the firm, would like to add bonds with embedded options to the firm's bond portfolio. Rayes has asked Mingfang Hsu, one of the firm's analysts, to assist her in selecting and analyzing bonds for possible inclusion in the firm's bond portfolio.

Hsu first selects two corporate bonds that are callable at par and have the same characteristics in terms of maturity, credit quality and call dates. Hsu uses the option adjusted spread (OAS) approach to analyse the bonds, assuming an interest rate volatility of 10%. The results of his analysis are presented in Exhibit 1.

Exhibit 1	Summary Results of Hsu's Analysis Using the OAS Approach
Bond	**OAS (in bps)**
Bond #1	25.5
Bond #2	30.3

Hsu then selects the four bonds issued by RW, Inc. given in Exhibit 2. These bonds all have a maturity of three years and the same credit rating. Bonds #4 and #5 are identical to Bond #3, an option-free bond, except that they each include an embedded option.

Exhibit 2	Bonds Issued by RW, Inc.	
Bond	**Coupon**	**Special Provision**
Bond #3	4.00% annual	
Bond #4	4.00% annual	Callable at par at the end of years 1 and 2
Bond #5	4.00% annual	Putable at par at the end of years 1 and 2
Bond #6	One-year Libor annually, set in arrears	

To value and analyze RW's bonds, Hsu uses an estimated interest rate volatility of 15% and constructs the binomial interest rate tree provided in Exhibit 3.

Exhibit 3   Binomial Interest Rate Tree Used to Value RW's Bonds

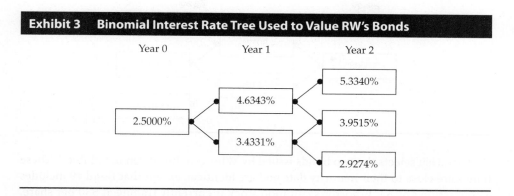

Rayes asks Hsu to determine the sensitivity of Bond #4's price to a 20 bps parallel shift of the benchmark yield curve. The results of Hsu's calculations are shown in Exhibit 4.

Exhibit 4   Summary Results of Hsu's Analysis about the Sensitivity of Bond #4's Price to a Parallel Shift of the Benchmark Yield Curve

	+20 bps	−20 bps
Magnitude of the Parallel Shift in the Benchmark Yield Curve	+20 bps	−20 bps
Full Price of Bond #4 (% of par)	100.478	101.238

Hsu also selects the two floating-rate bonds issued by Varlep, plc given in Exhibit 5. These bonds have a maturity of three years and the same credit rating.

Exhibit 5   Floating-Rate Bonds Issued by Varlep, plc

Bond	Coupon
Bond #7	One-year Libor annually, set in arrears, capped at 5.00%
Bond #8	One-year Libor annually, set in arrears, floored at 3.50%

To value Varlep's bonds, Hsu constructs the binomial interest rate tree provided in Exhibit 6.

Exhibit 6   Binomial Interest Rate Tree Used to Value Varlep's Bonds

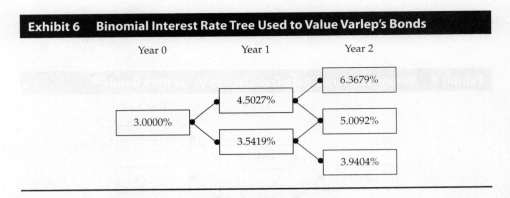

Last, Hsu selects the two bonds issued by Whorton, Inc. given in Exhibit 7. These bonds are close to their maturity date and are identical, except that Bond #9 includes a conversion option. Whorton's common stock is currently trading at $30 per share.

Exhibit 7   Bonds Issued by Whorton, Inc.

Bond	Type of Bond
Bond #9	Convertible bond with a conversion price of $50
Bond #10	Identical to Bond #9 except that it does not include a conversion option

11 Based on Exhibit 1, Rayes would *most likely* conclude that relative to Bond #1, Bond #2 is:

   A overpriced.

   B fairly priced.

   C underpriced.

12 The effective duration of Bond #6 is:

   A lower than or equal to 1.

   B higher than 1 but lower than 3.

   C higher than 3.

13 In Exhibit 2, the bond whose effective duration will lengthen if interest rates rise is:

   A Bond #3.

   B Bond #4.

   C Bond #5.

14 The effective duration of Bond #4 is *closest* to:

   A 0.76.

   B 1.88.

   C 3.77.

15 The value of Bond #7 is *closest* to:

   A 99.697% of par.

   B 99.936% of par.

   C 101.153% of par.

16 The value of Bond #8 is *closest* to:

   A 98.116% of par.

B 100.000% of par.

C 100.485% of par.

17 The value of Bond #9 is equal to the value of Bond #10:

A plus the value of a put option on Whorton's common stock.

B plus the value of a call option on Whorton's common stock.

C minus the value of a call option on Whorton's common stock.

18 The minimum value of Bond #9 is equal to the *greater* of:

A the conversion value of Bond #9 and the current value of Bond #10.

B the current value of Bond #10 and a call option on Whorton's common stock.

C the conversion value of Bond #9 and a call option on Whorton's common stock.

19 The factor that is currently *least likely* to affect the risk-return characteristics of Bond #9 is:

A Interest rate movements.

B Whorton's credit spreads.

C Whorton's common stock price movements.

SOLUTIONS

1 C is correct. The call option embedded in Bond #2 can be exercised only at two predetermined dates: 1 October 20X1 and 1 October 20X2. Thus, the call feature is Bermudan style.

2 C is correct. The bond that would most likely protect investors against a significant increase in interest rates is the putable bond, i.e., Bond #3. When interest rates have risen and higher-yield bonds are available, a put option allows the bondholders to put back the bonds to the issuer prior to maturity and to reinvest the proceeds of the retired bonds in higher-yielding bonds.

3 B is correct. A fall in interest rates results in a rise in bond values. For a callable bond such as Bond #2, the upside potential is capped because the issuer is more likely to call the bond. In contrast, the upside potential for a putable bond such as Bond #3 is uncapped. Thus, a fall in interest rates would result in a putable bond having more upside potential than an otherwise identical callable bond. Note that A is incorrect because the effective duration of a putable bond increases, not decreases, with a fall in interest rates—the bond is less likely to be put and thus behaves more like an option-free bond. C is also incorrect because the effective convexity of a putable bond is always positive. It is the effective convexity of a callable bond that will change from positive to negative if interest rates fall and the call option is near the money.

4 A is correct:

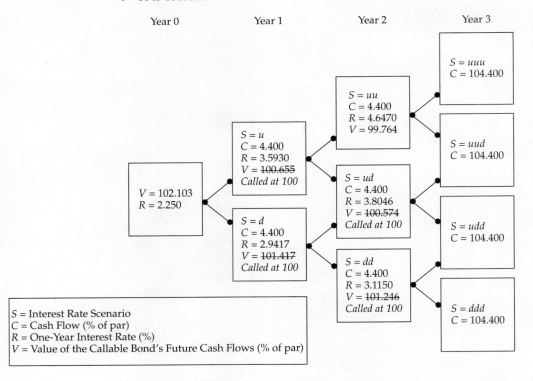

S = Interest Rate Scenario
C = Cash Flow (% of par)
R = One-Year Interest Rate (%)
V = Value of the Callable Bond's Future Cash Flows (% of par)

5 C is correct:

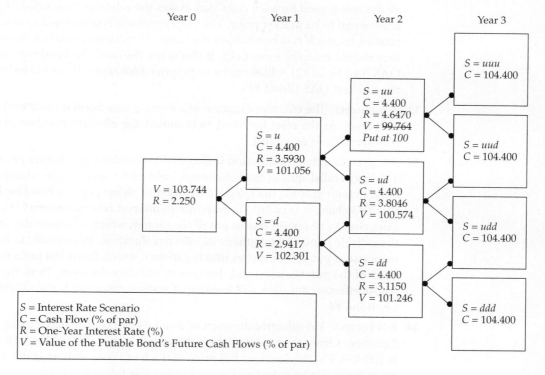

	Year 0	Year 1	Year 2	Year 3

Year 0:
V = 103.744
R = 2.250

Year 1:
S = u
C = 4.400
R = 3.5930
V = 101.056

S = d
C = 4.400
R = 2.9417
V = 102.301

Year 2:
S = uu
C = 4.400
R = 4.6470
V = 99.764
Put at 100

S = ud
C = 4.400
R = 3.8046
V = 100.574

S = dd
C = 4.400
R = 3.1150
V = 101.246

Year 3:
S = uuu
C = 104.400

S = uud
C = 104.400

S = udd
C = 104.400

S = ddd
C = 104.400

S = Interest Rate Scenario
C = Cash Flow (% of par)
R = One-Year Interest Rate (%)
V = Value of the Putable Bond's Future Cash Flows (% of par)

6 C is correct. Bond #3 is a putable bond, and the value of a put option increases as interest rates rise. At higher interest rates, the value of the underlying option-free bond (straight bond) declines, but the decline is offset partially by the increase in the value of the embedded put option, which is more likely to be exercised.

7 C is correct. Regardless of the type of option, an increase in interest rate volatility results in an increase in option value. Because the value of a putable bond is equal to the value of the straight bond *plus* the value of the embedded put option, Bond #3 will increase in value if interest rate volatility increases. Put another way, an increase in interest rate volatility will most likely result in more scenarios where the put option is exercised, which increases the values calculated in the interest rate tree and, thus, the value of the putable bond.

8 C is correct. Bond #2 is a callable bond, and the value of the embedded call option increases as the yield curve flattens. When the yield curve is upward sloping, the one-period forward rates on the interest rate tree are high and opportunities for the issuer to call the bond are fewer. When the yield curve flattens or inverts, many nodes on the tree have lower forward rates, which increases the opportunities to call and, thus, the value of the embedded call option.

9 B is correct. The conversion price of a convertible bond is equal to the par value divided by the conversion ratio—that is, $1,000/31= $32.26 per share.

10 B is correct. The market price on 19 October 20X0 ($37.50) is above the conversion price of $1,000/31 = $32.26 per share. Thus, the convertible bond exhibits mostly stock risk-return characteristics, and a fall in the stock price will result in a fall in the convertible bond price. However, the change in the convertible bond price is less than the change in the stock price because the convertible bond has a floor—that floor is the value of the straight bond.

11 C is correct. The option-adjusted spread (OAS) is the constant spread added to all the one-period forward rates that makes the arbitrage-free value of a risky bond equal to its market price. The OAS approach is often used to assess bond relative values. If two bonds have the same characteristics and credit quality, they should have the same OAS. If this is not the case, the bond with the largest OAS (i.e., Bond #2) is likely to be underpriced (cheap) relative to the bond with the smallest OAS (Bond #1).

12 A is correct. The effective duration of a floating-rate bond is close to the time to next reset. As the reset for Bond #6 is annual, the effective duration of this bond is lower than or equal to 1.

13 B is correct. Effective duration indicates the sensitivity of a bond's price to a 100 bps parallel shift of the benchmark yield curve assuming no change in the bond's credit spread. The effective duration of an option-free bond such as Bond #3 changes very little in response to interest rate movements. As interest rates rise, a call option moves out of the money, which increases the value of the callable bond and lengthens its effective duration. In contrast, as interest rates rise, a put option moves into the money, which limits the price depreciation of the putable bond and shortens its effective duration. Thus, the bond whose effective duration will lengthen if interest rates rise is the callable bond, i.e., Bond #4.

14 B is correct. The effective duration of Bond #4 can be calculated using Equation 3 from the reading, where ΔCurve is 20 bps, PV_- is 101.238, and PV_+ is 100.478. PV_0, the current full price of the bond (i.e., with no shift), is not given but it can be calculated using Exhibit 3 as follows:

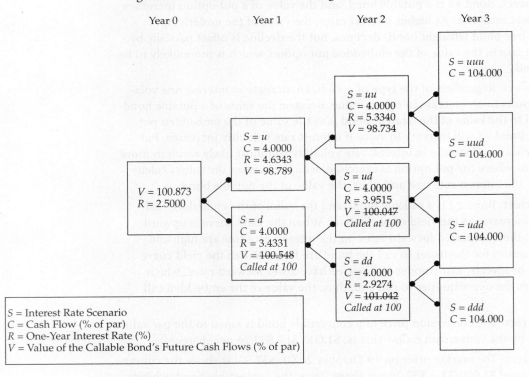

Thus, the effective duration of Bond #4 is:

$$\text{Effective duration} = \frac{101.238 - 100.478}{2 \times (0.0020) \times (100.873)} = 1.88$$

15 A is correct:

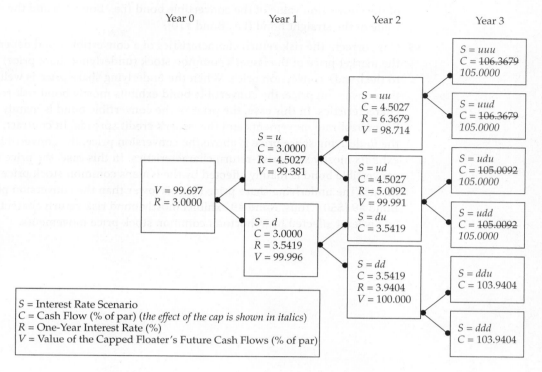

S = Interest Rate Scenario
C = Cash Flow (% of par) *(the effect of the cap is shown in italics)*
R = One-Year Interest Rate (%)
V = Value of the Capped Floater's Future Cash Flows (% of par)

16 C is correct:

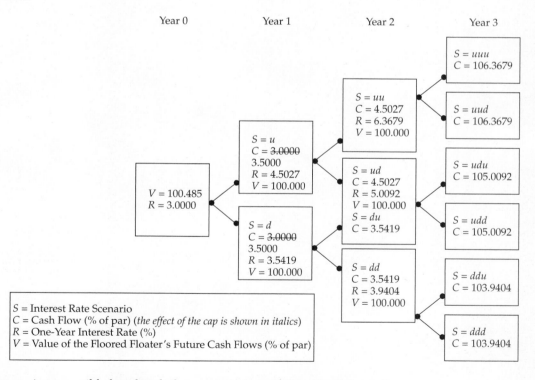

S = Interest Rate Scenario
C = Cash Flow (% of par) *(the effect of the cap is shown in italics)*
R = One-Year Interest Rate (%)
V = Value of the Floored Floater's Future Cash Flows (% of par)

17 B is correct. A convertible bond includes a conversion option, which is a call option on the issuer's common stock. This conversion option gives the bond-holders the right to convert their debt into equity. Thus, the value of Bond #9, the convertible bond, is equal to the value of Bond #10, the underlying option-free bond (straight bond), plus the value of a call option on Whorton's common stock.

18 A is correct. The minimum value of a convertible bond is equal to the greater of the conversion value of the convertible bond (i.e., Bond #9) and the current value of the straight bond (i.e., Bond #10).

19 C is correct. The risk-return characteristics of a convertible bond depend on the market price of the issuer's common stock (underlying share price) relative to the bond's conversion price. When the underlying share price is well below the conversion price, the convertible bond exhibits mostly bond risk-return characteristics. In this case, the price of the convertible bond is mainly affected by interest rate movements and the issuer's credit spreads. In contrast, when the underlying share price is above the conversion price, the convertible bond exhibits mostly stock risk-return characteristics. In this case, the price of the convertible bond is mainly affected by the issuer's common stock price movements. The underlying share price ($30) is lower than the conversion price of Bond #9 ($50). Thus, Bond #9 exhibits mostly bond risk-return characteristics and is least affected by Whorton's common stock price movements.

38

Credit Analysis Models

by Robert A. Jarrow, PhD, and Donald R. van Deventer, PhD

Robert A. Jarrow, PhD, is at the Samuel Curtis Johnson Graduate School of Management at Cornell University (USA). Donald R. van Deventer, PhD, is at Kamakura Corporation (USA).

LEARNING OUTCOMES

Mastery	The candidate should be able to:
☐	a. explain probability of default, loss given default, expected loss, and present value of the expected loss and describe the relative importance of each across the credit spectrum;
☐	b. explain credit scoring and credit ratings, including why they are called ordinal rankings;
☐	c. explain strengths and weaknesses of credit ratings;
☐	d. explain structural models of corporate credit risk, including why equity can be viewed as a call option on the company's assets;
☐	e. explain reduced form models of corporate credit risk, including why debt can be valued as the sum of expected discounted cash flows after adjusting for risk;
☐	f. explain assumptions, strengths, and weaknesses of both structural and reduced form models of corporate credit risk;
☐	g. explain the determinants of the term structure of credit spreads;
☐	h. calculate and interpret the present value of the expected loss on a bond over a given time horizon;
☐	i. compare the credit analysis required for asset-backed securities to analysis of corporate debt.

1   INTRODUCTION

Since 1990, credit-related financial crises have spurred developments in credit risk analysis. These crises include the following:

■ The collapse of the Japanese bubble and its aftermath (1989–present), which originated with overvalued Japanese real estate and equity prices. The collapse was a slow process, lasting for over a decade, and resulted in sluggish growth in the Japanese economy for years to follow.

■ The Mexican "tequila crisis" of 1994–1995, which originated with the devaluation of the Mexican peso in December 1994, causing significant losses on Mexican government bonds.

■ The Asian crisis, also known as the Asian contagion (1997–1998), which originated with the crash of the Thai baht in July 1997 and spread to equity markets globally.

■ The Russian debt crisis (1998), which originated with Russia defaulting on its debt in August 1998, causing significant losses on Russian securities that spread to equity markets globally.

■ The 2008 global financial crisis, which was first identified as such in 2008 although it lasted beyond 2008. It originated in part with a decline in housing prices and resulted in significant losses on securitized instruments based on home mortgages. It spread globally to other markets, including equity markets.

Dramatic shifts in key macroeconomic factors caused a wide array of countries', companies', and individuals' default risk to increase during these crises. Traditional credit ratings were only partially effective in capturing the changes in these correlated default risks. As a result, additional tools to quantify and manage risks have been developed. These tools include methods for estimating correlated default probabilities and recovery rates based on macroeconomic factors. These new models are purposefully constructed to incorporate systemic default risk similar to that experienced in the recent financial crisis. This reading describes different approaches to credit risk analysis, the strengths and weaknesses of each approach, and the application of the approaches to credit risk evaluation.

Section 2 presents an overview of four basic measures relevant to credit risk: the probability of default, the loss given default, the expected loss, and the present value of the expected loss. Section 3 discusses two traditional approaches to credit risk management: credit scoring and credit ratings. Both approaches are still widely used. Credit scoring provides an ordinal ranking of the credit risk for retail borrowers (small owner-operated businesses and individuals). Credit ratings provide an ordinal ranking of a borrower's credit riskiness. Credit ratings are used for securities issued by financial and non-financial companies (corporate issuers), sovereigns, and sub-sovereign governments, for the companies and governments themselves, and for asset-backed securities.

Sections 4 and 5 discuss structural and reduced form approaches or models for analyzing credit risk. The structural model is based on insights obtained from option pricing methodology.[1] The reduced form model overcomes limitations inherent in the structural approach and enables the inclusion of systemic default risk into the modeling methodology.[2]

---

1 Merton (1974).
2 The reduced form model of Jarrow and Turnbull (1992, 1995) is based on the Heath–Jarrow–Morton (1992) model for pricing interest rate derivatives. Useful explanatory references include Jarrow (2009) for credit risk models and Chava and Jarrow (2004) for the estimation of the reduced form model's parameters.

How to use structural and reduced form models to price risky debt and to determine the probability of default and the expected loss is shown. For practical applications, the estimation of each models' parameters is described. Strengths and weaknesses of both the structural and reduced form credit risk models are also described.

Section 6 discusses the term structure of credit spreads and shows how to use credit spreads to estimate the present value of the expected loss. Numerous examples are provided to help the reader understand this procedure. Section 7 discusses credit analysis of asset-backed securities (ABS). A summary and practice problems conclude the reading.

MEASURES OF CREDIT RISK

2

This section discusses, in an intuitive fashion, some basic credit risk measures for fixed-income securities: the probability of default, the loss given default, the expected loss, and the present value of the expected loss.

For the purposes of this discussion, consider a bond issued by Company XYZ with a principal of F dollars, a fixed coupon of $c\%$ of the principal paid semiannually, and a maturity of T years. The bond is in default if any of the bond's covenants (promises) are violated. The most common cause of default is the omission of a coupon or principal payment. Credit risk is the risk that such a default may occur and result in the partial or total loss of the remaining coupon and principal payments.

To quantify this credit risk, four measures are often estimated. The first is the probability that the bond will default before maturity, called the **probability of default** or **default probability**. Obviously, the higher the probability of default, the more risky the bond, everything else held constant. The second measure is the **loss given default**, the amount of the remaining coupon and principal payments lost in the event of default. The loss given default is often expressed as a percentage of the position or exposure. A related measure is the **recovery rate**, which is the percentage of the position received or recovered in default. The loss given default plus the expected recovery rate when each is expressed as a percentage of the position equals 100%. In the simplest and most extreme case, the loss given default is 100%. In other words, there is no amount recovered.

The third measure is the **expected loss** on the bond. The expected loss is equal to the probability of default multiplied by the loss given default. Calculation of the expected loss is complicated for various reasons, but an important reason is that both the probability of default and the loss given default can depend on the health of the economy, in addition to company-specific balance sheet considerations. Indeed, in a healthy and growing economy, one would expect that the probability of default would be smaller and that if default occurs, the loss given default would be smaller as well. In such a situation, when computing the expected loss, both the default probability and loss given default need to be made dependent on the state of the economy and the weighted average of these state-dependent expected losses need to be calculated. The weights used in this average correspond to the probabilities that the different possible states of the economy occur.

The fourth credit risk measure is the **present value of the expected loss**. The present value of the expected loss is conceptually the largest price one would be willing to pay on a bond to a third party (e.g., an insurer) to entirely remove the credit risk of purchasing and holding the bond. Paying this fee transforms a "credit risky" bond to a "riskless bond," assuming, of course, that the third-party insurer is free of default risk.

The present value of the expected loss is the most complex credit risk measure to calculate because it involves two modifications to the expected loss. The first modification is to explicitly adjust the probabilities to account for the risk of the cash flows (the risk premium). Recall from your studies of option pricing that an option can be valued using "risk-neutral valuation," where one takes the expected value of the option's payoffs discounted to the present by the risk-free rate. In taking this expectation, "risk-neutral" probabilities are used instead of the actual probabilities. The difference between the actual and risk-neutral probabilities is that the risk-neutral probabilities adjust for risk. The actual probabilities are those from "nature." The second modification is to include the time value of money in the calculation—that is, the discounting of the future cash flows to the present. Of course, the loss of the bond's principal 10 years from now has a smaller present value than the loss of the bond's principal 1 year from now. These two adjustments—using the risk-neutral probabilities and discounting—can either decrease or increase the present value of the expected loss relative to the expected loss itself. Of the credit risk measures considered, the present value of the expected loss is perhaps the most important. This is because when one considers the purchase or sale of the bond, one is interested in the exact dollar difference one should pay or receive on the bond, relative to an otherwise identical and riskless government bond. This difference is the single measure that most succinctly captures the credit risk in the bond.

EXAMPLE 1

A bond portfolio manager has $500,000 to invest in a bond portfolio. From his credit risk analysis department he collects the following information on four (hypothetical) debt issues:

Name of Company	Probability of Default (% per year)	Expected Loss (dollars per 100 par)	Present Value of the Expected Loss (dollars per 100 par)
Green Company	1.15	$15.00	$13.50
Sleepy Company	0.85	$20.00	$14.00
Red Fruit Corp.	2.25	$37.00	$32.00
Slot Machines Inc.	0.05	$1.00	$0.75

Rank the companies in terms of the different credit risk measures. Do they give the same ranking? Which measure would you use and why?

Solution:

The rankings are as follows:

Ranking	Probability of Default (% per year)	Expected Loss (dollars per 100 par)	Present Value of the Expected Loss (dollars per 100 par)
Least Risky	Slot Machines Inc.	Slot Machines Inc.	Slot Machines Inc.
.	Sleepy Company	Green Company	Green Company
.	Green Company	Sleepy Company	Sleepy Company
Most Risky	Red Fruit Corp.	Red Fruit Corp.	Red Fruit Corp.

The probability of default gives a different ranking from either the expected loss or the present value of the expected loss. The difference in rankings based on these two measures is due to the loss given default. By measures of expected loss, Green Company ranks as less risky than Sleepy Company. Given the higher probability of default for Green Company than Sleepy Company, Green Company's loss given default must be smaller than it is for Sleepy Company. Note that the expected loss and the present value of the loss give the same rankings.

A simple example clarifies this distinction. Consider a company, called XYZ, whose one-year default probability is 1. Hence, XYZ is sure to default over the next year. For the purpose of this example, let us also suppose that its loss given default is zero. That is, when XYZ defaults, the debt holders incur no losses. Hence, its expected loss and the present value of the expected loss are zero as well. Then, when ranking XYZ according to the probability of default, it is the most risky company possible; however, according to its expected loss or the present value of the expected loss, it is the least risky company possible. The key difference, of course, between these different measures is due to the loss given default. The present value of the expected loss is the preferred measure because it includes the probability of default, the loss given default, the time value of money, and the risk premium in its computation. The expected loss is second best, including both the default probability and loss given default. The default probability is the least inclusive measure.

The difference between a risky bond's yield to maturity and the yield to maturity of a government bond with similar features is the credit spread. This implies that the credit spread includes within its value the probability of default, the loss given default, and the time value of money, including adjusting for the risk of the cash flows lost in default (the risk premium). The larger the credit spread on a bond, the larger at least one of these underlying components is. To determine which of these components explains the credit spread, one needs a model. Using a model, one can compute which of these components is the largest. To understand credit risk, therefore, one needs to understand credit risk models.

Traditional credit models—credit scoring and credit ratings—can be viewed as a methodology for summarizing credit risk measures into a single measure. Structural and reduced form models are quantitative approaches constructed to enable the computation of the credit risk measures. We discuss each of these approaches next, starting with the traditional credit models.

TRADITIONAL CREDIT MODELS 3

Credit scoring and credit ratings, two traditional approaches to credit risk analysis, apply to different types of borrowers. Credit scoring is used for small owner-operated businesses and individuals. These small borrowers are often referred to as retail borrowers. Credit ratings are used for companies, sovereigns, sub-sovereigns, and those entities' securities, as well as asset-backed securities. An understanding of the traditional approaches to credit risk is useful because

- they are widely used and
- they provide a link between the traditional, financial statement–based credit analysis methods covered in Level I of the CFA Program and the structural and reduced form credit risk models, which are the primary focus of this reading.

Credit scoring ranks a borrower's credit riskiness. It does not provide an estimate of a borrower's default probability. It is called an *ordinal ranking* because it only orders borrowers' riskiness from highest to lowest. Credit scoring is not capable of determining whether Borrower A is twice as risky as Borrower B, a *cardinal ranking*.

Probabilities of default provide a cardinal ranking of credit: For example, if Borrower A has a default probability of 2% and Borrower B has a default probability of 4%, then Borrower B is twice as risky as Borrower A.

Credit scoring is performed in most countries around the world, and it is typically applied to individuals and very small businesses where the owner-manager provides his personal guarantee on any borrowings. A retail borrower's credit score from a credit bureau or a financial institution may not be representative of the borrower's credit worthiness. The retail borrower may be borrowing from many institutions in many forms, including credit cards, auto loans, first mortgage loans, second mortgage loans, and home equity lines of credit. Because there are no *cross-default*[3] clauses for retail borrowers, it is possible for a retail borrower to be more likely to default on one type of loan than on another. That means credit scores have different implications for an individual's default probability on different types of loans.

A credit score has the following characteristics:

■ Credit scores provide an ordinal ranking of a borrower's credit risk. The higher the score, the less risky the borrower. If Borrower A has a credit score of 800 and Borrower B has a credit score of 400, Borrower A is less likely to default than Borrower B, but it does not mean that Borrower A is half as likely to default as Borrower B.

■ Credit scores do not explicitly depend on current economic conditions. For example, if Borrower A has a credit score of 800 and the economy deteriorates, Borrower A's credit score does not adjust unless Borrower A's behavior or financial circumstances change.

■ Credit scores are not percentile rankings of the borrower among a universe of borrowers. There can be many borrowers with the same credit score, and the percentage of borrowers with a particular score can change over time. The following chart is based on information from www.creditscoring.com. It summarizes the distribution of credit scores from the US credit specialist FICO as of 8 August 2011. This distribution is representative of credit scores available from credit agencies around the world, including Equifax, Experian, and TransUnion. The delinquency rate is the probability of being more than 90 days past due in the next 24 months:

Percentile	Percentage of People	Score	Delinquency Rate
2nd	2%	300–499	87%
7th	5%	500–549	71%
15th	8%	550–599	51%
27th	12%	600–649	31%
42nd	15%	650–699	15%
60th	18%	700–749	5%
87th	27%	750–799	2%
100th	13%	800–850	1%

3 A cross-default clause states that the borrower is in default on Loan 1 if the borrower is in default on any other loan or form of borrowing, say, Loan 2. This is a standard provision for most corporate lending that is intended to prevent the borrower from treating lenders differently when the borrower is in financial distress. Cross-default clauses are rare in sovereign lending, but that is changing rapidly. The clauses are very rare in retail lending.

- Many lenders prefer stability in credit scores over accuracy, so there is some pressure on credit bureaus to take this into account when generating credit scores.

- Credit scores have different implications for the probability of default depending on the borrower and the nature of the loan that has been extended. For example, a retail borrower in financial distress may pay on her home mortgage and default on credit card debt because the consequences for credit card default are less serious. The default probabilities for a given credit score are therefore likely higher on credit card lending than they are on home mortgages.

Credit scores are used in many countries in the world, but scoring varies considerably across countries. In some countries, only negative information, such as a default, is reported. Therefore, no score or information is positive because it means no news has been reported about the borrower. In other countries, factors such as payment history and debt outstanding are used to develop a credit score, but the weighting of the factors can differ across countries. Assuming you are a borrower in the United States, the Federal Trade Commission identifies the following factors that affect your credit score in the United States.[4]

- Have you paid your bills on time? Payment history is a significant factor. If you have paid bills late, had an account referred to collections, or declared bankruptcy, it is likely to affect your score negatively.

- Are you maxed out? Many scoring systems evaluate the amount of debt you have compared with your credit limits. If the amount you owe is close to your credit limit, it's likely to have a negative effect on your score.

- How long have you had credit? The length of your credit track record is important. A short credit history may affect your score negatively, but such factors as timely payments and low balances can offset that.

- Have you applied for new credit lately? Many scoring systems consider whether you have applied for credit recently. If you have applied for too many new accounts recently, it could have a negative effect on your score.

- How many credit accounts do you have and what kinds of accounts are they? Although it is generally considered a plus to have established credit accounts, too many credit card accounts or certain types of loans may have a negative effect on your score.

EXAMPLE 2

A bank analyst is considering the loan applications of three individuals. Each is requesting a personal loan of $55,000. The bank can lend to only one of them. The bank's criteria emphasize the FICO score. Which individual is the bank analyst *most likely* to recommend lending to?

A Individual A has a salary of $157,000, a net worth of $300,000, five credit cards, and a FICO score of 550.

B Individual B has a salary of $97,000, a net worth of $105,000, two credit cards, and a FICO score of 700.

C Individual C has a salary of $110,000, a net worth of $300,000, no credit cards, and a FICO score of 600.

---

4 See www.ftc.gov.

Solution:

The bank analyst is most likely to recommend lending to Individual B. Individual B has the highest FICO score, 700. Individual C appears to be an attractive candidate for a loan but has not built up a credit score by judicious use of credit and repayment, as evidenced by no credit cards.

Credit ratings rank the credit risk of a company, government (sovereign), quasi-government, or asset-backed security. Credit ratings do not provide an estimate of the loan's default probability. Credit ratings have a history that dates back more than a century. Standard & Poor's (S&P) was established in 1860, and Moody's Investors Service was founded in 1909. As of August 2012, 10 credit-rating agencies are recognized by the US Securities and Exchange Commission as "nationally recognized statistical rating organizations." The 10 credit-rating agencies are A.M. Best Company, Inc., DBRS Ltd., Egan-Jones Rating Company, Fitch, Inc., Japan Credit Rating Agency, LACE Financial Corp., Moody's Investors Service, Rating and Investment Information, Inc., RealPoint LLC, and Standard & Poor's Rating Services. Many non-US-based credit-rating agencies are included in the list. As of October 2011, the UK Financial Services Authority[5] had registered the following credit-rating agencies: A.M. Best Europe Rating Services Ltd., DBRS Ratings Limited, Fitch Ratings Limited, Fitch Ratings CIS Limited, Moody's Investors Service Ltd., and Standard & Poor's Credit Market Services Europe Ltd. Regulators around the world have established similar lists of recognized credit-rating agencies.

In addition to the credit ratings issued by third-party rating agencies, **internal ratings** are also created and heavily used by financial institutions to control their credit risk. The number of rating grades and their definitions vary among third-party rating agencies and among financial services firms, but their objective is the same: to create an ordinal ranking of borrowers by riskiness as an aid to portfolio selection and risk management.

Rating agencies like Standard & Poor's and Moody's Investors Service use more than 20 rating grades. Exhibit 1 shows the ratings assigned by these two agencies to debt issues. For Standard & Poor's ratings, *investment-grade* bonds are those rated BBB– and above. All other rating classes are considered *non-investment-grade*, *speculative-grade*, or *junk bonds*. For Moody's Investors Service, investment-grade bonds are those rated Baa3 and above. Large financial institutions define their own rating scales, but 10–20 risk levels are common.

Exhibit 1	Sample Rating Scales Ranked from Best to Worst Rating		
Rating Category	**Moody's Investors Service**	**Standard & Poor's**	**Example of a Bank Internal Rating**
1	Aaa	AAA	20
2	Aa1	AA+	19
3	Aa2	AA	18
4	Aa3	AA–	17
5	A1	A+	16
6	A2	A	15
7	A3	A–	14

---

5 In 2013, the Financial Services Authority was replaced by two new regulatory authorities, the Financial Conduct Authority (FCA) and the Prudential Regulation Authority (PRA).

Exhibit 1   (Continued)

Rating Category	Moody's Investors Service	Standard & Poor's	Example of a Bank Internal Rating
8	Baa1	BBB+	13
9	Baa2	BBB	12
10	Baa3	BBB−	11
11	Ba1	BB+	10
12	Ba2	BB	9
13	Ba3	BB−	8
14	B1	B+	7
15	B2	B	6
16	B3	B−	5
17	Caa1	CCC+	4
18	Caa2	CCC	3
19	Caa3	CCC−	2
20	Ca	CC	1
21	C	D	

Both third-party and internal credit ratings are measures that summarize an extensive analysis of a borrower's credit history. For example, a bank's credit file on a typical corporate borrower may have 100 pages of history and analysis on the borrower's relationship with the bank. Saying that the borrower is BBB+ or rated a 9 is an efficient way to communicate the conclusions of this extensive analysis with respect to the borrower's credit risk in relation to other potential borrowers.

Rating agencies arose because there are economies of scale in the collection of credit-related information. Indeed, there are large fixed costs in obtaining financial information, but fewer costs in distributing the collected information to others. Collecting financial information requires significant time and resources. This was especially true before the advent of the internet, when information was available only in paper form and had to be obtained by visiting companies one by one. Even today, however, credit-rating agencies still profit by reducing the costs of obtaining and analyzing credit information to the eventual end-user, the lender. This is the economic basis of their business franchise.

Some rating agencies, such as Egan-Jones Rating Company, are compensated by subscribers. However, rating agencies are often compensated using an *issuer-pays model*, where the issuer (borrower) pays the credit-rating agency to rate their debt. The rating is then distributed free of charge to potential lenders. If detail is desired on the underlying analysis, an investor/lender has to subscribe. Potential investors/lenders may rely on credit ratings rather than doing their own credit analyses or in conjunction with their own credit analyses. A high credit rating may result in more funds being potentially available to a borrower. The problem with an issuer-pays model is that there is an incentive conflict. To obtain more business, credit-rating agencies have an incentive to give higher ratings than may be deserved. Recent events associated with the 2008 global financial crisis have drawn attention to the potential seriousness of this problem; ratings that were subsequently judged to be higher than justified have resulted in regulators questioning the wisdom of relying on and referring to credit-rating agencies in financial regulations.

Another issue is that rating agencies may be motivated to keep their ratings stable over time to reduce unnecessary volatility in debt market prices. Unfortunately, there is an inherent conflict between stability and accuracy. Stable ratings can only be accurate "on average" because, by design, they change infrequently while information arrives incrementally and continuously with the changing business cycle. This desire for stability in the ratings gives rise to a non-constant relationship over time between credit ratings and default probabilities. To see this phenomenon, consider Exhibit 2 showing historical annual default rate percentages from Standard & Poor's for companies rated CCC.

Exhibit 2	Actual Default Rate on Companies Rated CCC by Standard & Poor's, 1981–2010		
Year	Default Rate (%)	Year	Default Rate (%)
1981	0	1996	4.17
1982	21.43	1997	12.00
1983	6.67	1998	42.86
1984	25.00	1999	32.35
1985	15.38	2000	34.12
1986	23.08	2001	44.55
1987	12.28	2002	44.12
1988	20.37	2003	32.93
1989	33.33	2004	15.33
1990	31.25	2005	8.94
1991	33.87	2006	12.38
1992	30.19	2007	15.09
1993	13.33	2008	26.26
1994	16.67	2009	48.68
1995	28.00	2010	22.27

Source: Standard & Poor's Corporation, *Default, Transition, and Recovery: 2010 Annual Global Corporate Default Study and Rating Transitions* (30 March 2011).

As shown in Exhibit 2, although the credit rating is constant, at CCC, over time, the actual percentage of defaults is not. For example, when the economy was healthy in 1981, the default rate was 0%, but in the recession of 2009, it was 48.68%. The default probability of a CCC company appears to change over time with the business cycle, whereas the rating does not.

Strengths and weaknesses of the traditional credit ratings (both traditional third-party and internal ratings) can be summarized as follows.

Rating Strengths

- They provide a simple statistic that summarizes a complex credit analysis of a potential borrower.

- They tend to be stable over time and across the business cycle, which reduces debt market price volatility.

Rating Weaknesses

- They tend to be stable over time, which reduces the correspondence to a debt offering's default probability.

- They do not explicitly depend on the business cycle, whereas a debt offering's default probability does.

- The issuer-pays model for compensating credit-rating agencies has a potential conflict of interest that may distort the accuracy of credit ratings. (This weakness applies to third-party ratings only.)

EXAMPLE 3

A bond portfolio manager has $500,000 to invest in two bonds. He collects the S&P credit ratings and yields to maturity on four hypothetical debt issues:

- Green Company, AA–, 5%
- Sleepy Company, B–, 7%
- Red Fruit Corp, BBB+, 6.5%
- Slot Machines Incorporated, CCC, 9%

Rank the companies in terms of their credit risk. Which companies are investment grade?

Solution:

Using Exhibit 1, the ranking is Green Company, Red Fruit Corp, Sleepy Company, and Slot Machines Inc. The investment-grade bonds are Green Company and Red Fruit Corp.

Traditional credit ratings are applied to corporate debt, government debt, quasi-government debt, and asset-backed securities. Asset-backed securities have some unique characteristics and are discussed in Section 7 of this reading.

STRUCTURAL MODELS

4

Credit-rating agencies use a number of analytical tools to develop their ratings. Structural models underlie the default probabilities and credit analytics provided by Moody's KMV and other vendors, including Kamakura Corporation. **Structural models** were originated to understand the economics of a company's liabilities and build on the insights of option pricing theory. They are called structural models because they are based on the *structure* of a company's balance sheet.

To understand structural models, it is easiest to start with a company with a simple financing structure. The balance sheet of this hypothetical company is shown in Exhibit 3.

Exhibit 3   Balance Sheet of a Simple Company at Time t

Assets A_t	Debt $D(t,T)$
	Zero-coupon bond

(continued)

Exhibit 3   (Continued)

- maturity T
- face value K

_____

Equity S_t

The company illustrated in Exhibit 3 has assets, liabilities, and equity on its balance sheet. The assets have a time t value of A_t dollars. The liabilities consist of a single debt issue, which is a zero-coupon bond with a face value of K dollars that matures at time T. The time t value of the zero-coupon bond is denoted $D(t,T)$. Finally, the time t value of the company's equity is denoted S_t. The value of the company's assets must equal the total value of its liabilities and equity:

$$A_t = D(t,T) + S_t$$

The company's owners (equity holders) have *limited liability*; the equity holders' liability to the debt holders extends only to the company's assets and not their personal wealth. Alternatively stated, if the equity holders default on the debt payment at time T, the debt holders' only recourse is to take over the company and assume ownership of the company's assets. They have no additional claim on the equity holders' personal wealth. This limited liability is the basis for the analogy between the company's equity and a call option.

4.1 The Option Analogy

To illustrate the option analogy, let us consider the equity holders' decision to pay off the debt at time T. The equity holders will pay off the debt at time T only if it is in their best interests to do so. Because at time T the value of the company's assets is A_T, the equity holders will pay off the debt only if the value of the assets at time T exceeds what is owed—that is, $A_T \geq K$. After the payment, they keep what's left over $(A_T - K)$. If $A_T < K$, the equity holders will default on the debt issue. Consequently, the time T value of the equity is:

$$S_T = \begin{cases} A_T - K & \text{if} \quad A_T \geq K \\ 0 & \text{if} \quad A_T < K \end{cases} = \max[A_T - K, 0]$$

It is now easy to see the *call option analogy* for equity. The company's equity has the same payoff as a European call option on the company's assets with strike price K and maturity T. Hence, holding the company's equity is economically equivalent to owning a European call option on the company's assets. This is the key insight of the structural model.

The time T value of the company's debt is:

$$D(T,T) = \begin{cases} K & \text{if} \quad A_T \geq K \\ A_T & \text{if} \quad A_T < K \end{cases} = \min[K, A_T]$$

This expression states that the debt holders get the face value, K, back if the time T asset value exceeds this payment. Otherwise, the equity holders default and the bondholders take over the company and collect the value of the company's assets. The implication is that:

- the probability that the debt defaults at time T is equal to the probability that the asset's value falls below the face value of the debt—that is, $\text{prob}(A_T < K)$—and

- the loss given default is the quantity $K - A_T$.

To determine these quantities for practical usage, we need to make some assumptions, which are discussed in Section 4.2. Before doing this, we can express $D(T,T)$ in an alternative way by adding K before the bracket and subtracting K inside the bracket on the right side of the previous expression. Doing so gives:

$$D(T,T) = K - \begin{cases} 0 & \text{if} \quad A_T \geq K \\ K - A_T & \text{if} \quad A_T < K \end{cases} = K - \max[K - A_T, 0]$$

In this equation, we see that the debt's time T payoff is equivalent to getting K dollars with certainty less the payoff to a European put option on the company's assets with strike price K and maturity T. We now have a *debt option analogy*:

> Owning the company's debt is economically equivalent to owning a riskless bond that pays K dollars with certainty at time T, and simultaneously selling a European put option on the assets of the company with strike price K and maturity T.

The debt option analogy explains why risky debt is less valuable than riskless debt. The difference in value is equal to the short put option's price. In essence, the debt holders lend the equity holders K dollars and simultaneously sell them an insurance policy for K dollars on the value of their assets. If the assets fall below K, the debt holders take the assets in exchange for their loan. This possibility creates the credit risk.

4.2 Valuation

To use the structural model to determine a company's credit risk, we need to add assumptions that enable us to explicitly value the implied call and put options. To do this, the standard application of the structural model imposes the same assumptions used in option pricing models. These assumptions are

1 the company's assets trade in frictionless markets that are arbitrage free,

2 the riskless rate of interest, r, is constant over time, and

3 the time T value of the company's assets has a lognormal distribution with mean uT and variance $\sigma^2 T$.

The first assumption implies that there are no transaction costs and states that the company's assets are traded in markets that are arbitrage free. "Frictionless markets" means that the markets are *liquid*, with no bid–ask spreads and no quantity impact of a trade on the market price. It also implies that the company's asset value is observable at all times. This implication is significant, and we will return to its importance later in the reading. The no-arbitrage argument is needed to price the option.

The second assumption is that the riskless rate of interest is a constant over time. In other words, there is no interest rate risk in the model. When studying fixed-income securities whose values change with movements in interest rates, this assumption is unrealistic. Because this assumption is not satisfied in actual markets, it is a weakness of this model's formulation.

The third assumption states that the company's asset value evolves over time according to a lognormal distribution with an expected return equal to $u\%$ per year and a volatility equal to $\sigma\%$ per year. Consequently, the expected return and volatility of the company's assets over the time period $[0,T]$ are uT and $\sigma^2 T$, respectively.

These three assumptions are identical to those for stock price behavior in the original Black–Scholes option pricing model. Hence, the Black–Scholes option pricing formula applies to the equity's time t value because it is a European call option on the company's assets. The formula is:

$$S_t = A_t N(d_1) - Ke^{-r(T-t)}N(d_2)$$

where

$$d_1 = \frac{\ln\left(\frac{A_t}{K}\right) + r(T-t) + \frac{1}{2}\sigma^2(T-t)}{\sigma\sqrt{T-t}}$$

$$d_2 = d_1 - \sigma\sqrt{T-t}$$

$N(.)$ = the cumulative standard normal distribution function with mean 0 and variance 1.

The value of the debt can be obtained using the accounting identity $A_t = D(t,T) + S_t$. Substitution of the formula for S_t into this accounting identity gives:

$$D(t,T) = A_t N(-d_1) + Ke^{-r(T-t)}N(d_2)$$

The first term in this expression, $A_t N(-d_1)$, corresponds to the present value of the payoff on the company's debt if default occurs. The second term in this expression, $Ke^{-r(T-t)}N(d_2)$, corresponds to the present value of the payoff on the company's debt if default does not occur. A close examination of the second term shows that the risk-neutral probability of the company's debt not defaulting, $\text{prob}(A_T \geq K)$, is equal to $N(d_2)$. The sum of these two terms, therefore, gives the present value of the company's debt.

This valuation formula is useful for understanding the probability of default, the expected loss, and the present value of the expected loss as shown in the next section.

4.3 Credit Risk Measures

For the evaluation of credit risk, the structural model enables one to explicitly calculate the credit risk measures discussed in Section 2. The following formulas are obtained from the formula for the company's debt, $D(t,T)$, as given in the previous expression.

▪ The probability of the debt defaulting is:

$$\text{prob}(A_T < K) = 1 - \text{prob}(A_T \geq K) = 1 - N(e_2),$$

where

$$e_1 = \frac{\ln\left(\frac{A_t}{K}\right) + u(T-t) + \frac{1}{2}\sigma^2(T-t)}{\sigma\sqrt{T-t}}$$

$$e_2 = e_1 - \sigma\sqrt{T-t}$$

This expression follows from noting that $\text{prob}(A_T \geq K) = N(e_2)$.

▪ The expected loss is:

$$KN(-e_2) - A_t e^{u(T-t)}N(-e_1)$$

- The present value of the expected loss is obtained by subtracting the value of the debt, $D(t,T)$, from the value of a default-free (riskless) zero-coupon bond:

$$KP(t,T) - D(t,T) = Ke^{-r(T-t)}N(-d_2) - A_tN(-d_1)$$

where $P(t,T) = e^{-r(T-t)}$ is the time t price of a default-free zero-coupon bond paying a dollar at time T.

It is important for the reader to note the following facts about the formulas in this section:

- The present value of the expected loss is the difference between the value of a riskless zero-coupon bond paying K dollars at maturity and the value of the risky debt:

$$Ke^{-r(T-t)} - D(t,T)$$

Alternatively, the present value of the expected loss is also given by the risk-neutral expected discounted loss:

$$\tilde{E}\big(K - D(T,T)\big)e^{-r(T-t)}$$

where $\tilde{E}(.)$ denotes taking an expectation using the risk-neutral probabilities.

- In this computation, the riskless rate is used to discount the future cash flows. The cash flows' risks are captured in this computation by replacing the actual probabilities with the risk-neutral probabilities. The difference between the use of $\{d_1,d_2\}$ in the present value of the loss and $\{e_1,e_2\}$ in the probability of a loss is due to the difference between the risk-neutral and the actual probabilities. The risk-neutral probabilities are determined by assuming that the asset value's expected return is the riskless rate r (see $\{d_1,d_2\}$), whereas the actual probabilities use the asset value's real expected return of u% per year (see $\{e_1,e_2\}$).

- The probability of default depends explicitly on the company's assumed liability structure. We mention this fact here for subsequent comparison with the reduced form model. This explicit dependency of the probability of default on the company's liability structure is a limitation of the structural model.

These credit risk measures can be calculated given the inputs $\{A_t, u, r, \sigma, K, T\}$.

EXAMPLE 4

Interpreting Structural Model Credit Risk Measures

Assume a company has the following values:

- Time t asset value: A_t = $1000.
- Expected return on assets: u = 0.03 per year.
- Risk-free rate: r = 0.01 per year.
- Face value of debt: K = $700.
- Time to maturity of debt: $T - t$ = 1 year.
- Asset return volatility: σ = 0.30 per year.

The company's credit risk measures can now be computed. We first need to compute some intermediate quantities:

$$d_1 = \frac{\ln\left(\frac{1{,}000}{700}\right) + 0.01(1) + \frac{1}{2}(0.3)^2(1)}{0.3\sqrt{1}} = 1.37225$$

$$d_2 = 1.37225 - 0.3\sqrt{1} = 1.07225$$

$$N(-d_1) = 0.0850$$

$$N(-d_2) = 0.1418$$

$$e_1 = \frac{\ln\left(\frac{1{,}000}{700}\right) + 0.03(1) + \frac{1}{2}(0.3)^2(1)}{0.3\sqrt{1}} = 1.43892$$

$$e_2 = 1.43892 - 0.3\sqrt{1} = 1.13892$$

$$N(-e_1) = 0.0751$$

$$N(-e_2) = 0.1274$$

The probability of default is $\text{prob}(A_T < K) = N(-e_2) = 0.1274$, or 12.74% over the debt's time to maturity, which is one year.

The expected loss is:

$$KN(-e_2) - A_t e^{u(T-t)} N(-e_1) = 700(0.1274) - 1{,}000 e^{0.03}(0.0751) = \$11.78$$

The present value of the expected loss is:

$$KP(t,T) - D(t,T) = Ke^{-r(T-t)} N(-d_2) - A_t N(-d_1)$$
$$= 700 e^{-0.01(1)}(0.1418) - 1{,}000(0.0850) = \$13.28$$

In this example, the present value of the expected loss on the $700 bond is $13.28. This value is how much an investor would pay to a third party (an insurer) to remove the risk of default from holding this bond. The expected loss itself is only $11.78.

The difference between the expected loss and the present value of the expected loss includes:

A a premium for the risk of credit loss only.

B a discount for the time value of money only.

C both a discount for the time value of money and a premium for the risk of credit loss.

Solution:

C is correct. The $1.50 difference includes both a discount for the time value of money and the risk premium required by the market to bear the risk of credit loss. In this case, the present value of the expected loss exceeds the expected loss. This means that the risk premium must dominate the difference because the time-value-of-money discount will reduce the present value of the expected loss compared with the expected loss. In other words, in the absence of a risk premium, the present value of the expected loss will be less than the expected loss.

We now discuss estimating the inputs to the model.

4.4 Estimation

Before discussing the estimation of these inputs to the structural model, it is helpful to discuss parameter estimation in option pricing models more generally. There are two ways to estimate the parameters of any option pricing model: *historical* and *implicit*.

Historical estimation is where one uses past time-series observations of the underlying asset's price and standard statistical procedures to estimate the parameters. For example, to estimate the asset's expected return and volatility in the structural model using historical estimation, one obtains past time-series observations of the asset's value, A_t, (say, daily prices for one year) and then computes the mean return over the year and the return's standard deviation.

Implicit estimation, also called *calibration*, uses market prices of the options themselves to find the value of the parameter that equates the market price to the formula's price. In other words, calibration finds the implied value of the parameter. For example, consider using the standard Black-Scholes call option pricing model for a stock option. To estimate the underlying stock's volatility using implicit estimation, one would observe the market value of the call option and find the volatility that equates the Black-Scholes formula to the call's market price, called the *implied volatility*. This procedure is standard in equity option markets. As illustrated by this example, implicit estimation always involves solving an equation, or a set of equations, for an unknown—in this case, the implied volatility.

For the structural model, one cannot use historical estimation. The reason is that the company's assets (which include buildings and non-traded investments), in contrast to our initial assumption, do not trade in frictionless markets. Consequently, the company's asset value is *not observable*. Because one cannot observe the company's asset value, one cannot use standard statistics to compute a mean return or the asset return's standard deviation.

This leaves implicit estimation as the only alternative for the structural model. Implicit estimation is a complex estimation procedure and underlies some commercial vendors' default probability estimates, including Moody's KMV. This procedure requires that the company's equity be actively traded so that a time series of market prices for the company's equity is available, which enables the computation of the company's asset value parameters using the company's debt-to-equity ratio. Here is a step-by-step description of the procedure for computing the company's asset value parameters $\{A_t, \sigma\}$.

- Collect a time series of equity market prices, S_t, for $t = 1, ..., n$ (for example, daily prices over the last year).

- From these equity prices, compute the equity's volatility, which is the sample standard derivation, denoted $\sqrt{var\left(\dfrac{dS}{S}\right)}$.

- For each time t, set up the following two equations:

$$S_t = A_t N(d_1) - Ke^{-r(T-t)}N(d_2)$$

and

$$\sqrt{var\left(\frac{dS}{S}\right)} = N(d_1)\frac{A_t}{S_t}$$

- Solve these *2n* equations for the $(n + 1)$ unknowns: $\{A_t$ for $t = 1, ..., n$; and $\sigma\}$.

The only remaining parameter to estimate is the company's asset expected return per year, u. Standard practice is to use an equilibrium capital asset pricing model (CAPM) in conjunction with an estimate for the riskless rate, r, to determine u. In the simplest CAPM (a static one-period model), one can write the company's asset return as equal to the risk-free rate plus a risk premium determined by the company's asset beta:

$$u = r + \beta(u_m - r)$$

where β is the beta of the company's asset, u_m is the expected return per year on the market portfolio, and $(u_m - r)$ is the market's equity risk premium. Of course, to use this estimate, one must first determine the company's asset beta and the expected return on the market portfolio. Modern portfolio theory provides the methods for doing this. Standard statistics can be used to estimate the market portfolio's mean return, and linear regression can be used to estimate the company's equity beta. Given an estimate of the company's equity beta, the company's asset beta can be deduced by unlevering the company's equity beta. Estimation of the market's equity risk premium is more challenging because there is no observable expected return on the market portfolio. There is no agreement in the financial community on which method to use to estimate the market's equity risk premium. Many finance professionals advocate the use of a more realistic multi-period CAPM that includes multiple risk factors in the risk premium rather than a single-factor CAPM. However, there is no consensus on how many and which risk factors to include.

A positive attribute of the Black–Scholes model is that it does not require an estimate of a risk premium. It made the formula usable in practice. The fact that one needs to estimate the market's equity risk premium in the computation of the company's default probability is a weakness of the structural model.

A well-known problem with implicit estimation, or calibration more generally, is that if the model's assumptions are not reasonable approximations of the market's actual structure, then the implicit estimate will incorporate the model's error and not represent the true parameter. This bias will, in turn, introduce error into the resulting probability of default and the expected loss, thereby making the resulting estimates unreliable. Unfortunately, this criticism applies to the structural model because its assumptions are not a good representation of reality. This is true for the following reasons:

- A typical company's balance sheet will have a liability structure much more complex than just the simple zero-coupon bond structure represented in Exhibit 3.

- Interest rates are not constant over time. This issue is serious because when dealing with fixed-income securities that involve significant interest rate risk, assuming that interest rates are constant is equivalent to assuming interest rate risk is irrelevant.

- The assumed lognormal distribution for asset prices implies a "thin" tail for the company's loss distribution. There is significant evidence that a company's loss distribution has a left tail "fatter" than those implied by a lognormal distribution.

- It is assumed that the asset's return volatility is constant over time, independent of changing economic conditions and business cycles.

- In contrast to a key assumption, the company's assets do not trade in frictionless markets; examples include buildings and non-traded investments.

The strength of the structural model is the useful economic intuition it provides for understanding the risks involved in a company's debt and equity, which is a primary value of learning this model. Although the structural model underlies some credit risk estimates used in practice, the implausibility of the assumptions underlying structural models brings the models into question. Although many of the structural model's assumptions can be relaxed or modified, the assumption that assets trade in frictionless markets is a defining characteristic of structural models and cannot be relaxed. Generalizing the frictionless market assumption generates the reduced form model discussed in the next section.

Structural Model Strengths

- It provides an option analogy for understanding a company's default probability and recovery rate.
- It can be estimated using only current market prices.

Structural Model Weaknesses

- The default probability and recovery rate depend crucially on the assumed balance sheet of the company, and realistic balance sheets cannot be modeled.
- Its credit risk measures can be estimated only by using implicit estimation procedures because the company's asset value is unobservable.
- Its credit risk measures are biased because implicit estimation procedures inherit errors in the model's formulation.
- The credit risk measures do not explicitly consider the business cycle.

REDUCED FORM MODELS

5

Reduced form models were originated to overcome a key weakness of the structural model—the assumption that the company's assets trade. Reduced form models replace this assumption with a more robust one—that some of the company's debt trades. They are called reduced form models because they impose their assumptions on the outputs of a structural model—the probability of default and the loss given default—rather than on the balance sheet structure itself. Unlike structural models, this change in perspective gives reduced form models tremendous flexibility in matching actual market conditions.

To understand reduced form models, it is easiest to start with a company where one of the liabilities is a zero-coupon bond with face value K and maturity T. For easy comparison with the structural model in the previous section, we denote the time t value of this debt as $D(t,T)$. We divide the time period $[0,T]$ up into the time intervals $0, \Delta, 2\Delta, ..., T - \Delta$ of length Δ.

Reduced form models make the following assumptions:

1 The company's zero-coupon bond trades in frictionless markets that are arbitrage free;

2 The riskless rate of interest, r_t, is stochastic;

3 The state of the economy can be described by a vector of stochastic variables X_t that represent the *macroeconomic* factors influencing the economy at time t;

4 The company defaults at a random time t, where the probability of default over $[t,t + \Delta]$ when the economy is in state X_t is given by $\lambda(X_t)\Delta$;

5 Given the vector of macroeconomic state variables X_t, a company's default represents idiosyncratic risk; and

6 Given default, the percentage loss on the company's debt is $0 \le \iota(X_t) \le 1$.

The first assumption requires only that one of the company's liabilities, a zero-coupon bond, trades in frictionless and arbitrage-free markets. Reduced form models do not assume that the company's assets trade. They also do not assume that the company's remaining liabilities or even its equity trades. Other liabilities could be used in place of a zero-coupon bond. Finally, markets are assumed to be liquid, with no transaction costs or bid–ask spreads, and markets are assumed to be arbitrage free.

The second assumption allows interest rates to be stochastic. Allowing for this possibility is essential to capture the interest rate risk inherent in the pricing of fixed-income securities. Only the term structure evolution must be arbitrage free.

The third assumption is that the relevant state of the economy can be described by a vector of macroeconomic state variables X_t. For example, this set of state variables might include the riskless rate, the inflation rate, the level of unemployment, the growth rate of gross domestic product, and so forth. This set of macroeconomic state variables is stochastic, and its evolution is completely arbitrary. This assumption is not very restrictive.

The fourth, fifth, and sixth assumptions are imposed on the outputs of a structural model, which are the probability of default and the loss given default. The fourth assumption is that the default time can be modeled as a Cox process, with a *default intensity* of $\lambda(X_t)$. Given a company that has not yet defaulted, the **default intensity** gives the probability of default over the next instant $[t, t + \Delta]$ when the economy is in state X_t. The key advantage of this assumption is that the default probability explicitly depends on the business cycle through the macroeconomic state variables X_t. This allows, for example, for the probability that default increases in a recession and declines in a healthy economy. This is a very general method of modeling default over time. In fact, this formulation allows for systemic defaults across companies.

The fifth assumption states that, given the state of the economy, whether a particular company defaults depends only on company-specific considerations. For example, suppose that in a recession, the probability of default increases. Now consider two car companies, General Motors and Ford. In a recession, the probability that each car company defaults will increase. This happens via the dependence of the default intensity on the macroeconomic state variables X_t. The idiosyncratic risk assumption is different. It states that whether either of these two companies actually defaults in a recession depends on each company's actions and not the macroeconomic factors. A company-specific action could be that the company's management made an error in their debt choice in years past, which results in their defaulting now. Management error is idiosyncratic risk, not economy-wide or systematic risk.

An open research question is whether, conditioned on the state of the economy, default risk is idiosyncratic. Although this assumption can be easily relaxed, relaxing it introduces the necessity of estimating a default risk premium. Although it can be done, it introduces additional complexity into the estimation process. We include this assumption here because it is a reasonable first approximation and because it simplifies both the notation and subsequent explanations.

The sixth assumption states that if default occurs, debt is worth only $[1 - \iota(X_t)]$ of its face value. Here, $[1 - \iota(X_t)]$ is the percentage recovery rate on the debt in the event of default. The loss given default, $\iota(X_t)$, explicitly depends on the business cycle through the macroeconomic state variables. This allows, for example, that in a recession the loss given default is larger than it is in a healthy economy. This assumption is also very general and not restrictive.

These six assumptions underlying the reduced form model are very general, allowing the default probability and the loss given default to depend on the business cycle, as reflected in the macroeconomic state variables X_t. Given a proper specification of the functional forms for the default intensity and loss given default and stochastic processes for the spot rate of interest and the macroeconomic variables, they provide a reasonable approximation of actual debt markets.

5.1 Valuation

Under the assumption of no arbitrage, it can be shown that option pricing methodology when applied to a reduced form model implies that risk-neutral probabilities exist such that the debt's price is equal to the expected discounted payoff to the debt at maturity—that is,

$$D(t,T) = \tilde{E}\left[\frac{K}{(1 + r_t\Delta)(1 + r_{t+\Delta}\Delta)\ldots(1 + r_{T-\Delta}\Delta)}\right]$$

where $\tilde{E}(.)$ denotes taking an expectation using the risk-neutral probabilities.

The expression shows that the debt's value is given by the expected discounted value of the K dollars promised at time t. The discounting is done using the risk-free rate over the time intervals $0, \Delta, \ldots, T - \Delta$. The adjustment for the risk of the debt's cash flows occurs through the use of the risk-neutral probabilities when taking the expectation.

Although the lengthy and challenging proof is not shown here, this expression can be written as:

$$D(t,T) = \tilde{E}\left\langle\frac{K}{\{1 + [r_t + \lambda(X_t)]\Delta\}\{1 + [r_{t+\Delta} + \lambda(X_{t+\Delta})]\}\ldots\{1 + [r_{T-\Delta} + \lambda(X_{T-\Delta})]\Delta\}}\right\rangle +$$

$$\sum_{i=t}^{T-\Delta}\tilde{E}\left\langle\frac{K[1 - \iota(X_i)]}{\{1 + [r_t + \lambda(X_t)]\Delta\}\{1 + [r_{t+\Delta} + \lambda(X_{t+\Delta})]\}\ldots\{1 + [r_i + \lambda(X_i)]\Delta\}}\lambda(X_i)\Delta\right\rangle$$

This expression decomposes the value of the company's debt into two parts. The first term on the right side of this expression represents the debt's expected discounted payoff K given that *there is no default* on the company's debt. Note that the discount rate on the right side of this expression, $[r_u + \lambda(X_u)]$ has been increased for the risk of default. The second term on the right side of this expression represents the debt's expected discounted payoff *if default occurs*. This is equal to the payoff if default occurs *at time i*, $K[1 - i(X_i)]$, multiplied by the probability of default at time i, $\lambda(X_i)$ Δ, discounted, and then summed across all the times $0, \Delta, \ldots, T - \Delta$. In this last term, observe that the loss is subtracted from the debt's promised face value. In conjunction, these observations prove that the valuation formula explicitly incorporates both the loss given default and the intensity process.

This form of the debt's price is very abstract and very general. In any application, a particular evolution for both the interest rate and macroeconomic state variable vector needs to be specified. Many such structures have been used in the literature and practice. We illustrate one useful choice later in this section as an example. The study of more complex specifications is outside the scope of this reading and left for independent reading.

For this reading, we are especially interested in quantifying the credit risk measures discussed in Section 2.

5.2 Credit Risk Measures

In the reduced form model, the credit risk measures are quantified as follows:

■ The probability of the debt defaulting over $[0,T]$ is:

$$\text{prob}(\tau \leq T) = 1 - E\left\{\frac{1}{[1 + \lambda(X_0)\Delta][1 + \lambda(X_\Delta)]\ldots[1 + \lambda(X_{T-\Delta})\Delta]}\right\}$$

where $E(.)$ denotes taking an expectation using the actual probabilities.

- The expected loss is:

$$\sum_{i=0}^{T-\Delta} E\left\{ \frac{\iota(X_i)K}{\left[1 + \lambda(X_0)\Delta\right]\left[1 + \lambda(X_\Delta)\right]\cdots\left[1 + \lambda(X_i)\Delta\right]} \lambda(X_i)\Delta \right\}$$

- The present value of the expected loss is:

$$KP(t,T) - D(t,T)$$

where $D(t,T)$ is given in the formula in section 5.1.

All of these quantities can be easily computed given the required inputs and the probability distribution for the macroeconomic state variables and interest rates. Note that, unlike the structural model, the company's probability of default does not explicitly depend on the company's balance sheet. The same default probability applies to all of the company's liabilities because of the existence of cross-default clauses in corporate debt. In the event of default, reduced form models allow the company's different liabilities to have different loss rates. These are significant advantages of using a reduced form model.

Before discussing the estimation of these inputs, we discuss a simple scenario (constant default probability and loss given default) to illustrate the interpretation of these formulas. This discussion will also prove useful in a subsequent section to understand the term structure of credit spreads.

5.2.1 *Constant Default Probability and Loss Given Default Formulas*

This section illustrates the reduced form pricing formulas for a zero-coupon bond under the following special (and unrealistic) assumptions.

- The default probability is a constant—that is, $\lambda(X_t) = \lambda$.

    This assumption implies that the probability of default does not depend on the macroeconomic state of the economy.

- The dollar loss given default is a constant percentage of the zero-coupon bond's value just before default—that is, $\iota(X_\tau)K = \gamma D(\tau-,T)$.

    Here, the symbol $\tau-$ means the instant just before default. Note that, as with the probability of default, the loss given default also does not depend on the macroeconomic state of the economy under this assumption.

Combined, these two additional assumptions imply that the zero-coupon bond's price takes the following special form (see Jarrow 2009):

$$D(t,T) = Ke^{-\lambda\gamma(T-t)}P(t,T)$$

where $P(t,T)$ is the time t value of a default-free zero-coupon bond paying one dollar at time T.

The risky zero-coupon bond's price is equal to the fraction $0 < e^{-\lambda\gamma(T-t)} < 1$ of an otherwise equivalent, but riskless, zero-coupon bond's price $KP(t,T)$. The risky company's expected percentage loss per unit of time appears in the exponent of the fraction. To see this, note that

$\lambda\gamma$ = (Probability of default per year) × (Percentage loss given default)

= Expected percentage loss per yearUnder this structure, one can also show that the three credit risk measures are:

- the probability of the debt defaulting over $[0,T]$:

$$\text{prob}(\tau \le T) = 1 - e^{-\lambda(T-t)}$$

- the expected loss:

$$K[1 - e^{-\lambda\gamma(T-t)}] \text{ and}$$

- the present value of the loss given default:

$$KP(t,T) - D(t,T) = KP(t,T)[1 - e^{-\lambda\gamma(T-t)}]$$

Note that in the expected loss and the present value of the expected loss, because the default probability does not depend on the macroeconomic state of the economy, the actual and risk-neutral default probabilities are equal and depend only on λ. Later in this reading, we will use these simple formulas to help understand the term structure of credit spreads and to provide a simple method to estimate expected losses.

EXAMPLE 5

Interpreting Reduced Form Model Credit Risk Measures

Assume a company has the following values for its debt issue:

- Face value: $K = \$700$,
- Time to maturity: $T - t = 1$ year,
- Default intensity (the approximate probability of default per year): $\lambda = 0.01$, and
- Loss given default: $\gamma = 0.4$ (40%).

Let the one-year default-free zero-coupon bond's price, $P(t,T)$, equal 0.96. The company's probability of default, expected loss, and present value of the expected loss using the constant intensity and loss given default formulas are as follows:

Probability of default:

$$\text{prob}(\tau \leq T) = 1 - e^{-0.01(1)} = 0.00995$$

Expected loss:

$$K[1 - e^{-\lambda\gamma(T-t)}] = 700[1 - e^{-0.004(1)}] = \$2.79$$

Present value of the expected loss:

$$KP(t,T) - D(t,T) = 700(0.96)[1 - e^{-0.004(1)}] = \$2.68$$

The probability of default over the life of the bond is 0.995%. The expected loss on the $700 bond is $2.79. The present value of the expected loss is $2.68.

1 The largest amount a bondholder would pay to a third party (an insurer) to remove the credit risk of the bond is:

A $0.11.

B $2.68.

C $2.79.

2 In this case, the premium for the risk of credit loss:

A dominates the discount for the time value of money.

B balances out the discount for the time value of money.

C is dominated by the discount for the time value of money.

Solution to 1:

B is correct. The present value of the expected loss is $2.68. This is the largest amount one would pay to a third party (an insurer) to remove the credit risk from the bond.

Solution to 2:

In this case, the present value of the expected loss is less than the expected loss. The time value of money dominates the risk premium. In other words, the risk premium is dominated by the time value of money.

5.3 Estimation

As explained in the previous section, there are two approaches that can be used to estimate a model's parameters: historical and implicit. As with structural models, implicit estimation is possible. Unlike with structural models, however, historical estimation can be used for a reduced form model because the economy's macroeconomic state variables and the company's debt prices are both observable. This ability to use historical estimation with a reduced form model is a significant advantage of this approach to credit modeling. This section studies both approaches to estimating the parameters of a reduced form model.

5.3.1 *Implicit Estimation*

To use implicit estimation, one must completely specify the inputs to the reduced form model and the probability distributions for the macroeconomic state variables. Many such choices are possible. An illustration of such a choice is given in the previous example. Once a choice is made, the resulting formula for the zero-coupon bond's price will depend on a set of parameters θ—that is, $D(t,T \mid \theta)$. Using this price formula, the goal is to estimate the parameters θ. For example, in the previous example, the parameters θ equal the constant recovery rate and default probability.

For the moment, let us assume that we can directly observe the risky company's zero-coupon bond prices. Although these zero-coupon bonds may not trade in practice, we will show in the next section how to estimate these zero-coupon bond prices from observable risky coupon bond prices, which do trade.

Following is a step-by-step description of the procedure for computing the reduced form model's parameters:

■ Collect a time series of risky debt market prices, $D_{market}(t,T)$ for $t = 1, 2, ..., n$ (for example, daily prices over the last year).

■ For each time t, set up the equation $D_{market}(t,T) = D(t,T \mid \theta)$.

■ Solve these n equations for the parameters θ.

The problem with implicit estimation, of course, is that if one uses a misspecified model—a model that is inconsistent with the market structure—then the resulting estimates will be biased. For example, in the previous illustration, *by assumption*, the default probability and loss given default do not depend on the macroeconomic state of the economy. This is not true in practice. If one uses this model to estimate these parameters, one will get different estimates depending on the state of the economy—economic expansion or recession—in contradiction to the model's assumptions. This contradiction implies that the parameter estimates obtained by this procedure are unreliable. This problem can be avoided by historical estimation, which we discuss next.

5.3.2 *Historical Estimation*

Estimating a reduced form model's parameters using historical estimation is an application of **hazard rate estimation**. Hazard rate estimation is a technique for estimating the probability of a binary event, like default/no default, mortality/no mortality, car crash/no car crash, prepay/no prepay, and so on. It is widely used in medical research and is applicable to enterprise risk management for the full spectrum of insurance-type events. Credit risk is one of those applications.

In theory, default can occur continuously in time. In practice, however, we have default data corresponding only to discrete time intervals. Hence, reduced form credit models must be estimated and implemented using discrete time statistical procedures. We will now illustrate how to estimate the default probability using a hazard rate estimation procedure.

Exhibit 4 shows typical default data for corporate debt. The first column gives the name of a company. In this example, we only list two: Citigroup and Lehman Brothers. Of course in the actual database, all existing companies need to be included. The second column gives the *default flag*, which equals 1 if the given company defaults during the time period indicated and 0 if no default occurred. The time period under consideration is given in the third column. Here, the time period corresponds to a month. Note that Lehman Brothers defaulted on its debt in September 2008, whereas Citigroup did not default over this sample period.

The remaining columns give the macroeconomic state variables X_t, augmented to include company-specific measures, collectively called the *explanatory variables*. They can include borrower-specific balance sheet items, dummy variables for calendar year effects, or other variables. In Exhibit 4, the explanatory variables are market leverage, the stock's return less the riskless rate (called the excess return), the stock's volatility, the Chicago Board Options Exchange Volatility Index (VIX, an index that measures the implied volatility of the S&P 500 Index), the net income to total assets ratio, and the unemployment rate. Other variables could have been included.

Once the default database has been assembled, as in Exhibit 4, the next step is to select a functional form for the intensity process. A convenient choice is the logistic function:

$$\text{prob}(t) = \frac{1}{1 + e^{-\alpha - \sum_{i=1}^{N} b_i X_t^i}}$$

where prob(t) is the probability of default over $[t, t + \Delta]$, $X_t = \left(X_t^1, ..., X_t^N \right)$ represents the N state variables, and $\{\alpha, b_i \text{ for } i = 1, ..., N\}$ are constants.

Exhibit 4	Sample Default Data for Public Company Default Database							
	Dependent Variable			**Explanatory Variables**				
Company	**Default Flag**	**Date**	**Market Leverage**	**Excess Return**	**Stock Volatility**	**VIX**	**Net Income/ Total Assets**	**Unemployment Rate**
Citigroup	0	6/30/2010	0.944985	0.144827	0.571061	34.54	0.002212	9.7
Citigroup	0	7/30/2010	0.937445	0.18934	0.511109	23.5	0.001392	9.5
Citigroup	0	8/31/2010	0.943071	−0.28633	0.43267	26.05	0.001392	9.5
Citigroup	0	9/30/2010	0.940171	−0.27173	0.353897	23.7	0.001392	9.6
Citigroup	0	10/29/2010	0.937534	−0.14237	0.343142	21.2	0.001093	9.6

(continued)

Exhibit 4 (Continued)

Company	Default Flag	Date	Market Leverage	Excess Return	Stock Volatility	VIX	Net Income/ Total Assets	Unemployment Rate
Citigroup	0	11/30/2010	0.937113	−0.05561	0.371965	23.54	0.001093	9.6
Citigroup	0	12/31/2010	0.929734	0.301176	0.369208	17.75	0.001093	9.8
Citigroup	0	1/31/2011	0.925846	0.254157	0.355727	19.53	0.000684	9.4
Citigroup	0	2/28/2011	0.927821	0.174812	0.322558	18.35	0.000684	9.0
Citigroup	0	3/31/2011	0.931556	−0.04238	0.312913	17.74	0.000684	8.9
Citigroup	0	4/29/2011	0.929757	−0.12338	0.254542	14.75	0.00154	8.8
Citigroup	0	5/31/2011	0.936565	−0.19566	0.244869	15.45	0.00154	9.0
Citigroup	0	6/30/2011	0.935858	−0.17385	0.293736	16.52	0.00154	9.1
Lehman	0	1/31/2008	0.984411	−0.30473	0.376592	28.655	0.0012528	6.8
Lehman	0	2/28/2008	0.983969	−0.17537	0.362842	26.07	0.0012528	6.7
Lehman	0	3/31/2008	0.976221	−0.08861	0.329009	23.32	0.0012528	6.7
Lehman	0	4/30/2008	0.972138	0.268176	0.319171	25.894	0.0009837	6.7
Lehman	0	5/31/2008	0.974212	0.221157	0.259633	19.525	0.0009837	6.7
Lehman	0	6/30/2008	0.978134	0.141812	0.249766	21.483	0.0009837	6.7
Lehman	0	7/31/2008	0.976245	−0.07538	0.299611	20.185	0.0006156	6.9
Lehman	1	8/31/2008	0.983393	−0.15638	0.384124	19.514	0.0006156	6.6

In this equation, prob(t) represents the probability of default over the time period $[t, t + \Delta]$ and $\{\alpha, b_i$ for $i = 1, ..., N\}$ are the parameters to be estimated. The time period Δ is measured in years, so a month corresponds to $\Delta = 1/12$.

The parameters can be estimated using maximum likelihood estimation.[6] This can be a complex computational exercise. It can be shown that this maximum likelihood estimation is equivalent to running the following simple *linear regression* to estimate the coefficients:

$$\ln\left(\frac{d_t}{1 - d_t}\right) = \alpha + \sum_{i=1}^{N} b_i X_t^i$$

where the dependent variable (the left side of the regression) includes the default flag

$d_t = \{1$ if default, 0 if no default$\}$.

This is called a *logistic regression* because of the function on the left side of this expression. Exhibit 5 shows the outputs from running a logistic regression based on data similar to those given in Exhibit 4 but using only four explanatory variables. The first one, unemployment, is a macroeconomic variable that is the same for all companies. The last three variables—the market leverage ratio (accounting liabilities divided by the market value of equity), the net income to assets ratio, and the cash to assets ratio—are specific to the company.

---

6 The maximum likelihood estimator is the estimator that maximizes the probability (the "likelihood") that the observed data was generated by the model. In addition to intuitive appeal, maximum likelihood estimators have good statistical properties.

Exhibit 5 Sample Logistic Regression Results

Coefficient Name	Coefficient Value	Input Value	Input Name
Alpha	−3		
b1	0.8	0.072	Unemployment (decimal)
b2	1.5	0.9	Market leverage ratio (decimal)
b3	−2	0.01	Net income/assets (decimal)
b4	−1	0.05	Cash/assets (decimal)

Given the coefficients in Exhibit 5, for any time period t, one can substitute the explanatory variables in the logistic function equation to get an estimate of the default probability, prob(t), for the time period considered. In Exhibit 4, we used monthly observation periods, so the default probability given is an estimate for the default probability over the next month. For example, substituting the specific input values shown in Exhibit 5 in the logistic function produces a monthly default probability estimate of

$$\text{prob}(t) = \frac{1}{1 + e^{3 - 0.8(0.072) - 1.5(0.9) + 2(0.01) + 1(0.05)}} = 0.1594, \text{ or } 15.94\%$$

EXAMPLE 6

Assume that the credit analysis department has derived a new logistic regression model for the one-year default probability. The coefficients of the model and the inputs for Easy Company are given in Exhibit 6.

Exhibit 6 Logistic Regression

Coefficient Name	Coefficient Value	Input Value	Input Name
Alpha	−4		Constant term
b1	0.07	0.091	Unemployment (decimal)
b2	1.3	0.93	Market leverage ratio (decimal)
b3	−1.96	0.0045	Net income/Assets (decimal)
b4	0.5	0.0315	US Treasury 10-year (decimal)
b5	−0.93	0.043	Cash/Assets (decimal)

What is the one-year probability of default for Easy Company?

Solution:

$$\text{prob}(t) = \frac{1}{1 + e^{4 - 0.07(0.091) - 1.3(0.93) + 1.96(0.0045) - 0.5(0.0315) + 0.93(0.043)}}$$
$$= 0.05638, \text{ or } 5.638\%$$

Estimation of the default probability using the hazard rate estimation methodology is very flexible. The default probabilities generated correspond to default over the next time period, and they depend explicitly on the state of the economy and the company, as represented by the choice of the explanatory variables included in the estimation. The default probabilities are for all of the company's liabilities because of the cross-default clauses present in corporate debt.

To estimate the loss given default process $\{\iota(X_s)\}$, one can use a similar procedure. First, one needs to specify the function form of $\iota(X_s)$. For example, one could assume that

$$\iota(X_t) = c_0 + \sum_{i=1}^{N} c_i X_t^i$$

where $\{c_i \text{ for } i = 1, ..., N\}$ are constants.

Other functional forms are also possible. To estimate such an equation, one needs historical observations of losses on defaulted debt issues (the left side of the equation). These losses are often available internally within a financial institution's records. The independent variables on the right side correspond to the relevant explanatory variables; for example, they could be the same state variables used in the hazard rate estimation. Given these data, the coefficients of the regression are obtained and the state conditional losses given default are estimated.

Reduced Form Model Strengths

- The model's inputs are observable, so historical estimation procedures can be used for the credit risk measures.
- The model's credit risk measures reflect the changing business cycle.
- The model does not require a specification of the company's balance sheet structure.

Reduced Form Model Weakness

- Hazard rate estimation procedures use past observations to predict the future. For this to be valid, the model must be properly formulated and back tested.

5.4 Comparison of Credit Risk Models

The previous sections have introduced three approaches for evaluating a debt's credit risk: credit ratings, structural models, and reduced form models. All three models have been empirically evaluated with respect to their accuracy in measuring a debt issue's default probability. Of the three approaches, credit ratings are the least accurate predictors. This is because credit ratings tend to lag changes in a debt issue's credit risk because of rating agencies' desire to keep ratings relatively stable over time, and consequently, they are relatively insensitive to changes in the business cycle.

Reduced form models perform better than structural models because structural models are computed using implicit estimation procedures whereas reduced form models are computed using historical estimation (hazard rate procedures). The improved performance is due to the flexibility of hazard rate estimation procedures—that is, both their ability to incorporate changes in the business cycle and their independence of a particular model specifying a company's balance sheet structure.

THE TERM STRUCTURE OF CREDIT SPREADS

This section covers the term structure of credit risk spreads, its composition, and how to use **credit spreads** to estimate the present value of the expected loss and the expected percentage loss per year. These estimates are used regularly by financial institutions in their fixed-income investment decisions and computation of their risk management measures. In practice, because risky coupon bonds trade, credit risk spreads are inferred from coupon bond prices. To understand this calculation, we must first understand the valuation of credit risky coupon bonds.

6.1 Coupon Bond Valuation

In this section, we discuss the arbitrage-free pricing theory for coupon bonds. First, consider a default-free coupon bond with coupons equal to C dollars paid at times $i = 1, 2, ..., T$, a face value of F dollars, and a maturity of time T. It is well known that under the assumptions of no arbitrage and frictionless markets, the price of this coupon bond can be written as:

$$B_G(t) = \sum_{i=1}^{T-1} CP(t,i) + (C + F)P(t,T)$$

where $B_G(t)$ is the time t price of the default-free coupon bond.

Unfortunately, for an otherwise credit risky coupon bond—with *promised* coupons equal to C dollars paid at times $i = 1, 2, ..., T$, a face value of F dollars, and a maturity of time T—and the corresponding risky zero-coupon bonds, a similar relation need not hold. The reason is that although the coupon and zero-coupon bonds may come from the same company, they can differ in their seniority and the percentage loss given default. To avoid this situation, we need to impose the following condition on the risky debt issued by the same company:

$B_G(t)$ and $D(t,T)$ for all T must be of *equal priority* in the event of default

where $D(t,T)$ is the time t price of a zero-coupon bond issued by the company. By "equal priority," we mean that in the event of default, the remaining promised cash flows on all these bonds have equal proportionate losses, where the equal proportionality loss factors across bonds can depend on the date of the promised payments. Under this equal priority condition, the following condition holds:

$$B_C(t) = \sum_{i=1}^{T-1} CD(t,i) + (C + F)D(t,T)$$

where $B_C(t)$ is the time t price of the risky coupon bond.

The proof of this pricing formula is straightforward. Because of equal priority, the coupon bond on the left side of this expression and the portfolio of zero-coupon bonds represented by the right side of this expression always have the same cash flows, regardless of default. Consequently, these two methods of obtaining the same future cash flows must have the same price at time t or an arbitrage opportunity exists. This completes the proof.

This sufficient condition is not very restrictive. When computing credit spreads, one wants to hold constant for credit risk. Because different seniority bonds from the same company can have different credit risk, one should always partition bonds into equal seniority before starting any credit risk computation.

6.2 The Term Structure of Credit Spreads

The term structure of credit spreads corresponds to the spread between the yields on default-free and credit risky zero-coupon bonds. In practice, because coupon bonds (rather than zero-coupon bonds) often trade for any given company, to compute the credit spreads one first needs to estimate the zero-coupon bond prices implied by the coupon bond prices. This estimation is done using the previous equations. The typical step-by-step procedure is as follows:

- At a given time t, collect N coupon bond prices $\{B_C(t)\}$ for a set of distinct bonds where the maximum-maturity bond in the collection has maturity $T_{max} < N$. This guarantees that there are more bonds than unknowns in the dataset.

- For each distinct bond, we have an equation:

$$B_C(t) = \sum_{i=1}^{T-1} CD(t,i) + (C + F)D(t,T)$$

  The unknowns $\{D(t,i)$ for $t = 1, ..., T_{max}\}$ are the same across all N equations.

- Solve the N equations for the T_{max} unknowns, $\{D(t,i)$ for $t = 1, ..., T_{max}\}$.

For the remainder of this section, without loss of generality, we will assume that at time t, we observe both the term structure of default-free and risky zero-coupon bond prices $\{P(t,T), D(t,T)$ for all $T\}$.

The next step is to compute the yields on these zero-coupon bonds. The yields on the risky $[y_D(t,T)]$ and riskless $[y_P(t,T)]$ zero-coupon bonds are defined by the following expressions:

$$D(t,T) = Ke^{-y_D(t,T)(T-t)} \text{ and}$$

$$P(t,T) = e^{-y_P(t,T)(T-t)}$$

Using these formulas, one generates a set of yields for a discrete set of maturities $\{T = 1, ..., T_{max}\}$, where T_{max} is the largest maturity of all the zero-coupon bonds considered. The credit spread is defined by *Credit spread*$(t) = y_D(t,T) - y_P(t,T)$.

From these discrete observations, one can obtain a smoothed yield curve using standard smoothing procedures.[7] A smoothed credit spread is illustrated in Exhibit 7. This credit spread is for Treasuries versus swaps (that have the risk of a highly rated European bank). For this exhibit, we used US Treasuries to illustrate these computations, although any sovereign's bonds could have been used instead.

---

7 van Deventer, Imai, and Mesler (2004).

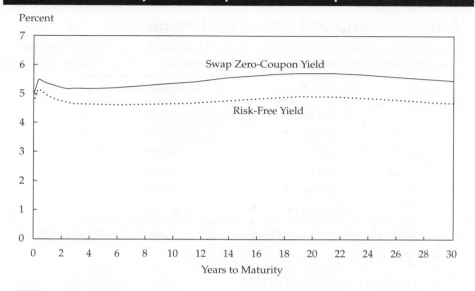

Exhibit 7   US Treasury and ABC Corporation Zero-Coupon Yields

Note: US Treasury and ABC Corporation zero-coupon yields are derived from the Federal Reserve H15 Statistical Release using maximum smoothness forward rate smoothing.
Sources: Kamakura Corporation; Board of Governors of the Federal Reserve.

Using either the structural or reduced form model, *under the frictionless market assumption*, the credit spread is entirely due to credit risk. To see this, it is easiest to use the constant default probability and loss given default formulas of Section 5.2.1.

Recall that the risky zero-coupon bond's price in this example is given by:

$$D(t,T) = Ke^{-\lambda\gamma(T-t)}P(t,T)$$

Performing some algebraic adjustments in the previous equation gives:

$$-\frac{\ln\left(\dfrac{d(t,T)}{K}\right)}{(T-t)} = \lambda\gamma - \frac{\ln\left[P(t,T)\right]}{(T-t)}$$

Using the definition of the yields, we see that the credit spread equals:

$$y_D(t,T) - y_P(t,T) = \lambda\gamma$$

Here, the credit spread is equal to the expected percentage loss per year on the risky zero-coupon bond. It is equal to difference between the average yields on the risky zero-coupon bond and the riskless zero-coupon bond.

This example enables us to estimate the expected percentage loss per year implied by the credit spread. It is a rough estimate because the assumption that the default probability and loss given default are constants is not true in practice.

The following is a basic description of the procedure for computing the "back-of-the-envelope" estimate of the expected percentage loss per year.

- Collect a time series of zero-coupon bond yields $\{y_D(t,T), y_P(t,T)\}$ for $t = 1, ..., n$.

- Compute the average yield spread, which gives the estimate:

$$\frac{\sum_{t=1}^{n} y_D(t,T) - y_P(t,T)}{n} = \lambda\gamma$$

EXAMPLE 7

Estimate of Expected Percentage Loss per Year

An analyst finds that the one-year yields on HandSoap Corporation (a Japanese company) and Japanese bonds over the past week are as shown below:

Japanese Bonds	HandSoap Corp.
0.0115	0.0357
0.0116	0.0358
0.0116	0.0359
0.0117	0.0360
0.0118	0.0360
Avg.: 0.01164	Avg.: 0.03588

Compute the expected percentage loss per year implied by these yields.

Solution:

$$\lambda\gamma = 0.03588 - 0.01164 = 0.02424.$$

6.3 Present Value of the Expected Loss

This section shows how to compute the present value of the expected loss using the term structure of credit spreads. From the term structure of credit spreads, one needs to compute the term structure of default-free and risky zero-coupon bond prices $\{P(t,T), D(t,T)$ for all $T\}$. The method for computing these zero-coupon bond prices was discussed in the previous section.

Consider a risky company that has a *promised* cash flow of X_T dollars at time T. The present value of the expected loss is given by:

$$[P(t,T) - D(t,T)]X_T$$

This represents the present value of the cash flow, if riskless, less the present value of the cash flow considering credit risk. Using this simple formula, it is easy to calculate the present value of the expected loss.

EXAMPLE 8

Present Value of the Expected Loss

1 Consider Powder Corporation, a German manufacturer, which has promised to pay investors 25 euros on 30 September 2014. Today is 11 August 2011. The risk-free zero-coupon yield on German bonds is 0.3718%. The Powder Corporation credit spread for payment due 30 September 2014 is 0.2739%. For convenience, we have made the assumption that the bonds of the German government are risk free and that there are 365 days in each year. All yields and spreads are continuously compounded.

What is the present value of Powder Corporation's promise to pay both on a credit risky basis and a risk-free basis? What is the present value of the expected loss implied by the credit spread?

Payment Date	Risk-Free Zero-Coupon Yields (%)	Credit Spread (%)	Total Yield (%)	Years to Maturity	Discount Factor	Cash Flow	Present Value	Risk-Free Discount Factor	Risk-Free Present Value	Present Value Difference
9/30/2014	0.3718	0.2739	0.6457	3.1397	0.979930	25	24.4983	0.9884	24.7099	−0.2116

Solution to 1:

The promise to pay 25.00 euros on 30 September 2014 is worth 24.4983 euros considering credit risk. It is worth 24.7099 on a risk-free basis, so the present value of the expected loss due to credit risk is 0.2116.

2   Suppose that Powder Corporation has also promised to pay 25 euros on 31 March 2016. Today is 11 August 2011. The risk-free yield from 11 August 2011 to that date is 0.8892%, and the credit spread is 0.5688%.

What are the credit-adjusted valuation, the risk-free valuation, and the present value of the expected loss due to credit risk?

Payment Date	Risk-Free Zero-Coupon Yields (%)	Credit Spread (%)	Total Yield (%)	Years to Maturity	Discount Factor	Cash Flow	Present Value	Risk-Free Discount Factor	Risk-Free Present Value	Present Value Difference
3/31/2016	0.8892	0.5688	1.4580	4.6411	0.934571	25	23.3643	0.9596	23.9893	−0.6250

Solution to 2:

The credit-adjusted valuation is 23.3643 euros, derived using the continuously compounded total yield. The value on a risk-free basis is 23.9893 euros, so the present value of the expected loss due to credit risk is 0.6250 euro.

3   Suppose now that Powder Corporation has made a promise to pay 1,025 euros on 30 September 2017. Today is 11 August 2011. The risk-free yield from 11 August 2011 to that date is 1.4258%, and the credit spread is 0.8747%. What are the credit-adjusted valuation, the risk-free valuation, and the present value of the expected loss due to credit risk?

Payment Date	Risk-Free Zero-Coupon Yields (%)	Credit Spread (%)	Total Yield (%)	Years to Maturity	Discount Factor	Cash Flow	Present Value	Risk-Free Discount Factor	Risk-Free Present Value	Present Value Difference
9/30/2017	1.4258	0.8747	2.3004	6.1425	0.868226	1025	889.9319	0.9161	939.0528	−49.1209

Solution to 3:

The credit-adjusted present value is 889.9319 euros, and the risk-free valuation is 939.0528 euros. The expected loss due to credit risk is 49.1209 euros.

4   Suppose now that Powder Corporation issues a ten-year 5% coupon bond with semi-annual payment dates and principal of 1,000 euros. The value of this bond at time t when there are n payments remaining is:

$$B_C(t) = \sum_{i=1}^{n} 25D(t,i) + (1,025)D(t,n)$$

The value if this bond were risk free is:

$$B_G(t) = \sum_{i=1}^{n} 25P(t,i) + (1,025)P(t,n)$$

The loss in value due to credit risk is $B_G(t) - B_C(t)$.

Today is 11 August 2011. Let the two payment dates be 30 September and 31 March. The bond, which was originally issued in 2007, matures on 30 September 2017. Using the risk-free yields and credit spreads prevailing on 11 August 2011, what are the credit-adjusted values, risk-free values, and present value of the expected loss due to credit risk on this bond? (Note that valuations will be net present values and accrued interest (an accounting concept) should be ignored.)

Coupon Rate	5.00%
Coupon Payments	Semi-annual
Principal Amount	1000

Payment Dates	Risk-Free Zero-Coupon Yields (%)	Credit Spread (%)	Total Yield (%)	Years to Maturity	Discount Factor	Cash Flow	Present Value	Risk-Free Discount Factor	Risk-Free Present Value	Present Value Difference
9/30/2011	0.0134	0.0696	0.0830	0.1370	0.999886	25	24.9972	1.0000	24.9995	−0.0024
3/31/2012	0.0947	0.1160	0.2107	0.6384	0.998565	25	24.9664	0.9994	24.9849	−0.0185
9/30/2012	0.1033	0.1209	0.2242	1.1397	0.997448	25	24.9362	0.9988	24.9706	−0.0344
3/31/2013	0.1463	0.1454	0.2917	1.6384	0.995233	25	24.8808	0.9976	24.9402	−0.0593
9/30/2013	0.2061	0.1795	0.3856	2.1397	0.991783	25	24.7946	0.9956	24.8900	−0.0954
3/31/2014	0.2723	0.2172	0.4895	2.6384	0.987167	25	24.6792	0.9928	24.8210	−0.1418
9/30/2014	0.3718	0.2739	0.6457	3.1397	0.979930	25	24.4983	0.9884	24.7099	−0.2116
3/31/2015	0.5160	0.3561	0.8722	3.6384	0.968765	25	24.2191	0.9814	24.5350	−0.3159
9/30/2015	0.6953	0.4583	1.1536	4.1397	0.953368	25	23.8342	0.9716	24.2907	−0.4565
3/31/2016	0.8892	0.5688	1.4580	4.6411	0.934571	25	23.3643	0.9596	23.9893	−0.6250
9/30/2016	1.0808	0.6781	1.7589	5.1425	0.913520	25	22.8380	0.9459	23.6484	−0.8104
3/31/2017	1.2597	0.7800	2.0397	5.6411	0.891310	25	22.2828	0.9314	23.2851	−1.0024
9/30/2017	1.4258	0.8747	2.3004	6.1425	0.868226	1025	889.9319	0.9161	939.0528	−49.1209
Total Value							1180.2228		1233.1174	−52.8945

Solution to 4:

Note that three of the payments on this bond were analyzed previously in Questions 1, 2, and 3.

The sum of all credit-adjusted values gives us the total net present value of the bond, 1,180.2228 euros. On a risk-free basis, the bond is worth 1,233.1174 euros, so the present value of the expected loss from credit risk is 52.8945 euros.

5 Consider XYZ Corporation (based in France), which issues a 20-year bond in euros in 2003. The bond has a 6% coupon, payable annually. The bond matures on 30 November 2023, and interest payments are due on 30 November of each year.

What is the credit-adjusted value, the risk-free value, and the present value of the expected loss on this bond if one uses the risk-free yields and credit spreads prevailing on XYZ bonds as of 11 August 2011?

Note that these yields are continuously compounded yields and we are assuming for simplicity that there are 365 days in each year.

Coupon Rate	6.00%
Coupon Payments	Annual
Principal Amount	1000

Payment Dates	Risk-Free Zero-Coupon Yields (%)	Credit Spread (%)	Total Yield (%)	Years to Maturity	Discount Factor	Cash Flow	Present Value	Risk-Free Discount Factor	Risk-Free Present Value	Present Value Difference
11/30/2011	0.0413	0.1323	0.1736	0.3041	0.9995	60	59.9683	0.9999	59.9925	−0.0241
11/30/2012	0.1132	0.2024	0.3156	1.3068	0.9959	60	59.7530	0.9985	59.9113	−0.1583
11/30/2013	0.2265	0.3128	0.5393	2.3068	0.9876	60	59.2582	0.9948	59.6874	−0.4291
11/30/2014	0.4153	0.4969	0.9123	3.3068	0.9703	60	58.2170	0.9864	59.1816	−0.9646
11/30/2015	0.7592	0.8322	1.5915	4.3068	0.9338	60	56.0252	0.9678	58.0698	−2.0446
11/30/2016	1.1423	1.2057	2.3480	5.3096	0.8828	60	52.9673	0.9412	56.4691	−3.5018
11/30/2017	1.4873	1.5333	3.0116	6.3096	0.8269	60	49.6165	0.9109	54.6566	−5.0401
11/30/2018	1.7705	1.8183	3.5888	7.3096	0.7693	60	46.1557	0.8786	52.7164	−6.5608
11/30/2019	2.0358	2.0770	4.1128	8.3096	0.7105	60	42.6313	0.8444	50.6619	−8.0306
11/30/2020	2.2786	2.3136	4.5922	9.3123	0.6520	60	39.1226	0.8088	48.5286	−9.4060
11/30/2021	2.4950	2.5247	5.0197	10.3123	0.5959	60	35.7553	0.7731	46.3884	−10.6331
11/30/2022	2.6842	2.7091	5.3934	11.3123	0.5433	60	32.5973	0.7381	44.2872	−11.6899
11/30/2023	2.8474	2.8682	5.7156	12.3123	0.4947	1060	524.4249	0.7043	746.5366	−222.1117
Total Value							1116.4926		1397.0873	−280.5947

Solution to 5:

XYZ Corporation's bond is analyzed in exactly the same way as the Powder Corporation bond analyzed in Example 4.

The credit-adjusted value is 1,116.4926 euros, and the risk-free value is 1,397.0873 euros. The expected loss due to credit losses is 280.5947 euros.

When considering the decomposition of the credit spread in either the structural or reduced form models, the assumption was made that markets are frictionless. This assumption implies, of course, that there is no quantity impact of a purchase or sale on the price of the security. Such a quantity impact on the purchase or sale price introduces *liquidity risk*, which was assumed away in both of these models. In reality, of course, markets are not frictionless and liquidity risk plays an important role.

In practical applications, one must recognize that the "true" credit spread will consist of both the expected percentage loss (as in the structural and reduced form models) and a liquidity risk premium—that is, $y_D(t,T) - y_P(t,T) = E(\text{Percentage loss}) + \text{Liquidity premium}$.

The liquidity premium will be positive in practice because sovereign government bonds trade in more liquid markets than do most corporate bonds.

7   ASSET-BACKED SECURITIES

In this section, we introduce **asset-backed securities** (ABS). They are discussed separately because they are distinct from either corporate or sovereign debt in the structure of their future cash flows. ABS can appear deceptively similar to corporate debt with similar stated provisions: coupon payments, face value, and maturity date. However, ABS are complex fixed-income instruments created through a process known as securitization.

An asset-backed security is a type of bond issued by a legal entity called a special purpose entity (SPE) or special purpose vehicle (SPV). An SPE is formed to own the pool of securitized assets from which the cash flows will be generated. The pool of securitized assets is typically referred to as the collateral for the ABS. The collateral usually consists of a collection of loans or receivables of a particular type. ABS are classified by the loans or receivables that are the collateral. For example, residential mortgage–backed securities (RMBS) have residential mortgages as their collateral, commercial mortgage–backed securities (CMBS) have commercial mortgages as their collateral, credit card receivables ABS have credit card receivables as their collateral, collateralized debt obligations (CDOs) hold a variety of asset types (corporate bonds, residential mortgages, commercial mortgages, or other ABS) as their collateral, and so forth. The loans and receivables in the pool of securitized assets generate cash flows from interest payments and scheduled and early repayments of principal. The pool of securitized assets can also incur losses if any of the loans or receivables default.

Similar to a company, an SPE is created by the equity holders. To finance the purchase of the collateral, the equity holders issue debt. The structure of the debt for an SPE is different from that of typical corporate debt. An SPE's debt is issued in various bond tranches. The bonds usually have a stated maturity, face value, and coupon payment. The bond tranches are differentiated by their seniority with respect to their receipt of the collateral's cash flows and losses.

The cash flows are paid first to the most senior bond tranches, then to the next senior, and so forth until all coupon payments are paid. Any residual cash flows go to the equity holders. The losses due to defaulting loans go in reverse order. Any losses are first covered by the equity holders, then the least senior bond tranche, and so forth up to the most senior bond tranche. This allocation of cash flows and losses is called the *waterfall*. In practice, the waterfall is often more complex, containing triggers based on the characteristics of the collateral to divert more cash flows to the most senior bond tranches if the collateral's cash flows decline significantly. These triggers are essentially embedded options. A typical SPE is illustrated in Exhibit 8.

Exhibit 8   A Typical Asset-Backed Security SPV

Assets	Liabilities	Waterfall	
Collateral pool (loans)	Senior bond tranche	Cash flows ↓	Losses ↑
	Mezzanine bond tranche		
	Junior bond tranche		
	. . .		
	Equity		

Unlike corporate debt, an ABS does not go into default when an interest payment is missed. A default in the pool of securitized assets does not cause a default to either the SPE or a bond tranche. For an ABS, the bond continues to trade until either its maturity date or all of its face value is eliminated because of the accumulated losses in the pool of securitized assets or through early loan prepayments. An ABS may be better characterized as a credit derivative than a simple bond because of the complexity of the cash flows.

To value the ABS bond tranches, as with the valuation of any credit derivative, either a structural model or a reduced form model can be used. The valuation must necessarily start with modeling the composition of the collateral pool and the cash flow waterfall. In practice, this exercise is very difficult and complex because different SPEs have different waterfalls. Monte Carlo simulation procedures are often used in practice. The valuation and hedging of ABS, and more generally credit derivatives, are left to future readings.

With respect to credit risk, the credit risk measures used for corporate or sovereign bonds can be applied: probability of loss, expected loss, and present value of the expected loss. As mentioned previously, in this case, the probability of default does not apply, so it is replaced by the probability of a loss. To calculate these measures, a model analogous to those used for corporate and sovereign debt is used. However, the calculations are much more complex.

With respect to the credit ratings of ABS, the credit-rating agencies use the same rating scale as that used for corporate and sovereign debt, although the fact that they are distinct in the structure of their future cash flows is always noted; they may be referred to as structured finance *debt* securities or structured debt. Given the complexity of ABS, the use of the same credit-rating scales may be inappropriate. Some have argued that the credit agencies mis-rated ABS prior to 2007 and that this mis-rating contributed to the 2008 global financial crisis and the subsequent losses.[8] The alleged mis-ratings of structured debt has raised questions about the validity and use of credit ratings. New regulatory reforms have since been introduced by governments around the world, and credit-rating companies have positively responded with changes to their rating methodologies.

SUMMARY

Credit risk analysis is extremely important to a well-functioning economy. Financial crises often originate in the mis-measuring of, and changes in, credit risk. Mis-rating can result in mispricing and misallocation of resources. This reading discusses a variety of approaches to credit risk analysis: credit scoring, credit rating, structural models, and reduced form models. In addition, the reading discusses asset-backed securities and explains why using approaches designed for credit risk analysis of debt may result in problematic measures. Key points of the reading include the following:

- There are four credit risk measures of a bond: the probability of default, the loss given default, the expected loss, and the present value of the expected loss. Of the four, the present value of the expected loss is the most important because it represents the highest price one is willing to pay to own the bond and, as such, it incorporates an adjustment for risk and the time value of money.

---

8 See "Wall Street and the Financial Crisis: Anatomy of a Financial Collapse," Majority and Minority Staff Report, US Senate Committee on Special Investigations (13 April 2011).

- Credit scoring and credit ratings are traditional approaches to credit risk assessment, used to rank retail borrowers.

- During the financial crisis, credit-rating agencies mis-rated debt issues, generating concern over the method in which credit-rating agencies are paid for their services.

- Structural models of credit risk assume a simple balance sheet for the company consisting of a single liability, a zero-coupon bond. Structural models also assume the assets of the company trade and are observable.

- In a structural model, the company's equity can be viewed as a European call option on the assets of the company, with a strike price equal to the debt's face value. This analogy is useful for understanding the debt's probability of default, its loss given default, its expected loss, and the present value of the expected loss.

- The structural model's inputs can only be estimated using calibration, where the inputs are inferred from market prices of the company's equity.

- Reduced form models of credit risk consider a company's traded liabilities. Reduced form models also assume a given process for the company's default time and loss given default. Both of these quantities can depend on the state of the economy as captured by a collection of macroeconomic factors.

- Using option pricing methodology, reduced form models provide insights into the debt's expected loss and the present value of the expected loss.

- The reduced form model's inputs can be estimated using either calibration or historical estimation. Historical estimation is the preferred methodology; it incorporates past time-series observations of company defaults, macroeconomic variables, and company balance sheet characteristics. Hazard rate estimation techniques are used in this regard.

- The term structure of credit spreads is the difference between yields on risky bonds versus default-free zero-coupon bonds. These yields can be estimated from the market prices of traded coupon bonds of both types.

- The present value of the expected loss on any bond can be estimated using the term structure of credit spreads.

- Asset-backed securities (ABS) are issued by a special purpose entity (SPE). The SPE's assets, called the collateral, consist of a collection of loans or receivables. To finance its assets, the SPE issues bonds (the ABS) in tranches that have different priorities with respect to cash flows and losses, called the waterfall.

- ABS do not default, but they can lose value as the SPE's pool of securitized assets incurs defaults. Modeling an ABS's credit risk—the probability of loss, the loss given default, the expected loss, and the present value of the loss—is a complex exercise.

REFERENCES

Chava, S., and R. Jarrow. 2004. "Bankruptcy Prediction with Industry Effects." *Review of Finance*, vol. 8, no. 4:537–569.

Heath, D., R. Jarrow, and A. Morton. 1992. "Bond Pricing and the Term Structure of Interest Rates: A New Methodology for Contingent Claims Valuation." *Econometrica: Journal of the Econometric Society*, vol. 60, no. 1 (January):77–105.

Jarrow, R. 2009. "Credit Risk Models." *Annual Review of Financial Economics*, vol. 1, no. December:37–68.

Jarrow, R., and S. Turnbull. 1992. "Credit Risk: Drawing the Analogy." *Risk Magazine*, 5 (9).

Jarrow, R., and S. Turnbull. 1995. "Pricing Derivatives on Financial Securities Subject to Credit Risk." *Journal of Finance*, vol. 50, no. 1 (March):53–85.

Merton, R.C. 1974. "On the Pricing of Corporate Debt: The Risk Structure of Interest Rates." *Journal of Finance*, vol. 29, no. 2 (May):449–470.

van Deventer, D.R., K. Imai, and M. Mesler. 2004. *Advanced Financial Risk Management: Tools and Techniques for Integrated Credit Risk and Interest Rate Risk Management.* Hoboken, NJ: John Wiley & Sons.

PRACTICE PROBLEMS

The following information relates to Questions 1–8

Campbell Fixed Income Analytics provides credit analysis services on a consulting basis to fixed income managers. A new hire, Liam Cassidy, has been asked by his supervisor, Malcolm Moriarty, to answer some questions and to analyze a corporate bond issued by Dousing Dragons (DD). Moriarty is trying to assess Cassidy's level of knowledge.

Moriarty asks Cassidy:

"Why are clients willing to pay for structural and reduced form model analytics when they can get credit ratings for free?"

Cassidy identifies the following limitations of credit ratings:

Limitation A   The issuer-pays model may distort the accuracy of credit ratings.

Limitation B   Credit ratings tend to vary across time and across the business cycle.

Limitation C   Credit ratings do not provide an estimate of a bond's default probability.

Cassidy is asked to consider the use of a structural model of credit risk to analyze DD's bonds. Cassidy knows that holding DD's equity is economically equivalent to owning a type of security that is linked to DD's assets. However, Cassidy cannot remember the type of security or why this is true. Moriarty provides a hint:

"It is true because equity shareholders have limited liability."

Moriarty asks Cassidy to analyze one of DD's bonds using data presented in Exhibit 1 and a reduced form model.

Exhibit 1   Dousing Dragons, Inc. Credit Analysis Worksheet

Coupon rate:	0.875%				Coupon Payments:	Semiannual				
Face value:	1,000									
Today's date:	August 15, 2014				Maturity date:	August 15, 2018				

Payment dates:	Risk-free Zero Coupon Yields (Percent)	Credit Spread (Percent)	Total Yield (Percent)	Years to Maturity	Discount Factor	Cash Flow	Present Value	Risk-free Discount Factor	Risk-free Present Value
2/15/2015	0.13	0.12	0.25	0.50	0.99880	4.38	4.3747	0.9994	4.3774
8/15/2015	0.20	0.24	0.44	1.00	0.99560	4.38	4.3607	0.9980	4.3712
2/15/2016	0.23	0.31	0.54	1.50	0.99200	4.38	4.3450	0.9966	4.3651
8/15/2016	0.28	0.37	0.65	2.00	0.98710	4.38	4.3235	0.9944	4.3555
2/15/2017	0.32	0.38	0.70	2.50	0.98270	4.38	4.3042	0.9920	4.3450
8/15/2017	0.35	0.39	0.74	3.00	0.97810	4.38	4.2841	0.9896	4.3344

Exhibit 1   (Continued)

Payment dates:	Risk-free Zero Coupon Yields (Percent)	Credit Spread (Percent)	Total Yield (Percent)	Years to Maturity	Discount Factor	Cash Flow	Present Value	Risk-free Discount Factor	Risk-free Present Value
2/15/2018	0.44	0.43	0.87	3.50	0.97010	4.38	4.2490	0.9848	4.3134
8/15/2018	0.47	0.46	0.93	4.00	0.96370	1,004.38	967.9210	0.9814	985.6985
Total value:							998.1623		1,016.1606

Moriarty also asks Cassidy to discuss the similarities and differences in the analysis of asset-backed securities (ABS) and corporate debt. Cassidy states that:

Statement 1   Credit analysis for ABS and corporate bonds incorporates the same credit measures: probability of default, expected loss, and present value of expected loss.

Statement 2   Credit analysis for ABS and corporate bonds is different due to their future cash flow structures.

Statement 3   Credit analysis for ABS and corporate bonds can be done using either a structural or a reduced form model.

1 Which of Cassidy's stated limitations of credit ratings is *incorrect*?

    A Limitation A

    B Limitation B

    C Limitation C

2 Given Moriarty's hint, Cassidy should *most likely* identify the type of security as a European:

    A put option.

    B call option.

    C debt option.

3 The model chosen by Moriarty to analyze one of DD's bonds requires that:

    A the equity of DD is traded.

    B the assets of DD are traded.

    C some of the debt of DD is traded.

4 Compared to a structural model, which of the following estimation approaches will Moriarty's choice of credit model allow him to use?

    A Implicit

    B Historical

    C Calibration

5 Compared to a structural model, an advantage of the model chosen by Moriarty to analyze DD's bond is *most likely* that:

    A its measures reflect the changing business cycle.

    B it requires a specification of the company's balance sheet.

    C it is possible to estimate the expected present value of expected loss.

6 Based on Exhibit 1, the present value of the expected loss due to credit risk on the bond is *closest* to:

   A   1.84.

   B   16.16.

   C   18.00.

7 Based on Exhibit 1, the present value of the expected loss due to credit risk relating to the single promised payment scheduled on February 15, 2017, is *closest* to:

   A   0.04.

   B   0.08.

   C   0.11.

8 Which of Cassidy's statements relating to the similarities and differences between the credit analysis of ABS and corporate bonds is *incorrect*?

   A   Statement 1

   B   Statement 2

   C   Statement 3

The following information relates to Questions 9–14

Elisabeta Borrego is a credit analyst for a large global pension fund. She and her colleagues conduct original research and also use research provided by outside analysts.

Borrego holds a weekly meeting with interns and junior analysts at which they discuss credit analysis topics. Her notes from the most recent meeting are shown in Exhibit 1.

Exhibit 1   Meeting Notes from Session with Interns and Junior Analysts

Following are two comments on the expected loss on a bond:

Comment 1	A sufficient condition for Company A to have a higher expected loss than Company B is that it has a higher probability of default than Company B.
Comment 2	A sufficient condition for Company X to have a higher present value of expected loss than Company Y is that it has a higher expected loss on its bond than Company Y.

Following are three comments on bond ratings:

Comment A	A company's bonds have maintained the same bond rating for two business cycles, which means the company has maintained the same probability of default.
Comment B	Suppose two firms have the same bond rating. If the bond rating for one firm improves one level and the bond rating for the other firm drops one level, the changes in the probability of default for the two bonds should be equal (but with different signs).
Comment C	The issuer-pays model, in which the bond issuer pays the credit rating agency to rate its debt, creates an incentive conflict.

Exhibit 1   (Continued)

Gehr Company case:

> Gehr Company's only debt is a zero-coupon bond maturing in one
> year with a promised payoff equal to 70% of the value of its assets
> today. Gehr sells some of its existing assets and purchases new assets
> with the same value but higher risk. How will these transactions affect
> the values of Gehr's outstanding bonds and common stock if we view
> the equity as a European call option?

Borrego and her colleagues use both structural models and reduced form models
to analyze bond risks. They use structural models, based on the insights of option
pricing theory, to estimate credit analytics and default probabilities. Borrego has
two concerns with using structural models: "First, historical estimation of inputs
is a problem if any of the assets of the firm do not trade in frictionless markets and
we cannot observe their values. Second, implicit estimation, the other way to obtain
inputs for structural models, also has its flaws. If the assumptions of the models used
to obtain the implicit estimates are not reasonable approximations of the market's
actual structure, it can cause errors in the estimates of the probability of default and
the expected loss."

Borrego and her team often use a reduced form model to estimate bond default
rates. Specifically, they use a logistic regression to predict defaults with historical
inputs. An advantage of the reduced form model, Borrego states, is the fact that the
input variables are observable. She states that its disadvantage is that past observations are used to predict the future, which means the model must be well formulated
and back tested.

Borrego's firm has invested in a mortgage-backed special purpose entity that has
four tranches: senior bond tranche, mezzanine bond tranche, junior bond tranche, and
equity. Borrego's colleague, Jeremy Maklin, advises her that the quality of the collateral
pool is important in evaluating the different tranches. He says, "The waterfall contains
triggers based on the characteristics of the collateral pool that divert more cash flows
to the most senior bond tranches if the collateral pool's cash flows decline significantly.
Furthermore, I do not consider the cash flows and risk of an asset-backed bond and
a corporate bond to be equivalent, even if they have the same coupon payments, face
value, maturity, and bond ratings."

9 Which comments from the meeting notes in Exhibit 1 about the expected loss
   on a bond are *correct*?

   A Only Comment 1

   B Only Comment 2

   C Neither Comment 1 nor 2

10 Which comment about bond ratings from the meeting notes in Exhibit 1 is
    correct?

   A Comment A

   B Comment B

   C Comment C

11 How will Gehr's sale and purchase of assets (noted in Exhibit 1) affect the val-
    ues of its bonds and common stock?

   A The values of Gehr's bonds and common stock will both decline.

    B   The value of the bonds will decline and the value of common stock will increase.

    C   The values of Gehr's bonds and common stock will both increase.

12 Are Borrego's concerns about the problems of historical or implicit estimation of the inputs for structural models correct?

    A   Yes

    B   No, only her first concern is correct

    C   No, only her second concern is correct

13 With regard to using a reduced form model to predict bond defaults, are the advantage and disadvantage stated by Borrego correct?

    A   Only the advantage is correct.

    B   Only the disadvantage is correct.

    C   Both the advantage and the disadvantage are correct.

14 Are Maklin's statements about the waterfall and the equivalence of asset-backed bonds and corporate bonds correct?

    A   Only his statement about the waterfall is correct.

    B   Only his statement about the equivalence of the types of bonds is correct.

    C   Both of his statements are correct.

The following information relates to Questions 15–20

Meg Chole, a senior credit analyst for a large commercial bank, recently hired Stacy Garzon as a junior credit analyst. As a part of Garzon's training, Chole reviews with Garzon the various credit analysis services provided by the bank.

Chole indicates that many financial institutions and rating agencies use structural models to assess credit risk. She provides Garzon with a simple balance sheet for a firm that has assets, debt consisting of a zero-coupon bond, and equity. Chole asks Garzon to describe characteristics associated with structural models. Garzon identifies the following characteristics:

    Characteristic 1   Structural models are based on the structure of the firm's balance sheet.

    Characteristic 2   In a structural model, the company's equity has the same payoff as a European call option on the company's assets.

    Characteristic 3   The structural model assumes that the probability of default is the probability that equity value is less than the face value of the zero-coupon bond at maturity.

Chole tells Garzon that many financial institutions prefer to assess credit risk by using reduced form models. She states that the reduced form model assumes that at least one of the company's liabilities trades in frictionless markets. Chole asks Garzon: "What is the effect on the credit spread if the assumption of frictionless markets is incorrect?"

Chole also asks Garzon to describe strengths associated with using a reduced form model to assess credit risk. Garzon states the following:

Statement 1   The reduced form model does not require a specification of the company's balance sheet structure.

Statement 2   The reduced form model's credit risk measures are not affected by the business cycle.

Chole then asks Garzon to use the reduced form model, which applies option pricing methodology, to value the debt of Company C. She indicates that the expected discounted payoff of Company C's debt is

- $500,000, assuming the company does not default on its debt, or
- $200,000, assuming the company defaults on its debt.

Chole next asks Garzon to use the term structure of credit spreads to assess the credit risk of a zero-coupon bond issued by Company D. She provides Garzon with the information in Exhibit 1. She tells Garzon to assume a 365-day year and that all yields and spreads are continuously compounded.

Exhibit 1   Company D Term Structure of Credit Spread Information

Today's date: 13 April 2014

Maturity date: 30 June 2017

Face value: $1,000

Credit spread: 0.40%

Risk-free zero-coupon yield: 0.25%

The final training topic addresses credit analysis for asset-backed securities. Chole asks Garzon, "What is the effect of an interest payment being missed in the collateral pool?"

15 Which of Garzon's stated characteristics associated with the structural model is *incorrect*?

   A Characteristic 1

   B Characteristic 2

   C Characteristic 3

16 The *most appropriate* response to Chole's question regarding credit spreads in frictionless markets is that if the stated assumption of reduced form models is incorrect, credit spreads will be:

   A less than the expected percentage loss.

   B equal to the expected percentage loss.

   C greater than the expected percentage loss.

17 Which of Garzon's statements about the strengths of the reduced form model is correct?

   A Statement 1 only

   B Statement 2 only

   C Both Statement 1 and Statement 2

18 Garzon should conclude that the value of Company C's debt is *closest* to:

   A $200,000.

   B $500,000.

   C $700,000.

19 Based on the information in Exhibit 1, the present value of expected loss because of credit risk for Company D's debt is *closest* to:

   A $4.80.

   B $7.90.

   C $12.70.

20 In response to Chole's question on asset-backed securities, Garzon should respond that the:

   A junior bond tranche will default.

   B probability of default will increase.

   C asset-backed security will not default.

SOLUTIONS

1   B is correct. Limitation B is incorrect. Credit ratings tend to be stable, not variable, across time and across the business cycle. Rating agencies may be motivated to keep their ratings stable across time to reduce unnecessary volatility in debt market prices. Credit ratings do not explicitly depend on the business cycle.

The issuer-pays model for compensating credit rating agencies has a potential conflict of interest that may distort the accuracy of credit ratings. Credit ratings do not provide an estimate of default probability. They are ordinal rankings. There is no constant relationship between credit ratings and default probabilities.

2   B is correct. Holding the company's equity is economically equivalent to owning a European call option on the firm's assets. Holding the company's equity has the same payoff as a European call option on the company's assets with a strike price equivalent to the face value of the company's debt.

3   C is correct. The reduced form model assumes that some of the company's debt is traded. Reduced form models do not assume that the company's assets, equity, or all its debt are traded. The structural model assumes that the company's assets trade.

4   B is correct. The ability to use historical estimation is a significant advantage of the reduced form model. Both structural and reduced form models can use implicit estimation (or calibration).

5   A is correct. The reduced form model produces credit risk measures that reflect the changing business cycle. The credit risk measures from structural models do not explicitly depend on the business cycle. Credit ratings are also generally insensitive to changes in the business cycle. Both reduced form and structural models can be used to estimate the expected present value of expected loss.

6   C is correct. The present value of the expected loss due to credit risk is closest to 18.00. It is the difference between the credit-adjusted valuation (present value) of 998.1623 and the risk free valuation (risk-free present value) of 1,016.1606. [1,016.1606 − 998.1623 = 17.9983 ≈ 18.00]

7   A is correct. The present value of the expected loss due to credit risk is 0.04 and is calculated as the risk-free present value of 4.3450 less the risk-adjusted present value of 4.3042, or 0.0408, or approximately 0.04. [4.3450 − 4.3042 = 0.0408 ≈ 0.04]

8   A is correct. Statement 1 is incorrect. The probability of default does not apply to ABS because asset-backed securities do not default when an interest payment is not made. Probability of loss is used in place of default. Credit analysis for both ABS and corporate bonds is different due to their future cash flow structures. Both structural and reduced form models can be used to analyze ABS and corporate bonds.

9   C is correct. Neither Comment 1 nor 2 are correct. Comment 1 is incorrect because the expected loss depends on the probability of default and the loss given default. Although Company A has a higher probability of default, a lower loss given default or a higher recovery rate could cause Company A's expected loss to be lower than that of Company B. Comment 2 is incorrect because two modifications to the expected loss are needed to determine the present value of the expected loss: a modification to adjust to risk-neutral probabilities and a

modification to discount for the time value of money. These two modifications can either increase or decrease the present value of the expected loss relative to the expected loss itself.

10 C is correct. Comment C is correct because the issuer-pays model creates an incentive conflict; the credit rating agency has an incentive to give a higher rating than may be justified. The credit rating agency has a conflict of interest that can reduce the accuracy of bond ratings.

11 B is correct. The value of the bonds will decline and the value of common stock will increase. The changes in the value of debt and equity can be considered using options analogies. Using a call option analogy for equity, a company's equity has the same payoff as a European call option on the company's assets with a strike price equal to the bond's promised payoff at time T. The increase in the volatility of assets increases the value of the company's equity, the call option on the company's asset. Using the debt option analogy, owning debt is equivalent to owning risk-free bonds with a certain payoff at time T and simultaneously selling European put options to shareholders with a strike price of the certain payoff at maturity T. The increase in asset volatility increases the value of the put and decreases the value of the bonds.

12 A is correct. Borrego's concerns about historical and implicit estimation of the inputs for structural models are correct. Historical estimation of inputs is not possible because the company's assets do not trade in frictionless markets, and their values are not observable. As a result, the returns and volatility of the assets cannot be determined using historical estimation. If the assumptions of the models used for implicit estimation are not reasonable approximations of the market's actual structure, the inputs derived from those models are unreliable.

13 C is correct. Both the stated advantage and disadvantage are correct. An advantage of a reduced form model is that the input variables are observable, so historical estimation procedures can be used. Models using historical data to predict the future must be properly formulated and back tested.

14 C is correct. Both of his statements are correct. The waterfall does allocate more cash flows to the most senior bond tranches if the collateral pool's cash flows decline significantly. His statement that asset-backed bonds and corporate bonds are not equivalent is also correct. Because of their complexity, asset-backed bonds are more difficult to analyze, and they are not substitutes even if they have the same coupons, principal, maturity, and bond rating. For example, an asset-backed security does not default when an interest payment is missed.

15 C is correct. Garzon's stated Characteristic 3 is incorrect. In the structural model, the company's equity can be viewed as a European call option on the company's assets with a strike price equal to the face value of debt. Using the option analogy, at maturity, the probability that a bond defaults is equal to the probability that the asset value falls below the face value of debt. The probability of default is the probability that asset value, not equity value, is less than the face value of the zero-coupon bond.

16 C is correct. Chole notes that reduced form models assume that markets are frictionless. In reality, markets are not frictionless. The presence of market friction introduces a positive liquidity risk premium. Credit spreads will consist of the expected percentage loss and a positive liquidity premium. Because of the positive liquidity premium, the credit spread will be greater than the expected percentage loss.

17 A is correct. Only Statement 1 is correct. The reduced form model does not require a specification of the company's balance sheet structure. The reduced form model assumes that some of the company's debt trades and imposes this assumption on the outputs of a structural model rather than on the balance sheet structure. This assumption allows for more realistic balance sheets to be modeled and gives reduced form models more flexibility in matching actual market conditions. An advantage of reduced form models is that their credit risk measures reflect the changing business cycle.

18 C is correct. The value of Company C's debt is closest to $700,000. Using the reduced form model, the value of debt is determined by calculating the expected discounted value of debt after adjusting for risk. The value of the company's debt can be decomposed into two parts: the expected discounted payoff of company debt, assuming there is no default, and the expected discounted payoff of debt if default occurs. The expected discounted payoff of Company C's debt is $500,000, assuming the company does not default, and the expected discounted payoff is $200,000, assuming default occurs. Therefore, the value of Company C's debt is $500,000 + $200,000 = $700,000.

19 C is correct. The present value of expected loss because of credit risk is closest to $12.70. The calculations for the present value of expected loss because of credit risk are as follows:

Total yield = Risk-free zero coupon yield + Credit spread
= 0.25% + 0.40% = 0.65%

Years to maturity = 1,174 days/365 days = 3.2164 years
Total yield discount factor = $e^{(\text{Total yield \%})(\text{Years to maturity})}$
= $e^{(0.0065)(3.2164)}$ = 0.9793

Credit-adjusted present value = (Cash flow)(Discount factor)
= $1,000(0.9793) = $979.30

Risk-free discount factor = $e^{(\text{Risk-free yield \%})(\text{Years to maturity})}$
= $e^{(0.0025)(3.2164)}$ = 0.9920

Risk-free present value = (Cash flow)(Discount factor)
= $1,000(0.9920) = $992.00

Difference in present value because of credit risk = Risk-free present value
− Credit-adjusted present value
= $992.00 − $979.30 =
$12.70

The credit-adjusted present value is $979.30, and the risk-free valuation is $992. Thus, the present value of expected loss because of credit risk is $12.70.

20 C is correct. The asset-backed security will not default. A default in the collateral pool does not cause a default to either the special purpose entity or a bond tranche. The asset-backed security will continue to trade until its maturity date or until all of its face value is eliminated. Consequently, Garzon should conclude that an asset-backed security will not default if it misses an interest payment or if there is a default in the collateral pool. The probability of default does not apply to an asset-backed security.

Credit Default Swaps

by Brian Rose and Don M. Chance, PhD, CFA

Brian Rose (USA). Don M. Chance, PhD, CFA, is at Louisiana State University (USA).

LEARNING OUTCOMES

Mastery	The candidate should be able to:
☐	a. describe credit default swaps (CDS), single-name and index CDS, and the parameters that define a given CDS product;
☐	b. describe credit events and settlement protocols with respect to CDS;
☐	c. explain the principles underlying, and factors that influence, the market's pricing of CDS;
☐	d. describe the use of CDS to manage credit exposures and to express views regarding changes in shape and/or level of the credit curve;
☐	e. describe the use of CDS to take advantage of valuation disparities among separate markets, such as bonds, loans, equities, and equity-linked instruments.

INTRODUCTION

1

A **credit derivative** is a derivative instrument in which the underlying is a measure of a borrower's credit quality. Four types of credit derivatives are (1) total return swaps, (2) credit spread options, (3) credit-linked notes, and (4) credit default swaps, or CDS.[1] The first three are not frequently encountered. CDS have clearly emerged as the primary type of credit derivative and, as such, are the topic of this reading. In a CDS, one party makes payments to the other and receives in return the promise of compensation if a third party defaults.

---

[1] We use the expression CDS in both singular and plural form, as opposed to CDSs or CDS's.

In any derivative, the payoff is based on (*derived from*) the performance of an underlying instrument, rate, or asset that we call the underlying.[2] For a CDS, the underlying is the credit quality of a borrower. At its most fundamental level, a CDS provides protection against default, but it also protects against changes in the market's perception of a borrower's credit quality well in advance of default. The value of a CDS will rise and fall as opinions change about the likelihood of default. The actual event of default might never occur.

Derivatives are characterized as *contingent claims*, meaning that their payoffs are dependent on the occurrence of a specific event or outcome. For an equity option, the event is that the stock price is above (for a call) or below (for a put) the exercise price at expiration. For a CDS, the credit event is more difficult to identify. In financial markets, whether a default has occurred is sometimes not clear. Bankruptcy would seem to be a default, but many companies declare bankruptcy and some ultimately pay all of their debts. Some companies restructure their debts, usually with creditor approval but without formally declaring bankruptcy. Creditors are clearly damaged when debts are not paid, not paid on time, or paid in a form different from what was promised, but they are also damaged when there is simply an increase in the likelihood that the debt will not be paid. The extent of damage to the creditor can be difficult to determine. A decline in the price of a bond when investors perceive an increase in the likelihood of default is a very real loss to the bondholder. Credit default swaps are designed to protect creditors against such credit events. As a result of the complexity of defining what constitutes default, the industry has expended great effort to provide clear guidance on what credit events are covered by a CDS contract. As with all efforts to write a perfect contract, however, no such device exists and disputes do occasionally arise. We will take a look at these issues later.

This reading is organized as follows: Section 2 explores basic definitions and concepts, and Section 3 covers the elements of valuation and pricing. Section 4 discusses applications. Section 5 provides a summary.

2   BASIC DEFINITIONS AND CONCEPTS

We start by defining a **credit default swap**:

> *A credit default swap is a derivative contract between two parties, a credit protection buyer and credit protection seller, in which the buyer makes a series of cash payments to the seller and receives a promise of compensation for credit losses resulting from the default—that is, a pre-defined credit event—of a third party.*

In a CDS contract there are two counterparties, the **credit protection buyer** and the **credit protection seller**. The buyer agrees to make a series of periodic payments to the seller over the life of the contract (which are determined and fixed at contract initiation) and receives in return a promise that if default occurs, the protection seller will compensate the protection buyer. If default occurs, the periodic payments made by the protection buyer to the protection seller terminate. Exhibit 1 shows the structure of payment flows.

---

2 Consistent with industry practice, we use the word underlying as a noun even though it generally requires a follower, such as in underlying asset. Because derivatives exist on credit and other non-assets, the word underlying has taken on the properties of a noun in the world of derivatives.

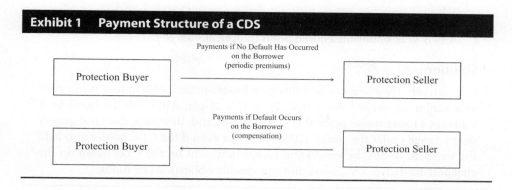

Exhibit 1   Payment Structure of a CDS

Credit default swaps are somewhat similar to put options. Put options effectively enable the option holder to sell (put) the underlying to the option seller if the underlying performs poorly relative to the exercise price. The option holder is thus compensated for the poor performance of the underlying. CDS act in a similar manner. If a default occurs, a loan or bond has clearly performed badly. The protection buyer is then compensated by the protection seller. How that compensation occurs and how much protection it provides are some points we will discuss.[3]

The majority of CDS are written on debt issued by corporate borrowers, which will be our focus in this reading. But note that CDS can be written on the debt of sovereign governments and state and local governments. In addition, CDS can be written on portfolios of loans, mortgages, or debt securities.

2.1 Types of CDS

There are three types of CDS; single-name CDS, index CDS, and tranche CDS.[4] A CDS on one specific borrower is called a **single-name CDS**. The borrower is called the **reference entity**, and the contract specifies a **reference obligation**, a particular debt instrument issued by the borrower that is the designated instrument being covered. The designated instrument is usually a senior unsecured obligation, which is often referred to as a senior CDS, but the reference obligation is not the only instrument covered by the CDS. Any debt obligation issued by the borrower that is *pari passu* (ranked equivalently in priority of claims) or higher relative to the reference obligation is covered. The payoff of the CDS is determined by the **cheapest-to-deliver** obligation, which is the debt instrument that can be purchased and delivered at the lowest cost but has the same seniority as the reference obligation.

EXAMPLE 1

Cheapest-to-Deliver Obligation

Assume that a company with several debt issues trading in the market files for bankruptcy (i.e., a credit event takes place). What is the cheapest-to-deliver obligation for a senior CDS contract?

A   A subordinated unsecured bond trading at 20% of par

---

3 Note that a CDS does not eliminate credit risk. It eliminates the credit risk of one party but substitutes the credit risk of the CDS seller. Although there are no guarantees that the CDS seller will not default, as was seen with several large financial institutions in the crisis that started in 2007, most CDS sellers are relatively high-quality borrowers. If they were not, they could not be active sellers of CDS.
4 In addition to CDS, there are also options on CDS, which are called CDS swaptions. We will not cover this instrument here. Swaptions in general are covered elsewhere in the derivatives material.

B   A five-year senior unsecured bond trading at 50% of par

C   A two-year senior unsecured bond trading at 45% of par

Solution:

C is correct. The cheapest-to-deliver, or lowest-priced, instrument is the two-year senior unsecured bond trading at 45% of par. Although the bond in A trades at a lower dollar price, it is subordinated and, therefore, does not qualify for coverage under the senior CDS. Note that even if the CDS holder also held the five-year bonds, he would still receive payment on the CDS based on the cheapest-to-deliver obligation, not the specific obligations he holds.

A second type of credit default swap, an **index CDS**, involves a combination of borrowers. These instruments have been created such that it is possible to trade indices of CDS. This type of instrument allows participants to take positions on the credit risk of a combination of companies, in much the same way that investors can trade index or exchange-traded funds that are combinations of the equities of companies. Correlation of returns is a strong determinant of a portfolio's behavior. For index CDS, this concept takes the form of a factor called **credit correlation**, and it is a key determinant of the value of an index CDS. Analyzing the effects of those correlations is a highly specialized subject beyond the CFA Program, but the reader should be aware that much effort is placed on modeling how defaults by certain companies are connected to defaults by other companies. The more correlated the defaults, the more costly it is to purchase protection for a combination of the companies. In contrast, for a diverse combination of companies whose defaults have low correlations, it will be much less expensive to purchase protection.

A third type of CDS is the **tranche CDS**, which covers a combination of borrowers but only up to pre-specified levels of losses—much in the same manner that asset-backed securities are divided into tranches, each covering particular levels of losses. The tranche CDS is only a small portion of the CDS market, and we will not cover it any further.

2.2 Important Features of CDS Markets and Instruments

As we will describe in more detail later, the CDS market is large, global, and well organized. The unofficial industry governing body is the International Swaps and Derivatives Association (ISDA), which publishes industry-supported conventions that facilitate the functioning of the market. Parties to CDS contracts generally agree that their contracts will conform to ISDA specifications. These terms are specified in a document called the **ISDA Master Agreement**, which the parties to a CDS sign. In Europe, the standard CDS contract is called the Standard Europe Contract, and in the United States and Canada, it is called the Standard North American Contract. Other standardized contracts exist for Asia, Australia, Latin America, and a few specific countries.

Each CDS contract specifies a **notional amount**, or "notional" for short, which is the amount of protection being purchased. For example, if a company has a bond issue of €100 million, a CDS could be constructed for any amount up to €100 million. The notional amount can be thought of as the *size* of the contract. It is important to understand that the total amount of CDS notional can exceed the amount of debt outstanding of the reference entity.[5] As we will discuss later, the credit protection buyer does not have to be an actual creditor holding exposure (i.e., owing a loan, bond, or other debt instrument). It can be simply a party that believes that there will be a change in the credit quality of the reference entity.

As with all derivatives, the CDS contract has an expiration or maturity date, and coverage is provided up to that date. The typical maturity range is 1 to 10 years, with 5 years being the most common and actively traded maturity, but the two parties can negotiate any maturity. Maturity dates are typically the last day of March, June, September, or December, with June and December being the most popular. As with bonds, a CDS contract of a particular maturity is really that maturity only for an instant. For example, a five-year CDS is technically no longer a five-year CDS just a day later. As the maturity of that CDS decreases, a new five-year CDS is created, and it begins to be referred to as the five-year CDS. Of course, this point is no different from ordinary bonds.

The buyer of a CDS pays a periodic premium to the seller, referred to as the **CDS spread**, which is a return over Libor required to protect against credit risk. It is sometimes referred to as a credit spread. Conceptually, it is the same as the credit spread on a bond, the compensation for bearing credit risk. This premium is determined based on valuation models that are beyond the scope of the CFA program. Nonetheless, it is important to understand the concept of the credit spread on a CDS, and we will have much more to say about it later in this reading.

An important advancement in the development of CDS in recent years has been in establishing standard annual coupon rates on CDS contracts.[6] Formerly, the rate was set at the credit spread. If a CDS required a rate of 4% to compensate the protection seller for the assumption of credit risk, the protection buyer made quarterly payments amounting to 4% annually. Now CDS rates are standardized, with the most common coupons being either 1% or 5%. The 1% rate typically is used for a CDS on an investment-grade company or index, and the 5% rate is used for a CDS on a high-yield company or index. Obviously, either standardized rate might not be the appropriate rate to compensate the seller. Clearly, not all investment-grade companies have equivalent credit risk, and not all high-yield companies have equivalent credit risk. In effect, the standard rate may be too high or too low. This discrepancy is accounted for by an **upfront payment**, commonly called the **upfront premium**. The differential between the credit spread and the standard rate is converted to a present value basis. Thus, a protection buyer paying a standard rate that is insufficient to compensate the protection seller will make a cash upfront payment. Similarly, a credit spread less than the standard rate would result in a cash payment from the protection seller to the protection buyer.

Regardless of whether either party makes an upfront payment, the reference entity's credit quality could change during the life of the contract, thereby resulting in changes in the value of the CDS. These changes are reflected in the price of the CDS in the market. Consider a high-yield company with a 5% credit spread and its CDS bears a coupon of 5%. Therefore, there is no upfront payment. The protection buyer

---

5 This point will be discussed in more detail later, but here we will address the obvious question of how the aggregate amount of protection can exceed the aggregate risk. As an analogy, consider the exercise of an option. Given the number of options created, at exercise the call option holders could have the right to buy more shares than exist or put option holders could have the right to sell more shares than exist. Such an event has never come close to happening. In the CDS market, the cash settlement feature, which is typically not used for options on stocks, solves this problem. We will describe how cash settlement works later.
6 The reader should be aware of the potential confusion over the term "coupon." The reference bond will make payments that are referred to collectively as the coupon. A CDS on the reference bond will have its own coupon rate, which is calculated based on the expected payoff. Furthermore, with standardization of CDS coupons, there is likely to be a third payment referred to as a coupon. The reader must be alert to the context.

simply agrees to make 5% payments over the life of the CDS. Now suppose that at some later date, the reference entity experiences a decrease in its credit quality. The credit protection buyer is thus paying 5% for risk that now merits a rate higher than 5%. The coverage and cost of protection are the same, but the risk being covered is greater. The value of the CDS to the credit protection buyer has, therefore, increased, and if desired, he could unwind the position to capture the gain. The credit protection seller has experienced a loss in value of the instrument because he is receiving 5% to cover a risk that is higher than it was when the contract was initiated. It should be apparent that absent any other exposure to the reference entity, if the credit quality of the reference entity decreases, the credit protection buyer gains and the credit protection seller loses.[7] The market value of the CDS reflects these gains and losses.

Because of these CDS characteristics, there is potential confusion regarding which party is long and which is short. Normally, we think of buyers as being long and sellers as being short, but in the CDS world, it is the opposite. Because the credit protection buyer promises to make a series of future payments, it is regarded as being short. This is consistent with the fact that in the financial world, "shorts" are said to benefit when things go badly. Credit quality is based on the underlying debt obligation, and when it improves, the credit protection seller benefits. When credit quality deteriorates, the credit protection buyer benefits. Hence, the CDS industry views the credit protection seller as the long and the buyer as the short. This point can lead to confusion because we effectively say the credit protection buyer is short and the credit protection seller is long.

2.3 Credit and Succession Events

The **credit event** is what defines default by the reference entity—that is, the outcome that triggers a payment from the credit protection seller to the credit protection buyer. This event must be unambiguous: Did it occur, or did it not? For the market to function well, the answer to this question must be clear.

There are three general types of credit events: bankruptcy, failure to pay, and restructuring. **Bankruptcy** is a declaration provided for by a country's laws that typically involves the establishment of a legal procedure that forces creditors to defer their claims. Bankruptcy essentially creates a temporary fence around the company through which the creditors cannot pass. During the bankruptcy process, the defaulting party works with its creditors and the court to attempt to establish a plan for repaying the debt. If that plan fails, there is likely to be a full liquidation of the company, at which time the court determines the payouts to the various creditors. Until liquidation occurs, the company normally continues to operate. Many companies do not liquidate and are able to emerge from bankruptcy. A bankruptcy filing by the reference entity is universally regarded as a credit event in CDS contracts.

Another credit event recognized in standard CDS contracts is **failure to pay**, which occurs when a borrower does not make a scheduled payment of principal or interest on any outstanding obligations after a grace period, without a formal bankruptcy filing. The third type of event, **restructuring**, refers to a number of possible events, including reduction or deferral of principal or interest, change in seniority or priority of an obligation, or change in the currency in which principal or interest is scheduled to be paid. To qualify as a credit event, the restructuring must be involuntary, meaning that it is forced on the borrower by the creditors who must accept the restructured

---

7 A key element of this point is the absence of any other exposure to the reference entity. The credit protection buyer could be holding the debt itself, and the CDS might cover only a portion of the debt. Thus, the credit protection buyer might be gaining on the CDS, as described in the text, but be losing on its overall position.

terms.[8] In the United States, restructuring is not considered a credit event because bankruptcy is typically the preferred route for US companies. Outside the United States, restructuring is more commonly used and is considered a credit event. The Greek debt crisis is a good example of a restructuring that triggered a credit event.

Determination of whether a credit event occurs is done by a 15-member group within the ISDA called the Determinations Committee (DC). Each region of the world has a Determinations Committee, which consists of 10 CDS dealer banks and 5 non-bank end users. To declare a credit event, there must be a supermajority vote of 12 members.

The determinations committees also play a role in determining whether a **succession event** occurred. A succession event arises when there is a change in the corporate structure of the reference entity, such as through a merger, divestiture, spinoff, or any similar action in which ultimate responsibility for the debt in question becomes unclear. For example, if a company acquires all of the shares of a target company, it ordinarily assumes the target company's debt as well. Many mergers, however, are more complicated and can involve only partial acquisition of shares. Spinoffs and divestitures can also involve some uncertainty about who is responsible for certain debts. When such a question arises, it becomes critical for CDS holders. The question is ordinarily submitted to a DC, and its resolution often involves complex legal interpretations of contract provisions and country laws. If a succession event is declared, the CDS contract is modified to reflect the DC's interpretation of whoever it believes becomes the obligor for the original debt. Ultimately, the CDS contract could be split among multiple entities.

2.4 Settlement Protocols

If the DC declares that a credit event has occurred, the two parties to a CDS have the right, but not the obligation, to settle. **Settlement** typically occurs 30 days after declaration of the credit event by the DC. CDS can be settled by **physical settlement** or by **cash settlement**. The former is less common and involves actual delivery of the debt instrument in exchange for a payment by the credit protection seller of the notional amount of the contract. In cash settlement, the credit protection seller pays cash to the credit protection buyer. Determining the amount of that payment is a critical factor because opinions can differ about how much money has actually been lost. The payment should essentially be the loss that the credit protection buyer has incurred, but determining that amount is not straightforward. Default on a debt does not mean that the creditor will lose the entire amount owed. A portion of the loss could be recovered. The percentage of the loss recovered is called the **recovery rate**. It then becomes the percentage received by the protection buyer relative to the amount owed. The complement is called the **payout ratio**, which is essentially an estimate of the expected credit loss. The **payout amount** is determined as the payout ratio multiplied by the notional.[9]

Payout ratio = 1 − Recovery rate (%)

Payout amount = Payout ratio × Notional

Actual recovery can be a very long process, however, and can occur much later than the payoff date of the CDS. To determine an appropriate payout ratio, the industry conducts an auction in which major banks and dealers submit bids and offers for the

---

[8] Although our focus is on corporate debt, sovereign and municipal governments sometimes declare a moratorium or, more drastically, a repudiation of debt, both of which typically qualify as credit events.
[9] Do not confuse this payout ratio with the payout ratio in equity analysis, which is the percentage of earnings paid out as dividends.

cheapest-to-deliver defaulted debt. This process identifies the market's expectation for the recovery rate and the complementary payout ratio, and the CDS parties agree to accept the outcome of the auction, even though the actual recovery rate can ultimately be quite different, which is an important point if the CDS protection buyer also holds the underlying debt.

EXAMPLE 2

Settlement Preference

A French company files for bankruptcy, triggering various CDS contracts. It has two series of senior bonds outstanding: Bond A trades at 30% of par, and Bond B trades at 40% of par. Investor X owns €10 million of Bond A and owns €10 million of CDS protection. Investor Y owns €10 million of Bond B and owns €10 million of CDS protection.

1 Determine the recovery rate for both CDS contracts.
2 Explain whether Investor X would prefer to cash settle or physically settle her CDS contract or whether she is indifferent.
3 Explain whether Investor Y would prefer to cash settle or physically settle his CDS contract or whether he is indifferent.

Solution to 1:

Bond A is the cheapest-to-deliver obligation, trading at 30% of par, so the recovery rate for both CDS contracts is 30%.

Solution to 2:

Investor X has no preference between settlement methods. She can cash settle for €7 million [(1 − 30%) × €10 million] and sell her bond for €3 million, for total proceeds of €10 million. Alternatively, she can physically deliver her entire €10 million face amount of bonds to the counterparty in exchange for €10 million in cash.

Solution to 3:

Investor Y would prefer a cash settlement because he owns Bond B, which is worth more than the cheapest-to-deliver obligation. He will receive the same €7 million payout on his CDS contract, but can sell Bond B for €4 million, for total proceeds of €11 million. If he were to physically settle his contract, he would receive only €10 million, the face amount of his bond.

2.5 CDS Index Products

So far, we have mostly been focusing on single-name CDS. As noted, there are also index CDS products. A company called Markit has been instrumental in producing CDS indices. Of course, a CDS index is not in itself a traded instrument any more than a stock index is a traded product. As with the major stock indices, however, the industry has created traded instruments based on the Markit indices. These instruments are CDS that generate a payoff based on any default that occurs on any entity covered by the index.

The Markit indices are classified by region and further classified (or divided) by credit quality. The two most commonly traded regions are North America and Europe. North American indices are identified by the symbol CDX, and European, Asian, and Australian indices are identified as iTraxx. Within each geographic category are investment-grade and high-yield indices. The former are identified as CDX IG and iTraxx Main, each comprising 125 entities. The latter are identified as CDX HY, consisting of 100 entities, and iTraxx Crossover, consisting of up to 50 high-yield entities.[10] Investment-grade index CDS are typically quoted in terms of spreads, whereas high-yield index CDS are quoted in terms of prices. Both types of products use standardized coupons. All CDS indices are equally weighted. Thus, if there are 125 entities, the settlement on one entity is 1/125 of the notional.[11]

Markit updates the components of each index every six months by creating new series while retaining the old series. The latest created series is called the **on-the-run** series, whereas the older series are called **off-the-run** series. When an investor moves from one series to a new one, the move is called a **roll**. When an entity within an index defaults, that entity is removed from the index and settled as a single-name CDS based on its relative proportion in the index. The index then moves forward with a smaller notional.

Index CDS are typically used to take positions on the credit risk of the sectors covered by the indices as well as to protect bond portfolios that consist of or are similar to the components of the indices. Standardization is generally undertaken to increase trading volume, which is somewhat limited in the single-name market with so many highly diverse entities. With CDS indices on standardized portfolios based on the credit risk of well-identified companies, market participants have responded by trading them in large volumes. Indeed, index CDS are typically more liquid than single-name CDS with average daily trading volume several times that of single-name CDS.

EXAMPLE 3

Hedging and Exposure Using Index CDS

Assume that an investor sells $500 million of protection on the CDX IG index. Concerned about the creditworthiness of a few of the components, the investor hedges a portion of the credit risk in each. For Company A, he purchases $3 million of single-name CDS protection, and Company A subsequently defaults.

1 What is the investor's net notional exposure to Company A?

2 What proportion of his exposure to Company A has he hedged?

3 What is the remaining notional on his index CDS trade?

Solution to 1:

The investor is long $4 million notional ($500 million/125) through the index CDS and is short $3 million notional through the single-name CDS. His net notional exposure is $1 million.

Solution to 2:

He has hedged 75% of his exposure ($3 million out of $4 million).

Solution to 3:

His index CDS has $496 million remaining notional.

---

10 Markit also creates other categories of CDS indices, including emerging markets, sovereigns, municipals, high-yield/high-beta companies, and high-volatility companies.

11 Some confusion might arise from quoting certain CDS as prices and some as spreads, but keep in mind that the bond market often quotes bonds as prices and sometimes as yields. For example, a Treasury bond can be described as having a price of 120 or a yield of 2¾%. Both terms, combined with the other characteristics of the bond, imply the same concept.

2.6 Market Characteristics

Credit default swaps trade in the over-the-counter market in a network of banks and other financial institutions. To better understand this market, we will first review how credit derivatives and specifically CDS were started.

As financial intermediaries, banks draw funds from savings-surplus sectors, primarily consumers, and channel them to savings-deficit sectors, primarily businesses. Corporate lending is indeed the core element of banking. When a bank makes a corporate loan, it assumes two primary risks. One is that the borrower will not repay principal and interest, and the other is that interest rates will change such that the return the bank is earning is not commensurate with returns on comparable instruments in the marketplace. The former is called **credit risk** or **default risk**, and the latter is called **interest rate risk**. There are many ways to manage interest rate risk.[12] Until around the mid-1990s, credit risk could be managed only by using traditional methods, such as analysis of the borrower, its industry, and the macroeconomy, as well as control methods, such as credit limits, monitoring, and collateral. These two groups of techniques defined what amounted only to internal credit risk management. In effect, the only defenses against credit risk were to not make a loan, to lend but require collateral (the value of which is also at risk), or to lend and closely monitor the borrower, hoping that any problems could be foreseen and dealt with before a default occurred.

Around 1995, credit derivatives were created to provide a new and potentially more effective method of managing credit risk.[13] They allow credit risk to be transferred from the lender to another party. In so doing, they facilitate the separation of interest rate risk from credit risk. Banks can then provide their most important service—lending—knowing that the credit risk can be transferred to another party if so desired. This ability to easily transfer credit risk allows banks to greatly expand their loan business. Given that lending is such a large and vital component of any economy, credit derivatives facilitate economic growth and have expanded to cover, and indeed are primarily focused on, the short-, intermediate-, and long-term bond markets. In fact, credit derivatives are more effective in the bond market, in which terms and conditions are far more standard, than in the bank loan market. Of the four types of credit derivatives, credit default swaps have clearly established themselves as the most widely used instrument. Indeed, in today's markets CDS are nearly the only credit derivative used to any great extent.

In principle, insurance contracts could be written that would allow the transfer of credit risk from one party to another. Credit insurance has existed for many years, but its growth has been constrained by the fact that insurance products are typically more consumer focused than commercially focused. Because it is such an important consumer product, insurance is very heavily regulated. It is very costly for insurance products to expand into new areas with different regulatory authorities. Thus, the ability of a relatively standard product to expand in similar form beyond its regulatory borders is limited. The CDS instrument arose and grew partly in response to this problem. By distinguishing CDS from insurance, the industry was able to effectively

---

12 These methods include duration-based strategies, gap management, and the use of interest rate derivatives.

13 There is some evidence that the first credit derivative was created by Blythe Masters, a managing director of J.P. Morgan, and was used to manage the potential risk of Exxon defaulting following its oil spill near Valdez, Alaska.

offer a product that entailed a buyer making a series of promised payments in return for which it received a promise of compensation for losses, a product almost economically identical to insurance but legally distinct.[14]

CDS transactions are executed in the over-the-counter market by phone, instant message, or the Bloomberg message service. Trade information is reported to the **Depository Trust and Clearinghouse Corporation**, which is a US-headquartered entity providing post-trade clearing, settlement, and information services for many kinds of securities in addition to asset custody and asset servicing. New regulations require that almost all CDS be centrally cleared, meaning that parties will send their contracts through clearinghouses that collect and distribute payments and impose margin requirements, as well as mark positions to market. In so doing, a considerable amount of systemic risk is eliminated.[15]

The Bank for International Settlements reported that as of June 2012, the gross notional amount of CDS was about $26.9 trillion with a market value of $1.2 trillion.[16] A rough estimate of the net notional, or promised payments if all possible defaults occur, is about 10% of the gross notional. Single-name CDS are about 60% of the credit derivatives market.

The size of the market today is considerably smaller than it was just a few years ago. For example, in December 2007 CDS gross notional was $57.9 trillion, about twice the size as in December 2011. The decline is accounted for by the fact that the use of CDS fell following the 2008 financial crisis. CDS had been widely used, and indeed overused and mismanaged, by many financial institutions that were ultimately bailed out by governments and central banks. Many of these institutions took credit risk exposures that they thought were diversified or controlled by complex models they had spent millions of dollars and many years developing. Notably, the financial crisis was largely brought about by a real estate crash and the widespread use of subprime mortgages. Credit risk proved to be globally systemic, a possibility not envisioned by risk managers of many well-known institutions, such as AIG. With so many of the large participants in the CDS market effectively out of business, bailed out or taken over, or having to pull back their lending substantially, the use of CDS declined greatly. Nonetheless, the CDS global market is extremely large and well worth our attention.

Until 2010, CDS were essentially unregulated over-the-counter financial instruments. Because of some of the problems discussed earlier, they are now under government regulations or securities and derivatives guidelines in virtually all countries. These regulations require that most CDS transactions be centrally reported and, as noted, most have to be cleared through an authorized clearinghouse.

BASICS OF VALUATION AND PRICING 3

Derivatives are typically valued by constructing a hedge between the derivative and the underlying that produces a risk-free position and merits a return of the risk-free rate. The price of the underlying and certain other variables jointly imply the price of

---

14 Probably the most important step in the development of credit default swaps was not calling them "insurance," which would have almost surely triggered a different set of regulations. It is unclear why they are called *swaps*. As presented elsewhere in the curriculum on the subject of derivatives, swaps involve a series of bilateral payments in which parties exchange a series of cash flows. A CDS is clearly a variation of an option and is not at all a swap.
15 The use and operations of clearinghouses are covered in Level I readings on derivatives.
16 By comparison, interest rate swap notional at that same time was about $379 trillion. These figures are obtained from the Bank for International Settlements' semi-annual surveys of derivatives usage.

the derivative that guarantees a risk-free return on the hedged position. In the context of CDS, pricing means determining the CDS spread or upfront payment given a particular coupon rate for a contract. In turn, this process implies the CDS price.[17]

This principle is fairly easy to apply for conventional derivatives but somewhat more difficult for credit derivatives. For conventional derivatives, the underlying is usually traded in active markets. For example, options on Royal Dutch Shell, futures on a German government bond, and swaps on the yen are relatively easy to value because the underlying instruments trade actively. But the underlying of a CDS is credit, which is a somewhat vague concept. Credit does not "trade" in the traditional sense but exists implicitly within the bond and loan market. The actual valuation of credit, which reveals the price at which credit risk can be sold, is much more difficult to obtain in relation to the valuation of derivatives driven by equities, interest rates, and currencies.

The exact application of these concepts in CDS pricing models is an advanced topic beyond the scope of the CFA Program. It is important, nonetheless, that CFA charterholders have a good grasp of the factors that determine CDS pricing, but the details are not necessary. Thus, we will cover this material at a high level.

3.1 Basic Pricing Concepts

The most important element of CDS pricing is the **probability of default**. With a few exceptions, a loan or bond involves a series of promised payments. Non-payment on any one of these obligations is a default. To illustrate, consider a simple example of a two-year, 5%, $1,000 loan, with one interest payment of $50 due in one year and a final interest and principal payment of $1,050 due in two years. Each of these payments is subject to the possibility of default.

It can be a bit confusing to refer to a general probability of default. There might be a 2% chance of defaulting on the first interest payment but a greater probability of default on the final interest and principal payment because the amount owed is larger and there is a longer period of time until the second payment. The probability of default is normally greater over a longer period of time.[18]

The relevant probability of default is referred to as a concept from statistics called the **hazard rate**. The hazard rate is the probability that an event will occur *given that it has not already occurred*. Once the event occurs, there is no further likelihood of its occurrence. A hazard rate can also be viewed as a conditional probability. It is the probability that something will occur, with the condition that it has not already occurred.

In the life insurance industry, the probability of death clearly meets the concept of a hazard rate. One cannot die if one has already died. Analogously, in the credit industry, default is treated this way.[19] In our example, let the hazard rates be 2% for the first interest payment and 4% for the final interest and principal payment. The 4% rate is the probability that default occurs in Year 2, given that it has not occurred in Year 1. We will assume a 40% recovery rate, which is a common assumption for

17 Recall that we have sometimes distinguished between valuation and pricing for forward, futures, and swaps but not options. Although credit default swaps may be called "swaps," they are really options. Valuation and pricing are, thus, the same concept.
18 The probability of default is typically greater over a longer period of time, because there is more time for the borrower's financial condition to worsen. But there are some exceptions. A borrower could be struggling financially in the short run but might have better prospects in the long run.
19 Technically, a company can default more than once. It can declare bankruptcy, reorganize, continue to operate and even emerge from bankruptcy only to default again, perhaps years later. For example, there are many instances of this occurring in the US airline and auto industries. Credit risk modeling typically does not consider such possibilities because they are fairly uncommon. For our purposes, a CDS terminates with the first credit event, so this event is the principal focus.

senior unsecured debt. Thus, if default occurs on the $50 payment, the bondholder will receive $20 ($50 × 40%), and if default occurs on the final $1,050 payment, the bondholder receives $420 ($1,050 × 40%). Exhibit 2 shows the possibilities. Note that there are three outcomes: the bondholder receives (1) $50 at Year 1 and $1,050 at Year 2 with a probability of 98% × 96% = 94.08%, (2) $50 at Year 1 and $420 at Year 2 with probability 98% × 4% = 3.92%, and (3) $20 at Year 1 and $420 at Year 2 with probability 2%.[20] These probabilities add up to 100%.

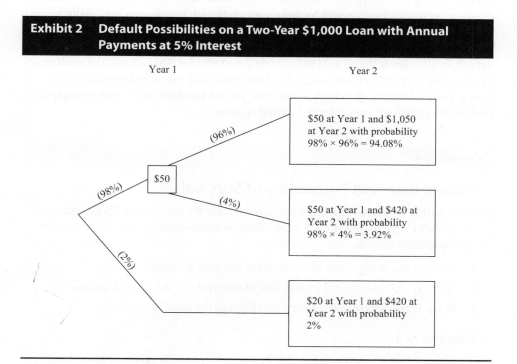

Exhibit 2   Default Possibilities on a Two-Year $1,000 Loan with Annual Payments at 5% Interest

Now, suppose we ask the question, "what is the probability of default?" There are several possible answers because there are really several questions. The probability of default is 2% on the first payment but 4% on the second. In a more general sense, we might like to know the probability of *any* default occurring or, in a complementary sense, the **probability of survival**. In this problem, the probability of survival is 0.98 multiplied by 0.96, approximately 94.08%. Thus, the probability of default occurring at some time in the life of the loan is 100% − 94.08% = 5.92%.

An important concept in credit analysis is the **loss given default**, which is the amount that will be lost if a default occurs. In the example, that amount cannot be precisely specified because it must refer to a particular default. If the borrower defaults on the first payment, the amount lost is $50 − $20 = $30 on the first payment and $1,050 − $420 = $630 on the second, for a total loss given default of $660. If the borrower defaults only on the second payment, the loss given default is $630. From the loss given default, it is possible to calculate the **expected loss**, which is simply the full amount owed minus the expected recovery, or the loss given default, multiplied by the probability of default:

Expected loss = Loss given default × Probability of default

---

[20] Although we say "at Year 1" and "at Year 2," we do not really know when during a year recovery will occur. In the exhibit, we simply assume that the cash flow occurs "at Year 1 (or 2)," but it could occur earlier in the year. Also, for the third outcome, we assume that if default occurs on the first payment, it will also occur on the second but that recovery on the second will be the same as if the first were made in full. This might not be the case in practice, but other estimates can be easily inserted.

In the example, there is a 2% chance of losing $660 and a (0.98) × (0.04) = 0.0392, or 3.92%, chance of losing $630. Thus, unadjusted for time value of money, the expected loss is (0.02) × ($660) + (0.0392) × ($630) = $37.90. This calculation shows that the expected loss is obtained by multiplying the losses given defaults ($660 and $630, respectively) by the probabilities of default (2% and 3.92%, respectively).

Now consider another possibility, a 10-year bond with an equivalent hazard rate of 2% each year.[21] Suppose we want to know the probability that the borrower will not default during the entire 10-year period. Of course, if we try to draw a 10-year tree diagram, as in Exhibit 2, it will become very cluttered, but we can still easily answer this question. The probability that a default will occur at some point during the 10 years is one minus the probability of no default in 10 years. The probability of no default in 10 years is (0.98) × (0.98) ... (0.98) = (0.98)^{10} = 0.817. Thus, the probability of default is 1 − 0.817 = 0.183, or 18.3%. This somewhat simplified example illustrates how a low probability of default in any one period can turn into a surprisingly high probability of default over a longer period of time.

EXAMPLE 4

Hazard Rate and Probability of Survival

Assume that a company's hazard rate is a constant 8% per year, or 2% per quarter. An investor sells five-year CDS protection on the company with the premiums paid quarterly over the next five years.

1 What is the probability of survival for the first quarter?

2 What is the conditional probability of survival for the second quarter?

3 What is the probability of survival through the second quarter?

Solution to 1:

The probability of survival for the first quarter is 98% (100% minus the 2% hazard rate).

Solution to 2:

The conditional probability of survival for the second quarter is also 98%, because the hazard rate is constant at 2%. In other words, *conditional on the company having survived the first quarter*, there is a 2% probability of default in the second quarter.

Solution to 3:

The probability of survival through the second quarter is 96.04%. The probability of survival through the first quarter is 98%, and the conditional probability of survival through the second quarter is also 98%. The probability of survival through the second quarter is thus 98% × 98% = 96.04%. Alternatively, 1 − 96.04% = 3.96% is the probability of default sometime during the first two quarters.

Understanding the concept of pricing a CDS is facilitated by recognizing that there are essentially two sides, or legs, of a contract. There is the **protection leg**, which is the contingent payment that the credit protection seller may have to make to the credit protection buyer, and the **premium leg**, which is the series of payments the credit protection buyer promises to make to the credit protection seller.

---

21 The hazard rate is unlikely to be the same each year, but we will use a simple case here to minimize the computations.

To estimate the value of the protection leg, the probability of each payment, the timing of each payment, and the discount rate must be taken into account.[22] In essence, we need to determine the expected payoff of each promised payment on the reference entity. Having estimated the probability of default for each payment, we find the expected payoff of a given payment on the reference entity by multiplying the payment adjusted for the expected recovery rate by the probability of survival and then discounted at an appropriate rate. The sum of all of these amounts is the expected payoff of the bond or loan, which should, of course, be the price at which the bond is trading in the market. Then, suppose we assume there is no default possibility on the bond. We could then discount all payments at the risk-free rate to obtain the hypothetical value of the bond if it had no credit risk. The difference between these two figures is the value of the credit exposure. In other words, what an investor would pay for the bond, which contains credit risk, minus what the investor would pay if the bond had no credit risk is what it would cost to eliminate the credit risk. This amount is, therefore, the value of the protection leg and is the present value of the contingent obligation of the credit protection seller to the credit protection buyer. Although we could obtain the value of the bond and implicitly the credit premium from the bond's price in the market, we would have to trust that the bond market is properly pricing the credit risk. That may not be the case, as we will discuss later.

Now, we must evaluate the premium leg or present value of the payments made by the protection buyer to the protection seller. With a fixed standardized coupon rate, this calculation would seem simple, but one complication must be considered. For example, for a five-year CDS, the credit protection buyer promises a set of payments over five years, but if the credit event occurs any time during that five-year period, the payments terminate. Hence, the various hazard rates must also be applied to the premium leg to obtain the expected payments promised by the CDS buyer to the seller.

The difference in value of the protection leg and premium leg determines the upfront payment. The party having a claim on the greater present value must make up the cash difference at the initiation date of the contract. Thus, we have

Upfront payment = Present value of protection leg − Present value of premium leg

and if the result is greater (less) than zero, the protection buyer (seller) pays the protection seller (buyer). The actual mechanics of these calculations are somewhat more complex than described here. As noted, for the CFA Program, we take a high-level view of credit default swaps and leave the details to credit derivatives specialists.

3.2 The Credit Curve

The credit spread of a debt instrument is the rate in excess of Libor that investors expect to receive to justify holding the instrument.[23] The credit spread can be expressed roughly as the probability of default multiplied by the loss given default, with the latter in terms of a percentage.[24] The credit spreads for a range of maturities of a

---

[22] There is a technical distinction between the true probability of default and the risk-neutral probability of default. Pricing is done using the risk-neutral probability of default, not the true probability of default. Risk-neutral probability is covered in the Level I readings on derivatives. In this reading, we will not make the distinction explicitly but it should be kept in mind.

[23] Libor is not a risk-free rate and contains some credit risk itself. Libor is the rate on loans made from one London bank to another. Given that London banks bear some default risk, Libor is typically higher than the rate on government debt.

[24] We previously showed that the expected loss is also the loss given default times the probability of default expressed in currency units. When expressed as a percentage of notional, this relationship is the credit spread. These are all rough approximations because the true relationships are complicated by multiple payments and discounting.

company's debt make up its **credit curve**. The credit curve is somewhat analogous to the term structure of interest rates, which is the set of rates on default-free debt over a range of maturities, but the credit curve applies to non-government borrowers and incorporates credit risk into each rate.

The CDS market for a given borrower is integrated with the credit curve of that borrower. In fact, given the evolution and high degree of efficiency of the CDS market, the credit curve is essentially determined by the CDS rates. The curve is affected by a number of factors, a key one of which is the set of aforementioned hazard rates. A constant hazard rate will tend to flatten the credit curve.[25] Upward-sloping credit curves imply a greater likelihood of default in later years, whereas downward-sloping credit curves imply a greater probability of default in the earlier years. Downward-sloping curves are less common and often a result of severe near-term stress in the financial markets.

EXAMPLE 5

Change in Credit Curve

A company's 5-year CDS trades at a credit spread of 300 bps, and its 10-year CDS trades at a credit spread of 500 bps.

1   The company's 5-year spread is unchanged, but the 10-year spread widens by 100 bps. Describe the implication of this change in the credit curve.

2   The company's 10-year spread is unchanged, but the 5-year spread widens by 500 bps. Describe the implication of this change in the credit curve.

Solution to 1:

This change implies that although the company is not any riskier in the short term, its longer-term creditworthiness is less attractive. Perhaps the company has adequate liquidity for the time being, but after five years it must begin repaying debt or it will be expected to have cash flow difficulties.

Solution to 2:

This change implies that the company's near-term credit risk is now much greater. In fact, the probability of default will decrease if the company can survive for the next five years. Perhaps the company has run into liquidity issues that must be resolved soon, and if not resolved, the company will default.

3.3 CDS Pricing Conventions

With corporate bonds, we typically refer to their values in terms of prices or spreads. The spread is a somewhat more informative measure than price. People are relatively familiar with a normal range of interest rates, so spreads can be easily compared with interest rates. It is more difficult to compare prices. A high-yield bond can be offered with a coupon equal to its yield and, therefore, a price of par value. At the same time, a low-yield bond with the same maturity can likewise be offered with a coupon equal to its yield, and therefore, its price is at par. These two bonds would have identical prices at the offering date, and their prices might even be close through much of their

---

25 Because of discounting, the credit curve would not be completely flat even if the hazard rates are constant. For example, for a company issuing 5- and 10-year zero-coupon bonds, there could be equally likely probabilities of default and hence equal expected payoffs. But the present values of the payoffs are not the same and hence the discount rates that equate the present value to the expected payoffs will not be the same. Constant hazard rates tend to flatten a curve but would not flatten it completely unless all rates were zero.

lives, but they are quite different bonds. Focusing on their prices would, therefore, provide little information. Their spreads are much more informative. With Libor or the risk-free rate as a benchmark, investors can get a sense for the amount of credit risk implied by their prices, maturities, and coupons. The same is true for CDS. Although CDS have their own prices, their spreads are far more informative.

As we briefly described earlier, the convention in the CDS market starting in recent years is for standardized coupons of 1% for investment-grade debt or 5% for high-yield debt. Clearly, the reference entity need not have debt that implies a credit spread of either of these rates. As such, the present value of the promised payments from the credit protection buyer to the credit protection seller can either exceed or be less than the expected payoff. In effect, the payments are either too large or too small for the risk. The present value difference is the upfront premium paid from one party to the other. Hence, the upfront premium is the present value of the credit spread minus the present value of the fixed coupon. Of course, this specification is quite general. A good rough approximation used by the industry is that the upfront premium is the (Credit spread − Fixed coupon) × Duration of the CDS.[26] Moreover, this specification is in terms of rates. The upfront premium must ultimately be converted to a price, which is done by subtracting the percentage premium from 100.

These relationships are summarized as follows:

$$\text{Present value of credit spread} = \text{Upfront premium} + \text{Present value of fixed coupon}$$

A good approximation of the present value of a stream of payments can be made by multiplying the payment rate by the duration:

$$\text{Upfront premium} \approx (\text{Credit spread} - \text{Fixed coupon}) \times \text{Duration}$$

$$\text{Credit spread} \approx (\text{Upfront premium/Duration}) + \text{Fixed coupon}$$

$$\text{Price of CDS in currency per 100 par} = 100 - \text{Upfront premium \%}$$

$$\text{Upfront premium \%} = 100 - \text{Price of CDS in currency per 100 par}$$

EXAMPLE 6

Premiums and Credit Spreads

1   Assume a high-yield company's 10-year credit spread is 600 bps, and the duration of the CDS is eight years. What is the approximate upfront premium required to buy 10-year CDS protection? Assume high-yield companies have 5% coupons on their CDS.

2   Imagine an investor sold five-year protection on an investment-grade company and had to pay a 2% upfront premium to the buyer of protection. Assume the duration of the CDS to be four years. What are the company's credit spreads and the price of the CDS per 100 par?

---

26 Recall that duration is a type of cash flow weighted-average maturity for a bond. For a CDS, if default occurs, the payments terminate. Thus, we cannot assume that all payments are made with certainty, and the duration must take this possibility into account for every payment. Normally, one should adjust the duration of a bond for credit losses, but it is not usually done unless the bond pricing model used takes into account the stochastic nature of the credit spread.

Solution to 1:

To buy 10-year CDS protection, an investor would have to pay a 500 bps coupon plus the present value of the difference between that coupon and the current market spread (600 bps). In this case, the upfront premium would be approximately 100 bps × 8 (duration), or 8% of the notional.

Solution to 2:

The value of the upfront premium is equal to the premium (−2%) divided by the duration (4), or −50 bps. The sign of the upfront premium is negative because the seller is paying the premium rather than receiving it. The credit spread is equal to the fixed coupon (100 bps) plus the running value of the upfront premium (−50 bps), or 50 bps. As a reminder, because the company's credit spread is less than the fixed coupon, the protection seller must pay the upfront premium to the protection buyer. The price in currency would be 100 minus the upfront premium, but the latter is negative, so the price is 100 − (−2) = 102.

3.4 Valuation Changes in CDS during Their Lives

As with any traded financial instrument, a CDS has a value that fluctuates during its lifetime. That value is determined in the competitive marketplace. Market participants constantly assess the current credit quality of the reference entity to determine its current value and (implied) credit spread. Clearly, many factors can change over the life of the CDS. By definition, the duration shortens through time. Likewise, the probability of default, the expected loss given default, and the shape of the credit curve will all change as new information is received. The exact valuation procedure of the CDS is precisely the same as it is when the CDS is first issued and simply incorporates the new inputs. The new market value of the CDS reflects gains and losses to the two parties.

Consider the following example of a five-year CDS with a fixed 1% coupon. The credit spread on the reference entity is 2.5%. In promising to pay 1% coupons to receive coverage on a company whose risk justifies 2.5% coupons, the present value of the protection leg exceeds the present value of the payment leg. The difference is the upfront premium, which will be paid by the CDS buyer to the CDS seller. During the life of the CDS, assume that the credit quality of the reference entity improves, such that the credit spread is now 2.1%. Now, consider a newly created CDS with the same remaining maturity and 1% coupon. The present value of the payment leg would still be less than the present value of the protection leg, but the difference would be less than it was when the original CDS was created because the risk is now less. Logically, it should be apparent that for the original CDS, the seller has gained and the buyer has lost. The difference between the original upfront premium and the new value is the seller's gain and buyer's loss. A rough approximation of the change in value of the CDS for a given change in spread is as follows:[27]

Profit for the buyer of protection ≈ Change in spread in bps × Duration × Notional

Alternatively, we might be interested in the CDS percentage price change, which is obtained as

% Change in CDS price = Change in spread in bps × Duration

[27] The relationships expressed in the two equations should be somewhat known to candidates from the fixed-income readings, which illustrate that the percentage change in the price of a bond is approximately the change in yield multiplied by the modified duration. In this case, the change in yield is analogous to the change in spread, measured in basis points. The duration of the CDS is analogous to the duration of the bond on which the CDS is written. The use of the term "modified" with respect to duration is a small adjustment requiring division by one plus the yield.

EXAMPLE 7

Profit and Loss from Change in Credit Spread

An investor buys $10 million of five-year CDS protection, and the CDS contract has a duration of four years. The company's credit spread was originally 500 bps and widens to 800 bps.

1   Does the investor (credit protection buyer) benefit or lose from the change in credit spread?

2   Estimate the CDS price change and estimated profit to the investor.

Solution to 1:

The investor owns protection, so he is economically short and benefits from an increase in the company's credit spread. He can sell the protection for a higher premium.

Solution to 2:

The percentage price change is estimated as the change in spread (300 bps) multiplied by the duration (4) or 12%. The profit to the investor is 12% times the notional ($10 million), or $1.2 million.

3.5 Monetizing Gains and Losses

As with any financial instrument, changes in the price of a CDS gives rise to opportunities to unwind the position, and either capture a gain or realize a loss. This process is called **monetizing** a gain or loss. Keep in mind that the protection seller is effectively long the reference entity. He has entered into a contract to insure the debt of the reference entity, for which he receives a series of promised payments and possibly an upfront premium. He clearly benefits if the reference entity's credit quality improves because he continues to receive the same compensation but bears less risk. Using the opposite argument, the credit protection buyer benefits from a deterioration of the reference entity's credit quality.[28] Thus, the seller is more or less long the company and the buyer is more or less short the company. As the company's credit quality changes through time, the market value of the CDS changes, giving rise to gains and losses for the CDS counterparties. The counterparties can realize those gains and losses by entering into new offsetting contracts, effectively selling their CDS positions to other parties.

Going back to the example in the previous section, assume that during the life of the CDS, the credit quality of the reference entity improves. The implied upfront premium on a new CDS that matches the terms of the original CDS with adjusted maturity is now the market value of the original CDS. In our example, this new CDS has an upfront premium that would be paid by the buyer to the seller, but that premium is smaller than on the original CDS.

Now, suppose that the buyer of the original CDS wants to unwind his position. He would then enter into this new CDS as a protection seller and receive the newly calculated upfront premium. As we noted, this value is less than what he paid originally. Likewise, the seller could offset his original position by entering into this new CDS as a protection buyer. He would pay an upfront premium that is less than what he originally received. The original protection buyer monetizes a loss and the seller

---

28   Again, it is important to remember that these statements are limited to the buyer or seller's position in the CDS and not any other instruments held by either party.

monetizes a gain. The transaction to unwind the CDS does not need to be done with the same original party, although doing so offers some advantages. As clearinghouses begin to be more widely used with CDS, unwind transactions should become even more common and easier to do.

At this point, we have identified two ways of realizing a profit or loss on a CDS. One is to effectively exercise the CDS in response to a default. The other is to unwind the position by entering into a new offsetting CDS in the market. A third, and the least common, method occurs if there is no default. A party can simply hold the position until expiration, at which time the credit protection seller has captured all of the premiums and has not been forced to make any payments, and the seller's obligation for any further payments is terminated. The spread of the CDS will go to zero, in much the same manner as a bond converges toward par as it approaches maturity. The CDS seller clearly gains, having been paid to bear the risk of default that is becoming increasingly unlikely, and the CDS buyer loses.[29]

4 APPLICATIONS OF CDS

Credit default swaps, as demonstrated, facilitate the transfer of credit risk. As simple as that concept seems, there are many different circumstances under which CDS are used. In this section, we consider some applications of this instrument.

Any derivative instrument has two general uses. One is to exploit an expected movement in the underlying. The derivative typically requires less capital and is usually an easier instrument in which to create a short economic exposure as compared with the underlying. The derivatives market can also be more efficient, meaning that it can react to information more rapidly and have more liquidity than the market for the underlying. Thus, information or an expectation of movement in the underlying can often be exploited much better with the derivative than with the underlying directly.

The other trading opportunity facilitated by derivatives is in valuation differences between the derivative and the underlying. If the derivative is mispriced relative to the underlying, one can take the appropriate position in the derivative and an offsetting position in the underlying. If the valuation assessment is correct and other investors come to the same conclusion, the values of the derivative and underlying will converge, and the investor will earn a return that is essentially free of risk because the risk of the underlying has been hedged away by the holding of long and short positions. Whether this happens as planned depends on both the efficiency of the market and the quality of the valuation model. Differences can also exist between the derivative and other derivatives on the same underlying.

These two general types of uses are also the major applications of CDS. We will refer to them as managing credit exposures, meaning the taking on or shedding of credit risk in light of changing expectations and/or valuation disparities. With valuation disparities, the focus is on differences in the pricing of credit risk in the CDS market relative to that of the underlying bonds.

---

[29] Indeed, the buyer loses on the CDS because it paid premiums to receive protection in the event of a default, which did not occur. Although technically a loss, the buyer might well be a creditor of the reference entity, so the buyer's overall position is not a loss. The CDS is, as we have mentioned, somewhat like insurance, so the buyer may not look at it as a loss in the same manner that an individual might not look at an expiring insurance contract on his house as a loss simply because it did not burn down.

4.1 Managing Credit Exposures

The most basic application of a CDS is to increase or decrease credit exposure. The most obvious such application is for a lender to buy a CDS to reduce its credit exposure to a borrower. For the CDS seller, the trade adds credit exposure. A lender's justification for using a CDS seems obvious. The lender may have assumed too much credit risk but does not want to sell the bond or loan because there can be significant transaction costs, because later it may want the bond or loan back, or because the market for the bond or loan is relatively illiquid. If the risk is temporary, it is almost always easier to temporarily reduce risk by using a CDS. Beyond financial institutions, any organization exposed to credit is potentially a candidate for using CDS.

The justification for selling credit protection is somewhat less obvious. The seller can be a CDS dealer, whose objective is to profit from making markets in CDS. A dealer typically attempts to manage its exposure by either diversifying its credit risks or hedging the risk by entering into a transaction with yet another party, such as by shorting the debt or equity of the reference entity, often accompanied by investment of the funds in a repurchase agreement, or repo. If the dealer manages the risk effectively, the risk assumed in selling the CDS is essentially offset when the payment for assuming the risk exceeds the cost of removing the risk. Achieving this outcome successfully requires sophisticated credit risk modeling, a topic beyond the scope of the CFA Program.

Although dealers make up a large percentage of CDS sellers, not all are dealers. Consider that any bondholder is a buyer of credit and interest rate risk. If the bondholder wants only credit risk, it can obtain it by selling a CDS, which would require far less capital and incur potentially lower overall transaction costs than buying the bond. Moreover, the CDS can easily be more liquid than the bond, so the position can be unwound much more easily.

As noted, it is apparent why a party making a loan might want credit protection. Consider, however, that a party with no exposure to the reference entity might also purchase credit protection. Such a position is called a **naked credit default swap**, and it has resulted in some controversy in regulatory and political circles. In buying a naked CDS, the investor is taking a position that the entity's credit quality will deteriorate, whereas the seller of a naked CDS is taking the position that the entity's credit quality will improve.[30] It is the position of the buyer that has caused some controversy. Some regulators and politicians believe it is inappropriate for a party with no exposure to a borrower to speculate that the borrower's financial condition will deteriorate. This controversy accelerated during the financial crises of 2008–2009 because many investors held these naked CDS and benefited from the crisis.

The counterargument, however, is that elsewhere in the financial markets, such bets are made all of the time in the form of long puts, short futures, and short sales of stocks and bonds. These instruments are generally accepted as a means of protecting oneself against weak if not bad performance in the financial markets. Likewise, a CDS is a means of protecting oneself against terrible economic conditions. Must everyone suffer during a financial crisis? Are there not ways to trade that would reward investors who go against the majority of investors and ultimately are proven correct? Moreover, not having a position in an entity does not mean one does not have exposure. In particular, the default of a sovereign entity or municipality imposes

---

[30] To be clear, a naked CDS does not mean that *both* parties have no exposure to the underlying. Either or both could have no exposure. A naked CDS simply refers to the position of one party. The counterparty may or may not have exposure.

costs on many citizens and organizations.[31] Other proponents of naked CDS argue that they bring liquidity to the credit market, potentially providing more stability, not less. Nonetheless, naked CDS trading is banned in Europe for sovereign debt, although generally permitted otherwise.

CDS trading strategies, with or without naked exposure, can take several forms. A party can take an outright long or short position, as we have previously discussed. Alternatively, the party can take a long position in one CDS and a short position in another, called a **long/short trade**.[32] One CDS would be on one reference entity, and the other would be on a different entity. This transaction is a bet that the credit position of one entity will improve relative to that of another. The two entities might be related in some way or might produce substitute goods. For example, one might take a position that because of competition and changes in the luxury car industry, the credit quality of Daimler will improve and that of BMW will weaken, so going long a Daimler CDS and short a BMW CDS would be appropriate. Another similar trade would be to take a long position in one CDS index and a short position in another. For example, the anticipation of a weakening economy could make one go short a high-yield CDS index and long an investment-grade CDS index. As another example, the expectation of strengthening in the Asian economy relative to the European economy could induce one to go short a European CDS index and long an Asian CDS index.[33]

Another type of long/short trade, called a **curve trade**, involves buying a CDS of one maturity and selling a CDS on the same reference entity with a different maturity. Consider two CDS maturities, which we will call the short term and the long term to keep things simple. We will assume the more common situation of an upward-sloping credit curve, meaning that long-term CDS rates are higher than short-term rates. If the curve changes shape, it becomes either steeper or flatter. A steeper (flatter) curve means that long-term credit risk increases (decreases) relative to short-term credit risk.[34] An investor who believes that long-term credit risk will increase relative to short-term credit risk (credit curve steepening) can go short a long-term CDS and long a short-term CDS. In the short run, a curve-steepening trade is bullish. It implies that the short-term outlook for the reference entity is better than the long-term outlook. In the short run, a curve-flattening trade is bearish. It implies that the short-run outlook for the reference entity looks worse than the long-run outlook and reflects the expectation of near-term problems for the reference entity.

---

31 Another apparent naked exposure to the reference entity arises from simply having large commercial deposits at a bank, either traditional deposits or collateral for another transaction. If the bank defaults, the funds could be at risk. Technically, this is not naked exposure, but it does not take the form of a traditional loan or bond.

32 In the world of options and futures trading, such a transaction is typically called a spread.

33 As a reminder, the CDS seller is long credit and the buyer is short credit. Improvements in credit quality benefit (hurt) the CDS seller (buyer).

34 The considerably less common starting scenario of a downward-sloping credit curve has the opposite interpretation. A steeper curve means that short-term credit risk increases relative to long-term credit risk. Even less common is that of a flat credit curve, in which case a steeper curve can occur either from an increase or decrease in long-term credit risk relative to short-term credit risk.

EXAMPLE 8

Curve Trading

An investor owns some intermediate-term bonds issued by a company and has become concerned about the risk of a near-term default, although he is not very concerned about a default in the long term. The company's two-year duration CDS currently trades at 350 bps, and the four-year duration CDS is at 600 bps.

1 Describe a potential curve trade that the investor could use to hedge the default risk.

2 Explain why an investor may prefer to use a curve trade as a hedge against the company's default risk rather than a straight short position in one CDS.

Solution to 1:

The investor anticipates a flattening curve and can exploit this possibility by positioning himself short (buying protection) in the two-year CDS while going long in the four-year CDS (selling protection).

Solution to 2:

Going short one CDS and long another reduces some of the risk because both positions will react similarly, although not equally, to information about the reference entity's default risk. Moreover, the cost of one position will be partially or more than wholly offset by the premium on the other.

Of course, there can be changes to the credit curve that take the form of simply shifts in the general level of the curve, whereby all rates go up or down by roughly equal amounts. As with long-duration bonds relative to short-duration bonds, the values of longer-term CDS will be more sensitive than those of shorter-term CDS. As an example, a trader who believes that all rates will go up will want to be short CDS but will realize that long-term CDS will move more than short-term CDS. Thus, he might want to be short in long-term CDS and hedge by going long in short-term CDS. He will balance the sizes of the positions so that the volatility of the position he believes will gain in value will be more than the other position. If more risk is desired, he might choose to trade only one leg, the more volatile one.

4.2 Valuation Differences and Basis Trading

Different investors will have different assessments of the price of credit risk. Such differences of opinion will lead to valuation disparities. Clearly, there can be only one appropriate price at which credit risk can be eliminated, but that price is not easy to determine. The party that has the best estimate of the appropriate price of credit risk can capitalize on its knowledge or ability at the expense of another party. Any such comparative advantage can be captured by trading the CDS against either the reference entity's debt or equity or derivatives on its debt or equity, but such trading is critically dependent on the accuracy of models that isolate the credit risk component of the debt or equity return. As noted, those models are beyond the scope of the CFA Program, but it is important to understand the basic ideas.

The yield on the bond issued by the reference entity to a CDS contains a factor that reflects the credit risk. In principle, the amount of yield attributable to credit risk on the bond should be the same as the credit spread on a CDS. It is, after all, the compensation paid to the party assuming the credit risk, regardless of whether that risk is borne by a bondholder or a CDS seller. But there may be a difference in the credit risk compensation in the bond market and CDS market. This differential pricing can arise from mere differences of opinions, differences in models used by participants in the two markets, differences in liquidity in the two markets, and supply and demand conditions in the repo market, which is a primary source of financing for bond purchases. A difference in the credit spreads in these two markets is the foundation of a strategy known as a **basis trade**.

The general idea behind most basis trades is that any such mispricing is likely to be temporary and the spreads should return to equivalence when the market recognizes the disparity. For example, suppose the bond market implies a 5% credit risk premium whereas the CDS market implies a 4% credit risk premium. The trader does not know which is correct but believes these two rates will eventually converge. From the perspective of the CDS, its premium is too low relative to the bond credit risk premium. From the perspective of the bond, its premium is too high relative to the CDS market, which means its price is too low. So, the CDS market could be pricing in too little credit risk, and/or the bond market could be pricing in too much credit risk. Either market could be correct, but it does not matter. The investor would buy the CDS, thereby purchasing credit protection at what appears to be an unjustifiably low rate, and buy the bond, thereby assuming credit risk and paying an unjustifiably low price for the bond. The risk is balanced because the default potential on the bond is protected by the CDS.[35] If convergence occurs, the trade would capture the 1% differential in the two markets.

To determine the profit potential of such a trade, it is necessary to decompose the bond yield into the risk-free rate plus the funding spread plus the credit spread.[36] The risk-free rate plus the funding spread is essentially Libor. The credit spread is then the excess of the yield over Libor and can be compared with the credit spread in the CDS market. If the spread is higher in the bond (CDS) market than the CDS (bond) market, it is said to be a negative (positive) basis.

EXAMPLE 9

Bonds vs. Credit Default Swaps

An investor wants to be long the credit risk of a given company. The company's bond currently yields 6% and matures in five years. A comparable five-year CDS contract has a credit spread of 3.25%. The investor can borrow in the market at a 2.5% interest rate.

1   Calculate the bond's credit spread.

2   Identify a basis trade that would exploit the current situation.

Solution to 1:

The bond's credit spread is equal to the yield (6%) minus the investor's cost of funding (2.5%). Therefore, the bond's credit spread is currently 3.5%.

---

35 The bondholder does bear interest rate risk on the bond, but this risk can be hedged with a duration strategy or interest rate derivatives. The general idea is to eliminate all risks and capitalize on the disparity between the price of credit risk in the bond and CDS markets.

36 In practice, this decomposition can be complicated by the existence of embedded options, such as with callable and convertible bonds or when the bond is not selling near par. Those factors would need to be removed in the calculations.

Solution to 2:

The bond and CDS markets imply different credit spreads. Credit risk is cheap in the CDS market (3.25%) relative to the bond market (3.5%). The investor should buy protection in the CDS market at 3.25% and go long the bond, thereby earning 3.5% for assuming the credit risk.

Another type of trade using CDS can occur within the instruments issued by a single entity. Credit risk is an element of virtually every unsecured debt instrument or the capital leases issued by a company. Each of these instruments is priced to reflect the appropriate credit risk. Investors can use the CDS market to first determine whether any of these instruments is incorrectly priced relative to the CDS and then buy the cheaper one and sell the more expensive one. Again, there is the assumption that the market will adjust. This type of trading is much more complex, however, because priority of claims means that not all of the instruments pay off equally if default occurs.

EXAMPLE 10

Using CDS to Trade on a Leveraged Buyout

An investor believes that a company will undergo a leveraged buyout (LBO) transaction, whereby it will issue large amounts of debt and use the proceeds to repurchase all of the publicly traded equity, leaving the company owned by management and a few insiders.

1 Why might the CDS spread change?
2 What equity-versus-credit trade might an investor execute in anticipation of such a corporate action?

Solution to 1:

Taking on the additional debt will almost surely increase the probability of default, thereby increasing the CDS spread.

Solution to 2:

The investor might consider buying the stock and buying CDS protection. Both legs will profit if the LBO occurs because the stock price rises and the CDS price rises as its spread widens to reflect the increased probability of default.

The CDS indices also permit some opportunities for a type of arbitrage trade. If the cost of the index is not equivalent to the aggregate cost of the index components, the opportunity exists to go long the cheaper instrument and short the more expensive instrument. Again, there is the implicit assumption that convergence will occur. Assuming it does, the investor gains the benefit while basically having neutralized the risk.

A collateralized debt obligation (CDO) is created by assembling a portfolio of debt securities and issuing claims against the portfolio in the form of tranches. These tranches have different priorities of claims, with some tranches responsible for credit losses before others. Yet another type of instrument, called a **synthetic CDO**, is created by combining a portfolio of default-free securities with a combination of credit default swaps undertaken as protection sellers. The default-free securities plus the CDS holdings are, thus, a synthetic CDO because they effectively contain securities subject to default. If an institution can assemble the synthetic CDO at a lower cost than the actual CDO, it can then buy the former and sell the latter, capturing a type of arbitrage profit.

SUMMARY

This reading on credit default swaps provides a basic introduction to these instruments and their markets. The following key points are covered:

- A credit default swap (CDS) is a contract between two parties in which one party purchases protection from another party against losses from the default of a borrower for a defined period of time.

- A CDS is written on the debt of a third party, called the reference entity, whose relevant debt is called the reference obligation, typically a senior unsecured bond.

- A CDS written on a particular reference obligation normally provides coverage for all obligations of the reference entity that have equal or higher seniority.

- The two parties to the CDS are the credit protection buyer, who is said to be short the reference entity's credit, and the credit protection seller, who is said to be long the reference entity's credit. The seller (buyer) is said to be long (short) because the seller is bullish (bearish) on the financial condition of the reference entity.

- The CDS pays off upon occurrence of a credit event, which includes bankruptcy, failure to pay, and, in some countries, restructuring.

- Settlement of a CDS can occur through a cash payment from the credit protection seller to the credit protection buyer as determined by the cheapest-to-deliver obligation of the reference entity, or by physical delivery of the reference obligation from the protection buyer to the protection seller in exchange for the CDS notional.

- A cash settlement payoff is determined by an auction of the reference entity's debt, which gives the market's assessment of the likely recovery rate. The credit protection buyer must accept the outcome of the auction even though the ultimate recovery rate could differ.

- CDS can be constructed on a single entity or as indices containing multiple entities.

- The fixed payments made from CDS buyer to CDS seller are customarily set at a fixed annual rate of 1% for investment-grade debt or 5% for high-yield debt.

- Valuation of a CDS is determined by estimating the present value of the protection leg, which is the payment from the protection seller to the protection buyer in event of default, and the present value of the payment leg, which is the series of payments made from the protection buyer to the protection seller. Any difference in the two series results in an upfront payment from the party having the greater present value to the counterparty.

- An important determinant of the value of the expected payments is the hazard rate, the probability of default given that default has not already occurred.

- CDS prices are often quoted in terms of credit spreads, the implied number of basis points that the credit protection seller receives from the credit protection buyer to justify providing the protection.

- Credit spreads are often expressed in terms of a credit curve, which expresses the relationship between the credit spreads on bonds of different maturities for the same borrower.

- CDS change in value over their lives as the credit quality of the reference entity changes, which leads to gains and losses for the counterparties, even though default may not have occurred or may never occur.

- Either party can monetize an accumulated gain or loss by entering into an off-setting position that matches the terms of the original CDS.

- CDS are used to increase or decrease credit exposures or to capitalize on different assessments of the cost of credit among different instruments tied to the reference entity, such as debt, equity, and derivatives of debt and equity.

PRACTICE PROBLEMS

The following information relates to Questions 1–6

UNAB Corporation

On 1 January 20X2, Deem Advisors purchased a $10 million six-year senior unsecured bond issued by UNAB Corporation. Six months later (1 July 20X2), concerned about the portfolio's credit exposure to UNAB, Doris Morrison, the chief investment officer at Deem Advisors, purchases a $10 million CDS with a standardized coupon rate of 5%. The reference obligation of the CDS is the UNAB bond owned by Deem Advisors.

On 1 January 20X3, Morrison asks Bill Watt, a derivatives analyst, to assess the current credit quality of UNAB bonds and the value of Deem Advisor's CDS on UNAB debt. Watt gathers the following information on the UNAB's debt issues currently trading in the market:

Bond 1: A two-year senior unsecured bond trading at 40% of par

Bond 2: A six-year senior unsecured bond trading at 50% of par

Bond 3: A six-year subordinated unsecured bond trading at 20% of par

With respect to the credit quality of UNAB, Watt makes the following statement:

> "There is severe near-term stress in the financial markets and UNAB's credit curve clearly reflects the difficult environment."

On 1 July 20X3, UNAB fails to make a scheduled interest payment on the outstanding subordinated unsecured obligation after a grace period; however, the company does not file for bankruptcy. Morrison asks Watt to determine if UNAB experienced a credit event and, if so, to recommend a settlement preference.

Kand Corporation

Morrison is considering purchasing a 10-year CDS on Kand Corporation debt to hedge its current portfolio position. She instructs Watt to determine if an upfront payment would be required and, if so, the amount of the premium. Watt presents the information for the CDS in Exhibit 1.

Exhibit 1	Summary Data for 10-year CDS on Kand Corporation
Credit spread	700 basis points
Duration	7 years
Coupon rate	5%

Morrison purchases the 10-year CDS on Kand Corporation debt. Two months later the credit spread for Kand Corp. has increased by 200 basis points. Morrison asks Watt to close out the firm's CDS position on Kand Corporation by entering into new offsetting contracts.

Tollunt Corporation

Deem Advisors' chief credit analyst recently reported that Tollunt Corporation's five-year bond is currently yielding 7% and a comparable CDS contract has a credit spread of 4.25%. Since Libor is 2.5%, Watt has recommended executing a basis trade to take advantage of the pricing of the Tollunt's bonds and CDS. The basis trade would consist of purchasing both the bond and the CDS contract.

1 If UNAB experienced a credit event on 1 July, Watt should recommend that Deem Advisors:

   A   prefer a cash settlement.

   B   prefer a physical settlement.

   C   be indifferent between a cash or a physical settlement.

2 According to Watt's statement, the shape of UNAB's credit curve is *most likely*:

   A   flat.

   B   upward-sloping.

   C   downward-sloping.

3 Should Watt conclude that UNAB experienced a credit event?

   A   Yes.

   B   No, because UNAB did not file for bankruptcy.

   C   No, because the failure to pay occurred on a subordinated unsecured bond.

4 Based on Exhibit 1, the upfront premium as a percent of the notional for the CDS protection on Kand Corp. would be *closest* to:

   A   2.0%.

   B   9.8%.

   C   14.0%.

5 If Deem Advisors enters into a new offsetting contract two months after purchasing the CDS protection on Kand Corporation, this action will *most likely* result in:

   A   a loss on the CDS position.

   B   a gain on the CDS position.

   C   neither a loss or a gain on the CDS position.

6 Based on basis trade for Tollunt Corporation, if convergence occurs in the bond and CDS markets, the trade will capture a profit *closest* to:

   A   0.25%.

   B   1.75%.

   C   2.75%.

SOLUTIONS

1   A is correct. Deem Advisors would prefer a cash settlement. Deem Advisors owns Bond 2 (trading at 50% of par), which is worth more than the cheapest-to-deliver obligation (Bond 1 trading at 40% of par). Deem Advisors can cash settle for $6 million [= (1 − 40%) × $10 million] on its CDS contract and sell Bond 2 it owns for $5 million, for total proceeds of $11 million. If Deem Advisors were to physically settle the contract, only $10 million would be received, the face amount of the bonds and they would deliver Bond 2.

B is incorrect because if Deem Advisors were to physically settle the contract, they would receive only $10 million, which is less than the $11 million that could be obtained from a cash settlement. C is incorrect because Deem Advisors would not be indifferent between settlement protocols as the firm would receive $1 million more with a cash settlement in comparison to a physical settlement.

2   C is correct. A downward-sloping credit curve implies a greater probability of default in the earlier years than in the later years. Downward-sloping curves are less common and often are the result of severe near-term stress in the financial markets.

A is incorrect because a flat credit curve implies a constant hazard rate (relevant probability of default). B is incorrect because an upward-sloping credit curve implies a greater probability of default in later years.

3   A is correct. UNAB experienced a credit event when it failed to make the scheduled coupon payment on the outstanding subordinated unsecured obligation. Failure to pay, a credit event, occurs when a borrower does not make a scheduled payment of principal or interest on *any* outstanding obligations after a grace period, even without a formal bankruptcy filing.

B is incorrect because a credit event can occur without filing for bankruptcy. There are three general types of credit events: bankruptcy, failure to pay, and restructuring.

C is incorrect because a credit event (failure to pay) occurs when a borrower does not make a scheduled payment of principal or interest on *any* outstanding obligations after a grace period, without a formal bankruptcy filing.

4   C is correct. An approximation for the upfront premium is the (Credit spread − Fixed coupon rate) × Duration of the CDS. To buy 10-year CDS protection, Deem Advisors would have to pay an approximate upfront premium of 1400 basis points [(700 − 500) × 7], or 14% of the notional.

A is incorrect because 200 basis points, or 2%, is derived by taking the simple difference between the credit spread and the fixed coupon rate (700 − 500). B is incorrect because 980 basis points, or 9.8%, is the result of dividing the credit spread by the fixed coupon rate and multiplying by the duration of the CDS [(700/500) × 7].

5   B is correct. Deem Advisors purchased protection, and therefore is economically short and benefits from an increase in the company's spread. Since putting on the protection, the credit spread increased by 200 basis points, and Deem Advisors realizes the gain by entering into a new offsetting contract (sells the protection for a higher premium to another party).

A is incorrect because a decrease (not increase) in the spread would result in a loss for the credit protection buyer. C is incorrect because Deem Advisors, the credit protection buyer, would profit from an increase in the company's credit spread, not break even.

6   A is correct. A difference in credit spreads in the bond market and CDS market is the foundation of the basis trade strategy. If the spread is higher in the bond market than the CDS market, it is said to be a negative basis. In this case, the bond credit spread is currently 4.50% (bond yield minus Libor) and the comparable CDS contract has a credit spread of 4.25%. The credit risk is cheap in the CDS market relative to the bond market. Since the protection and the bond were both purchased, if convergence occurs, the trade will capture the 0.25% differential in the two markets (4.50% − 4.25%).

B is incorrect because the bond market implies a 4.50% credit risk premium (bond yield minus Libor) and the CDS market implies a 4.25% credit risk premium. Convergence of the bond market credit risk premium and the CDS credit risk premium would result in capturing the differential, 0.25%. The 1.75% is derived by incorrectly subtracting Libor from the credit spread on the CDS (= 4.25% − 2.50%).

C is incorrect because convergence of the bond market credit risk premium and the CDS credit risk premium would result in capturing the differential, 0.25%. The 2.75% is derived incorrectly by subtracting the credit spread on the CDS from the current bond yield (= 7.00% − 4.25%).

Derivatives

TOPIC LEVEL LEARNING OUTCOME

The candidate should be able to estimate the value of futures, forwards, options, and swaps and demonstrate how they may be used in various strategies.

14

Derivative Instruments

Valuation and Strategies

This study session examines derivative investments: forwards and options. It focuses on pricing, valuation, and strategies.

READING ASSIGNMENTS

READING

40

Pricing and Valuation of Forward Commitments

by Robert E. Brooks, PhD, CFA, and Barbara Valbuzzi, CFA

Robert E. Brooks, PhD, CFA, is at the University of Alabama (USA). Barbara Valbuzzi, CFA (Italy).

LEARNING OUTCOMES

Mastery	The candidate should be able to:
☐	**a.** describe and compare how equity, interest rate, fixed-income, and currency forward and futures contracts are priced and valued;
☐	**b.** calculate and interpret the no-arbitrage value of equity, interest rate, fixed-income, and currency forward and futures contracts;
☐	**c.** describe and compare how interest rate, currency, and equity swaps are priced and valued;
☐	**d.** calculate and interpret the no-arbitrage value of interest rate, currency, and equity swaps.

INTRODUCTION

1

Forward commitments cover forwards, futures, and swaps. Pricing and valuation of forward commitments will be introduced here. A forward commitment is a derivative instrument in the form of a contract that provides the ability to lock in a price or rate at which one can buy or sell the underlying instrument at some future date or exchange an agreed-upon amount of money at a series of dates. As many investments can be viewed as a portfolio of forward commitments, this material is important to the practice of investment management.

The reading is organized as follows. Section 2 introduces the principles of the no-arbitrage approach to pricing and valuation of forward commitments. Section 3 presents the pricing and valuation of forwards and futures. Subsections address the cases of equities, interest rates, fixed-income instruments, and currencies as underlyings of forward commitments. Section 4 presents the pricing and valuation of swaps, addressing interest rate, currency, and equity swaps.

2   PRINCIPLES OF ARBITRAGE-FREE PRICING AND VALUATION OF FORWARD COMMITMENTS

In this section, we examine arbitrage-free pricing and valuation of forward commitments—also known as the no-arbitrage approach to pricing and valuing such instruments. We introduce some guiding principles that heavily influence the activities of arbitrageurs who are price setters in forward commitment markets.

There is a distinction between the pricing and the valuation of forward commitments. Forward commitment pricing involves determining the appropriate forward commitment price or rate when initiating the forward commitment contract. Forward commitment valuation involves determining the appropriate value of the forward commitment, typically after it has been initiated.

Our approach to pricing and valuation is based on the assumption that prices adjust to not allow arbitrage profits. Hence, the material will be covered from an arbitrageur's perspective. Key to understanding this material is to think like an arbitrageur. Specifically, like most people, the arbitrageur would rather have more money today than less. The arbitrageur abides by two fundamental rules:

Rule #1   Do not use your own money.

Rule #2   Do not take any price risk.

The arbitrageur often needs to borrow or lend money to satisfy Rule #1. If we buy the underlying, we borrow the money. If we sell the underlying, we lend the money. These transactions will synthetically create the identical cash flows to a particular forward commitment, but they will be opposite and, therefore, offsetting, which satisfies Rule #2. Note that for Rule #2, the concern is only market price risk related to the underlying and the derivatives used, as explained in detail later. Clearly, if we can generate positive cash flows today and abide by both rules, we have a great business; such is the life of an arbitrageur.

In an effort to demonstrate various pricing and valuation results based on the no-arbitrage approach, we will rely heavily on tables showing cash flows at Times 0 and T. From an arbitrage perspective, if an initial investment requires 100 euros, then we will present it as a −100 euro cash flow. Cash inflows to the arbitrageur have a positive sign, and outflows are negative.

Pricing and valuation tasks based on the no-arbitrage approach imply an inability to create a portfolio with no future liabilities and a positive cash flow today. In other words, if cash and forward markets are priced correctly with respect to each other, we cannot create such a portfolio. That is, we cannot create money today with no risk or future liability. This approach is built on the **law of one price**, which states that if two investments have the same or equivalent future cash flows regardless of what will happen in the future, then these two investments should have the same current price. Alternatively, if the law of one price is violated, someone could buy the cheaper asset and sell the more expensive, resulting in a gain at no risk and with no commitment of capital. The law of one price is built on the value additivity principle, which states that the value of a portfolio is simply the sum of the values of each instrument held in the portfolio.

Throughout this reading, the following key assumptions are made: (1) Replicating instruments are identifiable and investable, (2) market frictions are nil, (3) short selling is allowed with full use of proceeds, and (4) borrowing and lending are available at a known risk-free rate.

Analyses in this reading will rely on the **carry arbitrage model**, a no-arbitrage approach in which the underlying instrument is either bought or sold along with a forward position—hence the term "carry." Carry arbitrage models are also known as cost-of-carry arbitrage models or cash-and-carry arbitrage models. Typically, each type of forward commitment will result in a different model, but common elements will be observed. Carry arbitrage models are a great first approximation to explaining observed forward commitment prices in many markets.

The central theme here is that forward commitments are generally priced so as to preclude arbitrage profits. Section 3 demonstrates how to price and value equity, interest rate, fixed-income, and currency forward contracts. We also explain how these results apply to futures contracts.

PRICING AND VALUING FORWARD AND FUTURES CONTRACTS

3

In this section, we examine the pricing of forward and futures contracts based on the no-arbitrage approach. The resulting carry arbitrage models are based on the replication of the forward contract payoff with a position in the underlying that is financed through an external source. Although the margin requirements, mark-to-market features, and centralized clearing in futures markets result in material differences between forward and futures markets in some cases, we focus mainly on cases in which the particular carry arbitrage model can be used in both markets.

We start with a very simple setup to arrive at the primary insight that the current forward or futures price of a non-cash-paying instrument is simply equal to the price of the underlying adjusted upward for the amount that would be earned over the term of the contract by compounding the initial underlying price at the rate that incorporates costs and benefits related to the underlying instrument. Initially, we adopt a simplified approach in which we determine the forward price by compounding the underlying price at the risk-free rate. We then turn to examining the particular nuances of equity, interest rate, fixed-income, and currency forward and futures contracts. Mastery of the simple setup will make understanding the unique nuances in each market easier to comprehend. First, we examine selected introductory material.

3.1 Our Notation

In the following, notations are established for forward and futures contracts that will allow us to express concisely the key pricing and valuation relationships. **Forward price** or **futures price** refers to the price that is negotiated between the parties in the forward or futures contract. The market value of the forward or futures contract, termed **forward value** or **futures value** and sometimes just value, refers to the monetary value of an existing forward or futures contract. When the forward or futures contract is established, the price is negotiated so that the value of the contract on the initiation date is zero. Subsequent to the initiation date, the value can be significantly positive or negative.

Let S_t denote the price of the underlying instrument observed at Time t, where t is the time since the initiation of the forward contract and is expressed as a fraction of years.[1] Consider T as the initial time to expiration, expressed as a fraction of years. S_0 denotes the underlying price observed when the forward contract is initiated, and S_T denotes the underlying price observed when the forward contract expires. Also, let $F_0(T)$ denote the forward price established at the initiation date, 0, and expiring

---

1 Note that t can be greater than a year—for example t = 1.25. The variable t is expressed in years, not days or months, because interest rates, dividend yields, and most financial returns are expressed as yearly rates.

at date T, where T represents a period of time later. For example, suppose that on the initiation date (t = 0) a forward contract is negotiated for which $F_0(0.25) = €350$. Then the forward price for the forward contract is €350, with the contract expiration T = 0.25 years later. Similarly, let $f_0(T)$ denote the futures price for a contract established at the initiation date, 0, that expires at date T. Therefore, uppercase "F" denotes the forward price, whereas lowercase "f" denotes the futures price. Similarly, we let uppercase "V" denote the forward value, whereas lowercase "v" denotes the futures value. Many concepts in this reading apply equally to pricing and valuation of both forwards and futures. When they differ, we will emphasize the distinctions.

A key observation, to which we will return in greater detail, is that as a result of the no-arbitrage approach, when the forward contract is established, the forward price is negotiated so that the market value of the forward contract on the initiation date is zero. Most forward contracts are structured this way and are referred to as **at market**. No money changes hands, meaning that the initial value is zero. The forward contract value when initiated is expressed as $V_0(T) = v_0(T) = 0$. Again, we assume no margin requirements. Subsequent to the initiation date, the forward value can be significantly positive or negative.

At expiration, both the forward contract and the futures contract are equivalent to a spot transaction in the underlying. In fact, forward and futures contracts negotiated at Time T for delivery at Time T are by definition equivalent to a spot transaction at Time T. This property is often called **convergence**, and it implies that at Time T, both the forward price and the futures price are equivalent to the spot price—that is, $F_T(T) = f_T(T) = S_T$.

Let us define $V_t(T)$ as the forward contract value at Time t during the life of the futures contract. At expiration, T,

The market value of a long position in a forward contract value is $V_T(T) = S_T - F_0(T)$.

The market value of a short position in a forward contract value is $V_T(T) = F_0(T) - S_T$.

Let us define $v_t(T)$ as the futures contract value at Time t during the life of the futures contract. Note that as a result of marking to market, the value of a futures contract at expiration is simply the difference in the futures price from the previous day. Our time subscript is expressed in a fraction of a year; hence, we use (t−) to denote the fraction of the year that the previous trading day represents. At expiration, T:

The market value of a long position in a futures contract value before marking to market is $v_t(T) = f_t(T) - f_{t-}(T)$.

The market value of a short position in a futures contract value before marking to market is $v_t(T) = f_{t-}(T) - f_t(T)$.

The futures contract value after daily settlement is $v_t(T) = 0$.

As illustrated later, in this reading we adopt a simplified approach in which the valuation of forward and futures contracts is treated as the same, whereas the forward value and the futures value will be different because of futures contracts being marked to market and forward contracts not being marked to market.[2]

Exhibit 1 shows a forward contract at initiation and expiration. A long position in a forward contract will have a positive value at expiration if the underlying is above the initial forward price, whereas a short position in a forward contract will have a positive value at expiration if the underlying is below the initial forward price.

---

2 There are specific cases when $f_t(T) \neq F_t(T)$, but they are beyond the scope of this reading.

Exhibit 1	Value of a Forward Contract at Initiation and Expiration

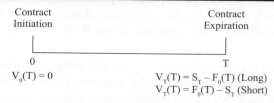

Contract Initiation   Contract Expiration

0   T

$V_0(T) = 0$

$V_T(T) = S_T - F_0(T)$ (Long)
$V_T(T) = F_0(T) - S_T$ (Short)

We turn now to focus on generic forward contracts.

3.2 No-Arbitrage Forward Contracts

We first consider a generic forward contract, meaning that we do not specify the underlying as anything more than just an asset. As we move through this section, we will continue to address specific additional factors to bring each carry arbitrage model closer to real markets. Thus, we will develop several different carry arbitrage models, each one applicable to specific forward commitment contracts.

3.2.1 Carry Arbitrage Model When There Are No Underlying Cash Flows

Carry arbitrage models receive their name from the literal interpretation of carrying the underlying over the life of the forward contract. If an arbitrageur enters a forward contract to sell an underlying instrument for delivery at Time T, then to hedge this exposure, one strategy is to buy the underlying instrument at Time 0 with borrowed funds and carry it to the forward expiration date so it can be sold under the terms of the forward contract as illustrated in Exhibit 2.

Exhibit 2	Cash Flows Related to Carrying the Underlying through Calendar Time

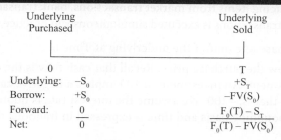

Underlying Purchased   Underlying Sold

0   T

Underlying:	$-S_0$	$+S_T$
Borrow:	$+S_0$	$-FV(S_0)$
Forward:	0	$F_0(T) - S_T$
Net:	0	$F_0(T) - FV(S_0)$

For now, we will keep the significant technical issues to a minimum. When possible, we will just use FV and PV to denote the future value and present value, respectively. We are not concerned now about compounding conventions, day count conventions, or even the appropriate risk-free interest rate proxy. We will address these complexities only when necessary.

Carry arbitrage models rest on the no-arbitrage assumptions given earlier. To understand carry arbitrage models, it is helpful to think like an arbitrageur. The arbitrageur seeks to exploit any pricing discrepancy between the futures or forward price and the underlying spot price. The arbitrageur is assumed to prefer more money compared to less money, assuming everything else is the same. We now expand on the two fundamental rules for the arbitrageur.

Rule #1   Do not use our own money. Specifically, the arbitrageur does not use
           his or her own money to acquire positions but borrows to purchase
           the underlying. Also, the arbitrageur does not spend proceeds from
           short selling transactions but invests them at the risk-free interest
           rate.

Rule #2   Do not take any price risk. In our discussion, the arbitrageur focuses
           here only on market price risk related to the underlying and the deriv-
           atives used. We do not consider other risks, such as liquidity risk and
           counterparty credit risk. These topics are covered in more advanced
           treatments.

Consider the following strategy in which an arbitrageur purchases the underlying
instrument with borrowed money in the spot market at price S_0 at Time 0 and later,
at Time T, contemporaneously sells the underlying at a price of S_T and repays the
loan. The cash flow from this strategy evaluated at Time T is the proceeds from the
sales of the underlying, S_T, less $FV_{0,T}(S_0)$ or, more simply, $FV(S_0)$, the price of the
underlying purchased at Time 0 grossed up by the finance cost, assumed to be the
risk-free interest rate. In other words, the arbitrageur borrows the money to buy the
asset, so he will pay back $FV(S_0)$ at Time T, based on the risk-free rate.

Clearly, when S_T is below $FV(S_0)$, this transaction will suffer a loss. Note that
breakeven will occur when the underlying value at T exactly equals the future price
of the underlying at 0 grossed up by the finance cost or $S_T = FV(S_0)$. If we assume
continuous compounding (r_c), then $FV(S_0) = S_0 e^{r_c T}$. If we assume annual compounding
(r), then $FV(S_0) = S_0(1 + r)^T$. Note that in practice, observed interest rates are derived
from market prices; it is not the other way around. Significant errors can occur if the
quoted interest rate is used with the wrong compounding convention.[3] When possible,
we just use the generic present value and future value to minimize confusion.

To help clarify, Exhibit 3 shows the cash flows from carrying the underlying, say,
stock, assuming $S_0 = 100$, r = 5%, T = 1, and $S_T = 90$ or 110.[4] Each step consists of
transactions that generate the cash flows shown at times 0 and T. Each row of cash flows
in tables such as the one below are termed "steps," and they will involve a wide array
of cash flow producing items from market transactions, bank transactions, and other
events. The set of transactions is executed simultaneously in practice, not sequentially.

Step 1   Purchase one unit of the underlying at Time 0.

Step 2   Borrow the purchase price. Recall that cash flow is the opposite of
          investment. An investment of 100 implies a negative cash flow of
          100—that is, −100. We assume the interest rate is quoted on an annual
          compounding basis and time is expressed in fractions of a year.

---

3 For many quantitative finance tasks, it is easier to do the analysis with continuous compounding even
though the underlying rate quotation conventions are based on another method.
4 Note that S_T can take on any value, but in the table we present just two values, one representing an up
move and one representing a down move.

Exhibit 3   Cash Flows for Financed Position in the Underlying Instrument

Steps	Cash Flows at Time 0	Cash Flows at Time T
1. Purchase underlying at 0 and sell at T	$-S_0 = -100$	$+S_T = 90$ or $+S_T = 110$
2. Borrow funds at 0 and repay with interest at T	$+S_0 = 100$	$-FV(S_0) = -100(1 + 0.05)^1 = -105$
Net cash flow	0	$+S_T - FV(S_0) = 90 - 105 = -15$ or $= 110 - 105 = 5$

Because the two outcomes are not the same, the strategy at this point fails to satisfy the arbitrageur's Rule #2: Do not take any price risk. Thus, to satisfy Rule #2, consider a third transaction that allows one to lock in the value of the underlying at Time T. This result can be achieved by selling, at Time 0, a forward contract on the underlying at price $F_0(T)$, where the underlying will be delivered at Time T.[5] Recall that the value of the forward contract at expiration will simply be the difference between the underlying, S_T, and the initial forward price, $F_0(T)$.

As seen in Exhibit 4, we add two additional steps, again executed simultaneously:

Step 3   Sell a forward contract. As we are seeking to determine the equilibrium forward price, we do not assume that the forward price is initially at market, meaning that the value is zero. Thus, the forward contract value at Time 0, $V_0(T)$, may be non-zero. We illustrate selected numerical values for clarity.

Step 4   Borrow the arbitrage profit in order to capture it today. If the transaction leads to an arbitrage profit at the Time T expiration, you borrow against it. In other words, suppose that in setting up the transaction, you know that it will produce an arbitrage profit of €5. Then you could borrow the present value of €5 and pay it back at expiration with the arbitrage profit. In effect, you are pre-capturing your arbitrage profit by bringing it to the present so as to receive it at Time 0. The amount you borrow will be the forward price minus the future value of the spot price when compounded at the risk-free rate. As we will see shortly, if the forward contract is priced correctly, there will be no arbitrage profit and, hence, no Step 4. Note also that we exclude the case of lending, because it would occur only if you executed a strategy to capture a certain loss, which we presume no one would do.

In this exhibit, the forward price is assumed to be trading at 105.

---

5 Note that when an arbitrageur needs to sell the underlying, it must be assumed that she does not hold it in inventory and thus must short sell it. When the transaction calls for selling a derivative instrument, such as a forward contract, it is always just selling—technically, not short selling.

Exhibit 4   Cash Flows for Financed Position in the Underlying Instrument Combined with a Forward Contract

Steps	Cash Flows at Time 0	Cash Flows at Time T
1. Purchase underlying at 0 and sell at T	$-S_0 = -100$	$+S_T = 90$ or $+S_T = 110$
2. Borrow funds at 0 and repay with interest at T	$+S_0 = 100$	$-FV(S_0) = -S_0(1 + r)^T$ $= -100(1 + 0.05)^1 = -105$
3. Sell forward contract at 0 when $F_0(T) = 105$	$+V_0(T)$	$V_T(T) = F_0(T) - S_T = 105 - 90 = 15$ or $V_T(T) = F_0(T) - S_T = 105 - 110 = -5$
4. Borrow arbitrage profit	$+PV[F_0(T)$ $- FV(S_0)]$	$-[F_0(T) - FV(S_0)]$ $= -[105 - 100(1 + 0.05)] = 0$
Net cash flow	$+V_0(T)$ $+ PV[F_0(T)$ $- FV(S_0)]$	$+S_T - FV(S_0) + F_0(T) - S_T$ $- [F_0(T) - FV(S_0)] = 0$ (For every underlying value)

Notice that at expiration the underlying is worth 90 or 110 and the forward contract is worth either 15 or −5. The combination of the underlying and the forward value is 90 + 15 = 105 or 110 − 5 = 105, and that 105 is precisely the amount necessary to pay off the loan. So, there is zero cash flow at expiration under any and all circumstances.

Based on the no-arbitrage approach, a portfolio offering zero cash flow in the future is expected to be valued at zero at Time 0. That is, based on Exhibit 4, the net cash flow at Time 0 can be expressed as $V_0(T) + PV[F_0(T) - FV(S_0)] = 0$. With this perspective, the value of a given short forward contract is, therefore, $V_0(T) = -PV[F_0(T) - FV(S_0)]$, which can be rearranged and denoted $V_0(T) = S_0 - PV[F_0(T)]$. Based on this result, we see that the no-arbitrage forward price is simply the future value of the underlying, or

$$F_0(T) = \text{Future value of underlying} = FV(S_0) \tag{1}$$

In our example, $F_0(T) = FV(S_0) = 105$. In fact, with annual compounding and T = 1, we have simply $F_0(1) = S_0(1 + r)^T = 100(1 + 0.05)^1$. The future value refers to the amount of money equal to the spot price invested at the compound risk-free interest rate during the time period. It is not to be confused with or mistaken for the mathematical expectation of the spot price at Time T.

To better understand the arbitrage mechanics, suppose we observe that $F_0(1) = 106$. Based on the prior information, we observe that the forward price is higher than that determined by the carry arbitrage model (recall $F_0(T) = FV(S_0) = 105$). Because the model value is lower than the market forward price, we conclude that the market forward price is too high and should be sold. An arbitrage opportunity exists, and it will involve selling the forward contract at 106. Because of Rule #2—the arbitrageur should not take any market price risk—the second transaction is to purchase the underlying instrument so that gains (or losses) on the underlying will be offset by losses (or gains) on the forward contract. Finally, because of Rule #1—the arbitrageur does not use his or her own money—the third transaction involves borrowing the purchase price of the underlying security. Based on a desire by the arbitrageur to receive future arbitrage profits today, the fourth transaction involves borrowing the known terminal profits. Note that all four transactions are done simultaneously. To summarize, the arbitrage transactions can be represented in the following four steps:

Step 1   Sell the forward contract on the underlying.

Step 2   Purchase the underlying.

Step 3   Borrow the funds for the underlying purchase.

Step 4   Borrow the arbitrage profit.[6]

Exhibit 5 shows the resulting cash flows from these transactions. This strategy is known as carry arbitrage because we are carrying—that is, we are long—the underlying instrument. Note that if the forward price were 106, the value of the forward contract would be 0.9524 at Time 0. In fact, $V_0(T) = PV[F_0(T) - FV(S_0)] = (106 - 105)/(1 + 0.05) = 0.9524$. But if the counterparty enters a long position in the forward contract at a forward price of 106, valuing it incorrectly, then the forward contract seller has the opportunity to receive the 0.9524 with no liability in the future. In Step 4, the arbitrageur borrows this amount. At Time T, the arbitrage profit of 1 will exactly offset the repayment of this loan. This opportunity represents a portfolio that will be pursued aggressively. It is a clear arbitrage opportunity.

Exhibit 5   Cash Flows with Forward Contract Market Price Too High Relative to Carry Arbitrage Model

Steps	Cash Flows at Time 0	Cash Flows at Time T
1. Sell forward contract on underlying at $F_0(T) = 106$	$V_0(T) = 0$	$V_T(T) = F_0(T) - S_T = 106 - 90 = 16$ or $V_T(T) = F_0(T) - S_T = 106 - 110 = -4$
2. Purchase underlying at 0 and sell at T	$-S_0 = -100$	$+S_T = 90$ or $+S_T = 110$
3. Borrow funds for underlying purchase	$+S_0 = 100$	$-FV(S_0) = -100(1 + 0.05) = -105$
4. Borrow arbitrage profit	$+PV[F_0(T) - FV(S_0)]$ $= (106 - 105)/(1+0.05)$ $= 0.9524$	$-[F_0(T) - FV(S_0)]$ $= -[106 - 100(1+0.05)] = -1$
Net cash flow	0.9524	$16 + 90 - 105 - 1$ or $-4 + 110 - 105 - 1$ $= 0$

Suppose instead we observe a lower forward price of $F_0(T) = 104$. Based on the prior information, we conclude that the forward price is too low when compared to the forward price determined by the carry arbitrage model. In fact, the carry arbitrage model forward price is again $F_0(T) = FV(S_0) = 105$. Thus, Step 1 here is to buy a forward contract, and the value at T is $S_T - F_0(T)$. Because of Rule #2—the arbitrageur not taking any risk—Step 2 is to sell short the underlying instrument. Because of Rule #1—the arbitrageur not using her own money, or technically here spending another entity's money—Step 3 involves lending the short sale proceeds. Finally, to capture the arbitrage profit today, you borrow its present value. Again, to summarize, the arbitrage transactions involve the following four steps:

Step 1   Buy the forward contract on the underlying.

Step 2   Sell the underlying short.

Step 3   Lend the short sale proceeds.

Step 4   Borrow the arbitrage profit.

---

6 Remember that you are bringing the arbitrage profit from the future, time T, to the present, time 0, by borrowing against it and paying back the loan at T with the arbitrage profit. We exclude the case of lending, because it involves an arbitrage loss and would mean that the arbitrageur invests some of his own money at time 0 and pays out its value at T to cover the arbitrage loss.

Note that this set of transactions is the exact opposite of the prior case in Exhibit 5. This strategy is known as **reverse carry arbitrage** because we are doing the opposite of carrying the underlying instrument; that is, we are short selling the underlying instrument.

Therefore, unless $F_0(T) = FV(S_0)$, there is an arbitrage opportunity. Notice that if $F_0(T) > FV(S_0)$, then the forward contract is sold and the underlying is purchased. Thus, arbitrageurs drive down the forward price and drive up the underlying price until $F_0(T) = FV(S_0)$ and a risk-free positive cash flow today no longer exists. Further, if $F_0(T) < FV(S_0)$, then the forward contract is purchased and the underlying is sold short. In this case, the forward price is driven up and the underlying price is driven down. Arbitrageurs' market activities will drive forward prices to equal the future value of the underlying, bringing the law of one price into effect once again. Most importantly, if the forward contract is priced at its equilibrium price, there will be no arbitrage profit and thus no Step 4.

EXAMPLE 1

Forward Contract Price

An Australian stock paying no dividends is trading in Australian dollars for A\$63.31, and the annual Australian interest rate is 2.75% with annual compounding.

1 Based on the current stock price and the no-arbitrage approach, which of the following values is *closest* to the equilibrium three-month forward price?

  A A\$63.31

  B A\$63.74

  C A\$65.05

2 If the interest rate immediately falls 50 bps to 2.25%, the three-month forward price will:

  A decrease.

  B increase.

  C be unchanged.

Solution to 1:

B is correct. Based on the information given, we know $S_0 = $ A\$63.31, r = 2.75% (annual compounding), and T = 0.25. Therefore,

$$F_0(T) = FV_{0,T}(S_0) = 63.31(1 + 0.0275)^{0.25} = \text{A\$63.7408}.$$

Solution to 2:

A is correct, and we know this is true because the forward price is directly related to the interest rate. Specifically,

$$F_0(T) = FV_{0,T}(S_0) = 63.31(1 + 0.0225)^{0.25} = \text{A\$63.6632}.$$

Therefore, we see in this case a fall in interest rates resulted in a decrease in the forward price. This relationship between forward prices and interest rates will generally hold so long as the underlying is not also influenced by interest rates.

As we see here, remember that one significant implication of this arbitrage activity is that the quoted forward price does not directly reflect expectations of future underlying prices. The only factors that matter are the interest rate and time to expiration. Other factors will be included later as we make the carry arbitrage model more realistic, but we will not be including expectations of future underlying prices. So, in other words, an opinion that the underlying will increase in value, perhaps even substantially, has no bearing on the forward price.

We now turn to the task of understanding the value of an existing forward contract. There are many circumstances in which, once a forward contract has been entered, one wants to know the contract's fair value. The goal is to calculate the position's value at current market prices. It may be due to market-based accounting, in which the accounting statements need to reflect the current fair value of various instruments. Finally, it is simply important to know whether a position in a forward contract is making money or losing money.

The forward value, based on arbitrage, can best be understood by referring to Exhibit 6. Suppose the first transaction involves buying a forward contract with a price of $F_0(T)$ at Time 0 with expiration of Time T. Now consider selling a new forward contract with price $F_t(T)$ at Time t again with expiration of Time T. Exhibit 6 shows the potential cash flows. Remember the equivalence at expiration between the forward price, the futures price, and the underlying price, meaning $F_T(T) = f_T(T) = S_T$. Note that the column labeled "Value at Time t" represents the value of the forward contracts. Note that we are seeking the forward value; hence, this transaction would result in cash flows only if it is actually executed. We need not actually execute the transaction; we just need to see what it would produce if we did. This point is analogous to the fact that if holding a liquid asset, we need not sell it to determine its value; we can simply observe its market price, which gives us an estimate of the price at which we could sell it.

Exhibit 6   Cash Flows for the Valuation of a Long Forward Position

Steps	Cash Flow at Time 0	Value at Time t	Cash Flow at Time T
1. Buy forward contract at 0 at $F_0(T)$	0	$V_t(T)$	$V_T(0, T) = S_T - F_0(T)$
2. Sell forward contract at t at $F_t(T)$	NA	0	$V_T(t, T) = F_t(T) - S_T$
Net cash flows/Value	0	$V_t(T)$	$+F_t(T) - F_0(T)$

There are now three different points in time to consider: Time 0, Time t, and Time T. For clarity, we explicitly state the period for present value, $PV_{t,T}()$ rather than $PV()$, which means the present value at point t of an amount paid in T − t years, and for future value, $FV_{t,T}()$ rather than $FV()$, which means the future value in T − t years of an amount paid at point t.

Note that once the offsetting forward is entered, the net position is not subject to market risk in that the cash flow at Time T is not influenced by what happens to the spot price. The position is completely hedged. Therefore, the value observed at Time t of the original forward contract initiated at Time 0 and expiring at Time T is simply the present value of the difference in the forward prices, $PV_{t,T}[F_t(T) - F_0(T)]$. Based on Exhibit 6, the forward value at Time t for a long position in the forward contract entered at Time 0 is the present value of the difference in forward prices, or

$V_t(T) =$ Present value of difference in forward prices

$$= PV_{t,T}\left[F_t(T) - F_0(T)\right]$$

(2)

Thus, there is the old forward price, which is the price the participants agreed on when the contract was started, and now there is also the new forward price, which is the price at which any two participants would agree to deliver the underlying at the same date as in the original contract. Of course, now the spot price has changed and some time has elapsed, so the new forward price will likely not equal the old forward price. The value of the contract is simply the present value of the difference in these two prices, with the present value calculated over the remaining life of the contract.

Alternatively, $V_t(T) = S_t - PV_{t,T}[F_0(T)]$.[7] Thus, the long forward contract value can be viewed as the present value, determined using the given interest rate, of the difference in forward prices—the original one and a new one that is priced at the point of valuation. If we know the underlying price at Time t, S_t, then we can estimate the forward price, $F_t(T) = FV_{t,T}(S_t)$. Based on Equation 2, we then solve for the forward value. Note that the short position is simply the negative value of Equation 2.

EXAMPLE 2

Forward Contract Value

Assume that at Time 0 we entered into a one-year forward contract with price $F_0(T) = 105$. Nine months later, at Time t = 0.75, the observed price of the stock is $S_{0.75} = 110$ and the interest rate is 5%. The value of the existing forward contract expiring in three months will be *closest* to:

A   −6.34.

B   6.27.

C   6.34.

Solution:

B is correct. Note that, based on $F_0(T) = 105$, $S_{0.75} = 110$, r = 5%, and T − t = 0.25, the three-month forward price at Time t is equal to $F_t(T) = FV_{t,T}(S_t) = 110(1 + 0.05)^{0.25} = 111.3499$. Therefore, we find that the value of the existing forward entered at Time 0 valued at Time t using the difference method is

$$V_t(T) = PV_{t,T}[F_t(T) - F_0(T)] = (111.3499 - 105)/(1 + 0.05)^{0.25} = 6.2729.$$

Now that we have the basics of forward pricing and forward valuation, we introduce some other realistic carrying costs that influence pricing and valuation.

3.2.2 *Carry Arbitrage Model When Underlying Has Cash Flows*

We have seen that forward pricing and valuation is driven by arbitrageurs seeking to exploit mispricing by either carrying or reverse carrying the underlying instrument. Carry arbitrage requires paying the interest cost, whereas reverse carry arbitrage results in receiving the interest benefit. For many instruments, there are other significant carry costs and benefits. We will now incorporate into forward pricing various costs and benefits related to the underlying instrument. For this reason, we need to introduce some notation.

Let γ (Greek lowercase gamma) denote the **carry benefits** (for example, dividends, foreign interest, and bond coupon payments that would arise from certain underlyings). Let $\gamma_T = FV_{0,T}(\gamma_0)$ denote the future value of underlying carry benefits and

---

[7] From Equation 1 and assuming annual compounding, $F_t(T) = S_t(1 + r)^{(T-t)}$, so $PV_{t,T}[F_t(T)] = PV_{t,T}[S_t(1 + r)^{(T-t)}] = S_t$.

$\gamma_0 = PV_{0,T}(\gamma_T)$ denote the present value of underlying carry benefits. Let θ (Greek lowercase theta) denote the **carry costs**. For financial instruments, these costs are essentially zero. For commodities, these costs include such factors as waste, storage, and insurance. Let $\theta_T = FV_{0,T}(\theta_0)$ denote the future value of underlying costs and $\theta_0 = PV_{0,T}(\theta_T)$ denote the present value of underlying costs. We do not cover commodities in this reading, but you should be aware of this cost. Moreover, you should note that carry costs are similar to financing costs. Holding a financial asset does not generate direct carry costs, but it does result in the opportunity cost of the interest that could be earned on the money tied up in the asset. Thus, the financing costs that come from the rate of interest and the carry costs that are common to physical assets are equivalent concepts.

The key forward pricing equation, based on these notations, can be expressed as

$$F_0(T) = \text{Future value of underlying adjusted for carry cash flows}$$

$$= FV_{0,T}(S_0 + \theta_0 - \gamma_0) \qquad \text{(3)}$$

Thus, the forward price is the future value of the underlying adjusted for carry cash flows. Carry costs, like the rate of interest, increase the burden of carrying the underlying instrument through time; hence, these costs are added in the forward pricing equation. Alternatively, carry benefits decrease the burden of carrying the underlying instrument through time; hence, these benefits are subtracted in the forward pricing equation.

In the following discussion, we follow the arbitrage procedure discussed previously, but now we also consider that the underlying pays some form of benefit during the life of the forward contract. Because of the types of instruments considered here, underlying benefits will be our focus. Note, however, that costs are handled in exactly the same way except there is a sign change.

The arbitrageur purchases the underlying with borrowed money at Time 0 and then sells it at Time T. Notice that any benefits from owning the underlying are placed in a risk-free investment. The risk again is that the underlying value (S_T) will decrease between 0 and T, when the position is unwound. Note that breakeven will occur when the underlying value at T exactly equals the future value of the underlying at 0 adjusted for any benefits, or $S_T = FV(S_0) - \gamma_T = FV(S_0 - \gamma_0)$. Thus, based on this breakeven expression, the underlying benefits (γ) have the effect of lowering the cost of carrying the underlying, and therefore, the forward price is lower.

To help clarify, we illustrate in Exhibit 7 the same example as before in which $S_0 = 100$, $r = 5\%$, $T = 1$, and $S_T = 90$ or 110. We now assume the underlying is known to distribute 2.9277 at Time $t = 0.5$: $\gamma_t = 2.9277$. Thus, the time until the distribution of 2.9277 is t, and hence, the present value is $\gamma_0 = 2.9277/(1 + 0.05)^{0.5} = 2.8571$. The time between the distribution and the forward expiration is $T - t = 0.5$, and thus, the future value is $\gamma_T = 2.9277(1 + 0.05)^{0.5} = 3$.

Remember that the steps in these tables simply refer to cash flow producing events and are initiated simultaneously.

Step 1   Purchase the underlying at Time 0, receive the dividend at Time t = 0.5, and sell the underlying at Time T.

Step 2   Reinvest the dividend received at Time t = 0.5 at the risk-free interest rate until Time T.

Step 3   Borrow the initial cost of the underlying. The strategy again at this point fails to satisfy Rule #2 of the arbitrageur: Do not take any price risk. If the underlying falls in value, then there is price risk.

Step 4   Sell a forward contract. This transaction addresses Rule #2. Specifically, we sell a forward contract at Time 0 and the underlying will be delivered at Time T.

Step 5 Borrow the arbitrage profit.

Exhibit 7	Cash Flows for Financed Position in the Underlying with Forward		
Steps	Cash Flow at Time 0	Cash Flow at Time t	Cash Flow at Time T
1. Purchase underlying at 0, sell at T	$-S_0 = -100$	$+\gamma_t = 2.9277$	$+S_T = 90$ or $+S_T = 110$
2. Reinvest distribution		$-\gamma_t = -2.9277$	$+\gamma_T = 2.9277(1 + 0.05)^{0.5} = 3$
3. Borrow funds	$+S_0 = 100$		$-FV(S_0) = -100(1 + 0.05)^1 = -105$
4. Sell forward contract	$V_0(T)$		$V_T(T) = F_0(T) - S_T = 102 - 90 = 12$ or $102 - 110 = -8$
5. Borrow arbitrage profit	$+PV[F_0(T) + \gamma_T - FV(S_0)]$		$-[F_0(T) + \gamma_T - FV(S_0)]$
Net cash flows	$V_0(T) + PV[F_0(T) + \gamma_T - FV(S_0)]$	0	$+S_T + \gamma_T - FV(S_0) + F_0(T) - S_T - [F_0(T) + \gamma_T - FV(S_0)] = 0$

We know in equilibrium the value of the cash flow at Time 0 is zero, or $V_0(T) + PV[F_0(T) + \gamma_T - FV(S_0)] = 0$, and thus $V_0(T) = -PV[F_0(T) + \gamma_T - FV(S_0)]$. If the forward contract has zero value, then the forward price is simply the future value of the underlying less the future value of carry benefits, or

$F_0(T)$ = Future value of underlying − Future value of carry benefits

$= FV(S_0) - \gamma_T$

As the carry benefits increase, the forward price decreases. In short, benefits reduce the cost of carrying the asset, and that reduces the forward price. In this example, the equilibrium forward price is $FV_{0,T}(S_0) - \gamma_T = 105 - 3 = 102$. This is the rationale for the carry arbitrage model adjusted for underlying benefits paid, or $F_0(T) = FV_{0,T}(S_0) - \gamma_T$. Note that because $\gamma_T = FV_{0,T}(\gamma_0)$, we can also express the carry benefit adjusted model as $F_0(T) = FV_{0,T}(S_0 - \gamma_0)$. In words, the initial forward price is equal to the future value of the underlying minus the value of any ownership benefits at expiration. Carry benefits lower the carry burden of the arbitrageur. In effect, because the underlying benefits reduce the burden of carrying the underlying, the forward price is lower. We see that the cost of carrying the underlying is now $F_0(T) = 102$, which is lower than the previous example in which $F_0(T) = 105$.

The forward value for a long position when the underlying has carry benefits or carry costs is found in the same way as described previously except that the new forward price, as well as the old, is adjusted to account for these benefits and costs. Specifically,

$V_t(T)$ = Present value of difference in forward prices

$$= PV_{t,T}[F_t(T) - F_0(T)] \qquad (4)$$

The forward value is equal to the present value of the difference in forward prices. The benefits and costs are reflected in this valuation equation because they are incorporated in the forward price: $F_t(T) = FV_{t,T}(S_t + \theta_t - \gamma_t)$. Again, the forward value is simply the present value of the difference in forward prices.

Before examining equity, interest rate, fixed-income bond, and currency underlyings, we review an important technical issue related to compounding convention. Assume the underlying is a common stock quoted in euros (€) with an initial price of €100 (S_0 = €100), the European risk-free interest rate is 5% (r = 0.05, annual compounding), T = 1 year, and the known dividend payment in t = 0.5 years is γ_t = €2.9277 or in future value terms is γ_T = €3.0. As illustrated previously, the no-arbitrage forward price is €102, which is determined as follows:

$$F_0(T) = FV_{0,T}(S_0 + \theta_0 - \gamma_0)$$
$$= [100 + 0 - 2.9277/(1 + 0.05)^{0.5}](1 + 0.05)^1$$
$$= 105 - 3 = €102$$

Recall that γ_0 denotes the present value of carry benefits. In this case, the carry benefits are not paid until t = 0.5; hence, discounting is required. Thus, γ_0 = 2.9277/(1 + 0.05)$^{0.5}$ = 2.8571.

Now let us consider stock indexes, such as the EURO STOXX 50 or the US Russell 3000. With stock indexes, it is difficult to account for the numerous dividend payments paid by underlying stocks that vary in timing and amount. Dividend index point is a measure of the quantity of dividends attributable to a particular index. It is a useful measure of the amount of dividends paid; a very useful number for arbitrage trading. To simplify the problem, a continuous dividend yield is often assumed. What this means is that it is assumed that dividends accrue continuously over the period in question rather than on specific discrete dates, which is not an unreasonable assumption for an index with a large number of component stocks.

Before turning to this carry arbitrage model variation, we will review continuous compounding in general, based on the previous example, because it is a perennial source of confusion. The equivalence between annual compounding and continuous compounding can be expressed as $(1 + r)^T = e^{r_c T}$ or $r_c = \ln[(1 + r)^T]/T = \ln(1 + r)$;[8] "ln" refers to the natural log of the function. Note that in the marketplace, zero coupon bond prices or bank deposit amounts are the underlying instrument and interest rates are derived from prices. Though we often refer to these instruments in terms of quoted rates, ultimately investors are concerned with the resulting cash flows. Therefore, if the quoted interest rate is 5% based on annual compounding as shown in the previous example, then we can solve for the implied interest rate based on continuous compounding, or $r_c = \ln(1 + r) = \ln(1 + 0.05) = 0.0488$, or 4.88%. In most cases, the context makes clear when the rate being used is continuous; hence, we use the subscript c only when clarity is required.

We see that compounding continuously results in a lower quoted rate. What this implies is that a cash flow compounded at 5% annually is equivalent to being compounded at 4.88% continuously. Based on the information in the previous example, the implied dividend yield can be derived. Specifically, the carry arbitrage model with continuous compounding is again the future value of the underlying adjusted for carry and can be expressed as

$$F_0(T) = S_0 e^{(r_c + \theta - \gamma)T} \text{ (Future value of the underlying adjusted for carry)}$$

Note that in this context r_c, θ, and γ are continuously compounded rates.

The carry arbitrage model can also be used when the underlying requires storage costs, needs to be insured, and suffers from spoilage. In these cases, rather than lowering the carrying burden, these costs make it more costly to carry and hence the forward price is higher.

We now apply these results to equity forward and futures contracts.

---

8 Recall that $\ln(a^x) = x\ln(a)$. Thus, $\ln[(1 + r)^T]/T = \ln(1 + r)$ and time to maturity does not influence this conversion from annual to continuous rates.

3.3 Equity Forward and Futures Contracts

Although we alluded to equity forward pricing and valuation in the last section, we illustrate with concrete examples the application of carry arbitrage models to equity forward and futures contracts. Remember that here we assume that forward contracts and futures contracts are priced in the same way. It is vital to treat the compounding convention of interest rates appropriately.

If the underlying is a stock, then the carry benefit is the dividend payments as illustrated in the next two examples.

EXAMPLE 3

Equity Futures Contract Price with Continuously Compounded Interest Rates

The continuously compounded dividend yield on the EURO STOXX 50 is 3%, and the current stock index level is 3,500. The continuously compounded annual interest rate is 0.15%. Based on the carry arbitrage model, the three-month futures price will be *closest* to:

A   3,473.85.

B   3,475.15.

C   3,525.03.

Solution:

B is correct. Based on the carry arbitrage model, the forward price is $F_0(T)$ = $S_0 e^{(r_c - \gamma)T}$. The future value of the underlying adjusted for carry, i.e., the dividend payments, over the next year would be $3,500 e^{(0.0015 - 0.03)(3/12)} = 3,475.15$.

EXAMPLE 4

Equity Forward Pricing and Forward Valuation with Discrete Dividends

Suppose Nestlé common stock is trading for CHF70 and pays a CHF2.20 dividend in one month. Further, assume the Swiss one-month risk-free rate is 1.0%, quoted on an annual compounding basis. Assume that the stock goes ex-dividend the same day the single stock forward contract expires. Thus, the single stock forward contract expires in one month.

1   The one-month forward price for Nestlé common stock will be *closest* to:

   A   CHF67.80.

   B   CHF67.86.

   C   CHF69.94.

2   An increase in which of the following parameters would result in an increase in the forward price?

   A   Dividends

   B   Risk-free interest rate

   C   Expected future stock price

Solution to 1:

B is correct. In this case, we have $S_0 = 70$, $r = 1.0\%$, $T = 1/12$, and $\gamma_T = 2.2$. Therefore, $F_0(T) = FV_{0,T}(S_0 + \theta_0 - \gamma_0) = FV_{0,T}(S_0) + FV_{0,T}(\theta_0) - FV_{0,T}(\gamma_0) = 70(1 + 0.01)^{1/12} + 0 - 2.2 = CHF67.86$.

Solution to 2:

B is correct. The forward price is not influenced by the expected spot price. It solely reflects carry costs and carry benefits. Being a carry benefit, the increase in dividends reduces the forward price. Thus, in the answers above, only an increase in the risk-free rate will result in an increase in the forward price.

The value of an equity forward contract entered earlier is simply the present value of the difference in the initial forward price and the current forward price as illustrated in the next example.

EXAMPLE 5

Equity Forward Valuation

Suppose we bought a one-year forward contract at 102 and there are now three months to expiration. The underlying is currently trading for 110, and interest rates are 5% on an annual compounding basis.

1 If there are no other carry cash flows, the forward value of the existing contract will be *closest* to:

   A −10.00.

   B 9.24.

   C 10.35.

2 If a dividend payment is announced between the forward's valuation and expiration dates, assuming the news announcement does not change the current underlying price, the forward value will *most likely*:

   A decrease.

   B increase.

   C be the same.

Suppose that instead of buying a forward contract, we buy a one-year *futures* contract at 102 and there are now three months to expiration. Today's futures price is 112.35. There are no other carry cash flows.

3 After marking to market, the futures value of the existing contract will be *closest* to:

   A −10.35.

   B 0.00.

   C 10.35.

4 Compared to the value of a forward contract, the value of a futures contract is *most likely*:

   A lower.

   B higher.

   C the same.

Solution to 1:

B is correct. For this case, we have $F_0(T) = 102$, $S_{0.75} = 110$, $r = 5\%$, and $T - t = 0.25$. Note that the new forward price at t is simply $F_t(T) = FV_{t,T}(S_t) = 110(1 + 0.05)^{0.25} = 111.3499$. Therefore, we have

$$V_t(T) = PV_{t,T}[F_t(T) - F_0(T)] = (111.3499 - 102)/(1 + 0.05)^{0.25} = 9.2365.$$

Thus, we see that the current forward value is greater than the difference between the current underlying value of 110 and the initial forward price of 102 as a result of interest costs resulting in the new forward price being 111.35.

Solution to 2:

A is correct. The old forward price is fixed. The discounted difference in the new forward price and the old forward price is the value. If we impose a new dividend, it would lower the new forward price and thus lower the value of the old forward contract.

Solution to 3:

B is correct. Futures contracts are marked to market daily, which implies that the market value, resulting in profits and losses, is received or paid at each daily settlement. Hence, the equity futures value is zero each day after settlement has occurred.

Solution to 4:

A is correct. After marking to market, the futures contract value is zero because profits and losses are taken daily. Thus, because we are long the futures or forward contract and the price has risen, the futures value will be lower than the forward value.

We turn now to the widely used interest rate forward and futures contracts.

3.4 Interest Rate Forward and Futures Contracts

Libor, which stands for London Interbank Offered Rate, is a widely used interest rate that serves as the underlying for many derivative instruments. It represents the rate at which London banks can borrow from other London banks. When these loans are in dollars, they are known as Eurodollar time deposits, with the rate referred to as dollar Libor. There are, however, Libor rates for all major non-dollar currencies. Average Libor rates are derived and posted each day at 11:30 a.m. London time. Lenders and participants in the interest rate derivatives market use these posted Libor rates to determine the interest payments on loans and the payoffs of various derivatives.[9] In addition to this London spot market, there are active forward and futures markets for

---

9 In 2008, financial regulators and many market participants began to suspect that the daily quoted Libor, which was compiled by the British Bankers Association (BBA), was being manipulated by certain banks that submitted their rates to the BBA for use in determining this average. In 2014, the BBA ceded control of the daily Libor reporting process to the Intercontinental Exchange.

derivatives based on Libor. Our focus will be on forward markets, as represented by forward rate agreements. In order to understand the forward market, however, let us first look at the Libor spot market. Assume the following notation:

$L_i(m)$ = Libor on an m-day deposit observed on day i

NA = notional amount, quantity of funds initially deposited

NTD = number of total days in a year, used for interest calculations (always 360 in the Libor market)

t_m = accrual period, fraction of year for m-day deposit—t_m = m/NTD

TA = terminal amount, quantity of funds repaid when the Libor deposit is withdrawn

For example, suppose day i is designated as Time 0, and we are considering a 90-day Eurodollar deposit (m = 90). Dollar Libor is quoted at 2%; thus, $L_i(m) = L_0(90) = 0.02$. If \$50,000 is initially deposited, then NA = \$50,000. Libor is stated on an actual over 360-day count basis (often denoted ACT/360) with interest paid on an add-on basis.[10] Hence, t_m = 90/360 = 0.25. Accordingly, the terminal amount can be expressed as TA = $NA[1 + L_0(m)t_m]$, and the interest paid is thus TA − NA = $NA[L_0(m)t_m]$. In this example, TA = \$50,000[1 + 0.02(90/360)] = \$50,250 and the interest is \$50,250 − \$50,000 = \$250.

Now let us turn to the forward market for Libor. A **forward rate agreement** (FRA) is an over-the-counter (OTC) forward contract in which the underlying is an interest rate on a deposit. An FRA involves two counterparties: the fixed receiver (short) and the floating receiver (long). Thus, being long the FRA means that you gain when Libor rises. The fixed receiver counterparty receives an interest payment based on a fixed rate and makes an interest payment based on a floating rate. The floating receiver counterparty receives an interest payment based on a floating rate and makes an interest payment based on a fixed rate. If we are the fixed receiver, then it is understood without saying that we also are the floating payer, and vice versa. Because there is no initial exchange of cash flows, to eliminate arbitrage opportunities, the FRA price is the fixed interest rate such that the FRA value is zero on the initiation date.

FRAs are identified in the form of "X × Y," where X and Y are months and the multiplication symbol, ×, is read as "by." To grasp this concept and the notion of exactly what is the underlying in an FRA, consider a 3 × 9 FRA, which is pronounced "3 by 9." The 3 indicates that the FRA expires in three months. The underlying is implied by the difference in the 3 and the 9. That is, the payoff of the FRA is determined by six-month Libor when the FRA expires in three months. The notation 3 × 9 is market convention, though it can seem confusing at first. We will see shortly that the rate on the FRA will be determined by the relationship between the spot rate on a nine-month Libor deposit and the spot rate on a three-month deposit when the FRA is initiated. A short (long) FRA will effectively replicate going short (long) a nine-month Libor deposit and long (short) a three-month FRA deposit. And although market convention quotes the time periods as months, the calculations use days based on the assumption of 30 days in a month.

The contract established between the two counterparties settles in cash the difference between a fixed interest payment established on the initiation date and a floating interest payment established on the FRA expiration date. The underlying of an FRA is neither a financial asset nor even a financial instrument; it is just an interest payment. It is also important to understand that the parties to an FRA are not necessarily engaged in a Libor deposit in the spot market. The Libor spot market

---

10 The add-on basis is one way to quote interest rates and the convention in the Libor market. The idea is that the interest is added on at the end—in contrast, for example, to the discount basis, in which the current price is discounted based on the amount paid at maturity.

is simply the benchmark from which the payoff of the FRA is determined. Although a party may use an FRA in conjunction with a Libor deposit, it does not have to do so any more than a party that uses a forward or futures on a stock index has to have a position in the stock index.

In Exhibit 8, we illustrate the key time points in an FRA transaction. The FRA is created and priced at Time 0, the initiation date, and expires h days later. The underlying instrument has m days to maturity as of the FRA expiration date. Thus, the FRA is on m-day Libor. We assume there is a point during the life of the FRA, day g, at which we wish to determine the value of the FRA. So, for example, a 30-day FRA on 90-day Libor would have h = 30, m = 90, and h + m = 120. If we wanted to value the FRA prior to expiration, g could be any day between 0 and 30. The FRA value is the market value on the evaluation date and reflects the fair value of the original position.

Exhibit 8   Important FRA Dates, Expressed in Days from Initiation

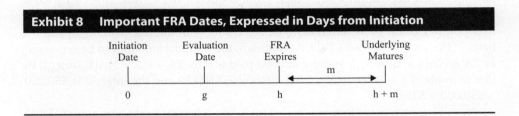

Using the notation in Exhibit 8, let FRA(0,h,m) denote the fixed forward rate set at Time 0 that expires at Time h wherein the underlying Libor deposit has m days to maturity at expiration of the FRA. Thus, the rate set at initiation of a contract expiring in 30 days in which the underlying is 90-day Libor is denoted FRA(0,30,90) and will be a number, such as 1% or 2.5%. Like all standard forward contracts, no money changes hands when an FRA is initiated, so our objective is to price the FRA, meaning to determine the fixed rate [FRA(0,30,90)] such that the value is zero on the initiation date.

When any interest rate derivative expires, there are technically two ways to settle at expiration: "advanced set, settled in arrears" and "advanced set, advanced settled." FRAs are typically settled based on advanced set, advanced settled, whereas swaps and interest rate options are normally based on advanced set, settled in arrears. Let us look at both approaches, because they are both used in the interest rate derivatives markets.

In the earlier example of a Libor deposit of $50,000 for 90 days at 2%, the rate was set when the money was deposited, interest accrued over the life of the deposit, and the interest was paid and the principal of $50,250 was repaid at maturity, 90 days later. The term **advanced set** is used because the reference interest rate is set at the time the money is deposited. The advanced set convention is almost always used, because most issuers and buyers of financial instruments want to know the rate on the instrument while they have a position in it.

In an FRA, the term "advanced" refers to the fact that the interest rate is set at Time h, the FRA expiration date, which is the time the underlying deposit starts. The term **settled in arrears** is used when the interest payment is made at Time h + m, the maturity of the underlying instrument. Thus, an FRA with advanced set, settled in arrears works the same way as a typical bank deposit as described in the previous example. At Time h, the interest rate is set, and the interest payment is made at Time h + m. Alternatively, when **advanced settled** is used, the settlement is made at Time h. Thus, in a FRA with the advanced set, advanced settled feature, the FRA expires and settles at the same time. Advanced set, advanced settled is almost always used in FRAs, though we will see advanced set, settled in arrears when we cover interest rate swaps, and it is also used in interest rate options. From this point forward in this reading, all FRAs will be advanced set, advanced settled, as they are in practice.

Mathematically, the settlement amounts for advanced set, advanced settled are determined in the following manner:

Settlement amount at h for receive-floating:

$$NA\left\{\left[L_h(m) - FRA(0,h,m)\right]t_m\right\}\Big/\left[1 + D_h(m)t_m\right]$$

Settlement amount at h for receive-fixed:

$$NA\left\{\left[FRA(0,h,m) - L_h(m)\right]t_m\right\}\Big/\left[1 + D_h(m)t_m\right]$$

Note the divisor, $1 + D_h(m)t_m$. This term is a discount factor applied to the FRA payoff. It reflects the fact that the rate on which the payoff is determined, $L_h(m)$, is obtained on day h from the Libor spot market, which uses settled in arrears. In the Libor spot market, this rate assumes that a Libor deposit has been made on day h at this rate with interest to be paid on day h + m—that is, settled in arrears. In the FRA market, the payment convention is advanced settle. The discount factor is, therefore, appropriately applied to the FRA payment because the payment is received in advance, not in arrears. Often it is assumed that $D_h(m) = L_h(m)$ and we will commonly do so here, but it can be different.[11]

Again, it is important to not be confused by the role played by the Libor spot market in an FRA. In the spot market, Libor deposits are made by various parties that are lending to banks. These rates are used as the benchmark for determining the payoffs of FRAs. The two parties to an FRA do not necessarily engage in any Libor spot transactions. Moreover, Libor spot deposits are settled in arrears, whereas FRA payoffs are settled in advance—hence the discounting.

EXAMPLE 6

Calculating Interest on Libor Spot and FRA Payments

In 30 days, a UK company expects to make a bank deposit of £10,000,000 for a period of 90 days at 90-day Libor set 30 days from today. The company is concerned about a possible decrease in interest rates. Its financial adviser suggests that it negotiate today, at Time 0, a 1 × 4 FRA, an instrument that expires in 30 days and is based on 90-day Libor. The company enters into a £10,000,000 notional amount 1 × 4 receive-fixed FRA that is advanced set, advanced settled. The appropriate discount rate for the FRA settlement cash flows is 0.40%. After 30 days, 90-day Libor in British pounds is 0.55%.

1 The interest actually paid at maturity on the UK company's bank deposit will be *closest* to:

   A £10,000.

   B £13,750.

   C £27,500.

2 If the FRA was initially priced at 0.60%, the payment received to settle it will be *closest* to:

   A −£2,448.75.

   B £1,248.75.

---

[11] For example, there is a current debate on whether the overnight index swap (OIS) rate is the appropriate discount rate for financial derivatives. Because Libor and the OIS rate are different, we need the capacity to incorporate different rates for the reference rate for settlement and the discount rate for valuation. We do not seek to resolve this debate here. Historically, there have been several candidate discount rates offered, and the popularity of each rate changes over time.

    C £1,250.00.

3 If the FRA was initially priced at 0.50%, the payment received to settle it will be *closest* to:

    A −£1,248.75.

    B £1,248.75.

    C £1,250.00.

Solution to 1:

B is correct. This is a simple Libor deposit of £10,000,000 for 90 days at 0.55%. Therefore, TA = 10,000,000[1 + 0.0055(0.25)] = £10,013,750. So the interest paid at maturity is £13,750.

Solution to 2:

B is correct. In this example, m = 90 (number of days in the deposit), t_m = 90/360 (fraction of year until deposit matures observed at the FRA expiration date), and h = 30 (number of days initially in the FRA). The settlement amount of the 1 × 4 FRA at h for receive-fixed is

$$NA\{[FRA(0,h,m) - L_h(m)]t_m\}/[1 + D_h(m)t_m]$$

$$= [10,000,000(0.0060 - 0.0055)(0.25)]/[1 + 0.0040(0.25)] = £1,248.75.$$

Because the FRA involves paying floating, its value benefited from a decline in rates.

Solution to 3:

A is correct. The data are similar to those in the previous question, but the initial FRA rate was 0.50% and not 0.60%. Thus, the settlement amount of the 1 × 4 FRA at h for receive-fixed is

$$NA\{[FRA(0,h,m) - L_h(m)]t_m\}/[1 + D_h(m)t_m]$$

$$= [10,000,000(0.0050 - 0.0055)(0.25)]/[1 + 0.0040(0.25)] = -£1,248.75$$

The FRA suffered from a rise in rates because it is again paying floating.

With this background, we turn to FRA pricing by illustrating the appropriate FRA(0,h,m) rate that makes the value of the FRA equal to zero on the initiation date. For our purposes, we assume that borrowing and lending can be done at Libor. Also, the notional amount is assumed to be one unit of the designated currency: NA = 1. Finally, we will assume that the discount rate on the FRA settlement is the FRA rate at that point in time.

Consider the following no-arbitrage strategy, depicted in Exhibit 9, in which numerical values are also provided as an aid to understanding the concepts. We illustrate a 3 × 6 FRA for which NA = 1, h = 90, m = 90, t_h = 90/360, $L_0(h) = L_0(90)$ = 1.5%, t_{h+m} = 180/360, $L_0(h + m) = L_0(180)$ = 2.0%, and t_m = 90/360. That is, today 90-day Libor is 1.5% and 180-day Libor is 2%. First, consider the following three arbitrage-related transactions all done at Time 0:

Step 1   Deposit funds for h + m days: At Time 0, deposit an amount equal to $1/[1 + L_0(h)t_h]$, the present value of 1 maturing in h days, in a bank for h + m days at an agreed upon rate of $L_0(h + m)$. After h + m days, withdraw an amount equal to $[1 + L_0(h + m)t_{h+m}]/[1 + L_0(h)t_h]$. Based on the data provided, the deposit amount is 1/[1 + 0.015(90/360)] = 0.996264. After h + m days, the withdrawn amount is equal to

0.996264[1 + 0.02(180/360)] = 1.006227. In other words, deposit 0.996264 for 180 days at 2%. One hundred eighty days later, withdraw 1.006227.

Step 2   Borrow funds for h days: At Time 0, borrow 0.996264, corresponding to $\{1/[1 + L_0(h)t_h]\}$, for h days so that the net cash flow at Time 0 is zero. In h days, this borrowing will be worth 1. In other words, borrow 0.996264 for 90 days at 1.5%. In 90 days, pay back 1.

Step 3   At Time h, roll over the maturing loan in Step 2 by borrowing funds for m days at the rate $L_h(m)$. Assume rates rise and $L_h(m)$ = 3.0%. Then at the end of m days, we will owe $[1 + L_h(m)t_m]$ = [1 + 0.03(90/360)] = 1.0075.

Recall the two rules of the arbitrageur: Rule #1: Do not use our own money. Rule #2: Do not take any price risk. In the transactions above, Rule #1 is satisfied. Unfortunately, Rule #2 is not satisfied because the future value at Time h + m of the borrowed cash flows may be more than the asset cash flows. Note that the risk is that the rate $L_h(m)$ will cause us to roll over the loan in Step 2 at a higher rate that more than offsets the gain from the loan we make in Step 1. This is the case here, because we will owe 1.0075 at the end of period m (Step 3) but will receive only 1.006227 from Step 1 if interest rates go up at Time h to 3%.

This risk can be eliminated by entering a receive-floating FRA on m-day Libor that expires at Time h and has the rate set at FRA(0,h,m). Now assume we roll the FRA payoff forward from h to h + m by investing any gain or borrowing to cover any loss at the rate $L_h(m)$. Let us assume the discount factor in the FRA payoff formula is $1 + L_h(m)t_m$. We see in Exhibit 9 that the following transaction enables us to satisfy Rule #2.

Step 4   Enter a receive-floating FRA and roll the payoff at h to h + m at the rate $L_h(m)$. The payoff at Time h will be $([L_h(m) - FRA(0,h,m)]t_m)/(1 + L_h(m)t_m)$. There will be no cash flow from this FRA at Time h because this amount will be rolled forward at the rate $L_h(m)t_m$. Therefore, the value realized at Time h + m will be $[L_h(m) - FRA(0,h,m)]t_m$.

Exhibit 9	**Cash Flow Table for Deposit and Lending Strategy with FRA**		
Steps	**Cash Flow at Time 0**	**Cash Flow at Time h**	**Cash Flow at Time h + m**
1. Make deposit for h + m days	$-1/[1 + L_0(h)t_h]$ $= -0.996264$	0	$+[1 + L_0(h + m)t_{h+m}]/[1 + L_0(h)t_h]$ $= 1.006227$
2. Borrow funds for h days	$+1/[1 + L_0(h)t_h]$ $= +0.996264$	-1	
3. Borrow funds for m days initiated at h		$+1$	$-[1 + L_h(m)t_m] = -1.0075$
4. Receive-floating FRA and roll payoff at $L_h(m)$ rate from h to h + m	0	0	$+[L_h(m) - FRA(0, h, m)]t_m$ $= [0.03 - FRA(0,h,m)](90/360)$
Net cash flows	0	0	$+[1 + L_0(h + m)t_{h+m}]/[1 + L_0(h)t_h] -$ $[1 + L_h(m)t_m]$ $+[L_h(m) - FRA(0,h,m)]t_m$

Recall that the goal is to identify the appropriate FRA(0,h,m) rate that makes the value of the FRA equal to zero on the initiation date. The terminal cash flows as expressed in the table can be used to solve for the FRA fixed rate. Because the transaction starts off with no initial investment or receipt of cash, the net cash flows at Time h + m should equal zero; thus,

$$+\left[1 + L_0(h + m)t_{h+m}\right]/\left[1 + L_0(h)t_h\right] -$$
$$\left[1 + L_h(m)t_m\right] + \left[L_h(m) - FRA(0,h,m)\right]t_m = 0$$

Solving for the FRA fixed rate, we have

$$FRA(0,h,m) = \left\{\left[1 + L_0(h + m)t_{h+m}\right]/\left[1 + L_0(h)t_h\right] - 1\right\}/t_m \qquad (5)$$

This equation looks complex, but it is really quite simple. In fact, it may well be quite familiar. It is essentially the compound value of $1 invested at the longer-term Libor for h + m days divided by the compound value of $1 invested at the shorter-term Libor for h days minus 1 and then annualized. The result is simply *the forward rate in the Libor term structure*. Recall that with simple interest, a one-period forward rate is found by solving the expression $[1 + y(1)][1 + f(1)] = [1 + y(2)]^2$, where y denotes the one- and two-period yield to maturity and f denotes the forward rate in the next period. The equation above is similar but simply addresses the unique features of add-on interest rate calculations. Based on the numbers used in the previous two tables, we note

$$FRA(0,90,90) = \{[1 + L_0(180)t_{180}]/[1 + L_0(90)t_{90}] - 1\}/t_{90}$$
$$= \{[1 + 0.02(180/360)]/[1 + 0.015(90/360)] - 1\}/(90/360)$$
$$= 0.024907 \text{ or } 2.49\%.[12]$$

EXAMPLE 7

FRA Fixed Rate

Based on market quotes on Canadian dollar (C$) Libor, the six-month C$ Libor and the nine-month C$ Libor are presently at 1.5% and 1.75%, respectively. Assume a 30/360-day count convention. The 6 × 9 FRA fixed rate will be *closest* to:

A 2.00%.

B 2.23%.

C 2.25%.

Solution:

B is correct. Based on the information given, we know L(180) = 1.5% and L(270) = 1.75%. The 6 × 9 FRA rate is thus

$$FRA(0,h,m) = \{[1 + L_0(h + m)t_{h+m}]/[1 + L_0(h)t_h] - 1\}/t_m$$
$$FRA(0,180,90) = \{[1 + 0.0175(270/360)]/[1 + 0.015(180/360)] - 1\}/(90/360)$$
$$FRA(0,180,90) = [(1.013125/1.0075) - 1]4 = 0.0223325, \text{ or } 2.23\%$$

---

[12] The result given in this example can be compared with the result from a simple approximation technique. Notice that for this FRA, 90 is half of 180. Thus, we can use the simple arithmetic average equation—here, (1/2)1.5% + (1/2)X = 2.0%—and solve for the missing variable X: X = 2.5%. Knowing this approximation will always be biased slightly high, we know we are looking for an answer that is a little less than 2.5%. This is a nice way to check your final answer.

We can now value an existing FRA using the same general approach as we did with the forward contracts previously covered; specifically, we can enter into an offsetting transaction at the new rate that would be set on an FRA that expires at the same time as our original FRA. By taking the opposite position, the new FRA offsets the old one. That is, if we are long the old FRA, we will receive the rate $L_h(m)$ at h. We will go short a new FRA that will force us to pay $L_h(m)$ at h. Consider the following strategy, illustrated in Exhibit 10, in which we again assume that NA = 1. Let us assume that we initiate an FRA that expires in 90 days and is based on 90-day Libor. The fixed rate at initiation is 2.49%. Thus, t_m = 90/360, and FRA(0,h,m) = FRA(0,90,90) = 2.49%. When the FRA expires and makes its payoff, assume that we do not collect or pay the payoff; instead, we roll it forward by lending it (if a gain) or borrowing it (if a loss) from period h to period h + m at the rate $L_h(m)$. We then collect or pay the rolled forward value at h + m. Thus, there is no cash realized at Time h.

Now having entered into the long FRA with the intention of rolling the payoff forward, let us now position ourselves 30 days later, at Time g, at which there are 60 days remaining in the life of the FRA. Assume that at this point, the rate on an FRA based on 90-day Libor that expires in 60 days is 2.59%. Thus, FRA(g,h − g,m) = FRA(30,60,90) = 2.59%. We go short this FRA, and as with the long FRA, we roll forward its payoff from Time h to h + m. Therefore, there is no cash realized from this FRA at Time h. This strategy is illustrated in Exhibit 10.

Exhibit 10 Cash Flows for FRA Valuation

Steps	Cash Flow at Time g	Cash Flow at Time h	Cash Flow at Time h + m
1. Receive-floating FRA (settled in arrears) at Time 0; roll forward at Rate $L_h(m)$ from h to h + m		0	$+\{[L_h(m) - FRA(0,h,m)]t_m\}$ $= +(L_h(m) - 0.0249)(90/360)$
2. Receive-fixed FRA (settled in arrears) at Time g; roll forward at Rate $L_h(m)$ from h to h + m	0	0	$+[FRA(g,h - g,m) - L_h(m)]t_m$ $= +[0.0259 - L_h(m)](90/360)$
Net cash flows	0	0	$+[FRA(g,h - g,m) - FRA(0,h,m)]t_m$ $= +(0.0259 - 0.0249)(90/360)$ $= 0.00025$

To recap, the original FRA that we wish to value had its fixed rate set at 2.49% when it was initiated. Now, 30 days later, a new offsetting FRA can be created at 2.59%. The value of the offset position is 10 bps (2.59% − 2.49%) times 90/360 paid at Time h + m, assuming we roll the FRA payoffs forward. We will receive this amount at h + m, so it must be discounted back to Time g in order to obtain the value.

Because the cash flows at h + m are now known with certainty at g, this offsetting transaction at Time g has completely eliminated all of the risk at Time h + m. Our task, however, is to determine the fair value of the original FRA at Time g. Therefore, we need the present value of this Time h + m cash flow at Time g. That is, the value of the old FRA is the present value of the difference in the new FRA rate and the old FRA rate. Specifically, we let $V_g(0,h,m)$ be the value of the FRA at Time g that was initiated at Time 0, expires at Time h, and is based on m-day Libor. Note that discounting will be over the period h + m − g. With $D_g(h + m - g)$ as the discount rate, the value is

$$V_g(0,h,m) =$$

$$\left\{[FRA(g,h - g,m) - FRA(0,h,m)]t_m\right\} / \left[1 + D_g(h + m - g)t_{h+m-g}\right] \quad (6)$$

where the new FRA rate is the formula we previously learned, simply applied to this new offsetting transaction:

$$FRA(g,h-g,m) = \{[1 + L_g(h + m - g)t_{h+m-g}]/[1 + L_g(h - g)t_{h-g}] - 1\}/t_m$$

Thus, the date g value of the receive-floating FRA initiated at date 0 is merely the present value of the difference in FRA rates, one entered on date g and one entered on date 0. Traditionally, it is assumed that the discount rate, $D_g(h + m - g)$, is equal to the underlying floating rate, $L_g(h + m - g)$, but that is not necessary.[13] Let us assume a 60-day rate of 3% on day g. Thus, $L_g(h - g) = L_{30}(60) = 3\%$. Then the value of the FRA would be

$$V_g(0,h,m) = V_{60}(0,90,90) = 0.00025/[1 + 0.03(60/360)] = 0.000249.$$

And of course, this amount is per notional of 1. Thus, the answer found here must be multiplied by the actual notional amount as demonstrated in the following example.

EXAMPLE 8

FRA Valuation

Suppose we entered a receive-floating 6 × 9 FRA at a rate of 0.86%, with notional amount of C$10,000,000 at Time 0. The six-month spot Canadian dollar (C$) Libor was 0.628%, and the nine-month C$ Libor was 0.712%. Also, assume the 6 × 9 FRA rate is quoted in the market at 0.86%. After 90 days have passed, the three-month C$ Libor is 1.25% and the six-month C$ Libor is 1.35%, which we will use as the discount rate to determine the value at g. We have h = 180 and m = 90.

Assuming the appropriate discount rate is C$ Libor, the value of the original receive-floating 6 × 9 FRA will be *closest* to:

A C$14,500.

B C$14,625.

C C$14,651.

Solution:

C is correct. Initially, we have $L_0(h) = L_0(180) = 0.628\%$, $L_0(h + m) = L_0(270) = 0.712\%$, and FRA(0,180,90) = 0.86%. After 90 days (g = 90), we have $L_g(h - g) = L_{90}(90) = 1.25\%$ and $L_g(h + m - g) = L_{90}(180) = 1.35\%$. Interest rates rose during this period; hence, the FRA likely has gained value because the position is receive-floating. First, we compute the new FRA rate at Time g and then estimate the fair FRA value as the discounted difference in the new and old FRA rates. The new FRA rate at Time g, denoted FRA(g,h − g,m) = FRA(90,90,90), is the rate on day 90 of an FRA to expire in 90 days in which the underlying is 90-day Libor. That rate is found as

$$FRA(g,h - g,m) = FRA(90,90,90)$$
$$= \{[1 + L_g(h + m - g)t_{h+m-g}]/[1 + L_g(h - g)t_{h-g}] - 1\}/t_m,$$

and based on the information in this example, we have

$$FRA(90,90,90) = \{[1 + L_{90}(180 + 90 - 90)(180/360)]/[1 + L_{90}(180 - 90)(90/360)] - 1\}/(90/360).$$

---

13 Again, there is a current debate on whether the OIS rate should be used for discounting; hence, we may have a different discount rate, but in any case, that rate would be known at time g.

Substituting the values given in this problem, we find

$$FRA(90,90,90) = \{[1 + 0.0135(180/360)]/[1 + 0.0125(90/360)] - 1\}/$$
$$(90/360) = [(1.00675/1.003125) - 1]4 = 0.0145, \text{ or } 1.45\%.$$

Therefore,

$$V_g(0,h,m) = V_{90}(0,180,90)$$
$$= 10,000,000[(0.0145 - 0.0086)(90/360)]/[1 + 0.0135(180/360)]$$
$$= 14,651.$$

Again, floating rates rose during this period; hence, the FRA enjoyed a gain. Notice that the FRA rate rose by roughly 59 bps (= 145 − 86), and 1 bp for 90-day money and a 1,000,000 notional amount is 25. Thus, we can also estimate the terminal value as $10 \times 25 \times 59 = 14,750$. As with all fixed-income strategies, understanding the value of a basis point is often helpful when estimating profits and losses and managing the risks of FRAs.

We now turn to the specific features of various forward and futures markets. The same general principles will apply, but the specifics will be different.

3.5 Fixed-Income Forward and Futures Contracts

Fixed-income forward and futures contracts have several unique issues that influence the specifics of the carry arbitrage model. First, in some countries the prices of fixed-income securities (termed "bonds" here) are quoted without the interest that has accrued since the last coupon date. The quoted price is sometimes known as the clean price. Naturally, when buying a bond, one must pay the full price, which is sometimes called the dirty price, so the accrued interest is included. Nonetheless, it is necessary to understand how the quoted bond price and accrued interest compose the true bond price and the effect this convention has on derivative pricing. The quote convention for futures contracts, whether based on clean or dirty prices, usually corresponds to the quote convention in the respective bond market. In this section, we will largely treat forwards and futures the same, except in certain places where noted.

In general, accrued interest is computed based on the following linear interpolation formula:

Accrued interest = Accrual period × Periodic coupon amount, or

$$AI = (NAD/NTD) \times (C/n)$$

where NAD denotes the number of accrued days since the last coupon payment, NTD denotes the number of total days during the coupon payment period, n denotes the number of coupon payments per year, and C is the stated annual coupon amount. For example, after two months (60 days), a 3% semi-annual coupon bond with par of 1,000 would have accrued interest of $AI = (60/180) \times (30/2) = 5$. Note that accrued interest is expressed in currency (not percent) and the number of total days (NTD) depends on the coupon payment frequency (semi-annual on 30/360 day count convention would be 180).

Second, fixed-income futures contracts often have more than one bond that can be delivered by the seller. Because bonds trade at different prices based on maturity and stated coupon, an adjustment known as the conversion factor is used in an effort to make all deliverable bonds roughly equal in price.

Third, when multiple bonds can be delivered for a particular maturity of a futures contract, a cheapest-to-deliver bond typically emerges after adjusting for the conversion factor. The conversion factor is a mathematical adjustment to the amount required when settling a futures contract that is supposed to make all eligible bonds equal the same amount. For example, the conversion factor may seek to adjust each bond to an equivalent 6% coupon bond. The conversion factor adjustment, however, is not precise. Thus, the seller will deliver the bond that is least expensive.

For bond markets in which the quoted price includes the accrued interest and in which futures or forward prices assume accrued interest is in the bond price quote, the futures or forward price simply conforms to the general formula we have previously discussed. Recall that the futures or forward price is simply the future value of the underlying in which finance costs, carry costs, and carry benefits are all incorporated or

$F_0(T)$ = Future value of underlying adjusted for carry cash flows

$\quad\quad = FV_{0,T}(S_0 + \theta_0 - \gamma_0)$

Again, Time 0 is the forward contract trade initiation date, and Time T is the contract expiration date. For the fixed-income bond, let T + Y denote the underlying instrument's current time to maturity. Therefore, Y is the time to maturity of the underlying bond at Time T, when the contract expires. Let $B_0(T + Y)$ denote the quoted price observed at Time 0 of a fixed-rate bond that matures at Time T + Y and pays a fixed coupon rate. For bonds quoted without accrued interest, let AI_0 denote the accrued interest at Time 0. The carry benefits are the bond's fixed coupon payments, $\gamma_0 = PVCI_{0,T}$, meaning the present value of all coupon interest paid over the forward contract horizon from Time 0 to Time T. The corresponding future value of these coupons is $\gamma_T = FVCI_{0,T}$. Finally, there are no carry costs, and thus $\theta_0 = 0$. To be consistent with prior notation, we have

S_0 = Quoted bond price + Accrued interest = $B_0(T + Y) + AI_0$

We could just insert this price into the previous equation, letting $\gamma_0 = PVCI_{0,T}$, and thereby obtain the futures price the simple and traditional way. But fixed-income futures contracts often permit delivery of more than one bond and use a conversion factor system to provide this flexibility. In these markets, the futures price, $F_0(T)$, is defined here as the quoted futures price, $QF_0(T)$, times the conversion factor, $CF(T)$. In fact, the futures contract settles against the quoted bond price without accrued interest. Thus, the total profit or loss on a long futures position is $B_T(T + Y) - F_0(T)$. Based on our notation above, we can represent this profit or loss as $(S_T - AI_T) - F_0(T)$. Therefore, the fixed-income forward or futures price including the conversion factor, termed the "adjusted price," can be expressed as[14]

$F_0(T) = QF_0(T)CF(T)$

$\quad\quad$ = Future value of underlying adjusted for carry cash flows $\quad\quad$ **(7)**

$\quad\quad = FV_{0,T}\left[S_0 - PVCI_{0,T}\right] = FV_{0,T}\left[B_0(T + Y) + AI_0 - PVCI_{0,T}\right]$

In other words, the actual futures price is $F_0(T)$, but in the market, the availability of multiple deliverable bonds gives rise to the adjustment factor. Hence, the price you would see quoted is QF_0.

Recall that the bracketed term $B_0(T + Y) + AI_0 - PVCI_{0,T}$ is just the full spot price minus the present value of the coupons over the life of the forward or futures contract. The fixed-income forward or futures price is thus the future value of the quoted bond price plus accrued interest less any coupon payments made during the life of the contract. Again, the quoted bond price plus the accrued interest is the spot price: It is in fact the price you would have to pay to buy the bond. Market conventions in some countries just happen to break this price out into the quoted price plus the accrued interest.

---

14 In this section, we will use the letter F to denote either the forward price or the futures price times the conversion factor.

Now let us explore carry arbitrage in the bond market, assuming that accrued interest is broken out and that multiple bonds are deliverable, thereby requiring the use of the conversion factor. Consider the following transactions:

Step 1 Buy the underlying bond, requiring S_0 cash flow.

Step 2 Borrow an amount equivalent to the cost of the underlying bond, S_0.

Step 3 Sell the futures contract at $F_0(T)$.

Step 4 Borrow the arbitrage profit.

Exhibit 11 shows the cash flow consequences for this portfolio in which the futures price is not in equilibrium. Note that $FVCI_{0,T}$ denotes the future value as of Time T of any coupons paid during the life of the futures contract. Again, for illustration purposes, we provide a numerical example: Suppose $T = 0.25$, $CF(T) = 0.8$, $B_0(T + Y) = 107$ (the quoted price), $FVCI_{0,T} = 0.0$ (meaning no accrued interest over the life of the contract), $AI_0 = 0.07$ (the accrued interest at Time 0), $AI_T = 0.20$ (the accrued interest at Time T), $QF_0(T) = 135$ (the quoted futures price), and $r = 0.2\%$. Thus, $S_0 = B_0(T + Y) + AI_0 = 107 + 0.07 = 107.07$ (the full or spot price), and $F_0(T) = CF(T) QF_0(T) = 0.8(135) = 108$ (the adjusted price). At Time T, suppose $B_T(T + Y) = 110$ and thus $S_T = B_T(T + Y) + AI_T = 110 + 0.20 = 110.20$. Because $FVCI_{0,T} = 0.0$, there are no coupons paid over the life of the futures. Note that the full (spot) price, S_0, is 108 whereas the future value adjusted for carry cash flows (Equation 7) is $(107 + 0.07)(1.002)^{0.25} = 107.12$. Adding the accrued interest at expiration ($AI_T = 0.20$) to the adjusted futures price gives 108.20. The difference between 108.20 and 107.12 is 1.08, which means that the futures contract is overpriced by 1.08. Thus, the arbitrage will involve borrowing the arbitrage profit, which is the present value of 1.08, or 1.0795—that is, $108(1.002)^{-0.25}$.

Exhibit 11	**Cash Flows for Fixed Rate Coupon Bond Futures Pricing**	
Steps	**Cash Flow at Time 0**	**Cash Flow at Time T**
1. Buy bond	$-S_0 = -[B_0(T + Y) + AI_0]$ $= -[107 + 0.07]$ $= -107.07$	$S_T + FVCI_{0,T}$ $= 110.20 + 0.0$ $= 110.20$
2. Borrow	$+S_0 = 107.07$	$-FV_{0,T}(S_0)$ $= -(1+0.002)^{0.25}(107.07)$ $= -107.12$
3. Sell futures	0	$F_0(T) - B_T(T + Y)$ $= 108 - 110$ $= -2$
4. Borrow arbitrage profit	$+PV_{0,T}[F_0(T) - FV_{0,T}(S_0) + AI_T + FVCI_{0,T}]$ $= (1 + 0.002)^{-0.25}[108 - 107.12 + 0.20 + 0.0]$ $= 1.0795$	$-[F_0(T) - FV_{0,T}(S_0) + AI_T + FVCI_{0,T}]$ $= -[108 - 107.12 + 0.20 + 0.0]$ $= -1.08$
Net cash flows	$+PV_{0,T}[F_0(T) - FV_{0,T}(S_0) + AI_T + FVCI_{0,T}]$ $= 1.0795$	0

Thus, the value of the Time 0 cash flows should be zero or else there is an arbitrage opportunity. The numerical example provided shows a 1.0795 cash flow at Time 0 per bond. If the value in the Time 0 column for net cash flows is positive, then conduct the carry arbitrage of buy bond, borrow, and sell futures (again, termed *carry arbitrage* because the underlying is "carried"). If the Time 0 column is negative, then conduct the reverse carry arbitrage of short sell bond, lend, and buy futures (termed *reverse carry arbitrage* because the underlying is not carried but is sold short).

Thus, in equilibrium, to eliminate an arbitrage opportunity, we expect

$$PV_{0,T}[F_0(T) - FV_{0,T}(S_0) + AI_T + FVCI_{0,T}] = 0$$

or

$$F_0(T) = FV_{0,T}(S_0) - AI_T - FVCI_{0,T}$$

For clarity, substituting for $F_0(T)$ and S_0 and solving for the quoted futures price, we have

$$QF_0(T) = \text{Conversion factor adjusted future}$$
$$\text{value of underlying adjusted for carry} \qquad (8)$$
$$= \left[1/CF(T)\right]\left\{FV_{0,T}\left[B_0(T + Y) + AI_0\right] - AI_T - FVCI_{0,T}\right\}$$

In the example above, we have

$$QF_0(T) = [1/CF(T)]\{FV_{0,T}[B_0(T + Y) + AI_0] - AI_T - FVCI_{0,T}\}$$
$$= (1/0.8)[(1 + 0.002)^{0.25}(107 + 0.07) - 0.20 - 0.0] = 133.65$$

Note that the futures price of 135 used for calculations in Exhibit 11 was higher than the equilibrium futures price of 133.65; hence, the arbitrage transaction of selling the futures contract resulted in a riskless positive cash flow.

EXAMPLE 9

Estimating the Euro-Bund Futures Price

Euro-bund futures have a contract value of €100,000, and the underlying consists of long-term German debt instruments with 8.5 to 10.5 years to maturity. They are traded on the Eurex. Suppose the underlying 2% German bund is quoted at €108 and has accrued interest of €0.083 (one-half of a month since last coupon). The euro-bund futures contract matures in one month. At contract expiration, the underlying bund will have accrued interest of €0.25, there are no coupon payments due until after the futures contract expires, and the current one-month risk-free rate is 0.1%. The conversion factor is 0.729535. In this case, we have $T = 1/12$, $CF(T) = 0.729535$, $B_0(T + Y) = 108$, $FVCI_{0,T} = 0$, $AI_0 = 0.5(2/12) = €0.083$, $AI_T = 1.5(2/12) = 0.25$, and $r = 0.1\%$. The equilibrium euro-bund futures price based on the carry arbitrage model will be *closest* to:

A   €147.57.

B   €147.82.

C   €148.15.

Solution:

B is correct. The carry arbitrage model for forwards and futures is simply the future value of the underlying with adjustments for unique carry features. With bond futures, the unique features include the conversion factor, accrued interest, and any coupon payments. Thus, the equilibrium euro-bund futures price can be found using the carry arbitrage model in which

$$F_0(T) = FV_{0,T}(S_0) - AI_T - FVCI_{0,T}$$

or

$$QF_0(T) = [1/CF(T)]\{FV_{0,T}[B_0(T + Y) + AI_0] - AI_T - FVCI_{0,T}\}$$

Thus, we have

$$QF_0(T) = [1/0.729535][(1 + 0.001)^{1/12}(108 + 0.083) - 0.25 - 0] = 147.82$$

In equilibrium, the euro-bund futures price should be approximately €147.82 based on the carry arbitrage model.

Because of the mark-to-market settlement procedure, the value of a bond futures is essentially the price change since the previous day's settlement. That value is captured at the settlement at the end of the day, at which time the value of a bond futures contract, like other futures contracts, is zero.

We now turn to the task of estimating the fair value of the bond forward contract at a point in time during its life. Forwards are not settled daily, so the value is not formally realized until expiration. Suppose the first transaction is buying an at-market bond forward contract at Time 0 with expiration of Time T. Now consider selling a new bond forward contract at Time t again with expiration of Time T. Exhibit 12 shows the potential cash flows. Because this is a bond forward contract, we assume either no conversion factor or effectively a conversion factor of 1. Suppose now $B_T(T + Y) = 108$, $F_0(T) = 107.12$, and $F_t(T) = 107.92$.

Exhibit 12   Cash Flows for Offsetting a Long Forward Position

Steps	Cash Flow at Time 0	Cash Flow at Time t	Cash Flow at Time T
1. Buy bond forward contract at 0	0	$V_t(T)$	$V_T(0,T) = B_T(T + Y) - F_0(T)$ $= 108 - 107.12 = 0.88$
2. Sell bond forward contract at t	NA	0	$V_T(t,T) = F_t(T) - B_T(T + Y)$ $= 107.92 - 108 = -0.08$
Net cash flows	0	$V_t(T)$	$F_t(T) - F_0(T)$ $= 107.92 - 107.12 = 0.8$

Note that the net position from these bond forward transactions is risk free. It is independent of the underlying bond value, $B_T(T + Y)$. Therefore, the forward value observed at Time t of a Time T maturity bond forward contract is simply the present value—denoted $PV_{t,T}()$—of the difference in forward prices. That is,

$$V_t(T) = \text{Present value of difference in forward prices} = PV_{t,T}[F_t(T) - F_0(T)]$$

Based on our example in the table and assuming $T - t = 0.1$ and $r = 0.15\%$, we have $V_t(T) = (107.92 - 107.12)/(1 + 0.0015)^{0.1} = 0.79988$. Note that this is the same result as the generic case with a simple conversion factor adjustment. Recall that the conversion factor is an adjustment to make all bonds roughly equal in value.

EXAMPLE 10

Estimating the Value of a Euro-Bund Forward Position

Suppose that one month ago, we purchased five euro-bund forward contracts with two months to expiration and a contract notional of €100,000 each at a price of 145 (quoted as a percentage of par). The euro-bund forward contract now has one month to expiration. Again, assume the underlying is a 2% German bund quoted at 108 and has accrued interest of 0.0833 (one-half of a month since last coupon). At the contract expiration, the underlying bund will have accrued interest of 0.25, there are no coupon payments due until after the forward contract expires, and the current annualized one-month risk-free rate is 0.1%.

Based on the current forward price of 148, the value of the euro-bund forward position will be *closest* to:

A   €2,190.

B   €14,998.

C   €15,000.

Solution:

B is correct. Because we are given both forward prices, the solution is simply

$$V_t(T) = PV_{t,T}[F_t(T) - F_0(T)] = (148 - 145)/(1 + 0.001)^{1/12} = 2.9997$$

which is 2.9997 per €100 par value because this forward price was quoted as a percentage of par. Because five contracts each with €100,000 par were entered, we have $0.029997(€100,000)5 = €14,998.50$. Note that when interest rates are so low and the forward contract has a short maturity, then the present value effect is minimal.

3.6 Currency Forward and Futures Contracts

Currency derivative contracts require careful attention to the unit of value. For example, if we are discussing bond futures, then the underlying is perceived in currency per unit of par value. If we are trading gold futures, then the quotation will be in currency per troy ounce. If trading a common stock, then it will be in currency per share. When trading currency itself, great care must be taken to know which currency is the base currency. When quoting an exchange rate, we will say that the foreign currency is trading for a certain number of units of domestic currency. For example, we could say, "The euro is trading for $1.30," meaning that €1 is worth $1.30. We use the shorthand notation of DC/FC to refer to the price of one unit of foreign currency expressed in terms of domestic currency units when embedded in an equation.[15] With currency, perspective makes a significant difference. Thus, when pricing and valuing currency forwards and futures contracts, a clear perspective requires considerable care. The carry arbitrage model with foreign exchange presented here is also known as **covered interest rate parity** and sometimes just **interest rate parity**.

Recall that currency forward contracts are agreements to exchange one currency for another on a future date at an exchange rate the counterparties agree on today. One approach to pricing is based on a forward exchange rate satisfying an arbitrage relationship that equates the investment return on two alternative but equivalent investment strategies. We illustrate these two strategies assuming the domestic currency is British pounds (£) and the foreign currency is the euro (€).

Strategy #1:

We simply invest one currency unit in a domestic risk-free bond. Thus, at Time T, we have the original investment grossed up at the domestic interest rate or the future value of 1DC, denoted FV(1DC). For example, the future value at Time T of this strategy can be expressed as $FV_{£,T}(1)$, given British pounds as the domestic currency.

Strategy #2:

---

15 Some practitioners prefer to express the discussion here as FC/DC, contradicting normal mathematics as well as contradicting standard market quotations, such as $ per bushel of wheat or $ per ounce of gold.

We engage in three simultaneous transactions termed *steps* here. In Step 1, the domestic currency is converted at the current spot exchange rate, $S_0(FC/DC)$, into the foreign currency (FC). At this point, 1 domestic currency unit is being converted to the foreign currency; hence, we use $S_0(FC/DC)$ generically or $S_0(€/£)$ in our example. Note that the final answer will express the spot exchange rate as the reciprocal $1/S_0(FC/DC) = S_0(DC/FC)$. In Step 2, FC is invested at the foreign risk-free rate until Time T. For example, the future value at Time T of this strategy can be expressed as $FV_{€,T}(1)$, given that the euro is the foreign currency. In Step 3, a forward foreign exchange contract is entered to sell the foreign currency at Time T in exchange for domestic currency with the forward rate denoted $F_0(DC/FC,T)$. So, for example, $F_0(£/€,T)$ is the rate on a forward commitment at Time 0 to sell one euro for British pounds at Time T. This transaction can be looked at as being short the euro in pound terms or being long the pound in euro terms for delivery at Time T.

We are examining two ways to invest British pounds at Time 0, and both strategies should result in the same value in domestic currency units at Time T. If not, then an arbitrage opportunity exists. Remember that the current spot exchange rate, $S_0(£/€)$, is the number of British pounds for one euro. Again, in our example, $FV_{£,T}(1)$ denotes the future value of one British pound and $FV_{€,T}(1)$ denotes the future value of one euro.[16] Based on the two strategies, the value at Time T follows:

Strategy 1. Future value at Time T of investing £1: $FV_{£,T}(1)$

Strategy 2. Future value at Time T of investing £1: $F_0(£/€,T)FV_{€,T}(1)S_0(€/£)$

Assuming both strategies lead to the same number of British pounds at Time T, we have $FV_{£,T}(1) = F_0(£/€)FV_{€,T}(1)S_0(€/£)$. Note that $S_0(£/€) = 1/S_0(€/£)$, simply reflecting the reciprocal of the exchange rate. Thus, solving for the forward foreign exchange rate, the forward rate can be expressed as

$F_0(£/€,T)$ = Future value of spot exchange rate adjusted for foreign rate

$$= FV_{£,T}(1)/\left[FV_{€,T}(1)S_0(€/£)\right] = S_0(£/€)FV_{£,T}(1)/FV_{€,T}(1) \qquad (9)$$

The carry adjustment, though it looks different, is similar to what we did in other carry models. In the numerator, we have simply the future value of the spot exchange rate. Rather than subtracting the carry benefit of foreign interest—the euro here—we divide by the future value of one euro, based on the euro interest rate. The effect is similar: The higher the foreign interest rate, the greater the benefit, and hence, the lower the forward or futures price will be.

If the two strategies result in different values at Time T, then the arbitrageur would buy the strategy offering the higher value at Time T and sell the strategy offering the lower value at Time T. This arbitrage activity would result in no cash flow today and positive cash flow at expiration. As with previous examples, we could borrow the arbitrage profit today and pay the loan back when the profit is captured at T.

---

16 Note that the interest could be compounded annually, continuously, or by any other method at this point; hence, we use the generic future value specification.

EXAMPLE 11

Pricing Forward Foreign Exchange Contracts

Suppose the current spot exchange rate, $S_0(£/€)$, is £0.792 (what 1€ is trading for in £). Further assume that the annual compounded annualized risk-free rates are 1% for the British pound and 0.3% for the euro.

1 The arbitrage-free one-year foreign exchange forward rate, $F_0(£/€,T)$ (expressed as the number of £ per 1€), will be *closest* to:

   A 0.792.

   B 0.794.

   C 0.798.

2 Now suppose the foreign exchange forward rate, $F_0(£/€,T)$, is observed to be below the foreign exchange spot rate, $S_0(£/€)$. Based on the carry arbitrage model, compared to British interest rates, the eurozone interest rate will *most likely* be:

   A lower.

   B higher.

   C the same.

Solution to 1:

C is correct. Based on the information given, we have $S_0(£/€) = 0.792$, T = 1 year, $r_£ = 1.0\%$, and $r_€ = 0.3\%$ (both with annual compounding). Therefore,

$$F_0(£/€,1) = S_0(£/€)FV_{£,1}(1)/FV_{€,1}(1) = 0.792(1 + 0.01)^1/(1 + 0.003)^1 = 0.798,$$

or £0.798/€.

Solution to 2:

B is correct. Note that if we observe that $F_0(£/€,T)$ is smaller than $S_0(£/€)$, then the carry arbitrage model provides a simple explanation: The British interest rate is lower than the eurozone interest rate. Based on the carry arbitrage model, foreign exchange forward rates solely reflect interest-related carry costs. Specifically, $F_0(£/€,T) < S_0(£/€)$ if and only if $r_£ < r_€$.

Note that the future value expressions in Equation 9 are in the same pattern as the spot exchange rate. If the spot exchange rate is expressed as 1€ is trading for £—denoted $S_0(£/€)$ and $F_0(£/€,T)$—then the future value ratio is $FV_{£,T}(1)/FV_{€,T}(1)$. If we assume annual compounding and denote the risk-free rates $r_£$ and $r_€$, respectively, we have

$$F_0(£/€,T) = S_0(£/€)(1 + r_£)^T/(1 + r_€)^T \text{ (Annually compounded version)}$$

If we assume continuous compounding and denote these risk-free rates in domestic (UK) and eurozone as $r_{£,c}$ and $r_{€,c}$, respectively, we have

$$F_0(£/€,T) = S_0(£/€) e^{(r_{£,c} - r_{€,c})T} \text{ (Continuously compounded version)}$$

To summarize, we identify several ways we get tripped up in understanding currency forward and futures contracts. First, if we let DC denote generically domestic currency and FC denote generically foreign currency, then there are two representations of the carry arbitrage model based on $S_0(FC/DC) = 1/S_0(DC/FC)$ and $F_0(FC/DC) = 1/F_0(DC/FC)$. If we assume annual compounding, we have either

$$F_0(DC/FC,T) = S_0(DC/FC)\frac{(1 + r_{DC})^T}{(1 + r_{FC})^T} \text{ or } F_0(FC/DC,T) = S_0(FC/DC)\frac{(1 + r_{FC})^T}{(1 + r_{DC})^T}$$

A good way to remember this relationship is that the interest rate in the numerator should be the rate for the country whose currency is specified in the spot rate quote. Thus, if the spot rate quote is in euros, the numerator should be the euro interest rate. Then the interest rate in the denominator is the rate in the other country.

Second, interest rates can be quoted in a wide variety of ways, including annual compounding (previous equation) and continuous compounding (following equation).

$$F_0(DC/FC,T) = S_0(DC/FC)e^{(r_{DC,c} - r_{FC,c})T} \text{ or } F_0(FC/DC,T) = S_0(FC/DC)e^{(r_{FC,c} - r_{DC,c})T}$$

Here, likewise, the currency quote should match the first interest rate. Thus, if the spot rate is quoted in euros, then the first interest rate in the exponential will be the euro rate.

In equilibrium, $F_0(£/€,T) = S_0(£/€)FV_£(1)/FV_€(1)$; otherwise, positive future cash flow can be generated with no initial investment, which is an arbitrage profit.

We now turn to the task of estimating the fair value of the foreign exchange forward contract. The forward value, based on arbitrage, can best be understood by referring to Exhibit 13. Suppose the first transaction is buying a foreign exchange forward contract at Time 0 with expiration of Time T. Now consider selling a new foreign exchange forward contract at Time t also with expiration of Time T. Exhibit 13 shows the potential cash flows again using British pounds (£) as the domestic currency and euros (€) as the foreign currency. Suppose $T = 1$, $T - t = 0.5$, $F_0(£/€,T) = 0.804$, $F_t(£/€,T) = 0.901$, $S_T(£/€) = 1.2$, and $r_{£,t} = 1.2\%$. In other words, six months ago we bought a forward contract at 0.804, and the new forward price is 0.901.

Exhibit 13   Cash Flows for Offsetting a Long Forward Position

Steps	Cash Flow at Time 0	Cash Flow at Time t	Cash Flow at Time T
1. Buy forward contract at 0	0	$V_t(T)$	$V_T(0,T) = S_T(£/€) - F_0(£/€,T)$ $= 1.2 - 0.804 = 0.396$
2. Sell forward contract at t	NA	0	$V_T(t,T) = F_t(£/€,T) - S_T(£/€)$ $= 0.901 - 1.2 = -0.299$
Net cash flows	0	$V_t(T)$	$+F_t(£/€,T) - F_0(£/€,T)$ $= 0.901 - 0.804 = 0.097$

Note that the net position is again risk free. Therefore, the forward value observed at t of a T maturity forward contract is simply the present value of the difference in foreign exchange forward prices. That is,

$V_t(T)$ = Present value of the difference in forward prices

$$= PV_{£,t,T}\left[F_t(£/€,T) - F_0(£/€,T)\right]$$

(10)

Based on our numerical example, we have $V_t(T) = (0.901 - 0.804)/(1 + 0.012)^{0.5} = £0.0964/€$.

> ### EXAMPLE 12
>
> ## Computing the Foreign Exchange Forward Contract Value
>
> A corporation sold €10,000,000 against a British pound forward at a forward rate of £0.8000 for €1 at Time 0. The current spot market at Time t is such that €1 is worth £0.7500, and the annually compounded risk-free rates are 0.80% for the British pound and 0.40% for the euro. Assume at Time t there are three months until the forward contract expiration.
>
> 1 The forward price $F_t(£/€,T)$ at Time t will be *closest* to:
>
>   A 0.72.
>
>   B 0.74.
>
>   C 0.75.
>
> 2 The value of the foreign exchange forward contract at Time t will be *closest* to:
>
>   A £492,000.
>
>   B £495,000.
>
>   C £500,000.
>
> **Solution to 1:**
>
> C is correct. Note that the forward price at Time t is
>
> $$F_t(£/€,T) = S_t(£/€)FV_{£,t,T}(1)/FV_{€,t,T}(1)$$
> $$= 0.75(1 + 0.008)^{0.25}/(1 + 0.004)^{0.25}$$
> $$= 0.7507.$$
>
> **Solution to 2:**
>
> A is correct. The value per euro to the seller of the foreign exchange futures contract at Time t is simply the present value of the difference between the initial forward price and the £/€ forward price at Time t or
>
> $$V_t(T) = PV_{£,t,T}[F_0(£/€,T) - F_t(£/€,T)]$$
> $$= (0.8000 - 0.7507)/(1 + 0.008)^{0.25}$$
> $$= £0.0492 \text{ per euro.}$$
>
> Note that the corporation has an initial short position, so the short position of a €10,000,000 notional amount has a positive value of €10,000,000(£0.0492/€) = £492,000 for the corporation because the forward rate fell between Time 0 and Time t.

We conclude this section with observations on the similarities and differences between forward and futures contracts.

3.7 Comparing Forward and Futures Contracts

For every market considered here, the carry arbitrage model provides an approach for both pricing and valuing forward contracts. Recall the two generic expressions:

$$F_0(T) = FV_{0,T}(S_0 + \theta_0 - \gamma_0) \text{ (Forward pricing)}$$

$$V_t(T) = PV_{t,T}[F_t(T) - F_0(T)] \text{ (Forward valuation)}$$

Carry costs (θ_0) increase the forward price, and carry benefits (γ_0) decrease the forward price. The arbitrageur is carrying the underlying, and costs increase the burden whereas benefits decrease the burden. The forward value can be expressed as either the present value of the difference in forward prices or as a function of the current underlying price adjusted for carry cash flows and the present value of the initial forward price.

Futures prices are generally found using the same model, but futures values are different because of the daily marking to market. Recall that the futures values are zero at the end of each day because profits and losses are taken daily.

In summary, the carry arbitrage model provides a compelling way to price and value forward and futures contracts. In short, the forward or futures price is simply the future value of the underlying adjusted for any carry cash flows. The forward value is simply the present value of the difference in forward prices at an intermediate time in the contract. The futures value is zero after marking to market. We turn now to pricing and valuing swaps.

PRICING AND VALUING SWAP CONTRACTS

4

Based on the foundational materials in the last section on using the carry arbitrage model for pricing and valuing forward and futures contracts, we now apply this approach to pricing and valuing swap contracts. Swap contracts can be synthetically created by either a portfolio of underlying instruments or a portfolio of forward contracts. We focus here solely on the portfolio of underlying instruments approach.

We consider a receive-floating and pay-fixed interest rate swap. The swap will involve a series of n future cash flows at points in time represented simply here as 1, 2, ..., n. Let S_i denote the generic floating interest rate cash flow based on some underlying, and let FS denote the cash flow based on some fixed interest rate. We assume that the last cash flow occurs at the swap expiration. Exhibit 14 shows the cash flows of a generic swap. Later we will let S_i denote the floating cash flows tied to currency movements or equity movements.

Exhibit 14   Generic Swap Cash Flows: Receive-Floating, Pay-Fixed

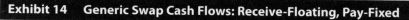
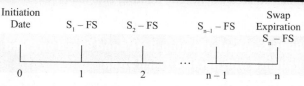

We again will rely on the arbitrage approach for determining the pricing of a swap. This procedure involves finding the fixed swap rate such that the value of the swap at initiation is zero. Recall that the goal of the arbitrageur is to generate positive cash flows with no risk and no investment of one's own capital. Thus, it is helpful to be able to synthetically create a swap with a portfolio of other instruments. A receive-floating, pay-fixed swap is equivalent to being long a floating-rate bond and short a fixed-rate bond. Assuming both bonds were purchased at par, the initial cash flows are zero and the par payments at the end offset each other. Thus, the fixed bond payment should be equivalent to the fixed swap payment. Exhibit 15 shows the view of a swap as a pair of bonds. Note that the coupon dates on the bonds match the settlement dates on the swap and the maturity date matches the expiration date of the swap.[17]

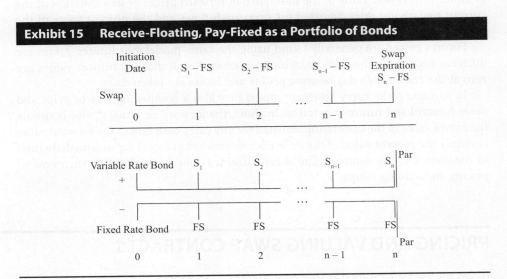

Exhibit 15   Receive-Floating, Pay-Fixed as a Portfolio of Bonds

As futures contracts can be viewed as marketable forward contracts, swaps can also be viewed as a portfolio of futures contracts.[18] In addition, because a single forward contract can be viewed as a portfolio of a call and a put option, a swap can also be viewed as a portfolio of options.[19]

Market participants often use swaps to transform one series of cash flows into another. For example, suppose that because of the relative ease of issuance, REB, Inc. sells a fixed-rate bond to investors. Based on careful analysis of the interest rate sensitivity of the company's assets, REB's leadership deems a Libor-based variable rate bond to be more appropriate. By entering a receive-fixed, pay-floating interest rate swap, REB can create a synthetic floating-rate bond, as illustrated in Exhibit 16. REB issues fixed-rate bonds and thus must make periodic fixed-rate-based payments, denoted FIX. REB then enters a receive-fixed (FIX) and pay-floating (FLT) interest rate swap. The two fixed rate payments cancel, leaving on net the floating-rate payments. Thus, we say that REB has created a synthetic floating-rate loan.

Exhibit 16   REB's Synthetic Floating-Rate Bond Based on Fixed-Rate Bond Issuance with Receive-Fixed Swap

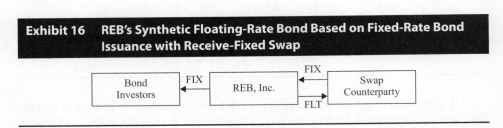

---

17 As with all derivative instruments, there are numerous technical details that have been simplified here. We will explore some of these details shortly.

18 In practice, futures have standardized characteristics, so there is rarely a set of futures contracts that can perfectly replicate a swap.

19 For example, a long forward contract is equivalent to a long call and a short put with the strike price equal to the forward price.

The example in Exhibit 16 is for a swap in which the underlying is an interest rate. There are also currency swaps and equity swaps. Currency swaps can be used in a similar fashion, but the risks being addressed are both interest rate and currency exposures. Equity swaps can also be used in a similar fashion, but the risk being addressed is equity exposure.

Swaps have several technical nuances that can have a significant influence on pricing and valuation. Differences in payment frequency and day count methods often have a material impact on pricing and valuation. Another difficult issue is identifying the appropriate discount rate to apply to the future cash flows. We turn now to examining three types of swap contracts—interest rate, currency, and equity—with a focus on pricing and valuation.

4.1 Interest Rate Swap Contracts

One approach to pricing and valuing interest rate swaps is based on a pair of bonds. We first need to introduce some basic notation and typical structures. It is important to understand that because they are OTC products in which the characteristics are agreed upon by the counterparties, swaps can be designed with an infinite number of variations. For example, a plain vanilla Libor-based interest rate swap can involve different frequencies of cash flow settlements and day count conventions. In fact, a swap can have both semi-annual payments and quarterly payments, as well as actual day counts and day counts based on 30 days per month. Also, the notional amount can vary across the maturities, such as would occur when aligning a swap with an amortizing loan. Thus, it is important to build in our models the flexibility to handle these variations and issues. Unless stated otherwise, we will assume the notional amounts are all equal to one (NA = 1); hence, we do not consider amortizing swaps here. Swap values per 1 notional amount can be simply multiplied by the actual notional amount to arrive at the swap's fair market value.

Interest rate swaps have two legs, typically a floating leg (FLT) and a fixed leg (FIX). The floating leg cash flow (denoted S_i to be consistent with other underlying instruments) can be expressed as

$$S_i = CF_{FLT,i} = AP_{FLT,i} r_{FLT,i} = \left(\frac{NAD_{FLT,i}}{NTD_{FLT,i}} \right) r_{FLT,i}$$

and the fixed leg cash flow (denoted FS) can be expressed as

$$FS = CF_{FIX,i} = AP_{FIX,i} r_{FIX} = \left(\frac{NAD_{FIX,i}}{NTD_{FIX,i}} \right) r_{FIX}$$

where CF_i simply reminds us that our focus is on cash flows, AP_i denotes the accrual period, $r_{FLT,i}$ denotes the observed floating rate appropriate for Time i, NAD_i denotes the number of accrued days during the payment period, NTD_i denotes the total number of days during the year applicable to cash flow i, and r_{FIX} denotes the fixed swap rate. The accrual period accounts for the payment frequency and day count methods. The two most popular day count methods are known as 30/360 and ACT/ACT. As the name suggests, 30/360 treats each month as having 30 days, and thus a year has 360 days. ACT/ACT treats the accrual period as having the actual number of days divided by the actual number of days in the year (365 or 366). Finally, the convention in the swap market is that the floating interest rate is assumed to be advanced set and settled in arrears; thus, $r_{FLT,i}$ is set at the beginning of period i and paid at the end.[20] If we assume constant accrual periods, the receive-fixed, pay-floating net cash flow can be expressed as

$$FS - S_i = AP(r_{FIX} - r_{FLT,i})$$

and the receive-floating, pay-fixed net cash flow can be expressed as

$$S_i - FS = AP(r_{FLT,i} - r_{FIX})$$

As a simple example, if the fixed rate is 5%, the floating rate is 5.2%, and the accrual period is 30 days based on a 360 day year, the payment of a receive-fixed, pay-floating swap is calculated as $(30/360)(0.05 - 0.052) = -0.000167$ per notional of 1. Because the floating rate exceeds the fixed rate, the party that pays floating (and receives fixed) would pay this amount to the party that receives floating (and pays fixed). In other words, there is only a single payment made from one party to the other.

We now turn to swap pricing. Exhibit 17 shows the cash flows for an interest rate swap along with a pair of bonds each with the same par amount.[21] Suppose the arbitrageur enters a receive-fixed, pay-floating interest rate swap with some initial value V. Because we are exploring the equilibrium fixed swap rate, we do not first assume the swap value is in fact zero or in equilibrium. Because this swap will lose value when floating rates rise, the arbitrageur purchases a variable rate bond whose value is denoted VB—satisfying Rule #2 of not taking any risk. Note that the terms of the variable rate bond are selected to match exactly the floating payments of the swap. To satisfy Rule #1 of not spending money, a fixed-rate bond is sold short—equivalent to borrowing funds—with terms to match exactly the fixed payments of the swap.

Exhibit 17   Cash Flows for Receive-Fixed Swap Hedge with Bonds

Steps	Time 0	Time 1	Time 2	...	Time n
1. Receive fixed swap	−V	$+FS - S_1$	$+FS - S_2$	...	$+FS - S_n$
2. Buy floating-rate bond	−VB	$+S_1$	$+S_2$	...	$+S_n +$ Par
3. Short sell fixed-rate bond	+FB	−FS	−FS	...	−(FS + Par)
Net cash flows	−V − VB + FB	0	0	0	0

Thus, the fixed coupon such that the floating-rate bond price equals the fixed-rate bond price is the equilibrium fixed swap rate. That is, in equilibrium we must have $-V - VB + FB = 0$ or else there is an arbitrage opportunity. For a receiver of a fixed rate and payer of a floating rate, the value of the swap is

$$V = \text{Value of fixed bond} - \text{Value of floating bond} = FB - VB \qquad (11)$$

---

20 Often, interest rate swaps are used to convert floating-rate loans to synthetic fixed rate loans. These floating-rate loans are advanced set, settled in arrears. Otherwise, while interest is accruing, we have no idea what rate is being applied until the end. Thus, with advanced set, settled in arrears, the interest begins accruing at a known rate and then the interest is paid at the end of the period, whereupon the interest rate is reset once again.

21 The underlying bonds have a designated par value on which their interest payments are based, whereas swaps are based on a notional amount that is never paid. The notional amount determines the size of the swap interest payments. Thus, a swap is like an offsetting pair of bonds with interest payments but no principal payments. In general, the notional amount of the swap will equal the par value of the underlying bonds.

The value of a receive-fixed, pay-floating interest rate swap is simply the value of buying a fixed-rate bond and issuing a floating-rate bond.[22] If we further stipulate that pricing the swap means to determine the fixed rate such that the value of the swap at initiation is zero, then the value of the fixed bond must equal the value of the floating bond.

The value of a floating-rate bond, assuming we are on a reset date and the interest payment matches the discount rate, is par, assumed to be 1 here. The value of a fixed bond is as follows:

$$\text{Fixed bond rate: } FB = C\sum_{i=1}^{n} PV_{0,t_i}(1) + PV_{0,t_n}(1) \tag{12}$$

where C denotes the coupon amount for the fixed-rate bond and $PV_{0,t_i}(1)$ is the appropriate present value factor for the ith fixed cash flow.

Based on the value of these bonds and noting that the fixed coupon amount is equivalent to the fixed swap rate, r_{FIX}, we obtain the swap pricing equation:

$$\text{Swap pricing equation: } r_{FIX} = \frac{1 - PV_{0,t_n}(1)}{\sum_{i=1}^{n} PV_{0,t_i}(1)} \tag{13}$$

The fixed swap rate is simply one minus the final present value term divided by the sum of present values. Therefore, one interpretation of the fixed swap rate is that it should be equal to the fixed rate on a par bond, which is the ratio one minus the present value of the final cash flow all divided by an annuity.[23]

The fixed swap leg cash flow for a unit of notional amount is simply the fixed swap rate adjusted for the accrual period, or $FS_i = AP_{FIX,i}r_{FIX}$. Alternatively, the annualized fixed swap rate is equal to the fixed swap leg cash flow divided by the fixed rate accrual period, or $r_{FIX,i} = FS/AP_{FIX,i}$. Note that if the accrual period varies across the swap payments, then the fixed swap payment will also vary. Thus, when relevant, a subscript i will be used. Often the fixed leg accrual period is constant; hence, the subscript can be safely omitted.

EXAMPLE 13

Solving for the Fixed Swap Rate Based on Present Value Factors

Suppose we are pricing a five-year Libor-based interest rate swap with annual resets (30/360 day count). The estimated present value factors, $PV_{0,t_i}(1)$, are given in the following table.

Maturity (years)	Present Value Factors
1	0.990099
2	0.977876
3	0.965136
4	0.951529
5	0.937467

---

22 In Exhibit 17, the trades illustrated in Steps 2 and 3 are synthetically creating an offsetting position; hence, the floating bond is purchased and the fixed bond is short sold.
23 The denominator of Equation 13 is simply the sum of the present values of receiving one currency unit on each payment date or an annuity.

The fixed rate of the swap will be *closest* to:

A   1.0%.

B   1.3%.

C   1.6%.

Solution:

B is correct. Note that the sum of present values is

$$\sum_{i=1}^{n} PV_{0,t_i}(1) = 0.990099 + 0.977876 + 0.965136 + 0.951529 + 0.937467$$

$$= 4.822107$$

Therefore, the solution for the fixed swap rate is

$$r_{FIX} = \frac{1 - PV_{0,t_n}(1)}{\sum_{i=1}^{n} PV_{0,t_i}(1)} = \frac{1 - 0.937467}{4.822107} = 0.012968, \text{ or } 1.2968\%$$

We now turn to interest rate swap valuation. Following a similar pattern as forward contracts, Exhibit 18 shows the cash flows for a receive-fixed interest rate swap initiated at Time 0 but that needs to be valued at Time t expressed per unit of the underlying currency. We achieve this valuation through entering an offsetting swap—receive-floating, pay-fixed. The floating sides offset, leaving only the difference in the fixed rates. We assume n' remaining cash flows. At Time t, the swap value is represented as the funds need to generate the appropriate future cash flows.

Exhibit 18   Cash Flows for Receive-fixed Swap Valued at Time t

Steps	Time t	Time 1	Time 2	...	Time n'
1. Receive fixed swap (Time 0)	$-V$	$+FS_0 - S_1$	$+FS_0 - S_2$	...	$+FS_0 - S_{n'}$
2. Receive floating swap (Time t)	0	$S_1 - FS_t$	$S_2 - FS_t$	...	$S_{n'} - FS_t$
Net cash flows	$-V$	$FS_0 - FS_t$	$FS_0 - FS_t$	...	$FS_0 - FS_t$

Thus, the value of a fixed rate swap at some future point in Time t is simply the sum of the present value of the difference in fixed swap rates times the stated notional amount (denoted NA), or

$$V = NA(FS_0 - FS_t)\sum_{i=1}^{n'} PV_{t,t_i} \tag{14}$$

It is important to be clear on which side this value applies. The rate FS_0 is the fixed rate established at the start of the swap and goes to the party receiving fixed. Thus, when Equation 14 with FS_0 having a positive sign is used, it provides the value to the party receiving fixed. The negative of this amount is the value to the fixed rate payer.

The examples illustrated here show swap valuation only on a payment date. If a swap is being valued between payment dates, some adjustments are necessary. We do not pursue this topic here.

EXAMPLE 14

Solving for the Swap Value Based on Present Value Factors

Suppose two years ago we entered a €100,000,000 seven-year receive-fixed Libor-based interest rate swap with annual resets (30/360 day count). The fixed rate in the swap contract entered two years ago was 2%. Again, the estimated present value factors, $PV_{0,t_i}(1)$, are repeated from the previous example.

Maturity (years)	Present Value Factors
1	0.990099
2	0.977876
3	0.965136
4	0.951529
5	0.937467

From the previous example, we know the current equilibrium fixed swap rate is 1.3% (two years after the swap was originally entered).

1 The value (in thousands) for the party receiving the fixed rate will be *closest* to:

   A −€5,000.

   B €3,375.

   C €4,822.

2 The value (in thousands) for the party in the swap receiving the floating rate will be *closest* to:

   A −€4,822.

   B −€3,375.

   C €5,000.

Solution to 1:

B is correct. Recall the sum of present values is 4.822107. Thus, the swap value per dollar notional is

$$V = \left(FS_0 - FS_t\right)\sum_{i=1}^{n'} PV_{t,t_i}$$

$$= (0.02 - 0.013)4.822107$$

$$= 0.03375$$

Thus, the swap value is €3,375,000.

Solution to 2:

B is correct. The equivalent receive-floating swap value is simply the negative of the receive-fixed swap value.

4.2 Currency Swap Contracts

A currency swap is a contract in which two counterparties agree to exchange future interest payments in different currencies. These interest payments can be based on either a fixed interest rate or a floating interest rate. Thus, with the addition of day count options and payment frequencies, there are many different ways to set up a currency swap. There are four major types of currency swaps: fixed-for-fixed, floating-for-fixed, fixed-for-floating, and floating-for-floating.

Currency swaps come in a wide array of types and structures. We review a few key features. First, currency swaps often but not always involve an exchange of notional amounts at both the initiation of the swap and at the expiration of the swap. Second, the payment on each leg of the swap is in a different currency unit, such as euros and Japanese yen, and the payments are not netted. Third, each leg of the swap can be either fixed or floating. To understand the pricing and valuation of currency swaps, we need a general approach that is flexible enough to handle each of these situations. We first focus on the fixed-for-fixed currency swaps with a very simple structure and only then consider other variations.

Currency swap pricing has three key variables: two fixed interest rates and one notional amount. Pricing a currency swap involves solving for the appropriate notional amount in one currency, given the notional amount in the other currency, as well as two fixed interest rates such that the currency swap value is zero at initiation. Because one notional amount is given, there are three swap pricing variables.

Because we are focused on fixed-for-fixed currency swaps, we need notation that reflects the different generic currency units. Thus, we let k = a and b to reflect two different currency units, such as euros and yen. Letters are used rather than numbers to avoid confusion with calendar time. The value of a fixed-rate bond in Currency k can be expressed generically as

$$FB_k = C_k \sum_{i=1}^{n} PV_{0,t_i,k}(1) + PV_{0,t_n,k}(Par_k)$$

where k = a or b, C_k denotes the periodic fixed coupon amount in Currency k, $\sum_{i=1}^{n} PV_{0,t_i,k}(1)$ denotes the present value from Time 0 to Time t_i discounting at the Currency k risk-free rate, and Par_k denotes the k currency unit par value. We do not assume par equals 1 because the notional amounts are typically different in each currency within the currency swap.

Exhibit 19 shows the cash flows for a fixed-for-fixed currency swap along with an offsetting pair of fixed-rate bonds. In this case, notice that the two bonds are in different currencies.[24] We assume the arbitrage cash flows will be evaluated in currency unit a. Therefore, all cash flows are converted to Currency a in the cash flow table based on the exchange rate denoted S_i—expressed as the number of units of Currency a for one unit of Currency b at Time i. We again ignore the technical nuances and assume the same accrual periods on both legs of the swap. Note that all the future cash flows, expressed in Currency a, are zero because the coupon rates on the fixed-rate bonds were selected to equal the fixed swap rates. Because we are demonstrating swap pricing, we do not assume the currency swap is initially valued correctly; hence, V can be either positive or negative. We initially use a negative sign, because an investment usually involves negative cash flows. We assume the par value of each bond is the same as the notional amount of each leg of the swap. From the arbitrageur's perspective, whether there is an exchange of notional amounts on the initiation date is not relevant because this exchange will be done at the current foreign exchange rate, and hence, it will have a fair value of zero. It is important, however, that this exchange of notional amounts is done at expiration. Because the swap notional amounts differ between the two currencies, it would be confusing to express these results per unit of Currency a. Therefore, each leg of the swap is assumed to have different notional amounts, but $Par_a = NA_a$ and $Par_b = NA_b$ in order to achieve zero cash flow at Time n.

---

24 Technically, we build these portfolios such that the initial value in each currency is par.

Exhibit 19 Cash Flows for Currency Swap Hedged with Bonds

Steps	Time 0	Time 1	Time 2	...	Time n
1. Enter currency swap	$-V_a$	$+FS_a - S_1FS_b$	$+FS_a - S_2FS_b$	...	$+FS_a + NA_a$ $- S_n(FS_b + NA_b)$
2. Short sell bond in Currency a	$+FB_a(C_a = FS_a)$	$-FS_a$	$-FS_a$	...	$-(FS_a + Par_a)$
3. Buy bond in Currency b	$-S_0FB_b(C_b = FS_b)$	$+S_1FS_b$	$+S_2FS_b$	...	$+S_n(FS_b + Par_b)$
Net cash flows	$-V_a + FB_a - S_0FB_b$	0	0	0	0

Based on this table, in equilibrium we must have

$$-V_a + FB_a - S_0FB_b = 0$$

and the fixed-for-fixed currency swap value is

$$V_a = FB_a - S_0FB_b$$

or else there is an arbitrage opportunity. Notice that the two-bond approach allows the arbitrageur to avoid having to convert one currency into another in the future. This approach mitigates all future currency exposure and basically identifies the current exchange rate that makes the value of the two bonds equal. Remember that the exchange rate S_0 is the number of Currency a units for one unit of Currency b at Time 0; thus, S_0FB_b is expressed in Currency a units.

Exhibit 20 provides a simple illustration of an at-market 10-year receive-fixed US$ and pay-fixed € swap, for which the annual reset coupon amount in US dollars is US$10 with par of US$1,300 and the annual reset coupon amount in euros is €9 with par of €1,000. Both bonds are assumed to be trading at par and have a 10-year maturity. This exhibit assumes a current spot exchange rate (S_0) at which €1 trades for US$1.3, and selected future spot exchange rates are $S_1 = \$1.5$, $S_2 = \$1.1$, and $S_{10} = \$1.2$. These future spot exchange rates are used to illustrate the conversion of future euro cash flows into US dollars, but notice that the cash flows are all zero regardless of the future spot exchange rates. In other words, we could have used any numbers for S_1, S_2, and S_{10}.

Exhibit 20 Numerical Example of Currency Swap Hedged with Bonds

Steps	Time 0	Time 1	Time 2	...	Time 10
1. Enter currency swap	0	$+\$10 - (\$1.5/€)€9 = -\$3.5$	$+\$10 - (\$1.1/€)€9 = \$0.1$	...	$+\$10 + \$1,300 -(\$1.2/€)(€9 + €1,000) = \$99.2$
2. Short sell US dollar bond	$+\$1,300$	$-\$10$	$-\$10$	...	$-(\$10 + \$1,300)$
3. Buy euro bond	$-(\$1.3/€)€1,000$	$+(\$1.5/€)€9$	$+(\$1.1/€)€9$	...	$+(\$1.2/€)(€9 + €1,000)$
Net cash flows	0	0	0	0	0

Clearly, if the initial swap value is not at market or zero, then there are arbitrage opportunities. If the initial swap value is positive, then this set of transactions would be implemented. If the initial swap value is negative, then the opposite set of transactions would be implemented. Specifically, enter a pay-US dollar, receive-euro swap, buy Currency a bonds, and short sell Currency b bonds. As before, the swap value after initiation is a simple variation of the expression above—specifically,

$$V_a = FB_a - S_0FB_b = 1{,}300 - 1.3(1{,}000) = 0$$

Note further that $C_a = FS_a$ and $C_b = FS_b$ are fixed swap payment amounts stipulated in the currency swap. One way to find the equilibrium currency swap price (that is, the two fixed rates) is to identify the initial coupon rates ($C_{0,a}$ and $C_{0,b}$) such that the two bonds trade at par—specifically,

$$FB_a(C_{0,a}, Par_a) = Par_a$$

and

$$FB_b(C_{0,b}, Par_b) = Par_b$$

In equilibrium, the notional amounts of the two legs of the currency swap are $NA_b = Par_b$ and $NA_a = Par_a = S_0Par_b$. That is, one first decides the par value desired in one currency and then solves for the implied notional amount in the other currency.

The goal is to determine the fixed rates of the swap such that the current swap value is zero; then we have

$$FB_a(C_{0,a}, Par_a) = S_0FB_b(C_{0,b}, Par_b)$$

Because the fixed swap rate does not depend on the notional amounts, the fixed swap rates are found in exactly the same manner as the fixed interest rate swap rate. For emphasis, we repeat the equilibrium fixed swap rate equations for each currency:

$$r_{FIX,a} = \frac{1 - PV_{0,t_n,a}(1)}{\sum\limits_{i=1}^{n} PV_{0,t_i,a}(1)}$$

and

$$r_{FIX,b} = \frac{1 - PV_{0,t_n,b}(1)}{\sum\limits_{i=1}^{n} PV_{0,t_i,b}(1)} \qquad (15)$$

Again, the fixed swap rate in each currency is simply one minus the final present value term divided by the sum of present values. We need to be sure that the present value terms are expressed on the basis of the appropriate currency.

We illustrate currency swap pricing with spot rates by way of an example.

EXAMPLE 15

Currency Swap Pricing with Spot Rates

A US company needs to borrow 100 million Australian dollars (A\$) for one year for its Australian subsidiary. The company decides to issue US-denominated bonds in an amount equivalent to A\$100 million. Then the company enters into a one-year currency swap with quarterly reset (30/360 day count) and the exchange of notional amounts at initiation and at maturity. At the swap's initiation, the US company receives the notional amount in Australian dollars and pays to the counterparty the notional amount in US dollars. At the swap's expiration, the US company pays the notional amount in Australian dollars and receives from the counterparty the notional amount in US dollars. Based on interbank rates, we observe the following spot rates today, at Time 0:

Days to Maturity	A$ Spot Interest Rates (%)	US$ Spot Interest Rates (%)
90	2.50	0.10
180	2.60	0.15
270	2.70	0.20
360	2.80	0.25

Assume that the counterparties in the currency swap agree to an A$/US$ spot exchange rate of 1.140 (expressed as number of Australian dollars for US$1).

1 The annual fixed swap rates for Australian dollars and US dollars, respectively, will be *closest* to:

   A 2.80% and 0.10%.

   B 2.77% and 0.25%.

   C 2.65% and 0.175%.

2 The notional amount (in US$ millions) will be *closest* to:

   A 88.

   B 100.

   C 114.

3 The fixed swap annual payments in the currency swap will be *closest* to:

   A A$692,000 and US$55,000.

   B A$220,000 and US$173,000.

   C A$720,000 and US$220,000.

Solution to 1:

B is correct. We first find the PV factors and then solve for the fixed swap rates. The present value expression based on spot rates (not forward rates) is $PV_{0,t_i}(1) = \dfrac{1}{1 + r_{Spot_i}\left(\dfrac{NAD_i}{NTD}\right)}$. Spot rates cover the entire period from 0 to t_i, unlike forward rates, which cover incremental periods. Based on the data given, we construct the following present value data table. The calculations are shown to the sixth decimal place in an effort to minimize rounding error. Rounding differences may occur in the solutions.

Days to Maturity	A$ Spot Interest Rates (%)	Present Value (A$1)	US$ Spot Interest Rates (%)	Present Value (US$1)
90	2.50	0.993789[a]	0.10	0.999750
180	2.60	0.987167	0.15	0.999251[b]
270	2.70	0.980152	0.20	0.998502
360	2.80	0.972763	0.25	0.997506
	Sum:	*3.933870*	*Sum:*	*3.995009*

[a] A$0.993789 = 1/[1 + 0.0250(90/360)].

[b] US$0.999251 = 1/[1 + 0.00150(180/360)].

Therefore, the Australian dollar periodic rate is

$$r_{\text{FIX.AUD}} = \frac{1 - PV_{0,t_4,\text{AUD}}(1)}{\sum_{i=1}^{4} PV_{0,t_i,\text{AUD}}(1)} = \frac{1 - 0.972763}{3.933870}$$

$$= 0.00692381 \text{ or } 0.692381\%$$

and the US dollar periodic rate is

$$r_{\text{FIX.USD}} = \frac{1 - PV_{0,t_4,\text{USD}}(1)}{\sum_{i=1}^{4} PV_{0,t_i,\text{USD}}(1)} = \frac{1 - 0.997506}{3.995009}$$

$$= 0.00062422 \text{ or } 0.062422\%$$

The annualized rate is simply (360/90) times the period results: 2.7695% for Australian dollars and 0.2497% for US dollars.

Solution to 2:

A is correct. The US dollar notional amount is calculated as A$100 million divided by the current spot exchange rate at which US$1 dollar trades for A$1.1400. This exchange is equal to US$87,719,298 (= A$100,000,000/1.14).

Solution to 3:

A is correct. The fixed swap payments in currency units equal the periodic swap rate times the appropriate notional amounts. From the answers to 1 and 2, we have

$$FS_{A\$} = NA_{A\$}(AP)r_{\text{FIX,A\$}}$$
$$= A\$100,000,000(90/360)(0.027695)$$
$$= A\$692,375$$

and

$$FS_{US\$} = NA_{US\$}(AP)r_{\text{FIX,US\$}}$$
$$= US\$87,719,298(90/360)(0.002497)$$
$$= US\$54,759.$$

Therefore, one approach to pricing currency swaps is to view the swap as a pair of fixed-rate bonds. The main advantage of this approach is that all foreign exchange considerations are moved to the initial exchange rate. We do not need to address future foreign currency transactions. Also, note that a fixed-for-floating currency swap is simply a fixed-for-fixed currency swap paired with a floating-for-fixed interest rate swap. Also, we do not technically "price" a floating-rate swap, because we do not designate a single coupon rate, and the value of such a swap is par on any reset date. Thus, we have the capacity to price any variation of currency swaps.

We now turn to currency swap valuation. Recall that with currency swaps, there are two main sources of risk: interest rates and exchange rates. Exhibit 21 shows the cash flows from three transactions. Note this exhibit is similar to the currency swap pricing exhibit, but the currency swap was initiated at Time 0 and here we are evaluating it at Time t. Step 1 shows the cash flows for a fixed-for-fixed currency swap expressed in units of Currency a. Step 2 is borrowing or short selling a bond in Currency a to generate sufficient funds to exactly offset the currency swap cash flows that are in units of Currency a. Step 3 is lending or buying a bond in Currency b to generate sufficient funds to exactly offset the currency swap cash flows that are in units of Currency b. The net cash flows at each future point in time are zero. Recall that S_i denotes the spot exchange rate in units of Currency a for each unit of Currency b at Time t_i. Thus, $S_tFS_{b,0}$ is the value of the Currency b fixed cash flow expressed in Currency a at Time t. From a value perspective, $FS_{b,0}$ is equivalent in value in Currency b to $S_tFS_{b,0}$ in Currency a. Hence, the future net cash flows are all zero.

Exhibit 21   Cash Flows for Currency Swap Hedged with Bonds

Steps	Time t	Time 1	Time 2	...	Time n′
1. Currency swap	$-V_a$	$+FS_{a,0} - S_1FS_{b,0}$	$+FS_{a,0} - S_2FS_{b,0}$	...	$+FS_{a,0} + NA_{a,0}$ $- S_{n}{}'(FS_{b,0} + NA_{b,0})$
2. Short sell bond (a)	$+FB_a$	$-FS_{a,0}$	$-FS_{a,0}$	...	$-(FS_{a,0} + NA_{a,0})$
3. Buy bond (b)	$-S_tFB_b$	$+S_1FS_{b,0}$	$+S_2FS_{b,0}$	...	$-S_{n}{}'(FS_{b,0} + NA_{b,0})$
Net cash flows	0	0	0		0

The value of a fixed-for-fixed currency swap at some future point in time, Time t, is simply the difference in a pair of fixed-rate bonds, one expressed in Currency a and one expressed in Currency b. To express the bonds in the same currency units, we convert the Currency b bond into units of Currency a through a spot foreign exchange transaction. Hence, we have

$$V_a = FB_a - S_0FB_b$$
$$= FS_{a,0}\sum_{i=1}^{n'}PV_{t,t_i,a} + NA_{a,0}PV_{t,t_{n'},a} - S_t\left(FS_{b,0}\sum_{i=1}^{n'}PV_{t,t_i,b} + NA_{b,0}PV_{t,t_{n'},b}\right)$$

Note that the fixed swap amount (FS) is the per-period fixed swap rate times the notional amount. Therefore, the currency swap valuation equation can be expressed as

$$V_a = NA_{a,0}\left(r_{FIX,a,0}\sum_{i=1}^{n'}PV_{t,t_i,a} + PV_{t,t_{n'},a}\right) -$$
$$S_t NA_{b,0}\left(r_{FIX,b,0}\sum_{i=1}^{n'}PV_{t,t_i,b} + PV_{t,t_{n'},b}\right)$$

(16)

EXAMPLE 16

Currency Swap Valuation with Spot Rates

This example builds on the previous example addressing currency swap pricing. Recall that a US company needed to borrow 100 million Australian dollars (A$) for one year for its Australian subsidiary. The company decided to borrow in US dollars (US$) an amount equivalent to A$100 million by issuing US-denominated bonds. The company entered into a one-year currency swap with quarterly reset (30/360 day count) and exchange of notional amounts at initiation and at maturity. At the swap's expiration, the US company pays the notional amount in Australian dollars and receives from the counterparty the notional amount in US dollars. The fixed rates were 2.7695% for Australian dollars and 0.2497% for US dollars. The notional amount in US dollars was US$87,719,298.

Assume 60 days have passed and we observe the following market information:

Days to Maturity	A$ Spot Interest Rates (%)	Present Value (A$1)	US$ Spot Interest Rates (%)	Present Value (US$1)
30	2.00	0.998336	0.50	0.999584
120	1.90	0.993707	0.40	0.998668
210	1.80	0.989609	0.30	0.998253
300	1.70	0.986031	0.20	0.998336
	Sum:	3.967683	*Sum:*	3.994841

The currency spot exchange rate is now A$1.13 for US$1.

The current value of the currency swap entered into 60 days ago will be *closest* to:

A   −AD$2,000,000.

B   AD$2,000,000.

C   AD$9,644,970.

Solution:

C is correct. Based on the data given, the currency swap value is

$$V_a = NA_{a,0}\left(r_{FIX,a,0}\sum_{i=1}^{n'}PV_{t,t_i,a} + PV_{t,t_{n'},a}\right) - S_0 NA_{b,0}\left(r_{FIX,b,0}\sum_{i=1}^{n'}PV_{t,t_i,b} + PV_{t,t_{n'},b}\right)$$

$$= 100,000,000[0.027695(3.967683) + 0.986031] - 1.13(87,719,298)$$
$$[0.002497(3.994841) + 0.998336]$$
$$= 9,644,970$$

In other words, the value of the payments to be received exceeds the value of the payments to be made by this amount. This value incorporates the change in the exchange rate and changes in interest rates in both countries since the start of the swap.

4.3 Equity Swap Contracts

Drawing on our prior definition of a swap, we define an equity swap in the following manner: An **equity swap** is an OTC derivative contract in which two parties agree to exchange a series of cash flows whereby one party pays a variable series that will be determined by an equity and the other party pays either (1) a variable series determined by a different equity or rate or (2) a fixed series. An equity swap is used to convert the returns from an equity investment into another series of returns, which, as noted, either can be derived from another equity series or can be a fixed rate. Equity swaps are widely used in equity portfolio investment management to modify returns and risks.

We examine three types of equity swaps: receive-equity return, pay-fixed; receive-equity return, pay-floating; and receive-equity return, pay-another equity return. Like interest rate swaps and currency swaps, there are several unique nuances for equity swaps. We highlight just a few. First, the underlying reference instrument for the equity leg of an equity swap can be an individual stock, a published stock index, or a custom portfolio. Second, the equity leg cash flow can be with or without dividends. Third, all the interest rate swap nuances exist with equity swaps that have a fixed or floating interest rate leg.

We focus here on viewing an equity swap as a portfolio of an equity position and a bond. The equity swap cash flows can be expressed as follows:

NA(Equity return − Fixed rate) (for receive-equity, pay-fixed),

NA(Equity return − Floating rate) (for receive-equity, pay-floating), and

NA(Equity return$_a$ − Equity return$_b$) (for receive-equity, pay-equity),

where a and b denote different equities. Note that an equity-for-equity swap can be viewed simply as a receive-equity a, pay-fixed swap combined with a pay-equity b, receive-fixed swap. The fixed payments cancel out, and we have synthetically created an equity-for-equity swap.

EXAMPLE 17

Equity Swap Cash Flows

Suppose we entered into a receive-equity index and pay-fixed swap. It is quarterly reset, 30/360 day count, €5,000,000 notional amount, pay-fixed (1.6% annualized, quarterly pay, or 0.4% per quarter).

1   If the equity index return was 4.0% for the quarter (not annualized), the equity swap cash flow will be *closest* to:

    A −€220,000.

    B −€180,000.

    C €180,000.

2   If the equity index return was −6.0% for the quarter (not annualized), the equity swap cash flow will be closest to:

    A −€320,000.

    B −€180,000.

    C €180,000.

Solution to 1:

C is correct. Note that the equity index return is reported on a quarterly basis. It is not an annualized number. The fixed leg is often reported on an annual basis. Thus, one must carefully interpret the different return conventions. In this case, receive-equity index counterparty cash flows are as follows:

    €5,000,000(0.04 − 0.004) = €180,000 (Receive 4%, pay 0.4% for the quarter)

Solution to 2:

A is correct. Similar to 1, we have

    €5,000,000(−0.06 − 0.004) = −€320,000 (Receive −6%, pay 0.4% for the quarter)

When the equity leg of the swap is negative, then the receive-equity counterparty must pay both the equity return as well as the fixed rate (or whatever the payment terms are). Note, also, that equity swaps may cause liquidity problems. As seen here, if the equity return is negative, then the receive-equity return, pay-floating or pay-fixed swap may result in a large negative cash flow.

The cash flows for the equity leg of an equity swap can be expressed as

$$S_i = NA_E R_{E_i}$$

where R_{E_i} denotes the periodic return of the equity either with or without dividends as specified in the swap contract and NA_E denotes the notional amount. The cash flows for the fixed interest rate leg of the equity swap are the same as those of an interest rate swap, or

$$FS = NA_E AP_{FIX} r_{FIX}$$

where AP_{FIX} denotes the accrual period for the fixed leg for which we assume the accrual period is constant and r_{FIX} here denotes the fixed rate on the equity swap.

For equity swaps, the equity position could be a wide variety of claims, including the return on a stock index with or without dividends and the return on an individual stock with or without dividends. For our objectives here, we ignore the influence of dividends by assuming the equity swap leg assumes all dividends are reinvested in the equity position.[25] The equity leg of the swap is produced by selling the equity position on a reset date and reinvesting the original equity notional amount, leaving a remaining balance that is the cash flow required of the equity swap leg.[26] Exhibit 22 shows the cash flows from an equity swap arbitrage transaction.

Exhibit 22   Cash Flows for Receive-Fixed Equity Swap Hedged with Equity and Bond

Steps	Time 0	Time 1	Time 2	...	Time n
1. Enter equity swap	$-V$	$+FS - S_1$	$+FS - S_2$	...	$+FS - S_n$
2. Buy NA_E equity	$-NA_E$	$+S_1$	$+S_2$	...	$+S_n + NA_E$
3. Short sell fixed-rate bond	$+FB(C = FS)$	$-FS$	$-FS$	...	$-(FS + Par)$
4. Borrow arbitrage profit	$-PV(Par - NA_E)$				$Par - NA_E$
Net cash flows	$-V - NA_E + FB$ $- PV(Par - NA_E)$	0	0	0	0

Let us examine the Time 1 cash flow. The equity swap is receive-fixed, pay-equity. For Step 1, if the equity-related cash flow S_1 is less than the fixed-leg cash flow, then the swap generates a positive cash flow to this counterparty. For Step 2, the cash flow is simply the cash flow related to the equity movement and dividends, if applicable. Essentially, if the position value is greater than NA_E, then the excess value is sold off, but if the position value is less than NA_E, then an additional equity position is acquired. For Step 3, the short bond position requires the payment of coupons. Note that these coupons, by construction, equal the fixed leg cash flows. The sum of these three transactions is always zero.

Note the final cash flow for the long position in the equity includes the final sale of the underlying equity position. The final periodic return on the equity plus the original equity value will equal the proceeds from the final sale of the underlying equity position. Note that for the terminal cash flows to equal zero, we must either set the bond par value to equal the initial equity position or finance this difference. In this case, the bond par value could be different from the notional amount of equity. Therefore, in equilibrium, we have $-V - NA_E + FB - PV(Par - NA_E) = 0$, and hence, the equity swap value is $V = -NA_E + FB - PV(Par - NA_E)$.

---

25 The arbitrage transactions for an equity swap when dividends are not included are extremely complex and beyond our objectives.
26 Technically, we just sell off any equity value in excess of NA_E or purchase additional shares to return the equity value to NA_E, effectively generating S_i.

The fixed swap rate can be expressed as the r_{FIX} rate such that $FB_0 = NA_E + PV(Par - NA_E)$. Note that assuming $NA_E = Par = 1$,

$$r_{FIX} = \frac{1 - PV_{0,t_n}(1)}{\sum_{i=1}^{n} PV_{0,t_i}(1)}$$

You should recognize that the pricing of an equity swap is identical to the pricing of a comparable interest rate swap even though the future cash flows are dramatically different. If the swap required a floating payment, there would be no need to price the swap, as the floating side effectively prices itself at par automatically at the start. If the swap involves paying one equity return against another, there would also be no need to price it. You could effectively view this arrangement as paying equity a and receiving a fixed rate as specified above and receiving equity b and paying the same fixed rate. The fixed rates would cancel.

Valuing an equity swap after the swap is initiated (V_t) is similar to valuing an interest rate swap except that rather than adjust the floating-rate bond for the last floating rate observed (remember, advanced set), we adjust the value of the notional amount of equity, or

$$V_t = FB_t(C_0) - (S_t/S_{t_-})NA_E - PV(Par - NA_E) \qquad \textbf{(17)}$$

where $FB_t(C_0)$ denotes the Time t value of a fixed-rate bond initiated with coupon C_0 at Time 0, S_t denotes the current equity price, S_{t_-} denotes the equity price observed at the last reset date, and $PV()$ denotes the present value function from Time t to the swap maturity time.

EXAMPLE 18

Equity Swap Pricing

In Examples 13 and 14 related to interest rate swaps, we considered a five-year, annual reset, 30/360 day count, Libor-based swap. The following table provides the present values per €1.

Maturity (years)	Present Value Factors
1	0.990099
2	0.977876
3	0.965136
4	0.951529
5	0.937467

Assume an annual reset Libor floating-rate bond trading at par. The fixed rate was previously found to be 1.2968%. Given these same data, the fixed interest rate in the EURO STOXX 50 equity swap is *closest* to:

A   0.0%.

B   1.1%.

C   1.3%.

Solution:

C is correct. The fixed rate on an equity swap is the same as that on an interest rate swap or 1.2968% as in Example 13. That is, the fixed rate on an equity swap is simply the fixed rate on a comparable interest rate swap.

EXAMPLE 19

Equity Swap Valuation

Suppose six months ago we entered a receive-fixed, pay-equity five-year annual reset swap in which the fixed leg is based on a 30/360 day count. At the time the swap was entered, the fixed swap rate was 1.5%, the equity was trading at 100, and the notional amount was 10,000,000. Now all spot interest rates have fallen to 1.2% (a flat term structure), and the equity is trading for 105.

1   The fair value of this equity swap is *closest* to:

    A   −€300,000.

    B   −€500,000.

    C   €500,000.

2   The value of the equity swap will be *closest* to zero if the stock price is:

    A   100.

    B   102.

    C   105.

Solution to 1:

A is correct. Because we have not yet passed the first reset date, there are five remaining cash flows for this equity swap. The fair value of this swap is found by solving for the fair value of the implied fixed-rate bond. We then adjust for the equity value. The fixed rate of 1.5% results in fixed cash flows of 150,000 at each settlement. Applying the respective present value factors, which are based on the new spot rates of 1.2%, gives us the following:

Date (in years)	Present Value Factors (PV)	Fixed Cash Flow	PV(Fixed Cash Flow)*
0.5	0.994036	150,000	149,105
1.5	0.982318	150,000	147,348
2.5	0.970874	150,000	145,631
3.5	0.959693	150,000	143,954
4.5	0.948767	10,150,000	9,629,981
		Total:	10,216,019

* Answers may differ due to rounding.

Therefore, the fair value of this equity swap is 10,216,019 less 10,500,000 [= (105/100)10,000,000], or a loss of 283,981.

Solution to 2:

B is correct. The stock price at which this equity swap's fair value is zero would require (Par = NA_E in this case)

$$V_t = FB_t(C_0) - (S_t/S_{t-})NA_E$$

The value of the fixed leg is now approximately 102% of par; a stock price of 102 will result in a value of zero,

$$V_t = 102 - (S_t/100)100 = 0$$

where S_t is 102.

SUMMARY

This reading on forward commitment pricing and valuation provides a foundation for understanding how forwards, futures, and swaps are both priced and valued.

Key points include the following:

- The arbitrageur would rather have more money than less and abides by two fundamental rules: Do not use your own money, and do not take any price risk.

- The no-arbitrage approach is used for the pricing and valuation of forward commitments and is built on the key concept of the law of one price, which states that if two investments have the same future cash flows, regardless of what happens in the future, these two investments should have the same current price.

- Throughout this reading, the following key assumptions are made:
  - Replicating instruments are identifiable and investable.
  - Market frictions are nil.
  - Short selling is allowed with full use of proceeds.
  - Borrowing and lending is available at a known risk-free rate.

- Carry arbitrage models used for forward commitment pricing and valuation are based on the no-arbitrage approach.

- With forward commitments, there is a distinct difference between pricing and valuation; pricing involves the determination of the appropriate fixed price or rate, and valuation involves the determination of the contract's current value expressed in currency units.

- Forward commitment pricing results in determining a price or rate such that the forward contract value is equal to zero.

- The price of a forward commitment is a function of the price of the underlying instrument, financing costs, and other carry costs and benefits.

- With equities, currencies, and fixed-income securities, the forward price is determined such that the initial forward value is zero.

- With forward rate agreements, the fixed interest rate is determined such that the initial value of the FRA is zero.

- Futures contract pricing here can essentially be treated the same as forward contract pricing.

- Because of daily marking to market, futures contract values are zero after each daily settlement.

- The general approach to pricing and valuing swaps as covered here is using a replicating or hedge portfolio of comparable instruments.
- With a basic understanding of pricing and valuing a simple interest rate swap, it is a straightforward extension to pricing and valuing currency swaps and equity swaps.
- With interest rate swaps and some equity swaps, pricing involves solving for the fixed interest rate.
- With currency swaps, pricing involves solving for the two fixed rates as well as the notional amounts in each currency.

Valuation of Contingent Claims

by Robert E. Brooks, PhD, CFA, and David Maurice Gentle, MEc, BSc, CFA

Robert E. Brooks, PhD, CFA, is at the University of Alabama (USA). David Maurice Gentle, MEc, BSc, CFA, is at Omega Risk Consulting (Australia).

LEARNING OUTCOMES

Mastery	The candidate should be able to
☐	**a.** describe and interpret the binomial option valuation model and its component terms;
☐	**b.** calculate the no-arbitrage values of European and American options using a two-period binomial model;
☐	**c.** identify an arbitrage opportunity involving options and describe the related arbitrage;
☐	**d.** describe how interest rate options are valued using a two-period binomial model;
☐	**e.** calculate and interpret the value of an interest rate option using a two-period binomial model;
☐	**f.** describe how the value of a European option can be analyzed as the present value of the option's expected payoff at expiration;
☐	**g.** identify assumptions of the Black–Scholes–Merton option valuation model;
☐	**h.** interpret the components of the Black–Scholes–Merton model as applied to call options in terms of a leveraged position in the underlying;
☐	**i.** describe how the Black–Scholes–Merton model is used to value European options on equities and currencies;
☐	**j.** describe how the Black model is used to value European options on futures;
☐	**k.** describe how the Black model is used to value European interest rate options and European swaptions;
☐	**l.** interpret each of the option Greeks;
☐	**m.** describe how a delta hedge is executed;
☐	**n.** describe the role of gamma risk in options trading;
☐	**o.** define implied volatility and explain how it is used in options trading.

1   INTRODUCTION

A contingent claim is a derivative instrument that provides its owner a right but not an obligation to a payoff determined by an underlying asset, rate, or other derivative. Contingent claims include options, the valuation of which is the objective of this reading. Because many investments contain embedded options, understanding this material is vital for investment management.

Our primary purpose is to understand how the values of options are determined. Option values, as with the values of all financial instruments, are typically obtained using valuation models. Any financial valuation model takes certain inputs and turns them into an output that tells us the fair value or price. Option valuation models, like their counterparts in the forward, futures, and swaps markets, are based on the principle of no arbitrage, meaning that the appropriate price of an option is the one that makes it impossible for any party to earn an arbitrage profit at the expense of any other party. The price that precludes arbitrage profits is the value of the option. Using that concept, we then proceed to introduce option valuation models using two approaches. The first approach is the binomial model, which is based on discrete time, and the second is the Black–Scholes–Merton (BSM) model, which is based on continuous time.

The reading is organized as follows. Section 2 introduces the principles of the no-arbitrage approach to pricing and valuation of options. In Section 3, the binomial option valuation model is explored, and in Section 4, the BSM model is covered. In Section 5, the Black model, being a variation of the BSM model, is applied to futures options, interest rate options, and swaptions. Finally, in Section 6, the Greeks are reviewed along with implied volatility. Section 7 provides a summary.

2   PRINCIPLES OF A NO-ARBITRAGE APPROACH TO VALUATION

Our approach is based on the concept of arbitrage. Hence, the material will be covered from an arbitrageur's perspective. Key to understanding this material is to think like an arbitrageur. Specifically, like most people, the arbitrageur would rather have more money than less. The arbitrageur, as will be detailed later, follows two fundamental rules:

Rule #1   Do not use your own money.

Rule #2   Do not take any price risk.

Clearly, if we can generate positive cash flows today and abide by both rules, we have a great business—such is the life of an arbitrageur. If traders could create a portfolio with no future liabilities and positive cash flow today, then it would essentially be a money machine that would be attractive to anyone who prefers more cash to less. In the pursuit of these positive cash flows today, the arbitrageur often needs to borrow to satisfy Rule #1. In effect, the arbitrageur borrows the arbitrage profit to capture it today and, if necessary, may borrow to purchase the underlying. Specifically, the arbitrageur will build portfolios using the underlying instrument to synthetically replicate the cash flows of an option. The underlying instrument is the financial instrument whose later value will be referenced to determine the option value. Examples of underlying instruments include shares, indexes, currencies, and interest rates. As we will see, with options we will often rely on a specific trading strategy that changes over time based on the underlying price behavior.

Based on the concept of comparability, the no-arbitrage valuation approach taken here is built on the concept that if two investments have the same future cash flows regardless of what happens, then these two investments should have the same current price. This principle is known as the **law of one price**. In establishing these foundations of option valuation, the following key assumptions are made: (1) Replicating instruments are identifiable and investable. (2) There are no market frictions, such as transaction costs and taxes. (3) Short selling is allowed with full use of proceeds. (4) The underlying instrument follows a known statistical distribution. (5) Borrowing and lending at a risk-free interest rate is available. When we develop the models in this reading, we will be more specific about what these assumptions mean, in particular what we mean by a known statistical distribution.

In an effort to demonstrate various valuation results based on the absence of arbitrage, we will rely heavily on cash flow tables, which are a representation of the cash flows that occur during the life of an option. For example, if an initial investment requires €100, then from an arbitrageur's perspective, we will present it as a −€100 cash flow. If an option pays off ¥1,000, we will represent it as a +¥1,000 cash flow. That is, cash outflows are treated as negative and inflows as positive.

We first demonstrate how to value options based on a two-period binomial model. The option payoffs can be replicated with a dynamic portfolio of the underlying instrument and financing. A dynamic portfolio is one whose composition changes over time. These changes are important elements of the replicating procedure. Based on the binomial framework, we then turn to exploring interest rate options using a binomial tree. Although more complex, the general approach is shown to be the same.

The multiperiod binomial model is a natural transition to the BSM option valuation model. The BSM model is based on the key assumption that the value of the underlying instrument follows a statistical process called geometric Brownian motion. This characterization is a reasonable way to capture the randomness of financial instrument prices while incorporating a pre-specified expected return and volatility of return. Geometric Brownian motion implies a lognormal distribution of the return, which implies that the continuously compounded return on the underlying is normally distributed.

We also explore the role of carry benefits, meaning the reward or cost of holding the underlying itself instead of holding the derivative on the underlying.

Next we turn to Fischer Black's futures option valuation model (Black model) and note that the model difference, versus the BSM model, is related to the underlying futures contract having no carry costs or benefits. Interest rate options and swaptions are valued based on simple modifications of the Black model.

Finally, we explore the Greeks, otherwise known as delta, gamma, theta, vega, and rho. The Greeks are representations of the sensitivity of the option value to changes in the factors that determine the option value. They provide comparative information essential in managing portfolios containing options. The Greeks are calculated based on an option valuation model, such as the binomial model, BSM model, or the Black model. This information is model dependent, so managers need to carefully select the model best suited for their particular situation. In the last section, we cover implied volatility, which is a measure derived from a market option price and can be interpreted as reflecting what investors believe is the volatility of the underlying.

The models presented here are useful first approximations for explaining observed option prices in many markets. The central theme is that options are generally priced to preclude arbitrage profits, which is not only a reasonable theoretical assumption but is sufficiently accurate in practice.

We turn now to option valuation based on the binomial option valuation model.

3   BINOMIAL OPTION VALUATION MODEL

The binomial model is a valuable tool for financial analysts. It is particularly useful as a heuristic device to understand the unique valuation approach used with options. This model is extensively used to value path-dependent options, which are options whose values depend not only on the value of the underlying at expiration but also how it got there. The path-dependency feature distinguishes this model from the Black–Scholes–Merton option valuation model (BSM model) presented in the next section. The BSM model values only path-independent options, such as European options, which depend on only the values of their respective underlyings at expiration. One particular type of path-dependent option that we are interested in is American options, which are those that can be exercised prior to expiration. In this section, we introduce the general framework for developing the binomial option valuation models for both European and American options.

The binomial option valuation model is based on the no-arbitrage approach to valuation. Hence, understanding the valuation of options improves if one can understand how an arbitrageur approaches financial markets. An arbitrageur engages in financial transactions in pursuit of an initial positive cash flow with no possibility of a negative cash flow in the future. As it appears, it is a great business if you can find it.[1]

To understand option valuation models, it is helpful to think like an arbitrageur. The arbitrageur seeks to exploit any pricing discrepancy between the option price and the underlying spot price. The arbitrageur is assumed to prefer more money compared with less money, assuming everything else is the same. As mentioned earlier, there are two fundamental rules for the arbitrageur.

Rule #1   Do not use your own money. Specifically, the arbitrageur does not use his or her own money to acquire positions. Also, the arbitrageur does not spend proceeds from short selling transactions on activities unrelated to the transaction at hand.

Rule #2   Do not take any price risk. The focus here is only on market price risk related to the underlying and the derivatives used. We do not consider other risks, such as liquidity risk and counterparty credit risk.

We will rely heavily on these two rules when developing option valuation models. Remember, these rules are general in nature, and as with many things in finance, there are nuances.

In Exhibit 1, the two key dates are the option contract initiation date (identified as Time 0) and the option contract expiration date (identified as Time T). Based on the no-arbitrage approach, the option value from the initiation date onward will be estimated with an option valuation model.

---

1 There is not a one-to-one correspondence between arbitrage and great investment opportunities. An arbitrage is certainly a great investment opportunity because it produces a risk-free profit with no investment of capital, but all great investment opportunities are not arbitrage. For example, an opportunity to invest €1 today in return for a 99% chance of receiving €1,000,000 tomorrow or a 1% chance of receiving €0 might appear to be a truly great investment opportunity, but it is not arbitrage because it is not risk free and requires the investment of capital.

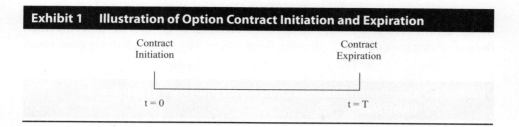

Exhibit 1   Illustration of Option Contract Initiation and Expiration

Contract Initiation

Contract Expiration

t = 0   t = T

Let S_t denote the underlying instrument price observed at Time t, where t is expressed as a fraction of a year. Similarly, S_T denotes the underlying instrument price observed at the option expiration date, T. For example, suppose a call option had 90 days to expiration when purchased (T = 90/365), but now only has 35 days to expiration (t = 55/365). Further, let c_t denote a European-style call price at Time t and with expiration on Date t = T, where both t and T are expressed in years. Similarly, let C_t denote an American-style call price. At the initiation date, the subscripts are omitted, thus c = c_0. We follow similar notation with a put, using the letter p, in place of c. Let X denote the exercise price.[2]

For example, suppose on 15 April a 90-day European-style call option contract with a 14 July expiration is initiated with a call price of c = €2.50 and T = 90/365 = 0.246575.

At expiration, the call and put values will be equal to their intrinsic value or exercise value. These **exercise values** can be expressed as

$c_T = Max(0,S_T - X)$ and
$p_T = Max(0,X - S_T)$,

respectively. If the option values deviate from these expressions, then there will be arbitrage profits available. The option is expiring, there is no uncertainty remaining, and the price must equal the market value obtained from exercising it or letting it expire.

Technically, European options do not have exercise values prior to expiration because they cannot be exercised until expiration. Nonetheless, the notion of the value of the option if it could be exercised, $Max(0,S_t - X)$ for a call and $Max(0,X - S_t)$ for a put, forms a basis for understanding the notion that the value of an option declines with the passage of time. Specifically, option values contain an element known as time value, which is just the market valuation of the potential for higher exercise value relative to the potential for lower exercise value. The time value is always non-negative because of the asymmetry of option payoffs at expiration. For example, for a call, the upside is unlimited, whereas the downside is limited to zero. At expiration, time value is zero.

Although option prices are influenced by a variety of factors, the underlying instrument has a particularly significant influence. At this point, the underlying is assumed to be the only uncertain factor affecting the option price. We now look in detail at the one-period binomial option valuation model. The one-period binomial model is foundational for the material that follows.

3.1 One-Period Binomial Model

Exhibit 2 illustrates the one-period binomial process for an asset priced at S. In the figure on the left, each dot represents a particular outcome at a particular point in time in the binomial lattice. The dots are termed nodes. At the Time 0 node, there are only two possible future paths in the binomial process, an up move and a down

---

2 In financial markets, the exercise price is also commonly called the strike price.

move, termed arcs. The figure on the right illustrates the underlying price at each node. At Time 1, there are only two possible outcomes: S^+ denotes the outcome when the underlying goes up, and S^- denotes the outcome when the underlying goes down.

Exhibit 2   One-Period Binomial Lattice with Underlying Distribution Illustrated

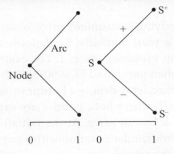

At Time 1, there are only two possible outcomes and two resulting values of the underlying, S^+ (up occurs) and S^- (down occurs). Although the one-period binomial model is clearly unrealistic, it will provide key insights into the more realistic multi-period binomial as well as the BSM model.

We further define the total returns implied by the underlying movements as

$$u = \frac{S^+}{S} \text{ (up factor) and}$$

$$d = \frac{S^-}{S} \text{ (down factor).}$$

The up factors and down factors are the total returns; that is, one plus the rate of return. The magnitudes of the up and down factors are based on the volatility of the underlying. In general, higher volatility will result in higher up values and lower down values.

We briefly review option valuation within a one-period binomial tree. With this review, we can move quickly to option valuation within a two-period binomial lattice by performing the one-period exercise three times.

We consider the fair value of a two-period call option value measured at Time 1 when an up move occurs, that is c^+. Based on arbitrage forces, we know this option value at expiration is either

$$c^{++} = Max(0, S^{++} - X) = Max(0, u^2 S - X), \text{ or}$$
$$c^{+-} = Max(0, S^{+-} - X) = Max(0, udS - X).$$

At this point, we assume that there are no costs or benefits from owning the underlying instrument. Now consider the transactions illustrated in Exhibit 3. These transactions are presented as cash flows. Thus, if we write a call option, we receive money at Time Step 0 and may have to pay out money at Time Step 1. Suppose the first trade is to write or sell one call option within the single-period binomial model. The value of a call option is positively related to the value of the underlying. That is, they both move up or down together. Hence, by writing a call option, the trader will lose money if the underlying goes up and make money if the underlying falls. Therefore, to execute a hedge, the trader will need a position that will make money if the underlying goes up. Thus, the second trade needs to be a long position in the underlying. Specifically, the trader buys a certain number of units, h, of the underlying. The symbol h is used because it represents a hedge ratio.

Note that with these first two trades, neither arbitrage rule is satisfied. The future cash flow could be either $-c^- + hS^-$ or $-c^+ + hS^+$ and can be positive or negative. Thus, the cash flows at the Time Step 1 could result in the arbitrageur having to pay out money if one of these values is less than zero. To resolve both of these issues, we set the Time Step 1 cash flows equal to each other—that is, $-c^+ + hS^+ = -c^- + hS^-$—and solve for the appropriate hedge ratio:

$$h = \frac{c^+ - c^-}{S^+ - S^-} \geq 0 \qquad\qquad (1)$$

We determine the hedge ratio such that we are indifferent to the underlying going up or down. Thus, we are hedged against moves in the underlying. A simple rule for remembering this formula is that the hedge ratio is the value of the call if the underlying goes up minus the value of the call if the underlying goes down divided by the value of the underlying if it goes up minus the value of the underlying if it goes down. The up and down patterns are the same in the numerator and denominator, but the numerator contains the option and the denominator contains the underlying.

Because call prices are positively related to changes in the underlying price, we know that h is non-negative. As shown in Exhibit 3, we will buy h underlying units as depicted in the second trade, and we will finance the present value of the net cash flows as depicted in the third trade. If we assume r denotes the per period risk-free interest rate, then the present value calculation, denoted as PV, is equal to $1/(1 + r)$. We need to borrow or lend an amount such that the future net cash flows are equal to zero. Therefore, we finance today the present value of $-hS^- + c^-$ which also equals $-hS^+ + c^+$. At this point we do not know if the finance term is positive or negative, thus we may be either borrowing or lending, which will depend on c, h, and S.

Exhibit 3	Writing One Call Hedge with h Units of the Underlying and Finance		
Strategy	**Time Step 0**	**Time Step 1 Down Occurs**	**Time Step 1 Up Occurs**
1) Write one call option	$+c$	$-c^-$	$-c^+$
2) Buy h underlying units	$-hS$	$+hS^-$	$+hS^+$
3) Borrow or lend	$-PV(-hS^- + c^-)$ $= -PV(-hS^+ + c^+)$	$-hS^- + c^-$	$-hS^+ + c^+$
Net Cash Flow	$+c - hS$ $-PV(-hS^- + c^-)$	0	0

The value of the net portfolio at Time Step 0 should be zero or there is an arbitrage opportunity. If the net portfolio has positive value, then arbitrageurs will engage in this strategy, which will push the call price down and the underlying price up until the net is no longer positive. We assume the size of the borrowing will not influence interest rates. If the net portfolio has negative value, then arbitrageurs will engage in the opposite strategy—buy calls, short sell the underlying, and lend—pushing the call price up and the underlying price down until the net cash flow at Time 0 is no longer positive. Therefore, within the single-period binomial model, we have

$$+c - hS - PV(-hS^- + c^-) = 0$$

or, equivalently,

$$+c - hS - PV(-hS^+ + c^+) = 0.$$

Therefore, the **no-arbitrage approach** leads to the following single-period call option valuation equation:

$$c = hS + PV(-hS^- + c^-) \qquad\qquad (2)$$

or, equivalently, $c = hS + PV(-hS^+ + c^+)$. In words, long a call option is equal to owning h shares of stock partially financed, where the financed amount is $PV(-hS^- + c^-)$, or using the per period rate, $(-hS^- + c^-)/(1 + r)$.[3]

We will refer to Equation 2 as the no-arbitrage single-period binomial option valuation model. This equation is foundational to understanding the two-period binomial as well as other option valuation models. The option can be replicated with the underlying and financing, a point illustrated in the following example.

EXAMPLE 1

Long Call Option Replicated with Underlying and Financing

Identify the trading strategy that will generate the payoffs of taking a long position in a call option within a single-period binomial framework.

A   Buy $h = (c^+ + c^-)/(S^+ + S^-)$ units of the underlying and financing of $-PV(-hS^- + c^-)$

B   Buy $h = (c^+ - c^-)/(S^+ - S^-)$ units of the underlying and financing of $-PV(-hS^- + c^-)$

C   Short sell $h = (c^+ - c^-)/(S^+ - S^-)$ units of the underlying and financing of $+PV(-hS^- + c^-)$

Solution:

B is correct. The following table shows the terminal payoffs to be identical between a call option and buying the underlying with financing.

Strategy	Time Step 0	Time Step 1 Down Occurs	Time Step 1 Up Occurs
Buy 1 call option	$-c$	$+c^-$	$+c^+$
OR A REPLICATING PORTFOLIO			
Buy h underlying units	$-hS$	$+hS^-$	$+hS^+$
Borrow or lend	$-PV(-hS^- + c^-)$ $= -PV(-hS^+ + c^+)$	$-hS^- + c^-$	$-hS^+ + c^+$
Net	$-hS - PV(-hS^- + c^-)$	$+c^-$	$+c^+$

Recall that by design, h is selected such that $-hS^- + c^- = -hS^+ + c^+$ or $h = (c^+ - c^-)/(S^+ - S^-)$. Therefore, a call option can be replicated with the underlying and financing. Specifically, the call option is equivalent to a leveraged position in the underlying.

---

3 Or, by the same logic, $PV(-hS^+ + c^+)$, which is $(-hS^+ + c^+)/(1 + r)$.

Thus, the no-arbitrage approach is a replicating strategy: A call option is synthetically replicated with the underlying and financing. Following a similar strategy with puts, the no-arbitrage approach leads to the following no-arbitrage single-period put option valuation equation:

$$p = hS + PV(-hS^- + p^-)$$ (3)

or, equivalently, $p = hS + PV(-hS^+ + p^+)$ where

$$h = \frac{p^+ - p^-}{S^+ - S^-} \leq 0$$ (4)

Because p^+ is less than p^-, the hedge ratio is negative. Hence, to hedge a long put position, the arbitrageur will short sell the underlying and lend a portion of the proceeds. Note that a long put position would be hedged by trading h units of the underlying. With h negative, this trade is a short sale, and because $-h$ is positive, the value $-hS$ results in a positive cash flow at Time Step 0.

EXAMPLE 2

Long Put Option Replicated with Underlying and Financing

Identify the trading strategy that will generate the payoffs of taking a long position in a put option within a single-period binomial framework.

A Short sell $-h = -(p^+ - p^-)/(S^+ - S^-)$ units of the underlying and financing of $-PV(-hS^- + p^-)$

B Buy $-h = (p^+ - p^-)/(S^+ - S^-)$ units of the underlying and financing of $-PV(-hS^- + p^-)$

C Short sell $h = (p^+ - p^-)/(S^+ - S^-)$ units of the underlying and financing of $+PV(-hS^- + p^-)$

Solution:

A is correct. Before illustrating the replicating portfolio, we make a few observations regarding the hedge ratio. Note that by design, h is selected such that $-hS^- + p^- = -hS^+ + p^+$ or $h = (p^+ - p^-)/(S^+ - S^-)$. Unlike calls, the put hedge ratio is not positive (note that $p^+ < p^-$ but $S^+ > S^-$). Remember that taking a position in $-h$ units of the underlying is actually short selling the underlying rather than buying it. The following table shows the terminal payoffs to be identical between a put option and a position in the underlying with financing.

Strategy	Time Step 0	Time Step 1 Down Occurs	Time Step 1 Up Occurs
Buy 1 Put Option	$-p$	$+p^-$	$+p^+$
OR A REPLICATING PORTFOLIO			
Short sell $-h$ Underlying Units	$-hS$	$+hS^-$	$+hS^+$
Borrow or Lend	$-PV(-hS^- + p^-)$ $= -PV(-hS^+ + p^+)$	$-hS^- + p^-$	$-hS^+ + p^+$
Net	$-hS - PV(-hS^- + p^-)$	$+p^-$	$+p^+$

> Therefore, a put option can be replicated with the underlying and financing. Specifically, the put option is simply equivalent to a short position in the underlying with financing in the form of lending.

What we have shown to this point is the no-arbitrage approach. Before turning to the expectations approach, we mention, for the sake of completeness, that the transactions for writing options are the reverse for those of buying them. Thus, for writing a call option, the writer will be selling stock short and investing proceeds, whereas for a put, the writer will be purchasing stock on margin. Once again, we see the powerful result that the same basic conceptual structure is used for puts and calls, whether written or purchased. Only the exercise and expiration conditions vary.

The no-arbitrage results that have been presented can be expressed as the present value of a unique expectation of the option payoffs.[4] Specifically, the **expectations approach** results in an identical value as the no-arbitrage approach, but it is usually easier to compute. The formulas are viewed as follows:

$$c = PV[\pi c^+ + (1 - \pi)c^-] \text{ and} \tag{5}$$

$$p = PV[\pi p^+ + (1 - \pi)p^-] \tag{6}$$

where the probability of an up move is

$$\pi = [FV(1) - d]/(u - d)$$

Recall the future value is simply the reciprocal of the present value or $FV(1) = 1/PV(1)$. Thus, if $PV(1) = 1/(1 + r)$, then $FV(1) = (1 + r)$. Note that the option values are simply the present value of the expected terminal option payoffs. The expected terminal option payoffs can be expressed as

$$E(c_1) = \pi c^+ + (1 - \pi)c^- \text{ and}$$

$$E(p_1) = \pi p^+ + (1 - \pi)p^-$$

where c_1 and p_1 are the values of the options at Time 1. The present value and future value calculations are based on the risk-free rate, denoted r.[5] Thus, the option values based on the expectations approach can be written and remembered concisely as

$$c = PV_r[E(c_1)] \text{ and}$$

$$p = PV_r[E(p_1)]$$

The expectations approach to option valuation differs in two significant ways from the discounted cash flow approach to securities valuation. First, the expectation is not based on the investor's beliefs regarding the future course of the underlying. That is, the probability, π, is objectively determined and not based on the investor's personal view. This probability has taken several different names, including risk-neutral (RN) probability. Importantly, we did not make any assumption regarding the arbitrageur's risk preferences: The expectations approach is a result of this arbitrage process, not an assumption regarding risk preferences. Hence, they are called risk-neutral probabilities. Although we called them probabilities from the very start, they are not the true probabilities of up and down moves.

---

4 It takes a bit of algebra to move from the no-arbitrage expression to the present value of the expected future payoffs, but the important point is that both expressions yield exactly the same result.
5 We will suppress "r" most of the time and simply denote the calculation as PV. The "r" will be used at times to reinforce that the present value calculation is based on the risk-free interest rate.

Second, the discount rate is *not* risk adjusted. The discount rate is simply based on the estimated risk-free interest rate. The expectations approach here is often viewed as superior to the discounted cash flow approach because both the subjective future expectation as well as the subjective risk-adjusted discount rate have been replaced with more objective measures.

EXAMPLE 3

Single-Period Binomial Call Value

A non-dividend-paying stock is currently trading at €100. A call option has one year to mature, the periodically compounded risk-free interest rate is 5.15%, and the exercise price is €100. Assume a single-period binomial option valuation model, where u = 1.35 and d = 0.74.

1   The optimal hedge ratio will be *closest* to:

   A   0.57.

   B   0.60.

   C   0.65.

2   The call option value will be *closest* to:

   A   €13.

   B   €15.

   C   €17.

Solution to 1:

A is correct. Given the information provided, we know the following:

$$S^+ = uS = 1.35(100) = 135$$

$$S^- = dS = 0.74(100) = 74$$

$$c^+ = Max(0, uS - X) = Max(0, 135 - 100) = 35$$

$$c^- = Max(0, dS - X) = Max(0, 74 - 100) = 0$$

With this information, we can compute both the hedge ratio as well as the call option value. The hedge ratio is:

$$h = \frac{c^+ - c^-}{S^+ - S^-} = \frac{35 - 0}{135 - 74} = 0.573770$$

Solution to 2:

C is correct. The risk-neutral probability of an up move is

$$\pi = [FV(1) - d]/(u - d) = (1.0515 - 0.74)/(1.35 - 0.74) = 0.510656,$$

where FV(1) = (1 + r) = 1.0515.

Thus the call value by the expectations approach is

$$c = PV[\pi c^+ + (1 - \pi)c^-] = 0.951022[(0.510656)35 + (1 - 0.510656)0] = €16.998,$$

where PV(1) = 1/(1 + r) = 1/(1.0515) = 0.951022.

Note that the call value by the no-arbitrage approach yields the same answer:

$$c = hS + PV(-hS^- + c^-) = 0.573770(100) + 0.951022[-0.573770(74) + 0] = €16.998.$$

The value of a put option can also be found based on put–call parity. Put–call parity can be remembered as simply two versions of portfolio insurance, long stock and long put or lend and long call, where the exercise prices for the put and call are identical. Put–call parity with symbols is

$$S + p = PV(X) + c \tag{7}$$

Put–call parity holds regardless of the particular valuation model being used. Depending on the context, this equation can be rearranged. For example, a call option can be expressed as a position in a stock, financing, and a put, or

$$c = S - PV(X) + p$$

EXAMPLE 4

Single-Period Binomial Put Value

You again observe a €100 price for a non-dividend-paying stock with the same inputs as the previous box. That is, the call option has one year to mature, the periodically compounded risk-free interest rate is 5.15%, the exercise price is €100, u = 1.35, and d = 0.74. The put option value will be *closest* to:

A €12.00.

B €12.10.

C €12.20.

Solution:

B is correct. For puts, we know the following:

$$p^+ = Max(0,100 - uS) = Max(0,100 - 135) = 0$$

$$p^- = Max(0,100 - dS) = Max(0,100 - 74) = 26$$

With this information, we can compute the put option value based on risk-neutral probability from the previous example or [recall that PV(1) = 0.951022]

$$p = PV[\pi p^+ + (1 - \pi)p^-] = 0.951022[(0.510656)0 + (1 - 0.510656)26] = €12.10$$

Therefore, in summary, option values can be expressed either in terms of replicating portfolios or as the present value of the expected future cash flows. Both expressions yield the same valuations.

3.2 Two-Period Binomial Model

The two-period binomial lattice can be viewed as three one-period binomial lattices, as illustrated in Exhibit 4. Clearly, if we understand the one-period model, then the process can be repeated three times. First, we analyze Box 1 and Box 2. Finally, based on the results of Box 1 and Box 2, we analyze Box 3.

Exhibit 4   Two-Period Binomial Lattice as Three One-Period Binomial Lattices

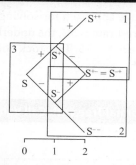

At Time 2, there are only three values of the underlying, S^{++} (an up move occurs twice), S^{--} (a down move occurs twice), and $S^{+-} = S^{-+}$ (either an up move occurs and then a down move or a down move occurs and then an up move). For computational reasons, it is extremely helpful that the lattice recombines—that is, $S^{+-} = S^{-+}$, meaning that if the underlying goes up and then down, it ends up at the same price as if it goes down and then up. A recombining binomial lattice will always have just one more ending node in the final period than the number of time steps. In contrast, a non-recombining lattice of n time steps will have 2^n ending nodes, which poses a tremendous computational challenge even for powerful computers.

For our purposes here, we assume the up and down factors are constant throughout the lattice, ensuring that the lattice recombines—that is $S^{+-} = S^{-+}$. For example, assume u = 1.25, d = 0.8, and S_0 = 100. Note that S^{+-} = 1.25(0.8)100 = 100 and S^{-+} = 0.8(1.25)100 = 100. So the middle node at Time 2 is 100 and can be reached from either of two paths.

The two-period binomial option valuation model illustrates two important concepts, self-financing and dynamic replication. Self-financing implies that the replicating portfolio will not require any additional funds from the arbitrageur during the life of this dynamically rebalanced portfolio. If additional funds are needed, then they are financed externally. Dynamic replication means that the payoffs from the option can be exactly replicated through a planned trading strategy. Option valuation relies on self-financing, dynamic replication.

Mathematically, the no-arbitrage approach for the two-period binomial model is best understood as working backward through the binomial tree. At Time 2, the payoffs are driven by the option's exercise value.
For calls:

$$c^{++} = Max(0, S^{++} - X) = Max(0, u^2 S - X),$$
$$c^{+-} = Max(0, S^{+-} - X) = Max(0, udS - X), \text{ and}$$
$$c^{--} = Max(0, S^{--} - X) = Max(0, d^2 S - X)$$

For puts:

$$p^{++} = Max(0, X - S^{++}) = Max(0, X - u^2 S),$$
$$p^{+-} = Max(0, X - S^{+-}) = Max(0, X - udS), \text{ and}$$
$$p^{--} = Max(0, X - S^{--}) = Max(0, X - d^2 S)$$

At Time 1, the option values are driven by the arbitrage transactions that synthetically replicate the payoffs at Time 2. We can compute the option values at Time 1 based on the option values at Time 2 using the no-arbitrage approach based on

Equations 1 and 2. At Time 0, the option values are driven by the arbitrage transactions that synthetically replicate the value of the options at Time 1 (again based on Equations 1 and 2).

We illustrate the no-arbitrage approach for solving the two-period binomial call value. Suppose the annual interest rate is 3%, the underlying stock is S = 72, u = 1.356, d = 0.541, and the exercise price is X = 75. The stock does not pay dividends. Exhibit 5 illustrates the results.

Exhibit 5   Two-Period Binomial Tree with Call Values and Hedge Ratios

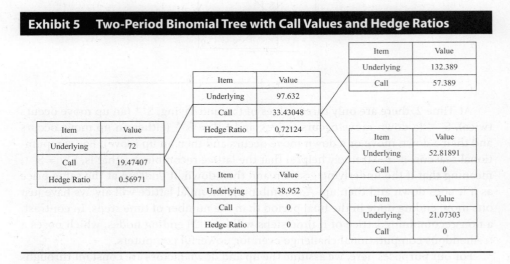

Item	Value
Underlying	72
Call	19.47407
Hedge Ratio	0.56971

Item	Value
Underlying	97.632
Call	33.43048
Hedge Ratio	0.72124

Item	Value
Underlying	38.952
Call	0
Hedge Ratio	0

Item	Value
Underlying	132.389
Call	57.389

Item	Value
Underlying	52.81891
Call	0

Item	Value
Underlying	21.07303
Call	0

We now verify selected values reported in Exhibit 5. At Time Step 2 and assuming up occurs twice, the underlying stock value is $u^2S = (1.356)^272 = 132.389$, and hence, the call value is 57.389 [= Max(0,132.389 – 75)]. The hedge ratio at Time Step 1, assuming up occurs once, is

$$h^+ = \frac{c^{++} - c^{+-}}{S^{++} - S^{+-}} = \frac{57.389 - 0}{132.389 - 52.819} = 0.72124$$

The RN probability of an up move throughout this tree is

$$\pi = [FV(1) - d]/(u - d) = (1.03 - 0.541)/(1.356 - 0.541) = 0.6$$

With this information, we can compute the call price at Time 1 when an up move occurs as

$$c = PV[\pi c^{++} + (1 - \pi)c^{+-}] = (1/1.03)[(0.6)57.389 + (1 - 0.6)0] = 33.43048$$

and at Time Step 0,

$$h = \frac{c^+ - c^-}{S^+ - S^-} = \frac{33.43048 - 0}{97.632 - 38.952} = 0.56971$$

Thus, the call price at the start is

$$c = PV[\pi c^+ + (1 - \pi)c^-] = (1/1.03)[(0.6)33.43048 + (1 - 0.6)0] = 19.47$$

From the no-arbitrage approach, the call payoffs can be replicated by purchasing h shares of the underlying and financing $-PV(-hS^- + c^-)$. Therefore, we purchase 0.56971 shares of stock for 41.019 [= 0.56971(72)] and borrow 21.545 {or in cash flow terms, $-21.545 = (1/1.03)[-0.56971(38.952) + 0]$}, replicating the call values at Time 1. We then illustrate Time 1 assuming that an up move occurs. The stock position will now be worth 55.622 [= 0.56971(97.632)], and the borrowing must be repaid with interest or 22.191 [= 1.03(21.545)]. Note that the portfolio is worth 33.431 (55.622 – 22.191), the same value as the call except for a small rounding error. Therefore, the portfolio of stock and the financing dynamically replicates the value of the call option.

The final task is to demonstrate that the portfolio is self-financing. Self-financing can be shown by observing that the new portfolio at Time 1, assuming an up move occurs, is equal to the old portfolio that was formed at Time 0 and liquidated at Time 1. Notice that the hedge ratio rose from 0.56971 to 0.72124 as we moved from Time 0 to Time 1, assuming an up move occurs, requiring the purchase of additional shares. These additional shares will be financed with additional borrowing. The total borrowing is 36.98554 $\{= -PV(-hS^{+-} + c^{+-}) = -(1/1.03)[-0.72124(52.81891) + 0]\}$. The borrowing at Time 0 that is due at Time 1 is 22.191. The funds borrowed at Time 1 grew to 36.98554. Therefore, the strategy is self-financing.

The two-period binomial model can also be represented as the present value of an expectation of future cash flows. Based on the one-period results, it follows by repeated substitutions that

$$c = PV[\pi^2 c^{++} + 2\pi(1 - \pi)c^{+-} + (1 - \pi)^2 c^{--}] \tag{8}$$

and

$$p = PV[\pi^2 p^{++} + 2\pi(1 - \pi)p^{+-} + (1 - \pi)^2 p^{--}] \tag{9}$$

Therefore, the two-period binomial model is again simply the present value of the expected future cash flows based on the RN probability. Again, the option values are simply the present value of the expected terminal option payoffs. The expected terminal option payoffs can be expressed as

$$E(c_2) = \pi^2 c^{++} + 2\pi(1 - \pi)c^{+-} + (1 - \pi)^2 c^{--}$$

and

$$E(p_2) = \pi^2 p^{++} + 2\pi(1 - \pi)p^{+-} + (1 - \pi)^2 p^{--}$$

Thus, the two-period binomial option values based on the expectations approach can be written and remembered concisely as

$$c = PV_r[E\pi(c_2)] \text{ and}$$

$$p = PV_r[E\pi(p_2)]$$

It is vital to remember that this present value is over two periods, so the discount factor with discrete rates is $PV = [1/(1 + r)^2]$. Recall the subscript "r" just emphasizes the present value calculation and is based on the risk-free interest rate.

EXAMPLE 5

Two-Period Binomial Model Call Valuation

You observe a €50 price for a non-dividend-paying stock. The call option has two years to mature, the periodically compounded risk-free interest rate is 5%, the exercise price is €50, u = 1.356, and d = 0.744. Assume the call option is European-style.

1 The probability of an up move based on the risk-neutral probability is *closest* to:

   A 30%.

   B 40%.

   C 50%.

2 The current call option value is *closest* to:

   A €9.53.

   B €9.71.

   C €9.87.

3 The current put option value is *closest* to:

   A €5.06.

   B €5.33.

   C €5.94.

Solution to 1:

C is correct. Based on the RN probability equation, we have:

$$\pi = [FV(1) - d]/(u - d) = [(1 + 0.05) - 0.744]/(1.356 - 0.744) = 0.5 \text{ or } 50\%$$

Solution to 2:

B is correct. The current call option value calculations are as follows:

$$c^{++} = Max(0, u^2 S - X) = Max[0, 1.356^2(50) - 50] = 41.9368$$

$$c^{-+} = c^{+-} = Max(0, udS - X) = Max[0, 1.356(0.744)(50) - 50] = 0.44320$$

$$c^{--} = Max(0, d^2 S - X) = Max[0, 0.744^2(50) - 50] = 0.0$$

With this information, we can compute the call option value:

$$c = PV[E(c_2)] = PV[\pi^2 c^{++} + 2\pi(1 - \pi)c^{+-} + (1 - \pi)^2 c^{--}]$$

$$= [1/(1 + 0.05)]^2[0.5^2 41.9368 + 2(0.5)(1 - 0.5)0.44320 + (1 - 0.5)^2 0.0]$$

$$= 9.71$$

It is vital to remember that the present value is over two periods, hence the single-period PV is squared. Thus, the current call price is €9.71.

Solution to 3:

A is correct. The put option value can be computed simply by applying put–call parity or $p = c + PV(X) - S = 9.71 + [1/(1 + 0.05)]^2 50 - 50 = 5.06$. Thus, the current put price is €5.06.

We now turn to consider American-style options. It is well-known that non-dividend-paying call options on stock will not be exercised early because the minimum price of the option exceeds its exercise value. To illustrate by example, consider a call on a US$100 stock, with an exercise price of US$10 (that is, very deep in the money). Suppose the call is worth its exercise value of only US$90. To get stock exposure, one could fund and pay US$100 to buy the stock, or fund and pay only US$90 for the call and pay the last US$10 at expiration only if the stock is at or above US$100 at that time. Because the latter choice is preferable, the call must be worth more than the US$90 exercise value. Another way of looking at it is that it would make no sense to exercise this call because you do not believe the stock can go any higher and you would thus simply be obtaining a stock that you believe would go no higher. Moreover, the stock would require that you pay far more money than you have tied up in the call. It is always better to just sell the call in this situation because it will be trading for more than the exercise value.

The same is not true for put options. By early exercise of a put, particularly a deep in-the-money put, the sale proceeds can be invested at the risk-free rate and earn interest worth more than the time value of the put. Thus, we will examine how early exercise influences the value of an American-style put option. As we will see, when early exercise has value, the no-arbitrage approach is the only way to value American-style options.

Suppose the periodically compounded interest rate is 3%, the non-dividend-paying underlying stock is currently trading at 72, the exercise price is 75, u = 1.356, d = 0.541, and the put option expires in two years. Exhibit 6 shows the results for a European-style put option.

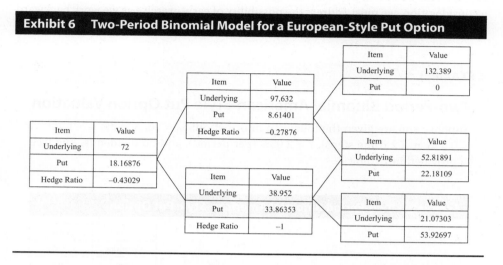

Exhibit 6   Two-Period Binomial Model for a European-Style Put Option

The Time 1 down move is of particular interest. The exercise value for this put option is 36.048 [= Max(0,75 − 38.952)]. Therefore, the exercise value is higher than the put value. So, if this same option were American-style, then the option would be worth more exercised than not exercised. Thus, the put option should be exercised. Exhibit 7 illustrates how the analysis changes if this put option were American-style. Clearly, the right to exercise early translates into a higher value.

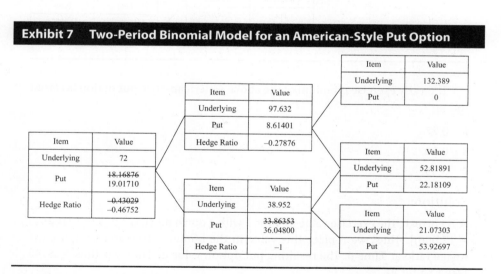

Exhibit 7   Two-Period Binomial Model for an American-Style Put Option

American-style option valuation requires that one work backward through the binomial tree and address whether early exercise is optimal at each step. In Exhibit 7, the early exercise premium at Time 1 when a down move occurs is 2.18447 (36.048 − 33.86353). Also, if we replace 33.86353 with 36.048—in bold below for emphasis—in the Time 0 calculation, we obtain a put value of

$$p = PV[\pi p^+ + (1 - \pi)p^-] = (1/1.03)[(0.6)8.61401 + (1 - 0.6)\textbf{36.048}] = 19.02$$

Thus, the early exercise premium at Time 0 is 0.85 (19.02 − 18.17). From this illustration, we see clearly that in a multiperiod setting, American-style put options cannot be valued simply as the present value of the expected future option payouts, as shown in Equation 9. American-style put options can be valued as the present value of the expected future option payout in a single-period setting. Hence, when early exercise is a consideration, we must address the possibility of early exercise as we work backward through the binomial tree.

EXAMPLE 6

Two-Period Binomial American-Style Put Option Valuation

Suppose you are given the following information: $S_0 = 26$, $X = 25$, $u = 1.466$, $d = 0.656$, $n = 2$ (time steps), $r = 2.05\%$ (per period), and no dividends. The tree is provided in Exhibit 8.

Exhibit 8   Two-Period Binomial American-Style Put Option

Item	Value
Underlying	55.87806
Put	0

Item	Value
Underlying	38.116
Put	0
Hedge Ratio	0

Item	Value
Underlying	25.00410
Put	0

Item	Value
Underlying	26
Put	4.01174
Hedge Ratio	−0.35345

Item	Value
Underlying	17.056
Put	7.44360
Hedge Ratio	−0.99970

Item	Value
Underlying	11.18874
Put	13.81126

The early exercise premium of the above American-style put option is *closest* to:

A   0.27.

B   0.30.

C   0.35.

Solution:

A is correct. The exercise value at Time 1 with a down move is 7.944 [= Max(0,25 − 17.056)]. Thus, we replace this value in the binomial tree and compute the hedge ratio at Time 0. The resulting put option value at Time 0 is thus 4.28143 (see Exhibit 9).

Exhibit 9   Solution

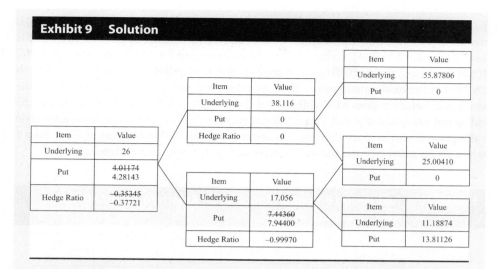

Item	Value
Underlying	26
Put	4.01174 ~~4.01174~~ 4.28143
Hedge Ratio	~~−0.35345~~ −0.37721

Item	Value
Underlying	38.116
Put	0
Hedge Ratio	0

Item	Value
Underlying	17.056
Put	~~7.44360~~ 7.94400
Hedge Ratio	−0.99970

Item	Value
Underlying	55.87806
Put	0

Item	Value
Underlying	25.00410
Put	0

Item	Value
Underlying	11.18874
Put	13.81126

In Exhibit 9, the early exercise premium at Time 1 when a down move occurs is 0.5004 (7.944 − 7.44360). Thus, if we replace 7.44360 with 7.944—in bold below for emphasis—in the Time 0 calculation, we have the put value of

$$p = PV[\pi p^+ + (1 - \pi)p^-] = (1/1.0205)[(0.45)0 + (1 - 0.45)\mathbf{7.944}] = 4.28$$

Thus, the early exercise premium at Time 0 when a down move occurs 0.27 (= 4.28 − 4.01).

We now briefly introduce the role of dividend payments within the binomial model. Our approach here is known as the escrow method. Because dividends lower the value of the stock, a call option holder is hurt. Although it is possible to adjust the option terms to offset this effect, most option contracts do not provide protection against dividends. Thus, dividends affect the value of an option. We assume dividends are perfectly predictable; hence, we split the underlying instrument into two components: the underlying instrument without the known dividends and the known dividends. For example, the current value of the underlying instrument without dividends can be expressed as

$$\hat{S} = S - \gamma$$

where γ denotes the present value of dividend payments. We use the ^ symbol to denote the underlying instrument without dividends. In this case, we model the uncertainty of the stock based on $\hat{S}$ and not S. At expiration, the underlying instrument value is the same, $\hat{S}_T = S_T$, because we assume any dividends have already been paid. The value of an investment in the stock, however, would be $S_T + \gamma_T$, which assumes the dividend payments are reinvested at the risk-free rate.

To illustrate by example, consider a call on a US$100 stock with exercise price of US$95. The periodically compounded interest rate is 1.0%, the stock will pay a US$3 dividend at Time Step 1, u = 1.224, d = 0.796, and the call option expires in two years. Exhibit 10 shows some results for an American-style call option. The computations in Exhibit 10 involve several technical nuances that are beyond the scope of our objectives. The key objective here is to see how dividend-motivated early exercise influences American options.

The Time 1 up move is particularly interesting. At Time 0, the present value of the US$3 dividend payment is US$2.970297 (= 3/1.01). Therefore, 118.7644 = (100 − 2.970297)1.224 is the stock value without dividends at Time 1, assuming an up move occurs. The exercise value for this call option, including dividends, is 26.7644

[= Max(0,118.7644 + 3 – 95)], whereas the value of the call option per the binomial model is 24.9344. In other words, the stock price just before it goes ex-dividend is 118.7644 + 3 = 121.7644, so the option can be exercised for 121.7644 – 95 = 26.7644. If not exercised, the stock drops as it goes ex-dividend and the option becomes worth 24.9344 at the ex-dividend price. Thus, by exercising early, the call buyer acquires the stock just before it goes ex-dividend and thus is able to capture the dividend. If the call is not exercised, the call buyer will not receive this dividend. The American-style call option is worth more than the European-style call option because at Time Step 1 when an up move occurs, the call is exercised early, capturing additional value.

Exhibit 10   Two-Period Binomial Model for an American-Style Call Option with Dividends

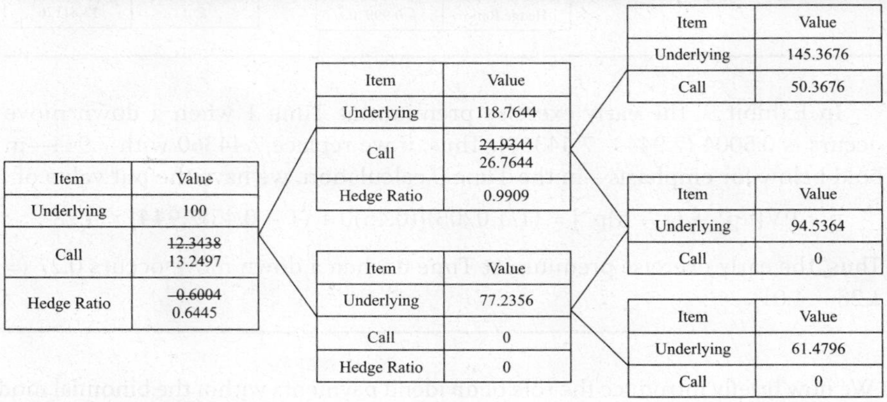

We now provide a comprehensive binomial option valuation example. In this example, we contrast European-style exercise with American-style exercise.

EXAMPLE 7

Comprehensive Two-Period Binomial Option Valuation Model Exercise

Suppose you observe a non-dividend-paying Australian equity trading for A$7.35. The call and put options have two years to mature, the periodically compounded risk-free interest rate is 4.35%, and the exercise price is A$8.0. Based on an analysis of this equity, the estimates for the up and down moves are u = 1.445 and d = 0.715, respectively.

1   Calculate the European-style call and put option values at Time Step 0 and Time Step 1. Describe and interpret your results.

2   Calculate the European-style call and put option hedge ratios at Time Step 0 and Time Step 1. Based on these hedge ratios, interpret the component terms of the binomial option valuation model.

3   Calculate the American-style call and put option values and hedge ratios at Time Step 0 and Time Step 1. Explain how your results differ from the European-style results.

Solution to 1:

The expectations approach requires the following preliminary calculations:

$$\text{RN probability: } \pi = [FV(1) - d]/(u - d)$$
$$= [(1 + 0.0435) - 0.715]/(1.445 - 0.715) = 0.45$$
$$c^{++} = Max(0, u^2 S - X)$$
$$= Max[0, 1.445^2(7.35) - 8.0] = 7.347$$
$$c^{+-} = Max(0, udS - X)$$
$$= Max[0, 1.445(0.715)7.35 - 8.0] = 0$$
$$c^{--} = Max(0, d^2 S - X)$$
$$= Max[0, 0.715^2(7.35) - 8.0] = 0$$
$$p^{++} = Max(0, X - u^2 S)$$
$$= Max[0, 8.0 - 1.445^2(7.35)] = 0$$
$$p^{+-} = Max(0, X - udS)$$
$$= Max[0, 8.0 - 1.445(0.715)7.35] = 0.406$$
$$p^{--} = Max(0, X - d^2 S)$$
$$= Max[0, 8.0 - 0.715^2(7.35)] = 4.24$$

Therefore, at Time Step 1, we have (note that $c_2\big|_1^+$ is read as the call value expiring at Time Step 2 observed at Time Step 1, assuming an up move occurs)

$$E\left(c_2\big|_1^+\right) = \pi c^{++} + (1 - \pi)c^{+-} = 0.45(7.347) + (1 - 0.45)0 = 3.31$$

$$E\left(c_2\big|_1^-\right) = \pi c^{-+} + (1 - \pi)c^{--} = 0.45(0.0) + (1 - 0.45)0.0 = 0.0$$

$$E\left(p_2\big|_1^+\right) = \pi p^{++} + (1 - \pi)p^{+-} = 0.45(0.0) + (1 - 0.45)0.406 = 0.2233$$

$$E\left(p_2\big|_1^-\right) = \pi p^{-+} + (1 - \pi)p^{--} = 0.45(0.406) + (1 - 0.45)4.24 = 2.51$$

Thus, because $PV_{1,2}(1) = 1/(1 + 0.0435) = 0.958313$, we have the Time Step 1 option values of

$$c^+ = PV_{1,2}\left[E\left(c_2\big|_1^+\right)\right] = 0.958313(3.31) = 3.17$$

$$c^- = PV_{1,2}\left[E\left(c_2\big|_1^-\right)\right] = 0.958313(0.0) = 0.0$$

$$p^+ = PV_{1,2}\left[E\left(p_2\big|_1^+\right)\right] = 0.958313(0.2233) = 0.214$$

$$p^- = PV_{1,2}\left[E\left(p_2\big|_1^-\right)\right] = 0.958313(2.51) = 2.41$$

At Time Step 0, we have

$$E\left(c_2\big|_0\right) = \pi^2 c^{++} + 2\pi(1 - \pi)c^{+-} + (1 - \pi)^2 c^{--}$$
$$= 0.45^2(7.347) + 2(0.45)(1 - 0.45)0 + (1 - 0.45)^2 0 = 1.488$$

$$E\left(p_2\big|_0\right) = \pi^2 p^{++} + 2\pi(1 - \pi)p^{+-} + (1 - \pi)^2 p^{--}$$
$$= 0.45^2(0) + 2(0.45)(1 - 0.45)0.406 + (1 - 0.45)^2 4.24 = 1.484$$

Thus,

$$c = PV_{rf,0,2}\left[E\left(c_2\big|0\right)\right] = 0.91836(1.488) = 1.37 \text{ and}$$

$$p = PV_{rf,0,2}\left[E\left(p_2\big|0\right)\right] = 0.91836(1.484) = 1.36$$

With the two-period binomial model, the call and put values based on the expectations approach are simply the present values of the expected payoffs. The present value of the expected payoffs is based on the risk-free interest rate and the expectations approach is based on the risk-neutral probability. The parameters in this example were selected so that the European-style put and call would have approximately the same value. Notice that the stock price is less than the exercise price by roughly the present value factor or $7.35 = 8.0/1.0435^2$. One intuitive explanation is put–call parity, which can be expressed as $c - p = S - PV(X)$. Thus, if $S = PV(X)$, then $c = p$.

Solution to 2:

The computation of the hedge ratios at Time Step 1 and Time Step 0 will require the option values at Time Step 1 and Time Step 2. The terminal values of the options are given in Solution 1.

$$
\begin{aligned}
S^{++} &= u^2S = 1.445^2(7.35) = 15.347 \\
S^{+-} &= udS = 1.445(0.715)7.35 = 7.594 \\
S^{--} &= d^2S = 0.715^2(7.35) = 3.758 \\
S^{+} &= uS = 1.445(7.35) = 10.621 \\
S^{-} &= dS = 0.715(7.35) = 5.255
\end{aligned}
$$

Therefore, the hedge ratios at Time 1 are

$$h_c^+ = \frac{c^{++} - c^{+-}}{S^{++} - S^{+-}} = \frac{7.347 - 0.0}{15.347 - 7.594} = 0.9476$$

$$h_c^- = \frac{c^{-+} - c^{--}}{S^{-+} - S^{--}} = \frac{0.0 - 0.0}{7.594 - 3.758} = 0.0$$

$$h_p^+ = \frac{p^{++} - p^{+-}}{S^{++} - S^{+-}} = \frac{0.0 - 0.406}{15.347 - 7.594} = -0.05237$$

$$h_p^- = \frac{p^{-+} - p^{--}}{S^{-+} - S^{--}} = \frac{0.406 - 4.24}{7.594 - 3.758} = -1.0$$

In the last hedge ratio calculation, both put options are in the money (p^{-+} and p^{--}). In this case, the hedge ratio will be -1, subject to a rounding error. We now turn to interpreting the model's component terms. Based on the no-arbitrage approach, we have for the call price, assuming an up move has occurred, at Time Step 1,

$$c^+ = h_c^+S^+ + PV_{1,2}\left(-h_c^+S^{+-} + c^{+-}\right)$$

$$= 0.9476(10.621) + (1/1.0435)[-0.9476(7.594) + 0.0] = 3.1684$$

Thus, the call option can be interpreted as a leveraged position in the stock. Specifically, long 0.9476 shares for a cost of 10.0645 [= 0.9476(10.621)] partially financed with a 6.8961 {= (1/1.0435)[−0.9476(7.594) + 0.0]} loan. Note that the loan amount can be found simply as the cost of the position in shares less the option value [6.8961 = 0.9476(10.621) − 3.1684]. Similarly, we have

$$c^- = h_c^- S^- + PV_{1,2}\left(-h_c^- S^{--} + c^{--}\right)$$

$$= 0.0(5.255) + (1/1.0435)[-0.0(3.758) + 0.0] = 0.0$$

Specifically, long 0.0 shares for a cost of 0.0 [= 0.0(5.255)] with no financing. For put options, the interpretation is different. Specifically, we have

$$p^+ = PV_{1,2}\left(-h_p^+ S^{++} + p^{++}\right) + h_p^+ S^+$$

$$= (1/1.0435)[-(-0.05237)15.347 + 0.0] + (-0.05237)10.621 = 0.2140$$

Thus, the put option can be interpreted as lending that is partially financed with a short position in shares. Specifically, short 0.05237 shares for a cost of 0.55622 [= (−0.05237)10.621] with financing of 0.77022 {= (1/1.0435)[−(−0.05237)15.347 + 0.0]}. Note that the lending amount can be found simply as the proceeds from the short sale of shares plus the option value [0.77022 = (0.05237)10.621 + 0.2140]. Again, we have

$$p^- = PV_{1,2}\left(-h_p^- S^{-+} + p^{-+}\right) + h_p^- S^-$$

$$= (1/1.0435)[-(-1.0)7.594 + 0.406] + (-1.0)5.255 = 2.4115$$

Here, we short 1.0 shares for a cost of 5.255 [= (−1.0)5.255] with financing of 7.6665 {= (1/1.0435)[−(−1.0)7.594 + 0.406]}. Again, the lending amount can be found simply as the proceeds from the short sale of shares plus the option value [7.6665 = (1.0)5.255 + 2.4115].

Finally, we have at Time Step 0

$$h_c = \frac{c^+ - c^-}{S^+ - S^-} = \frac{3.1684 - 0}{10.621 - 5.255} = 0.5905$$

$$h_p = \frac{p^+ - p^-}{S^+ - S^-} = \frac{0.2140 - 2.4115}{10.621 - 5.255} = -0.4095$$

The interpretations remain the same at Time Step 0:

$$c = h_c S + PV_{0,1}(-h_c S^- + c^-)$$
$$= 0.5905(7.35) + (1/1.0435)[-0.5905(5.255) + 0.0] = 1.37$$

Here, we are long 0.5905 shares for a cost of 4.3402 [=0.5905(7.35)] partially financed with a 2.97 {= (1/1.0435)[−0.5905(5.255) + 0.0] or = 0.5905(7.35) − 1.37} loan.

$$p = PV_{0,1}(-h_p S^+ + p^+) + h_p S$$
$$= (1/1.0435)\{-[0.4095(10.621)] + 0.214\} + (-0.4095)7.35 = 1.36$$

Here, we short 0.4095 shares for a cost of 3.01 [= (−0.4095)7.35] with financing of 4.37 (= (1/1.0435){−[0.4095(10.621)] + 0.214} or = (0.4095)7.35 + 1.36).

Solution to 3:

We know that American-style call options on non-dividend-paying stock are worth the same as European-style call options because early exercise will not occur. Thus, as previously computed, $c^+ = 3.17$, $c^- = 0.0$, and $c = 1.37$. Recall that the call exercise value (denoted with EV) is simply the maximum of zero or the stock price minus the exercise price. We note that the EVs are less than or equal to the call model values; that is,

$$c_{EV}^+ = \text{Max}(0, S^+ - X) = \text{Max}(0, 10.621 - 8.0) = 2.621 \; (< 3.1684)$$

$$c_{EV}^- = \text{Max}(0, S^- - X) = \text{Max}(0, 5.255 - 8.0) = 0.0 \; (= 0.0)$$

$$c_{EV} = \text{Max}(0, S - X) = \text{Max}(0, 7.35 - 8.0) = 0.0 \; (< 1.37)$$

Therefore, the American-style feature for non-dividend-paying stocks has no effect on either the hedge ratio or the option value. The binomial model for American-style calls on non-dividend-paying stocks can be described and interpreted the same as a similar European-style call. This point is consistent with what we said earlier. If there are no dividends, a European-style call will not be exercised early.

This result is not true for puts. We know that American-style put options on non-dividend-paying stock may be worth more than the analogous European-style put options. The hedge ratios at Time Step 1 will be the same as European-style puts because there is only one period left. Therefore, as previously shown, p^+ = 0.214 and p^- = 2.41.

The put exercise values are

$$p_{EV}^+ = \text{Max}(0, X - S^+) = \text{Max}(0, 8.0 - 10.621) = 0 \; (< 0.214)$$

$$p_{EV}^- = \text{Max}(0, X - S^-) = \text{Max}(0, 8.0 - 5.255) = 2.745 \; (> 2.41)$$

Because the exercise value for the put at Time Step 1, assuming a down move occurred, is greater than the model value, we replace the model value with the exercise value. Hence,

$$p^- = 2.745$$

and the hedge ratio at Time Step 0 will be affected. Specifically, we now have

$$h_p = \frac{p^+ - p^-}{S^+ - S^-} = \frac{0.2140 - 2.745}{10.621 - 5.255} = -0.4717$$

and thus the put model value is

$$p = (1/1.0435)[0.45(0.214) + 0.55(2.745)] = 1.54$$

Clearly, the early exercise feature has a significant impact on both the hedge ratio and the put option value in this case. The hedge ratio goes from −0.4095 to −0.4717. The put value is raised from 1.36 to 1.54.

We see through the simple two-period binomial model that an option can be viewed as a position in the underlying with financing. Furthermore, this valuation model can be expressed as the present value of the expected future cash flows, where the expectation is taken under the RN probability and the discounting is at the risk-free rate.

Up to this point, we have focused on equity options. The binomial model can be applied to any underlying instrument though often requiring some modifications. For example, currency options would require incorporating the foreign interest rate. Futures options would require a binomial lattice of the futures prices. Interest rate options, however, require somewhat different tools that we now examine.

3.3 Interest Rate Options

In this section, we will briefly illustrate how to value interest rate options. There are a wide variety of approaches to valuing interest rate options. We do not delve into how arbitrage-free interest rate trees are generated. The particular approach used here assumes the RN probability of an up move at each node is 50%.

Exhibit 11 presents a binomial lattice of interest rates covering two years along with the corresponding zero-coupon bond values. The rates are expressed in annual compounding. Therefore, at Time 0, the spot rate is (1.0/0.970446) − 1 or 3.04540%.[6] Note that at Time 1, the value in the column labeled "Maturity" reflects time to maturity not calendar time. The lattice shows the rates on one-period bonds, so all bonds have a maturity of 1. The column labeled "Value" is the value of a zero-coupon bond with the stated maturity based on the rates provided.

Exhibit 11   Two-Year Binomial Interest Rate Lattice by Year

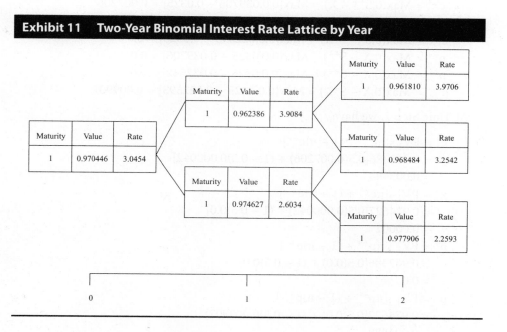

The underlying instrument for interest rate options here is the spot rate. A call option on interest rates will be in the money when the current spot rate is above the exercise rate. A put option on interest rates will be in the money when the current spot rate is below the exercise rate. Thus, based on the notation in the previous section, the current spot rate is denoted S. Option valuation follows the expectations approach discussed in the previous section but taken only one period at a time. The procedure is illustrated with an example.

---

6 The values in the first box from the left are observed at t = 0. The values in the remainder of the lattice are derived by using a technique that is outside the scope of this reading.

EXAMPLE 8

Option on Interest Rates

This example is based on Exhibit 11. Suppose we seek to value two-year European-style call and put options on the periodically compounded one-year spot interest rate (the underlying). Assume the notional amount of the options is US$1,000,000 and the call and put exercise rate is 3.25% of par. Assume the RN probability is 50%.

Solution:

Using the expectations approach introduced in the last section, we have (per US$1) at Time Step 2

$$c^{++} = Max(0, S^{++} - X) = Max[0, 0.039706 - 0.0325] = 0.007206$$
$$c^{+-} = Max(0, S^{+-} - X) = Max[0, 0.032542 - 0.0325] = 0.000042$$
$$c^{--} = Max(0, S^{--} - X) = Max[0, 0.022593 - 0.0325] = 0.0$$
$$p^{++} = Max(0, X - S^{++}) = Max[0, 0.0325 - 0.039706] = 0.0$$
$$p^{+-} = Max(0, X - S^{+-}) = Max[0, 0.0325 - 0.032542] = 0.0$$
$$p^{--} = Max(0, X - S^{--}) = Max[0, 0.0325 - 0.022593] = 0.009907$$

At Time Step 1, we have

$$c^{+} = PV_{1,2}[\pi c^{++} + (1 - \pi)c^{+-}]$$
$$= 0.962386[0.5(0.007206) + (1 - 0.5)0.000042]$$
$$= 0.003488$$
$$c^{-} = PV_{1,2}[\pi c^{+-} + (1 - \pi)c^{--}]$$
$$= 0.974627[0.5(0.000042) + (1 - 0.5)0.0]$$
$$= 0.00002$$
$$p^{+} = PV_{1,2}[\pi p^{++} + (1 - \pi)p^{+-}]$$
$$= 0.962386[0.5(0.0) + (1 - 0.5)0.0]$$
$$= 0.0$$
$$p^{-} = PV_{1,2}[\pi p^{+-} + (1 - \pi)p^{--}]$$
$$= 0.974627[0.5(0.0) + (1 - 0.5)0.009907]$$
$$= 0.004828$$

Notice how the present value factors are different for the up and down moves. At Time Step 1 in the + outcome, we discount by a factor of 0.962386, and in the − outcome, we discount by the factor 0.974627. Because this is an option on interest rates, it should not be surprising that we have to allow the interest rate to vary.

Therefore, at Time Step 0, we have

$$c = PV_{rf,0,1}[\pi c^{+} + (1 - \pi)c^{-}]$$
$$= 0.970446[0.5(0.003488) + (1 - 0.5)0.00002]$$
$$= 0.00170216$$
$$p = PV_{rf,0,1}[\pi p^{+} + (1 - \pi)p^{-}]$$
$$= 0.970446[0.5(0.0) + (1 - 0.5)0.004828]$$
$$= 0.00234266$$

Because the notional amount is US$1,000,000, the call value is US$1,702.16 [= US$1,000,000(0.00170216)] and the put value is US$2,342.66 [= US$1,000,000(0.00234266)]. The key insight is to just work a two-period binomial model as three one-period binomial models.

We turn now to briefly generalize the binomial model as it leads naturally to the Black–Scholes–Merton option valuation model.

3.4 Multiperiod Model

The multiperiod binomial model provides a natural bridge to the Black–Scholes–Merton option valuation model presented in the next section. The idea is to take the option's expiration and slice it up into smaller and smaller periods. The two-period model divides the expiration into two periods. The three-period model divides expiration into three periods and so forth. The process continues until you have a large number of time steps. The key feature is that each time step is of equal length. Thus, with a maturity of T, if there are n time steps, then each time step is T/n in length.

For American-style options, we must also test at each node whether the option is worth more exercised or not exercised. As in the two-period case, we work backward through the binomial tree testing the model value against the exercise value and always choosing the higher one.

The binomial model is an important and useful methodology for valuing options. The expectations approach can be applied to European-style options and will lead naturally to the BSM model in the next section. This approach simply values the option as the present value of the expected future payoffs, where the expectation is taken under the risk-neutral probability and the discounting is based on the risk-free rate. The no-arbitrage approach can be applied to either European-style or American-style options because it provides the intuition for the fair value of options.

BLACK–SCHOLES–MERTON OPTION VALUATION MODEL

4

The BSM model, although very complex in its derivation, is rather simple to use and interpret. The objective here is to illustrate several facets of the BSM model with the objective of highlighting its practical usefulness. After a brief introduction, we examine the assumptions of the BSM model and then delve into the model itself.

4.1 Introductory material

Louis Bachelier published the first known mathematically rigorous option valuation model in 1900. By the late 1960s, there were several published quantitative option models. Fischer Black, Myron Scholes, and Robert Merton introduced the BSM model in 1973 in two published papers, one by Black and Scholes and the other by Merton. The innovation of the BSM model is essentially the no-arbitrage approach introduced in the previous section but applied with a continuous time process, which is equivalent to a binomial model in which the length of the time step essentially approaches zero. It is also consistent with the basic statistical fact that the binomial process with a "large" number of steps converges to the standard normal distribution. Myron Scholes and Robert Merton won the 1997 Nobel Prize in Economics based, in part, on their work related to the BSM model.[7] Let us now examine the BSM model assumptions.

---

7 Fischer Black passed away in 1995 and the Nobel Prize is not awarded posthumously.

4.2 Assumptions of the BSM model

The key assumption for option valuation models is how to model the random nature of the underlying instrument. This characteristic of how an asset evolves randomly is called a stochastic process. Many financial instruments enjoy limited liability; hence, the values of instruments cannot be negative, but they certainly can be zero. In 1900, Bachelier proposed the normal distribution. The key advantages of the normal distribution are that zero is possible, meaning that bankruptcy is allowable, it is symmetric, it is relatively easy to manipulate, and it is additive (which means that sums of normal distributions are normally distributed). The key disadvantage is that negative stock values are theoretically possible, which violates the limited liability principal of stock ownership. Based on research on stock prices in the 1950s and 1960s, a preference emerged for the lognormal distribution, which means that log returns are distributed normally. Black, Scholes, and Merton chose to use the lognormal distribution.

Recall that the no-arbitrage approach requires self-financing and dynamic replication; we need more than just an assumption regarding the terminal distribution of the underlying instrument. We need to model the value of the instrument as it evolves over time, which is what we mean by a stochastic process. The stochastic process chosen by Black, Scholes, and Merton is called geometric Brownian motion (GBM).

Exhibit 12 illustrates GBM, assuming the initial stock price is S = 50. We assume the stock will grow at 3% (μ = 3% annually, geometrically compounded rate). This GBM process also reflects a random component that is determined by a volatility (σ) of 45%. This volatility is the annualized standard deviation of continuously compounded percentage change in the underlying, or in other words, the log return. Note that as a particular sample path drifts upward, we observe more variability on an absolute basis, whereas when the particular sample path drifts downward, we observe less variability on an absolute basis. For example, examine the highest and lowest lines shown in Exhibit 12. The highest line is much more erratic than the lowest line. Recall that a 10% move in a stock with a price of 100 is 10 whereas a 10% move in a stock with a price of 10 is only 1. Thus, GBM can never hit zero nor go below it. This property is appealing because many financial instruments enjoy limited liability and cannot be negative. Finally, note that although the stock movements are rather erratic, there are no large jumps—a common feature with marketable financial instruments.

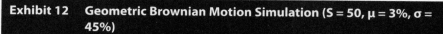

Exhibit 12   Geometric Brownian Motion Simulation (S = 50, μ = 3%, σ = 45%)

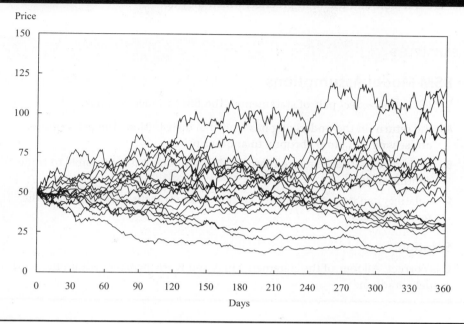

Within the BSM model framework, it is assumed that all investors agree on the distributional characteristics of GBM except the assumed growth rate of the underlying. This growth rate depends on a number of factors, including other instruments and time. The standard BSM model assumes a constant growth rate and constant volatility. The specific assumptions of the BSM model are as follows:

- The underlying follows a statistical process called geometric Brownian motion, which implies a lognormal distribution of the return, meaning that the logarithmic return, which is the continuously compounded return, is normally distributed.

- Geometric Brownian motion implies continuous prices, meaning that the price of underlying instrument does not jump from one value to another; rather, it moves smoothly from value to value.

- The underlying instrument is liquid, meaning that it can be easily bought and sold.

- Continuous trading is available, meaning that in the strictest sense one must be able to trade at every instant.

- Short selling of the underlying instrument with full use of the proceeds is permitted.

- There are no market frictions, such as transaction costs, regulatory constraints, or taxes.

- No-arbitrage opportunities are available in the marketplace.

- The options are European-style, meaning that early exercise is not allowed.

- The continuously compounded risk-free interest rate is known and constant; borrowing and lending is allowed at the risk-free rate.

- The volatility of the return on the underlying is known and constant.

- If the underlying instrument pays a yield, it is expressed as a continuous known and constant yield at an annualized rate.

Naturally, the foregoing assumptions are not absolutely consistent with real financial markets, but, as in all financial models, the question is whether they produce models that are tractable and useful in practice, which they do.

EXAMPLE 9

BSM Model Assumptions

Which is the *correct* pair of statements? The BSM model assumes:

A the return on the underlying has a normal distribution. The price of the underlying can jump abruptly to another price.

B brokerage costs are factored into the BSM model. It is impossible to trade continuously.

C volatility can be predicted with certainty. Arbitrage is non-existent in the marketplace.

Solution:

C is correct. All four of the statements in A and B are incorrect within the BSM model paradigm.

We turn now to a careful examination of the BSM model.

4.3 BSM model

The BSM model is a continuous time version of the discrete time binomial model. Given that the BSM model is based on continuous time, it is customary to use a continuously compounded interest rate rather than some discretely compounded alternative. Thus, when an interest rate is used here, denoted simply as r, we mean solely the annualized continuously compounded rate.[8] The volatility, denoted as σ, is also expressed in annualized percentage terms. Initially, we focus on a non-dividend-paying stock. The BSM model, with some adjustments, applies to other underlying instruments, which will be examined later.

The BSM model for stocks can be expressed as

$$c = SN(d_1) - e^{-rT}XN(d_2) \qquad (10)$$

and

$$p = e^{-rT}XN(-d_2) - SN(-d_1) \qquad (11)$$

where

$$d_1 = \frac{\ln(S/X) + \left(r + \sigma^2/2\right)T}{\sigma\sqrt{T}}$$

$$d_2 = d_1 - \sigma\sqrt{T}$$

N(x) denotes the standard normal cumulative distribution function, which is the probability of obtaining a value of less than x based on a standard normal distribution. In our context, x will have the value of d_1 or d_2. N(x) reflects the likelihood of observing values less than x from a random sample of observations taken from the standard normal distribution.

---

8 Note $e^r = 1 + r_d$, where r_d is the annually compounded rate.

Although the BSM model appears very complicated, it has straightforward interpretations that will be explained. N(x) can be estimated by a computer program or a spreadsheet or approximated from a lookup table. The normal distribution is a symmetric distribution with two parameters, the mean and standard deviation. The standard normal distribution is a normal distribution with a mean of 0 and a standard deviation of 1.

Exhibit 13 illustrates the standard normal probability density function (the standard bell curve) and the cumulative distribution function (the accumulated probability and range of 0 to 1). Note that even though GBM is lognormally distributed, the N(x) functions in the BSM model are based on the standard normal distribution. In Exhibit 13, we see that if x = −1.645, then N(x) = N(−1.645) = 0.05. Thus, if the model value of d is −1.645, the corresponding probability is 5%. Clearly, values of d that are less than 0 imply values of N(x) that are less than 0.5. As a result of the symmetry of the normal distribution, we note that N(−x) = 1 − N(x).

Exhibit 13   Standard Normal Distribution

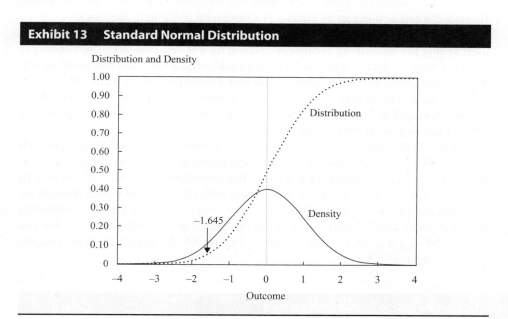

The BSM model can be described as the present value of the expected option payoff at expiration. Specifically, we can express the BSM model for calls as $c = PV_r[E(c_T)]$ and for puts as $p = PV_r[E(p_T)]$, where $E(c_T) = Se^{rT}N(d_1) - XN(d_2)$ and $E(p_T) = XN(-d_2) - Se^{rT}N(-d_1)$. The present value term in this context is simply e^{-rT}. As with most valuation tasks in finance, the value today is simply the present value of the expected future cash flows. It is important to note that the expectation is based on the risk-neutral probability measure defined in Section 3.1. The expectation is not based on the investor's subjective beliefs, which reflect an aversion to risk. Also, the present value function is based on the risk-free interest rate not on the investor's required return on invested capital, which of course is a function of risk.

Alternatively, the BSM model can be described as having two components: a stock component and a bond component. For call options, the stock component is $SN(d_1)$ and the bond component is $e^{-rT}XN(d_2)$. The BSM model call value is the stock component minus the bond component. For put options, the stock component is $SN(-d_1)$ and the bond component is $e^{-rT}XN(-d_2)$. The BSM model put value is the bond component minus the stock component.

The BSM model can be interpreted as a dynamically managed portfolio of the stock and zero-coupon bonds.[9] The goal is to replicate the option payoffs with stocks and bonds. For both call and put options, we can represent the initial cost of this replicating strategy as

Replicating strategy cost = $n_S S + n_B B$

where the equivalent number of underlying shares is $n_S = N(d_1) > 0$ for calls and $n_S = -N(-d_1) < 0$ for puts. The equivalent number of bonds is $n_B = -N(d_2) < 0$ for calls and $n_B = N(-d_2) > 0$ for puts. The price of the zero-coupon bond is $B = e^{-rT}X$. Note, if n is positive, we are buying the underlying and if n is negative we are selling (short selling) the underlying. The cost of the portfolio will exactly equal either the BSM model call value or the BSM model put value.

For calls, we are simply buying stock with borrowed money because $n_S > 0$ and $n_B < 0$. Again the cost of this portfolio will equal the BSM model call value, and if appropriately rebalanced, then this portfolio will replicate the payoff of the call option. Therefore, a call option can be viewed as a leveraged position in the stock.

Similarly, for put options, we are simply buying bonds with the proceeds from short selling the underlying because $n_S < 0$ and $n_B > 0$. The cost of this portfolio will equal the BSM model put value, and if appropriately rebalanced, then this portfolio will replicate the payoff of the put option. Note that a short position in a put will result in receiving money today and $n_S > 0$ and $n_B < 0$. Therefore, a short put can be viewed as an over-leveraged or over-geared position in the stock because the borrowing exceeds 100% of the cost of the underlying.

Exhibit 14 illustrates the direct comparison between the no-arbitrage approach to the single-period binomial option valuation model and the BSM option valuation model. The parallel between the h term in the binomial model and $N(d_1)$ is easy to see. Recall that the term hedge ratio was used with the binomial model because we were creating a no-arbitrage portfolio. Note for call options, $-N(d_2)$ implies borrowing money or short selling $N(d_2)$ shares of a zero-coupon bond trading at $e^{-rT}X$. For put options, $N(-d_2)$ implies lending money or buying $N(-d_2)$ shares of a zero-coupon bond trading at $e^{-rT}X$.

Exhibit 14   BSM and Binomial Option Valuation Model Comparison

	Call Option		Put Option	
Option Valuation Model Terms	**Underlying**	**Financing**	**Underlying**	**Financing**
Binomial Model	hS	$PV(-hS^- + c^-)$	hS	$PV(-hS^- + p^-)$
BSM Model	$N(d_1)S$	$-N(d_2)e^{-rT}X$	$-N(-d_1)S$	$N(-d_2)e^{-rT}X$

If the value of the underlying, S, increases, then the value of $N(d_1)$ also increases because S has a positive effect on d_1. Thus, the replicating strategy for calls requires continually buying shares in a rising market and selling shares in a falling market.

Within the BSM model theory, the aggregate losses from this "buy high/sell low" strategy, over the life of the option, adds up exactly to the BSM model option premium received for the option at inception.[10] This result must be the case; otherwise there would be arbitrage profits available. Because transaction costs are not, in fact, zero,

---

9 When covering the binomial model, the bond component was generically termed financing. This component is typically handled with bank borrowing or lending. With the BSM model, it is easier to understand as either buying or short selling a risk-free zero-coupon bond.

10 The validity of this claim does not rest on the validity of the BSM model assumptions; rather the validity depends only on whether the BSM model accurately predicts the replication cost.

the frequent rebalancing by buying and selling the underlying adds significant costs for the hedger. Also, markets can often move discontinuously, contrary to the BSM model's assumption that prices move continuously, thus allowing for continuous hedging adjustments. Hence, in reality, hedges are imperfect. For example, if a company announces a merger, then the company's stock price may jump substantially higher, contrary to the BSM model's assumption.

In addition, volatility cannot be known in advance. For these reasons, options are typically more expensive than they would be as predicted by the BSM model theory. In order to continue using the BSM model, the volatility parameter used in the formula is usually higher (by, say, 1% or 2%, but this can vary a lot) than the volatility of the stock actually expected by market participants. We will ignore this point for now, however, as we focus on the mechanics of the model.

EXAMPLE 10

Illustration of BSM Model Component Interpretation

Suppose we are given the following information on call and put options on a stock: $S = 100$, $X = 100$, $r = 5\%$, $T = 1.0$, and $\sigma = 30\%$. Thus, based on the BSM model, it can be demonstrated that $PV(X) = 95.123$, $d_1 = 0.317$, $d_2 = 0.017$, $N(d_1) = 0.624$, $N(d_2) = 0.507$, $N(-d_1) = 0.376$, $N(-d_2) = 0.493$, $c = 14.23$, and $p = 9.35$.

1 The initial trading strategy required by the no-arbitrage approach to replicate the call option payoffs for a buyer of the option is:

   A buy 0.317 shares of stock and short sell −0.017 shares of zero-coupon bonds.

   B buy 0.624 shares of stock and short sell 0.507 shares of zero-coupon bonds.

   C short sell 0.317 shares of stock and buy 0.017 shares of zero-coupon bonds.

2 Identify the initial trading strategy required by the no-arbitrage approach to replicate the put option payoffs for a buyer of the put.

   A Buy 0.317 shares of stock and short sell −0.017 shares of zero-coupon bonds.

   B Buy 0.624 shares of stock and short sell 0.507 shares of zero-coupon bonds.

   C Short sell 0.376 shares of stock and buy 0.493 shares of zero-coupon bonds.

Solution to 1:

B is correct. The no-arbitrage approach to replicating the call option involves purchasing $n_S = N(d_1) = 0.624$ shares of stock partially financed with $n_B = -N(d_2) = -0.507$ shares of zero-coupon bonds priced at $B = Xe^{-rT} = 95.123$ per bond. Note that by definition the cost of this replicating strategy is the BSM call model value or $n_S S + n_B B = 0.624(100) + (-0.507)95.123 = 14.17$. Without rounding errors, the option value is 14.23.

Solution to 2:

C is correct. The no-arbitrage approach to replicating the put option is similar. In this case, we trade $n_S = -N(-d_1) = -0.376$ shares of stock—specifically, short sell 0.376 shares—and buy $n_B = N(-d_2) = 0.493$ shares of zero-coupon bonds. Again, the cost of the replicating strategy is $n_S S + n_B B = -0.376(100) + (0.493)95.123 =$

9.30. Without rounding errors, the option value is 9.35. Thus, to replicate a call option based on the BSM model, we buy stock on margin. To replicate a put option, we short sell stock and lend part of the proceeds.

Note that the $N(d_2)$ term has an additional important interpretation. It is a unique measure of the probability that the call option expires in the money, and correspondingly, $1 - N(d_2) = N(-d_2)$ is the probability that the put option expires in the money. Specifically, the probability based on the RN probability of being in the money, not one's own estimate of the probability of being in the money nor the market's estimate. That is, $N(d_2) = \text{Prob}(S_T > X)$ based on the unique RN probability.

We now turn to incorporating various carry benefits into the BSM model. Carry benefits include dividends for stock options, foreign interest rates for currency options, and coupon payments for bond options. For other underlying instruments, there are carry costs that can easily be treated as negative carry benefits, such as storage and insurance costs for agricultural products. Because the BSM model is established in continuous time, it is common to model these carry benefits as a continuous yield, denoted generically here as γ^c or simply γ.

The BSM model requires a few adjustments to accommodate carry benefits. The carry benefit-adjusted BSM model is

$$c = Se^{-\gamma T}N(d_1) - e^{-rT}XN(d_2) \qquad (12)$$

and

$$p = e^{-rT}XN(-d_2) - Se^{-\gamma T}N(-d_1) \qquad (13)$$

where

$$d_1 = \frac{\ln(S/X) + \left(r - \gamma + \sigma^2/2\right)T}{\sigma\sqrt{T}}$$

Note that d_2 can be expressed again simply as $d_2 = d_1 - \sigma\sqrt{T}$. The value of a put option can also be found based on the carry benefit-adjusted put–call parity:

$$p + Se^{-\gamma T} = c + e^{-rT}X \qquad (14)$$

The carry benefit-adjusted BSM model can again be described as the present value of the expected option payoff at expiration. Now, however, $E(c_T) = Se^{(r-\gamma)T}N(d_1) - XN(d_2)$ and $E(p_T) = XN(-d_2) - Se^{(r-\gamma)T}N(-d_1)$. The present value term remains simply e^{-rT}. Carry benefits will have the effect of lowering the expected future value of the underlying

Again, the carry benefit adjusted BSM model can be described as having two components, a stock component and a bond component. For call options, the stock component is $Se^{-\gamma T}N(d_1)$ and the bond component is again $e^{-rT}XN(d_2)$. For put options, the stock component is $Se^{-\gamma T}N(-d_1)$ and the bond component is again $e^{-rT}XN(-d_2)$. Although both d_1 and d_2 are reduced by carry benefits, the general approach to valuation remains the same. An increase in carry benefits will lower the value of the call option and raise the value of the put option.

Note that $N(d_2)$ term continues to be interpreted as the RN probability of a call option being in the money. The existence of carry benefits has the effect of lowering d_1 and d_2, hence the probability of being in the money with call options declines as the carry benefit rises. This RN probability is an important element to describing how the BSM model is used in various valuation tasks.

For stock options, $\gamma = \delta$, which is the continuously compounded dividend yield. The dividend-yield BSM model can again be interpreted as a dynamically managed portfolio of the stock and zero coupon bonds. Based on the call model above applied to a dividend yielding stock, the equivalent number of units of stock is now $n_S = e^{-\delta T}N(d_1)$

> 0 and the equivalent number of units of bonds remains $n_B = -N(d_2) < 0$. Similarly with puts, the equivalent number of units of stock is now $n_S = -e^{-\delta T}N(-d_1) < 0$ and the equivalent number of units of bonds again remains $n_B = N(-d_2) > 0$.

With dividend paying stocks, the arbitrageur is able to receive the benefits of dividend payments when long the stock and has to pay dividends when short the stock. Thus, the burden of carrying the stock is diminished for a long position. The key insight is that dividends influence the dynamically managed portfolio by lowering the number of shares to buy for calls and lowering the number of shares to short sell for puts. Higher dividends will lower the value of d_1, thus lowering $N(d_1)$. Also, higher dividends will lower the number of bonds to short sell for calls and lower the number of bonds to buy for puts.

EXAMPLE 11

BSM Model Applied to Equities

Suppose we are given the following information on an underlying stock and options: $S = 60$, $X = 60$, $r = 2\%$, $T = 0.5$, $\delta = 2\%$, and $\sigma = 45\%$. Assume we are examining European-style options.

1 Which answer *best* describes how the BSM model is used to value a call option with the parameters given?

   A The BSM model call value is the exercise price times $N(d_1)$ less the present value of the stock price times $N(d_2)$.

   B The BSM model call value is the stock price times $e^{-\delta T}N(d_1)$ less the exercise price times $e^{-rT}N(d_2)$.

   C The BSM model call value is the stock price times $e^{-\delta T}N(-d_1)$ less the present value of the exercise price times $e^{-rT}N(-d_2)$.

2 Which answer *best* describes how the BSM model is used to value a put option with the parameters given?

   A The BSM model put value is the exercise price times $N(d_1)$ less the present value of the stock price times $N(d_2)$.

   B The BSM model put value is the exercise price times $e^{-\delta T}N(-d_2)$ less the stock price times $e^{-rT}N(-d_2)$.

   C The BSM model put value is the exercise price times $e^{-rT}N(-d_2)$ less the stock price times $e^{-\delta T}N(-d_1)$.

3 Suppose now that the stock does not pay a dividend—that is, $\delta = 0\%$. Identify the correct statement.

   A The BSM model option value is the same as the previous problems because options are not dividend adjusted.

   B The BSM model option values will be different because there is an adjustment term applied to the exercise price, that is $e^{-\delta T}$, which will influence the option values.

   C The BSM model option value will be different because d_1, d_2, and the stock component are all adjusted for dividends.

Solution to 1:

B is correct. The BSM call model for a dividend-paying stock can be expressed as $Se^{-\delta T}N(d_1) - Xe^{-rT}N(d_2)$.

Solution to 2:

C is correct. The BSM put model for a dividend-paying stock can be expressed as $Xe^{-rT}N(-d_2) - Se^{-\delta T}N(-d_1)$.

Solution to 3:

C is correct. The BSM model option value will be different because d_1, d_2, and the stock component are all adjusted for dividends.

EXAMPLE 12

How the BSM Model Is Used to Value Stock Options

Suppose that we have some Bank of China shares that are currently trading on the Hong Kong Stock Exchange at HKD4.41. Our view is that the Bank of China's stock price will be steady for the next three months, so we decide to sell some three-month out-of-the-money calls with exercise price at 4.60 in order to enhance our returns by receiving the option premium. Risk-free government securities are paying 1.60% and the stock is yielding HKD 0.24%. The stock volatility is 28%. We use the BSM model to value the calls.

Which statement is correct? The BSM model inputs (underlying, exercise, expiration, risk-free rate, dividend yield, and volatility) are:

A   4.60, 4.41, 3, 0.0160, 0.0024, and 0.28.

B   4.41, 4.60, 0.25, 0.0160, 0.0024, and 0.28.

C   4.41, 4.41, 0.3, 0.0160, 0.0024, and 0.28.

Solution:

B is correct. The spot price of the underlying is HKD4.41. The exercise price is HKD4.60. The expiration is 0.25 years (three months). The risk-free rate is 0.016. The dividend yield is 0.0024. The volatility is 0.28.

For foreign exchange options, $\gamma = r^f$, which is the continuously compounded foreign risk-free interest rate. When quoting an exchange rate, we will give the value of the domestic currency per unit of the foreign currency. For example, Japanese yen (¥) per unit of the euro (€) will be expressed as the euro trading for ¥135 or succinctly 135¥/€. This is called the foreign exchange spot rate. Thus, the foreign currency, the euro, is expressed in terms of the Japanese yen, which is in this case the domestic currency. This is logical, for example, when a Japanese firm would want to express its foreign euro holdings in terms of its domestic currency, Japanese yen.

With currency options, the underlying instrument is the foreign exchange spot rate. Again, the carry benefit is the interest rate in the foreign country because the foreign currency could be invested in the foreign country's risk-free instrument. Also, with currency options, the underlying and the exercise price must be quoted in the same currency unit. Lastly, the volatility in the model is the volatility of the log return of the spot exchange rate. Each currency option is for a certain quantity of foreign currency, termed the notional amount, a concept analogous to the number of shares of stock covered in an option contract. The total cost of the option would be obtained by multiplying the formula value by the notional amount in the same way that one would multiply the formula value of an option on a stock by the number of shares the option contract covers.

The BSM model applied to currencies can be described as having two components, a foreign exchange component and a bond component. For call options, the foreign exchange component is $Se^{-r^f T}N(d_1)$ and the bond component is $e^{-rT}XN(d_2)$, where r is the domestic risk-free rate. The BSM call model applied to currencies is simply the foreign exchange component minus the bond component. For put options, the foreign exchange component is $Se^{-r^f T}N(-d_1)$ and the bond component is $e^{-rT}XN(-d_2)$. The BSM put model applied to currencies is simply the bond component minus the foreign exchange component. Remember that the underlying is expressed in terms of the domestic currency.

EXAMPLE 13

BSM Model Applied to Value Options on Currency

A Japanese camera exporter to Europe has contracted to receive fixed euro (€) amounts each quarter for his goods. The spot price of the currency pair is 135¥/€. If the exchange rate falls to, say, 130¥/€, then the yen will have strengthened because it will take fewer yen to buy one euro. The exporter is concerned that the yen will strengthen because in this case, his forthcoming fixed euro will buy fewer yen. Hence, the exporter is considering buying an at-the-money spot euro put option to protect against this fall; this in essence is a call on yen. The Japanese risk-free rate is 0.25% and the European risk-free rate is 1.00%.

1. What are the underlying and exercise prices to use in the BSM model to get the euro put option value?

   A 1/135; 1/135

   B 135; 135

   C 135; 130

2. What are the risk-free rate and the carry rate to use in the BSM model to get the euro put option value?

   A 0.25%; 1.00%

   B 0.25%; 0.00%

   C 1.00%; 0.25%

Solution to 1:

B is correct. The underlying is the spot FX price of 135 ¥/€. Because the put is at-the-money spot, the exercise price equals the spot price.

Solution to 2:

A is correct. The risk-free rate to use is the Japanese rate because Japan is the domestic economy. The carry rate is the foreign currency's risk-free rate, which is the European rate.

We turn now to examine a modification of the BSM model when the underlying is a forward or futures contract.

5 BLACK OPTION VALUATION MODEL

In 1976, Fischer Black introduced a modified version of the BSM model approach that is applicable to options on underlying instruments that are costless to carry, such as options on futures contracts—for example, equity index futures—and options on forward contracts. The latter include interest rate-based options, such as caps, floors, and swaptions.

5.1 European Options on Futures

We assume that the futures price also follows geometric Brownian motion. We ignore issues like margin requirements and marking to market. Black proposed the following model for European-style futures options:

$$c = e^{-rT}[F_0(T)N(d_1) - XN(d_2)] \tag{15}$$

and

$$p = e^{-rT}[XN(-d_2) - F_0(T)N(-d_1)] \tag{16}$$

where

$$d_1 = \frac{\ln[F_0(T)/X] + (\sigma^2/2)T}{\sigma\sqrt{T}} \text{ and}$$

$$d_2 = d_1 - \sigma\sqrt{T}$$

Note that $F_0(T)$ denotes the futures price at Time 0 that expires at Time T, and σ denotes the volatility related to the futures price. The other terms are as previously defined. Black's model is simply the BSM model in which the futures contract is assumed to reflect the carry arbitrage model. Futures option put–call parity can be expressed as

$$c = e^{-rT}[F_0(T) - X] + p \tag{17}$$

As we have seen before, put–call parity is a useful tool for describing the valuation relationship between call and put values within various option valuation models.

The Black model can be described in a similar way to the BSM model. The Black model has two components, a futures component and a bond component. For call options, the futures component is $F_0(T)e^{-rT}N(d_1)$ and the bond component is again $e^{-rT}XN(d_2)$. The Black call model is simply the futures component minus the bond component. For put options, the futures component is $F_0(T)e^{-rT}N(-d_1)$ and the bond component is again $e^{-rT}XN(-d_2)$. The Black put model is simply the bond component minus the futures component.

Alternatively, futures option valuation, based on the Black model, is simply computing the present value of the difference between the futures price and the exercise price. The futures price and exercise price are appropriately adjusted by the N(d) functions. For call options, the futures price is adjusted by $N(d_1)$ and the exercise price is adjusted by $-N(d_2)$ to arrive at difference. For put options, the futures price is adjusted by $-N(-d_1)$ and the exercise price is adjusted by $+N(-d_2)$.

EXAMPLE 14

European Options on Futures Index

The S&P 500 Index (a spot index) is presently at 1,860 and the 0.25 expiration futures contract is trading at 1,851.65. Suppose further that the exercise price is 1,860, the continuously compounded risk-free rate is 0.2%, time to expiration is 0.25, volatility is 15%, and the dividend yield is 2.0%. Based on this information, the following results are obtained for options on the futures contract.[11]

Options on Futures	
Calls	**Puts**
$N(d_1) = 0.491$	$N(-d_1) = 0.509$
$N(d_2) = 0.461$	$N(-d_2) = 0.539$
$c = US\$51.41$	$p = US\$59.76$

1   Identify the statement that *best* describes how the Black model is used to value a European call option on the futures contract just described.

   A   The call value is the present value of the difference between the exercise price times 0.461 and the current futures price times 0.539.

   B   The call value is the present value of the difference between the current futures price times 0.491 and the exercise price times 0.461.

   C   The call value is the present value of the difference between the current spot price times 0.491 and the exercise price times 0.461.

2   Which statement *best* describes how the Black model is used to value a European put options on the futures contract just described?

   A   The put value is the present value of the difference between the exercise price times 0.539 and the current futures price times 0.509.

   B   The put value is the present value of the difference between the current futures price times 0.491 and the exercise price times 0.461.

   C   The put value is the present value of the difference between the current spot price times 0.491 and the exercise price times 0.461.

3   What are the underlying and exercise prices to use in the Black futures option model?

   A   1,851.65; 1,860

   B   1,860; 1,860

   C   1,860; 1,851.65

Solution to 1:

B is correct. Recall Black's model for call options can be expressed as $c = e^{-rT}[F_0(T)N(d_1) - XN(d_2)]$.

Solution to 2:

A is correct. Recall Black's model for put options can be expressed as $p = e^{-rT}[XN(-d_2) - F_0(T)N(-d_1)]$.

---

11 We ignore the effect of the multiplier. As of this writing, the S&P 500 futures option contract has a multiplier of 250. The prices reported here have not been scaled up by this amount. In practice, the option cost would by 250 times the option value.

> **Solution to 3:**
>
> A is correct. The underlying is the futures price of 1,851.65 and the exercise price was given as 1,860.

5.2 Interest Rate Options

With interest rate options, the underlying instrument is a reference interest rate, such as three-month Libor. An interest rate call option gains when the reference interest rate rises and an interest rate put option gains when the reference interest rate falls. Interest rate options are the building blocks of many other instruments.

For an interest rate call option on three-month Libor with one year to expiration, the underlying interest rate is a forward rate agreement (FRA) rate that expires in one year. This FRA is observed today and is the underlying rate used in the Black model. The underlying rate of the FRA is a 3-month Libor deposit that is investable in 12 months and matures in 15 months. Thus, in one year, the FRA rate typically converges to the three-month spot Libor.

Interest rates are typically set in advance, but interest payments are made in arrears, which is referred to as advanced set, settled in arrears. For example, with a bank deposit, the interest rate is usually set when the deposit is made, say t_{j-1}, but the interest payment is made when the deposit is withdrawn, say t_j. The deposit, therefore, has $t_m = t_j - t_{j-1}$ time until maturity. Thus, the rate is advanced set, but the payment is settled in arrears. Likewise with a floating rate loan, the rate is usually set and the interest accrues at this known rate, but the payment is made later. Similarly, with some interest rate options, the time to option expiration (t_{j-1}) when the interest rate is set does not correspond to the option settlement (t_j) when the cash payment is made, if any. For example, if an interest rate option payment based on three-month Libor is US$5,000 determined on January 15th, the actual payment of the US$5,000 would occur on April 15.

Interest rates are quoted on an annual basis, but the underlying implied deposit is often less than a year. Thus, the annual rates must be adjusted for the accrual period. Recall that the accrual period for a quarterly reset 30/360 day count FRA is 0.25 (= 90/360). If the day count is on an actual (ACT) number of days divided by 360 (ACT/360), then the accrual period may be something like 0.252778 (= 91/360), assuming 91 days in the period. Typically, the accrual period in FRAs is based on 30/360 whereas the accrual period based on the option is actual number of days in the contract divided by the actual number of days in the year (identified as ACT/ACT or ACT/365).

The model presented here is known as the standard market model and is a variation of Black's futures option valuation model. Again, let t_{j-1} denote the time to option expiration (ACT/365), whereas let t_j denote the time to the maturity date of the underlying FRA. Note that the interest accrual on the underlying begins at the option expiration (Time t_{j-1}). Let $FRA(0,t_{j-1},t_m)$ denote the fixed rate on a FRA at Time 0 that expires at Time t_{j-1}, where the underlying matures at Time t_j (= $t_{j-1} + t_m$), with all times expressed on an annual basis. We assume the FRA is 30/360 day count. For example, $FRA(0,0.25,0.5) = 2\%$ denotes the 2% fixed rate on a forward rate agreement that expires in 0.25 years with settlement amount being paid in 0.75 (= 0.25 + 0.5) years.[12] Let R_X denote the exercise rate expressed on an annual basis. Finally, let σ denote the interest rate volatility. Specifically, σ is the annualized standard deviation of the continuously compounded percentage change in the underlying FRA rate.

---

12 Note that in other contexts the time periods are expressed in months. For example with months, this FRA would be expressed as FRA(0,3,6). Note that the third term in parentheses denotes the maturity of the underlying deposit from the expiration of the FRA.

Interest rate options give option buyers the right to certain cash payments based on observed interest rates. For example, an interest rate call option gives the call buyer the right to a certain cash payment when the underlying interest rate exceeds the exercise rate. An interest rate put option gives the put buyer the right to a certain cash payment when the underlying interest rate is below the exercise rate.

With the standard market model, the prices of interest rate call and put options can be expressed as

$$c = (AP)e^{-r(t_{j-1}+t_m)}\left[FRA(0,t_{j-1},t_m)N(d_1) - R_X N(d_2)\right] \tag{18}$$

and

$$p = (AP)e^{-r(t_{j-1}+t_m)}\left[R_X N(-d_2) - FRA(0,t_{j-1},t_m)N(-d_1)\right] \tag{19}$$

where

AP denotes the accrual period in years

$$d_1 = \frac{\ln\left[FRA(0,t_{j-1},t_m)/R_X\right] + \left(\sigma^2/2\right)t_{j-1}}{\sigma\sqrt{t_{j-1}}}$$

$$d_2 = d_1 - \sigma\sqrt{t_{j-1}}$$

The formulas here give the value of the option for a notional amount of 1. In practice, the notional would be more than one, so the full cost of the option is obtained by multiplying these formula amounts by the notional amount. Of course, this point is just the same as finding the value of an option on a single share of stock and then multiplying that value by the number of shares covered by the option contract.

Immediately, we note that the standard market model requires an adjustment when compared with the Black model for the accrual period. In other words, a value such as $FRA(0,t_{j-1},t_m)$ or the strike rate, R_X, as appearing in the formula given earlier, is stated on an annual basis, as are interest rates in general. The actual option premium would have to be adjusted for the accrual period. After accounting for this adjustment, this model looks very similar to the Black model, but there are important but subtle differences. First, the discount factor, $e^{-r(t_{j-1}+t_m)}$, does not apply to the option expiration, t_{j-1}. Rather, the discount factor is applied to the maturity date of the FRA or $t_j (= t_{j-1} + t_m)$. We express this maturity as $(t_{j-1} + t_m)$ rather than t_j to emphasize the settlement in arrears nature of this option. Second, rather than the underlying being a futures price, the underlying is an interest rate, specifically a forward rate based on a forward rate agreement or $FRA(0,t_{j-1},t_m)$. Third, the exercise price is really a rate and reflects an interest rate, not a price. Fourth, the time to the option expiration, t_{j-1}, is used in the calculation of d_1 and d_2. Finally, both the forward rate and the exercise rate should be expressed in decimal form and not as percent (for example, 0.02 and not 2.0). Alternatively, if expressed as a percent, then the notional amount adjustment could be divided by 100.

As with other option models, the standard market model can be described as simply the present value of the expected option payoff at expiration. Specifically, we can express the standard market model for calls as $c = PV[E(c_{tj})]$ and for puts as $p = PV[E(p_{tj})]$, where $E(c_{tj}) = (AP)[FRA(0,t_{j-1},t_m)N(d_1) - R_X N(d_2)]$ and $E(p_{tj}) = (AP)[R_X N(-d_2) - FRA(0,t_{j-1},t_m)N(-d_1)]$. The present value term in this context is simply $e^{-rt_j} = e^{-r(t_{j-1}+t_m)}$. Again, note we discount from Time t_j, the time when the cash flows are settled on the FRA.

There are several interesting and useful combinations that can be created with interest rate options. We focus on a few that will prove useful for understanding swaptions in the next section. First, if the exercise rate is selected so as to equal the current FRA rate, then long an interest rate call option and short an interest rate put option is equivalent to a receive-floating, pay-fixed FRA.

Second, if the exercise rate is again selected so it is equal to the current FRA rate, then long an interest rate put option and short an interest rate call option is equivalent to a receive-fixed, pay-floating FRA. Note that FRAs are the building blocks of interest rate swaps.

Third, an interest rate cap is a portfolio or strip of interest rate call options in which the expiration of the first underlying corresponds to the expiration of the second option and so forth. The underlying interest rate call options are termed caplets. Thus, a set of floating-rate loan payments can be hedged with a long position in an interest rate cap encompassing a series of interest rate call options.

Fourth, an interest rate floor is a portfolio or strip of interest rate put options in which the expiration of the first underlying corresponds with the expiration of the second option and so forth. The underlying interest rate put options are termed floorlets. Thus, a floating-rate bond investment or any other floating-rate lending situation can be hedged with an interest rate floor encompassing a series of interest rate put options.

Fifth, similar to the put–call parity discussed earlier, long an interest rate cap and short an interest rate floor with the same exercise rate is equal to a receive-floating, pay-fixed interest rate swap. When the cap is in the money, the receive-floating counterparty will also receive an identical net payment. When the floor is in the money, the receive-floating counterparty will also pay an identical net payment.

Sixth, long an interest rate floor and short an interest rate cap with the same exercise rate is equal to a receive-fixed, pay-floating interest rate swap. When the floor is in the money, the receive-fixed counterparty will also receive an identical net payment. When the cap is in the money, the receive-floating counterparty will also pay an identical net payment.

Finally, if the exercise rate is set equal to the swap rate, then the value of the cap must be equal to the value of the floor. When an interest rate swap is initiated, its current value is zero and is known as an at-market swap. When an exercise rate is selected such that the cap equals the floor, then the initial cost of being long a cap and short the floor is also zero.

EXAMPLE 15

European Interest Rate Options

Suppose you are a speculative investor in Singapore. On 15 May, you anticipate that some regulatory changes will be enacted, and you want to profit from this forecast. On 15 June, you intend to borrow 10,000,000 Singapore dollars to fund the purchase of an asset, which you expect to resell at a profit three months after purchase, say on 15 September. The current three-month Sibor (that is, Singapore Libor) is 0.55%. The appropriate FRA rate over the period of 15 June to 15 September is currently 0.68%. You are concerned that rates will rise, so you want to hedge your borrowing risk by purchasing an interest rate call option with an exercise rate of 0.60%.

1   In using the Black model to value this interest rate call option, what would the underlying rate be?

A   0.55%

B   0.68%

C   0.60%

2 The discount factor used in pricing this option would be over what period of time?

    A 15 May–15 June

    B 15 June–15 September

    C 15 May–15 September

Solution to 1:

B is correct. In using the Black model, a forward or futures price is used as the underlying. This approach is unlike the BSM model in which a spot price is used as the underlying.

Solution to 2:

C is correct. You are pricing the option on 15 May. An option expiring 15 June when the underlying is three-month Sibor will have its payoff determined on 15 June, but the payment will be made on 15 September. Thus, the expected payment must be discounted back from 15 September to 15 May.

Interest rate option values are linked in an important way with interest rate swap values through caps and floors. As we will see in the next section, an interest rate swap serves as the underlying for swaptions. Thus, once again, we see that important links exist between interest rate options, swaps, and swaptions.

5.3 Swaptions

A swap option or swaption is simply an option on a swap. It gives the holder the right, but not the obligation, to enter a swap at the pre-agreed swap rate—the exercise rate. Interest rate swaps can be either receive fixed, pay floating or receive floating, pay fixed. A payer swaption is an option on a swap to pay fixed, receive floating. A receiver swaption is an option on a swap to receive fixed, pay floating. Note that the terms "call" and "put" are often avoided because of potential confusion over the nature of the underlying. Notice also that the terminology focuses on the fixed swap rate.

A payer swaption buyer hopes the fixed rate goes up before the swaption expires. When exercised, the payer swaption buyer is able to enter into a pay-fixed, receive-floating swap at the predetermined exercise rate, R_X. The buyer can then immediately enter an offsetting at-market receive-fixed, pay-floating swap at the current fixed swap rate. The floating legs of both swaps will offset, leaving the payer swaption buyer with an annuity of the difference between the current fixed swap rate and the swaption exercise rate. Thus, swaption valuation will reflect an annuity.

Swap payments are advanced set, settled in arrears. Let the swap reset dates be expressed as t_0, t_1, t_2, ..., t_n. Let R_{FIX} denote the fixed swap rate starting when the swaption expires, denoted as before with T, quoted on an annual basis, and R_X denote the exercise rate starting at Time T, again quoted on an annual basis. As before, we will assume a notional amount of 1.

Because swap rates are quoted on an annual basis, let AP denote the accrual period. Finally, we need some measure of uncertainty. Let σ denote the volatility of the forward swap rate. More precisely, σ denotes annualized, standard deviation of the continuously compounded percentage changes in the forward swap rate.

The swaption model presented here is a modification of the Black model. Let the present value of an annuity matching the forward swap payment be expressed as

$$PVA = \sum_{j=1}^{n} PV_{0,t_j} \quad (1)$$

This term is equivalent to what is sometimes referred to as an annuity discount factor. It applies here because a swaption creates a series of equal payments of the difference in the market swap rate at expiration and the chosen exercise rate. Therefore, the payer swaption valuation model is

$$PAY_{SWN} = (AP)PVA[R_{FIX}N(d_1) - R_X N(d_2)] \tag{20}$$

and the receiver swaption valuation model

$$REC_{SWN} = (AP)PVA[R_X N(-d_2) - R_{FIX}N(-d_1)] \tag{21}$$

where

$$d_1 = \frac{\ln(R_{FIX}/R_X) + (\sigma^2/2)T}{\sigma\sqrt{T}}, \text{ and as always,}$$

$$d_2 = d_1 - \sigma\sqrt{T}$$

As noted with interest rate options, the actual premium would need to be scaled by the notional amount. Once again, we can see the similarities to the Black model. We note that the swaption model requires two adjustments, one for the accrual period and one for the present value of an annuity. After accounting for these adjustments, this model looks very similar to the Black model but there are important subtle differences. First, the discount factor is absent. The payoff is not a single payment but a series of payments. Thus, the present value of an annuity used here embeds the option-related discount factor. Second, rather than the underlying being a futures price, the underlying is the fixed rate on a forward interest rate swap. Third, the exercise price is really expressed as an interest rate. Finally, both the forward swap rate and the exercise rate should be expressed in decimal form and not as percent (for example, 0.02 and not 2.0).

As with other option models, the swaption model can be described as simply the present value of the expected option payoff at expiration. Specifically, we can express the payer swaption model value as

$$PAY_{SWN} = PV[E(PAY_{SWN,T})]$$

and the receiver swaption model value as

$$REC_{SWN} = PV[E(REC_{SWN,T})],$$

where

$$E(PAY_{SWN,T}) = e^{rT}PAY_{SWN} \text{ and}$$
$$E(REC_{SWN,T}) = e^{rT}REC_{SWN}.$$

The present value term in this context is simply e^{-rT}. Because the annuity term embedded the discounting over the swaption life, the expected swaption values are the current swaption values grossed up by the current risk-free interest rate.

Alternatively, the swaption model can be described as having two components, a swap component and a bond component. For payer swaptions, the swap component is $(AP)PVA(R_{FIX})N(d_1)$ and the bond component is $(AP)PVA(R_X)N(d_2)$. The payer swaption model value is simply the swap component minus the bond component. For receiver swaptions, the swap component is $(AP)PVA(R_{FIX})N(-d_1)$ and the bond component is $(AP)PVA(R_X)N(-d_2)$. The receiver swaption model value is simply the bond component minus the swap component.

As with nearly all derivative instruments, there are many useful equivalence relationships. Recall that long an interest rate cap and short an interest rate floor with the same exercise rate is equal to a receive-floating, pay-fixed interest rate swap. Also, short an interest rate cap and long an interest rate floor with the same exercise rate is equal to a pay-floating, receive-fixed interest rate swap. There are also equivalence relationships with swaptions. In a similar way, long a receiver swaption and short a payer swaption with the same exercise rate is equivalent to entering a receive-fixed, pay-floating forward swap. Long a payer swaption and short a receiver swaption with the same exercise rate is equivalent to entering a receive-floating, pay-fixed forward swap. Note that if the exercise rate is selected such that the receiver and payer swaptions have the same value, then the exercise rate is equal to the at-market forward swap rate. Thus, there is again a put–call parity relationship important for valuation.

In addition, being long a callable fixed-rate bond can be viewed as being long a straight fixed-rate bond and short a receiver swaption. A receiver swaption gives the buyer the right to receive a fixed rate. Hence, the seller will have to pay the fixed rate when this right is exercised in a lower rate environment. Recall that the bond issuer has the right to call the bonds. If the bond issuer sells a receiver swaption with similar terms, then the bond issuer has essentially converted the callable bond into a straight bond. The bond issuer will now pay the fixed rate on the underlying swap and the floating rate received will be offset by the floating-rate loan created when the bond was refinanced. Specifically, the receiver swaption buyer will benefit when rates fall and the swaption is exercised. Thus, the embedded call feature is similar to a receiver swaption.

EXAMPLE 16

European Swaptions

Suppose you are an Australian company and have ongoing floating-rate debt. You have profited for some time by paying at a floating rate because rates have been falling steadily for the last few years. Now, however, you are concerned that within three months the Australian central bank may tighten its monetary policy and your debt costs will thus increase. Rather than lock in your borrowing via a swap, you prefer to hedge by buying a swaption expiring in three months, whereby you will have the choice, but not the obligation, to enter a five-year swap locking in your borrowing costs. The current three-month forward, five-year swap rate is 2.65%. The current five-year swap rate is 2.55%. The current three-month risk-free rate is 2.25%.

With reference to the Black model to value the swaption, which statement is correct?

A The underlying is the three-month forward, five-year swap rate.

B The discount rate to use is 2.55%.

C The swaption time to expiration, T, is five years.

Solution:

A is correct. The current five-year swap rate is not used as a discount rate with swaptions. The swaption time to expiration is 0.25, not the life of the swap.

6   OPTION GREEKS AND IMPLIED VOLATILITY

With option valuation models, such as the binomial model, BSM model, and Black's model, we are able to estimate a wide array of comparative information, such as how much the option value will change for a small change in a particular parameter.[13] We will explore this derived information as well as implied volatility in this section. These topics are essential for those managing option positions and in general in obtaining a solid understanding of how option prices change. Our discussion will be based on stock options, though the material covered in this section applies to all types of options.

The measures examined here are known as the Greeks and include, delta, gamma, theta, vega, and rho. With these calculations, we seek to address how much a particular portfolio will change for a given small change in the appropriate parameter. These measures are sometimes referred to as static risk measures in that they capture movements in the option value for a movement in one of the factors that affect the option value, while holding all other factors constant.

Our focus here is on European stock options in which the underlying stock is assumed to pay a dividend yield (denoted δ). Note that for non-dividend-paying stocks, $\delta = 0$.

6.1 Delta

Delta is defined as the change in a given instrument for a given small change in the value of the stock, holding everything else constant. Thus, the delta of long one share of stock is by definition +1.0, and the delta of short one share of stock is by definition −1.0. The concept of the option delta is similarly the change in an option value for a given small change in the value of the underlying stock, holding everything else constant. The option deltas for calls and puts are, respectively,

$$\text{Delta}_c = e^{-\delta T} N(d_1) \tag{22}$$

and

$$\text{Delta}_p = -e^{-\delta T} N(-d_1) \tag{23}$$

Note that the deltas are a simple function of $N(d_1)$. The delta of an option answers the question of how much the option will change for a given change in the stock, holding everything else constant. Therefore, delta is a static risk measure. It does not address how likely this particular change would be. Recall that $N(d_1)$ is a value taken from the cumulative distribution function of a standard normal distribution. As such, the range of values is between 0 and 1. Thus, the range of call delta is 0 and $e^{-\delta T}$ and the range of put delta is $-e^{-\delta T}$ and 0. As the stock price increases, the call option goes deeper in the money and the value of $N(d_1)$ is moving toward 1. As the stock price decreases, the call option goes deeper out of the money and the value of $N(d_1)$ is moving toward zero. When the option gets closer to maturity, the delta will drift either toward 0 if it is out of the money or drift toward 1 if it is in the money. Clearly, as the stock price changes and as time to maturity changes, the deltas are also changing.

Delta hedging an option is the process of establishing a position in the underlying stock of a quantity that is prescribed by the option delta so as to have no exposure to very small moves up or down in the stock price. Hence, to execute a single option delta hedge, we first calculate the option delta and then buy or sell delta units of stock. In practice, rarely does one have only one option position to manage. Thus, in general, delta hedging refers to manipulating the underlying portfolio delta by

---

[13] Parameters in the BSM model, for example, include the stock price, exercise price, volatility, time to expiration, and the risk-free interest rate.

appropriately changing the positions in the portfolio. A delta neutral portfolio refers to setting the portfolio delta all the way to zero. In theory, the delta neutral portfolio will not change in value for small changes in the stock instrument. Let N_H denote the number of units of the hedging instrument and Delta_H denote the delta of the hedging instrument, which could be the underlying stock, call options, or put options. Delta neutral implies the portfolio delta plus $N_H\text{Delta}_H$ is equal to zero. The optimal number of hedging units, N_H, is

$$N_H = -\frac{\text{Portfolio delta}}{\text{Delta}_H}$$

Note that if N_H is negative, then one must short the hedging instrument, and if N_H is positive, then one must go long the hedging instrument. Clearly, if the portfolio is options and the hedging instrument is stock, then we will buy or sell shares to offset the portfolio position. For example, if the portfolio consists of 100,000 shares of stock at US$10 per share, then the portfolio delta is 100,000. The delta of the hedging instrument, stock, is +1. Thus, the optimal number of hedging units, N_H, is −100,000 (= −100,000/1) or short 100,000 shares. Alternatively, if the portfolio delta is 5,000 and a particular call option with delta of 0.5 is used as the hedging instrument, then to arrive at a delta neutral portfolio, one must sell 10,000 call options (= −5,000/0.5). Alternatively, if a portfolio of options has a delta of −1,500, then one must buy 1,500 shares of stock to be delta neutral [= −(−1,500)/1]. If the hedging instrument is stock, then the delta is +1 per share.

EXAMPLE 17

Delta Hedging

Apple stock is trading at US$125. We write calls (that is, we sell calls) on 1,000 Apple shares and now are exposed to an increase in the price of the Apple stock. That is, if Apple rises, we will lose money because the calls we sold will go up in value, so our liability will increase. Correspondingly, if Apple falls, we will make money. We want to neutralize our exposure to Apple. Say the call delta is 0.50, which means that if Apple goes up by US$0.10, a call on one Apple share will go up US$0.05. We need to trade in such a way as to make money if Apple goes up, to offset our exposure. Hence, we buy 500 Apple shares to hedge. Now, if Apple goes up US$0.10, the sold calls will go up US$50 (our liability goes up), but our long 500 Apple hedge will profit by US$50. Hence, we are delta hedged.

Identify the *incorrect* statement:

A   If we sell Apple puts, we need to buy Apple stock to delta hedge.

B   Call delta is non-negative (≥ 0); put delta is non-positive (≤ 0).

C   Delta hedging is the process of neutralizing exposure to the underlying.

Solution:

A is the correct answer because statement A is incorrect. If we sell puts, we need to short sell stock to delta hedge.

One final interpretation of option delta is related to forecasting changes in option prices. Let $\hat{c}$, $\hat{p}$, and $\hat{S}$ denote some new value for the call, put, and stock. Based on an approximation method, the change in the option price can be estimated with a concept known as a delta approximation or

$$\hat{c} - c \cong Delta_c\left(\hat{S} - S\right) \text{ for calls and}$$

$$\hat{p} - p \cong Delta_p\left(\hat{S} - S\right) \text{ for puts.}[14]$$

We can now illustrate the actual call values as well as the estimated call values based on delta. Exhibit 15 illustrates the call value based on the BSM model and the call value based on the delta approximation,

$$\hat{c} = c + Delta_c\left(\hat{S} - S\right)$$

Notice for very small changes in the stock, the delta approximation is fairly accurate. For example, if the stock value rises from 100 to 101, notice that both the call line and the call (delta) estimated line are almost the same value. If, however, the stock value rises from 100 to 150, the call line is now significantly above the call (delta) estimated line. Thus, we see that as the change in the stock increases, the estimation error also increases. The delta approximation is biased low for both a down move and an up move.

Exhibit 15   Call Values and Delta Estimated Call Values (S = 100 = X, r = 5%, σ = 30%, δ = 0)

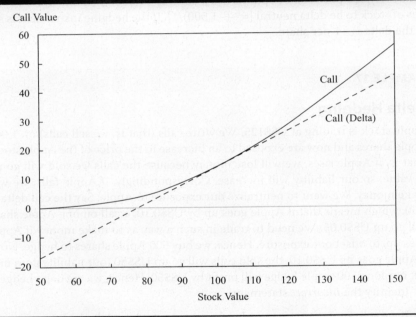

We see that delta hedging is imperfect and gets worse as the underlying moves further away from its original value of 100. Based on the graph, the BSM model assumption of continuous trading is essential to avoid hedging risk. This hedging risk is related to the difference between these two lines and the degree to which the underlying price experiences large changes.

---

14 The symbol $\cong$ denotes approximately. The approximation method is known as a Taylor series. Also note that the put delta is non-positive (≤ 0).

EXAMPLE 18

Delta Hedging

Suppose we know S = 100, X = 100, r = 5%, T = 1.0, σ = 30%, and δ = 5%. We have a short position in put options on 10,000 shares of stock. Based on this information, we note Delta$_c$ = 0.532, and Delta$_p$ = −0.419. Assume each stock option contract is for one share of stock.

1 The appropriate delta hedge, assuming the hedging instrument is stock, is executed by which of the following transactions? Select the *closest* answer.

  A Buy 5,320 shares of stock.

  B Short sell 4,190 shares of stock.

  C Buy 4,190 shares of stock.

2 The appropriate delta hedge, assuming the hedging instrument is calls, is executed by which of the following transactions? Select the *closest* answer.

  A Sell 7,876 call options.

  B Sell 4,190 call options.

  C Buy 4,190 call options.

3 Identify the correct interpretation of an option delta.

  A Option delta measures the curvature in the option price with respect to the stock price.

  B Option delta is the change in an option value for a given small change in the stock's value, holding everything else constant.

  C Option delta is the probability of the option expiring in the money.

Solution to 1:

B is correct. Recall that $N_H = -\dfrac{\text{Portfolio delta}}{\text{Delta}_H}$. The put delta is given as −0.419, thus the short put delta is 0.419. In this case, Portfolio delta = 10,000(0.419) = 4,190 and Delta$_H$ = 1.0. Thus, the number of number of hedging units is −4,190 [= −(4,190/1)] or short sell 4,190 shares of stock.

Solution to 2:

A is correct. Again the Portfolio delta = 4,190 but now Delta$_H$ = 0.532. Thus, the number of hedging units is −7,875.9 [= −(4,190/0.532)] or sell 7,876 call options.

Solution to 3:

B is correct. Delta is defined as the change in a given portfolio for a given small change in the stock's value, holding everything else constant. Option delta is defined as the change in an option value for a given small change in the stock's value, holding everything else constant.

6.2 Gamma

Recall that delta is a good approximation of how an option price will change for a small change in the stock. For larger changes in the stock, we need better accuracy. **Gamma** is defined as the change in a given instrument's delta for a given small change in the stock's value, holding everything else constant. Option gamma is similarly defined as the change in a given option delta for a given small change in the stock's value, holding everything else constant. Option gamma is a measure of the curvature in the option price in relationship to the stock price. Thus, the gamma of a long or short position in one share of stock is zero because the delta of a share of stock never changes. A stock always moves one-for-one with itself. Thus, its delta is always +1 and, of course, −1 for a short position in the stock. The gamma for a call and put option are the same and can be expressed as

$$\text{Gamma}_c = \text{Gamma}_p = \frac{e^{-\delta T}}{S\sigma\sqrt{T}}n(d_1) \tag{24}$$

where $n(d_1)$ is the standard normal probability density function. The lowercase "n" is distinguished from the cumulative normal distribution—which the density function generates—and that we have used elsewhere in this reading denoted by uppercase "N". The gamma of a call equals the gamma of a similar put based on put–call parity or $c - p = S_0 - e^{-rT}X$. Note that neither S_0 nor $e^{-rT}X$ is a direct function of delta. Hence, the right-hand side of put–call parity has a delta of 1. Thus, the right-hand side delta is not sensitive to changes in the underlying. Therefore, the gamma of a call must equal the gamma of a put.

Gamma is always non-negative. Gamma takes on its largest value near at the money. Options deltas do not change much for small changes in the stock price if the option is either deep in or deep out of the money. Also, as the stock price changes and as time to expiration changes, the gamma is also changing.

Gamma measures the rate of change of delta as the stock changes. Gamma approximates the estimation error in delta for options because the option price with respect to the stock is non-linear and delta is a linear approximation. Thus, gamma is a risk measure; specifically, gamma measures the non-linearity risk or the risk that remains once the portfolio is delta neutral. A gamma neutral portfolio implies the gamma is zero. For example, gamma can be managed to an acceptable level first and then delta is neutralized as a second step. This hedging approach is feasible because options have gamma but a stock does not. Thus, in order to modify gamma, one has to include additional option trades in the portfolio. Once the revised portfolio, including any new option trades, has the desired level of gamma, then the trader can get the portfolio delta to its desired level as step two. To alter the portfolio delta, the trader simply buys or sells stock. Because stock has a positive delta, but zero gamma, the portfolio delta can be brought to its desired level with no impact on the portfolio gamma.

One final interpretation of gamma is related to improving the forecasted changes in option prices. Again, let $\hat{c}$, $\hat{p}$, and $\hat{S}$ denote new values for the call, put, and stock. Again based on an approximation method, the change in the option price can be estimated by a delta-plus-gamma approximation or

$$\hat{c} - c \approx \text{Delta}_c\left(\hat{S} - S\right) + \frac{\text{Gamma}_c}{2}\left(\hat{S} - S\right)^2 \text{ for calls and}$$

$$\hat{p} - p \approx \text{Delta}_p\left(\hat{S} - S\right) + \frac{\text{Gamma}_p}{2}\left(\hat{S} - S\right)^2 \text{ for puts.}$$

Exhibit 16 illustrates the call value based on the BSM model; the call value based on the delta approximation,

$$\hat{c} = c + \text{Delta}_c\left(\hat{S} - S\right)$$

and the call value based on the delta-plus-gamma approximation,

$$\hat{c} = c + \text{Delta}_c\left(\hat{S} - S\right) + \frac{\text{Gamma}_c}{2}\left(\hat{S} - S\right)^2$$

Notice again that for very small changes in the stock, the delta approximation and the delta-plus-gamma approximations are fairly accurate. If the stock value rises from 100 to 150, the call line is again significantly above the delta estimated line but is below the delta-plus-gamma estimated line. Importantly, the call delta-plus-gamma estimated line is significantly closer to the BSM model call values. Thus, we see that even for fairly large changes in the stock, the delta-plus-gamma approximation is accurate. As the change in the stock increases, the estimation error also increases. From Exhibit 16, we see the delta-plus-gamma approximation is biased low for a down move but biased high for an up move. Thus, when estimating how the call price changes when the underlying changes, we see how the delta-plus-gamma approximation is an improvement when compared with using the delta approximation on its own.

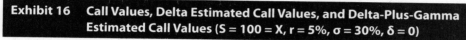

Exhibit 16   Call Values, Delta Estimated Call Values, and Delta-Plus-Gamma Estimated Call Values (S = 100 = X, r = 5%, σ = 30%, δ = 0)

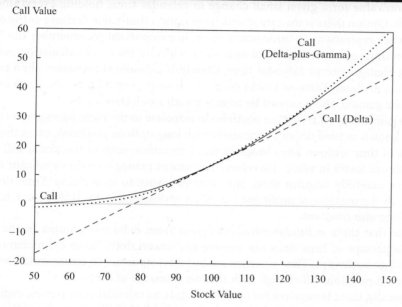

If the BSM model assumptions hold, then we would have no risk in managing option positions. In reality, however, stock prices often jump rather than move continuously and smoothly, which creates "gamma risk." Gamma risk is so-called because gamma measures the risk of stock prices jumping when hedging an option position, and thus leaving us suddenly unhedged.

EXAMPLE 19

Gamma Risk in Option Trading

Suppose we are options traders and have only one option position—a short call option. We also hold some stock such that we are delta hedged. Which one of the following statements is true?

A We are gamma neutral.

B Buying a call will increase our overall gamma.

C Our overall position is a positive gamma, which will make large moves profitable for us, whether up or down.

Solution:

B is correct. Buying options (calls or puts) will always increase net gamma. A is incorrect because we are short gamma, not gamma neutral. C is also incorrect because we are short gamma. We can only become gamma neutral from a short gamma position by purchasing options.

6.3 Theta

Theta is defined as the change in a portfolio for a given small change in calendar time, holding everything else constant. Option theta is similarly defined as the change in an option value for a given small change in calendar time, holding everything else constant. Option theta is the rate at which the option time value declines as the option approaches expiration. To understand theta, it is important to remember the "holding everything else constant" assumption. Specifically, the theta calculation assumes nothing changes except calendar time. Clearly, if calendar time passes, then time to expiration declines. Because stocks do not have an expiration date, the stock theta is zero. Like gamma, theta cannot be adjusted with stock trades.

The gain or loss of an option portfolio in response to the mere passage of calendar time is known as time decay. Particularly with long options positions, often the mere passage of time without any change in other variables, such as the stock, will result is significant losses in value. Therefore, investment managers with significant option positions carefully monitor theta and their exposure to time decay. Time decay is essentially the measure of profit and loss of an option position as time passes, holding everything else constant.

Note that theta is fundamentally different from delta and gamma in the sense that the passage of time does not involve any uncertainty. There is no chance that time will go backward. Time marches on, but it is important to understand how your investment position will change with the mere passage of time.

Typically, theta is negative for options. That is, as calendar time passes, expiration time declines and the option value also declines. Exhibit 17 illustrates the option value with respect to time to expiration. Remember, as calendar time passes, the time to expiration declines. Both the call and the put option are at the money and eventually are worthless if the stock does not change. Notice, however, how the speed of the option value decline increases as time to expiration decreases.

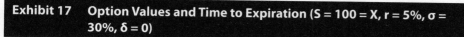

Exhibit 17   Option Values and Time to Expiration (S = 100 = X, r = 5%, σ = 30%, δ = 0)

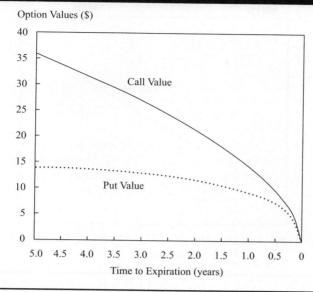

Option Values ($)

Time to Expiration (years)

6.4 Vega

Vega is defined as the change in a given portfolio for a given small change in volatility, holding everything else constant. Vega measures the sensitivity of a given portfolio to volatility. The vega of an option is positive. An increase in volatility results in an increase in the option value for both calls and puts.

The vega of a call equals the vega of a similar put based on put–call parity or $c - p = S_0 - e^{-rT}X$. Note that neither S_0 nor $e^{-rT}X$ is a direct function of volatility. Therefore, the vega of a call must offset the vega of a put so that the vega of the right-hand side is zero.

Unlike the Greeks we have already discussed, vega is based on an unobservable parameter, future volatility. Although historical volatility can be calculated, there is no objective measure of future volatility. Similar to the concept of expected value, future volatility is subjective. Thus, vega measures the sensitivity of a portfolio to changes in the volatility used in the option valuation model. Option values are generally quite sensitive to volatility. In fact, of the five variables in the BSM, an option's value is most sensitive to volatility changes.

At extremely low volatility, the option values tend toward their lower bounds. The lower bound of a European-style call option is zero or the stock less the present value of the exercise price, whichever is greater. The lower bound of a European-style put option is zero or the present value of the exercise price less the stock, whichever is greater. Exhibit 18 illustrates the option values with respect to volatility. In this case, the call lower bound is 4.88 and the put lower bound is 0. The difference between the call and put can be explained by put–call parity.

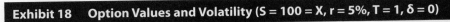

Exhibit 18   Option Values and Volatility (S = 100 = X, r = 5%, T = 1, δ = 0)

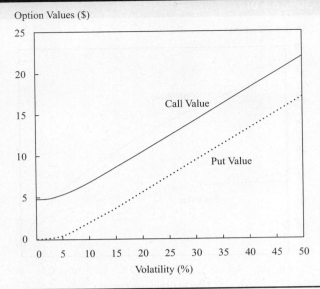

Vega is very important in managing an options portfolio because option values can be very sensitive to volatility changes. Vega is high when options are at or near the money and are short dated. Volatility is usually only hedged with other options and volatility itself can be quite volatile. Volatility is sometimes considered a separate asset class or a separate risk factor. Because it is rather exotic and potentially dangerous, exposure to volatility needs to be managed, bearing in mind that risk managers, board members, and clients may not understand or appreciate losses if volatility is the source.

6.5 Rho

Rho is defined as the change in a given portfolio for a given small change in the risk-free interest rate, holding everything else constant. Thus, rho measures the sensitivity of the portfolio to the risk-free interest rate.

The rho of a call is positive. Intuitively, buying an option avoids the financing costs involved with purchasing the stock. In other words, purchasing a call option allows an investor to earn interest on the money that otherwise would have gone to purchasing the stock. The higher the interest rate, the higher the call value.

The rho of a put is negative. Intuitively, the option to sell the stock delays the opportunity to earn interest on the proceeds from the sale. For example, purchasing a put option rather than selling the stock deprives an investor of the potential interest that would have been earned from the proceeds of selling the stock. The higher the interest rate, the lower the put value.

When interest rates are zero, the call and put option values are the same for at-the-money options. Recall that with put–call parity, we have $c - p = S_0 - e^{-rT}X$, and when interest rates are zero, then the present value function has no effect. As interest rates rise, the difference between call and put options increases as illustrated in

Exhibit 19. The impact on option prices when interest rates change is relatively small when compared with that for volatility changes and that for changes in the stock. Hence, the influence of interest rates is generally not a major concern.[15]

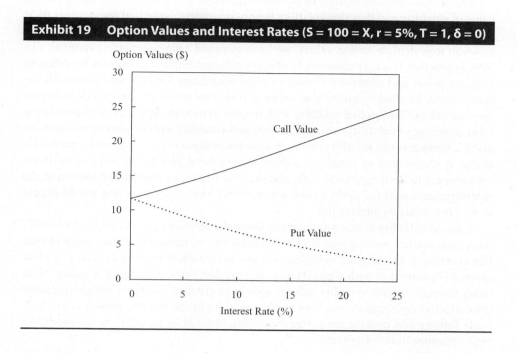

Exhibit 19   Option Values and Interest Rates (S = 100 = X, r = 5%, T = 1, δ = 0)

6.6 Implied Volatility

As we have already touched on in Section 6.4, for most options, the value is particularly sensitive to volatility. Unlike the price of the underlying, however, volatility, is not an observable value in the marketplace. Volatility can be, and often is estimated, based on a sample of historical data. For example, for a three-month option, we might look back over the last three months and calculate the actual historical stock volatility. We can then use this figure as an estimate of volatility over the next three months. The volatility parameter in the BSM model, however, is the *future* volatility. As we know, history is a very frail guide of the future, so the option may appear to be "mispriced" with respect to the actual future volatility experienced. Different investors will have different views of the future volatility. The one with the most accurate forecast will have the most accurate assessment of the option value.

   Much like yield to maturity with bonds, volatility can be inferred from option prices. This inferred volatility is called the **implied volatility**. Thus, one important use of the BSM model is to invert the model and estimate implied volatility. The key advantage is that implied volatility provides information regarding the perceived uncertainty going forward and thereby allows us to gain an understanding of the collective opinions of investors on the volatility of the underlying and the demand for options. If the demand for options increases and the no-arbitrage approach is not perfectly reflected

---

15 An exception to this rule is that with interest rate options, the interest rate is not constant and serves as the underlying. The relationship between the option value and the underlying interest rate is, therefore, captured by the delta, not the rho. Rho is really more generally the relationship between the option value and the rate used to discount cash flows.

in market prices—for example, because of transaction costs—then the preference for buying options will drive option prices up, and hence, the observed implied volatility. This kind of information is of great value to traders in options.

Recall that one assumption of the BSM model is that all investors agree on the value of volatility and that this volatility is non-stochastic. Note that the original BSM model assumes the underlying instrument volatility is constant in our context. That is, when we calculate option values, we have assumed a single volatility number, like 30%. In practice, it is very common to observe different implied volatilities for different exercise prices and observe different implied volatilities for calls and puts with the same terms. Implied volatility also varies across time to expiration as well as across exercise prices. The implied volatility with respect to time to expiration is known as the term structure of volatility, whereas the implied volatility with respect to the exercise price is known as the volatility smile or sometimes skew depending on the particular shape. It is common to construct a three dimensional plot of the implied volatility with respect to both expiration time and exercise prices, a visualization known as the volatility surface. If the BSM model assumptions were true, then one would expect to find the volatility surface flat.

Implied volatility is also not constant through calendar time. As implied volatility increases, market participants are communicating an increased market price of risk. For example, if the implied volatility of a put increases, it is more expensive to buy downside protection with a put. Hence, the market price of hedging is rising. With index options, various volatility indexes have been created, and these indexes measure the collective opinions of investors on the volatility in the market. Investors can now trade futures and options on various volatility indexes in an effort to manage their vega exposure in other options.

Exhibit 20 provides a look at a couple of decades of one such volatility index, the Chicago Board Options Exchange S&P 500 Volatility Index, known as the VIX. The VIX is quoted as a percent and is intended to approximate the implied volatility of the S&P 500 over the next 30 days. VIX is often termed the fear index because it is viewed as a measure of market uncertainty. Thus, an increase in the VIX index is regarded as greater investor uncertainty. From this figure, we see that the implied volatility of the S&P 500 is not constant and goes through periods when the VIX is low and periods when the VIX is high. In the recent financial crisis, the VIX was extremely high, indicating great fear and uncertainty in the equity market. Remember that implied volatility reflects both beliefs regarding future volatility as well as a preference for risk mitigating products like options. Thus, during the crisis, the higher implied volatility reflected both higher expected future volatility as well as increased preference for buying rather than selling options.

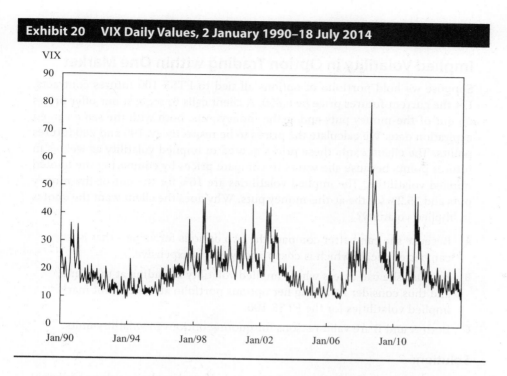

Exhibit 20   VIX Daily Values, 2 January 1990–18 July 2014

Implied volatility has several uses in option trading. An understanding of implied volatility is essential in managing an options portfolio. This reading explains the valuation of options as a function of the value of the underlying, the exercise price, the expiration date, the risk-free rate, dividends or other benefits paid by the underlying, and the volatility of the underlying. Note that each of these parameters is observable except the volatility of the underlying over the option term looking ahead. This volatility has to be estimated in some manner, such as by calculating historical volatility. But as noted, historical volatility involves looking back in time. There are, however, a vast number of liquid options traded on exchanges around the world so that a wide variety of option prices are observable. Because we know the price and all the parameters except the volatility, we can back out the volatility needed by the option valuation model to get the known price. This volatility is the implied volatility.

Hence, implied volatility can be interpreted as the market's view of how to value options. In the option markets, participants use volatility as the medium in which to quote options. The price is simply calculated by the use of an agreed model with the quoted volatility. For example, rather than quote a particular call option as trading for €14.23, it may be quoted as 30.00, where 30.00 denotes in percentage points the implied volatility based on a €14.23 option price. Note that there is a one-to-one relationship between the implied volatility and the option price, ignoring rounding errors.

The benefit of quoting via implied volatility (or simply volatility), rather than price, is that it allows volatility to be traded in its own right. Volatility is the "guess factor" in option pricing. All other inputs—value of the underlying, exercise price, expiration, risk-free rate, and dividend yield—are agreed.[16] Volatility is often the same order of magnitude across exercise prices and expiration dates. This means that traders can compare the values of two options, which may have markedly different exercise prices and expiration dates, and therefore, markedly different prices in a common unit of measure, specifically implied volatility.

---

16 The risk-free rate and dividend yield may not be entirely agreed, but the impact of variations to these parameters is generally very small compared with the other inputs.

EXAMPLE 20

Implied Volatility in Option Trading within One Market

Suppose we hold portfolio of options all tied to FTSE 100 futures contracts. Let the current futures price be 6,850. A client calls to request our offer prices on out-of-the-money puts and at-the-money puts, both with the same agreed expiration date. We calculate the prices to be respectively, 190 and 280 futures points. The client wants these prices quoted in implied volatility as well as in futures points because she wants to compare prices by comparing the quoted implied volatilities. The implied volatilities are 16% for the out-of-the-money puts and 15.2% for the at-the-money puts. Why does the client want the quotes in implied volatility?

A   Because she can better compare the two options for value—that is, she can better decide which is cheap and which is expensive.

B   Because she can assess where implied volatility is trading at that time, and thus consider revaluing her options portfolio at the current market implied volatilities for the FTSE 100.

C   Both A and B are valid reasons for quoting options in volatility units.

Solution:

C is correct. Implied volatility can be used to assess the relative value of different options, neutralizing the moneyness and time to expiration effects. Also, implied volatility is useful for revaluing existing positions over time.

EXAMPLE 21

Implied Volatility in Option Trading Across Markets

Suppose an options dealer offers to sell a three-month at-the-money call on the FTSE index option at 19% implied volatility and a one-month in-the-money put on Vodaphone (VOD) at 24%. An option trader believes that based on the current outlook, FTSE volatility should be closer to 25% and VOD volatility should be closer to 20%. What actions might the trader take to benefit from her views?

A   Buy the FTSE call and the VOD put.

B   Buy the FTSE call and sell the VOD put.

C   Sell the FTSE call and sell the VOD puts.

Solution:

B is correct. The trader believes that the FTSE call volatility is understated by the dealer and that the VOD put volatility is overstated. Thus, the trader would expect FTSE volatility to rise and VOD volatility to fall. As a result, the FTSE call would be expected to increase in value and the VOD put would be expected to decrease in value. The trader would take the positions as indicated in B.

Regulators, banks, compliance officers, and most option traders use implied volatilities to communicate information related to options portfolios. This is because implied volatilities, together with standard pricing models, give the "market consensus" valuation, in the same way that other assets are valued using market prices.

In summary, as long as all market participants agree on the underlying option model and how other parameters are calculated, then implied volatility can be used as a quoting mechanism. Recall that there are calls and puts, various exercise prices, various maturities, American and European, and exchange-traded and OTC options. Thus, it is difficult to conceptualize all these different prices. For example, if two call options on the same stock had different prices, but one had a longer expiration and lower exercise price and the other had a shorter expiration and higher exercise, which should be the higher priced option? It is impossible to tell on the surface. But if one option implied a higher volatility than the other, we know that after taking into account the effects of time and exercise, one option is more expensive than the other. Thus, by converting the quoted price to implied volatility, it is easier to understand the current market price of various risk exposures.

SUMMARY

This reading on the valuation of contingent claims provides a foundation for understanding how a variety of different options are valued. Key points include the following:

- The arbitrageur would rather have more money than less and abides by two fundamental rules: Do not use your own money and do not take any price risk.

- The no-arbitrage approach is used for option valuation and is built on the key concept of the law of one price, which says that if two investments have the same future cash flows regardless of what happens in the future, then these two investments should have the same current price.

- Throughout this reading, the following key assumptions are made:
  - Replicating instruments are identifiable and investable.
  - Market frictions are nil.
  - Short selling is allowed with full use of proceeds.
  - The underlying instrument price follows a known distribution.
  - Borrowing and lending is available at a known risk-free rate.

- The two-period binomial model can be viewed as three one-period binomial models, one positioned at Time 0 and two positioned at Time 1.

- In general, European-style options can be valued based on the expectations approach in which the option value is determined as the present value of the expected future option payouts, where the discount rate is the risk-free rate and the expectation is taken based on the risk-neutral probability measure.

- Both American-style options and European-style options can be valued based on the no-arbitrage approach, which provides clear interpretations of the component terms; the option value is determined by working backward through the binomial tree to arrive at the correct current value.

- For American-style options, early exercise influences the option values and hedge ratios as one works backward through the binomial tree.

- Interest rate option valuation requires the specification of an entire term structure of interest rates, so valuation is often estimated via a binomial tree.

- A key assumption of the Black–Scholes–Merton option valuation model is that the return of the underlying instrument follows geometric Brownian motion, implying a lognormal distribution of the return.

- The BSM model can be interpreted as a dynamically managed portfolio of the underlying instrument and zero-coupon bonds.

- BSM model interpretations related to $N(d_1)$ are that it is the basis for the number of units of underlying instrument to replicate an option, that it is the primary determinant of delta, and that it answers the question of how much the option value will change for a small change in the underlying.

- BSM model interpretations related to $N(d_2)$ are that it is the basis for the number of zero-coupon bonds to acquire to replicate an option and that it is the basis for estimating the risk-neutral probability of an option expiring in the money.

- The Black futures option model assumes the underlying is a futures or a forward contract.

- Interest rate options can be valued based on a modified Black futures option model in which the underlying is a forward rate agreement (FRA), there is an accrual period adjustment as well as an underlying notional amount, and that care must be given to day-count conventions.

- An interest rate cap is a portfolio of interest rate call options termed caplets, each with the same exercise rate and with sequential maturities.

- An interest rate floor is a portfolio of interest rate put options termed floorlets, each with the same exercise rate and with sequential maturities.

- A swaption is an option on a swap.

- A payer swaption is an option on a swap to pay fixed and receive floating.

- A receiver swaption is an option on a swap to receive fixed and pay floating.

- Long a callable fixed-rate bond can be viewed as long a straight fixed-rate bond and short a receiver swaption.

- Delta is a static risk measure defined as the change in a given portfolio for a given small change in the value of the underlying instrument, holding everything else constant.

- Delta hedging refers to managing the portfolio delta by entering additional positions into the portfolio.

- A delta neutral portfolio is one in which the portfolio delta is set and maintained at zero.

- A change in the option price can be estimated with a delta approximation.

- Because delta is used to make a linear approximation of the non-linear relationship that exists between the option price and the underlying price, there is an error that can be estimated by gamma.

- Gamma is a static risk measure defined as the change in a given portfolio delta for a given small change in the value of the underlying instrument, holding everything else constant.

- Gamma captures the non-linearity risk or the risk—via exposure to the underlying—that remains once the portfolio is delta neutral.

- A gamma neutral portfolio is one in which the portfolio gamma is maintained at zero.

- The change in the option price can be better estimated by a delta-plus-gamma approximation compared with just a delta approximation.

- Theta is a static risk measure defined as the change in the value of an option given a small change in calendar time, holding everything else constant.

- Vega is a static risk measure defined as the change in a given portfolio for a given small change in volatility, holding everything else constant.

- Rho is a static risk measure defined as the change in a given portfolio for a given small change in the risk-free interest rate, holding everything else constant.

- Although historical volatility can be estimated, there is no objective measure of future volatility.

- Implied volatility is the BSM model volatility that yields the market option price.

- Implied volatility is a measure of future volatility, whereas historical volatility is a measure of past volatility.

- Option prices reflect the beliefs of option market participant about the future volatility of the underlying.

- The volatility smile is a two dimensional plot of the implied volatility with respect to the exercise price.

- The volatility surface is a three dimensional plot of the implied volatility with respect to both expiration time and exercise prices.

- If the BSM model assumptions were true, then one would expect to find the volatility surface flat, but in practice, the volatility surface is not flat.

READING

42

Derivatives Strategies

by Robert A. Strong, PhD, CFA, and Russell A. Rhoads, CFA

Robert A. Strong, PhD, CFA, is at the University of Maine (USA). Russell A. Rhoads, CFA, is at The Options Institute at CBOE (USA).

LEARNING OUTCOMES

Mastery	The candidate should be able to:
☐	a. describe how interest rate, currency, and equity swaps, futures, and forwards can be used to modify risk and return;
☐	b. describe how to replicate an asset by using options and by using cash plus forwards or futures;
☐	c. describe the investment objectives, structure, payoff, and risk(s) of a covered call position;
☐	d. describe the investment objectives, structure, payoff, and risks(s) of a protective put position;
☐	e. calculate and interpret the value at expiration, profit, maximum profit, maximum loss, and breakeven underlying price at expiration for covered calls and protective puts;
☐	f. contrast protective put and covered call positions to being long an asset and short a forward on the asset;
☐	g. describe the investment objective(s), structure, payoffs, and risks of the following option strategies: bull spread, bear spread, collar, and straddle;
☐	h. calculate and interpret the value at expiration, profit, maximum profit, maximum loss, and breakeven underlying price at expiration of the following option strategies: bull spread, bear spread, collar, and straddle;
☐	i. describe uses of calendar spreads;
☐	j. identify and evaluate appropriate derivatives strategies consistent with given investment objectives.

1   INTRODUCTION

There are many ways in which investors and financial managers routinely use put and call options, futures, forward contracts, and various types of swap contracts to modify their investment positions or to implement market strategies. Some derivative strategies are purely speculative, designed to profit if a particular market change occurs. Other strategies are defensive, providing protection against an adverse event or removing the uncertainty around future events.

The purpose of this reading is to illustrate ways in which derivatives might be used in typical investment situations. Few financial managers or individual investors will ever use all of the strategies described here. That does not mean that some strategies are not important. An informed investment professional should still be aware of them and understand the associated risk–return trade-off. Although part of the medical school curriculum, many physicians will never treat a patient for frostbite or malaria. Regardless, patients have a right to expect that their doctors have an idea about how these conditions might be treated or, better yet, prevented. Someone who is travelling to an area where malaria is prevalent wants to acquire protection before the trip, and we expect doctors to know how to prescribe something for that even if they have never done it before. The doctor may also choose to refer the patient to a specialist, just as an investment manager may need to confer with a derivatives specialist.

An investment manager may not currently use derivatives but should be sufficiently familiar with them that he or she can answer questions about them and explain how they might logically be used to benefit a corporate treasury or protect an investment portfolio. When a financial adviser deals with a client's money, the adviser is dealing with the long-term financial health of the client. Physicians are expected to be current and knowledgeable, and investors have a right to expect the same of their financial advisers.

Section 2 of this reading shows how swaps, futures, and forwards can be used to change the risk exposure of an existing position. Section 3 shows how certain combinations of securities are equivalent to others. Section 4 is a discussion of two of the most widely used derivative strategies, covered calls and protective puts. In Section 5, we look at popular option strategies used by investors. Section 6 demonstrates a series of applications showing ways in which a money manager might solve a problem with derivatives.

2   CHANGING RISK EXPOSURES WITH SWAPS, FUTURES, AND FORWARDS

Financial managers use the derivatives markets to quickly and efficiently alter the underlying risk exposure of their asset portfolios or forthcoming business transactions. This section covers a variety of common examples that use various derivative products.

2.1   Interest Rate Swap/Futures Examples

Interest rate swaps and futures can be used to modify the risk and return of a fixed-income portfolio and can also be used in conjunction with an equity portfolio, as we will show later in this reading. Both interest rate swaps and futures are interest-sensitive instruments, and by adding them to a portfolio, either as long or short positions, they can increase or decrease the exposure of the portfolio to interest rates.

2.1.1 *Interest Rate Swap*

Interest rate swaps are an indispensable tool for many corporate treasurers, especially at a financial institution. In an interest rate swap, the two parties involved agree that on specified payment dates they will exchange cash flows, one based on a *variable* (floating) interest rate and the other based on a *fixed* rate determined at the time the swap is initiated. This fixed rate is called the swap rate.[1] Both interest rates are applied to the swap's notional value to determine the size of the payment. The period of time over which the payments are exchanged is called the swap tenor. At the end of this period, the swap is said to expire. The notional value is needed to determine the size of the payments, but the notional value does not actually change hands, nor is it borrowed or lent between the parties. Typically no funds change hands when the parties enter into the agreement. Normally, the resulting two payments (one fixed, one floating) will not be equal, so they are typically netted, with the party owing the greater amount sending the difference to the other party.

Let us examine how swaps can be used by looking at an application in fixed-income portfolio management. One way to measure interest rate risk is by using the concept of duration.[2] Consider a portfolio manager with an investment portfolio containing $500 million of fixed-rate US Treasury bonds with an average duration of five years. Suppose the manager wants to reduce this duration to three over the next year but does not want to sell any of the securities.

One way to do this would be with a pay-fixed interest rate swap. Because the portfolio is currently receiving a fixed rate, the manager will want to exchange part of this fixed-rate income stream for a floating-rate stream in order to lower the overall duration. This approach means the appropriate swap would pay the fixed rate and receive the floating rate.

Suppose the duration of the swap used by the manager is 1.5.[3] This duration is less than the existing portfolio duration, so adding the swap to the portfolio will reduce the overall average duration. By properly choosing the notional value of the swap, the portfolio manager can achieve a combination of the existing portfolio duration and the swap duration that sets the overall duration to the target duration.

2.1.2 *Interest Rate Futures*

A swap is an over-the-counter derivative that is subject to counterparty risk on the interest payment dates, although as stated previously, the notional value is not at risk. Because one party will owe money to the other, there is the possibility of default by one side of the trade. An alternative would be to use exchange-traded interest rate futures contracts, which are guaranteed by a clearinghouse and are virtually free of concerns about counterparty risk. These contracts are also sometimes referred to as bond futures because the underlying asset is often a bond. Because there are usually many different bonds that could be used to satisfy the delivery requirement, the hedge calculation can be complicated. Here we will provide a general description of how interest rate futures are used in adjusting portfolio duration.

Because most interest rate futures contracts are futures contracts in which the underlying is a bond, this type of contract would have a duration that is consistent with the forward behavior of the underlying deliverable bond. That is, the interest rate futures price will move as though it was the forward price of the bond on the expiration date. The price sensitivity of the futures will, therefore, reflect a type of

---

1 The swap price is also sometimes called the swap rate.
2 Although there are various duration measures, the most important is modified duration, which is an approximate measure of how a bond price changes given a small change in the level of interest rates, adjusted for the level of interest rates.
3 The duration of an interest rate swap is the duration of the fixed-rate component minus the duration of the floating-rate component.

forward duration that is based on the underlying bond. Thus, the futures price will move fairly consistently and proportionately with the yield that drives the underlying bond. Continuing with the example earlier in which the manager whose portfolio has a duration of five years wants to lower the duration to three years, the general principle is the same: By selling bond futures, a portfolio manager "adds negative duration" to the portfolio, and if done in the right quantity, the overall duration can be reduced to the target level.[4]

In general, anything done with an interest rate *futures* contract could also be done with an interest rate *forward* contract. Forwards, like swaps, have counterparty risk and can be customized. Futures are standardized and come with greater regulatory oversight and with a clearinghouse that makes counterparty risk virtually zero.[5]

2.2 Currency Swap/Futures Examples

Currency swaps and futures can be used effectively to alter risk exposures. We provide examples of how it is done in the next two sub-sections.

2.2.1 Currency Swap

A currency swap is different from an interest rate swap in two ways: 1) The interest rates are associated with different currencies, and 2) the notional value may be exchanged at the beginning and end of the swap's life.[6] As an example, suppose Assicurazioni Generali, the largest insurance company in Italy, wants to fund its operations in Switzerland, and for that, it needs Swiss francs. But it discovers that it can borrow cheaper in the euro market. The company decides to fund itself in euros and swap the cash flow into Swiss francs. Assicurazioni contacts a dealer and requests a quote on a pay-fixed €50 million three-year swap with semi-annual interest payments. The swap agreement provides that both parties pay a fixed rate. After entering into the swap agreement the dealer will hedge the swap with another party, possibly through a trade in the futures markets.

Exhibit 1 shows the direction of the cash flows. With the "block and arrow" diagram, it is easy to see how the cash flows net out. For instance, at origination Assicurazioni receives euros from the eurozone lender and passes them on to the swap dealer, so they are a pass through cash flow. Assicurazioni receives Swiss francs from the dealer just as if the firm had borrowed them. At each payment date, Assicurazioni receives a fixed-rate euro payment and passes it on to the eurozone lender.[7] The firm is left with a net outflow in fixed Swiss francs, which is the firm's preferred payment option. At maturity Assicurazioni returns the Swiss francs notional amount to the dealer and in return receives the notional amount in euros, which it uses to pay off its creditor.

---

4 It is important to note that the portfolio manager would sell the futures in this example because he wants to reduce the duration. If he bought futures, he would be increasing duration.

5 Regulatory changes in global markets are moving both over-the-counter swaps and forward contracts toward a clearing process as well.

6 Although an exchange of notional is often the case, the parties may agree not to do this. Some types of hedge transactions are designed to hedge only foreign cash flows and not principal payments, so a principal exchange on a currency swap would not be necessary.

7 The rate paid to the creditors on the euro loan will not exactly equal the rate paid to the firm on the swap. Also, when a company uses a swap, it can elect to receive either a fixed or a floating rate and will want to align the cash receipt with the floating or fixed rate on the loan.

Exhibit 1.   Currency Swap Cash Flows

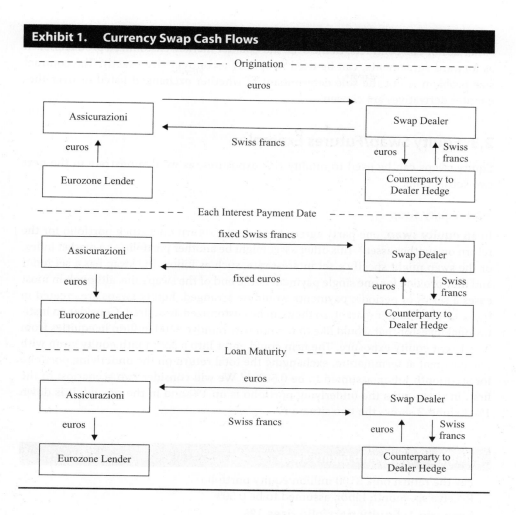

2.2.2 *Currency Futures*

Foreign currency futures are another useful tool in risk management.[8] For example, Swiss Re, a reinsurance company, might have a €25.18 million liability due to be paid in 15 months. If the euro were to appreciate versus the Swiss franc before the payment date, Swiss Re's effective borrowing cost would be higher. The firm could largely eliminate the foreign exchange risk associated with this debt by fixing the price of the euros now. One way to do this would be via a futures contract in which Swiss Re promises to buy the euros in 15 months at a Swiss franc price determined now. In 15 months, the firm needs the euros to pay the bill, so it wants to *buy* the euros and promises to pay for them in Swiss francs. At a futures exchange, contracts are standardized by size, so Swiss Re would determine the number of contracts needed to fund the liability. If, for instance, the contract size is €125,000, the firm would need

$$\frac{€25,180,000}{€125,000/\text{contract}} = 201.44 \text{ contracts}$$

---

8 Many firms prefer to hedge with currency *forward* contracts rather than futures because the forward contract trades in the over-the-counter market and can be customized to any size and any payment date. Exchange-traded futures are somewhat limited by standardized expiration dates and fixed notional sizes.

Fractional contracts are not allowed, so to fully hedge the risk the firm would buy either 201 or 202 contracts. In the over-the-counter market, customized products, such as forward agreements, can be used to specify a contract size exactly. The contract size problem is not the sole determinant of whether exchanged-listed or over-the-counter derivatives are chosen.

2.3 Equity Swap/Futures Examples

Equity swaps can be used to modify risk exposures, as we demonstrate in the next two subsections.

2.3.1 Equity Swap

In an **equity swap**, one party agrees to trade the return on a stock portfolio for the return on another asset.[9] This other asset might be another portfolio or a market index, or the swap might specify a set interest rate, such as Libor. The swap has a set tenor and may provide for one single payment at the end of the swap's life, although in most cases a series of periodic payments would be arranged. Equity swaps are created in the over-the-counter market, so they can be customized as desired. Consider an institutional investor that would like to temporarily remove $100 million in equities from its current equity exposure. The firm could enter into a six-month equity swap with one payment at termination, exchanging the total return on the underlying portfolio for six-month Libor, assumed to be 0.50%.[10] We will consider two scenarios: In the first, in six months the underlying portfolio is up 1%, and in the second, it is down 1%. Exhibit 2 shows the two situations.

Exhibit 2   Six-Month Equity Swap

Pay the return on a $100 million equity portfolio
Receive six-month Libor, assumed to be 0.50%

Scenario 1: Equity portfolio rises 1%

Pay: $100 million × 1% =	$1,000,000
Receive: $100 million × 0.50% × 0.50 =	250,000
Net payment =	$750,000

Scenario 2: Equity portfolio declines 1%

Pay: $100 million × –1% =	($1,000,000)
Receive: $100 million × 0.50% × 0.50 =	250,000
Net receipt =	$1,250,000

In the first scenario, the institutional investor would have an obligation to pay 1% × $100 million, or $1 million. On the Libor portion of the swap the investor would receive 0.50% × 0.50 × $100 million, or $250,000. The two parties would net the payments and provide for a single payment of $750,000, which the institutional investor would pay. The second scenario is slightly more complicated because the return the institutional investor must pay is *negative*, which means it will receive money both

---

9 The same principles discussed in this section apply to assets other than equities. When applied to bonds, loans, or an equity index, this arrangement may be called a "total return" swap.
10 This rate is stated on an annual basis, so for six months, one would earn half this amount.

from "paying" a negative return and from the Libor rate. It would receive $1 million from the "negative payment" and $250,000 from Libor, for a total of $1.25 million. At the end of the swap the institutional investor is in the same position in which it started, with the equity portfolio fully invested and again subject to market risk.

2.3.2 Stock Index Futures

Stock index futures are one of the most successful financial innovations of all time. The contract on the S&P 500's stock index began trading in 1982, and today this product is an indispensable tool for many money managers. Stock index futures differ from most other futures contracts in that they are **cash settled** at expiration. That is, it would not be feasible to actually transfer the underlying securities from one party to another, so instead the cash value changes hands. Rather than using the equity swap in the previous example, the institutional investor could temporarily remove market risk by selling stock index futures. If done in the correct quantity, this "short" position will largely offset the institution's long position.

One S&P 500 stock index futures contract is standardized as $250 times the index level. Assume that a one-month futures contract trades at 2,000.00 and that the portfolio carries average market risk, meaning a beta of 1.0.[11] To fully hedge the $100,000,000 portfolio, the portfolio manager would want to sell 200 contracts:

$$\frac{\$100,000,000}{(\$250 \times 2000.00)} = 200 \text{ contracts}$$

Suppose the S&P 500 stock index *rises* by 0.5% such that at the futures delivery time, the index is at 2,010.00. The institution sold the futures at 2,000.00 and cash settles the contract at 2,010.00. There is a "loss" of 10 index points, each point being worth $250, on 200 contracts for a total cash outflow of $500,000:

$$-10 \text{ points per contract} \times \$250 \text{ per point} \times 200 \text{ contracts} = \$500,000 \text{ loss}$$

If the stock index rises by 0.5%, the portfolio would also be expected to rise by this amount:

$$\$100,000,000 \times 0.5\% = \$500,000 \text{ gain}$$

If instead the market *fell* by 0.5%, the numbers would be the same, but the signs would change; there would be a $500,000 gain on the futures contract and a corresponding loss on the stock portfolio. Either way, the portfolio value is essentially "fixed" by selling the futures contracts. The market risk is hedged away.

EXAMPLE 1

Using Swaps to Manage Risk

1   A US bond portfolio manager who wants to hedge a bond portfolio against a potential rise in domestic interest rates could *best* hedge by:

   A   buying Treasury bond futures.

   B   paying a fixed rate in an interest rate swap.

   C   selling foreign currency futures on the home currency.

2   A typical currency swap used to hedge a bond portfolio differs from an interest rate swap with respect to the:

---

11 If the portfolio carried above market risk, say with a beta of 1.10, the number of contracts needed to hedge would increase by this factor. Similarly, a lower-risk portfolio would require proportionately fewer contracts.

    A tenor of the swap.

    B size of the initial cash flows.

    C presence of counterparty risk.

3 A stock portfolio manager who enters into a Libor-based equity swap and pays the equity return would owe money to the counterparty under which of the following conditions?

    A Portfolio return > Libor

    B Portfolio return = Libor

    C Portfolio return < minus Libor

Solution to 1:

B is correct. In an interest rate swap, if someone pays the fixed rate he or she would receive the floating rate. A floating-rate asset would most likely have a lower duration than a fixed-rate asset, and duration is a direct measure of interest rate risk. The swap would lower the portfolio duration.

Solution to 2:

B is correct. In an interest rate swap, there is no initial cash flow; the notional value is not exchanged. In a currency swap hedging a bond portfolio, both currencies change hands at the initiation and termination of the swap.

Solution to 3:

A is correct. The portfolio manager is agreeing to exchange the return on the portfolio for the Libor rate. If the portfolio earns more than Libor, the manager must remit the difference.

3   POSITION EQUIVALENCIES

It is useful to think of derivatives as building blocks that can be combined to create a particular end product with the desired risk exposure, much in the same way that a cook combines ingredients in preparing a meal. The risk manager's "spice rack" has puts and calls, each with many different expirations and exercise prices, as well as futures, forwards, and swaps. Often there is more than one way to create the desired risk–return exposure. Stated another way, certain collections of derivatives are economically equivalent to other assets or asset portfolios. A few of these relationships are especially important and are covered in the following pages.

3.1 Synthetic Long Asset

An outright long position in an asset is a common situation and easily understood. Suppose an investor buys shares of stock at a price of 50: She makes money when prices go up and is hurt when prices decline. What happens if she buys a call and writes a put, and both options have the same expiration date and the same exercise price of, say, 50?[12] Exhibit 3 shows the values of these two options and the overall position at expiration in comparison with the value of the stock at that same time.

---

[12] The exercise price is the price at which the option holder has the right to buy (with a call) or sell (with a put) and is also commonly called the *strike* or *striking* price. We will occasionally use terminology such as a "50-strike call" meaning a call option with an exercise price of 50.

Remember that at expiration, a call is worth the greater of zero or the stock price minus the exercise price, and a put is worth the greater of zero or the exercise price minus the stock price. This combination of options is equivalent to a long position in the stock and is often called a **synthetic long position**.[13]

Exhibit 3	Synthetic Long Position						
Stock price at expiration:	0	20	40	50	60	80	100
Alternative 1:							
Long 50-strike call payoff	0	0	0	0	10	30	50
Short 50-strike put payoff	−50	−30	−10	0	0	0	0
Total value	−50	−30	−10	0	10	30	50
Alternative 2: Long stock at 50							
Value	−50	−30	−10	0	10	30	50

The reason a long call and a short put synthetically replicate a long position in the underlying is that the long call creates the upside and the short put creates the downside of the underlying. The call exercises when the underlying is higher than the strike and turns into a synthetic position in the upside of the underlying. A short put obligates the writer to compensate the put buyer for downside moves by purchasing the stock at a higher price than its value. Thus, as a result of exercise by the buyer, a put writer incurs losses on the downside. These combined effects synthetically replicate the payoffs of the underlying.

3.2 Synthetic Short Asset

If instead of buying the call and writing the same-strike put to get a synthetic long stock position the investor did the opposite, logically the resulting position would be a **synthetic short position**. Indeed, that is exactly what happens, as Exhibit 4 shows. The explanation is the exact opposite of the explanation for the synthetic long.

Exhibit 4	Synthetic Short Position						
Stock price at expiration:	0	20	40	50	60	80	100
Alternative 1:							
Long 50-strike put payoff	50	30	10	0	0	0	0
Short 50-strike call payoff	0	0	0	0	−10	−30	−50
Total payoff	50	30	10	0	−10	−30	−50
Alternative 2: Short stock at 50							
Payoff	50	30	10	0	−10	−30	−50

---

13 Technically, the position is not precisely equal to a long position in a stock. From put–call parity, a long position in a stock equals a long call, short put, and a long position in a risk-free zero-coupon bond. With the options strategy, you must pay the exercise price at expiration, whereas with the stock strategy, the analog is the value of the stock price when the options are put in place. Adding a zero-coupon bond to the options strategy or setting the present value of the exercise price to the stock price would make it precisely the same as the stock strategy.

3.3 Synthetic Assets with Futures/Forwards

One very common use of futures or forward contracts is to eliminate future price risk. Consider an investor who owns a dividend-paying stock and wants to lock in a future selling price. The investor might enter into a forward or futures contract requiring him to deliver the shares at a future date in exchange for a cash amount determined today. Because the initial and final stock prices are known, this investment should earn the risk-free rate. What actually happens is that the dividends earned on the stock plus the return from the forward or futures contract together equal the risk-free rate. Thinking of this as an equation, Long stock + Short futures = Risk-free rate, or rearranging the equation, Stock − Futures = Risk-free rate.[14] This strategy is sometimes called a "synthetic risk-free rate," or occasionally "synthetic cash."

This result also means that someone can create a synthetic long position by investing in the risk-free asset and using the remaining funds to margin a long futures position: Stock = Risk-free rate + Futures.

3.4 Synthetic Put

When the Chicago Board Options Exchange opened in 1973, there were exchange-traded calls but no puts. Regulators were concerned about approving a financial instrument that benefited from falling prices. Informed market participants, however, knew that a put could easily be created by combining a short stock position with a long call. Suppose, for instance, an investor wants a put with an exercise price of 50. Exhibit 5 shows the payoffs from the put at various stock prices at option expiration, along with the payoffs from a stock shorted at a price of 50 and held simultaneously with a long call with an exercise price of 50. Regardless of the stock price at option expiration, the two alternatives have the same economic characteristics.[15]

Exhibit 5 Synthetic Put							
Stock price at expiration:	0	20	40	50	60	80	100
Alternative 1: Long 50-strike put							
Payoff	50	30	10	0	0	0	0
Alternative 2: Short stock at 50; buy 50-strike call							
Profit from short stock	50	30	10	0	−10	−30	−50
Payoff from long call	0	0	0	0	10	30	50
Net payoff	50	30	10	0	0	0	0

The creation of synthetic puts was widespread in the early days of option trading, and in 1975 the regulatory authorities allowed a pilot project authorizing puts on 25 different underlying stock issues. These puts were actively traded, no major problems

14 When the underlying asset on the futures contract is an equity security, the asset may pay dividends. If the dividend yield on the stock is higher than the interest rate, the futures price will be less than the spot price. The futures price will rise to converge at the spot price at the end of the futures contract, resulting in a loss on the short futures position. This loss offsets part of the gain from the dividend yield. Regardless, if held to the delivery date, the long stock/short futures position nets the risk-free interest rate.
15 As discussed in an earlier footnote, the addition of a risk-free bond is technically required to make the alternatives precisely equal, but they do have the same economic characteristics.

were caused, and the exchanges gradually were able to increase the number of listed puts. Nonetheless, it is important to know how to synthetically replicate a put because mispricing may make a replicated put cheaper or more expensive than a direct put.

3.5 Synthetic Call

In similar fashion, an investor can replicate a call from a long stock position combined with a long put. See Exhibit 6. The long put eliminates much of the downside risk whereas the long stock leaves the profit potential unlimited. As will be shown shortly, the popular "protective put" strategy has a profit and loss diagram similar to that of a long call.

Exhibit 6	Synthetic Call						
Stock price at expiration:	0	20	40	50	60	80	100
Alternative 1: Long 50-strike call							
Payoff	0	0	0	0	10	30	50
Alternative 2:Long stock at 50; buy 50-strike put							
Profit from long stock	−50	−30	−10	0	10	30	50
Payoff from long put	50	30	10	0	0	0	0
Net payoff	0	0	0	0	10	30	50

3.6 Foreign Currency Options

Suppose the treasurer of a multinational corporation with the euro as the home currency has an obligation to pay ¥145 million in one month. This obligation might arise, for example, from a commitment to purchase some Japanese products. The treasurer wants to protect against an appreciation of the yen relative to the euro, but at the same time does not want to lock in the exchange rate because of a belief that the yen may depreciate. Because the obligation is denominated in yen, however, the nature of the problem requires careful attention. Suppose the spot exchange rate is EUR/JPY = 136.99.[16] If the yen appreciates, this number will go down, and if the yen depreciates, this number will go up.

An appreciating yen means the euro is weakening and thus the home currency, the euro, would buy fewer yen. A futures contract or a forward contract could eliminate the risk but would also eliminate the potential for gains if the yen depreciates. With forwards or futures, the returns are symmetrical around the fixed price, but with options, only one side of the return distribution is affected. If the treasurer wants to benefit from an appreciating yen but not be locked in to a fixed rate, as with a futures or forward, he might buy a one-month call option on yen. Because the spot rate is quoted in yen, the strike will typically be quoted in yen.

Now, perhaps seemingly strange, we have a situation in which the treasurer would exercise the call option when the spot rate at expiration is *below* the strike. For example, at the strike rate of ¥136.99, exercise would require that the treasurer deliver ¥145 million/¥136.99 = €1,058,471 to obtain the necessary yen. If the spot rate at expiration rises to ¥140, a weakening of the yen (strengthening of the euro), he could deliver ¥145 million/¥140 = €1,035,714 to obtain the yen cheaper in the

---

16 This quote convention means that one euro is worth 136.99 yen.

spot market—that is, without exercising the call. If the spot rate at expiration falls to ¥130, a strengthening of the yen (weakening of the euro), he would have to deliver ¥145 million/¥130 = €1,115,385 to obtain the necessary yen in the market. Clearly it would be cheaper to exercise the option, thereby paying €1,058,471 to get the yen.

Note that the treasurer would exercise the foreign currency call when the yen was below the strike, but that is because the yen is quoted in relation to the euro in terms of yen per euro. This fact connects us to an important point about foreign currency options. A foreign currency call option always has a put option that is an identical twin. Instead of the yen call, suppose the treasurer had purchased an at-the-money put on €1,058,471 with the same expiration and exercise price as the call. This gives him the right to deliver euros in exchange for yen. This put option provides for exactly the same cash flows as the call option in the same circumstances. If he exercises his right to sell euros, he would deliver €1,058,471 and receive ¥145,000,000.

In either case, after receiving the ¥145,000,000 from the option counterparty the treasurer would use it to cover the company's obligation. With a set exercise price, the right to deliver euros in exchange for yen is exactly the same as the right to buy yen in exchange for euros.[17]

EXAMPLE 2

Option Position Equivalencies

1 Which of the following is *most* similar to a long put position?

  A Buy stock, write call

  B Short stock, buy call

  C Short stock, write call

2 Which of the following is *most* similar to a long call position?

  A Buy stock, buy put

  B Buy stock, write put

  C Short stock, write put

3 Which option portfolio with the same exercise price for both options is *most* similar to a long stock position?

  A Short call, long put

  B Long call, short put

  C Short call, short put

Solution to 1:

B is correct. The long call "cuts off" the unlimited losses from the short stock position.

Solution to 2:

A is correct. The long put provides a floor value to the position, making the maximum loss flat below the exercise price. The profit and loss diagram is the same shape as a long call.

---

17 This mirror-image nature of puts and calls is actually true for any underlying asset. A call giving the holder the right to buy stock can also be thought of as a put giving the right to sell a currency in exchange for stock. Such an arrangement would imply thinking of that currency as being worth a certain number of shares of stock. For example, we could say that a stock priced at €50 implies that €1 = 1/50 = 0.02 share. This is an unconventional way of thinking about stock, bonds, or commodities, but is perfectly natural for currencies.

Solution to 3:

B is correct. When both options have the same exercise price, a short put and long call produce a profit and loss diagram that is the same as a long stock position.

COVERED CALLS AND PROTECTIVE PUTS

4

Writing a **covered call** is a very common option strategy used by both individual and institutional investors. In this strategy, someone who already owns shares sells a call option giving someone else the right to buy their shares at the exercise price.[18] The investor owns the shares and has taken on the potential obligation to deliver the shares to the option buyer and accept the exercise price as the price at which he sells the shares. For his willingness to do this, the investor receives the premium on the option.

When someone simultaneously holds a long position in an asset and a long position in a put option on that asset, the put is often called a **protective put**. The name comes from the fact that the put protects against losses in the value of the underlying asset.

The examples that follow use the convention of identifying an option by the underlying asset, expiration, exercise price, and option type. For example, in Exhibit 7, the PBR October 16 call option sells for 1.42. The underlying asset is Petróleo Brasileiro (PBR) common stock, the expiration is October, the exercise price is 16, the option is a call, and the call price is 1.42. It is important to note that even though we will refer to this as the October 16 option, it does not expire on 16 October; 16 is the price at which the call owner has the right to buy, otherwise known as the exercise price or strike.

PBR	October	16	Call
Underlying asset	*expiration*	*exercise price*	*option type*

On some exchanges, certain options may have weekly expirations in addition to a monthly expiration, which means investors need to be careful in specifying the option of interest. For a given underlying asset and exercise price, there may be several weekly and one monthly option expiring in October. The examples that follow all assume a single monthly expiration.

4.1 Investment Objectives of Covered Calls

Consider the option data in Exhibit 7. Suppose there is one month until the September expiration. By convention, option listings show data for a single call or put, but in practice the smallest trading unit for an exchange-traded option is one contract covering 100 shares. Consider three different market participants that might logically use covered calls.

---

[18] If someone creates a call without owning the underlying asset, it is a *naked* call.

Exhibit 7		PBR Option Premiums: Current PBR share price = 15.84					
Calls			**Exercise Price**	**Puts**			
SEP	**OCT**	**NOV**		**SEP**	**OCT**	**NOV**	
1.64	1.95	2.44	15	0.65	0.99	1.46	
0.97	1.42	1.90	16	1.14	1.48	1.96	
0.51	1.02	1.44	17	1.76	2.09	2.59	

4.1.1 *Market Participant #1: Income Generation*

The most common motivation for writing covered calls is income generation. When someone writes an option they keep the option premium regardless of what happens in the future. Some investors view this premium as an additional source of income in the same way they view cash dividends. It is important to recognize that when someone writes a call option, however, he is essentially selling part of the return distribution associated with the underlying asset. See the illustration of the return distribution in Exhibit 8. The largest returns are those on the far right of the distribution. Someone who writes a call with an exercise price of 17 is giving up all returns above the strike price in exchange for the option premium. So, in Exhibit 8, the portion of the underlying return distribution that lies above a stock price of 17 belongs to the call buyer.

Perhaps an individual investor owns PBR and believes the stock price is likely to remain relatively flat over the next few months. With the stock currently trading at just under 16, the investor might think it unlikely that the stock will rise above 17. Exhibit 7 shows that the premium for a call option expiring in September with an exercise price of 17, referred to as the SEP 17 call, is 0.51. He could write that call and receive this premium. Alternatively, he could write a different call, say the NOV 17 call and receive 1.44. There is a clear trade-off between the size of the option premium and the likelihood of option exercise. The option writer would get more income from writing the longer-term option, but there is a greater chance that the option would move in the money, resulting in the option being exercised by the buyer and, therefore, the stock being called away from the writer.

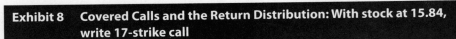

Exhibit 8   Covered Calls and the Return Distribution: With stock at 15.84, write 17-strike call

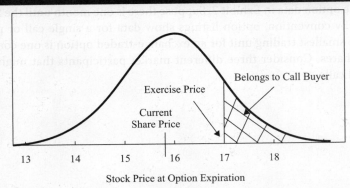

Stock Price at Option Expiration

Although it may be acceptable to think of the option premium as income, it is important to remember that the call writer has given up the most desirable part of the expected return distribution. For someone who believes significant price increases in the underlying are unlikely over the option's life, however, writing covered calls can be very attractive.

4.1.2 *Market Participant #2: Improving on the Market*

Next, consider Sofia Porto, a retail portfolio manager with a portfolio that has become overweight in energy companies. She wants to reduce this imbalance. She holds 5,000 shares of PBR, an energy company, and she expects the price of this stock to remain relatively stable over the next month. Porto might decide to write 10 exchange-traded PBR SEP 15 call contracts. This means she is creating 10 option contracts, each of which covers 100 shares. These 10 contracts give the buyer the right to purchase 1,000 shares of PBR stock at 15 per share anytime between the time of purchase and expiration in September. In exchange for this contingent claim, she receives the option premium of 1.64/call × 100 calls/contract × 10 contracts = 1,640. This income remains in her account regardless of what happens to the future PBR stock price or whether or not the option is exercised by its holder. Because the current PBR stock price (15.84) is above the exercise price of 15, the options she wrote are in the money. Given her expectation that the stock price will be stable over the next month, there is a high likelihood that the option will be exercised: The holder of the right to buy at 15 will certainly exercise this right if the option is in the money at the September option expiration. Because Porto wants to reduce the overweighting in energy stocks, this outcome is desirable. If the option is exercised, she has effectively sold the stock at 16.64. She gets 1.64 when she writes the option, and she gets 15 when the option is exercised. She could have simply sold the shares at their original price of 15.84, but in this specific situation the option strategy gave her an additional 800, or 5%, in a month's time.[19]

The option premium is composed of two parts: exercise value (also called intrinsic value) and time value.[20] Exercise value is the price advantage the option gives the buyer. In this case, the right to buy at 15 when the stock price is 15.84 is clearly worth 0.84. The option premium is 1.64, which is 0.80 more than the exercise value. This difference of 0.80 is called time value. Someone who writes covered calls to improve on the market is capturing the time value, which augments the stock selling price. Remember, though, that giving up part of the return distribution would result in an opportunity loss if the underlying goes up.

4.1.3 *Market Participant #3: Target Price Realization*

A third popular use of options is really a hybrid of the first two objectives. This strategy involves writing calls with an exercise price near the target price for the stock. Suppose a bank trust department holds PBR in many of its accounts and that its research team believes the stock would be properly priced at 16/share, which is just slightly higher than its current price. In those accounts for which the investment policy statement permits option activity, the manager might choose to write near-term calls with an exercise price near the target price, 16 in this case. Suppose an account holds 500 shares of PBR. Writing 5 SEP 16 call contracts at 0.97 brings in 485 in cash. If the stock is

---

19 Her effective selling price of 16.64 is 0.80 higher than the original price of 15.84: 0.80/15.84 = 5.05%.
20 Although the term "intrinsic value" is widely used among option practitioners, it is an unfortunate word choice. Those familiar with option pricing know that in the absence of arbitrage even an out-of-the-money option must have a certain positive value, but in practice that is not called intrinsic value. In addition to exercise value, some use the term "economic value" for intrinsic value because it is the value of the option if the investor were to exercise it at this very moment and trade out of the stock position.

above 16 in a month, the stock will be sold at its target price, with the option premium adding an additional 6% positive return to the account.[21] If PBR fails to rise to 16, the manager might write a new OCT expiration call with the same objective in mind.

Although popular, the investor should not view this strategy as a source of free money. The stock is currently very close to the target price, and the manager could simply sell it and be satisfied. Although the covered call writing program potentially adds to the return, there is also the chance that the stock could experience bad news or the overall market might pull back, resulting in an opportunity loss relative to the outright sale of the stock. The investor also would have an opportunity loss if the stock rises sharply above the exercise price and it was called away at a lower-than-market price.

4.1.4 Profit and Loss at Expiration

In the process of learning option strategies, it is always helpful to look at a graphical display of the profit and loss possibilities at the option expiration. Suppose an investor owns PBR, currently trading at 15.84, and chooses to write the NOV 17 call at 1.44. If the stock is above 17 at expiration, the option holder will exercise the call option and the investor will deliver the shares in exchange for the exercise price of 17. The maximum gain with a covered call is the appreciation to the exercise price plus the option premium.[22]

Some symbols will be helpful in learning these relationships:

S_0 = Stock price when option position opened
S_T = Stock price at option expiration
X = Option exercise price
c_0 = Call premium received or paid

The maximum gain = $(X - S_0) + c_0$. With a starting price of 15.84, a sale price of 17 results in 1.16 of price appreciation. The option writer would keep the option premium of 1.44 for a total gain of 1.16 + 1.44 = 2.60. This is the maximum gain from this strategy because all price appreciation above 17 belongs to the call holder. The call writer keeps the option premium regardless of what the stock does, so if it were to drop, the overall loss is reduced by the option premium received. Exhibit 9 shows the situation. The breakeven price for a covered call is the stock price minus the premium, or $S_0 - c_0$. In other words, the breakeven point occurs when the stock falls by the premium received; in this example, 15.84 − 1.44 = 14.40. The maximum loss would occur if the stock became worthless; it equals the original stock price minus the option premium received, or $S_0 - c_0$.[23] In this single unlikely scenario, the investor would lose 15.84 on the stock position, but still keep the premium of 1.44 for a total loss of 14.40.

At option expiration, the *value* of the covered call position is the stock price minus the exercise value of the call. Any appreciation beyond the exercise price belongs to the option buyer, so the covered call writer does not earn any gains beyond that point. Symbolically,

Covered call expiration value = $S_T - Max[(S_T - X),0]$

The *profit* at option expiration is the covered call value plus the option premium received minus the original price of the stock:

Covered call profit at expiration = $S_T - Max[(S_T - X,0]) + c_0 - S_0$

---

21 Relative to a stock price of 16, the option premium of 0.97 is 0.97/16 = 6.06%.
22 If someone writes an in-the-money covered call, there is "depreciation" to the exercise price, so the difference would be subtracted. For instance, if the stock price is 50 and a 45 call sells for 7, the maximum gain is (45 − 50) + 7 = 2.
23 Note that with a covered call, the breakeven price and the maximum loss are the same value.

In summary:

Maximum gain = $(X - S_0) + c_0$

Maximum loss = $S_0 - c_0$

Breakeven point = $S_0 - c_0$

Expiration value = $S_T - Max[(S_T - X,0]$

Profit at expiration = $S_T - Max[(S_T - X),0]_+ c_0 - S_0$

Exhibit 9 Covered Call Profit and Loss Diagram: With stock at 15.84, write 17 call at 1.44

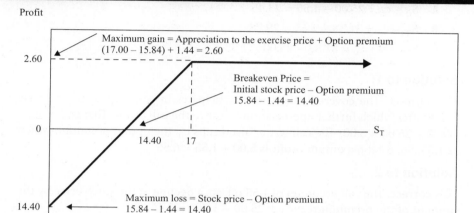

It is important to remember that these profit and loss diagrams depict the situation only at the end of the option's life.[24] Most equity covered call writing occurs with exchange-traded options, so the call writer always has the ability to buy the option back before expiration. If, for instance, the PBR stock price were to decline by one shortly after writing the covered call, the call value would most likely also decline. If this investor believed the decline was temporary, he might buy the call back at the new lower option premium, making a profit on that trade, and then write the option again after the share price recovered.

EXAMPLE 3

Characteristics of Covered Calls

S_0 = Stock price when option position opened = 25.00

X = Option exercise price = 30.00

S_T = Stock price at option expiration = 31.33

c_0 = Call premium received = 1.55

1 Which of the following correctly calculates the maximum profit from writing a covered call?

---

24 It is also important to note that the general shape of the profit and loss diagram for a covered call is the same as that of writing a put. Covered call writing is the most common use of options by individual investors, whereas writing puts is the least common.

A $(S_T - X) + c_0 = 31.33 - 30.00 + 1.55 = 2.88$

B $(S_T - S_0) - c_0 = 31.33 - 25.00 - 1.55 = 4.78$

C $(X - S_0) + c_0 = 30.00 - 25.00 + 1.55 = 6.55$

2 Which of the following correctly calculates the breakeven stock price from writing a covered call?

   A $S_0 - c_0 = 25.00 - 1.55 = 23.45$

   B $S_T - c_0 = 31.33 - 1.55 = 29.78$

   C $X + c_0 = 30.00 + 1.55 = 31.55$

3 Which of the following correctly calculates the maximum loss from writing a covered call?

   A $S_0 - c_0 = 25.00 - 1.55 = 23.45$

   B $S_T - c_0 = 31.33 - 1.55 = 29.78$

   C $S_T - X + c_0 = 31.33 - 25.00 + 1.55 = 7.88$

Solution to 1:

C is correct. The covered call writer participates in gains up to the exercise price, after which further appreciation is lost to the call buyer. That is, $X - S_0 = 30.00 - 25.00 = 5.00$. The call writer also keeps c_0, the option premium, which is 1.55. So, total maximum profit is $5.00 + 1.55 = 6.55$.

Solution to 2:

A is correct. The call premium of 1.55 offsets a decline in the stock price by the amount of the premium received: $25.00 - 1.55 = 23.45$.

Solution to 3:

A is correct. The stock price can fall to zero, causing a loss of the entire investment, but the option writer still gets to keep the option premium received: $25.00 - 1.55 = 23.45$

4.2 Investment Objective of Protective Puts

The primary motivation for the purchase of a protective put is to protect against loss when the asset falls in value. A protective put is similar to buying insurance, as we shall see in the next section.

4.2.1 Protecting Profits

Suppose a portfolio manager has a client with a 50,000 share position in PBR. His research suggests there may be a negative shock to the stock price in the next four to six weeks, and he wants to guard against a price decline. Buying a put while owning the stock is analogous to buying insurance. See Exhibit 10.

Exhibit 10   Protective Put and Insurance Analogies

Insurance Policy	Put Option
Premium	Time value
Value of asset	Price of stock
Face value	Exercise price

Insurance Policy	Put Option
Term of policy	Time until option expiration
Likelihood of loss	Volatility of stock

As with insurance policies, a put implies a deductible, which is the amount of the loss the insured is willing to bear. In this analogy, the stock price minus the exercise price is the deductible. [25]

With PBR stock at 15.84, Exhibit 7 indicates the portfolio manager could buy a one-month (SEP) 15-strike put for 0.65. This option is out of the money, so the premium is entirely time value. In this example, the deductible is 15.84 − 15.00 = 0.84. In other words, the stock can fall by 0.84 and the stock holder suffers this loss, but once the stock falls to 15.00 the put becomes valuable and offsets further losses on the stock. See Exhibit 11, which shows how the put cuts off the lower part of the return distribution. The protective put insures against the portion of the underlying return distribution that is below 15. Alternatively, the portfolio manager could buy a two-month option, paying 0.99 for an OCT 15 put, or he could buy a three-month option, paying 1.46 for a NOV 15 put. Note that there is not a linear relationship between the put value and its time until expiration. A two-month option does not sell for twice the price of a one-month option, nor does a three-month option sell for three times the price of a one-month option. The portfolio manager can also reduce the cost of insurance by increasing the size of the deductible, perhaps by using a put option with a 14 exercise price. A put option with an exercise price of 14 would have a lower premium, but would not protect against losses in the stock until it falls to 14.00 per share. The option price is cheaper, but on a 50,000 share position, the deductible would be 50,000 more than if the exercise price of 15 were selected.

Because of the uncertainty about the timing of the "shock event" he anticipates, the manager might decide to buy the NOV 15 put. Here is why. If he were to buy the cheaper SEP put, there is a good chance this option would expire before the anticipated stock price shock occurred. Given the four- to six-week time horizon, the OCT put would be appropriate, but there is still the potential to lose the premium without realizing any benefit. With a 0.99 premium for the OCT 15 put and 50,000 shares to protect, the cost to the account would be almost 50,000. The advantage of the NOV option is that although it is more expensive, it has the greater likelihood of not having expired before the news hits. As the stock drops, the value of the put would increase. Although he could hold onto the put position until its expiration, he might find it preferable to close out the option prior to maturity and recover some of the premium paid.[26]

---

25 Unlike typical insurance policies, however, it is possible to use a put to insure an asset for more than its current value. One simply sets the exercise price higher than the current stock price. Such a put will have a higher price.

26 A price shock to the underlying asset might increase the market's expectations of future volatility, thereby likely increasing the put premium. By selling the option early, the investor would capture this increase. Also, once the adverse event occurred, there may not be a reason to continue to hold the insurance policy. If the investor no longer needs it, he should cancel it and get part of the purchase price back. In other words, he should sell the put and recapture some of its cost.

Exhibit 11   Protective Puts and the Return Distribution

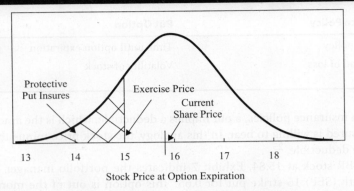

4.2.2 *Profit and Loss at Expiration*

Exhibit 12 shows the profit and loss diagram for the protective put.[27] The stock can rise to any level, and the position would benefit fully from the appreciation; the maximum gain is unlimited. On the downside, losses are "cut off" once the stock price falls to the exercise price. With a protective put, the maximum loss is the depreciation to the exercise price plus the premium paid, or $S_0 - X + p_0$. At the option expiration, the value of the protective put is the greater of the stock price or the exercise price. The reason is because the stock can rise to any level but has a floor value of the put exercise price. In symbols, the value of the combination of put and stock at expiration = $Max(S_T,X)$. The profit or loss at expiration is the ending value minus the beginning value. The initial value of the protective put is the starting stock price plus the put premium. In symbols, Profit of protective put at expiration = $Max(S_T,X) - S_0 - p_0$.

Exhibit 12   Protective Put Profit and Loss Diagram: With stock at 15.84, buy 15 put at 1.46

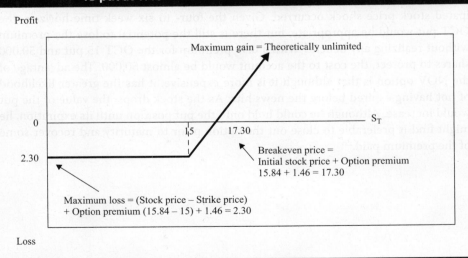

---

[27] Note that the profit and loss diagram for a protective put has a shape similar to a long call position, which is the result of put–call parity. Long the asset and long the put is equivalent to long a call plus long a risk-free bond. The bond has no impact on the shape of the profit and loss diagram.

In order to break even, the underlying asset must rise by enough to offset the price of the put that was purchased. The breakeven point is the initial stock price plus the option premium. In symbols, Breakeven point = $S_0 + p_0$.

In summary:

Maximum profit = $S_T - S_0 - p_0$ = Unlimited

Maximum loss = $S_0 - X + p_0$

Breakeven point = $S_0 + p_0$

Expiration value = $Max(S_T, X)$

Profit at expiration = $Max(S_T, X) - S_0 - p_0$

EXAMPLE 4

Characteristics of Protective Puts

S_0 = Stock price when option position opened = 25.00

X = Option exercise price = 20.00

S_T = Stock price at option expiration = 31.33

p_0 = Put premium paid = 1.15

1 Which of the following correctly calculates the profit with the protective put?

   A $S_T - S_0 - p_0 = 31.33 - 25.00 - 1.15 = 5.18$

   B $S_T - S_0 + p_0 = 31.33 - 25.00 + 1.15 = 7.48$

   C $S_T - X - p_0 = 31.33 - 20.00 - 1.15 = 10.18$

2 Which of the following correctly calculates the breakeven stock price with the protective put?

   A $S_0 - p_0 = 25.00 - 1.15 = 23.85$

   B $S_0 + p_0 = 25.00 + 1.15 = 26.15$

   C $S_T + p_0 = 31.33 - 1.15 = 30.18$

3 Which of the following correctly calculates the maximum loss with the protective put?

   A $S_0 - X + p_0 = 25.00 - 20.00 + 1.15 = 6.15$

   B $S_T - X - p_0 = 31.33 - 20.00 - 1.15 = 10.18$

   C $S_0 - p_0 = 25.00 - 1.15 = 23.85$

Solution to 1:

A is correct. If the stock price is above the put exercise price at expiration, the put will expire worthless. The profit is the gain on the stock ($S_T - S_0$) minus the cost of the put. Note that the maximum profit with a protective put is theoretically unlimited because the stock can rise to any level, and the entire profit is earned by the stockholder.

Solution to 2:

B is correct. Because the option buyer pays the put premium, he does not begin to make money until the stock rises by enough to recover the premium paid.

> **Solution to 3:**
>
> A is correct. Once the stock falls to the put exercise price, further losses are eliminated. The investor paid the option premium, so the total loss is the "deductible" plus the cost of the insurance.

4.3 Equivalence to Long Asset/Short Forward Position

All investors who consider option strategies should understand that some options are more sensitive to changes in the underlying asset than others. This relationship is measured by **delta**, an indispensable tool to a sophisticated options user. Delta measures how the option price changes as the underlying asset price changes.[28] Because a call increases in value and a put decreases in value as the underlying asset increases in price, call deltas range from 0 to 1 and put deltas range from 0 to −1. A long position in the underlying asset has a delta of 1.0, whereas a short position has a delta of −1.0. A rough rule of thumb is that an at-the-money option will have a delta that is approximately 0.5 (for a call) or −0.5 (for a put).

Suppose on the Tokyo Stock Exchange, Honda Motor Company stock sells for ¥3,500. A portfolio contains 100 shares, and the manager writes one exchange-traded covered call contract with a ¥3,500 strike. Because the call is at the money, meaning that the stock price and exercise price are equal, it will have a delta of about 0.5. The portfolio, however, is not long the call. The manager wrote it, and someone else owns it. From the portfolio's perspective, the delta is −0.5. A short call *loses* money as the underlying price rises. So, this covered call has an overall or **position delta** of 50: 100 points for the stock and −50 for the short call. Compare this call with a protective put in which someone buys 100 shares of stock and one contract of an at-the-money put. Its position delta would also be 50: 100 points for the stock and −50 points for the long put.

Finally, consider a long stock position of 100 shares and a short forward position of 50 shares. Because futures and forwards are essentially proxies for the stock, their deltas are also 1.0 for a long position and −1.0 for a short position. In this example, the short forward position "cancels" half the long stock position, so the position delta is also 50. These examples show three different positions: an at-the-money covered call, an at-the-money protective put, and a long stock/short forward position that all have the same delta. For small movements in the price of the underlying asset, these positions will show very similar gains and losses.

4.4 Writing Cash-Secured Puts

If someone writes a put option and simultaneously deposits an amount of money equal to the exercise price into a designated account, it is called writing a **cash-secured put**.[29] This strategy is appropriate for someone who is bullish on a stock or who wants to acquire shares at a particular price. The fact that the option exercise price is escrowed provides assurance that the put writer will be able to purchase the stock if the option holder chooses to exercise. Think of the cash in a cash-secured put as being similar to the stock part of a covered call. When an investor sells a call, she takes on the obligation to sell a stock, and this obligation is covered by ownership

---

28 Delta is the calculus first derivative of the option price with respect to the underlying asset price.
29 This strategy is also called a *fiduciary put*. When someone writes a put but does not escrow the exercise price, it is sometimes called a *naked put*. Note that this is a slightly different use of the adjective "naked" than with a naked call. When writing a naked call, the call writer does not have the underlying *asset* to deliver if the call is exercised. When an investor writes a naked put, the investor has not set aside the *cash* necessary to buy the asset if the put is exercised.

in the shares. When a put option is sold to create a new position, the obligation that accompanies this position is to purchase shares. In order to cover the obligation to purchase shares, the portfolio should have enough cash in the account to make good on this obligation. The short put position is covered or secured by cash in the account.

Now consider two slightly different scenarios using the price data from Exhibit 7. One investor might be bullish on PBR and, with the stock at 15.84, believes it very likely that the stock will remain above 15 at the September option expiration. Suppose the investor writes the SEP 15 put for 0.65. As is always the case, the investor will keep the option premium regardless of what the stock price does. If, as expected, the stock is above 15 at expiration, the option holder will not want to sell at the lower price, so the put option will expire unexercised. If the stock is below 15 at expiration, the put would be exercised and the option writer would be obliged to purchase shares at the exercise price of 15. Netting out the option premium means that the effective purchase price would be 15 − 0.65 = 14.35.

In another scenario, an institutional investor might be interested in purchasing PBR. Suppose the investor wrote the SEP 17 put for 1.76. If the stock is below 17 at expiration, the puts will be exercised and the investor would pay 17 for the shares, resulting in a net price of 17 − 1.76 = 15.24. Anytime someone writes an option, the maximum gain is the option premium received, so in this case, the maximum gain is 1.76. The maximum loss when writing a put occurs when the stock falls to zero. The option writer pays the exercise price for worthless stock, but still keeps the premium. In this example, the maximum loss would be 17 − 1.76 = 15.24. Exhibit 13 shows the corresponding profit and loss diagram.

Exhibit 13   Short Put Profit and Loss Diagram: Write SEP 17 put at 1.76

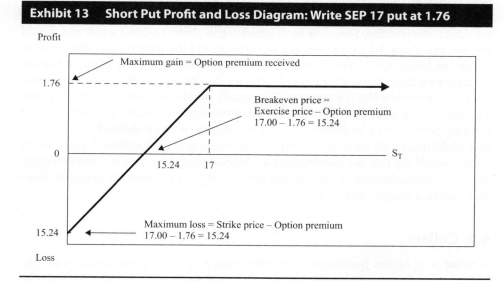

Note the similar shape of the covered call position in Exhibit 9 and the short put in Exhibit 13. Writing a covered call and writing a put are very similar with regard to their risk and reward characteristics.[30]

---

30 The two strategies are very similar because of put–call parity.

4.5 The Risk of Covered Calls and Protective Puts

Some market observers believe that any derivative activity is inherently risky and inappropriate in accounts with conservative objectives. It is easy to show that this belief is not true.

4.5.1 Covered Calls

Consider the individual who owns 100 shares of a stock, with a position delta of 100. Suppose the investor now writes calls against this entire position, and suppose that each of these options has a delta of 0.4. This covered call position has a position delta of $(100 \times 1.0) - (100 \times 0.4) = 60$. A position delta of 60 is equivalent to owning 60 shares of the underlying asset. An investor can lose more money on a 100-share position than on a 60-share position. Even if the stock declines to nearly zero, the loss is less with the covered call because the option writer always gets to keep the option premium. Viewed this way, the covered call position is less risky than the underlying asset held alone.

There is, however, an important aspect of risk with covered calls. This is the risk that the underlying asset moves substantially above the option exercise price, in which case there can be a significant opportunity cost. Remember Exhibit 8 and the implication the short call has on the return distribution. The call writer sells the potential for "big gains" to the option buyer and is likely to experience regret if the stock price advances sharply. When the share price is 100, having to sell at 75 is not pleasant.

4.5.2 Protective Puts

Similar logic applies to the use of protective puts. An investor who buys a put is essentially buying insurance on the stock. The put provides protection from the left tail of the return distribution. Someone buys insurance to protect against a risk and should not feel bad if the risk event does not materialize and the policyholder does not get to use the insurance. Stated another way, a homeowner should be happy if the fire insurance on their house goes unused. Still, we do not want to buy insurance we do not need, especially if it is expensive. Continually purchasing puts to protect against a possible stock price decline is an expensive strategy that would wipe out most of the long-term gain on an otherwise good investment. If risk is defined as something that could negatively affect the ability to achieve long-term investment goals, many people would say that the continuous purchase of protective puts is a risky strategy. The occasional purchase of a protective put to deal with a temporary situation, however, can be a sensible risk-reducing activity.

4.6 Collars

A **collar** is an option position in which the investor is long shares of stock and then buys a put with an exercise price below the current stock price and writes a call with an exercise price above the current stock price.[31] Collars allow a shareholder to acquire downside protection through a protective put but reduce the cash outlay by writing a covered call. By carefully selecting the options, an investor can often offset most of the put premium paid by the call premium received. In Exhibit 7, for instance, the

---

31 A collar is also called a *fence* or a *hedge wrapper*. In a foreign exchange transaction, it might be called a *risk reversal*.

NOV 15 put costs 1.46 and the NOV 17 call is 1.44, very nearly the same. A collar written in the over-the-counter market can be easily structured to provide a precise offset of the put premium with the call premium.[32]

4.6.1 *Collars on an Existing Holding*

Consider the risk–return trade-off for a shareholder who previously bought PBR stock at 12 and now buys the NOV 15 put for 1.46 and simultaneously writes the NOV 17 covered call for 1.44. Exhibit 14 shows a profit and loss worksheet for the three positions. Exhibit 15 shows the profit and loss diagram.

Exhibit 14	Collar Profit and Loss Worksheet: Stock purchased at 12, NOV 15 put purchased at 1.46, NOV 17 call written at 1.44					
Stock price at expiration →	**5**	**10**	**15**	**16**	**17**	**20**
Profit/loss from long stock	−7.00	−2.00	3.00	4.00	5.00	8.00
Profit/loss from long 15 put	8.54	3.54	−1.46	−1.46	−1.46	−1.46
Profit/loss from short 17 call	1.44	1.44	1.44	1.44	1.44	−1.56
Total	2.98	2.98	2.98	3.98	4.98	4.98

At or below the put exercise price of 15, the collar locks in a profit of 2.98. At or above the call exercise price of 17, the profit is constant at 4.98.

In this example, because the stock price had appreciated before establishing the collar, the position locks in a profit of at least 2.98. Investors typically establish a collar on a position that is already outstanding.

---

32 Most collars are structured so that the call and put premiums completely offset each other. If the investor starts with the put at a specific exercise price, he then sells a call that has the same premium. There is one specific call with the same premium, and it has a particular exercise price, which is above the exercise price of the put. An algorithm can be used to search for the exercise price on the call that has the same premium as that of the put, which is then the call that the investor should sell. Most collars are done in the over-the-counter market because the exercise price on the call must be a specific one. Exchange-traded options have standardized exercise prices, whereas the exercise prices of over-the-counter options can be set at whatever the investor wants.

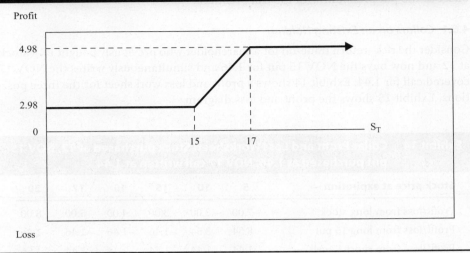

Exhibit 15   Collar Profit and Loss Diagram: Stock purchased at 12, NOV 15 put purchased at 1.46, NOV 17 call written at 1.44

4.6.2 Same-Strike Collar

What happens if an investor combines a same-strike collar with a long position in the underlying asset? Exhibit 16 shows that regardless of the stock price at option expiration, the combined position is worth the option exercise price. There is essentially no risk, and the position is protected from a decline in market value. As previously shown, long a put and short a call is a synthetic short position. When a long position is combined with a synthetic short position, logically the risk is completely neutralized.

Exhibit 16   Long Position plus Same-Strike Collar

Stock price at expiration →	0	20	40	50	60	80	100
Long 50-strike put payoff	50	30	10	0	0	0	0
Short 50-strike call payoff	0	0	0	0	−10	−30	−50
Long stock	0	20	40	50	60	80	100
Total payoff	50	50	50	50	50	50	50

4.6.3 The Risk of a Collar

We have already discussed the risks of covered calls and protective puts. The collar is essentially the simultaneous holding of both of these. See Exhibit 17 for the return distribution of a collar. A collar sacrifices the positive part of the return distribution in exchange for the removal of the adverse portion. With the short call option, the option writer sold the right side of the return distribution, which includes the most desirable outcomes. With the long put, the investor is protected against the left side of the distribution and the associated losses. The cost of the put is largely and often precisely offset by the income from writing the call. The collar dramatically narrows the distribution of possible investment outcomes, which is risk reducing. In exchange for the risk reduction, the return potential is limited.

Exhibit 17   Collars and the Return Distribution: With stock at 15.84, write 17 call and buy 15 put

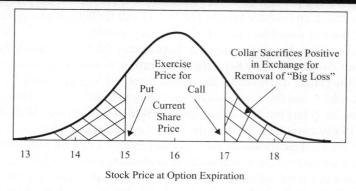

SPREADS AND COMBINATIONS

Option spreads and combinations can be useful option strategies. In a typical **option spread**, the investor buys one call and writes another or buys one put and writes another.[33] Someone might, for instance, buy a NOV 16 call and simultaneously write a NOV 17 call, or one might buy a SEP 17 put and write a SEP 15 put. An **option combination** typically uses both puts and calls. The most important option combination is the straddle, which is the only combination we cover in this reading. We will investigate spreads first.

5.1 Bull Spreads and Bear Spreads

Spreads are classified in two ways: by market sentiment and by the direction of the initial cash flows. A spread that becomes more valuable when the price of the underlying asset rises is a **bull spread**; a spread that becomes more valuable when the price declines is a **bear spread**. Because the investor buys one option and sells another, there is typically a net cash outflow or inflow. If establishing the spread requires a cash payment, it is referred to as a debit spread. Debit spreads are effectively long because the long option value exceeds the short option value. If the spread initially results in a cash inflow, it is referred to as a credit spread. Credit spreads are effectively short because the short option value exceeds the long option value. Any of these strategies can be created with puts or calls. The motivation for a spread is usually to place a directional bet, giving up part of the profit potential in exchange for a lower cost of the position. Some examples will help make this clear.

5.1.1 Bull Spread

Regardless of whether someone constructs a bull spread with puts or with calls, the strategy requires buying one option and writing another with a *higher* exercise price. Suppose, for instance, an investor thought it likely that by the September option expiration, PBR would rise to around 17 from its current level of 15.84. Based on the price data in Exhibit 7, what option strategy would capitalize on this anticipated

---

33 One important exception to the typical option spread is a *butterfly spread*, which is really two simultaneous spreads and can be done using only calls, only puts, or both puts and calls.

price movement? If someone were to buy the SEP 15 call for 1.64 and the stock rose to 17, at expiration the call would be worth $S_T - X = 17 - 15 = 2$. If the price of the option was 1.64, the profit is 0.36. The maximum loss is the price paid for the option, or 1.64. If, instead, an investor bought the SEP 16 call for 0.97, at an expiration stock price of 17, the call would be worth 1.00 for a gain of 0.03.

A spread could make more sense with these option values. If someone believes the stock will not rise above 17 by September expiration, it may make sense to "sell off" the part of the return distribution above that price. He would receive 0.51 for each SEP 17 call sold. Consider two alternatives: 1) buy the SEP 15 call as the other "leg" of the spread, or 2) buy the SEP 16 call instead. Which is preferred? With Alternative 1, the SEP 15 call costs 1.64. Writing the SEP 17 call brings in 0.51, so the net cost is 1.64 − 0.51 = 1.13. Traders would refer to this position as a PBR SEP 15/17 bull call spread. The maximum profit would occur at or above the exercise price of 17 because all gains above this level belong to the owner of the 17 call. At an underlying price of 17 or higher, from the trader's perspective, the position is worth 2, which represents the appreciation from 15 to 17. Having paid 1.13 for the spread, the maximum profit is 2.00 − 1.13 = 0.87. Another way to look at it is that at a price above 17, the trader exercises the long call, buying the stock at 15, and is forced to sell the stock at 17 to the holder of his short call.

With Alternative 2, the investor buys the SEP 16 call and pays 0.97 for it. Writing the SEP 17 call brings in 0.51, so the net cost would be 0.97 − 0.51 = 0.46. At an underlying price of 17 or higher, the spread would be worth 1.00, so the maximum profit is 1.00 − 0.46 = 0.54. Again, at 17 or higher, the trader exercises the call struck at 15, thereby buying the call, and has the other call exercised on him, thereby forcing him to sell the stock at 17. Exhibit 18 compares the profit and loss diagrams for these two alternatives.[34]

To determine the breakeven price with a spread, find the underlying asset price that will cause the exercise value of the two options combined to equal the initial cost of the spread. A spread has two exercise prices, which we can denote as X_L for the lower exercise price and X_H for the higher exercise price. There are also two option premiums, which we can denote as c_L for the lower-strike call and c_H for the higher-strike call. Mathematically, the breakeven price for a call bull spread is $X_L + (c_L - c_H)$, which represents the lower exercise price plus the cost of the spread. In the examples here, Alternative 1 costs 1.13. If at option expiration the stock is 16.13, the 15-strike option would be worth 1.13 and the 17-strike call would be worthless. The breakeven price is 15.00 + 1.13 = 16.13 as Exhibit 18 shows.

---

[34] Note that the shape of the profit and loss diagram is similar for a bull spread and for a collar.

Exhibit 18   Bull Spreads: Current PBR stock price = 15.84

Alternative 1: Buy SEP 15 call at 1.64, write SEP 17 call at 0.51

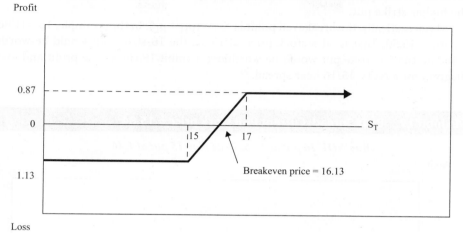

Alternative 2: Buy SEP 16 call at 0.97, write SEP 17 call at 0.51

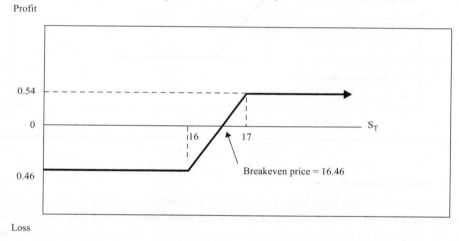

Which of the alternatives is preferable? There is no clear-cut answer. The SEP 15/17 spread becomes profitable with a smaller price rise in PBR stock.[35] With Alternative 1, the breakeven point of 16.13 is less than 2% above the current level, whereas with Alternative 2, reaching the breakeven point requires almost a 4% rise in the stock price. By carefully selecting the expiration and exercise prices for the two legs of the spread, an investor can choose the risk–return mix that most closely matches his investment outlook.

5.1.2 *Bear Spread*

With a bull spread, the investor buys the lower exercise price and writes the higher exercise price. It is the opposite with a bear spread: buy the higher exercise price and sell the lower. If someone believed PBR stock would be below 15 by the November expiration, one strategy would be to buy the PBR NOV 16 put at 1.96 and write the NOV 15 put at 1.46. This spread has a net cost of 0.50; this amount is the maximum loss, and it occurs at a PBR stock price of 16 or higher. The maximum gain is also

---

35 With a bull spread, this notation implies that the investor buys the 15 call and writes the 17 call.

0.50, which occurs at a stock price of 15 or lower. Finding the breakeven point uses the same logic as with a bull spread: find the underlying asset price at which the exercise value equals the initial cost. Let p_L represent the lower-strike put and p_H the higher-strike put.

Mathematically, the breakeven point is $X_H - (p_H - p_L)$. In this example, $16 - (1.96 - 1.46) = 15.50$. That is, at a stock price of 15.50, the 16-strike put would be worth 0.50 and the 15-strike put would be worthless. Exhibit 19 shows the profit and loss diagram for a NOV 15/16 bear spread.[36]

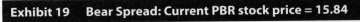

Exhibit 19   Bear Spread: Current PBR stock price = 15.84

Buy NOV 16 put at 1.96, write Nov 15 put at 1.46

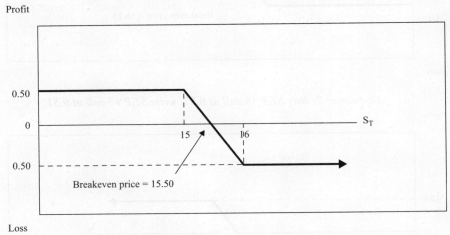

5.1.3 *Refining Spreads*

It is not necessary that both legs of a spread be established at the same time or maintained for the same period of time. Options are very versatile, and positions can be quickly adjusted as market conditions change. Here are a few examples of different tactical adjustments an option trader might consider.

5.1.3.1 Adding a Short Leg to a Long Position
Consider Carlos Aguila, a speculator who in September paid a premium of 1.50 for a NOV 40 call when the underlying stock was selling for 37. A month later, in October, the stock has risen to 48. He observes the following premiums for one-month call options.

Strike	Premium
40	8.30
45	4.42
50	1.91

---

36 Bull spreads can also be done with puts, and bear spreads can also be done with calls. If this is the case, the result is a credit spread with an initial cash inflow. Recall that American exercise-style options may be exercised at any time prior to expiration. Bull spreads with American puts have an additional risk, which is that the short put gets exercised early, whereas the long put is not yet in the money. If the bull spread uses American calls and the short call is exercised, the long call is deeper in the money, which offsets that risk. A similar point can be applied to bear spreads using calls. Thus, with American options, bull spreads with calls and bear spreads with puts are generally preferred but of course, not required.

This position has become very profitable. The call he bought is now worth 8.30. He paid 1.50, so his profit at this point is 8.30 − 1.50 = 6.80. He thinks the stock is likely to stabilize around its new level and doubts that it will go much higher. Aguila is considering writing another call option with an exercise price of either 45 or 50, thereby converting his long call position into a bull spread. Looking first at the NOV 50 call, he notes that the 1.91 premium would more than cover the initial cost of the NOV 40 call. If he were to write this call, the new profit and loss diagram would look like Exhibit 20. To review, consider the following points:

- At stock prices of 50 or higher, the exercise value of the spread is 10.00. The reason is because both options would be in the money, and a call with an exercise price of 40 would always be worth 10 more than a call with an exercise price of 50. The initial cost of the call with an exercise price of 40 was 1.50, and there was a 1.91 cash inflow after writing the call with an exercise price of 50. The profit is 10.00 − 1.50 + 1.91 = 10.41.

- At stock prices of 40 or lower, the exercise value of the spread is zero; both options would be out of the money. The initial cost of the call with an exercise price of 40 was 1.50, and there was a 1.91 cash inflow after writing the call with an exercise price of 50. The profit is 0 − 1.50 + 1.91 = 0.41.

- Between the two striking prices (40 and 50), the exercise value of the spread rises steadily as the stock price increases. For every unit increase up to the higher striking price, the exercise value of this spread increases by 1.0. For instance, if the stock price remains unchanged at 48, the exercise value of the spread is 8.00. The reason is because the call with an exercise price of 40 would be worth 8.00 and the call with an exercise price of 50 would be worthless. The initial cost of the 40-strike call was 1.50, and there was a 1.91 cash inflow when the 50-strike call was written. The profit is 8.00 − 1.50 + 1.91 = 8.41.

Now that he has written the NOV 50 call, Aguila needs to be careful how he views this new situation. No matter what happens to the stock price between now and expiration, the position is profitable, relative to his purchase price of the calls with an exercise price of 40. If the stock were to fall by any amount from its current level, however, he would have an opportunity loss: His profit would get progressively smaller if the price trended back to 40. Aguila would be correct in saying that the bull spread "locks in a profit," but it does not completely hedge against a decline in the value of his new strategy.

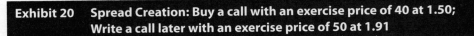

**Exhibit 20   Spread Creation: Buy a call with an exercise price of 40 at 1.50;
Write a call later with an exercise price of 50 at 1.91**

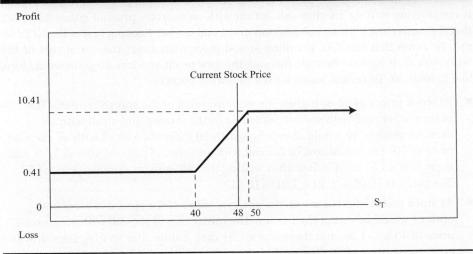

5.1.3.2 Multiple Strikes   Let us expand the prior example by assuming that Aguila owned 10 of the NOV 40 calls. He may choose to write higher-strike calls against just part of this position, which would leave additional upside potential if the stock were to continue to rise. Another choice would be writing a mix of two or more options, such as five of the Nov 50 options and five of the NOV 45 options. This approach would bring in premium income of

$$(5 \times 1.91) \qquad\qquad + (5 \times 4.42) \qquad\qquad = 31.65$$
$$\text{(50-strike call)} \qquad\qquad \text{(45-strike call)}$$

If the stock remains at 48 at option expiration, the NOV 50 call will expire worthless and the 45 call would be exercised. Aguila would receive a call notice indicating that he had been "assigned to sell" shares at 45 because of the call he wrote. Aguila owns 10 of the NOV 40 calls, so he could exercise 5 of these options and buy the shares he needs to deliver. Thus, for these five options, Aguila effectively buys the stock at 40 and sells at 45, making 5.00 per share. Remember, though, that he initially paid 1.50 for the 40 calls, so his profit is 3.50 per share. He makes $5 \times 3.50 = 17.50$. He still owns five of the NOV 40 calls, and these would each be worth their exercise value of the stock price minus the strike price: $48.00 - 40.00 = 8.00$. He paid 1.50 for them, so his gain is $5 \times (8.00 - 1.50) = 32.50$. He could sell these five contracts and close out his position, or exercise and sell the stock. His aggregate profit would be 81.65:

Option premium received:	31.65
Gain on five 40-strike calls used to deal with call exercise:	17.50
Gain on five 40-strike calls owned at option expiration:	32.50
Total:	81.65

If Aguila had kept the 10 NOV 40 contracts, their exercise value at expiration would have been $48.00 - 40.00 = 8.00$. Subtracting his purchase price of 1.50, his profit on 10 calls would have been $10 \times 6.50 = 65.00$. In this instance, the spread was a better performer than the long call by itself.

5.1.3.3 Spreads as a Volatility Play   A spread strategy may make sense with a volatile stock in a trending market. Suppose the market has been rising, and Lars Clive, an options speculator, expects this trend to continue. Hypothetical company ZKQ currently sells for 44. Suppose Clive buys a NOV 45 call for 5.25. Three days later the stock price has risen to 49. With this new price, a NOV 50 call sells for 5.74. Clive establishes a 45/50 bull call spread by writing the NOV 50 call. Now suppose five days pass and the stock price falls to 45. The new option values would be 5.41 for the NOV 45 call and 3.55 for the NOV 50 call. Clive closes out the Nov 50 leg of his spread by buying it back. He sold the call for 5.74, and bought it back for 3.55, so he makes 5.74 − 3.55 = 2.19, or 2.19 per contract. He still holds the long position in the NOV 45 call. Another four days pass, and ZKQ has risen to 48. The new price for the NOV 50 call would be 4.71; Clive then decides to write a call at this price. At this point, he has had two cash outflows totaling 8.80: the initial 5.25 plus the 3.55 to buy the NOV 50 call back. He has two inflows totaling 10.45: the premium income of 5.74 and then 4.71 from the two instances of writing the NOV 50 calls. Because the inflows of 10.45 exceed the outflows of 8.80, he has a resulting profit and loss diagram with a shape similar to the plot in Exhibit 20 that we saw in the previous example. The entire plot lies in profitable territory.

Time	Activity	Cash Out	Cash In
Day 1	Buy NOV 45 call	5.25	
Day 4	Sell NOV 50 call		5.74
Day 9	Buy NOV 50 call	3.55	
Day 13	Sell NOV 50 call		4.71
	Total	8.80	10.45
	Net Inflow		1.65

Spreads are primarily a directional play on the underlying spot price; still, spread traders can take advantage of changes in the level of volatility, and it is easy to create a hypothetical example like this one. There obviously is no guarantee that prices will continue to be volatile, or that any assumed price trend will continue. Still, the experienced option user knows to look for opportunistic plays that arise from price swings. Spreads are a relatively low-risk way to do so.

EXAMPLE 5

Spreads

$S_0 = 44.50$

OCT 45 call = 2.55 OCT 45 put = 2.92

OCT 50 call = 1.45 OCT 50 put = 6.80

1 What is the maximum gain with an OCT 45/50 bull call spread?

  A 1.10

  B 3.05

  C 3.90

2 What is the maximum loss with an OCT 45/50 bear put spread?

  A 1.12

  B 3.88

  C 4.38

3 What is the breakeven point with an OCT 45/50 bull call spread?

  A 46.10

      B   47.50

      C   48.88

Solution to 1:

C is correct. With a bull spread, the maximum gain occurs at the high exercise price. At an underlying price of 50 or higher, the spread is worth the difference in the strikes, or 50 − 45 = 5. The cost of establishing the spread is the price of the lower-strike option minus the price of the higher-strike option: 2.55 − 1.45 = 1.10. The maximum gain is 5.00 − 1.10 = 3.90.

Solution to 2:

B is correct. With a bear spread, you buy the higher exercise price and write the lower exercise price. When this strategy is done with puts, the higher exercise price option costs more than the lower exercise price option. Thus, you have a debit spread with an initial cash outlay, which is the most you can lose. The initial cash outlay is the cost of the OCT 50 put minus the premium received from writing the OCT 45 put: 6.80 − 2.92 = 3.88.

Solution to 3:

A is correct. You buy the OCT 45 call for 2.55 and sell the OCT 50 call for 1.45, for a net cost of 1.10. You breakeven when the position is worth the price you paid. The long call is worth 1.10 at a stock price of 46.10, and the OCT 50 call would expire out of the money and thus be worthless. The breakeven point is the lower exercise price of 45 plus the 1.10 cost of the spread, or 46.10.

5.1.4 *The Risk of Spreads*

Note that the shape of the profit and loss diagram for the bull spread in Exhibit 18 is similar to that of the collar in Exhibit 15. The upside return potential is limited, but so is the maximum loss. Just like the risk–return trade-off with the collar, an option spread takes the tails of the distribution out of play and leaves only price uncertainty between the option exercise prices. Looking at this another way, if someone were to simply buy a long call, the maximum gain would be unlimited and the maximum loss would be the option premium paid. If someone decides to convert this to a spread, it limits the maximum gain while simultaneously reducing the cost.

5.2 Calendar Spread

A strategy in which someone sells a near-dated call and buys a longer-dated one on the same underlying asset and with the same strike is commonly referred to as a **calendar spread**. When the investor buys the more distant option, it is a long calendar spread. The investor could also buy a near-term option and sell a longer-dated one, which would be a short calendar spread. Calendar spreads can also be done with puts; the investor would still buy one put and sell another put with a different expiration. As discussed previously, a portion of the option premium is time value. Time value decays over time and approaches zero as the option expiration date approaches. Taking advantage of this time decay is a primary motivation behind a calendar spread. Time decay is more pronounced for a short-term option than for one with a long time until expiration. A calendar spread trade seeks to exploit this characteristic by purchasing a longer-term option and writing a shorter-term option.

    Here is an example of how someone might use such a spread. Suppose XYZ stock is trading at 45 a share in August. XYZ has a new product that is to be introduced to the public early the following year. A trader believes this new product introduction is going to have a positive impact on the shares. Until the excitement associated with this announcement starts to affect the stock price, the trader believes that the stock will languish around the current level. See the option prices in Exhibit 21. Based on the bullish outlook for the stock going into January, the trader purchases the XYZ JAN 45 call at 3.81. Noting that the near-term price forecast is neutral, the trader also decides to sell a XYZ SEP 45 call for 1.55.

Now move forward to the September expiration and assume that XYZ is trading at 45. The September option will now expire with no value, which is a good outcome for the calendar spread trader. If the trader still believes that XYZ will stay around 45 into October before starting to move higher, the trader may continue to execute this strategy. An XYZ OCT 45 call might be sold for 1.55 with the hope that it also expires with no value.

Exhibit 21   Calendar Spread Call Option Prices

150 days until January option expiration
Underlying stock price = 45

Exercise Price	SEP	OCT	JAN
40	5.15	5.47	6.63
45	1.55	2.19	3.81
50	0.22	0.62	1.99

Just before September option expiration
Underlying stock price = 45

Exercise Price	SEP	OCT	JAN
40	5.00	5.15	6.39
45	0.00	1.55	3.48
50	0.00	0.22	1.69

In this example, the calendar spread trader has a directional opinion on the stock but does not believe that the price movement is imminent. Rather, the trader sees an opportunity to capture time value in one or more shorter-lived options that are expected to expire worthless.

5.3 Straddle

A long **straddle** is an option combination in which someone buys *both* puts and calls, with the same exercise price, on the same underlying asset.[37] If someone *writes* both options, it is a short straddle. Because a long call is bullish and a long put is bearish, this strategy may seem illogical. There are occasions, however, when a straddle might make sense. The classic example is in anticipation of some event in which the outcome is uncertain but likely to significantly affect the price of the underlying asset regardless of how the event gets resolved. From the shareholders' perspective for an option on a stock, if the news is bad, the stock price falls. If the news is good, it rises.

A straddle is an example of a directional play on the underlying volatility, expressing the view that volatility will either increase or decrease from its current level. A profitable outcome from a long straddle, however, usually requires a significant price movement in the underlying asset. The straddle buyer pays the premium for two

---

37 If someone buys puts and calls with different exercise prices, the position is called a strangle.

options, so to make a profit, the underlying asset has to move either above or below the option exercise price by the total amount spent on the straddle. As an example, suppose in the next few days there is a verdict expected in a liability lawsuit against an automobile manufacturer. An investor expects the stock to move sharply one way or the other once the verdict is revealed. Because a straddle is neither a bullish nor a bearish strategy, the chosen options usually have an exercise price close to the current stock price. With any other exercise price, there is a directional bias because initially one of the options will be in the money and one will be out of the money.

Experienced option traders know that it is difficult to make money with a straddle. In the example, other people will also be watching the court proceedings. The collective wisdom will predict higher volatility once the verdict is announced, and option prices rise when volatility expectations rise. This increased volatility means that both the puts and the calls become expensive well before the verdict is revealed, and the long straddle requires the purchase of both options. To make money, the straddle buyer has to be correct in his view that the "true" underlying volatility is higher than the market consensus. Essentially, the bet is that the straddle buyer is right and the other market participants, on average, are wrong about the volatility.

Suppose the underlying stock sells for 50, and an investor selects 30-day options with an exercise price of 50. The call sells for 2.29 and the put for 2.28, for a total investment of 4.57. To recover this cost, the underlying asset must either rise or fall by at least 4.57. At prices above 54.57 the call is in the money. At prices below 45.43 the put is in the money. See Exhibit 22. Theoretically, the stock can rise to any level, so the maximum profit with the long call is unlimited. If the stock declines, it can fall to no lower than zero. If that happens, the long put would be worth 50. Subtracting the 4.57 cost of the straddle gives a maximum profit of 45.43 from a stock drop.

For the straddle buyer, the worst outcome is if the stock closes exactly at 50, meaning both the put and the call would expire worthless. At any other price one of the options will have a positive exercise value. Note that at expiration, the straddle is not profitable if the stock price is in the range 45.43 to 54.57. It requires more than a 9% price move in one month to make money with this strategy. A speculator who believes such a move was unlikely might be inclined to *write* the straddle, in which case the profit and loss diagram in Exhibit 22 gets reversed, with a maximum gain of 4.57 and a theoretically unlimited loss if prices rise.

Exhibit 22	**Long Straddle: Current stock price = 50; Buy 50-strike call at 2.29, buy 50-strike put at 2.28**

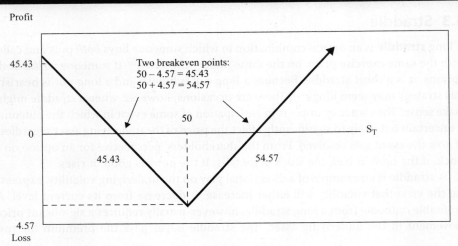

The risk of a long straddle is limited to the amount paid for the two option positions. At expiration, the only way both options expire worthless is if the stock price and exercise price are exactly equal; at any other final stock price, either the call or the put has a positive exercise value. Still, both options lose their time value, so it requires a significant price change in the underlying asset in order to move past one of the breakeven points.

5.4 Consequences of Exercise

When someone writes an option, it is important to remember that it creates a contingent claim, but the writer is not the owner of the claim. The writer sells the claim and has been paid to take on an obligation.

The option writer has an obligation to perform if the option holder chooses to exercise and has no control over whether or not exercise occurs. The consequences of exercise can be significant. When someone owns an option, they decide when and if to exercise. Unexpected exercise can be quite inconvenient.

Suppose, for instance, an investor buys a NOV 95 call and writes a NOV 105 call to form a 95/105 bull spread; later, the stock price rises to 113. At this price the spread has reached its maximum value of 10. Two weeks before expiration the owner of the 105 call exercises. Unless the investor already own these shares, it will be necessary to purchase them in the open market for 113. With a contract size of 100, it would cost $100 \times 113 = 11,300$ to make the purchase, and this purchase might be very inconvenient. Alternatively, depending on the brokerage firm's policies, it might be able to exercise the 95 call to acquire the needed shares. Even this approach may be undesirable because it is rarely a good idea to exercise an option very far ahead of the expiration date. Doing so essentially amounts to throwing away the time value.

For instance, suppose that with the underlying stock at 113 the NOV 95 call the investor owns sells for 18.75. The option is in the money by 18, so that is its exercise value. If the investor exercised the option, he would buy shares at this discount. But the economic gain would be just the 18, whereas the option given up in exchange for the shares was worth 18.75. If the investor wanted the shares, he would be better off selling the option for 18.75 and then buying shares on the open market for 113. The net price would be $113.00 - 18.75 = 94.25$, or 0.75 less than the strike price. With capital constraints, though, the investor might not be able to do this. The key point in this discussion is that an investor should think through the consequences of exercise before implementing any strategy that requires writing options.

INVESTMENT OBJECTIVES AND STRATEGY SELECTION

6

The risk of a derivative product depends on what you do with it. It is not the fork's fault if someone sticks it in an electric outlet and gets shocked. People should think of derivatives as *neutral products* that can be combined with other assets to create a more preferred risk–return trade-off. If used wisely, they can help an investor or a portfolio manager quickly adapt to changing market conditions or client needs.

6.1 The Necessity of Setting an Objective

Every trade should begin with an opinion of the underlying market. Only then can an informed trading decision be made. With stocks and most assets, one thinks about the direction of the market: Is it going up or down? With options, it is not enough to think about only market *direction*; it is also necessary to think about the volatility. In other words, what matters to users of options is not just the direction the underlying is headed, but the volatility of the underlying. For example, in a simple call option purchase, just having the underlying go up is not sufficient to make money. The underlying must go up enough that the option reaches breakeven. The gain in the value of the stock must be sufficient that the call overcomes the loss of its time value. A long call must have some upside volatility, and a long put must have some downside volatility.

Suppose an investor is neutral on market direction. Again, he should consider the volatility. A straddle buyer is neither bullish nor bearish but expects a sharp increase in volatility. Someone who is neutral directionally but does not anticipate a sudden price change may want to write the straddle. Spreads tend to be middle-of-the-road strategies that fit best in neutral, flat markets. A spread trade is often appropriate when the outlook for an underlying market is either neutral or non-trending, meaning that it does not have a strong bullish or bearish outlook. Exhibit 23 shows one way of looking at the interplay of direction and volatility.

Exhibit 23   Direction and Volatility with Options

		Direction		
		Bearish	**Neutral/No Bias**	**Bullish**
Volatility	High	Buy puts	Buy straddle	Buy calls
	Average	Write calls and buy puts	Spreads	Buy calls and write puts
	Low	Write calls	Write straddle	Write puts

Some option traders refer to the concept of volatility as *speed*, with a high volatility market being a *fast market* and a low volatility market being a *slow market*. Market speed can, however, also refer to the rate at which a market moves, so investors should take care to be aware of the distinction in the uses of these characterizations.

6.2 Spectrum of Market Risk

Derivatives enable market participants to take a position that is extremely bearish, extremely bullish, or somewhere in between and to quickly and efficiently shift along this continuum as desired. Suppose a pension fund owns one million shares of HSBC Holdings. For some reason, the portfolio manager would like to temporarily reduce the position by 10%, meaning to reduce the market exposure and convert the equivalent funds to cash. As this reading has already shown, there are a variety of ways in which this might be done. The portfolio manager could

1 sell 100,000 shares, which is 10% of the holding.
2 enter into a futures or forward contract to sell 100,000 shares.
3 write call contracts sufficient to generate minus 100,000 delta points.
4 buy put contracts sufficient to generate minus 100,000 delta points.
5 enter into a collar sufficient to generate minus 100,000 delta points.

Each of these alternatives has its own strengths and weaknesses. The first alternative (selling shares) has the advantage of clearly accomplishing the goal of a 10% reduction. For some investors, though, this solution could create a tax problem or result in inadvertently putting downward pressure on the stock price. Forward contracts are simple and effective, but they involve counterparty risk and are not easily canceled if later there is a desire to unwind the trade.[38] Writing calls brings in a cash premium, but leaves the writer subject to exercise risk. Buying puts requires a cash outlay but leaves the investor in control with respect to exercise risk. In short, all of the outcomes have advantages and disadvantages, but with derivatives, the investor has multiple choices instead of just one.

6.3 Analytics of the Breakeven Price

Investors often construct a profit and loss diagram for an option strategy that is under consideration. These diagrams are helpful in understanding the range of possible outcomes. It may also make sense to use option pricing theory to learn more about what the breakeven points on the profit and loss diagram really mean. The current option price is based on an outlook that takes into account an assumed future volatility of the prices of the underlying asset. Volatility is measured by standard deviation of percentage changes in the spot price of the underlying asset, and with an understanding of some basic statistical principles, this volatility can be used to estimate the likelihood of achieving a particular price target.

There are a variety of factors that come into play when determining the value of an option. The underlying market price, the exercise price of the option contract, the time left until option expiration, the current risk-free rate, and any dividends paid before expiration are all taken into account by the market when valuing an option. The exercise price is known, and the underlying market price and risk-free rate are easily accessible. The time remaining until expiration is consistently changing, but we always are aware of how much time is left until expiration. Dividends paid by companies are fairly stable as well.

There is another pricing factor that is taken into account, and that is the expected price movement or volatility of the underlying stock. The more volatility that is expected from the underlying over the life of an option, the higher the option premium. Consider two stocks, QRS and TUV, that are both trading at 50. QRS is a utility company that is expected to not have much volatility over the next month. TUV, however, is a biotech company that often experiences 5% price moves in a single day. All else being the same, options on QRS would have lower premiums than those on TUV. See the price data in Exhibit 24.

Exhibit 24	Volatility and Option Prices

30 days until March option expiration
QRS and TUV underlying stock price = 50

QRS Mar 50 Call = 1.00
QRS Mar 50 Put = 0.95
TUV Mar 50 Call = 2.50
TUV Mar 50 Put = 2.45

A trader buying a QRS Mar 50 call and QRS Mar 50 put would be purchasing a QRS Mar 50 straddle for 1.95. Buying a TUV Mar 50 straddle would involve purchasing the TUV Mar 50 call at 2.50 and TUV Mar 50 put at 2.45 for a net cost of 4.95. Breakeven at expiration for the QRS straddle occurs if the stock moves up or down 1.95 whereas

---

[38] It is possible to enter into an offsetting trade with the same counterparty, or a different counterparty, to net the position to zero. This approach is essentially the same as covering a futures contract position in which the counterparty is the clearinghouse. Offsetting a forward with a new forward is relatively easy to do.

breakeven for the TUV straddle would require a move of 4.95. In percentage terms, this means that breakeven for the QRS straddle is 3.90% (1.95/50.00) whereas TUV needs to rise or fall 9.90% (4.95/50.00) for the straddle just to break even.

We say that TUV options have a higher **implied volatility** than comparable QRS option contracts. Implied volatility is the standard deviation that causes an option pricing model to give the current option price. Option users, in fact, use implied volatility as a form of option currency, meaning that prices are quoted as implied volatilities. For instance, knowing that an option sells for 2.00 reveals nothing about its relative price because that depends on the moneyness (i.e., the extent to which the option is in or out of the money) and the remaining life of the option. If, instead, someone says an option sells for an annualized implied volatility of 45%, that is a standalone statistic that can be directly compared with other options. TUV option premiums are higher than QRS option premiums because the market expects greater potential price moves out of TUV than from QRS.

There are a few different perspectives on how we should measure the time periods with option volatility. There are usually 365 calendar days in a year, but the markets are not open on Saturdays or Sundays or official holidays, which vary by country. Because the stock price does not have the opportunity to change when the market is closed, most experts believe that those days should not count. For this reason, some people use 252 or some other appropriate number for the number of trading days in a year. Dispersion is a function of both the *size* of the "jumps" in the variable and the *number* of those jumps. We convert an annual variance (σ^2) to a daily variance by dividing by 252, and we convert an annual standard deviation (σ) to a daily standard deviation by dividing by $\sqrt{252}$. With options, volatility is measured by the annual standard deviation.

Suppose the underlying stock in Exhibit 22 typically has an annual volatility of 30%. An investor can obtain some information on the likelihood of reaching the breakeven points before entering into the trade. In order for the straddle to be profitable at expiration, the stock must move up or down by 4.57 units from the current price of 50, which is a 9.14% movement. Expiration is in 30 days, but this includes four weekends and possibly a holiday. Suppose there are only 21 trading days until expiration. We convert a 9.14% movement in 21 days to an annual volatility by multiplying by the square root of the number of 21-day periods in a 252-day "year":

$$\sigma_{annual} = 0.0914x\sqrt{\frac{252}{21}} = 32.6\%$$

The required price movement to the breakeven point represents an annual volatility that is only slightly greater than the historical level, so someone contemplating establishing the straddle might view this scenario favorably. If, instead, the straddle in Exhibit 22 costs 7 to establish, it would require a 14% move to reach a breakeven point. Using the formula just presented, this move is about 48.5% on an annual basis. You might not believe that such a price change could reasonably be expected in a 30-day period and thus elect not to enter into the strategy.[39]

EXAMPLE 6

Straddle Analytics

XYZ stock = 100.00

---

[39] As described, volatility for equity markets is typically defined as a relative price change (lognormal volatility) whereas in the interest rate market, market practice changes more and more to an absolute definition of volatility, using absolute movement in basis points per annum.

100-strike call = 8.00

100-strike put = 7.50

Options are three months until expiration

1 If Smith buys a straddle on XYZ stock, he is *best* described as expecting a:
  A high volatility market.
  B low volatility market.
  C average volatility market.

2 This strategy will break even at expiration stock prices of:
  A 92.50 and 108.50.
  B 92.00 and 108.00.
  C 84.50 and 115.50.

3 Reaching a breakeven point implies an annualized rate of return *closest* to:
  A 16%.
  B 31%.
  C 62%.

Solution to 1:

A is correct. A straddle is directionally neutral; it is neither bullish nor bearish. The straddle buyer wants volatility and wants it quickly, but does not care in which direction. The worst outcome is for the underlying asset to remain stable.

Solution to 2:

C is correct. To break even, the stock price must move enough to recover the cost of both the put and the call. These premiums total $15.50, so the stock must move up to $115.50 or down to $84.50.

Solution to 3:

C is correct. The price change to a breakeven point is 15.50 points, or 15.5% on a 100 stock. This is for three months. This outcome is equivalent to an annualized rate of 62%, found by multiplying by 4 (15.5% × 4 = 62%).

6.4 Applications

This section illustrates by means of mini cases some of the ways in which different market participants use derivative products as a tool to solve a problem or to alter a risk exposure. Note that with the wide variety of derivatives available there are almost always multiple ways in which derivatives might logically be used in a particular situation. These mini cases cover only a few of them.

6.4.1 *Writing Covered Calls*

Carlos Rivera is a portfolio manager in a small asset management firm focusing on high-net-worth clients. In mid-April he is preparing for an upcoming meeting with Dr. Mary Parker, a client whose daughter is about to get married. Dr. Parker and her husband have just decided to pay for their daughter's honeymoon and need to raise $30,000 relatively quickly. The client's portfolio is 100% invested in equities and, by policy, is aggressive. At the moment the Parkers are "asset rich and cash poor." They have largely depleted their cash reserves with the wedding expenses. The recently revised investment policy statement permits all option activity except the writing of naked calls. Over the next six months, Rivera's firm has a flat to slightly bearish market outlook. Dr. Parker's account contains 5,000 shares of Apple stock, a recent addition to the portfolio. Rivera is considering the following 30-day exchange-listed options, which expire in May.

Apple Options: Stock = $99.72		
Call	**Exercise Price**	**Put**
4.90	97	2.14
3.25	100	3.45
2.02	103	5.23

What strategy should Rivera recommend to Dr. Parker?

Solution: To generate income, Rivera will want to write options. The account permits the writing of covered, but not naked, calls and apparently also permits the writing of puts. Apple options trade on an organized exchange with a standard contract size of 100 options. With 5,000 shares in the account, 50 call contracts would be covered. If Rivera were to write either the MAY 100 or the MAY 103 calls, it would not generate the required income. Writing the MAY 97 calls would generate $4.90 × 100 × 50 = $24,500, but because this call is in the money, there is an increased risk of the option being in the money at expiration. Given the firm's market outlook, this risk might be acceptable. To make up the income shortfall of $30,000 − $24,500 = $5,500 Rivera could recommend writing a put.[40] To bring in the required premium, Rivera would have to write $5,500/$523 = 11 contracts of the MAY 103 put, or $5,500/$345 = 16 contracts of the MAY 100 put, or $5,500/$214 = 26 contracts of the MAY 97 put.[41] The puts with exercise prices of 100 and 103 are already in the money, and given the market outlook of Rivera's firm, they are likely to be exercised, resulting in a new cash demand on the portfolio. If Rivera writes 26 contracts of the MAY 97 puts, it will bring in the needed income, and if Apple remains above 97, the puts will expire worthless. If Apple closes below $97, the puts would be exercised and the account would require cash totaling $252,200 to pay for the exercise of 26 put contracts for $9,700/contract. The calls would have expired, so Rivera would be free to sell some of the Apple shares to raise cash if necessary. Rivera could recommend writing 50 contracts of the MAY 97 calls and 26 contracts of the MAY 97 puts. At the same time, it is important to note that writing puts is generally only appropriate for experienced, financially secure investors, and even for them, a financial adviser should review the adverse consequences of the puts being exercised.

6.4.2.1 Portfolio Protection Eliot Skaves manages a discretionary account with complete derivatives authority. The account holds 100,000 shares of Salar Limited, currently trading at HK$42.00. Salar has an earnings announcement scheduled in one week. Although Skaves expects an earnings increase, he expects the company to narrowly miss the consensus earnings estimate. He would like to protect the client's position in the company until the report is released but wants to keep the cost of the protection to a minimum. There are no exchange-traded options on Salar. Skaves contacts a Hong Kong dealer and receives the following quotes for one-month options.

---

[40] If Rivera also writes puts, he has written a straddle. Note, though, that the short calls are not naked because Rivera also owns the underlying shares. This means that his maximum loss from an increase in the price of the underlying asset is known and limited. He does not face the potentially unlimited losses associated with writing a naked call.

[41] The number of contracts is rounded up in order to get the required income.

Salar Options: Stock = HK$42.00		
Call	**Exercise Price**	**Put**
3.05	40.00	1.04
1.69	42.50	2.19
0.84	45.00	3.83

What strategy should Skaves use?

Solution: Given the need to keep the cost of the protection to a minimum, Skaves might first investigate writing calls against the stock. The option premium received provides limited downside protection. For instance, if Skaves wrote the call with an exercise price of 40.00, the 3.05 premium would offset a price decline down to 42.00 − 3.05 = 38.95. He would suffer the full loss of any decline below that. If he were to write the call with an exercise price of 42.50, he is protected down to 42.50 − 1.69 = 40.81. The disadvantages of obtaining protection this way are twofold: First, the protection is limited, and second, if the underlying stock rises above the exercise price, there is an opportunity cost. In this example, if Skaves is wrong about his earnings estimate and the company beats expectations, the stock is likely to rise, in which case he foregoes any gains from the rise above the option exercise price.

An alternative to writing the calls would be to purchase a protective put, perhaps the put with an exercise price of 40.00, with the intent of selling it shortly after the earnings announcement. If the earnings are less than market expectations, the stock is likely to fall, thereby increasing the put value and partially offsetting the loss. If the earnings meet market expectations, the put value may be sold at a price near its purchase price. If the earnings are better than expected and the stock price rises, the put will decline in value. Skaves no longer would need the "insurance" and could sell the put, recovering part of the purchase price.

6.4.2.2 Portfolio Protection: Adjustment

Assume that Salar's earnings turned out to be surprisingly good; they beat the consensus estimate by 7 cents. Immediately after the announcement the stock rose 10% to HK$46.20. Skaves believes this sharp jump in stock price is not justified by the new earnings level and expects the stock to give up about half this gain in the next few weeks. The new options prices are shown in the table. They reflect a jump in the anticipated volatility in the stock, which increases the value of both puts and calls.[42] Skaves notes that the put with an exercise price of 40.00 has declined from 1.04 to 0.83.

Salar Options Stock = HK$46.20		
Call	**Exercise Price**	**Put**
7.03	40.00	0.83
5.24	42.50	1.54
3.76	45.00	2.56
2.61	47.50	3.90

Now that the earnings announcement has been made, what should Skaves do?

---

42 The original table is based on an annual volatility of 40%; the new volatility is 60%.

Solution: Skaves no longer needs the protection from the put option, so he should stick with his original strategy and sell the put. Because of the increase in volatility, the price of the put with an exercise price of 40.00 has fallen from 1.04 to 0.83. Skaves can recover 80% of the "insurance premium" he paid. Given that Skaves has a rather specific short-term belief about Salar stock, he might also consider writing a call with an exercise price of either 45.00 or 47.50, especially because the volatility has risen. When options are expensive, writing them can be attractive. He believes the stock is likely to retreat to the HK$44.00 range soon. If he were to write the 47.50 call against all 100,000 shares, he would receive premium income of HK$261,000. This option would expire worthless as long as Salar stock is below HK$47.50 in 30 days. The call option with an exercise price of 45.00 would provide more income (HK$3,760), but if the stock does not fall as much as Skaves expects, he might face the inconvenience of the option being assigned and shares called away.

6.4.3 *Collar/Equity Swap*

Bernhard Steinbacher has a client with a 100,000 share holding in Targa, currently trading for €14. The client has a very low tax basis on this stock. Steinbacher wants to safeguard the value of the position but does not want to sell because of the substantial tax burden the sale would involve. He does not find exchange-traded options on the stock. He wants to present two different ways in which the client could protect an investment portfolio from a stock price decline.

Solution 1:   In the over-the-counter market, he might buy a put and then write a call to offset the put premium. This strategy is a collar. The put provides downside protection below the put exercise price, and the call brings in income to help offset the cost of the put. Recalling Exhibit 17 and the underlying return distribution, this strategy effectively sells the right tail of the distribution, which represents large gains, in exchange for eliminating the left tail, which represents large losses.

Solution 2:   Another possible solution is to enter into an equity swap trading the Targa return for Libor. The Targa shares are worth €1.4 million, so Steinbacher can agree to exchange the total return on the shares for the Libor return on this sum of money. He needs to decide the period of time for which the protection is needed and match the swap tenor to this. Perhaps he decides on six months, and six-month Libor is 0.34%, expressed as an annual rate.

Scenario A: Over the six months, Targa pays a €0.10 dividend and the share price rises 1%.

The total return on the stock is $\dfrac{(14 \times 1.01) - 14 + 0.10}{14} = 1.71\%$. For a six-month period, the Libor return would be half the annual rate, or 0.17%. The Targa stock return exceeds the Libor return, so Steinbacher would pay (1.71% − 0.17%) × €1.4 million = €21,560.

Scenario B: Over the six months Targa pays a €0.10 dividend and the share price falls 1%.

The total return on the stock is $\dfrac{(14 \times 0.99) - 14 + 0.10}{14} = -0.29\%$. The Targa stock return is less than the Libor return, so Steinbacher would "get paid" the negative return plus the Libor return and receive the difference (0.29% + 0.17%) × €1.4 million = €6,440.

6.4.4 *Writing Put Options*

Oscar Quintera is the chief financial officer for Tres Jotas, a private investment firm in Puerto Rico. Quintera wants to enter a new equity position, but the shares are trading above the price Quintera wants to pay. The company wants to acquire 500,000 shares, so a few dollars difference in the purchase price makes a big dollar difference. The current share price is $89.00, and Quintera is willing to buy the stock at a price of $87.50 or less.

Solution: Quintera can write in-the-money puts to effectively "get paid" to buy the stock. Quintera sells puts and keeps the cash regardless of what happens in the future. If the stock is above the exercise price at expiration, the option will not be exercised. Otherwise, the option is exercised, Quintera buys, and as desired, becomes an owner of the stock. With the stock at $89.00, a 30-day put option with an exercise price of 95.00 sells for 7.85. Quintera writes 5,000 contracts and receives premium income of $100 \times 5,000 \times \$7.85 = \$3,925,000$. The company keeps these funds regardless of future stock price movements. He is obligated to buy stock at $95.00 if the put holder chooses to exercise.

Scenario A: The stock is $92.00 per share on the option expiration day. With an exercise price of 95.00, the put is in the money and will be exercised. Quintera will be assigned to buy 500,000 shares at the exercise price of 95.00. The cost is $500,000 \times \$95.00 = \$47,500,000$. Quintera is satisfied with the outcome, though, because the firm keeps the premium income of $3,925,000, so the net cost of purchase is $47,500,000 − $3,925,000 = $43,575,000. On 500,000 shares, this means the effective purchase price is $43,575,000/500,000 = $87.15, which is below the $87.50 price Quintera was willing to pay.

Scenario B: The stock price is $97.00 on the option expiration day. With an exercise price of 95.00, the put is out of the money and would not be exercised. Quintera keeps the $3,925,000 premium received from writing the option. This adds to the company's profitability, but it did not acquire the shares and experienced an opportunity cost relative to an outright purchase of the stock at $89.00.

6.4.5 *Long Straddle*

Katrina Hamlet has been following McMillan Holdings for the past year. The company is involved in a potentially quite costly lawsuit, and she has been considering speculating with a straddle. The stock is currently trading for $75.00, and she is focused on at-the-money calls and puts selling for 2.58 and 2.57, respectively. After the market closed today, she hears a news story indicating that a jury decision is expected later tomorrow. Hamlet expects that the stock will move at least 10% either way once the verdict is read, making the straddle strategy potentially appropriate. The following morning after the market opens, she goes to place her trade and finds that although the stock price remains at $75.00, the option prices have adjusted to 6.00 for the call and 5.99 for the put. She wonders if these new option premiums have any implications for her intended strategy.

Solution: Hamlet is betting on a price movement in the underlying asset to make money with this trade. That price movement, up or down, must be large enough to recover the two premiums paid. In her early planning, that total was 2.58 + 2.57 = 5.15. She expects at least a 10% price movement, which on a stock selling for $75.00 would be an increase of $7.50. This price movement would be enough to cover the 5.15 cost and make her strategy profitable. The news report about the imminent verdict, however, increased the implied volatility in the options, raising their price and making it more difficult to achieve the breakeven points. The straddle now costs 6.00 + 5.99 =

11.99. To reach the breakeven point, she now needs the stock to move by almost 16%. If she expects a 10% price movement, she is not likely to be happy with the outcome of this trade.

6.4.6 Long Call

Olivier Akota believes a stock is going to move from £60 to £65 over the next 30 days. Akota checks the 30-day call options with an exercise price of 60 and believes they are overpriced at 4. He then looks at the 30-day call option with an exercise price of 65 and sees that he can sell it for 1.50.

Solution: Akota anticipates a sharp price increase in a short period of time, which is characteristic of a bullish, volatile market. The indicated strategy would be a long call position, but Akota believes the calls with an exercise price of 60 are overpriced. Also, at a premium of 4, if he is right and the stock advances to 65, his profit would be just 1 on an investment of 4. He might not like this risk–reward trade-off. If he were to buy the 60 call and also sell a call with an exercise price of 65 and form a call bull spread, his cost would be reduced by the 1.50 premium from writing the call, for a net cost of £2.50. Now, if the stock rises to £65 as he expects, he could earn a £2.50 profit on a £2.50 investment, doubling his money. In this case, a bull spread is reasonable, even though Akota believes the option he is buying is overpriced.

6.4.7 Calendar Spread

Britta Olofsson thinks that XYZ stock, which is trading at SEK30, is going to remain in a narrow range for the next month until a new product is announced. She then thinks the stock will take off on a bullish run. She wants to have long exposure in case the stock moves early but does not want to pay the premium for a two-month call.

Solution: Olofsson could benefit from a calendar spread. She expects little price movement in the next 30 days. For example, by writing a 15-day, at-the-money call with a strike of 30 for 1, she is essentially selling time value that would reduce the cost of, perhaps, a 45-day, 30-strike call that might sell for 1.50. So, assume she sells the 15-day call and buys the 45-day call. Her net cost would be SEK0.50. If the stock does not begin to advance until after the call she wrote expires, she participates fully in the rising stock through her long call position. If the stock fails to rise, her maximum loss is the SEK0.50 she paid. If the stock rises before the short option expires, both options would increase in value, and the net wealth effect on Mitchell would be modest. She would be inconvenienced, though, because when the shorter-term option was exercised she would be assigned to deliver shares that she might not have. This situation would require a significant cash outlay.

6.4.8 Currency Forward Contract

A Mexico-based firm anticipates receipt of a $4 million payment in three months. The firm wants to reduce the associated foreign exchange risk.

Solution: The firm could enter into a three-month forward contract in which it agrees to a future delivery of $4 million in exchange for pesos. Because the exchange rate is set today, the foreign exchange risk disappears.

6.4.9 Interest Rate Swap

Les Poiriers is the chief financial officer for Bonshaw Bank, a Canadian commercial bank. Because of a very successful marketing program by one of the bank's competitors, her bank has found it necessary to react to the competitive pressures by issuing a substantial number of long-term, fixed-rate mortgage loans. Although the bank has always done some of these, the current demand has resulted in unacceptable interest rate risk and has caused frequent violations of the bank's asset/liability management policy. Bonshaw Bank currently has C$400 million of these mortgages on its books, and Les Poiriers would like to reduce this amount by half.

Solution: Bonshaw needs to reduce its long-term, fixed-rate exposure to mortgage loans by C$200 million. The mortgages the bank owns are a receive-fixed product and can be hedged with an offsetting pay-fixed swap. Such a swap would reduce the duration of the loans, and hence, reduce the interest rate risk. Specifically, Les Poiriers could enter into a C$200 million notional value pay-fixed interest rate swap in which her bank pays the fixed rate to the counterparty and receives a floating rate. A floating-rate loan has a much lower duration than a long-term fixed-rate mortgage because the floating rate resets periodically as market interest rates change, bringing its market value back to par value.

SUMMARY

This reading on derivatives strategies shows a number of ways in which market participants might use derivatives to enhance returns or to reduce risk to better meet portfolio objectives. The following are the key points.

- Interest rate, currency, and equity futures and swaps can be used to modify risk and return by altering the characteristics of the cash flows of an investment portfolio.

- Buying a call and writing a put with the same exercise price creates a synthetic long position.

- A long position plus a short futures position in the same underlying asset creates a synthetic risk-free asset earning the risk-free rate.

- A covered call, in which the holder of a stock writes a call giving someone the right to buy the shares, is one of the most common uses of options by individual investors.

- Covered calls can be used to generate income, to acquire shares at a lower-than-market price, or to exit a position when the shares hit a target price.

- A covered call position has a limited maximum return because of the transfer of the right tail of the return distribution to the option buyer.

- The maximum loss of a covered call position is less than the maximum loss of the underlying shares alone, but the covered call carries the potential for an opportunity loss if the underlying shares rise sharply.

- A protective put is the simultaneous holding of a long stock position and a long put on the same asset. The put provides protection or insurance against a price decline.

- Although the continuous purchase of protective puts is expensive and probably suboptimal, the occasional purchase of a protective put to deal with a bearish short-term outlook can be a reasonable risk-reducing activity.

- The maximum loss with a protective put is limited because the downside risk is transferred to the option writer in exchange for the payment of the option premium.

- With an option spread, an investor buys one option and writes another of the same type. This reduces the position cost but caps the maximum payoff.

- A bull spread is normally constructed by buying a call option and writing another call option with a higher exercise price.

- A bear spread is normally constructed by buying a put option and writing another put option with a lower exercise price.

- With either a bull spread or a bear spread, both the maximum gain and the maximum loss are known and limited.

- A collar is an option position in which the investor is long shares of stock and simultaneously writes a covered call and buys a protective put.

- A calendar spread involves buying a long-dated option and writing a shorter-dated option of the same type with the same exercise price, or vice versa. The primary motivation for such a spread is to take advantage of the faster time decay with the shorter-term option.

- A straddle is an option combination in which the investor buys puts and calls with the same exercise price. The straddle holder typically needs a substantial price movement in the underlying asset in order to make a profit.

- The risk of a derivative product depends on how it is used. Derivatives should always be used in connection with a well-defined investment objective.

Glossary

Abandonment option   The ability to terminate a project at some future time if the financial results are disappointing.

Abnormal earnings   See *residual income*.

Abnormal return   The return on an asset in excess of the asset's required rate of return; the risk-adjusted return.

Absolute convergence   The idea that developing countries, regardless of their particular characteristics, will eventually catch up with the developed countries and match them in per capita output.

Absolute valuation model   A model that specifies an asset's intrinsic value.

Absolute version of PPP   The extension of the law of one price to the broad range of goods and services that are consumed in different countries.

Accounting estimates   Estimates used in calculating the value of assets or liabilities and in the amount of revenue and expense to allocate to a period. Examples of accounting estimates include, among others, the useful lives of depreciable assets, the salvage value of depreciable assets, product returns, warranty costs, and the amount of uncollectible receivables.

Accumulated benefit obligation   The actuarial present value of benefits (whether vested or non-vested) attributed, generally by the pension benefit formula, to employee service rendered before a specified date and based on employee service and compensation (if applicable) before that date. The accumulated benefit obligation differs from the projected benefit obligation in that it includes no assumption about future compensation levels.

Acquirer   The company in a merger or acquisition that is acquiring the target.

Acquiring company   The company in a merger or acquisition that is acquiring the target.

Acquisition   The purchase of some portion of one company by another; the purchase may be for assets, a definable segment of another entity, or the purchase of an entire company.

Active factor risk   The contribution to active risk squared resulting from the portfolio's different-than-benchmark exposures relative to factors specified in the risk model.

Active return   The return on a portfolio minus the return on the portfolio's benchmark.

Active risk   The standard deviation of active returns.

Active risk squared   The variance of active returns; active risk raised to the second power.

Active share   A measure of how similar a portfolio is to its benchmark. A manager who precisely replicates the benchmark will have an active share of zero; a manager with no holdings in common with the benchmark will have an active share of one.

Active specific risk   The contribution to active risk squared resulting from the portfolio's active weights on individual assets as those weights interact with assets' residual risk.

Adjusted funds from operations   Funds from operations (FFO) adjusted to remove any non-cash rent reported under straight-line rent accounting and to subtract maintenance-type capital expenditures and leasing costs, including leasing agents' commissions and tenants' improvement allowances.

Adjusted present value   (APV) As an approach to valuing a company, the sum of the value of the company, assuming no use of debt, and the net present value of any effects of debt on company value.

Adjusted R^2   A measure of goodness-of-fit of a regression that is adjusted for degrees of freedom and hence does not automatically increase when another independent variable is added to a regression.

Administrative regulations or administrative law   Rules issued by government agencies or other regulators.

Advanced set   The reference interest rate is set at beginning of the settlement period.

Advanced settled   An arrangement in which the settlement is made at the beginning of the settlement period.

Agency costs   Costs associated with the conflict of interest present when a company is managed by non-owners. Agency costs result from the inherent conflicts of interest between managers and equity owners.

Agency costs of equity   The smaller the stake that managers have in the company, the less is their share in bearing the cost of excessive perquisite consumption or not giving their best efforts in running the company.

Agency issues   Conflicts of interest that arise when the agent in an agency relationship has goals and incentives that differ from the principal to whom the agent owes a fiduciary duty. Also called *agency problems* or *principal–agent problems*.

Agency problem   A conflict of interest that arises when the agent in an agency relationship has goals and incentives that differ from the principal to whom the agent owes a fiduciary duty.

Alpha   The return on an asset in excess of the asset's required rate of return; the risk-adjusted return.

American Depositary Receipt   A negotiable certificate issued by a depositary bank that represents ownership in a non-US company's deposited equity (i.e., equity held in custody by the depositary bank in the company's home market).

Analysis of variance (ANOVA)   The analysis of the total variability of a dataset (such as observations on the dependent variable in a regression) into components representing different sources of variation; with reference to regression, ANOVA provides the inputs for an *F*-test of the significance of the regression as a whole.

Arbitrage   1) The simultaneous purchase of an undervalued asset or portfolio and sale of an overvalued but equivalent asset or portfolio, in order to obtain a riskless profit on the price differential. Taking advantage of a market inefficiency in a risk-free manner. 2) The condition in a financial market in which equivalent assets or combinations of assets sell for two different prices, creating an opportunity to profit at no risk with no commitment of money. In a well-functioning financial market, few arbitrage opportunities are possible. 3) A risk-free operation that earns an expected positive net profit but requires no net investment of money.

Arbitrage-free models   Term structure models that project future interest rate paths that emanate from the existing term structure. Resulting prices are based on a no-arbitrage condition.

Arbitrage-free valuation   An approach to valuation that determines security values that are consistent with the absence of arbitrage opportunities.

Arbitrage opportunity   An opportunity to conduct an arbitrage; an opportunity to earn an expected positive net profit without risk and with no net investment of money.

Arbitrage portfolio   The portfolio that exploits an arbitrage opportunity.

Asset-backed securities   A type of bond issued by a legal entity called a *special purpose vehicle* (SPV), on a collection of assets that the SPV owns. Also, securities backed by receivables and loans other than mortgage loans.

Asset-based approach   Approach that values a private company based on the values of the underlying assets of the entity less the value of any related liabilities.

Asset-based valuation   An approach to valuing natural resource companies that estimates company value on the basis of the market value of the natural resources the company controls.

Asset beta   The unlevered beta; reflects the business risk of the assets; the asset's systematic risk.

Asset purchase   An acquisition in which the acquirer purchases the target company's assets and payment is made directly to the target company.

Asymmetric information   The differential of information between corporate insiders and outsiders regarding the company's performance and prospects. Managers typically have more information about the company's performance and prospects than owners and creditors.

At market   When a forward contract is established, the forward price is negotiated so that the market value of the forward contract on the initiation date is zero.

At-the-money   An option in which the underlying value equals the exercise price.

Autocorrelation   The correlation of a time series with its own past values.

Autoregressive model (AR)   A time series regressed on its own past values, in which the independent variable is a lagged value of the dependent variable.

Available-for-sale investments   Debt and equity securities not classified as either held-to-maturity or fair value through profit or loss securities. The investor is willing to sell but not actively planning to sell. In general, available-for-sale securities are reported at fair value on the balance sheet.

Backward integration   A merger involving the purchase of a target ahead of the acquirer in the value or production chain; for example, to acquire a supplier.

Backwardation   A condition in futures markets in which the spot price exceeds the futures price; also, the condition in which the near-term (closer to expiration) futures contract price is higher than the longer-term futures contract price.

Bankruptcy   A declaration provided for by a country's laws that typically involves the establishment of a legal procedure that forces creditors to defer their claims.

Basic earnings per share   (EPS) Net earnings available to common shareholders (i.e., net income minus preferred dividends) divided by the weighted average number of common shares outstanding during the period.

Basis   The difference between the spot price and the futures price.

Basis trade   A trade based on the pricing of credit in the bond market versus the price of the same credit in the CDS market. To execute a basis trade, go long the "underpriced" credit and short the "overpriced" credit. A profit is realized when the price of credit between the short and long position converges.

Bear hug   A tactic used by acquirers to circumvent target management's objections to a proposed merger by submitting the proposal directly to the target company's board of directors.

Bear spread   A spread that becomes more valuable when the price of the underlying asset declines.

Benchmark   A comparison portfolio; a point of reference or comparison.

Benchmark value of the multiple   In using the method of comparables, the value of a price multiple for the comparison asset; when we have comparison assets (a group), the mean or median value of the multiple for the group of assets.

Bill-and-hold basis   Sales on a bill-and-hold basis involve selling products but not delivering those products until a later date.

Blockage factor   An illiquidity discount that occurs when an investor sells a large amount of stock relative to its trading volume (assuming it is not large enough to constitute a controlling ownership).

Bond indenture   A legal contract specifying the terms of a bond issue.

Bond yield plus risk premium method   An estimate of the cost of common equity that is produced by summing the before-tax cost of debt and a risk premium that captures the additional yield on a company's stock relative to its bonds. The additional yield is often estimated using historical spreads between bond yields and stock yields.

Bonding costs   Costs borne by management to assure owners that they are working in the owners' best interest (e.g., implicit cost of non-compete agreements).

Book value   Shareholders' equity (total assets minus total liabilities) minus the value of preferred stock; common shareholders' equity.

Book value of equity   Shareholders' equity (total assets minus total liabilities) minus the value of preferred stock; common shareholders' equity.

Book value per share   The amount of book value (also called carrying value) of common equity per share of common stock, calculated by dividing the book value of shareholders' equity by the number of shares of common stock outstanding.

Bootstrapping   A statistical method for estimating a sample distribution based on the properties of an approximating distribution.

Bottom-up approach   With respect to forecasting, an approach that usually begins at the level of the individual company or a unit within the company.

Bottom-up investing   An approach to investing that focuses on the individual characteristics of securities rather than on macroeconomic or overall market forecasts.

Breakup value   The value derived using a sum-of-the-parts valuation.

Breusch–Pagan test   A test for conditional heteroskedasticity in the error term of a regression.

Brokerage   The business of acting as agents for buyers or sellers, usually in return for commissions.

Bull spread   A spread that becomes more valuable when the price of the underlying asset rises.

Buy-side analysts   Analysts who work for investment management firms, trusts, and bank trust departments, and similar institutions.

Calendar spread   A strategy in which an investor sells (or buys) a near-dated call and buys (or sells) a longer-dated one on the same underlying asset and with the same strike.

Callable bond   Bond that includes an embedded call option that gives the issuer the right to redeem the bond issue prior to maturity, typically when interest rates have fallen or when the issuer's credit quality has improved.

Cannibalization   Cannibalization occurs when an investment takes customers and sales away from another part of the company.

Cap rate   See *capitalization rate*.

Capital charge   The company's total cost of capital in money terms.

Capital deepening   An increase in the capital-to-labor ratio.

Capital rationing   A capital rationing environment assumes that the company has a fixed amount of funds to invest.

Capital structure   The mix of debt and equity that a company uses to finance its business; a company's specific mixture of long-term financing.

Capitalization of earnings method   In the context of private company valuation, valuation model based on an assumption of a constant growth rate of free cash flow to the firm or a constant growth rate of free cash flow to equity.

Capitalization rate   The divisor in the expression for the value of perpetuity. In the context of real estate, the divisor in the direct capitalization method of estimating value. The cap rate equals net operating income divided by value.

Capitalized cash flow method   In the context of private company valuation, valuation model based on an assumption of a constant growth rate of free cash flow to the firm or a constant growth rate of free cash flow to equity. Also called *capitalized cash flow model*.

Capitalized cash flow model   In the context of private company valuation, valuation model based on an assumption of a constant growth rate of free cash flow to the firm or a constant growth rate of free cash flow to equity. Also called *capitalized cash flow method*.

Capitalized income method   In the context of private company valuation, valuation model based on an assumption of a constant growth rate of free cash flow to the firm or a constant growth rate of free cash flow to equity.

Capped floater   Floating-rate bond with a cap provision that prevents the coupon rate from increasing above a specified maximum rate. It protects the issuer against rising interest rates.

Carried interest   A share of any profits that is paid to the general partner (manager) of an investment partnership, such as a private equity or hedge fund, as a form of compensation designed to be an incentive to the manager to maximize performance of the investment fund.

Carry arbitrage model   A no-arbitrage approach in which the underlying instrument is either bought or sold along with an opposite position in a forward contract.

Carry benefits   Benefits that arise from owning certain underlyings; for example, dividends, foreign interest, and bond coupon payments.

Carry costs   Costs that arise from owning certain underlyings. They are generally a function of the physical characteristics of the underlying asset and also the interest forgone on the funds tied up in the asset.

Cash available for distribution   Funds from operations (FFO) adjusted to remove any non-cash rent reported under straight-line rent accounting and to subtract maintenance-type capital expenditures and leasing costs, including leasing agents' commissions and tenants' improvement allowances.

Cash-generating unit   The smallest identifiable group of assets that generates cash inflows that are largely independent of the cash inflows of other assets or groups of assets.

Cash offering   A merger or acquisition that is to be paid for with cash; the cash for the merger might come from the acquiring company's existing assets or from a debt issue.

Cash-secured put   An option strategy involving the writing of a put option and simultaneously depositing an amount of money equal to the exercise price into a designated account.

Cash settled   A procedure used in certain derivative transactions that specifies that the long and short parties engage in the equivalent cash value of a delivery transaction.

Cash settlement   A procedure used in certain derivative transactions that specifies that the long and short parties engage in the equivalent cash value of a delivery transaction.

Catalyst   An event or piece of information that causes the marketplace to re-evaluate the prospects of a company.

CDS spread   A periodic premium paid by the buyer to the seller that serves as a return over Libor required to protect against credit risk.

Chain rule of forecasting   A forecasting process in which the next period's value as predicted by the forecasting equation is substituted into the right-hand side of the equation to give a predicted value two periods ahead.

Cheapest-to-deliver   The debt instrument that can be purchased and delivered at the lowest cost yet has the same seniority as the reference obligation.

Clean surplus accounting   Accounting that satisfies the condition that all changes in the book value of equity other than transactions with owners are reflected in income. The bottom-line income reflects all changes in shareholders' equity arising from other than owner transactions. In the absence of owner transactions, the change in shareholders' equity should equal net income. No adjustments such as translation adjustments bypass the income statement and go directly to shareholders equity.

Clean surplus relation   The relationship between earnings, dividends, and book value in which ending book value is equal to the beginning book value plus earnings less dividends, apart from ownership transactions.

Clientele effect   The preference some investors have for shares that exhibit certain characteristics.

Club convergence   The idea that only rich and middle-income countries sharing a set of favorable attributes (i.e., are members of the "club") will converge to the income level of the richest countries.

Cobb–Douglas production function   A function of the form $Y = K^\alpha L^{1-\alpha}$ relating output (Y) to labor (L) and capital (K) inputs.

Cointegrated   Describes two time series that have a long-term financial or economic relationship such that they do not diverge from each other without bound in the long run.

Collar   An option position in which the investor is long shares of stock and then buys a put with an exercise price below the current underlying price and writes a call with an exercise price above the current underlying price.

Collateral return   The component of the total return on a commodity futures position attributable to the yield for the bonds or cash used to maintain the futures position. Also called *collateral yield*.

Commercial real estate properties   Income-producing real estate properties, properties purchased with the intent to let, lease, or rent (in other words, produce income).

Commodity swap   A type of swap involving the exchange of payments over multiple dates as determined by specified reference prices or indexes relating to commodities.

Common size statements   Financial statements in which all elements (accounts) are stated as a percentage of a key figure such as revenue for an income statement or total assets for a balance sheet.

Company fundamental factors   Factors related to the company's internal performance, such as factors relating to earnings growth, earnings variability, earnings momentum, and financial leverage.

Company share-related factors   Valuation measures and other factors related to share price or the trading characteristics of the shares, such as earnings yield, dividend yield, and book-to-market value.

Comparables   Assets used as benchmarks when applying the method of comparables to value an asset. Also called *comps*, *guideline assets*, or *guideline companies*.

Compiled financial statements   Financial statements that are not accompanied by an auditor's opinion letter.

Comprehensive income   All changes in equity other than contributions by, and distributions to, owners; income under clean surplus accounting; includes all changes in equity during a period except those resulting from investments by owners and distributions to owners; comprehensive income equals net income plus other comprehensive income.

Comps   Assets used as benchmarks when applying the method of comparables to value an asset.

Conditional convergence   The idea that convergence of per capita income is conditional on the countries having the same savings rate, population growth rate, and production function.

Conditional heteroskedasticity   Heteroskedasticity in the error variance that is correlated with the values of the independent variable(s) in the regression.

Conditional VaR (CVaR)   The average loss conditional on exceeding the VaR cutoff; sometimes referred to as the *expected tail loss* or *expected shortfall*.

Conglomerate discount   The discount possibly applied by the market to the stock of a company operating in multiple, unrelated businesses.

Conglomerate merger   A merger involving companies that are in unrelated businesses.

Consolidation   The combining of the results of operations of subsidiaries with the parent company to present financial statements as if they were a single economic unit. The assets, liabilities, revenues and expenses of the subsidiaries are combined with those of the parent company, eliminating intercompany transactions.

Constant dividend payout ratio policy   A policy in which a constant percentage of net income is paid out in dividends.

Constant returns to scale   The condition that if all inputs into the production process are increased by a given percentage, then output rises by that same percentage.

Contango   A condition in futures markets in which the spot price is lower than the futures price; also, the condition in which the near-term (closer to expiration) futures contract price is lower than the longer-term futures contract price.

Contingent consideration   Potential future payments to the seller that are contingent on the achievement of certain agreed on occurrences.

Continuing earnings   Earnings excluding nonrecurring components. Also referred to as *core earnings*, *persistent earnings*, or *underlying earnings*.

Continuing residual income   Residual income after the forecast horizon.

Continuing value   The analyst's estimate of a stock's value at a particular point in the future.

Control premium   An increment or premium to value associated with a controlling ownership interest in a company.

Conventional cash flow   A conventional cash flow pattern is one with an initial outflow followed by a series of inflows.

Convergence   The property of forward and futures contracts in which the derivative price becomes the spot price at expiration of the derivative.

Conversion period   For a convertible bond, the period during which bondholders have the right to convert their bonds into shares.

Conversion price   For a convertible bond, the price per share at which the bond can be converted into shares.

Conversion ratio   For a convertible bond, the number of shares of common stock that a bondholder receives from converting the bond into shares.

Conversion value   For a convertible bond, the value of the bond if it is converted at the market price of the shares. Also called *parity value*.

Convertible bond   Bond with an embedded conversion option that gives the bondholder the right to convert their bonds into the issuer's common stock during a pre-determined period at a pre-determined price.

Convexity   A measure of how interest rate sensitivity changes with a change in interest rates.

Core earnings   Earnings excluding nonrecurring components. Also referred to as *continuing earnings*, *persistent earnings*, or *underlying earnings*.

Corporate governance   The system of principles, policies, procedures, and clearly defined responsibilities and accountabilities used by stakeholders to overcome the conflicts of interest inherent in the corporate form.

Corporate raider   A person or organization seeking to profit by acquiring a company and reselling it, or seeking to profit from the takeover attempt itself (e.g., greenmail).

Corporation   A legal entity with rights similar to those of a person. The chief officers, executives, or top managers act as agents for the firm and are legally entitled to authorize corporate activities and to enter into contracts on behalf of the business.

Correlation analysis   The analysis of the strength of the linear relationship between two data series.

Cost approach   Approach that values a private company based on the values of the underlying assets of the entity less the value of any related liabilities. In the context of real estate, this approach estimates the value of a property based on what it would cost to buy the land and construct a new property on the site that has the same utility or functionality as the property being appraised.

Cost of debt The cost of debt financing to a company, such as when it issues a bond or takes out a bank loan.

Cost of equity The required rate of return on common stock.

Covariance stationary Describes a time series when its expected value and variance are constant and finite in all periods and when its covariance with itself for a fixed number of periods in the past or future is constant and finite in all periods.

Covered call An option strategy in which an investor who already owns the underlying asset sells a call option giving someone else the right to buy the asset at the exercise price.

Covered interest rate parity Relationship among the spot exchange rate, forward exchange rate, and the interest rates in two currencies that ensures that the return on a hedged (i.e., covered) foreign risk-free investment is the same as the return on a domestic risk-free investment. Also called *interest rate parity*.

Cox–Ingersoll–Ross model A partial equilibrium term structure model that assumes interest rates are mean reverting and interest rate volatility is directly related to the level of interest rates.

Credit correlation The correlation of credits contained in an index CDS.

Credit curve The credit spreads for a range of maturities of a company's debt; applies to non-government borrowers and incorporates credit risk into each rate.

Credit default swap A derivative contract between two parties in which the buyer makes a series of cash payments to the seller and receives a promise of compensation for credit losses resulting from the default.

Credit derivative A derivative instrument in which the underlying is a measure of the credit quality of a borrower.

Credit event The outcome that triggers a payment from the credit protection seller to the credit protection buyer.

Credit protection buyer One party to a credit default swap; the buyer makes a series of cash payments to the seller and receives a promise of compensation for credit losses resulting from the default.

Credit protection seller One party to a credit default swap; the buyer makes a series of cash payments to the seller and receives a promise of compensation for credit losses resulting from the default.

Credit ratings Ordinal rankings of the credit risk of a company, government (sovereign), quasi-government, or asset-backed security.

Credit risk The risk that the borrower will not repay principal and interest. Also called *default risk*.

Credit scoring Ordinal rankings of a retail borrower's credit riskiness. It is called an *ordinal ranking* because it only orders borrowers' riskiness from highest to lowest.

Credit spreads The difference between the yields on default-free and credit risky zero-coupon bonds.

Current exchange rate For accounting purposes, the spot exchange rate on the balance sheet date.

Current rate method Approach to translating foreign currency financial statements for consolidation in which all assets and liabilities are translated at the current exchange rate. The current rate method is the prevalent method of translation.

Curvature One of the three factors (the other two are level and steepness) that empirically explain most of the changes in the shape of the yield curve. A shock to the curvature factor affects mid-maturity interest rates, resulting in the term structure becoming either more or less hump-shaped.

Curve trade Buying a CDS of one maturity and selling a CDS on the same reference entity with a different maturity.

Cyclical businesses Businesses with high sensitivity to business- or industry-cycle influences.

Data mining The practice of determining a model by extensive searching through a dataset for statistically significant patterns.

"Dead-hand" provision A poison pill provision that allows for the redemption or cancellation of a poison pill provision only by a vote of continuing directors (generally directors who were on the target company's board prior to the takeover attempt).

Debt ratings An objective measure of the quality and safety of a company's debt based upon an analysis of the company's ability to pay the promised cash flows, as well as an analysis of any indentures.

Decision rule With respect to hypothesis testing, the rule according to which the null hypothesis will be rejected or not rejected; involves the comparison of the test statistic to rejection point(s).

Default intensity Gives the probability of default over the next instant $[t, t + \Delta]$ when the economy is in state X_t.

Default probability See *probability of default*.

Default risk See *credit risk*.

Defined benefit pension plans Plan in which the company promises to pay a certain annual amount (defined benefit) to the employee after retirement. The company bears the investment risk of the plan assets.

Defined contribution pension plans Individual accounts to which an employee and typically the employer makes contributions, generally on a tax-advantaged basis. The amounts of contributions are defined at the outset, but the future value of the benefit is unknown. The employee bears the investment risk of the plan assets.

Definition of value A specification of how "value" is to be understood in the context of a specific valuation.

Definitive merger agreement A contract signed by both parties to a merger that clarifies the details of the transaction, including the terms, warranties, conditions, termination details, and the rights of all parties.

Delta The relationship between the option price and the underlying price, which reflects the sensitivity of the price of the option to changes in the price of the underlying. Delta is a good approximation of how an option price will change for a small change in the stock.

Dependent variable The variable whose variation about its mean is to be explained by the regression; the left-hand-side variable in a regression equation.

Depository Trust and Clearinghouse Corporation A US-headquartered entity providing post-trade clearing, settlement, and information services.

Depreciated replacement cost In the context of real estate, the replacement cost of a building adjusted different types of depreciation.

Derivative A financial instrument whose value depends on the value of some underlying asset or factor (e.g., a stock price, an interest rate, or exchange rate).

Descriptive statistics The study of how data can be summarized effectively.

Diluted earnings per share   (diluted EPS) Net income, minus preferred dividends, divided by the weighted average number of common shares outstanding considering all dilutive securities (e.g., convertible debt and options); the EPS that would result if all dilutive securities were converted into common shares.

Dilution   A reduction in proportional ownership interest as a result of the issuance of new shares.

Diminishing marginal productivity   When each additional unit of an input, keeping the other inputs unchanged, increases output by a smaller increment.

Direct capitalization method   In the context of real estate, this method estimates the value of an income-producing property based on the level and quality of its net operating income.

Discount   To reduce the value of a future payment in allowance for how far away it is in time; to calculate the present value of some future amount. Also, the amount by which an instrument is priced below its face value.

Discount factor   The present value or price of a risk-free single-unit payment when discounted using the appropriate spot rate.

Discount for lack of control   An amount or percentage deducted from the pro rata share of 100 percent of the value of an equity interest in a business to reflect the absence of some or all of the powers of control.

Discount for lack of marketability   An amount of percentage deducted from the value of an ownership interest to reflect the relative absence of marketability.

Discount function   Discount factors for the range of all possible maturities. The spot curve can be derived from the discount function and vice versa.

Discount rate   Any rate used in finding the present value of a future cash flow.

Discounted abnormal earnings model   A model of stock valuation that views intrinsic value of stock as the sum of book value per share plus the present value of the stock's expected future residual income per share.

Discounted cash flow (DCF) analysis   In the context of merger analysis, it is an estimate of a target company's value found by discounting the company's expected future free cash flows to the present.

Discounted cash flow method   Income approach that values an asset based on estimates of future cash flows discounted to present value by using a discount rate reflective of the risks associated with the cash flows. In the context of real estate, this method estimates the value of an income-producing property based by discounting future projected cash flows.

Discounted cash flow model   A model of intrinsic value that views the value of an asset as the present value of the asset's expected future cash flows.

Discriminant analysis   A multivariate classification technique used to discriminate between groups, such as companies that either will or will not become bankrupt during some time frame.

Diversified REITs   REITs that own and operate in more than one type of property; they are more common in Europe and Asia than in the United States.

Divestiture   The sale, liquidation, or spin-off of a division or subsidiary.

Dividend coverage ratio   The ratio of net income to dividends.

Dividend discount model   (DDM) A present value model of stock value that views the intrinsic value of a stock as present value of the stock's expected future dividends.

Dividend displacement of earnings   The concept that dividends paid now displace earnings in all future periods.

Dividend imputation tax system   A taxation system which effectively assures that corporate profits distributed as dividends are taxed just once, at the shareholder's tax rate.

Dividend payout ratio   The ratio of cash dividends paid to earnings for a period.

Dividend policy   The strategy a company follows with regard to the amount and timing of dividend payments.

Dividend rate   the annualized amount of the most recent dividend.

Dominance   An arbitrage opportunity when a financial asset with a risk-free payoff in the future must have a positive price today.

Double taxation system   Corporate earnings are taxed twice when paid out as dividends. First, corporate earnings are taxed regardless of whether they will be distributed as dividends or retained at the G-13 corporate level, and second, dividends are taxed again at the individual shareholder level.

DOWNREIT   A variation of the UPREIT structure under which the REIT owns more than one partnership and may own properties at both the REIT level and the partnership level.

Downstream   A transaction between two related companies, an investor company (or a parent company) and an associate company (or a subsidiary) such that the investor company records a profit on its income statement. An example is a sale of inventory by the investor company to the associate or by a parent to a subsidiary company.

Due diligence   Investigation and analysis in support of a recommendation; the failure to exercise due diligence may sometimes result in liability according to various securities laws.

Dummy variable   A type of qualitative variable that takes on a value of 1 if a particular condition is true and 0 if that condition is false.

Duration   A measure of the approximate sensitivity of a security to a change in interest rates (i.e., a measure of interest rate risk).

Dutch disease   A situation in which currency appreciation driven by strong export demand for resources makes other segments of the economy (particularly manufacturing) globally uncompetitive.

Earnings surprise   The difference between reported EPS and expected EPS. Also referred to as *unexpected earnings*.

Earnings yield   EPS divided by price; the reciprocal of the P/E ratio.

Economic growth   The expansion of production possibilities that results from capital accumulation and technological change.

Economic obsolescence   In the context of real estate, a reduction in value due to current economic conditions.

Economic profit   See *residual income*.

Economic sectors   Large industry groupings.

Economic value added   (EVA®) A commercial implementation of the residual income concept; the computation of EVA® is the net operating profit after taxes minus the cost of capital, where these inputs are adjusted for a number of items.

Economies of scale A situation in which average costs per unit of good or service produced fall as volume rises. In reference to mergers, the savings achieved through the consolidation of operations and elimination of duplicate resources.

Edwards–Bell–Ohlson model A model of stock valuation that views intrinsic value of stock as the sum of book value per share plus the present value of the stock's expected future residual income per share.

Effective convexity Sensitivity of duration to changes in interest rates.

Effective duration Sensitivity of the bond's price to a 100 bps parallel shift of the benchmark yield curve, assuming no change in the bond's credit spread.

Embedded options Contingency provisions found in a bond's indenture or offering circular representing rights that enable their holders to take advantage of interest rate movements. They can be exercised by the issuer, by the bondholder, or automatically depending on the course of interest rates.

Enterprise value (EV) Total company value (the market value of debt, common equity, and preferred equity) minus the value of cash and investments.

Enterprise value multiple A valuation multiple that relates the total market value of all sources of a company's capital (net of cash) to a measure of fundamental value for the entire company (such as a pre-interest earnings measure).

Entry price The price paid to acquire an asset.

Equilibrium The condition in which supply equals demand.

Equity carve-out A form of restructuring that involves the creation of a new legal entity and the sale of equity in it to outsiders.

Equity charge The estimated cost of equity capital in money terms.

Equity REIT A REIT that owns, operates, and/or selectively develops income-producing real estate.

Equity swap A swap transaction in which at least one cash flow is tied to the return on an equity portfolio position, often an equity index.

Error autocorrelation The autocorrelation of the error term.

Error term The portion of the dependent variable that is not explained by the independent variable(s) in the regression.

Estimated parameters With reference to a regression analysis, the estimated values of the population intercept and population slope coefficient(s) in a regression.

Ex ante tracking error A measure of the degree to which the performance of a given investment portfolio might be expected to deviate from its benchmark; also known as *relative VaR*.

Ex ante version of PPP Hypothesis that expected changes in the spot exchange rate are equal to expected differences in national inflation rates. An extension of relative purchasing power parity to expected future changes in the exchange rate.

Ex-dividend Trading ex-dividend refers to shares that no longer carry the right to the next dividend payment.

Ex-dividend date The first date that a share trades without (i.e., "ex") the dividend.

Ex-dividend price The price at which a share first trades without (i.e., "ex") the right to receive an upcoming dividend.

Excess earnings method Income approach that estimates the value of all intangible assets of the business by capitalizing future earnings in excess of the estimated return requirements associated with working capital and fixed assets.

Exchange ratio The number of shares that target stockholders are to receive in exchange for each of their shares in the target company.

Exercise date The date when employees actually exercise stock options and convert them to stock.

Exercise value The value of an option if it were exercised. Also sometimes called *intrinsic value*.

Exit price The price received to sell an asset or paid to transfer a liability.

Expanded CAPM An adaptation of the CAPM that adds to the CAPM a premium for small size and company-specific risk.

Expectations approach A procedure for obtaining the value of an option derived from discounting at the risk-free rate its expected future payoff based on risk neutral probabilities.

Expected holding-period return The expected total return on an asset over a stated holding period; for stocks, the sum of the expected dividend yield and the expected price appreciation over the holding period.

Expected loss The probability of default multiplied by the loss given default; the full amount owed minus the expected recovery.

Expected shortfall See *conditional VaR*.

Expected tail loss See *conditional VaR*.

Exposure to foreign exchange risk The risk of a change in value of an asset or liability denominated in a foreign currency due to a change in exchange rates.

Extendible bond Bond with an embedded option that gives the bondholder the right to keep the bond for a number of years after maturity, possibly with a different coupon.

External growth Company growth in output or sales that is achieved by buying the necessary resources externally (i.e., achieved through mergers and acquisitions).

External sustainability approach An approach to assessing the equilibrium exchange rate that focuses on exchange rate adjustments required to ensure that a country's net foreign-asset/GDP ratio or net foreign-liability/GDP ratio stabilizes at a sustainable level.

Factor A common or underlying element with which several variables are correlated.

Factor betas An asset's sensitivity to a particular factor; a measure of the response of return to each unit of increase in a factor, holding all other factors constant.

Factor portfolio See *pure factor portfolio*.

Factor price The expected return in excess of the risk-free rate for a portfolio with a sensitivity of 1 to one factor and a sensitivity of 0 to all other factors.

Factor risk premium The expected return in excess of the risk-free rate for a portfolio with a sensitivity of 1 to one factor and a sensitivity of 0 to all other factors. Also called *factor price*.

Factor sensitivity See *factor betas*.

Failure to pay When a borrower does not make a scheduled payment of principal or interest on any outstanding obligations after a grace period.

Fair market value The market price of an asset or liability that trades regularly.

Fair value The amount at which an asset (or liability) could be bought (or incurred) or sold (or settled) in a current transaction between willing parties, that is, other than in a forced or liquidation sale; as defined in IFRS and US

GAAP, the price that would be received to sell an asset or paid to transfer a liability in an orderly transaction between market participants at the measurement date.

Financial contagion   A situation where financial shocks spread from their place of origin to other locales; in essence, a faltering economy infects other, healthier economies.

Financial distress   Heightened uncertainty regarding a company's ability to meet its various obligations because of lower or negative earnings.

Financial risk   The risk that environmental, social, or governance risk factors will result in significant costs or other losses to a company and its shareholders; the risk arising from a company's obligation to meet required payments under its financing agreements.

Financial transaction   A purchase involving a buyer having essentially no material synergies with the target (e.g., the purchase of a private company by a company in an unrelated industry or by a private equity firm would typically be a financial transaction).

First-differencing   A transformation that subtracts the value of the time series in period $t - 1$ from its value in period t.

First-order serial correlation   Correlation between adjacent observations in a time series.

Fitted parameters   With reference to a regression analysis, the estimated values of the population intercept and population slope coefficient(s) in a regression.

Fixed-rate perpetual preferred stock   Nonconvertible, noncallable preferred stock with a specified dividend rate that has a claim on earnings senior to the claim of common stock, and no maturity date.

Flip-in pill   A poison pill takeover defense that dilutes an acquirer's ownership in a target by giving other existing target company shareholders the right to buy additional target company shares at a discount.

Flip-over pill   A poison pill takeover defense that gives target company shareholders the right to purchase shares of the acquirer at a significant discount to the market price, which has the effect of causing dilution to all existing acquiring company shareholders.

Floored floater   Floating-rate bond with a floor provision that prevents the coupon rate from decreasing below a specified minimum rate. It protects the investor against declining interest rates.

Flotation cost   Fees charged to companies by investment bankers and other costs associated with raising new capital.

Forced conversion   For a convertible bond, when the issuer calls the bond and forces bondholders to convert their bonds into shares, which typically happens when the underlying share price increases above the conversion price.

Foreign currency transactions   Transactions that are denominated in a currency other than a company's functional currency.

Forward curve   The term structure of forward rates for loans made on a specific initiation date.

Forward dividend yield   A dividend yield based on the anticipated dividend during the next 12 months.

Forward integration   A merger involving the purchase of a target that is farther along the value or production chain; for example, to acquire a distributor.

Forward P/E   A P/E calculated on the basis of a forecast of EPS; a stock's current price divided by next year's expected earnings.

Forward price   The fixed price or rate at which the transaction scheduled to occur at the expiration of a forward contract will take place. This price is agreed to at the initiation date of the contract.

Forward pricing model   The model that describes the valuation of forward contracts.

Forward rate   An interest rate that is determined today for a loan that will be initiated in a future time period.

Forward rate agreement   A forward contract calling for one party to make a fixed interest payment and the other to make an interest payment at a rate to be determined at the contract expiration.

Forward rate model   The forward pricing model expressed in terms of spot and forward interest rates.

Forward value   The monetary value of an existing forward contract.

Franking credit   A tax credit received by shareholders for the taxes that a corporation paid on its distributed earnings.

Free cash flow   The actual cash that would be available to the company's investors after making all investments necessary to maintain the company as an ongoing enterprise (also referred to as free cash flow to the firm); the internally generated funds that can be distributed to the company's investors (e.g., shareholders and bondholders) without impairing the value of the company.

Free cash flow hypothesis   The hypothesis that higher debt levels discipline managers by forcing them to make fixed debt service payments and by reducing the company's free cash flow.

Free cash flow method   Income approach that values an asset based on estimates of future cash flows discounted to present value by using a discount rate reflective of the risks associated with the cash flows.

Free cash flow to equity   The cash flow available to a company's common shareholders after all operating expenses, interest, and principal payments have been made, and necessary investments in working and fixed capital have been made.

Free cash flow to equity model   A model of stock valuation that views a stock's intrinsic value as the present value of expected future free cash flows to equity.

Free cash flow to the firm   The cash flow available to the company's suppliers of capital after all operating expenses (including taxes) have been paid and necessary investments in working and fixed capital have been made.

Free cash flow to the firm model   A model of stock valuation that views the value of a firm as the present value of expected future free cash flows to the firm.

Friendly transaction   A potential business combination that is endorsed by the managers of both companies.

Functional currency   The currency of the primary economic environment in which an entity operates.

Functional obsolescence   In the context of real estate, a reduction in value due to a design that differs from that of a new building constructed for the intended use of the property.

Fundamental factor models   A multifactor model in which the factors are attributes of stocks or companies that are important in explaining cross-sectional differences in stock prices.

Fundamentals   Economic characteristics of a business such as profitability, financial strength, and risk.

Funds available for distribution   Funds from operations (FFO) adjusted to remove any non-cash rent reported under straight-line rent accounting and to subtract maintenance-type capital expenditures and leasing costs, including leasing agents' commissions and tenants' improvement allowances.

Funds from operations Accounting net earnings excluding (1) depreciation charges on real estate, (2) deferred tax charges, and (3) gains or losses from sales of property and debt restructuring.

Futures price The price at which the parties to a futures contract agree to exchange the underlying (or cash). In commodity markets, the price agreed on to deliver or receive a defined quantity (and often quality) of a commodity at a future date.

Futures value The monetary value of an existing futures contract.

FX carry trade An investment strategy that involves taking on long positions in high-yield currencies and short positions in low-yield currencies.

Gamma A measure of how sensitive an option's delta is to a change in the underlying. The change in a given instrument's delta for a given small change in the underlying's value, holding everything else constant.

Generalized least squares A regression estimation technique that addresses heteroskedasticity of the error term.

Going-concern assumption The assumption that the business will maintain its business activities into the foreseeable future.

Going-concern value A business's value under a going-concern assumption.

Goodwill An intangible asset that represents the excess of the purchase price of an acquired company over the value of the net identifiable assets acquired.

Grant date The day that stock options are granted to employees.

Gross domestic product A money measure of the goods and services produced within a country's borders over a stated time period.

Gross lease A lease under which the tenant pays a gross rent to the landlord who is responsible for all operating costs, utilities, maintenance expenses, and real estate taxes relating to the property.

Growth accounting equation The production function written in the form of growth rates. For the basic Cobb–Douglas production function, it states that the growth rate of output equals the rate of technological change plus α times the growth rate of capital plus $(1 - \alpha)$ times the growth rate of labor.

Growth capital expenditures Capital expenditures needed for expansion.

Growth option The ability to make additional investments in a project at some future time if the financial results are strong. Also called *expansion option*.

Guideline assets Assets used as benchmarks when applying the method of comparables to value an asset.

Guideline companies Assets used as benchmarks when applying the method of comparables to value an asset.

Guideline public companies Public-company comparables for the company being valued.

Guideline public company method A variation of the market approach; establishes a value estimate based on the observed multiples from trading activity in the shares of public companies viewed as reasonably comparable to the subject private company.

Guideline transactions method A variation of the market approach; establishes a value estimate based on pricing multiples derived from the acquisition of control of entire public or private companies that were acquired.

Harmonic mean A type of weighted mean computed by averaging the reciprocals of the observations, then taking the reciprocal of that average.

Hazard rate The probability that an event will occur, given that it has not already occurred.

Hazard rate estimation A technique for estimating the probability of a binary event, such as default/no default, mortality/no mortality, and prepay/no prepay.

Health care REITs REITs that invest in skilled nursing facilities (nursing homes), assisted living and independent residential facilities for retired persons, hospitals, medical office buildings, or rehabilitation centers.

Held for trading investments Debt or equity securities acquired with the intent to sell them in the near term.

Held-to-maturity investments Debt (fixed-income) securities that a company intends to hold to maturity; these are presented at their original cost, updated for any amortization of discounts or premiums.

Herfindahl–Hirschman Index (HHI) A measure of market concentration that is calculated by summing the squared market shares for competing companies in an industry; high HHI readings or mergers that would result in large HHI increases are more likely to result in regulatory challenges.

Heteroskedastic With reference to the error term of regression, having a variance that differs across observations.

Heteroskedasticity The property of having a nonconstant variance; refers to an error term with the property that its variance differs across observations.

Heteroskedasticity-consistent standard errors Standard errors of the estimated parameters of a regression that correct for the presence of heteroskedasticity in the regression's error term.

Historical exchange rates For accounting purposes, the exchange rates that existed when the assets and liabilities were initially recorded.

Historical simulation method The application of historical price changes to the current portfolio.

Ho–Lee model The first arbitrage-free term structure model. The model is calibrated to market data and uses a binomial lattice approach to generate a distribution of possible future interest rates.

Holding period return The return that an investor earns during a specified holding period; a synonym for total return.

Homoskedasticity The property of having a constant variance; refers to an error term that is constant across observations.

Horizontal merger A merger involving companies in the same line of business, usually as competitors.

Hostile transaction An attempt to acquire a company against the wishes of the target's managers.

Hotel REITs REITs that own hotel properties but, similar to health care REITs, in many countries they must refrain from operating their properties themselves to maintain their tax-advantaged REIT status.

Human capital The accumulated knowledge and skill that workers acquire from education, training, or life experience.

Hybrid approach With respect to forecasting, an approach that combines elements of both top-down and bottom-up analysis.

Hybrid REITs   REITs that own and operate income-producing real estate and invest in mortgages as well; REITs that have positions in both real estate assets and real estate debt.

I-spreads   Shortened form of "interpolated spreads" and a reference to a linearly interpolated yield.

Illiquidity discount   A reduction or discount to value that reflects the lack of depth of trading or liquidity in that asset's market.

Impairment   Diminishment in value as a result of carrying (book) value exceeding fair value and/or recoverable value.

Impairment of capital rule   A legal restriction that dividends cannot exceed retained earnings.

Implied volatility   The standard deviation that causes an option pricing model to give the current option price.

In-sample forecast errors   The residuals from a fitted time-series model within the sample period used to fit the model.

Income approach   Valuation approach that values an asset as the present discounted value of the income expected from it. In the context of real estate, this approach estimates the value of a property based on an expected rate of return; the estimated value is the present value of the expected future income from the property, including proceeds from resale at the end of a typical investment holding period.

Incremental cash flow   The cash flow that is realized because of a decision; the changes or increments to cash flows resulting from a decision or action.

Incremental VaR (IVaR)   A measure of the incremental effect of an asset on the VaR of a portfolio by measuring the difference between the portfolio's VaR while including a specified asset and the portfolio's VaR with that asset eliminated.

Indenture   A written contract between a lender and borrower that specifies the terms of the loan, such as interest rate, interest payment schedule, maturity, etc.

Independent projects   Independent projects are projects whose cash flows are independent of each other.

Independent regulators   Regulators recognized and granted authority by a government body or agency. They are not government agencies per se and typically do not rely on government funding.

Independent variable   A variable used to explain the dependent variable in a regression; a right-hand-side variable in a regression equation.

Index CDS   A type of credit default swap that involves a combination of borrowers.

Indexing   An investment strategy in which an investor constructs a portfolio to mirror the performance of a specified index.

Industrial REITs   REITs that hold portfolios of single-tenant or multi-tenant industrial properties that are used as warehouses, distribution centers, light manufacturing facilities, and small office or "flex" space.

Industry structure   An industry's underlying economic and technical characteristics.

Information ratio   (IR) Mean active return divided by active risk; or alpha divided by the standard deviation of diversifiable risk.

Informational frictions   Forces that restrict availability, quality, and/or flow of information and its use.

Initial public offering   (IPO) The initial issuance of common stock registered for public trading by a formerly private corporation.

Inter-temporal rate of substitution   The ratio of the marginal utility of consumption *s* periods in the future (the numerator) to the marginal utility of consumption today (the denominator).

Interest rate parity   See *covered interest rate parity.*

Interest rate risk   Risk that interest rates will change such that the return earned is not commensurate with returns on comparable instruments in the marketplace.

Internal rate of return   (IRR) Rate of return that discounts future cash flows from an investment to the exact amount of the investment; the discount rate that makes the present value of an investment's costs (outflows) equal to the present value of the investment's benefits (inflows).

Internal ratings   Credit ratings developed internally and used by financial institutions or other entities to manage risk.

International Fisher effect   Proposition that nominal interest rate differentials across currencies are determined by expected inflation differentials.

Intrinsic value   The value of an asset given a hypothetically complete understanding of the asset's investment characteristics; the value obtained if an option is exercised based on current conditions. The difference between the spot exchange rate and the strike price of a currency.

Inverse price ratio   The reciprocal of a price multiple, e.g., in the case of a P/E ratio, the "earnings yield" E/P (where P is share price and E is earnings per share).

Investment objectives   Desired investment outcomes; includes risk objectives and return objectives.

Investment strategy   An approach to investment analysis and security selection.

Investment value   The value to a specific buyer, taking account of potential synergies based on the investor's requirements and expectations.

ISDA Master Agreement   A standard or "master" agreement published by the International Swaps and Derivatives Association. The master agreement establishes the terms for each party involved in the transaction.

Judicial law   Interpretations of courts.

Justified (fundamental) P/E   The price-to-earnings ratio that is fair, warranted, or justified on the basis of forecasted fundamentals.

Justified price multiple   The estimated fair value of the price multiple, usually based on forecasted fundamentals or comparables.

Key rate durations   Sensitivity of a bond's price to changes in specific maturities on the benchmark yield curve. Also called *partial durations.*

kth order autocorrelation   The correlation between observations in a time series separated by *k* periods.

Labor force   Everyone of working age (ages 16 to 64) that either is employed or is available for work but not working.

Labor force participation rate   The percentage of the working age population that is in the labor force.

Labor productivity   The quantity of real GDP produced by an hour of labor. More generally, output per unit of labor input.

Labor productivity growth accounting equation   States that potential GDP growth equals the growth rate of the labor input plus the growth rate of labor productivity.

Lack of marketability discount   An extra return to investors to compensate for lack of a public market or lack of marketability.

Law of one price A principle that states that if two investments have the same or equivalent future cash flows regardless of what will happen in the future, then these two investments should have the same current price.

Leading dividend yield Forecasted dividends per share over the next year divided by current stock price.

Leading P/E A P/E calculated on the basis of a forecast of EPS; a stock's current price divided by next year's expected earnings.

Legal risk The risk that failures by company managers to effectively manage a company's environmental, social, and governance risk exposures will lead to lawsuits and other judicial remedies, resulting in potentially catastrophic losses for the company; the risk that the legal system will not enforce a contract in case of dispute or fraud.

Legislative and regulatory risk The risk that governmental laws and regulations directly or indirectly affecting a company's operations will change with potentially severe adverse effects on the company's continued profitability and even its long-term sustainability.

Level One of the three factors (the other two are steepness and curvature) that empirically explain most of the changes in the shape of the yield curve. A shock to the level factor changes the yield for all maturities by an almost identical amount.

Leveraged buyout (LBO) A transaction whereby the target company management team converts the target to a privately held company by using heavy borrowing to finance the purchase of the target company's outstanding shares.

Leveraged recapitalization A post-offer takeover defense mechanism that involves the assumption of a large amount of debt that is then used to finance share repurchases; the effect is to dramatically change the company's capital structure while attempting to deliver a value to target shareholders in excess of a hostile bid.

Libor–OIS spread The difference between Libor and the overnight indexed swap (OIS) rate.

Linear association A straight-line relationship, as opposed to a relationship that cannot be graphed as a straight line.

Linear regression Regression that models the straight-line relationship between the dependent and independent variable(s).

Linear trend A trend in which the dependent variable changes at a constant rate with time.

Liquidation To sell the assets of a company, division, or subsidiary piecemeal, typically because of bankruptcy; the form of bankruptcy that allows for the orderly satisfaction of creditors' claims after which the company ceases to exist.

Liquidation value The value of a company if the company were dissolved and its assets sold individually.

Liquidity preference theory A term structure theory that asserts liquidity premiums exist to compensate investors for the added interest rate risk they face when lending long term.

Liquidity premium The premium or incrementally higher yield that investors demand for lending long term.

Liquidity risk The risk that a financial instrument cannot be purchased or sold without a significant concession in price due to the size of the market.

Local currency The currency of the country where a company is located.

Local expectations theory A term structure theory that contends the return for all bonds over short time periods is the risk-free rate.

Locational obsolescence In the context of real estate, a reduction in value due to decreased desirability of the location of the building.

Lockout period Period during which a bond's issuer cannot call the bond.

Log-linear model With reference to time-series models, a model in which the growth rate of the time series as a function of time is constant.

Log-log regression model A regression that expresses the dependent and independent variables as natural logarithms.

Logit model A qualitative-dependent-variable multiple regression model based on the logistic probability distribution.

Long/short trade A long position in one CDS and a short position in another.

Look-ahead bias A bias caused by using information that was not available on the test date.

Lookback period The time period used to gather a historical data set.

Loss given default The amount that will be lost if a default occurs.

Macroeconomic balance approach An approach to assessing the equilibrium exchange rate that focuses on exchange rate adjustments needed to close the gap between the medium-term expectation for a country's current account balance and that country's normal (or sustainable) current account balance.

Macroeconomic factor model A multifactor model in which the factors are surprises in macroeconomic variables that significantly explain equity returns.

Macroeconomic factors Factors related to the economy, such as the inflation rate, industrial production, or economic sector membership.

Maintenance capital expenditures Capital expenditures needed to maintain operations at the current level.

Managerialism theories Theories that posit that corporate executives are motivated to engage in mergers to maximize the size of their company rather than shareholder value.

Marginal investor An investor in a given share who is very likely to be part of the next trade in the share and who is therefore important in setting price.

Marginal VaR (MVaR) A measure of the effect on portfolio VaR of a small change in a position size.

Market approach Valuation approach that values an asset based on pricing multiples from sales of assets viewed as similar to the subject asset.

Market conversion premium per share For a convertible bond, the difference between the market conversion price and the underlying share price, which allows investors to identify the premium or discount payable when buying a convertible bond rather than the underlying common stock.

Market conversion premium ratio For a convertible bond, the market conversion premium per share expressed as a percentage of the current market price of the shares.

Market efficiency A finance perspective on capital markets that deals with the relationship of price to intrinsic value. The **traditional efficient markets formulation** asserts that an asset's price is the best available estimate of its intrinsic value. The **rational efficient markets formulation** asserts that investors should expect to be rewarded for the costs of information gathering and analysis by higher gross returns.

Market timing Asset allocation in which the investment in the market is increased if one forecasts that the market will outperform T-bills.

Market value The estimated amount for which a property should exchange on the date of valuation between a willing buyer and a willing seller in an arm's-length transaction after proper marketing wherein the parties had each acted knowledgeably, prudently, and without compulsion.

Market value of invested capital The market value of debt and equity.

Mature growth rate The earnings growth rate in a company's mature phase; an earnings growth rate that can be sustained long term.

Maximum drawdown The worst-returning month or quarter for the portfolio or the worst peak-to-trough decline in a portfolio's returns.

Mean reversion The tendency of a time series to fall when its level is above its mean and rise when its level is below its mean; a mean-reverting time series tends to return to its long-term mean.

Merger The absorption of one company by another; two companies become one entity and one or both of the pre-merger companies ceases to exist as a separate entity.

Method based on forecasted fundamentals An approach to using price multiples that relates a price multiple to forecasts of fundamentals through a discounted cash flow model.

Method of comparables An approach to valuation that involves using a price multiple to evaluate whether an asset is relatively fairly valued, relatively undervalued, or relatively overvalued when compared to a benchmark value of the multiple.

Minority Interest The proportion of the ownership of a subsidiary not held by the parent (controlling) company.

Mispricing Any departure of the market price of an asset from the asset's estimated intrinsic value.

Mixed offering A merger or acquisition that is to be paid for with cash, securities, or some combination of the two.

Model specification With reference to regression, the set of variables included in the regression and the regression equation's functional form.

Molodovsky effect The observation that P/Es tend to be high on depressed EPS at the bottom of a business cycle, and tend to be low on unusually high EPS at the top of a business cycle.

Momentum indicators Valuation indicators that relate either price or a fundamental (such as earnings) to the time series of their own past values (or in some cases to their expected value).

Monetary assets and liabilities Assets and liabilities with value equal to the amount of currency contracted for, a fixed amount of currency. Examples are cash, accounts receivable, accounts payable, bonds payable, and mortgages payable. Inventory is not a monetary asset. Most liabilities are monetary.

Monetary/non-monetary method Approach to translating foreign currency financial statements for consolidation in which monetary assets and liabilities are translated at the current exchange rate. Non-monetary assets and liabilities are translated at historical exchange rates (the exchange rates that existed when the assets and liabilities were acquired).

Monetizing The conversion of the value of a financial transaction into currency.

Monitoring costs Costs borne by owners to monitor the management of the company (e.g., board of director expenses).

Monte Carlo simulation A method of estimating VaR in which the user develops his or her own assumptions about the statistical characteristics of the distribution and uses those characteristics to generate a distribution that represents hypothetical returns to a portfolio with the specified characteristics.

Mortgage-backed securities Asset-backed securitized debt obligations that represent rights to receive cash flows from portfolios of mortgage loans.

Mortgage REITs REITs that invest the bulk of their assets in interest-bearing mortgages, mortgage securities, or short-term loans secured by real estate.

Mortgages Loans with real estate serving as collateral for the loans.

Multi-family/residential REITs REITs that invest in and manage rental apartments for lease to individual tenants, typically using one-year leases.

Multicollinearity A regression assumption violation that occurs when two or more independent variables (or combinations of independent variables) are highly but not perfectly correlated with each other.

Multiple linear regression Linear regression involving two or more independent variables.

Multiple linear regression model A linear regression model with two or more independent variables.

Mutually exclusive projects Mutually exclusive projects compete directly with each other. For example, if Projects A and B are mutually exclusive, you can choose A or B, but you cannot choose both.

n-Period moving average The average of the current and immediately prior $n - 1$ values of a time series.

Naked credit default swap A position where the owner of the CDS does not have a position in the underlying credit.

Negative serial correlation Serial correlation in which a positive error for one observation increases the chance of a negative error for another observation, and vice versa.

Net asset balance sheet exposure When assets translated at the current exchange rate are greater in amount than liabilities translated at the current exchange rate. Assets exposed to translation gains or losses exceed the exposed liabilities.

Net asset value The difference between assets and liabilities, all taken at current market values instead of accounting book values.

Net asset value per share Net asset value divided by the number of shares outstanding.

Net lease A lease under which the tenant pays a net rent to the landlord as well as an additional amount based on the tenant's pro rata share of the operating costs, utilities, maintenance expenses, and real estate taxes relating to the property.

Net liability balance sheet exposure When liabilities translated at the current exchange rate are greater assets translated at the current exchange rate. Liabilities exposed to translation gains or losses exceed the exposed assets.

Net operating income Gross rental revenue minus operating costs, but before deducting depreciation, corporate overhead, and interest expense. In the context of real estate, a measure of the income from the property after deducting operating expenses for such items as property taxes, insurance, maintenance, utilities, repairs, and insurance but before deducting any costs associated with financing and before deducting federal income taxes. It is similar to earnings before interest, taxes, depreciation, and amortization (EBITDA) in a financial reporting context.

Net operating profit less adjusted taxes (NOPLAT) A company's operating profit with adjustments to normalize the effects of capital structure.

Net present value (NPV) The present value of an investment's cash inflows (benefits) minus the present value of its cash outflows (costs).

Net regulatory burden The private costs of regulation less the private benefits of regulation.

Net rent A rent that consists of a stipulated rent to the landlord and a further amount based on their share of common area costs for utilities, maintenance, and property taxes.

Network externalities The impact that users of a good, a service, or a technology have on other users of that product; it can be positive (e.g., a critical mass of users makes a product more useful) or negative (e.g., congestion makes the product less useful).

No-arbitrage approach A procedure for obtaining the value of an option based on the creation of a portfolio that replicates the payoffs of the option and deriving the option value from the value of the replicating portfolio.

No-growth company A company without positive expected net present value projects.

No-growth value per share The value per share of a no-growth company, equal to the expected level amount of earnings divided by the stock's required rate of return.

Non-cash rent An amount equal to the difference between the average contractual rent over a lease term (the straight-line rent) and the cash rent actually paid during a period. This figure is one of the deductions made from FFO to calculate AFFO.

Non-convergence trap A situation in which a country remains relative poor, or even falls further behind, because it fails to t implement necessary institutional reforms and/or adopt leading technologies.

Non-monetary assets and liabilities Assets and liabilities that are not monetary assets and liabilities. Non-monetary assets include inventory, fixed assets, and intangibles, and non-monetary liabilities include deferred revenue.

Non-renewable resources Finite resources that are depleted once they are consumed; oil and coal are examples.

Nonconventional cash flow In a nonconventional cash flow pattern, the initial outflow is not followed by inflows only, but the cash flows can flip from positive (inflows) to negative (outflows) again (or even change signs several times).

Nonearning assets Cash and investments (specifically cash, cash equivalents, and short-term investments).

Nonlinear relation An association or relationship between variables that cannot be graphed as a straight line.

Nonstationarity With reference to a random variable, the property of having characteristics such as mean and variance that are not constant through time.

Normal EPS The EPS that a business could achieve currently under mid-cyclical conditions. Also called *normalized EPS*.

Normalized earnings The expected level of mid-cycle earnings for a company in the absence of any unusual or temporary factors that affect profitability (either positively or negatively).

Normalized EPS The EPS that a business could achieve currently under mid-cyclical conditions. Also called *normal EPS*.

Normalized P/E P/E based on normalized EPS data.

Notional amount The amount of protection being purchased in a CDS.

NTM P/E Next twelve months P/E: current market price divided by an estimated next twelve months EPS.

Off-the-run A series of securities or indexes that were issued/created prior to the most recently issued/created series.

Office REITs REITs that invest in and manage multi-tenanted office properties in central business districts of cities and suburban markets.

On-the-run The most recently issued/created series of securities or indexes.

One-sided durations Effective durations when interest rates go up or down, which are better at capturing the interest rate sensitivity of bonds with embedded options that do not react symmetrically to positive and negative changes in interest rates of the same magnitude.

Operating risk The risk attributed to the operating cost structure, in particular the use of fixed costs in operations; the risk arising from the mix of fixed and variable costs; the risk that a company's operations may be severely affected by environmental, social, and governance risk factors.

Operational risk The risk of loss from failures in a company's systems and procedures, or from external events.

Opportunity cost The value that investors forgo by choosing a particular course of action; the value of something in its best alternative use.

Optimal capital structure The capital structure at which the value of the company is maximized.

Option-adjusted spread (OAS) Constant spread that, when added to all the one-period forward rates on the interest rate tree, makes the arbitrage-free value of the bond equal to its market price.

Option combination An option strategy that typically uses both puts and calls, an example of which is the straddle, which involves buying one call and one put.

Option spread The investor buys one call and writes another with a different exercise price or expiration or buys one put and writes another with a different exercise price or expiration.

Orderly liquidation value The estimated gross amount of money that could be realized from the liquidation sale of an asset or assets, given a reasonable amount of time to find a purchaser or purchasers.

Organic growth Company growth in output or sales that is achieved by making investments internally (i.e., excludes growth achieved through mergers and acquisitions).

Other comprehensive income Changes to equity that bypass (are not reported in) the income statement; the difference between comprehensive income and net income.

Other post-employment benefits Promises by the company to pay benefits in the future, such as life insurance premiums and all or part of health care insurance for its retirees.

Out-of-sample forecast errors The differences between actual and predicted value of time series outside the sample period used to fit the model.

Out-of-the-money Options that, if exercised, would require the payment of more money than the value received and therefore would not be currently exercised.

Pairs trading An approach to trading that uses pairs of closely related stocks, buying the relatively undervalued stock and selling short the relatively overvalued stock.

Par curve A hypothetical yield curve for coupon-paying Treasury securities that assumes all securities are priced at par.

Par swap A swap in which the fixed rate is set so that no money is exchanged at contract initiation.

Parameter instability The problem or issue of population regression parameters that have changed over time.

Parametric method A method of estimating VaR which uses the historical mean, standard deviation, and correlation of security price movements to estimate the portfolio VaR. Generally assumes a normal distribution, but can be adapted to non-normal distributions with the addition of skewness and kurtosis. Sometimes called the *variance–covariance method* or the *analytical method.*

Partial equilibrium models Term structure models that make use of an assumed form of interest rate process. Underlying risk factors, such as the impact of changing interest rates on the economy, are not incorporated in the model.

Partial regression coefficients The slope coefficients in a multiple regression. Also called *partial slope coefficients.*

Partial slope coefficients The slope coefficients in a multiple regression. Also called *partial regression coefficients.*

Partnership A business owned and operated by more than one individual.

Payout amount The payout ratio times the notional.

Payout policy The principles by which a company distributes cash to common shareholders by means of cash dividends and/or share repurchases.

Payout ratio An estimate of the expected credit loss.

Pecking order theory The theory that managers take into account how their actions might be interpreted by outsiders and thus order their preferences for various forms of corporate financing. Forms of financing that are least visible to outsiders (e.g., internally generated funds) are most preferable to managers and those that are most visible (e.g., equity) are least preferable.

PEG The P/E-to-growth ratio, calculated as the stock's P/E divided by the expected earnings growth rate.

Pension obligation The present value of future benefits earned by employees for service provided to date.

Perfect capital markets Markets in which, by assumption, there are no taxes, transactions costs, or bankruptcy costs, and in which all investors have equal ("symmetric") information.

Performance appraisal The evaluation of risk-adjusted performance; the evaluation of investment skill.

Perpetuity A perpetual annuity, or a set of never-ending level sequential cash flows, with the first cash flow occurring one period from now.

Persistent earnings Earnings excluding nonrecurring components. Also referred to as *core earnings, continuing earnings,* or *underlying earnings.*

Pet projects Projects in which influential managers want the corporation to invest. Often, unfortunately, pet projects are selected without undergoing normal capital budgeting analysis.

Physical deterioration In the context of real estate, a reduction in value due to wear and tear.

Physical settlement Involves actual delivery of the debt instrument in exchange for a payment by the credit protection seller of the notional amount of the contract.

Poison pill A pre-offer takeover defense mechanism that makes it prohibitively costly for an acquirer to take control of a target without the prior approval of the target's board of directors.

Poison puts A pre-offer takeover defense mechanism that gives target company bondholders the right to sell their bonds back to the target at a pre-specified redemption price, typically at or above par value; this defense increases the need for cash and raises the cost of the acquisition.

Pooling of interests method A method of accounting in which combined companies were portrayed as if they had always operated as a single economic entity. Called pooling of interests under US GAAP and uniting of interests under IFRS. (No longer allowed under US GAAP or IFRS).

Portfolio balance approach A theory of exchange rate determination that emphasizes the portfolio investment decisions of global investors and the requirement that global investors willingly hold all outstanding securities denominated in each currency at prevailing prices and exchange rates.

Position delta The overall delta of a position that contains some combination of assets and derivatives.

Positive serial correlation Serial correlation in which a positive error for one observation increases the chance of a positive error for another observation, and a negative error for one observation increases the chance of a negative error for another observation.

Potential GDP The maximum amount of output an economy can sustainably produce without inducing an increase in the inflation rate. The output level that corresponds to full employment with consistent wage and price expectations.

Preferred habitat theory A term structure theory that contends that investors have maturity preferences and require yield incentives before they will buy bonds outside of their preferred maturities.

Premise of value The status of a company in the sense of whether it is assumed to be a going concern or not.

Premium leg The series of payments the credit protection buyer promises to make to the credit protection seller.

Present value model A model of intrinsic value that views the value of an asset as the present value of the asset's expected future cash flows.

Present value of growth opportunities The difference between the actual value per share and the no-growth value per share. Also called *value of growth.*

Present value of the expected loss Conceptually, the largest price one would be willing to pay on a bond to a third party (e.g., an insurer) to entirely remove the credit risk of purchasing and holding the bond.

Presentation currency The currency in which financial statement amounts are presented.

Price momentum A valuation indicator based on past price movement.

Price multiples The ratio of a stock's market price to some measure of value per share.

Price return Measures the price appreciation or percentage change in price of a security or the securities in an index or portfolio.

Price-setting option The operational flexibility to adjust prices when demand varies from forecast. For example, when demand exceeds capacity, the company could benefit from the excess demand by increasing prices.

Priced risk Risk for which investors demand compensation for bearing (e.g., equity risk, company-specific factors, macroeconomic factors).

Principal–agent problem   A conflict of interest that arises when the agent in an agency relationship has goals and incentives that differ from the principal to whom the agent owes a fiduciary duty.

Principal components analysis   (PCA) A non-parametric method of extracting relevant information from high-dimensional data that uses the dependencies between variables to represent information in a more tractable, lower-dimensional form.

Principle of no arbitrage   In well-functioning markets, prices will adjust until there are no arbitrage opportunities.

Prior transaction method   A variation of the market approach; considers actual transactions in the stock of the subject private company.

Private market value   The value derived using a sum-of-the-parts valuation.

Probability of default   The probability that a bond issuer will not meet its contractual obligations on schedule.

Probability of survival   The probability that a bond issuer will meet its contractual obligations on schedule.

Probit model   A qualitative-dependent-variable multiple regression model based on the normal distribution.

Procedural law   The body of law that focuses on the protection and enforcement of the substantive laws.

Production-flexibility   The operational flexibility to alter production when demand varies from forecast. For example, if demand is strong, a company may profit from employees working overtime or from adding additional shifts.

Project sequencing   To defer the decision to invest in a future project until the outcome of some or all of a current project is known. Projects are sequenced through time, so that investing in a project creates the option to invest in future projects.

Prospective P/E   A P/E calculated on the basis of a forecast of EPS; a stock's current price divided by next year's expected earnings.

Protection leg   The contingent payment that the credit protection seller may have to make to the credit protection buyer.

Protective put   An option strategy in which a long position in an asset is combined with a long position in a put.

Proxy fight   An attempt to take control of a company through a shareholder vote.

Proxy statement   A public document that provides the material facts concerning matters on which shareholders will vote.

Prudential supervision   Regulation and monitoring of the safety and soundness of financial institutions to promote financial stability, reduce system-wide risks, and protect customers of financial institutions.

Purchasing power gain   A gain in value caused by changes in price levels. Monetary liabilities experience purchasing power gains during periods of inflation.

Purchasing power loss   A loss in value caused by changes in price levels. Monetary assets experience purchasing power loss during periods of inflation.

Purchasing power parity (PPP)   The idea that exchange rates move to equalize the purchasing power of different currencies.

Pure expectations theory   A term structure theory that contends the forward rate is an unbiased predictor of the future spot rate. Also called the *unbiased expectations theory*.

Pure factor portfolio   A portfolio with sensitivity of 1 to the factor in question and a sensitivity of 0 to all other factors.

Putable bond   Bond that includes an embedded put option, which gives the bondholder the right to put back the bonds to the issuer prior to maturity, typically when interest rates have risen and higher-yielding bonds are available.

Qualitative dependent variables   Dummy variables used as dependent variables rather than as independent variables.

Quality of earnings analysis   The investigation of issues relating to the accuracy of reported accounting results as reflections of economic performance; quality of earnings analysis is broadly understood to include not only earnings management, but also balance sheet management.

Random walk   A time series in which the value of the series in one period is the value of the series in the previous period plus an unpredictable random error.

Rational efficient markets formulation   See *market efficiency*.

Real estate investment trusts (REITS)   Tax-advantaged entities (companies or trusts) that typically own, operate, and—to a limited extent—develop income-producing real estate property.

Real estate operating companies   Regular taxable real estate ownership companies that operate in the real estate industry in countries that do not have a tax-advantaged REIT regime in place or are engaged in real estate activities of a kind and to an extent that do not fit within their country's REIT framework.

Real exchange rate   The relative purchasing power of two currencies, defined in terms of the *real* goods and services that each can buy at prevailing national price levels and nominal exchange rates. Measured as the ratio of national price levels expressed in a common currency.

Real interest rate parity   The proposition that real interest rates will converge to the same level across different markets.

Real options   Options that relate to investment decisions such as the option to time the start of a project, the option to adjust its scale, or the option to abandon a project that has begun.

Rebalance return   A return from rebalancing the component weights of an index.

Reconstitution   When dealers recombine appropriate individual zero-coupon securities and reproduce an underlying coupon Treasury.

Recovery rate   The percentage of the loss recovered.

Reduced form models   Models of credit analysis based on the outputs of a structural model but with different assumptions. The model's credit risk measures reflect changing economic conditions.

Reference entity   The borrower on a single-name CDS.

Reference obligation   A particular debt instrument issued by the borrower that is the designated instrument being covered.

Regime   With reference to a time series, the underlying model generating the times series.

Regression coefficients   The intercept and slope coefficient(s) of a regression.

Regulatory arbitrage   Entities identify and use some aspect of regulations that allows them to exploit differences in economic substance and regulatory interpretation or in foreign and domestic regulatory regimes to their (the entities) advantage.

Regulatory burden   The costs of regulation for the regulated entity.

Regulatory capture   Theory that regulation often arises to enhance the interests of the regulated.

Regulatory competition   Regulators may compete to provide a regulatory environment designed to attract certain entities.

Relative-strength indicators   Valuation indicators that compare a stock's performance during a period either to its own past performance or to the performance of some group of stocks.

Relative valuation models   A model that specifies an asset's value relative to the value of another asset.

Relative VaR   See *ex ante tracking error*.

Relative version of PPP   Hypothesis that changes in (nominal) exchange rates over time are equal to national inflation rate differentials.

Renewable resources   Resources that can be replenished, such as a forest.

Rental price of capital   The cost per unit of time to rent a unit of capital.

Replacement cost   In the context of real estate, the value of a building assuming it was built today using current construction costs and standards.

Reporting unit   For financial reporting under US GAAP, an operating segment or one level below an operating segment (referred to as a component).

Reputational risk   The risk that a company will suffer an extended diminution in market value relative to other companies in the same industry due to a demonstrated lack of concern for environmental, social, and governance risk factors.

Required rate of return   The minimum rate of return required by an investor to invest in an asset, given the asset's riskiness.

Residential properties   Properties that provide housing for individuals or families. Single-family properties may be owner-occupied or rental properties, whereas multi-family properties are rental properties even if the owner or manager occupies one of the units.

Residual autocorrelations   The sample autocorrelations of the residuals.

Residual dividend policy   A policy in which dividends are paid from any internally generated funds remaining after such funds are used to finance positive NPV projects.

Residual income   Earnings for a given time period, minus a deduction for common shareholders' opportunity cost in generating the earnings. Also called *economic profit* or *abnormal earnings*.

Residual income method   Income approach that estimates the value of all intangible assets of the business by capitalizing future earnings in excess of the estimated return requirements associated with working capital and fixed assets.

Residual income model   (RIM) A model of stock valuation that views intrinsic value of stock as the sum of book value per share plus the present value of the stock's expected future residual income per share. Also called *discounted abnormal earnings model* or *Edwards–Bell–Ohlson model*.

Residual loss   Agency costs that are incurred despite adequate monitoring and bonding of management.

Restructuring   Reorganizing the financial structure of a firm.

Retail REITs   REITs that invest in such retail properties as regional shopping malls or community/neighborhood shopping centers.

Return on capital employed   Operating profit divided by capital employed (debt and equity capital).

Return on invested capital   A measure of the after-tax profitability of the capital invested by the company's shareholders and debt holders.

Reverse carry arbitrage   A strategy in involving the short sale of the underlying and an offsetting opposite position in the derivative.

Reverse stress testing   A risk management approach in which the user identifies key risk exposures in the portfolio and subjects those exposures to extreme market movements.

Reviewed financial statements   A type of non-audited financial statements; typically provide an opinion letter with representations and assurances by the reviewing accountant that are less than those in audited financial statements.

Rho   The change in a given derivative instrument for a given small change in the risk-free interest rate, holding everything else constant. Rho measures the sensitivity of the option to the risk-free interest rate.

Riding the yield curve   A maturity trading strategy that involves buying bonds with a maturity longer than the intended investment horizon. Also called *rolling down the yield curve*.

Risk budgeting   The allocation of an asset owner's total risk appetite among groups or divisions (in the case of a trading organization) or among strategies and managers (in the case of an institutional or individual investor).

Risk decomposition   The process of converting a set of holdings in a portfolio into a set of exposures to risk factors.

Risk factors   Variables or characteristics with which individual asset returns are correlated. Sometimes referred to simply as *factors*.

Risk reversal   An option position that consists of the purchase of an out-of-the-money call and the simultaneous sale of an out-of-the-money put with the same "delta," on the same underlying currency or security, and with the same expiration date.

Robust standard errors   Standard errors of the estimated parameters of a regression that correct for the presence of heteroskedasticity in the regression's error term.

Roll   When an investor moves from one series to a new one.

Roll return   The component of the return on a commodity futures contract attributable to rolling long futures positions forward through time. Also called *roll yield*.

Rolling down the yield curve   A maturity trading strategy that involves buying bonds with a maturity longer than the intended investment horizon. Also called *riding the yield curve*.

Root mean squared error (RMSE)   The square root of the average squared forecast error; used to compare the out-of-sample forecasting performance of forecasting models.

Sales comparison approach   In the context of real estate, this approach estimates value based on what similar or comparable properties (comparables) transacted for in the current market.

Scaled earnings surprise   Unexpected earnings divided by the standard deviation of analysts' earnings forecasts.

Scatter plot   A two-dimensional plot of pairs of observations on two data series.

Scenario analysis   Analysis that involves changing multiple assumptions at the same time.

Screening   The application of a set of criteria to reduce a set of potential investments to a smaller set having certain desired characteristics.

Seasonality   A characteristic of a time series in which the data experiences regular and predictable periodic changes, e.g., fan sales are highest during the summer months.

Securities offering   A merger or acquisition in which target shareholders are to receive shares of the acquirer's common stock as compensation.

Security selection risk   See *active specific risk.*

Segmented markets theory   A term structure theory that contends yields are solely a function of the supply and demand for funds of a particular maturity.

Self-regulating organizations   Private, non-governmental organizations that both represent and regulate their members. Some self-regulating organizations are also independent regulators.

Sell-side analysts   Analysts who work at brokerages.

Sensitivity analysis   Analysis that shows the range of possible outcomes as specific assumptions are changed; involves changing one assumption at a time.

Serially correlated   With reference to regression errors, errors that are correlated across observations.

Service period   For employee stock options, usually the period between the grant date and the vesting date.

Settled in arrears   An arrangement in which the interest payment is made at the end of the settlement period.

Settlement   In the case of a credit event, the process by which the two parties to a CDS contract satisfy their respective obligations.

Shaping risk   The sensitivity of a bond's price to the changing shape of the yield curve.

Shareholders' equity   Total assets minus total liabilities.

Shark repellents   A pre-offer takeover defense mechanism involving the corporate charter (e.g., staggered boards of directors and supermajority provisions).

Shopping center   REITs that invest in such retail properties as regional shopping malls or community/neighborhood shopping centers.

Single-name CDS   Credit default swap on one specific borrower.

Sinking fund bond   A bond which requires the issuer to set aside funds over time to retire the bond issue, thus reducing credit risk.

Sole proprietorship   A business owned and operated by a single person.

Spin-off   A form of restructuring in which shareholders of a parent company receive a proportional number of shares in a new, separate entity; shareholders end up owning stock in two different companies where there used to be one.

Split-off   A form of restructuring in which shareholders of the parent company are given shares in a newly created entity in exchange for their shares of the parent company.

Split-rate tax system   In reference to corporate taxes, a split-rate system taxes earnings to be distributed as dividends at a different rate than earnings to be retained. Corporate profits distributed as dividends are taxed at a lower rate than those retained in the business.

Spot curve   The term structure of spot rates for loans made today.

Spot price   The current price of an asset or security. For commodities, the current price to deliver a physical commodity to a specific location or purchase and transport it away from a designated location.

Spot rate   The interest rate that is determined today for a risk-free, single-unit payment at a specified future date.

Spot yield curve   The term structure of spot rates for loans made today.

Spurious correlation   A correlation that misleadingly points toward associations between variables.

Stabilized NOI   In the context of real estate, the expected NOI when a renovation is complete.

Stable dividend policy   A policy in which regular dividends are paid that reflect long-run expected earnings. In contrast to a constant dividend payout ratio policy, a stable dividend policy does not reflect short-term volatility in earnings.

Standard deviation   The positive square root of the variance; a measure of dispersion in the same units as the original data.

Standard of value   A specification of how "value" is to be understood in the context of a specific valuation.

Standardized beta   With reference to fundamental factor models, the value of the attribute for an asset minus the average value of the attribute across all stocks, divided by the standard deviation of the attribute across all stocks.

Standardized unexpected earnings   (SUE) Unexpected earnings per share divided by the standard deviation of unexpected earnings per share over a specified prior time period.

Static trade-off theory of capital structure   A theory pertaining to a company's optimal capital structure; the optimal level of debt is found at the point where additional debt would cause the costs of financial distress to increase by a greater amount than the benefit of the additional tax shield.

Statistical factor model   A multifactor model in which statistical methods are applied to a set of historical returns to determine portfolios that best explain either historical return covariances or variances.

Statistically significant   A result indicating that the null hypothesis can be rejected; with reference to an estimated regression coefficient, frequently understood to mean a result indicating that the corresponding population regression coefficient is different from 0.

Statutes   Laws enacted by legislative bodies.

Statutory merger   A merger in which one company ceases to exist as an identifiable entity and all its assets and liabilities become part of a purchasing company.

Steady state rate of growth   The constant growth rate of output (or output per capita) which can or will be sustained indefinitely once it is reached. Key ratios, such as the capital–output ratio, are constant on the steady-state growth path.

Steepness   One of the three factors (the other two are level and curvature) that empirically explain most of the changes in the shape of the yield curve. A shock to the steepness factor changes short-term yields more than long-term yields.

Sterilized intervention   A policy measure in which a monetary authority buys or sells its own currency to mitigate undesired exchange rate movements and simultaneously offsets the impact on the money supply with transactions in other financial instruments (usually money market instruments).

Stock purchase   An acquisition in which the acquirer gives the target company's shareholders some combination of cash and securities in exchange for shares of the target company's stock.

Stop-loss limit   Constraint used in risk management that requires a reduction in the size of a portfolio, or its complete liquidation, when a loss of a particular size occurs in a specified period.

Storage REITs   REITs that own and operate self-storage properties, sometimes referred to as mini-warehouse facilities.

Straddle   An option strategy involving the purchase of a put and a call on the same underlying with the same exercise price and expiration date. If the put and call are held long, it is a long straddle; if they are held short, it is a short straddle.

Straight bond   An underlying option-free bond with a specified issuer, issue date, maturity date, principal amount and repayment structure, coupon rate and payment structure, and currency denomination.

Straight-line rent   The average annual rent under a multi-year lease agreement that contains contractual increases in rent during the life of the lease. For example if the rent is $100,000 in Year 1, $105,000 in Year 2, and $110,000 in Year 3, the average rent to be recognized each year as revenue under straight-line rent accounting is ($100,000 + $105,000 + $110,000)/3 = $105,000.

Straight-line rent adjustment   See *non-cash rent*.

Strategic transaction   A purchase involving a buyer that would benefit from certain synergies associated with owning the target firm.

Stress tests   A risk management technique which assesses the portfolio's response to extreme market movements.

Stripping   A dealer's ability to separate a bond's individual cash flows and trade them as zero-coupon securities.

Structural models   Structural models of credit analysis build on the insights of option pricing theory. They are based on the structure of a company's balance sheet.

Subsidiary merger   A merger in which the company being purchased becomes a subsidiary of the purchaser.

Substantive law   The body of law that focuses on the rights and responsibilities of entities and relationships among entities.

Succession event   A change of corporate structure of the reference entity, such as through a merger, divestiture, spinoff, or any similar action, in which ultimate responsibility for the debt in question is unclear.

Sum-of-the-parts valuation   A valuation that sums the estimated values of each of a company's businesses as if each business were an independent going concern.

Sunk cost   A cost that has already been incurred.

Supernormal growth   Above average or abnormally high growth rate in earnings per share.

Survivorship bias   Bias that may result when failed or defunct companies are excluded from membership in a group.

Sustainable growth rate   The rate of dividend (and earnings) growth that can be sustained over time for a given level of return on equity, keeping the capital structure constant and without issuing additional common stock.

Swap curve   The term structure of swap rates.

Swap rate   The interest rate for the fixed-rate leg of an interest rate swap.

Swap rate curve   The term structure of swap rates.

Swap spread   The difference between the fixed rate on an interest rate swap and the rate on a Treasury note with equivalent maturity; it reflects the general level of credit risk in the market.

Synthetic CDO   Created by combining a portfolio of default-free securities with a combination of credit default swaps undertaken as protection sellers.

Synthetic long position   A combination of options (buying a call and writing a put) having the same expiration date and the same exercise price, which is approximately equivalent to a long position in the stock.

Synthetic short position   A derivatives strategy that creates the same performance as a short position in the underlying.

Systematic risk   Risk that affects the entire market or economy; it cannot be avoided and is inherent in the overall market. Systematic risk is also known as non-diversifiable or market risk.

Systemic risk   The risk of failure of the financial system.

Tail risk   The risk that losses in extreme events could be greater than would be expected for a portfolio of assets with a normal distribution.

Takeover   A merger; the term may be applied to any transaction, but is often used in reference to hostile transactions.

Takeover premium   The amount by which the takeover price for each share of stock must exceed the current stock price in order to entice shareholders to relinquish control of the company to an acquirer.

Tangible book value per share   Common shareholders' equity minus intangible assets reported on the balance sheet, divided by the number of shares outstanding.

Target   The company in a merger or acquisition that is being acquired.

Target capital structure   A company's chosen proportions of debt and equity.

Target company   The company in a merger or acquisition that is being acquired.

Target payout ratio   A strategic corporate goal representing the long-term proportion of earnings that the company intends to distribute to shareholders as dividends.

Technical indicators   Momentum indicators based on price.

TED spread   A measure of perceived credit risk determined as the difference between Libor and the T-bill yield of matching maturity.

Temporal method   A variation of the monetary/non-monetary translation method that requires not only monetary assets and liabilities, but also non-monetary assets and liabilities that are measured at their current value on the balance sheet date to be translated at the current exchange rate. Assets and liabilities are translated at rates consistent with the timing of their measurement value. This method is typically used when the functional currency is other than the local currency.

Tender offer   A public offer whereby the acquirer invites target shareholders to submit ("tender") their shares in return for the proposed payment.

Term premium   The additional return required by lenders to invest in a bond to maturity net of the expected return from continually reinvesting at the short-term rate over that same time horizon.

Terminal price multiples   The price multiple for a stock assumed to hold at a stated future time.

Terminal share price   The share price at a particular point in the future.

Terminal value of the stock   The analyst's estimate of a stock's value at a particular point in the future. Also called *continuing value of the stock*.

Termination date   The date of the final payment on a swap; also, the swap's expiration date.

Theta   The change in a derivative instrument for a given small change in calendar time, holding everything else constant. Specifically, the theta calculation assumes nothing changes except calendar time. Theta also reflects the rate at which an option's time value decays.

Time series   A set of observations on a variable's outcomes in different time periods.

Tobin's *q*   The ratio of the market value of debt and equity to the replacement cost of total assets.

Top-down approach   With respect to forecasting, an approach that usually begins at the level of the overall economy. Forecasts are then made at more narrowly defined levels, such as sector, industry, and market for a specific product.

Top-down investing   An approach to investing that typically begins with macroeconomic forecasts.

Total factor productivity (TFP)   A multiplicative scale factor that reflects the general level of productivity or technology in the economy. Changes in total factor productivity generate proportional changes in output for any input combination.

Total invested capital   The sum of market value of common equity, book value of preferred equity, and face value of debt.

Tracking error   The standard deviation of the differences between a portfolio's returns and its benchmark's returns; a synonym of active risk. Also called *tracking risk*.

Tracking risk   The standard deviation of the differences between a portfolio's returns and its benchmark's returns; a synonym of active risk. Also called *tracking error*.

Trailing dividend yield   Current market price divided by the most recent annualized dividend.

Trailing P/E   A stock's current market price divided by the most recent four quarters of EPS (or the most recent two semi-annual periods for companies that report interim data semi-annually.) Also called *current P/E*.

Tranche CDS   A type of credit default swap that covers a combination of borrowers but only up to pre-specified levels of losses.

Transaction exposure   The risk of a change in value between the transaction date and the settlement date of an asset of liability denominated in a foreign currency.

Trend   A long-term pattern of movement in a particular direction.

Triangular arbitrage   An arbitrage transaction involving three currencies which attempts to exploit inconsistencies among pair wise exchange rates.

Unbiased expectations theory   A term structure theory that contends the forward rate is an unbiased predictor of the future spot rate. Also called the *pure expectations theory*.

Unconditional heteroskedasticity   Heteroskedasticity of the error term that is not correlated with the values of the independent variable(s) in the regression.

Uncovered interest rate parity   The proposition that the expected return on an uncovered (i.e., unhedged) foreign currency (risk-free) investment should equal the return on a comparable domestic currency investment.

Underlying earnings   Earnings excluding nonrecurring components. Also referred to as *continuing earnings, core earnings*, or *persistent earnings*.

Unexpected earnings   The difference between reported EPS and expected EPS. Also referred to as an *earnings surprise*.

Unit root   A time series that is not covariance stationary is said to have a unit root.

Uniting of interests method   A method of accounting in which combined companies were portrayed as if they had always operated as a single economic entity. Called pooling of interests under US GAAP and uniting of interests under IFRS. (No longer allowed under US GAAP or IFRS).

Unlimited funds   An unlimited funds environment assumes that the company can raise the funds it wants for all profitable projects simply by paying the required rate of return.

Unsterilized intervention   A policy measure in which a monetary authority buys or sells its own currency to mitigate undesired exchange rate movements and does not offset the impact on the money supply with transactions in other financial instruments.

Upfront payment   The difference between the credit spread and the standard rate paid by the protection if the standard rate is insufficient to compensate the protection seller. Also called *upfront premium*.

Upfront premium   See *upfront payment*.

UPREITs   An umbrella partnership REIT under which the REIT owns an operating partnership and serves as the general partner of the operating partnership. All or most of the properties are held in the operating partnership.

Upstream   A transaction between two related companies, an investor company (or a parent company) and an associate company (or a subsidiary company) such that the associate company records a profit on its income statement. An example is a sale of inventory by the associate to the investor company or by a subsidiary to a parent company.

Valuation   The process of determining the value of an asset or service on the basis of variables perceived to be related to future investment returns, or on the basis of comparisons with closely similar assets.

Value additivity   An arbitrage opportunity when the value of the whole equals the sum of the values of the parts.

Value at risk (VaR)   The minimum loss that would be expected a certain percentage of the time over a certain period of time given the assumed market conditions.

Value of growth   The difference between the actual value per share and the no-growth value per share.

Variance   The expected value (the probability-weighted average) of squared deviations from a random variable's expected value.

Vasicek model   A partial equilibrium term structure model that assumes interest rates are mean reverting and interest rate volatility is a constant.

Vega   The change in a given derivative instrument for a given small change in volatility, holding everything else constant. A sensitivity measure for options that reflects the effect of volatility.

Venture capital investors   Private equity investors in development-stage companies.

Vertical merger   A merger involving companies at different positions of the same production chain; for example, a supplier or a distributor.

Vested benefit obligation   The actuarial present value of vested benefits.

Vesting date   The date that employees can first exercise stock options.

Visibility   The extent to which a company's operations are predictable with substantial confidence.

Weighted average cost of capital   (WACC) A weighted average of the after-tax required rates of return on a company's common stock, preferred stock, and long-term debt, where the weights are the fraction of each source of financing in the company's target capital structure.

Weighted harmonic mean   See *harmonic mean*.

White-corrected standard errors   A synonym for robust standard errors.

White knight   A third party that is sought out by the target company's board to purchase the target in lieu of a hostile bidder.

White squire   A third party that is sought out by the target company's board to purchase a substantial minority stake in the target—enough to block a hostile takeover without selling the entire company.

Winner's curse The tendency for the winner in certain competitive bidding situations to overpay, whether because of overestimation of intrinsic value, emotion, or information asymmetries.

Write-down A reduction in the value of an asset as stated in the balance sheet.

Yield curve factor model A model or a description of yield curve movements that can be considered realistic when compared with historical data.

Z-spread The constant basis point spread that needs to be added to the implied spot yield curve such that the discounted cash flows of a bond are equal to its current market price.

Zero A bond that does not pay a coupon but is priced at a discount and pays its full face value at maturity.

Zero-coupon bond A bond that does not pay a coupon but is priced at a discount and pays its full face value at maturity.

Index